ROSARIO + VAMPIRE

Season II

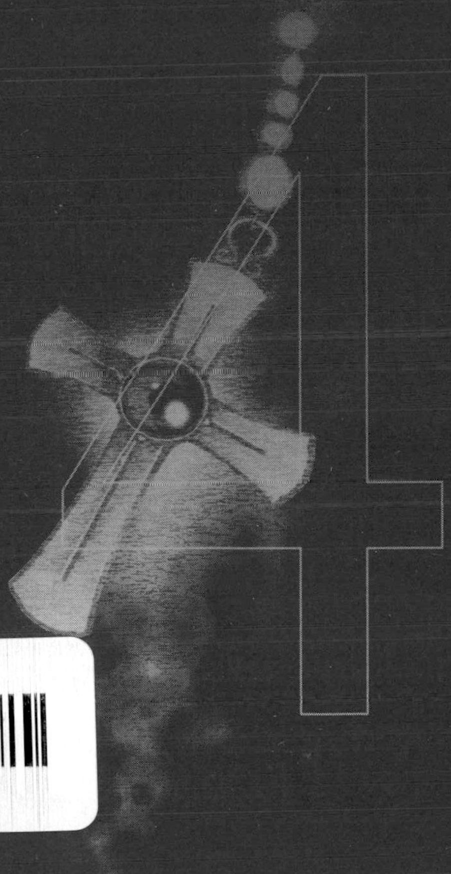

14

AKIHISA IKEDA

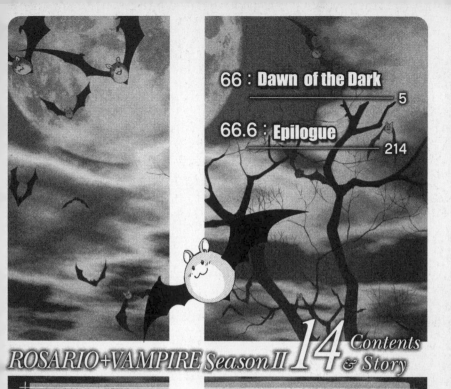

66 : Dawn of the Dark ——————— 5

66.6 : Epilogue ——————— 214

ROSARIO+VAMPIRE Season II 14 Contents & Story

Tsukune Aono accidentally enrolls in Yokai Academy, a high school for monsters! After befriending the school's cutest girl, Moka Akashiya, he decides to stay...even though Yokai has a zero-tolerance policy toward humans (a *fatal* policy). Tsukune survives with the help of his News Club friends—Moka (Vampire), Kurumu (Succubus), Yukari (Witch) and Mizore (Snow Fairy). Then they are attacked by Fairy Tale, an organization bent on destroying the human world by reviving Alucard, the First Ancestor of the Vampires. When Fairy Tale kidnaps Moka, her friends infiltrate the Hanging Garden, the enemy's flying fortress, to save her.

Fairy Tale's leader, Gyokuro, has taken control of Alucard through Moka's Rosario, which seals her powers. To fight Gyokuro, Tsukune breaks his spirit lock, turning himself into a ghoul! Before her defeat, Gyokuro sends the Hanging Garden on a trajectory to crash into the human world and merges with Alucard. But Moka's mother, Akasha, awakens from hibernation inside Alucard's body and...Alucard consumes Gyokuro. Tsukune's erstwhile friend Miyabi is revealed to be an embodiment of Alucard. And then Miyabi impales Moka and the Rosario with his tentacles in an attempt to free his main body from Akasha's seal...!

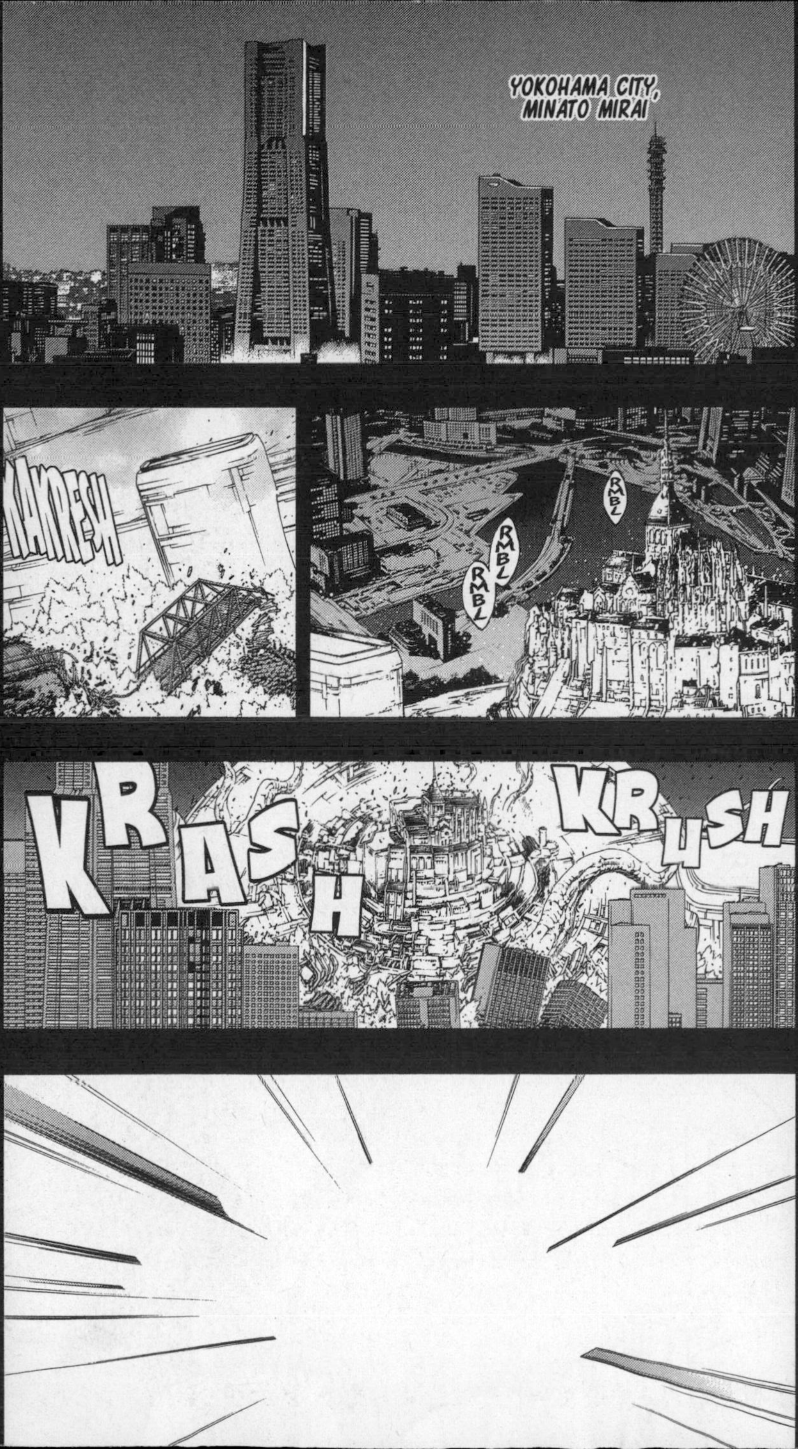
YOKOHAMA CITY, MINATO MIRAI
RMBL
RMBL
RMBL
RMBL
KRESH
KRUSH
KRASH

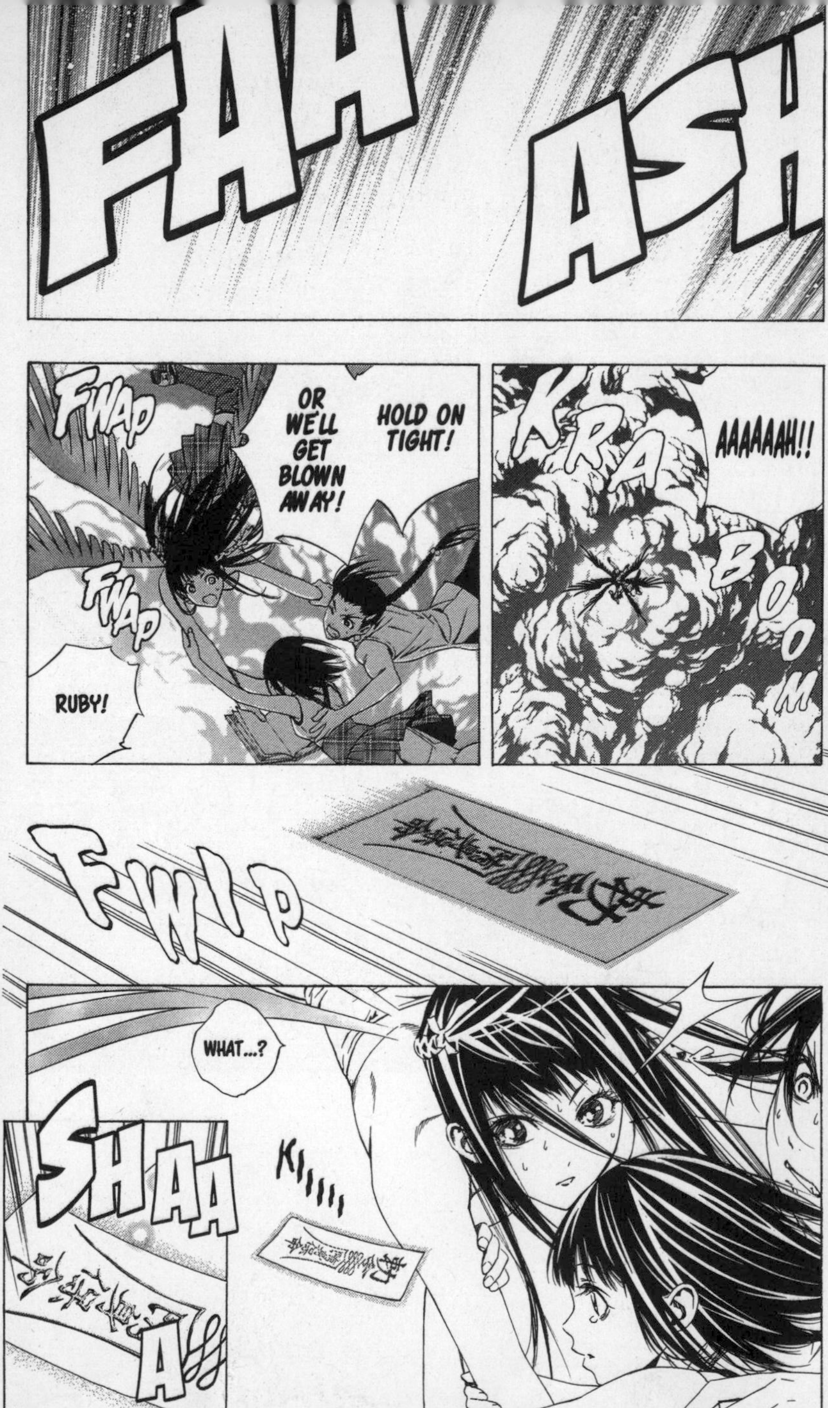
FAA
ASH
AAAAAAH!!
KRA
BOOM
HOLD ON TIGHT!
OR WE'LL GET BLOWN AWAY!
FWAP
FWAP
RUBY!
FWIP
WHAT...?
KI,,,,,
SHAA
A

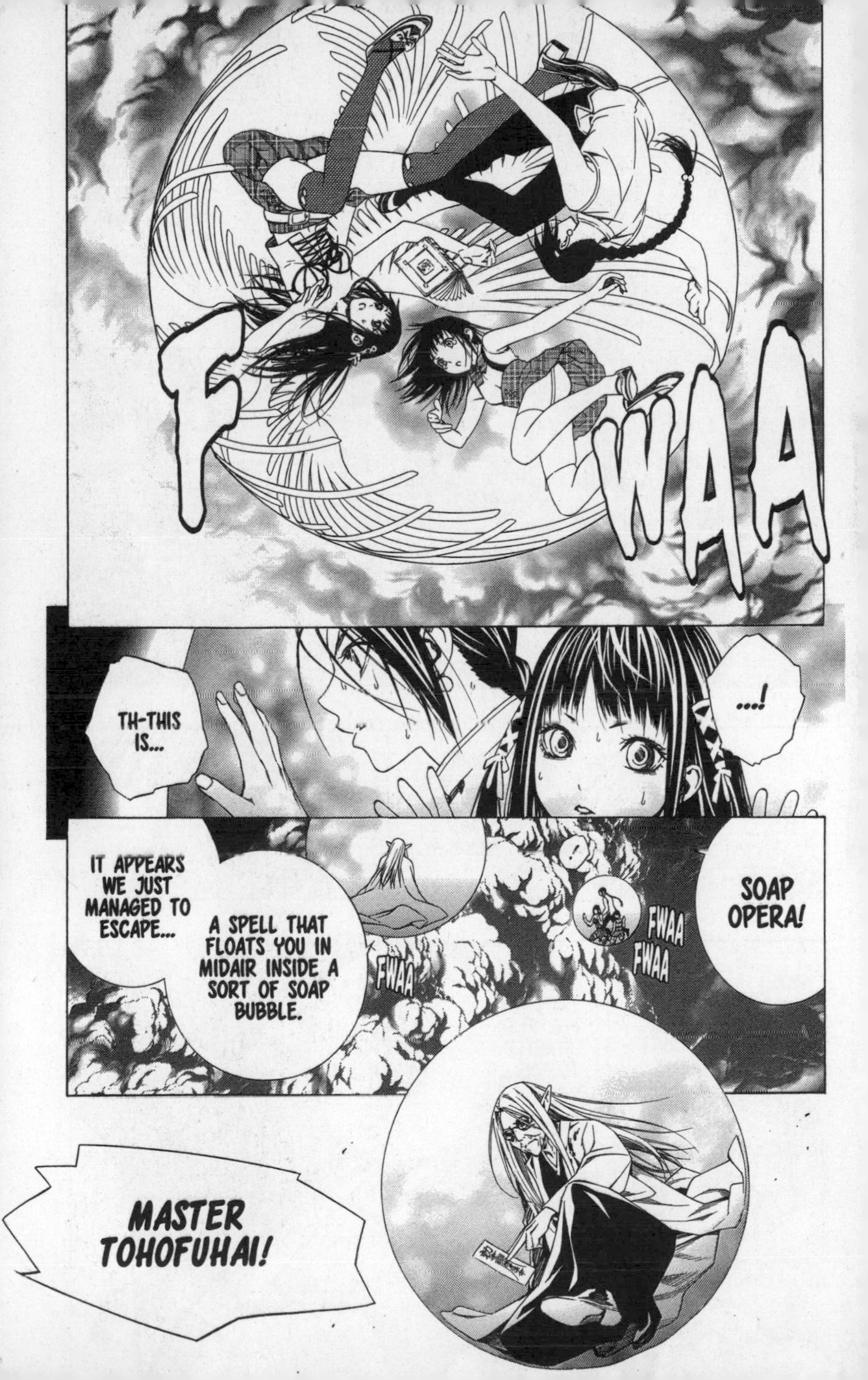
FWAA
...!
TH-THIS IS...
SOAP OPERA!
FWAA
FWAA
FWAA
A SPELL THAT FLOATS YOU IN MIDAIR INSIDE A SORT OF SOAP BUBBLE.
IT APPEARS WE JUST MANAGED TO ESCAPE...
MASTER TOHOFUHAI!

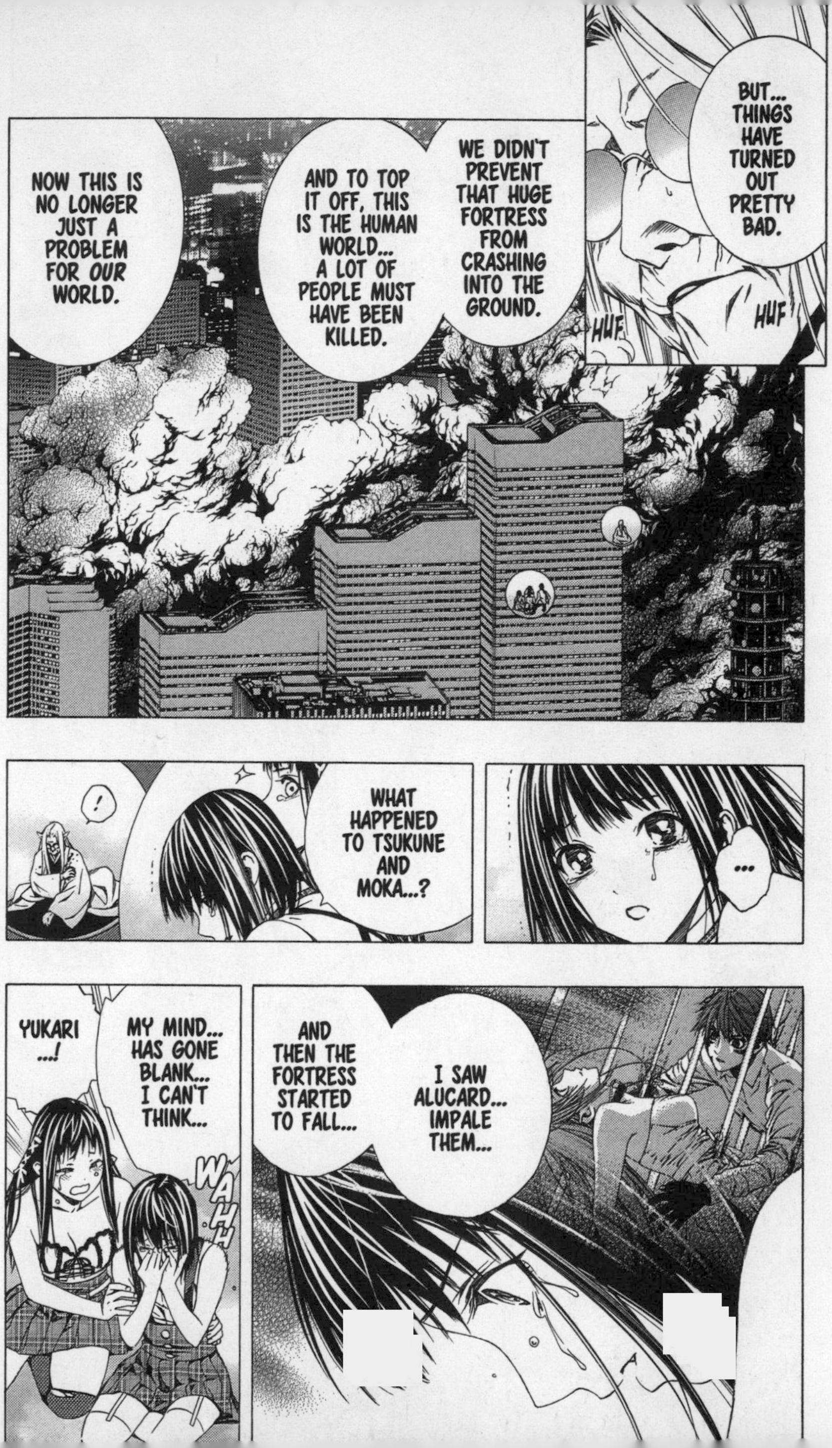
BUT... THINGS HAVE TURNED OUT PRETTY BAD.
HUF
HUF
WE DIDN'T PREVENT THAT HUGE FORTRESS FROM CRASHING INTO THE GROUND.
AND TO TOP IT OFF, THIS IS THE HUMAN WORLD... A LOT OF PEOPLE MUST HAVE BEEN KILLED.
NOW THIS IS NO LONGER JUST A PROBLEM FOR OUR WORLD.
...
WHAT HAPPENED TO TSUKUNE AND MOKA...?
!
I SAW ALUCARD... IMPALE THEM...
AND THEN THE FORTRESS STARTED TO FALL...
MY MIND... HAS GONE BLANK... I CAN'T THINK...
YUKARI ...!
WAHH

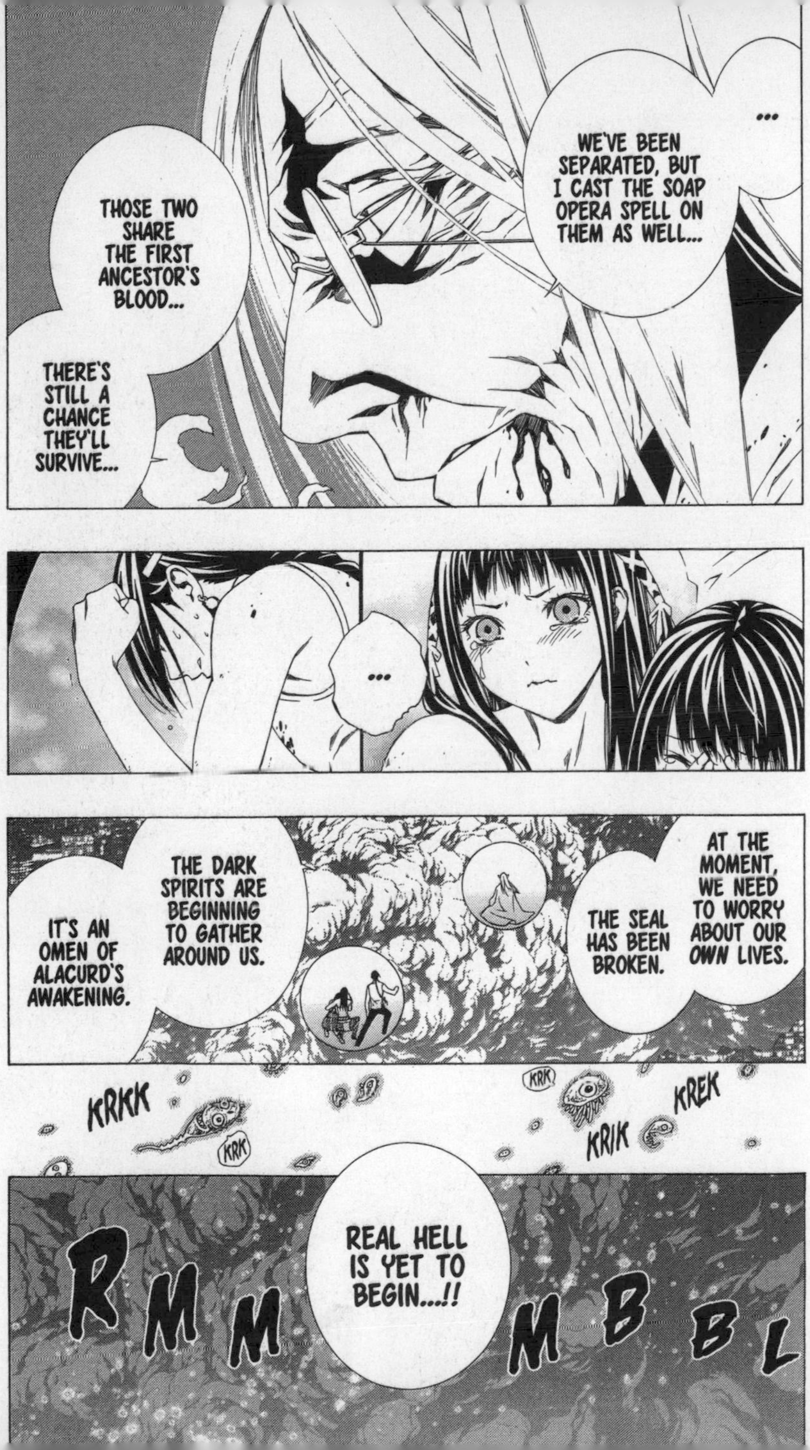
...
WE'VE BEEN SEPARATED, BUT I CAST THE SOAP OPERA SPELL ON THEM AS WELL...
THOSE TWO SHARE THE FIRST ANCESTOR'S BLOOD...
THERE'S STILL A CHANCE THEY'LL SURVIVE...
...
AT THE MOMENT, WE NEED TO WORRY ABOUT OUR OWN LIVES.
THE SEAL HAS BEEN BROKEN.
THE DARK SPIRITS ARE BEGINNING TO GATHER AROUND US.
IT'S AN OMEN OF ALACURD'S AWAKENING.
KREK
KRIK
KRK
KRK
KRKK
REAL HELL IS YET TO BEGIN...!!
RMM MBBL

Rosario+Vampire

of the Dark

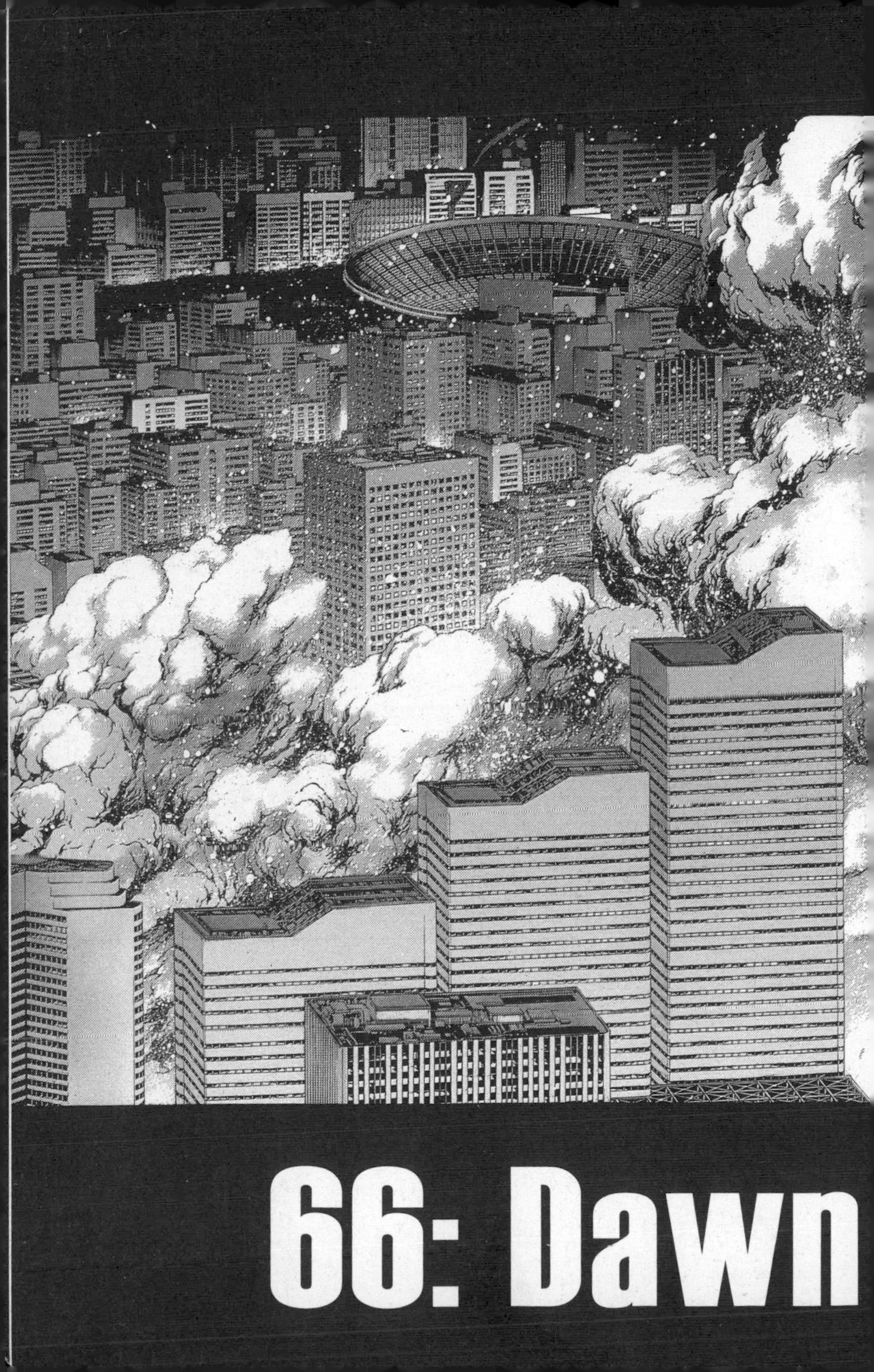

66: Dawn

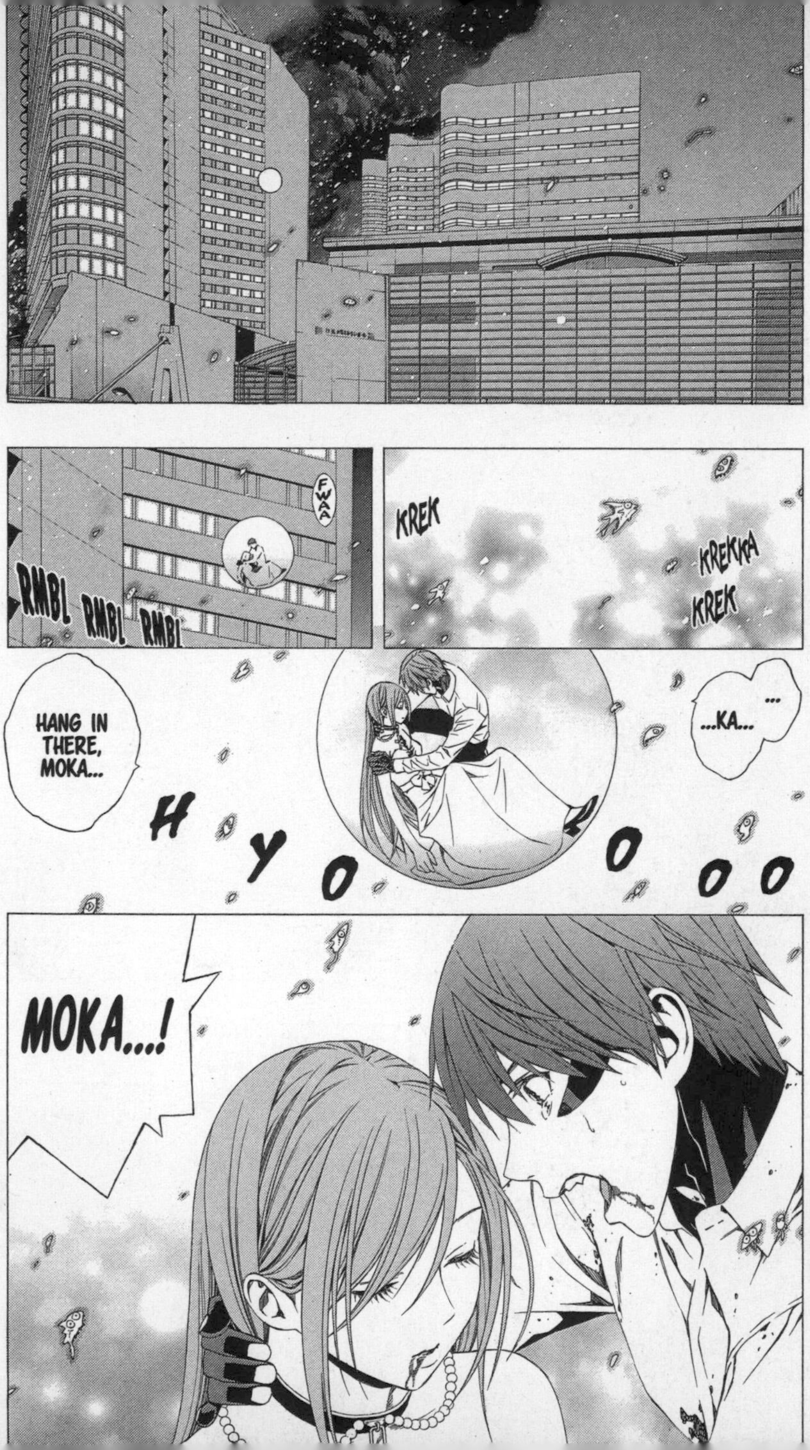
KREK
KREKKA
KREK
FWAA
RMBL RMBL RMBL
...
...KA...
HYOOOO
HANG IN THERE, MOKA...
MOKA...!

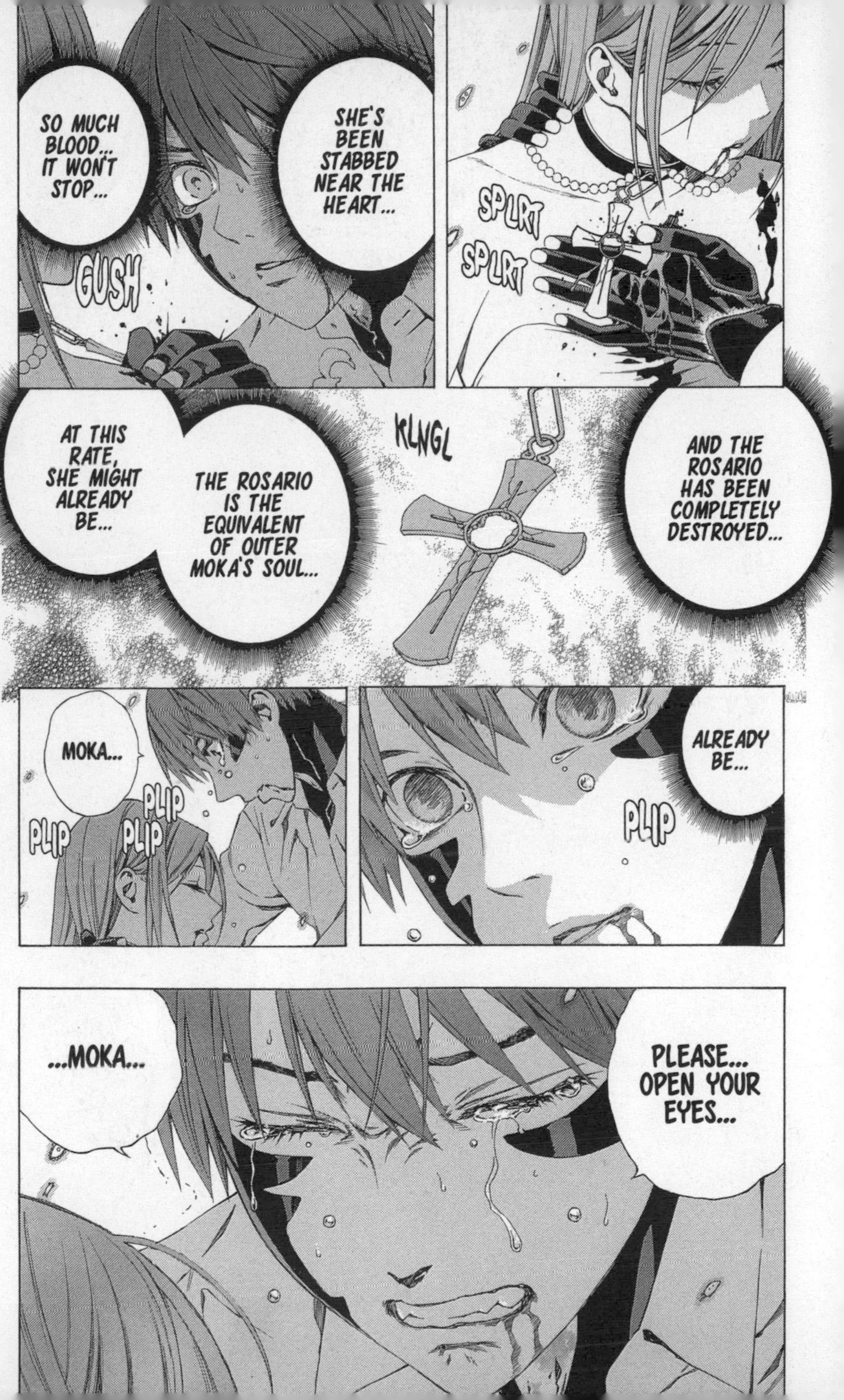
SPLRT
SPLRT
SHE'S BEEN STABBED NEAR THE HEART...
SO MUCH BLOOD... IT WON'T STOP...
GUSH
AND THE ROSARIO HAS BEEN COMPLETELY DESTROYED...
KLNGL
THE ROSARIO IS THE EQUIVALENT OF OUTER MOKA'S SOUL...
AT THIS RATE, SHE MIGHT ALREADY BE...
ALREADY BE...
PLIP
MOKA...
PLIP
PLIP
PLIP
PLEASE... OPEN YOUR EYES...
...MOKA...

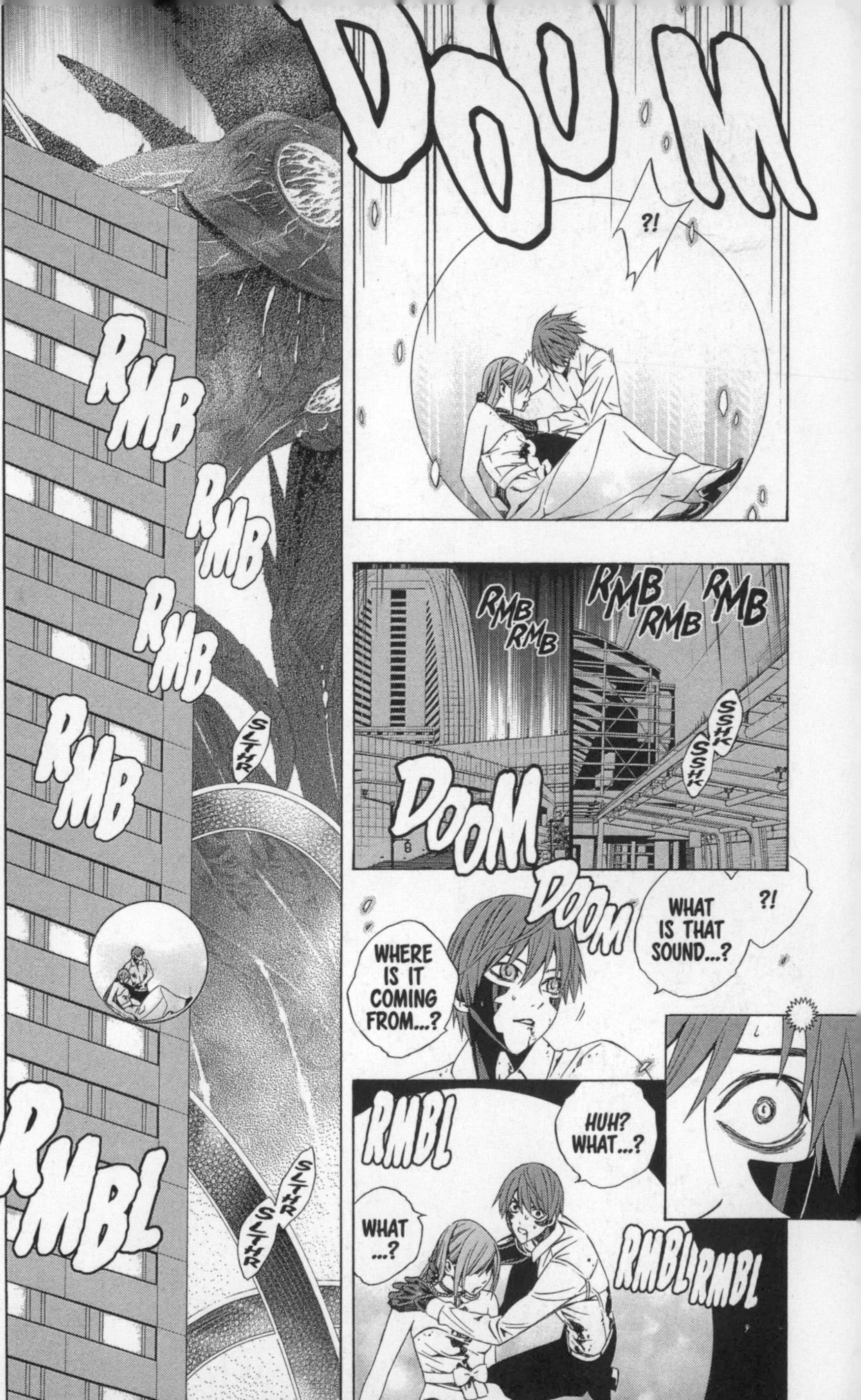
DOOM
?!
RMB RMB
RMB RMB RMB
SSHK SSHK
DOOM
DOOM
?!
WHAT IS THAT SOUND...?
WHERE IS IT COMING FROM...?
RMBL
HUH? WHAT...?
RMBL RMBL
WHAT ...?
RMB
RMB
RMB
RMB
SLTHR
RMBL
SLTHR SLTHR

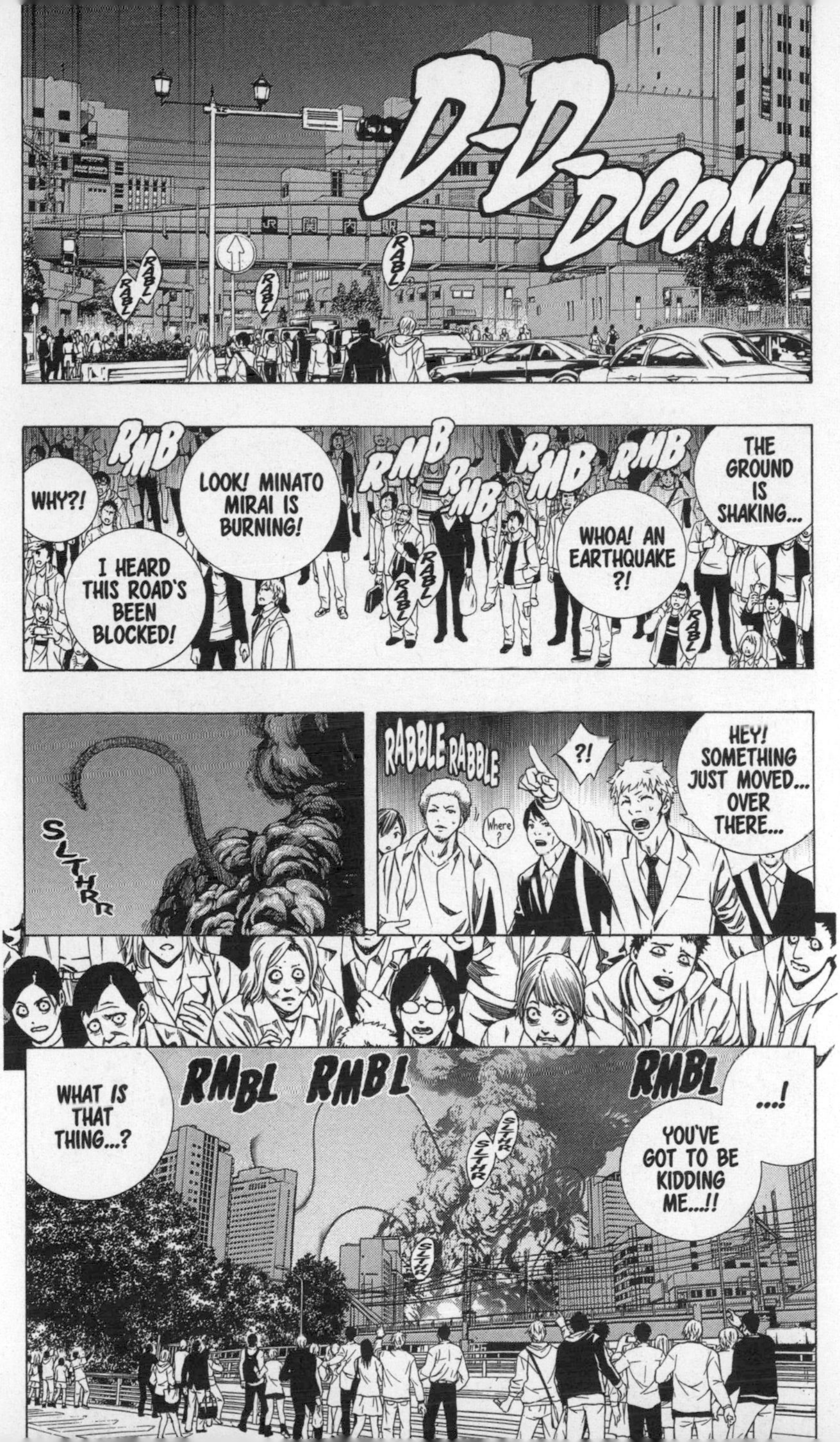
D-D-DOOM
JR 関内駅
RABL
RABL
RABL
RABL
THE GROUND IS SHAKING...
RMB
WHOA! AN EARTHQUAKE?!
RABL
RMB
RMB
RMB
RABL
RABL
LOOK! MINATO MIRAI IS BURNING!
RMB
WHY?!
I HEARD THIS ROAD'S BEEN BLOCKED!
HEY! SOMETHING JUST MOVED... OVER THERE...
?!
Where?
RABBLE RABBLE
SLTHRR
RMBL
...!
YOU'VE GOT TO BE KIDDING ME...!!
SLTHR
SLTHR
SLTHR
RMBL RMBL
WHAT IS THAT THING...?

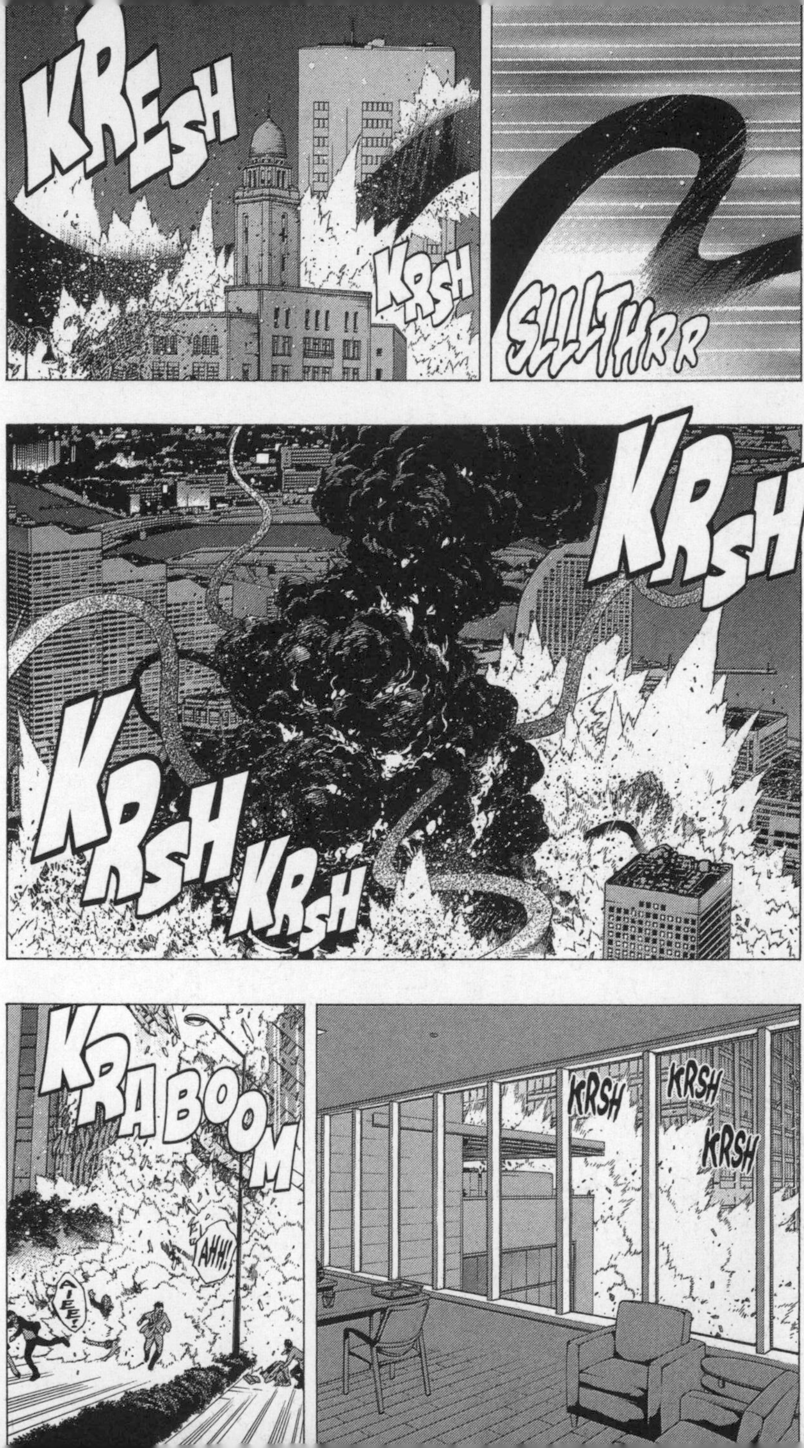
SLLLTHRR
KRESH
KRSH
KRSH
KRSH
KRSH
KRSH
KRSH
KRSH
KRABOOM
AHH!
AIEE!

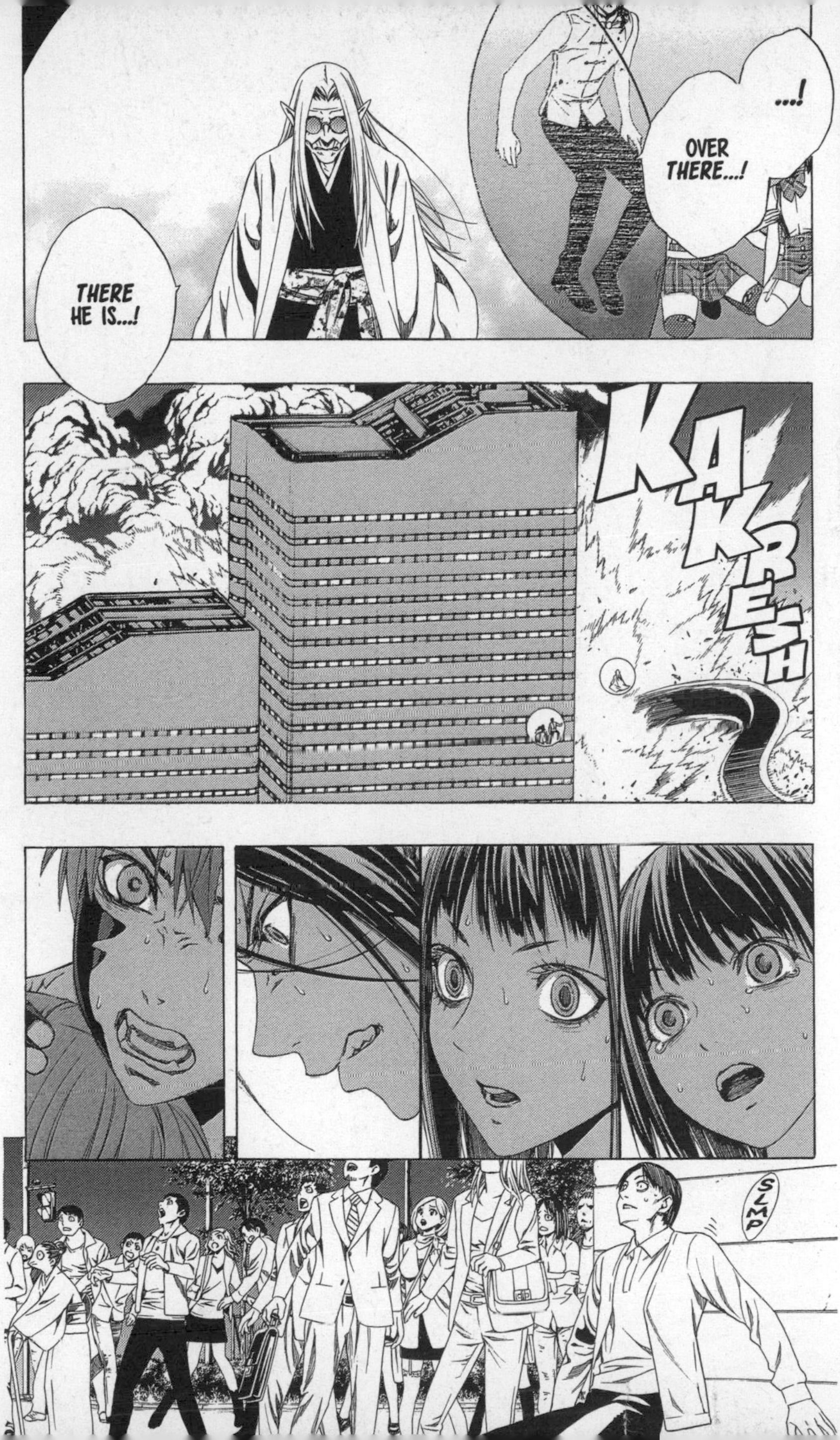
...!
OVER THERE...!
THERE HE IS...!
KAKRESH
SLMP

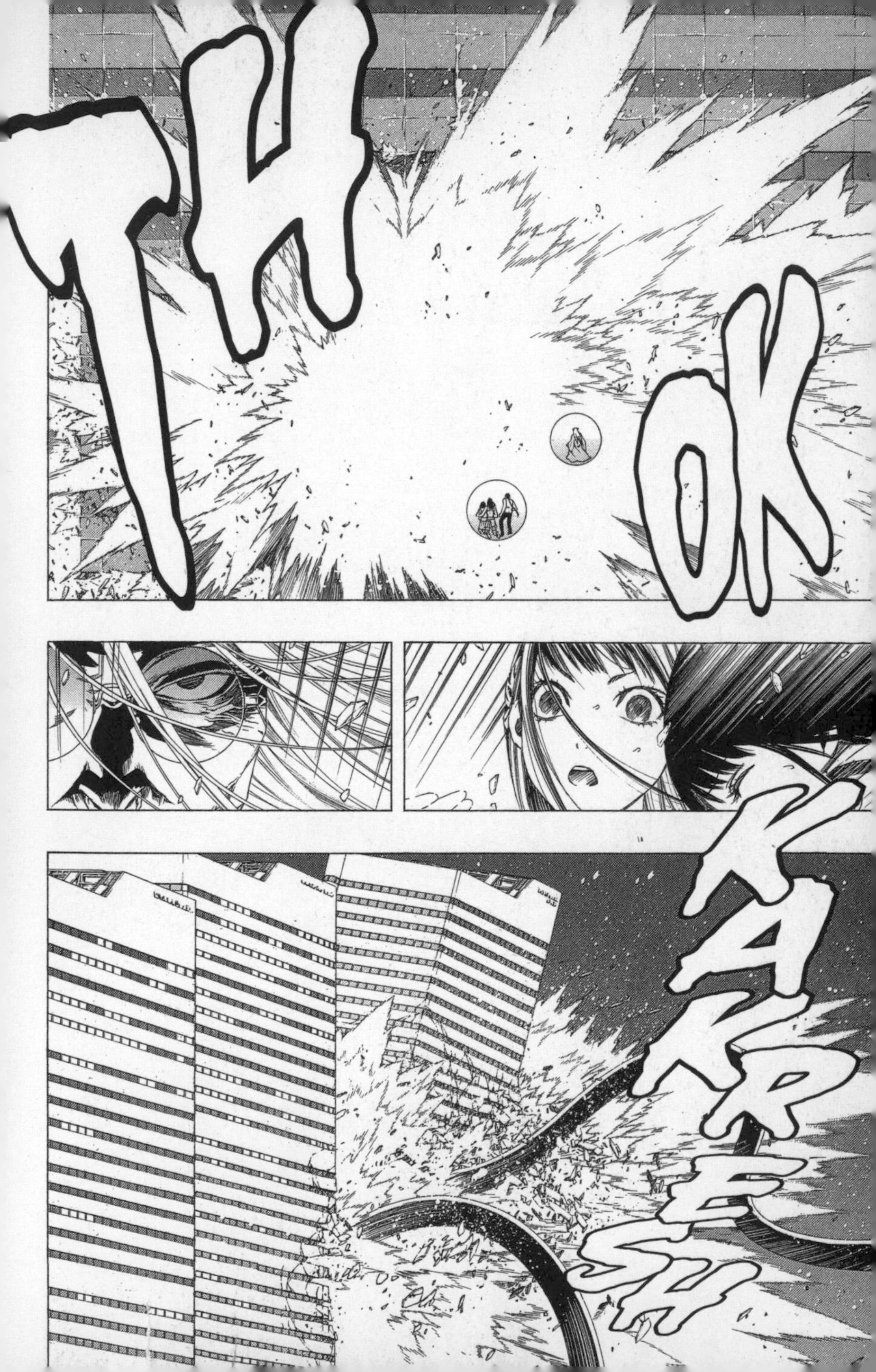
TH OK
KAKRESH

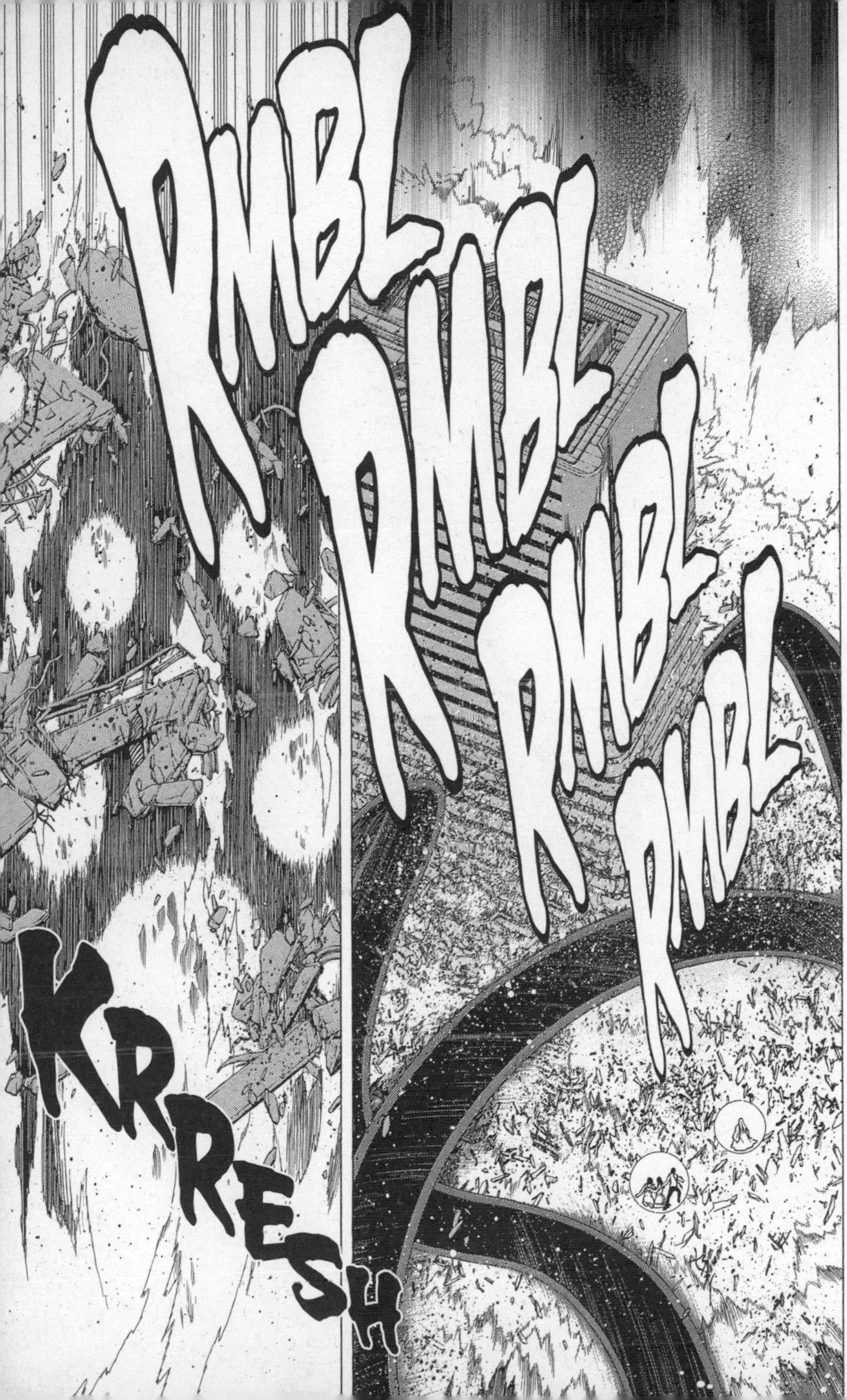
RMBL RMBL RMBL RMBL RMBL
KRRESH

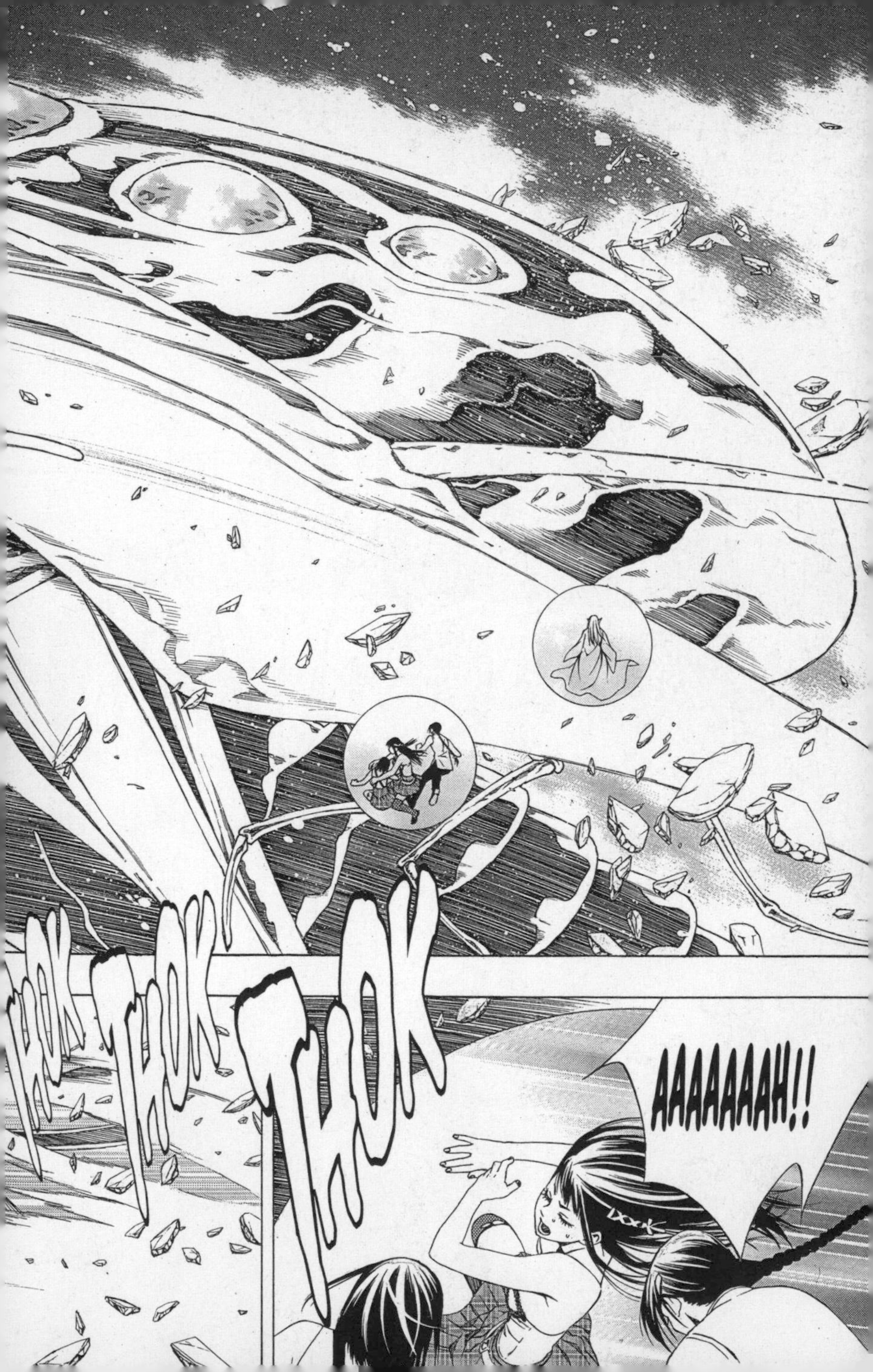
AAAAAAH!!
THOK
THOK
THOK

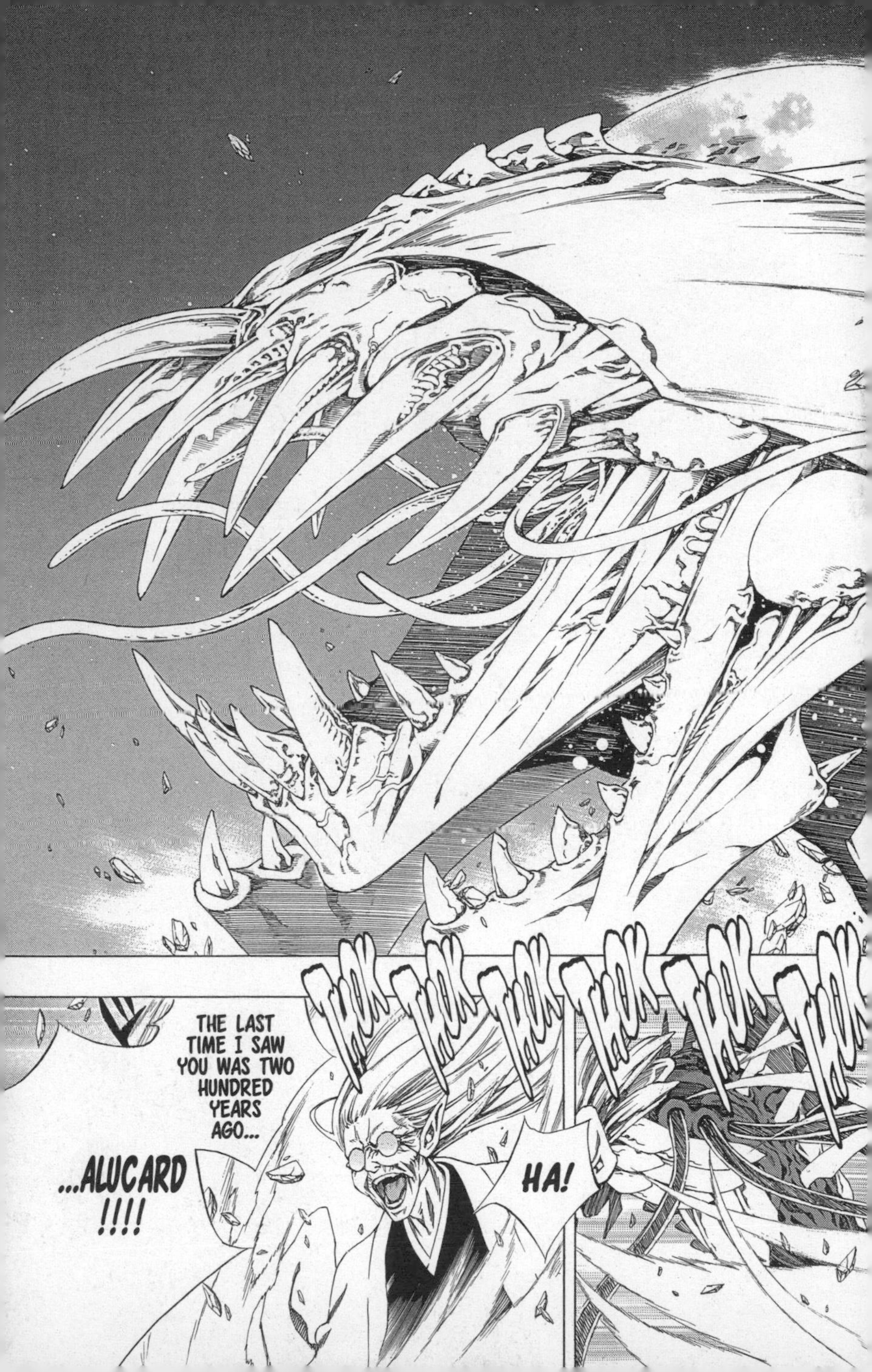
THOK THOK THOK THOK THOK THOK
HA!
THE LAST TIME I SAW YOU WAS TWO HUNDRED YEARS AGO...
...ALUCARD !!!!

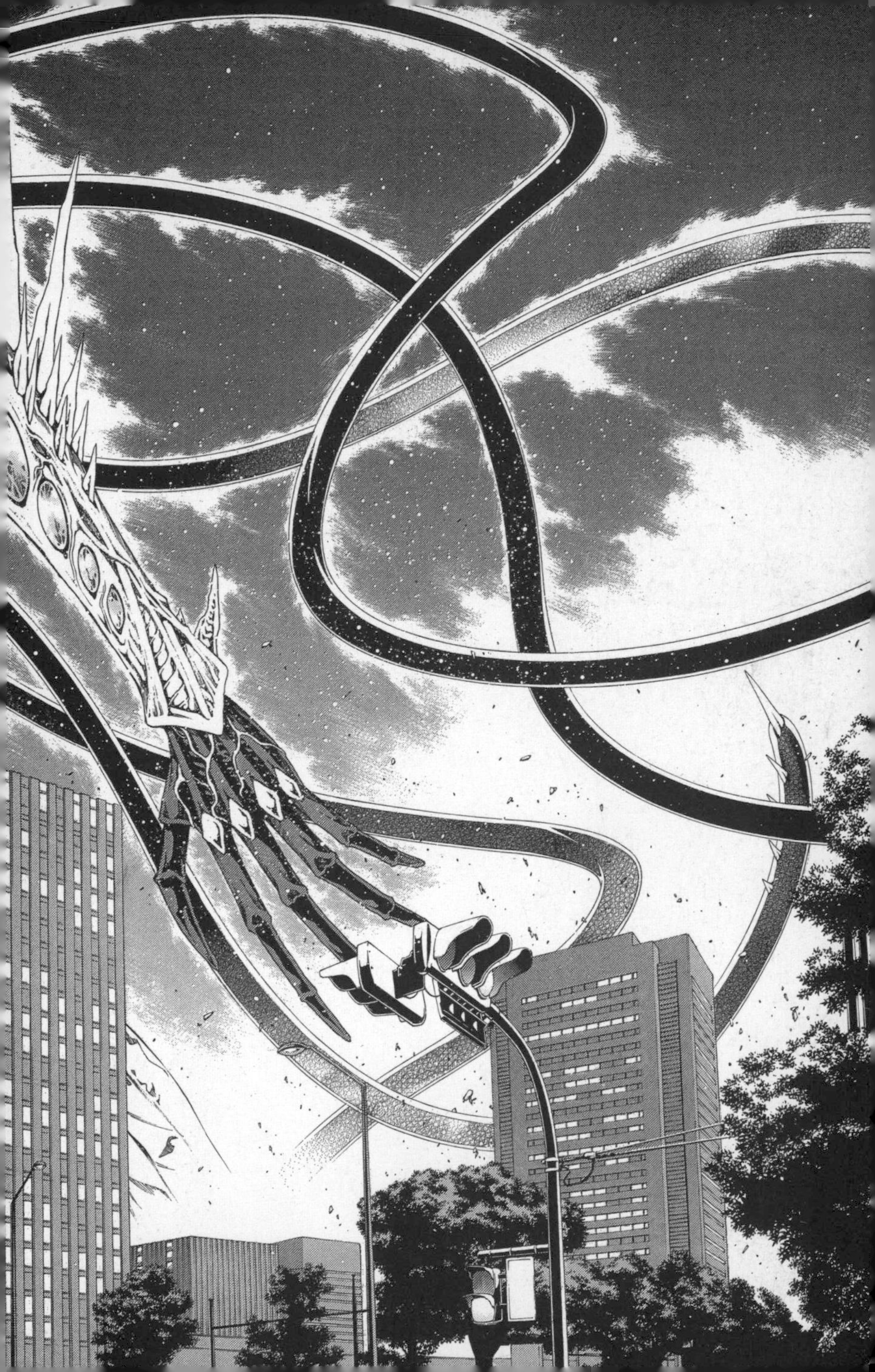

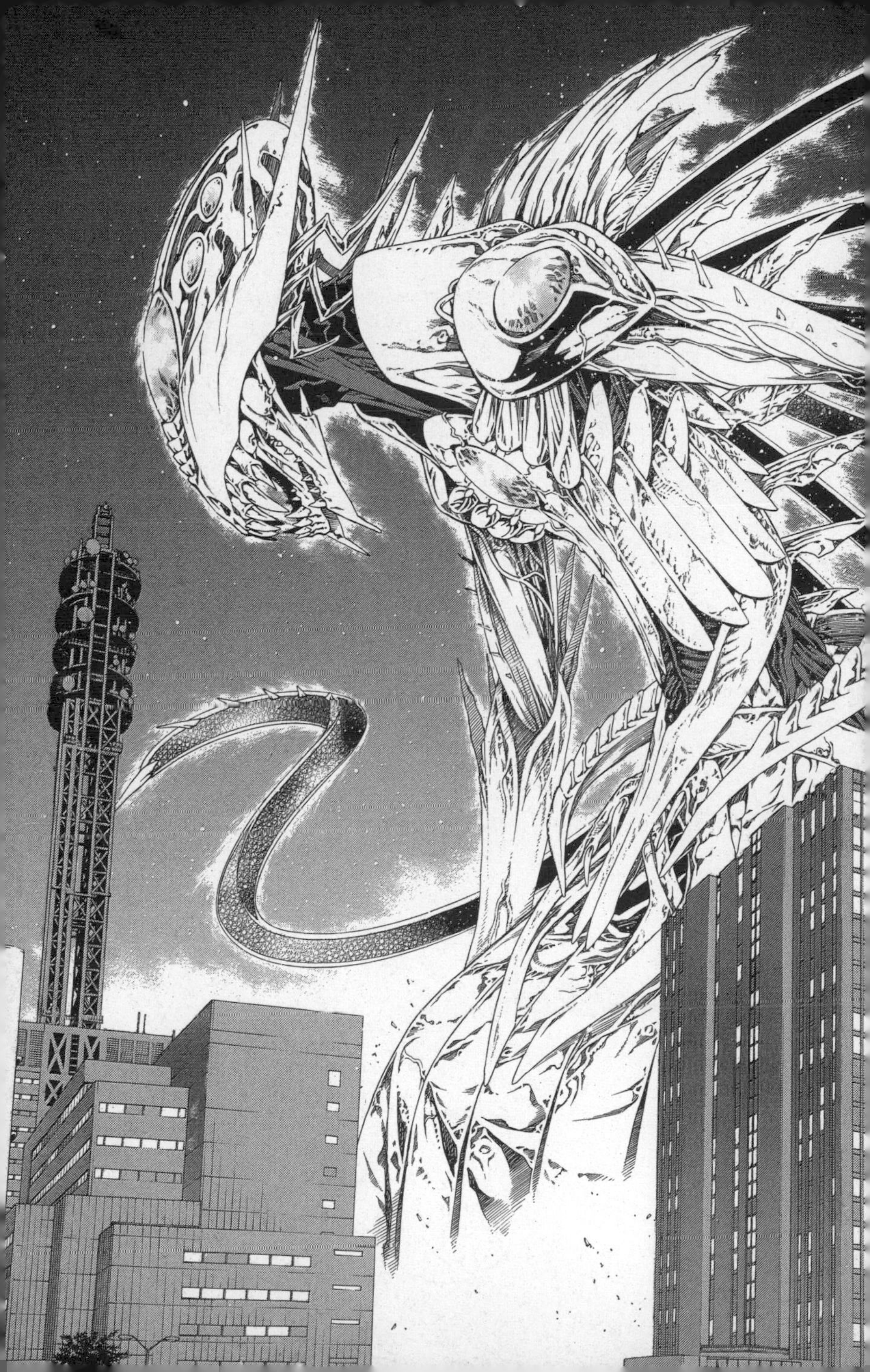

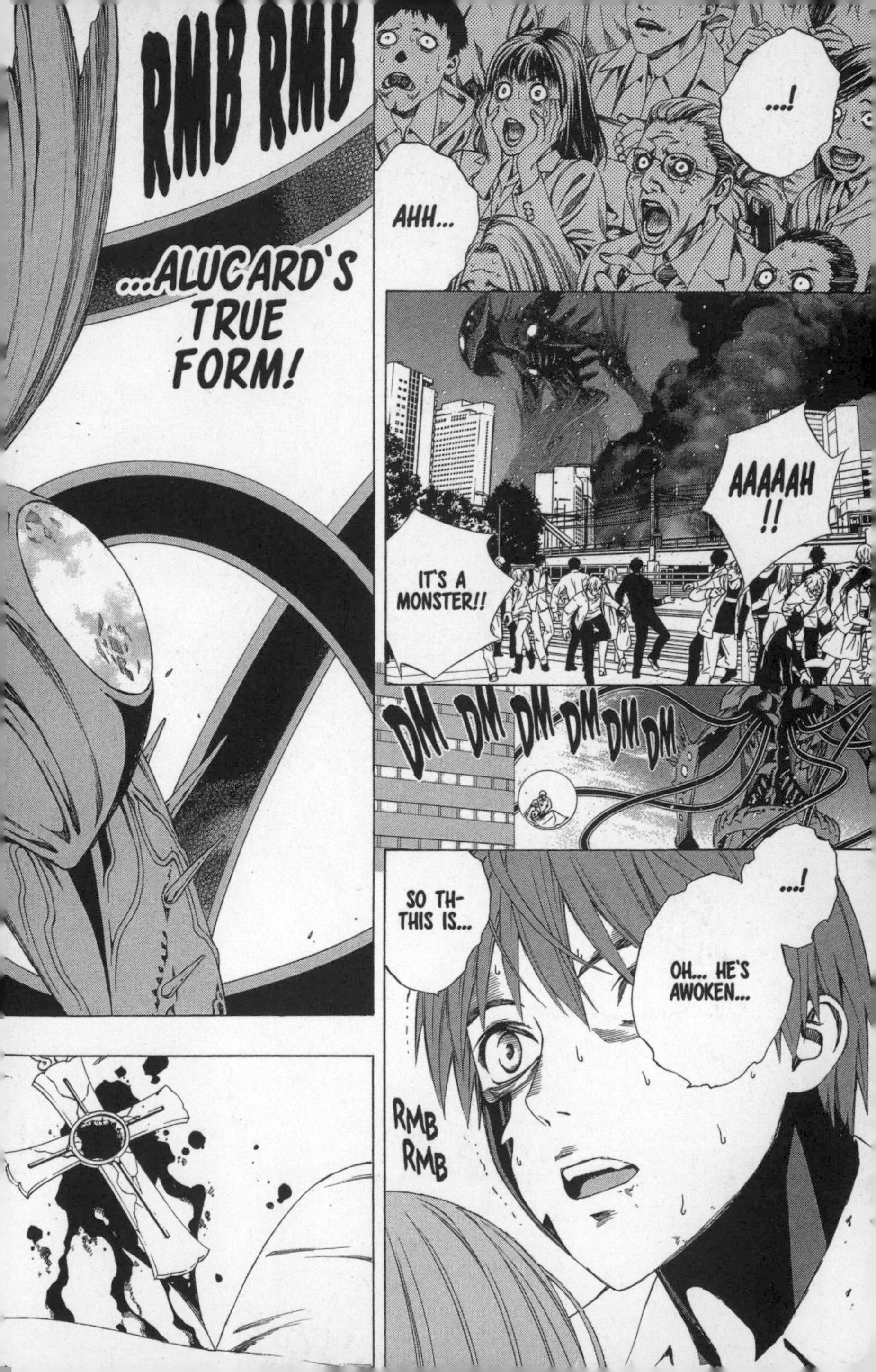
...!
AHH...
AAAAAH!!
IT'S A MONSTER!!
DM DM DM DM DM DM
...!
OH... HE'S AWOKEN...
SO TH-THIS IS...
RMB RMB
RMB RMB
...ALUCARD'S TRUE FORM!

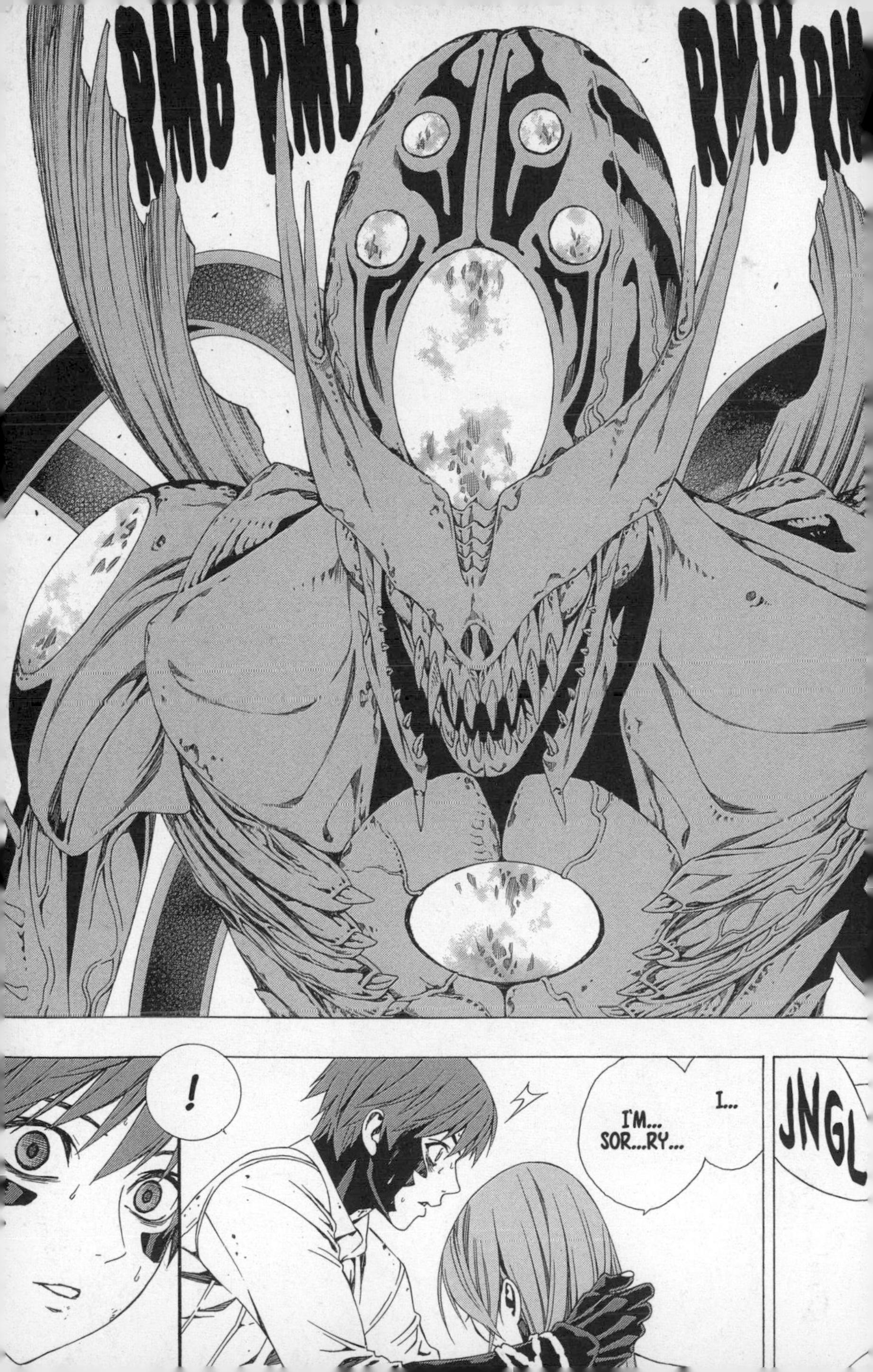
RMB RM
RMB RMB
JNGL
I...
I'M... SOR...RY...
!

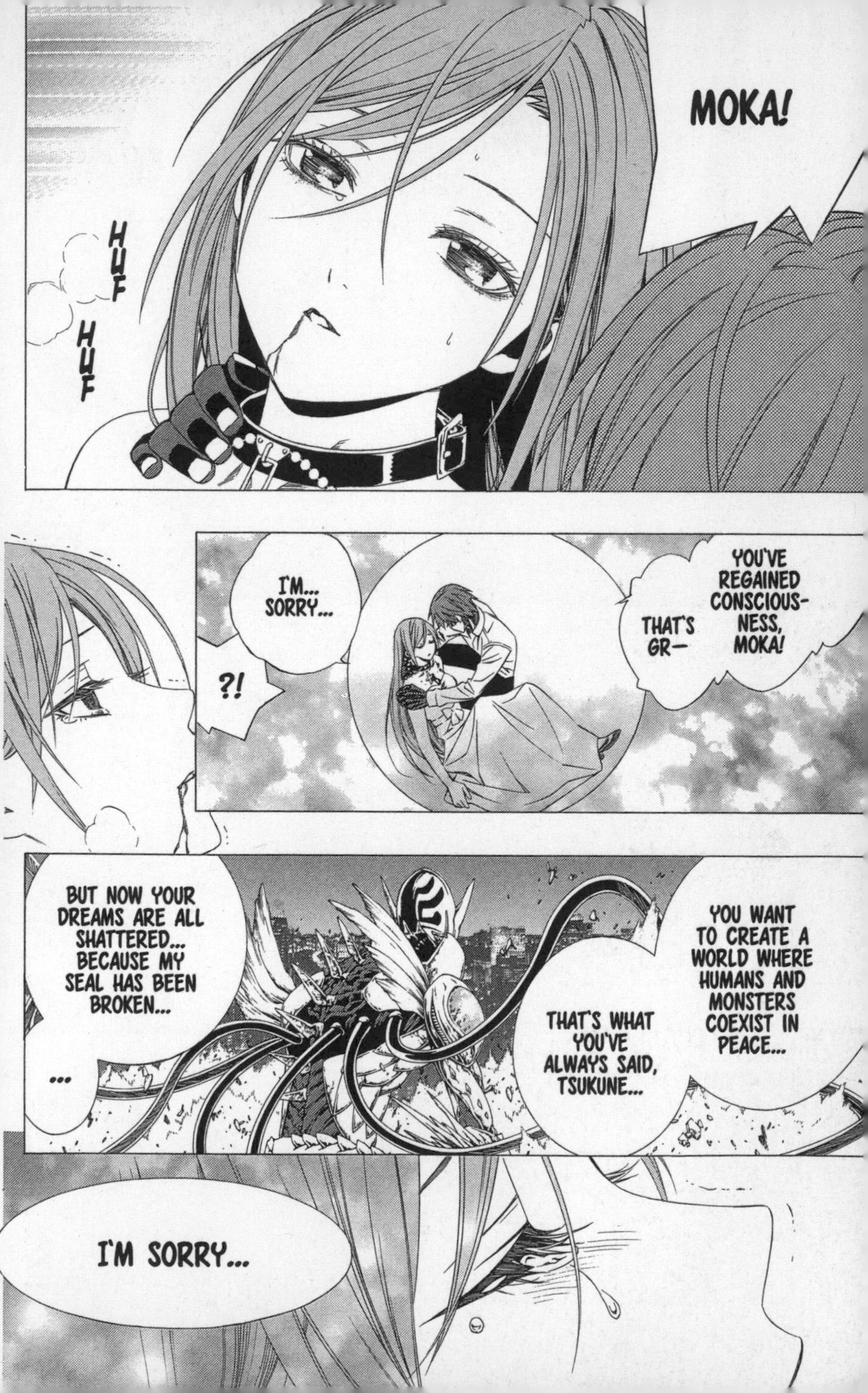
MOKA!
HUF HUF
YOU'VE REGAINED CONSCIOUSNESS, MOKA!
THAT'S GR—
I'M... SORRY...
?!
YOU WANT TO CREATE A WORLD WHERE HUMANS AND MONSTERS COEXIST IN PEACE...
THAT'S WHAT YOU'VE ALWAYS SAID, TSUKUNE...
BUT NOW YOUR DREAMS ARE ALL SHATTERED... BECAUSE MY SEAL HAS BEEN BROKEN...
...
I'M SORRY...

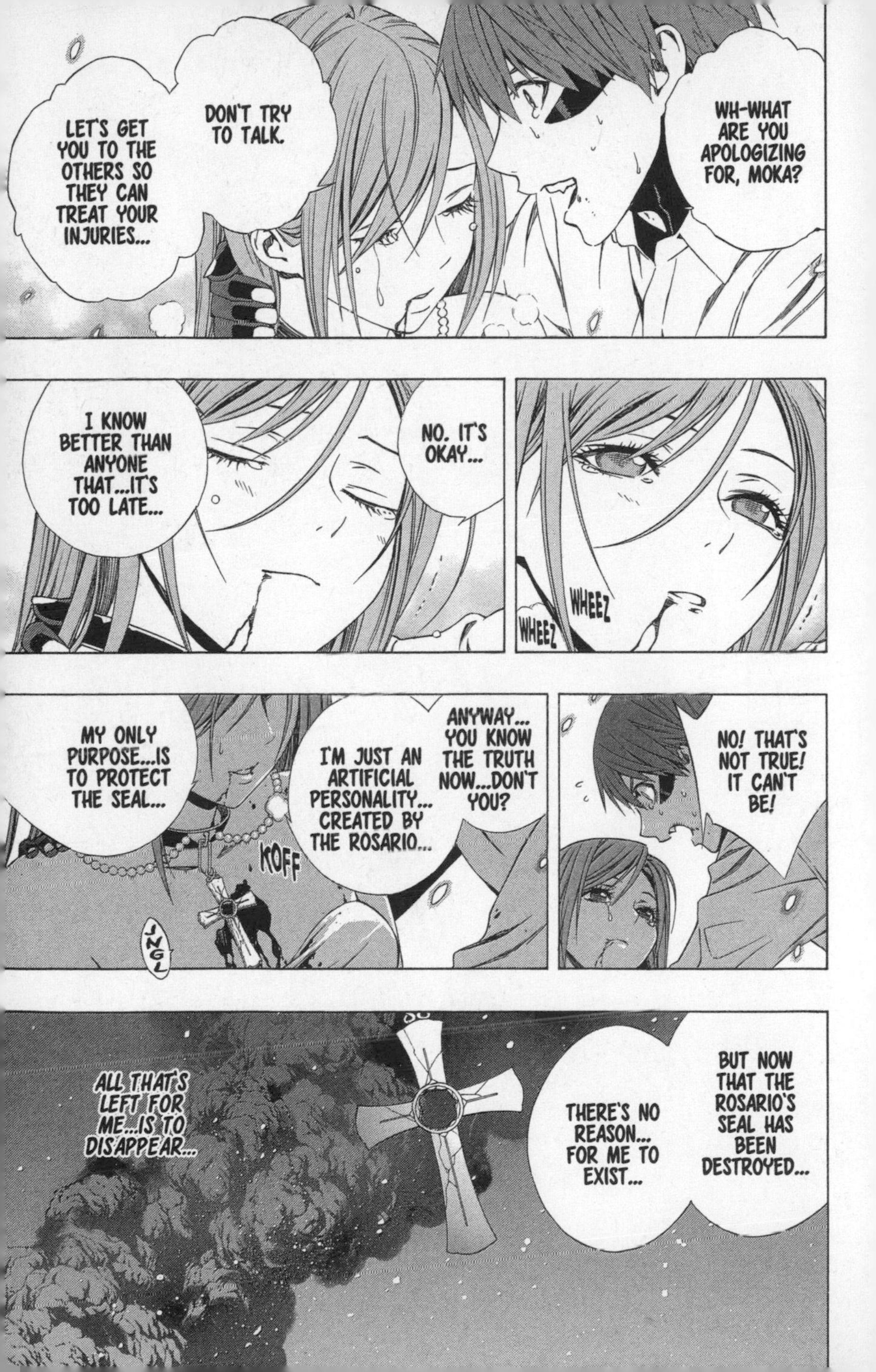
WH-WHAT ARE YOU APOLOGIZING FOR, MOKA?
DON'T TRY TO TALK.
LET'S GET YOU TO THE OTHERS SO THEY CAN TREAT YOUR INJURIES...
WHEEZ
WHEEZ
NO. IT'S OKAY...
I KNOW BETTER THAN ANYONE THAT...IT'S TOO LATE...
NO! THAT'S NOT TRUE! IT CAN'T BE!
ANYWAY... YOU KNOW THE TRUTH NOW...DON'T YOU?
I'M JUST AN ARTIFICIAL PERSONALITY... CREATED BY THE ROSARIO...
KOFF
MY ONLY PURPOSE...IS TO PROTECT THE SEAL...
JNGL
BUT NOW THAT THE ROSARIO'S SEAL HAS BEEN DESTROYED...
THERE'S NO REASON... FOR ME TO EXIST...
ALL THAT'S LEFT FOR ME...IS TO DISAPPEAR...

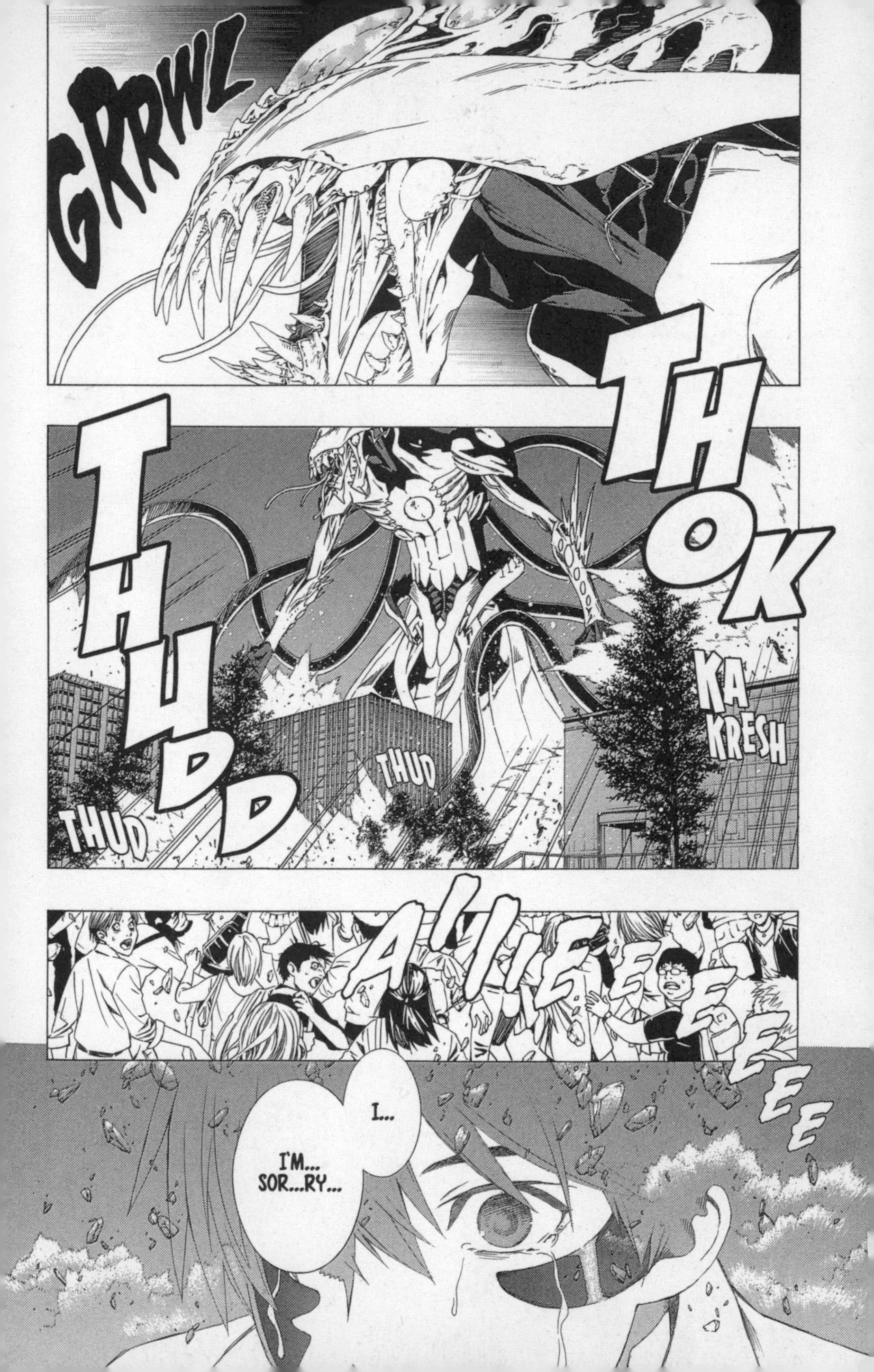
GRRWL
THOK
KA KRESH
THUD
THUDD
THUD
AIIIEEEEEEEE
I...
I'M... SOR...RY...

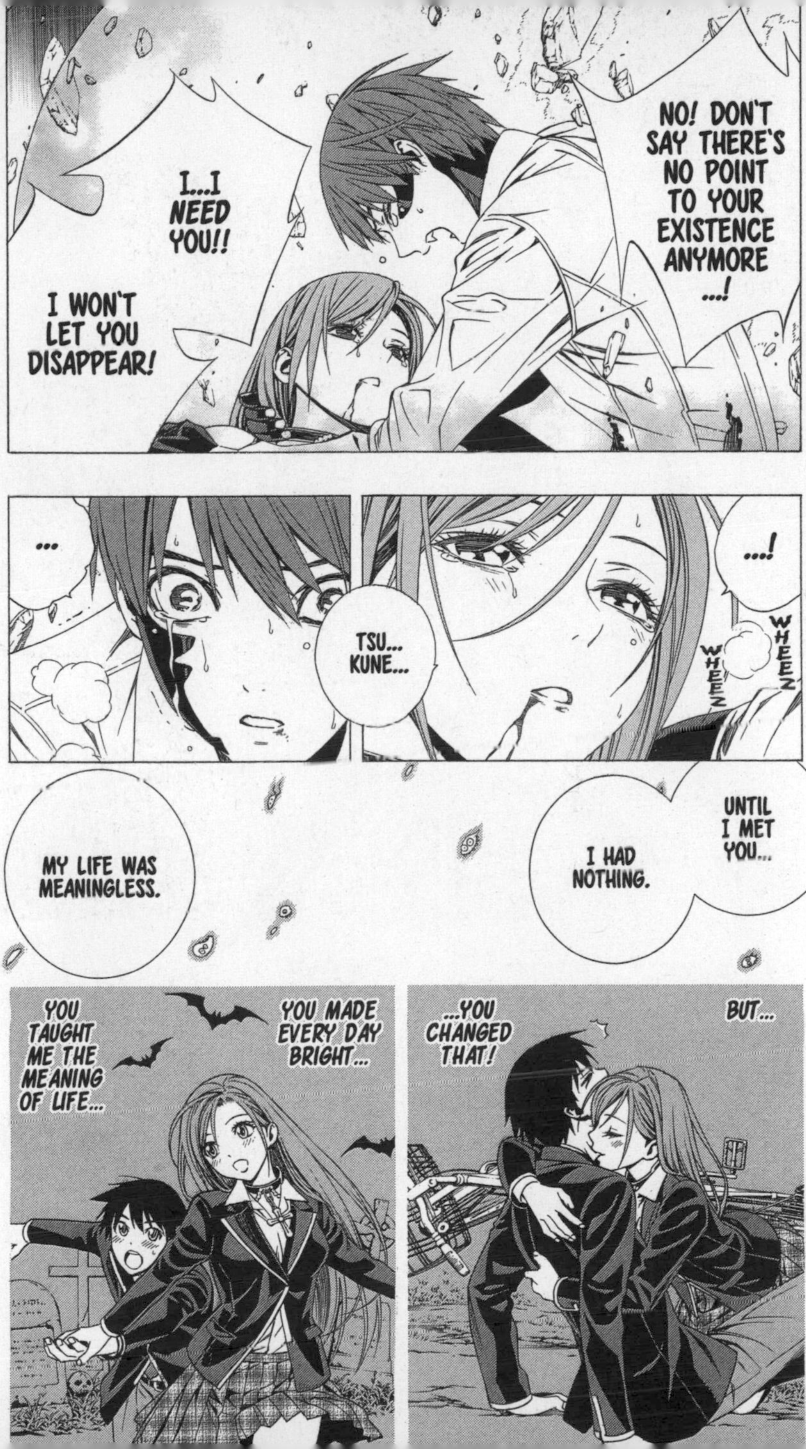
NO! DON'T SAY THERE'S NO POINT TO YOUR EXISTENCE ANYMORE ...!
I...I NEED YOU!!
I WON'T LET YOU DISAPPEAR!
...!
WHEEZ
WHEEZ
TSU... KUNE...
...
UNTIL I MET YOU...
I HAD NOTHING.
MY LIFE WAS MEANINGLESS.
BUT...
...YOU CHANGED THAT!
YOU MADE EVERY DAY BRIGHT...
YOU TAUGHT ME THE MEANING OF LIFE...

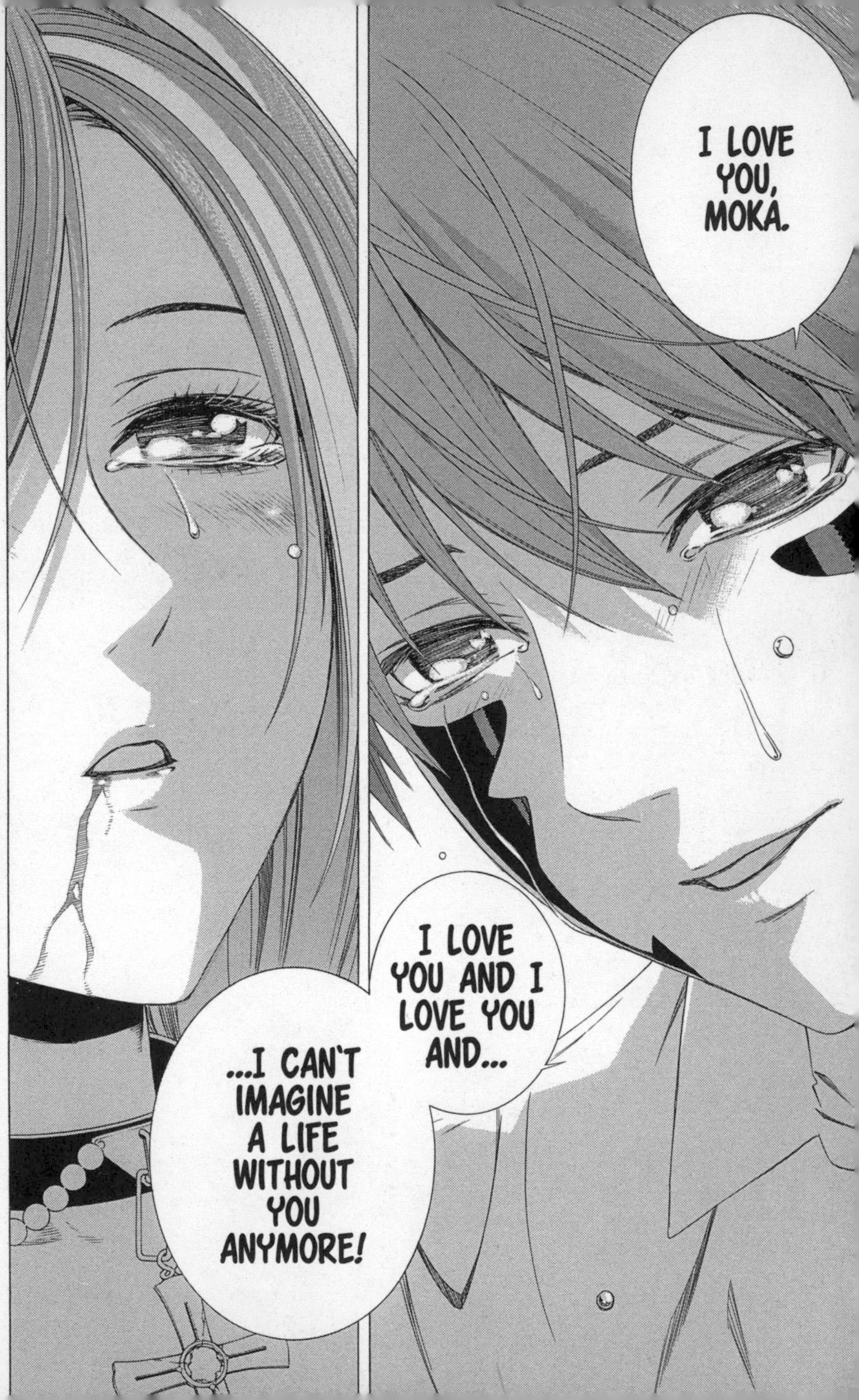
I LOVE YOU, MOKA.
I LOVE YOU AND I LOVE YOU AND...
...I CAN'T IMAGINE A LIFE WITHOUT YOU ANYMORE!

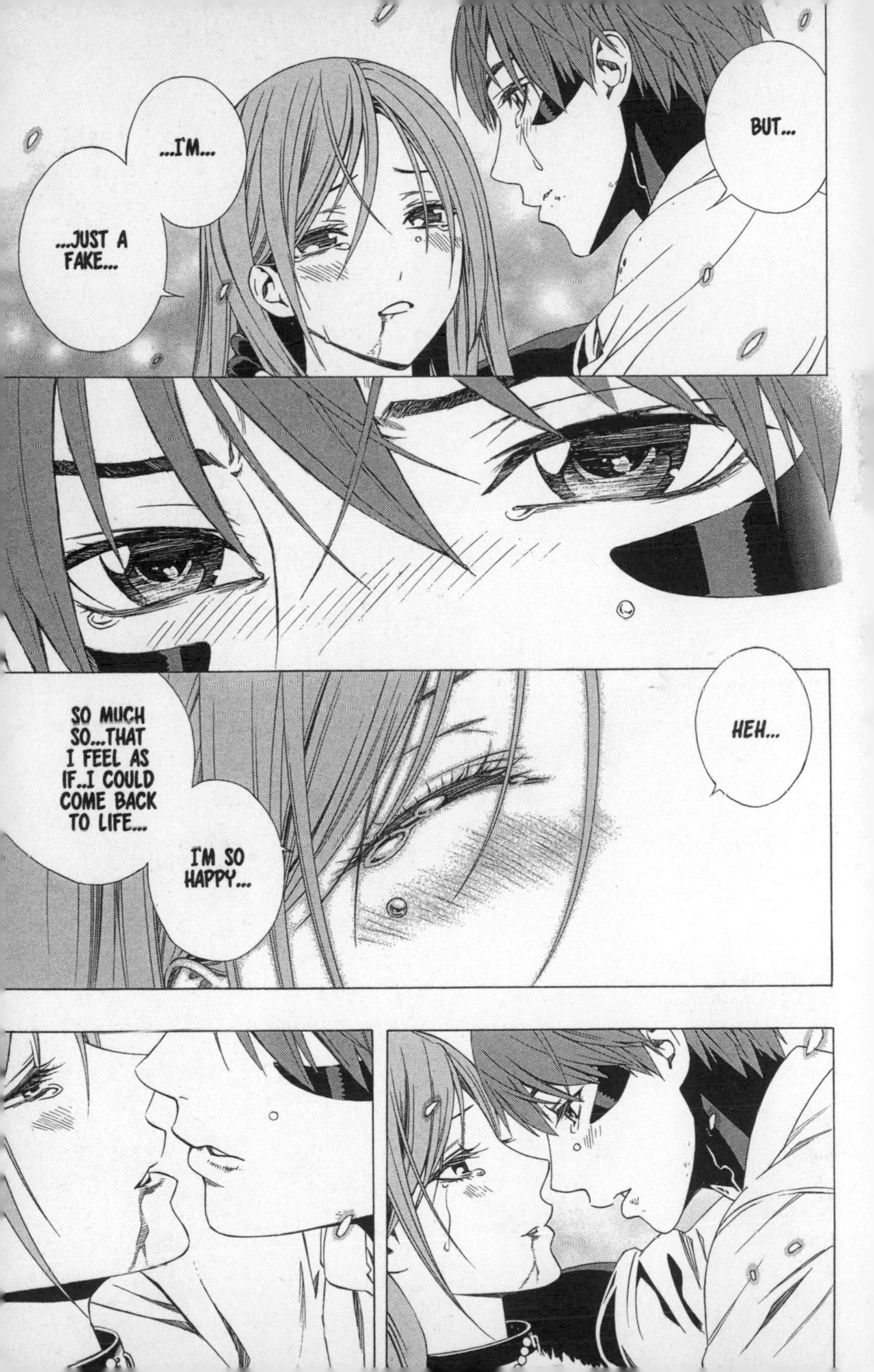
BUT...
...I'M...
...JUST A FAKE...
HEH...
I'M SO HAPPY...
SO MUCH SO...THAT I FEEL AS IF..I COULD COME BACK TO LIFE...

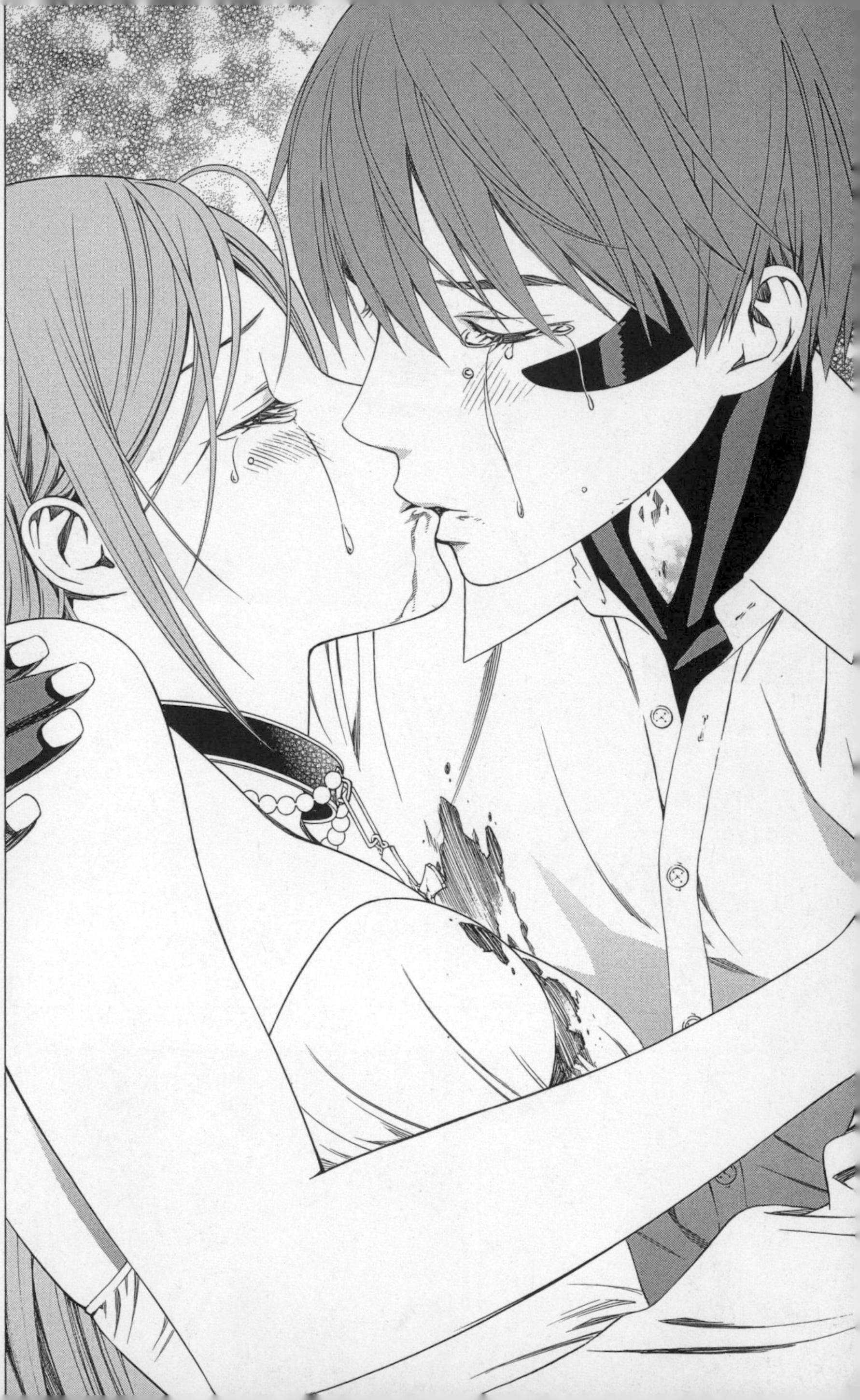

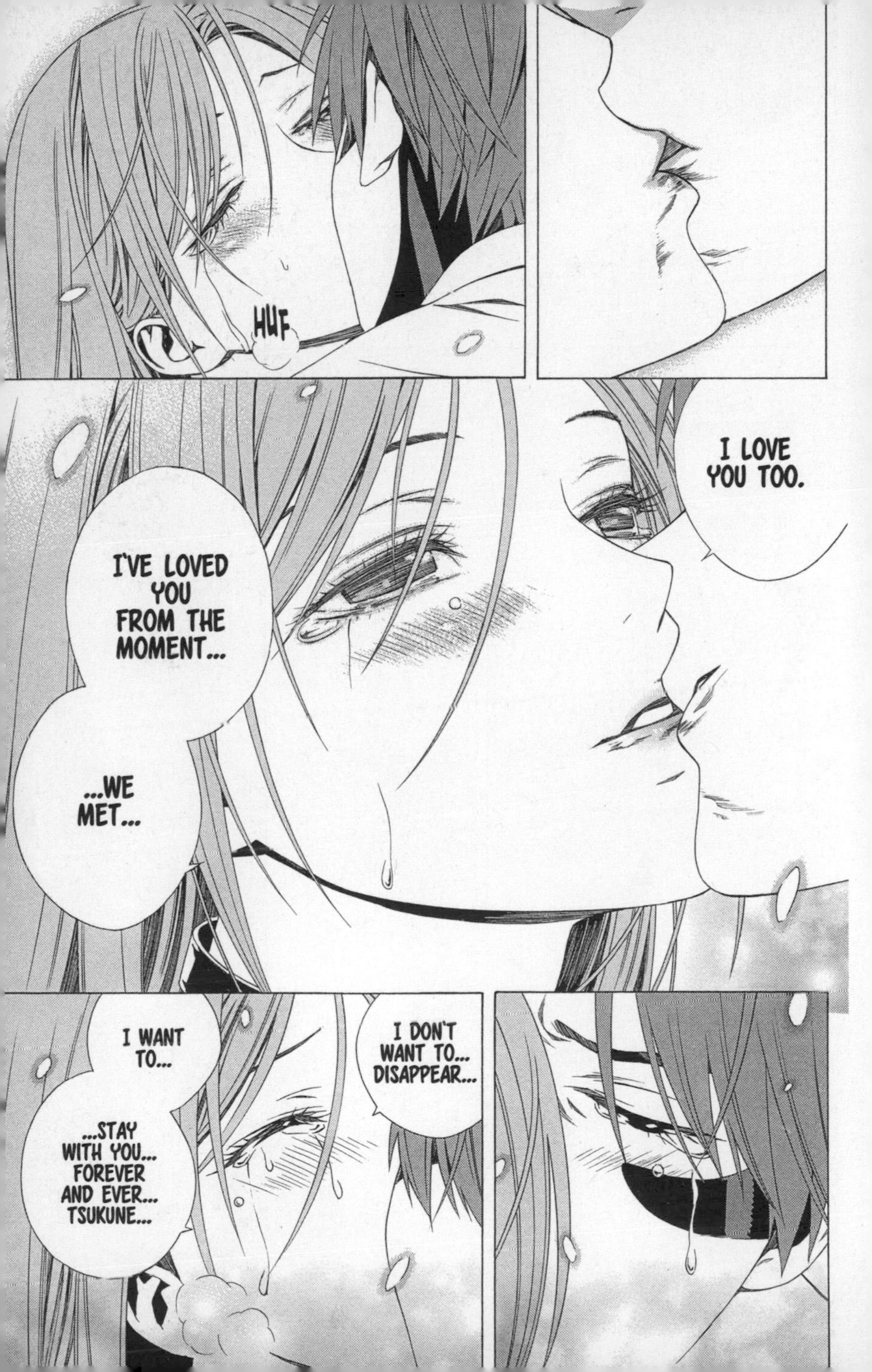
HUF
I LOVE YOU TOO.
I'VE LOVED YOU FROM THE MOMENT...
...WE MET...
I DON'T WANT TO... DISAPPEAR...
I WANT TO...
...STAY WITH YOU... FOREVER AND EVER... TSUKUNE...

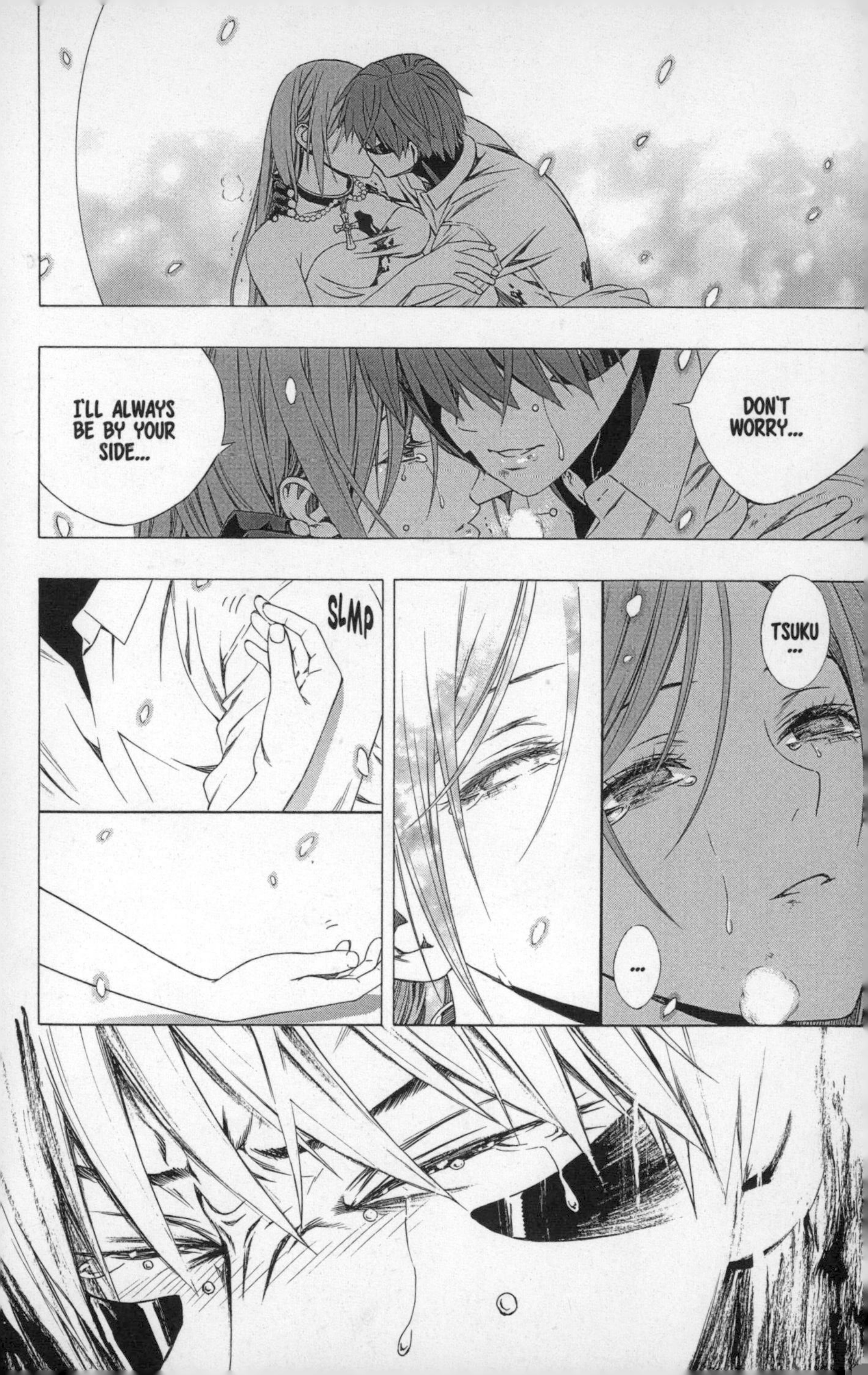
DON'T WORRY...
I'LL ALWAYS BE BY YOUR SIDE...
TSUKU...
...
SLMP

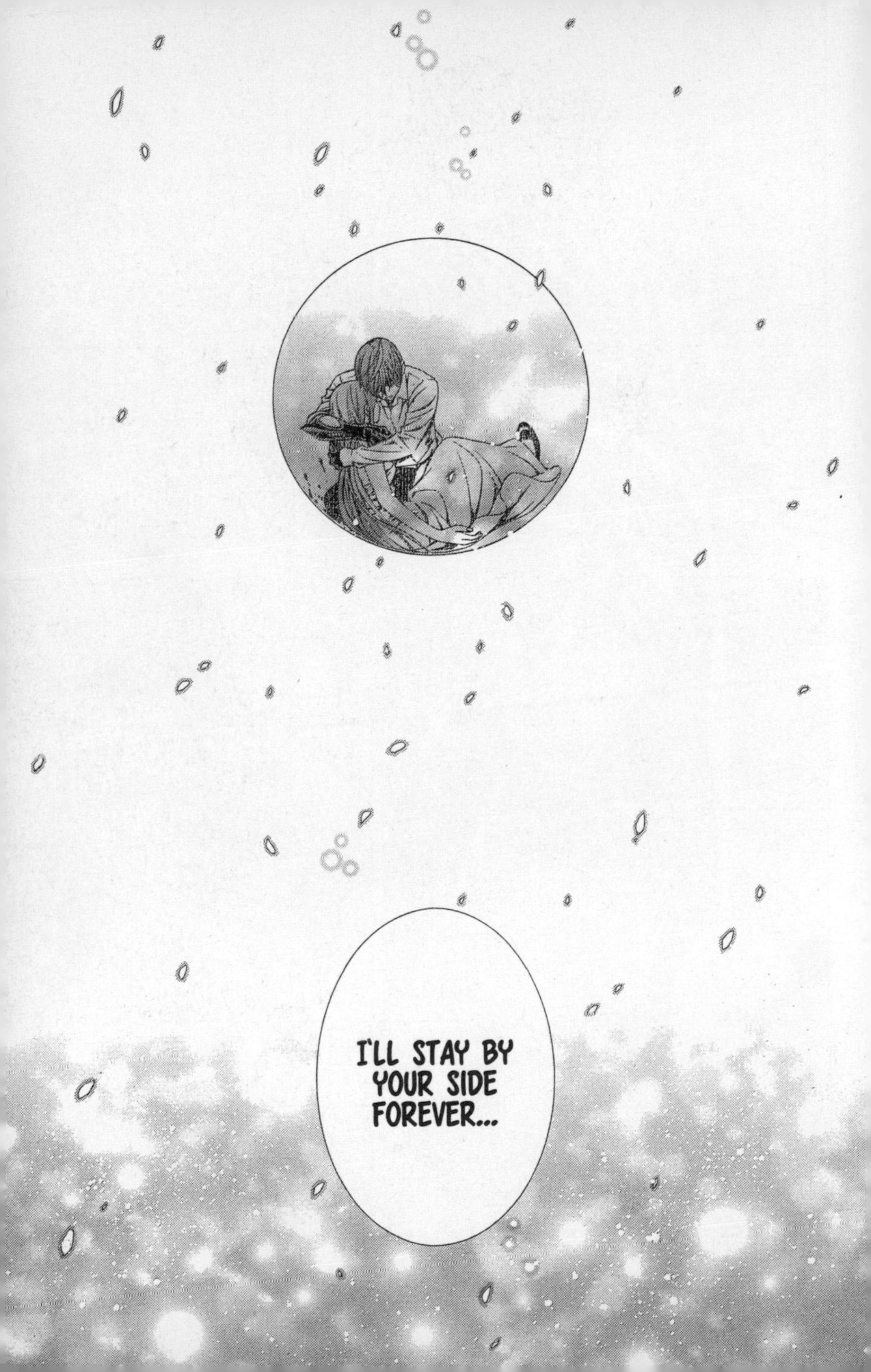
I'LL STAY BY YOUR SIDE FOREVER...

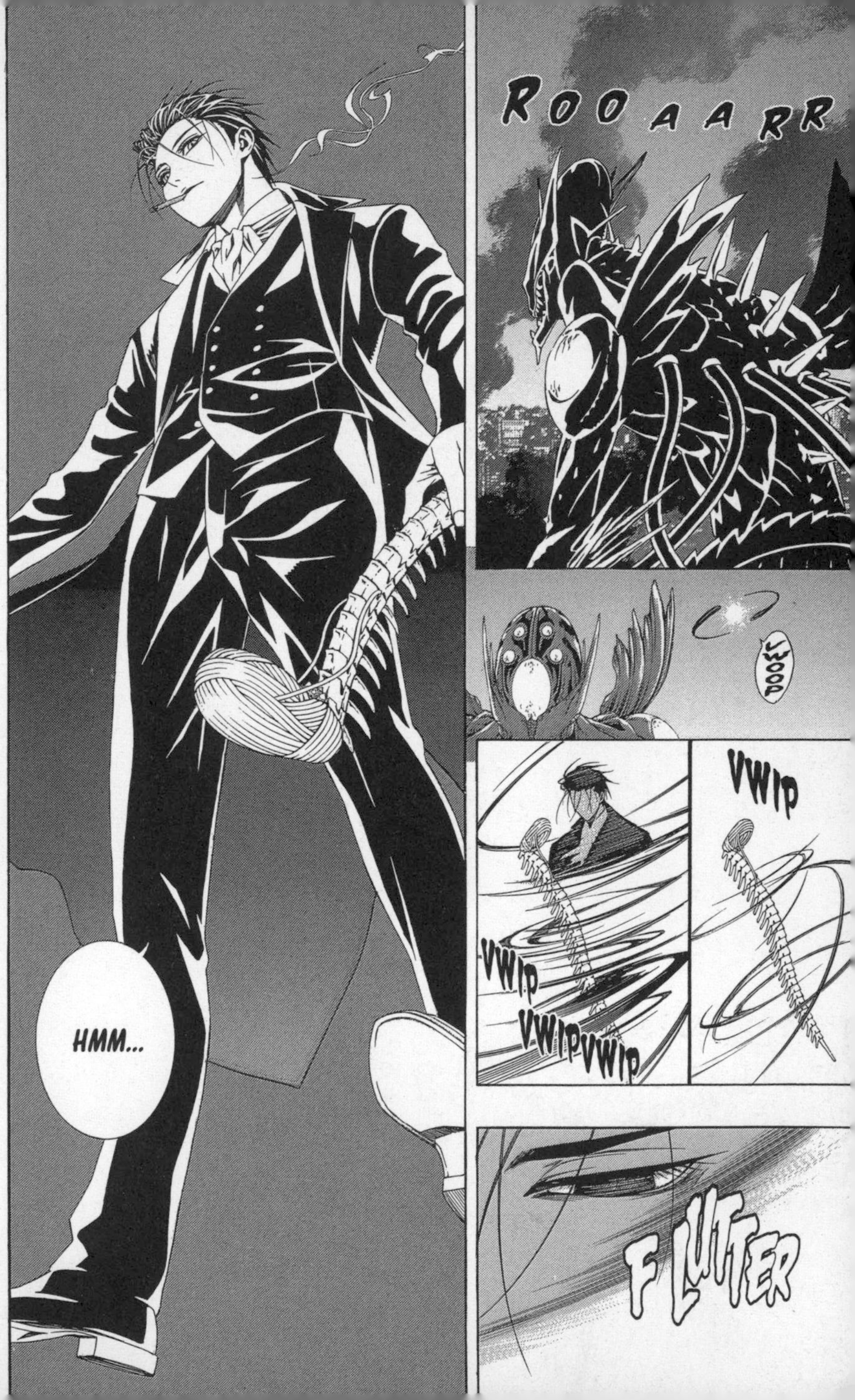
ROOAARR
JWOOP
VWIP
VWIP
VWIPVWIP
FLUTTER
HMM...

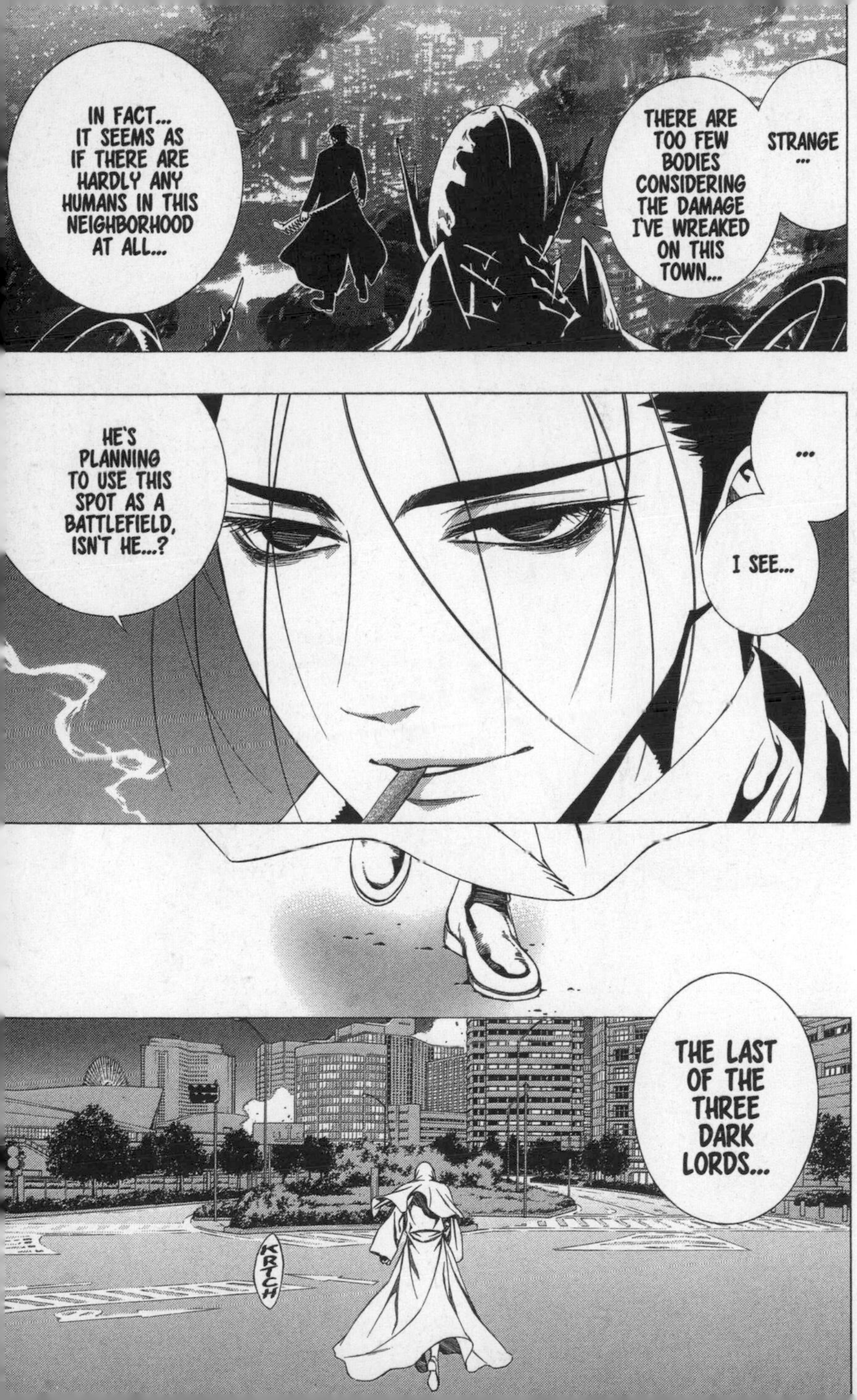
STRANGE ...
THERE ARE TOO FEW BODIES CONSIDERING THE DAMAGE I'VE WREAKED ON THIS TOWN...
IN FACT... IT SEEMS AS IF THERE ARE HARDLY ANY HUMANS IN THIS NEIGHBORHOOD AT ALL...
...
I SEE...
HE'S PLANNING TO USE THIS SPOT AS A BATTLEFIELD, ISN'T HE...?
THE LAST OF THE THREE DARK LORDS...
KRTCH

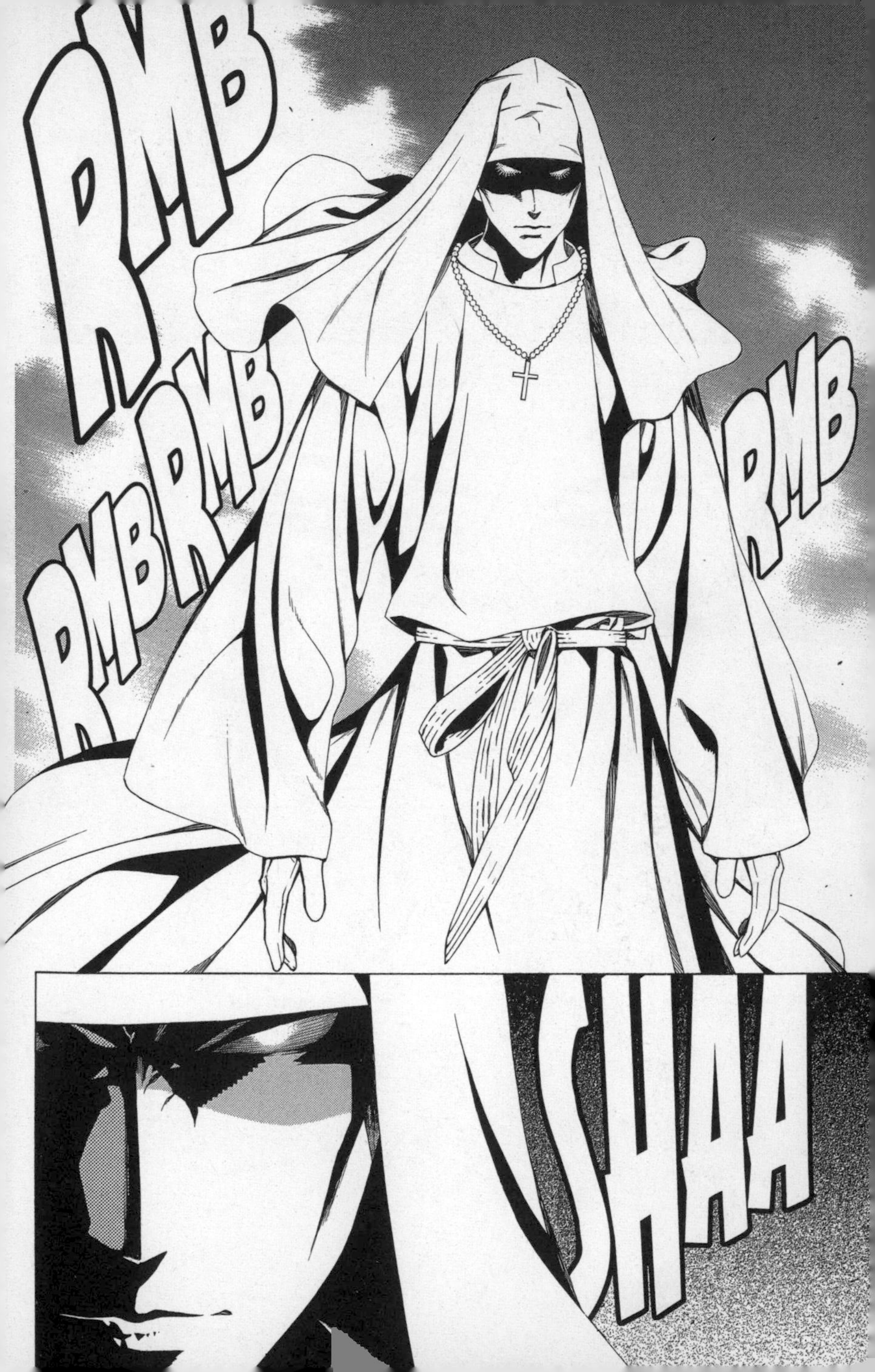
RMB
RMB
RMB
RMB
SHAA

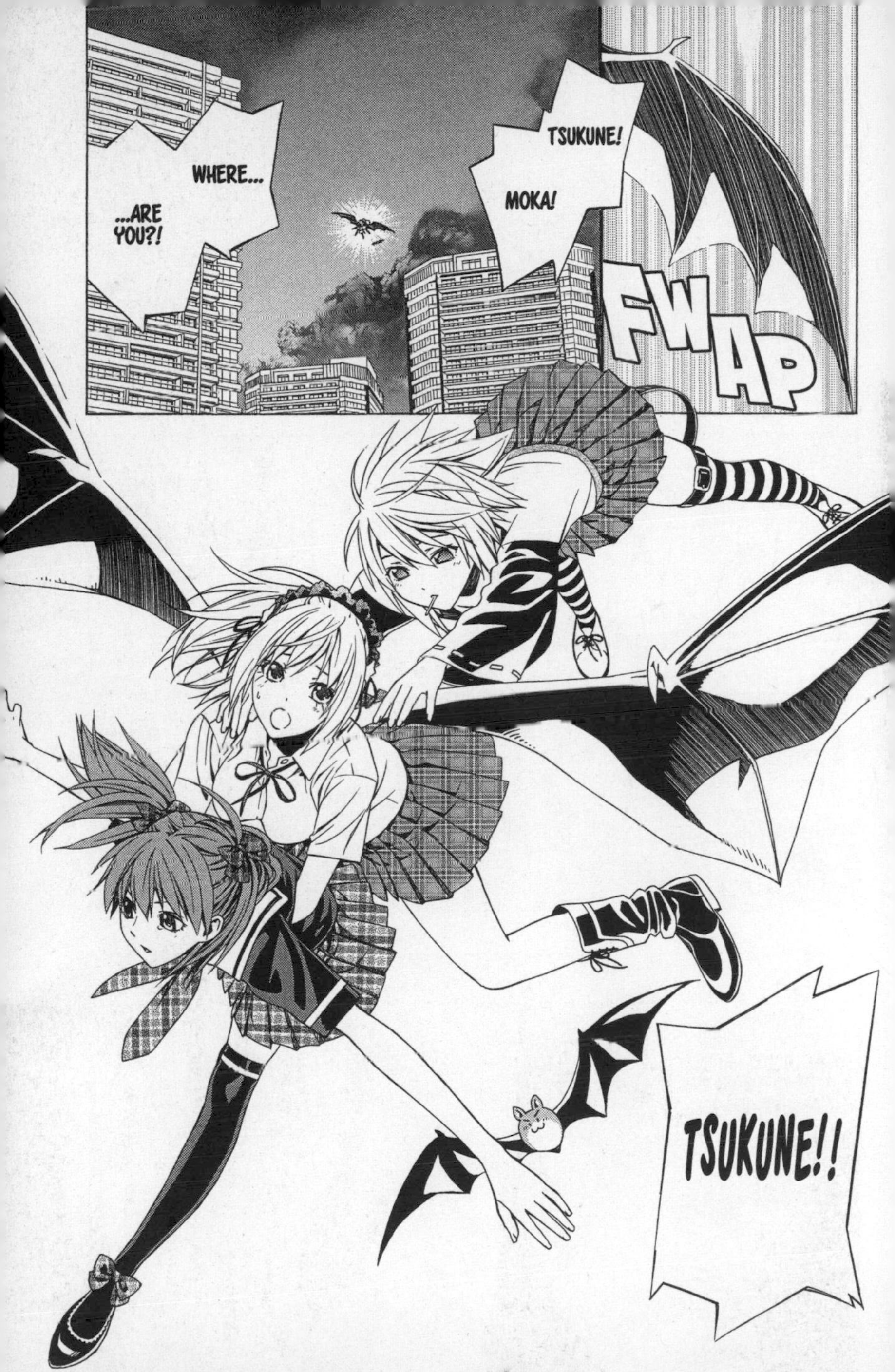
TSUKUNE! MOKA!
FWAP
WHERE... ...ARE YOU?!
TSUKUNE!!

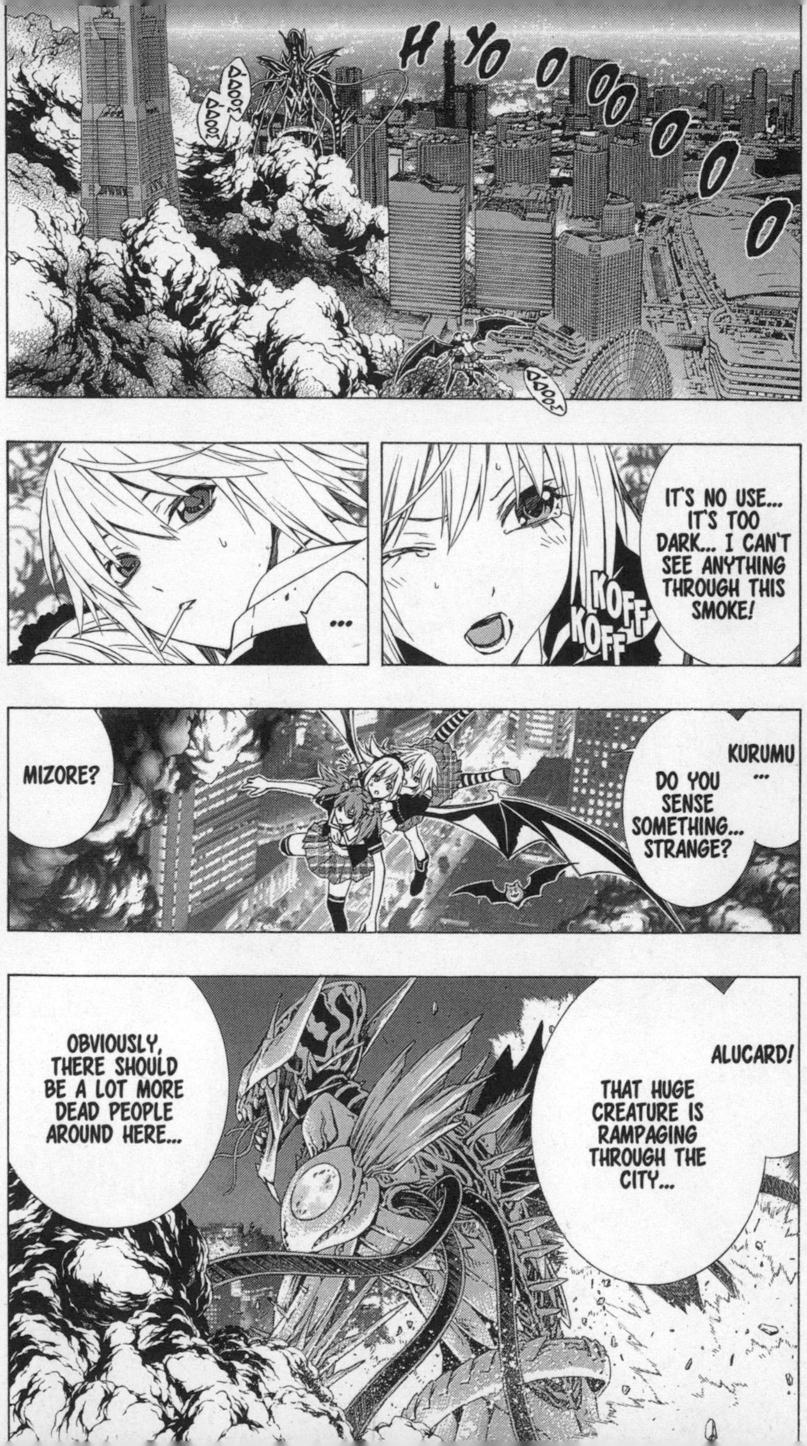

HYOOOOOOOOO
DOOM DOOM
DOOM
IT'S NO USE... IT'S TOO DARK... I CAN'T SEE ANYTHING THROUGH THIS SMOKE!
KOFF KOFF
...
KURUMU...
DO YOU SENSE SOMETHING... STRANGE?
MIZORE?
ALUCARD!
THAT HUGE CREATURE IS RAMPAGING THROUGH THE CITY...
OBVIOUSLY, THERE SHOULD BE A LOT MORE DEAD PEOPLE AROUND HERE...

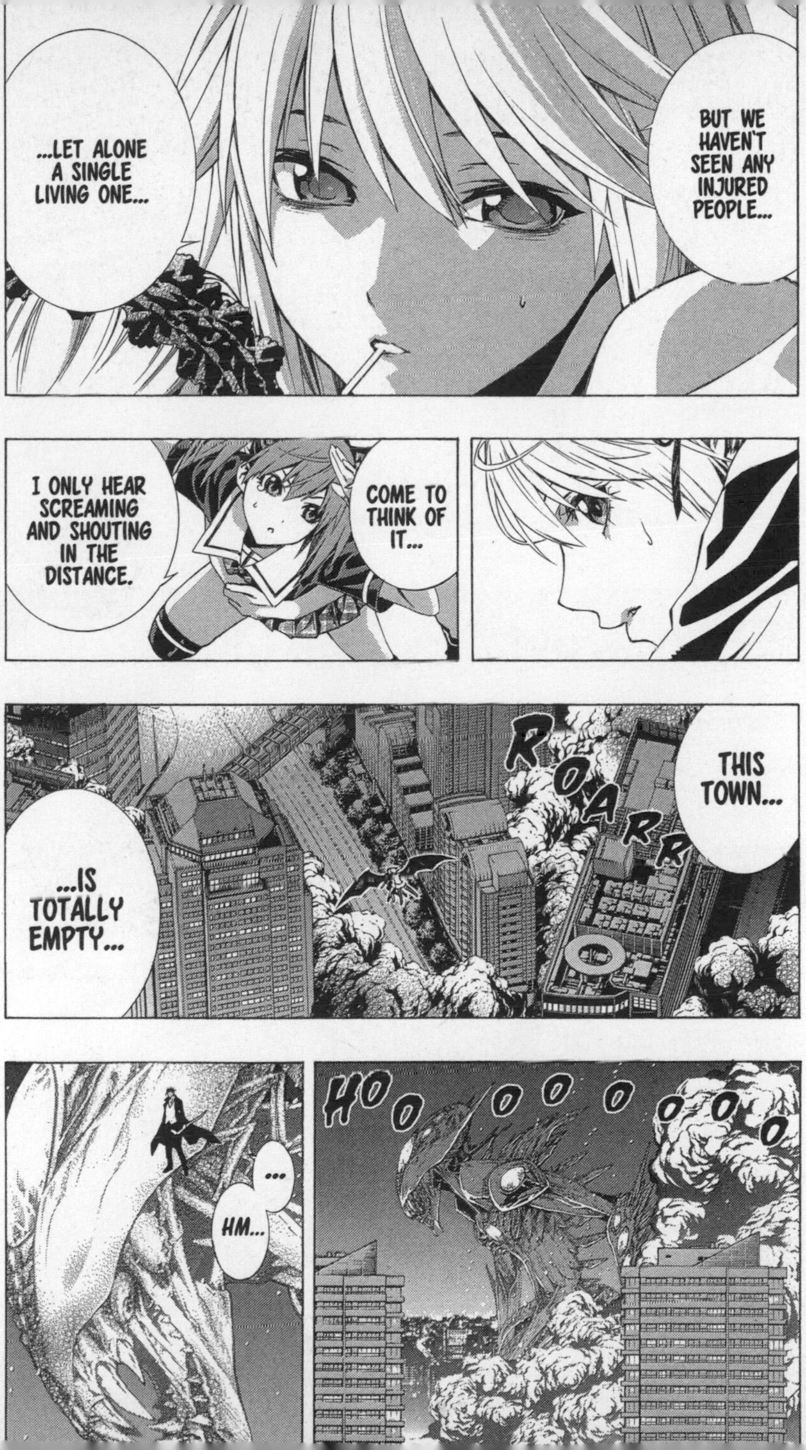
BUT WE HAVEN'T SEEN ANY INJURED PEOPLE...
...LET ALONE A SINGLE LIVING ONE...
COME TO THINK OF IT...
I ONLY HEAR SCREAMING AND SHOUTING IN THE DISTANCE.
THIS TOWN...
ROARR
...IS TOTALLY EMPTY...
HOOOOOOOOO
...
HM...

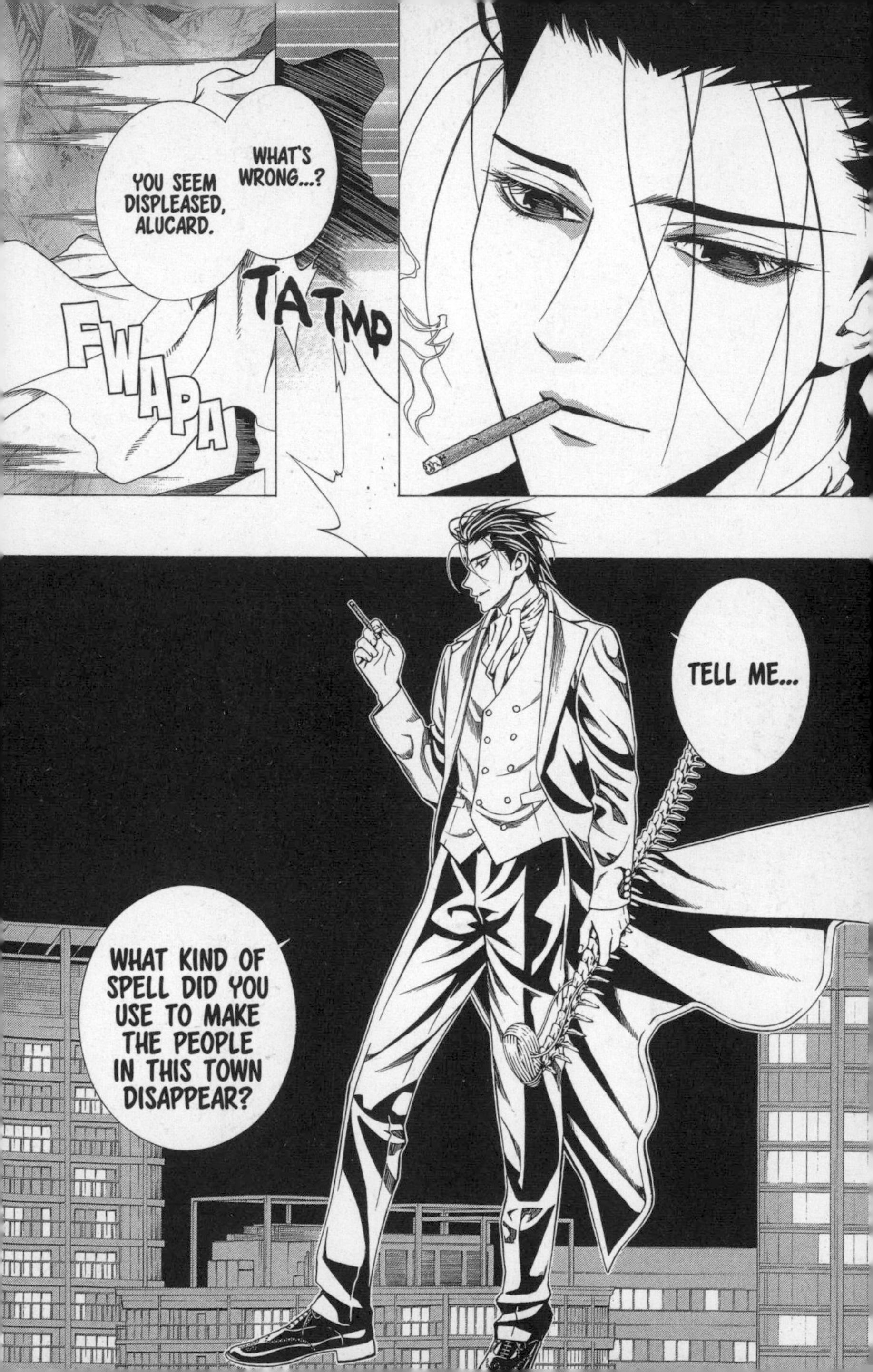
WHAT'S WRONG...?
YOU SEEM DISPLEASED, ALUCARD.
TATMP
F-WAPAPA
TELL ME...
WHAT KIND OF SPELL DID YOU USE TO MAKE THE PEOPLE IN THIS TOWN DISAPPEAR?

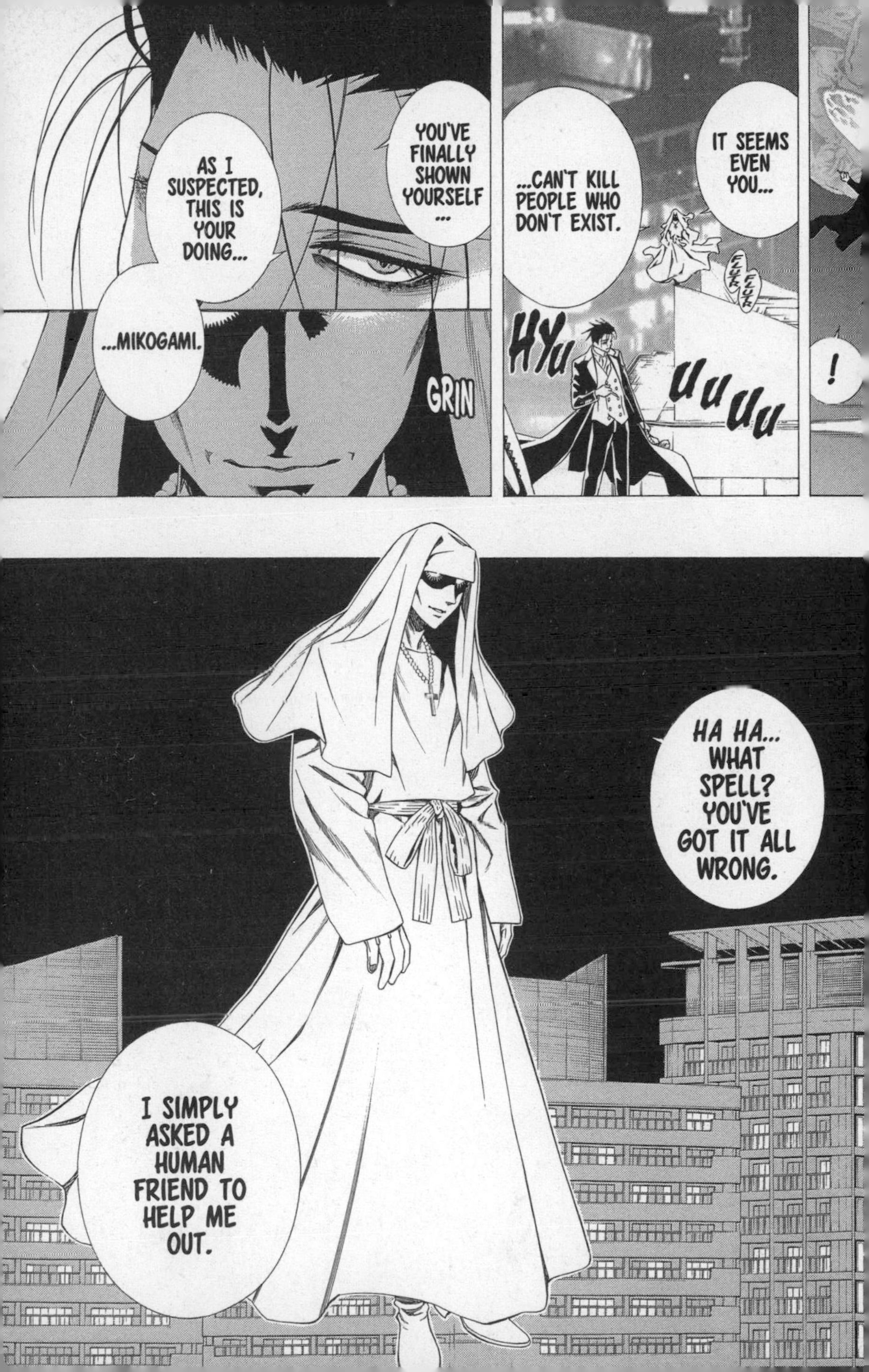
!
IT SEEMS EVEN YOU...
...CAN'T KILL PEOPLE WHO DON'T EXIST.
FLUTR
FLUTR
HYUUUUUU
YOU'VE FINALLY SHOWN YOURSELF...
AS I SUSPECTED, THIS IS YOUR DOING...
...MIKOGAMI.
GRIN
HA HA... WHAT SPELL? YOU'VE GOT IT ALL WRONG.
I SIMPLY ASKED A HUMAN FRIEND TO HELP ME OUT.

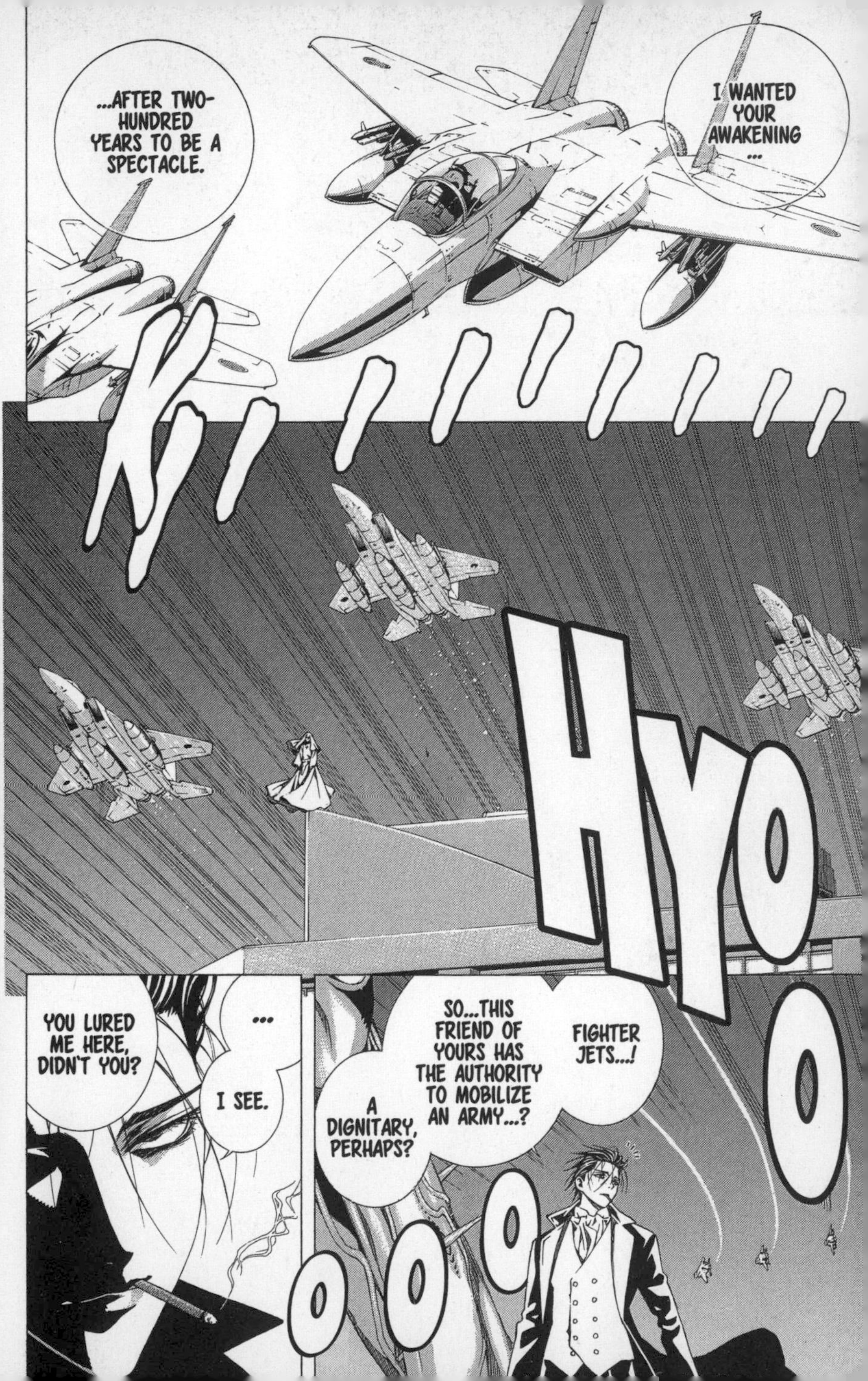
I WANTED YOUR AWAKENING...
...AFTER TWO-HUNDRED YEARS TO BE A SPECTACLE.
KIIIIIIIIII
HYOOOOO
FIGHTER JETS...!
SO...THIS FRIEND OF YOURS HAS THE AUTHORITY TO MOBILIZE AN ARMY...?
A DIGNITARY, PERHAPS?
...
I SEE.
YOU LURED ME HERE, DIDN'T YOU?

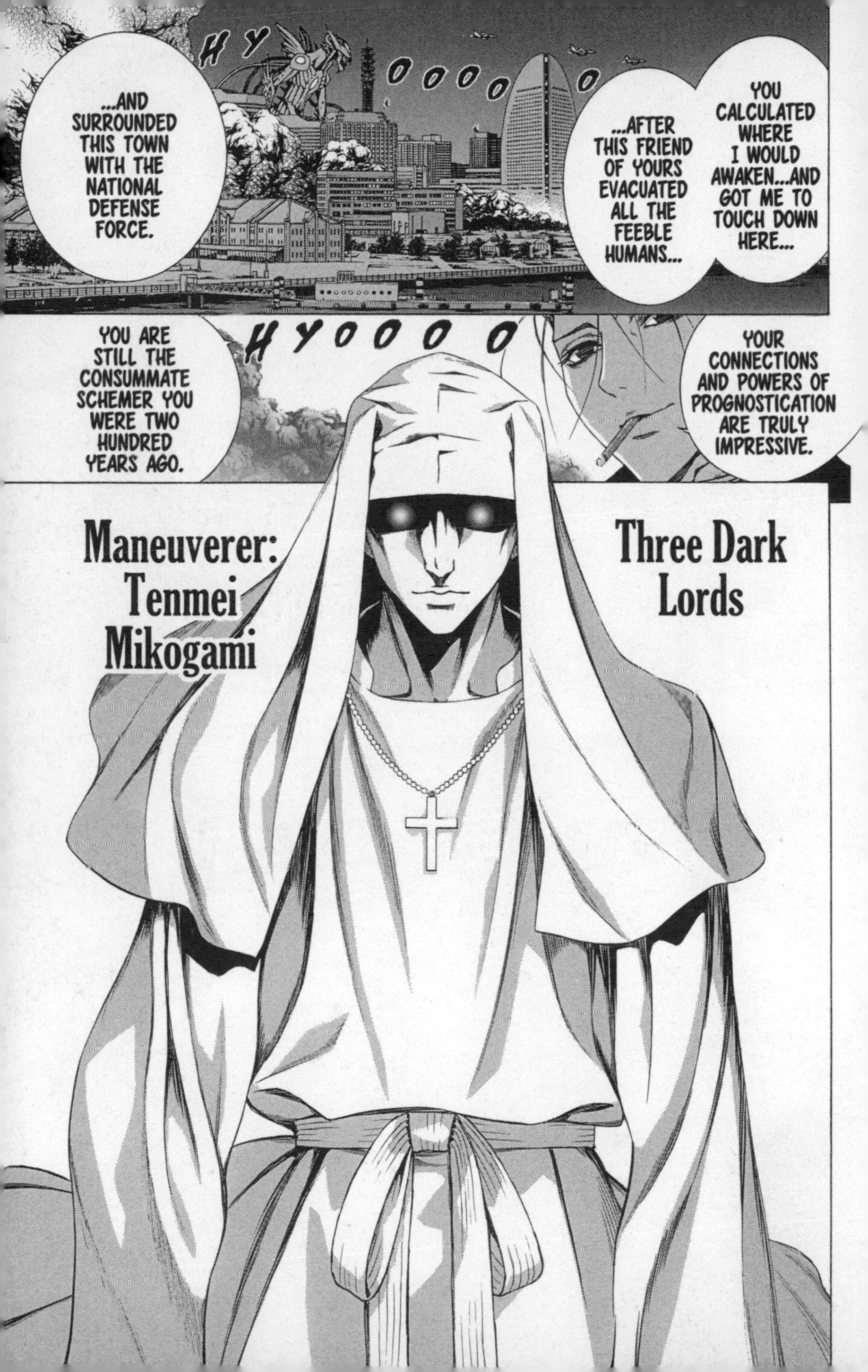
HYOOOOO
YOU CALCULATED WHERE I WOULD AWAKEN...AND GOT ME TO TOUCH DOWN HERE...
...AFTER THIS FRIEND OF YOURS EVACUATED ALL THE FEEBLE HUMANS...
...AND SURROUNDED THIS TOWN WITH THE NATIONAL DEFENSE FORCE.
HYOOOO
YOUR CONNECTIONS AND POWERS OF PROGNOSTICATION ARE TRULY IMPRESSIVE.
YOU ARE STILL THE CONSUMMATE SCHEMER YOU WERE TWO HUNDRED YEARS AGO.
Three Dark Lords
Maneuverer: Tenmei Mikogami

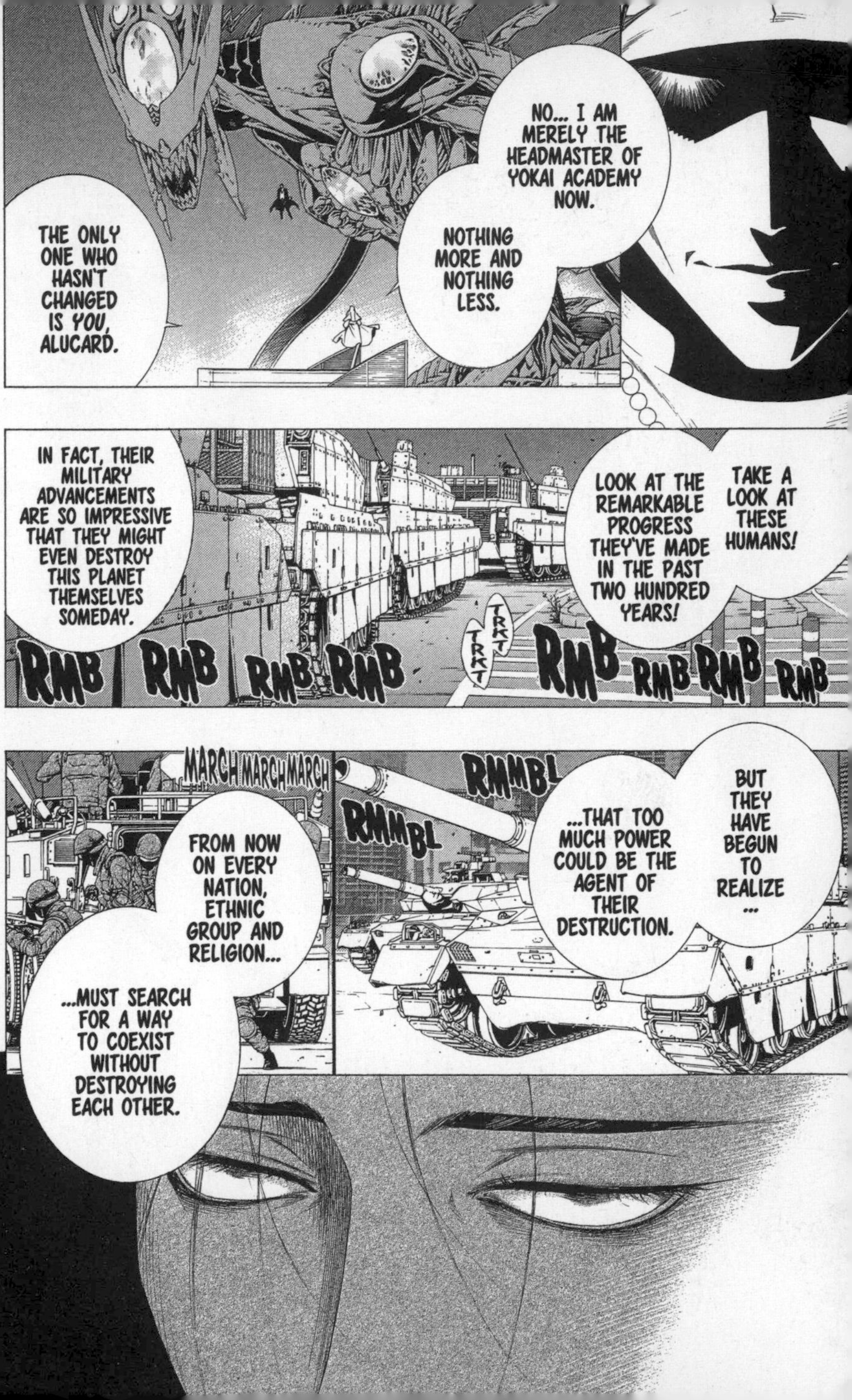
NO... I AM MERELY THE HEADMASTER OF YOKAI ACADEMY NOW.
NOTHING MORE AND NOTHING LESS.
THE ONLY ONE WHO HASN'T CHANGED IS *YOU*, ALUCARD.
TAKE A LOOK AT THESE HUMANS!
LOOK AT THE REMARKABLE PROGRESS THEY'VE MADE IN THE PAST TWO HUNDRED YEARS!
RMB RMB RMB RMB
TRKT TRKT
IN FACT, THEIR MILITARY ADVANCEMENTS ARE SO IMPRESSIVE THAT THEY MIGHT EVEN DESTROY THIS PLANET THEMSELVES SOMEDAY.
RMB RMB RMB RMB
BUT THEY HAVE BEGUN TO REALIZE...
...THAT TOO MUCH POWER COULD BE THE AGENT OF THEIR DESTRUCTION.
RMMBL
RMMBL
MARCH MARCH MARCH
FROM NOW ON EVERY NATION, ETHNIC GROUP AND RELIGION...
...MUST SEARCH FOR A WAY TO COEXIST WITHOUT DESTROYING EACH OTHER.

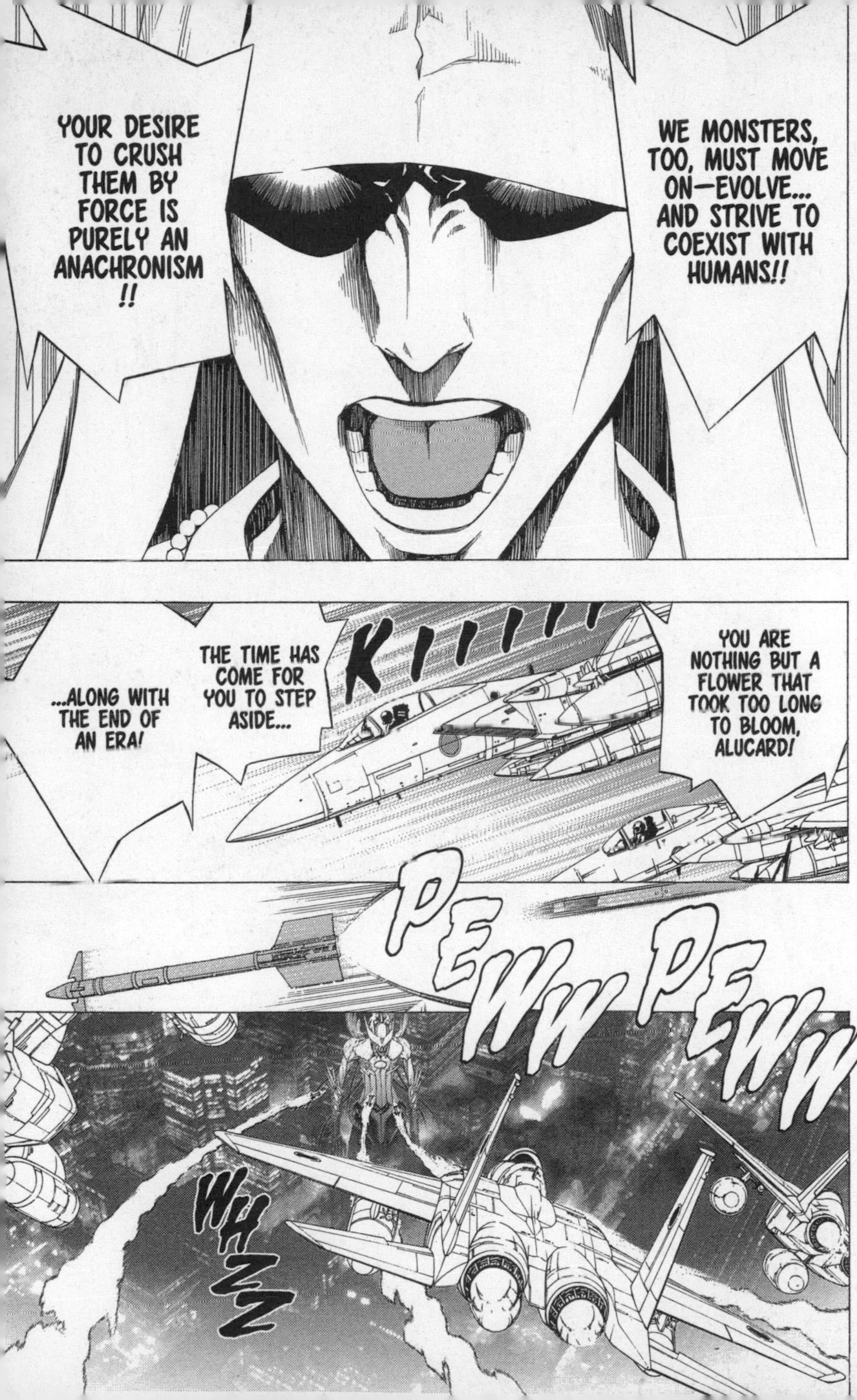
WE MONSTERS, TOO, MUST MOVE ON—EVOLVE... AND STRIVE TO COEXIST WITH HUMANS!!
YOUR DESIRE TO CRUSH THEM BY FORCE IS PURELY AN ANACHRONISM !!
YOU ARE NOTHING BUT A FLOWER THAT TOOK TOO LONG TO BLOOM, ALUCARD!
KIIIIII
THE TIME HAS COME FOR YOU TO STEP ASIDE...
...ALONG WITH THE END OF AN ERA!
PEWW PEWW
WHZZ

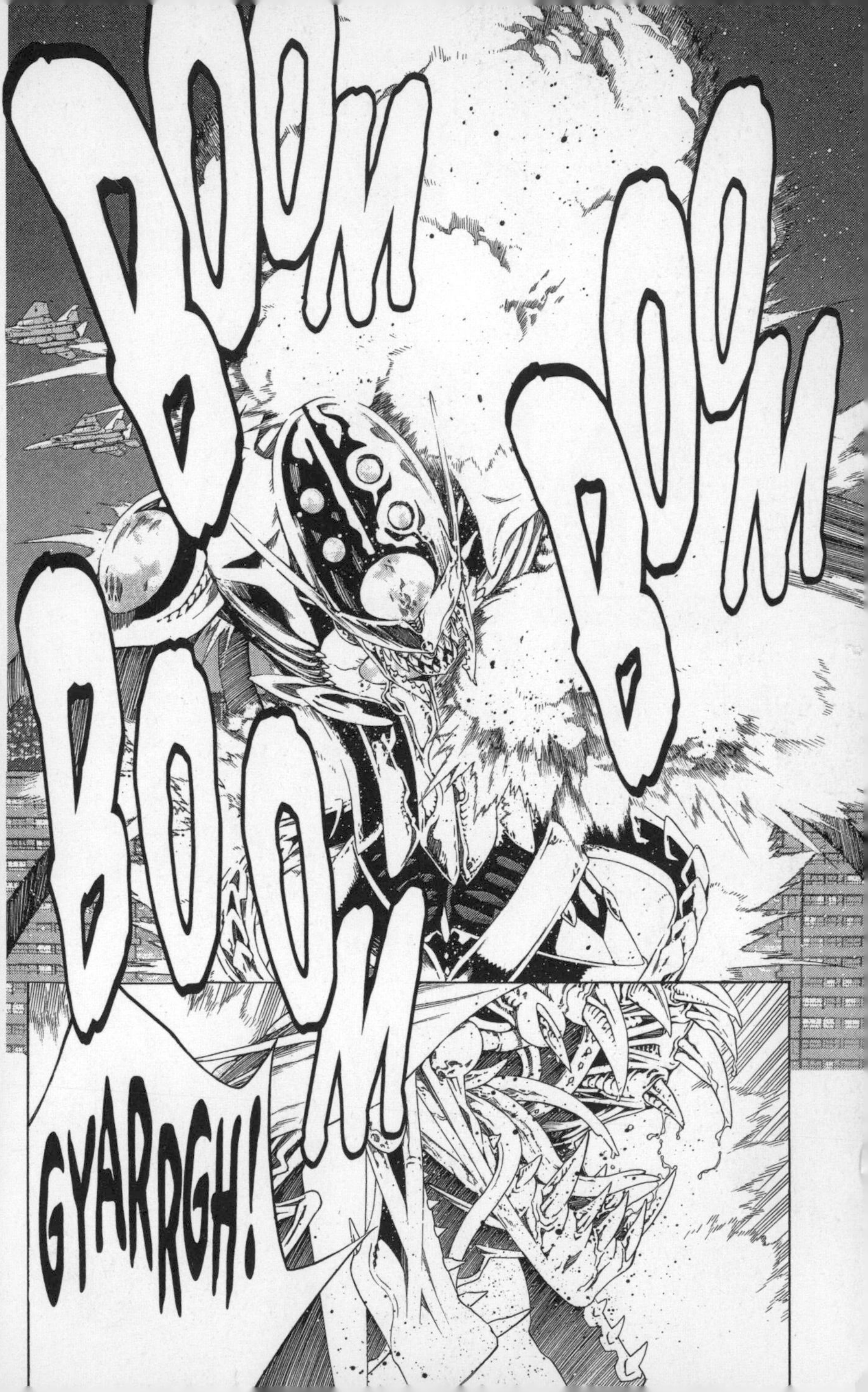
BOOM
BOOM
BOOM
GYARGH!

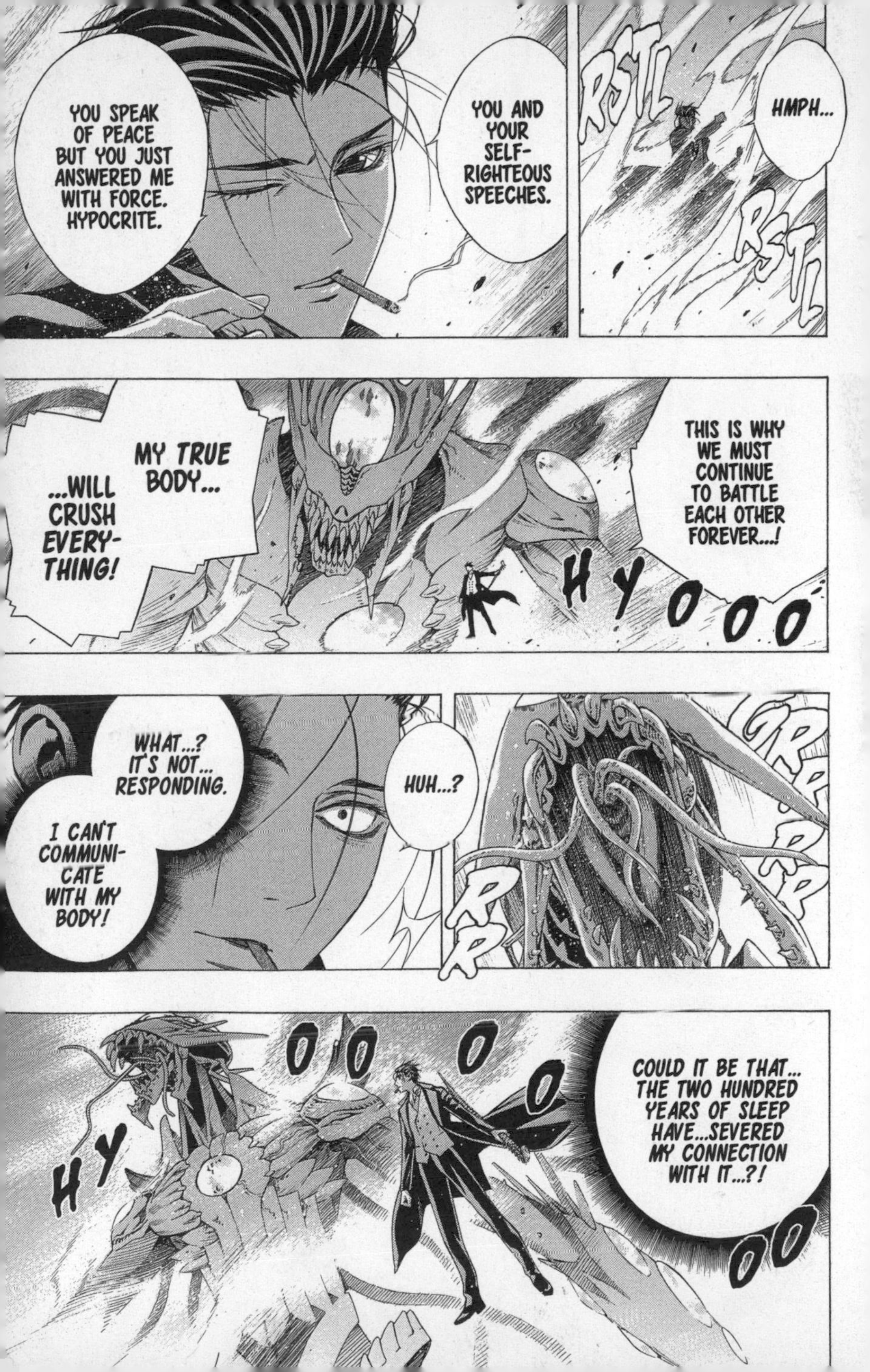
HMPH...
RSTL
RSTL
YOU AND YOUR SELF-RIGHTEOUS SPEECHES.
YOU SPEAK OF PEACE BUT YOU JUST ANSWERED ME WITH FORCE. HYPOCRITE.
THIS IS WHY WE MUST CONTINUE TO BATTLE EACH OTHER FOREVER...!
HYOOO
MY TRUE BODY...
...WILL CRUSH EVERY-THING!
GRR
RRR
HUH...?
WHAT...? IT'S NOT... RESPONDING.
I CAN'T COMMUNI-CATE WITH MY BODY!
COULD IT BE THAT... THE TWO HUNDRED YEARS OF SLEEP HAVE...SEVERED MY CONNECTION WITH IT...?!
HYOOOOOO

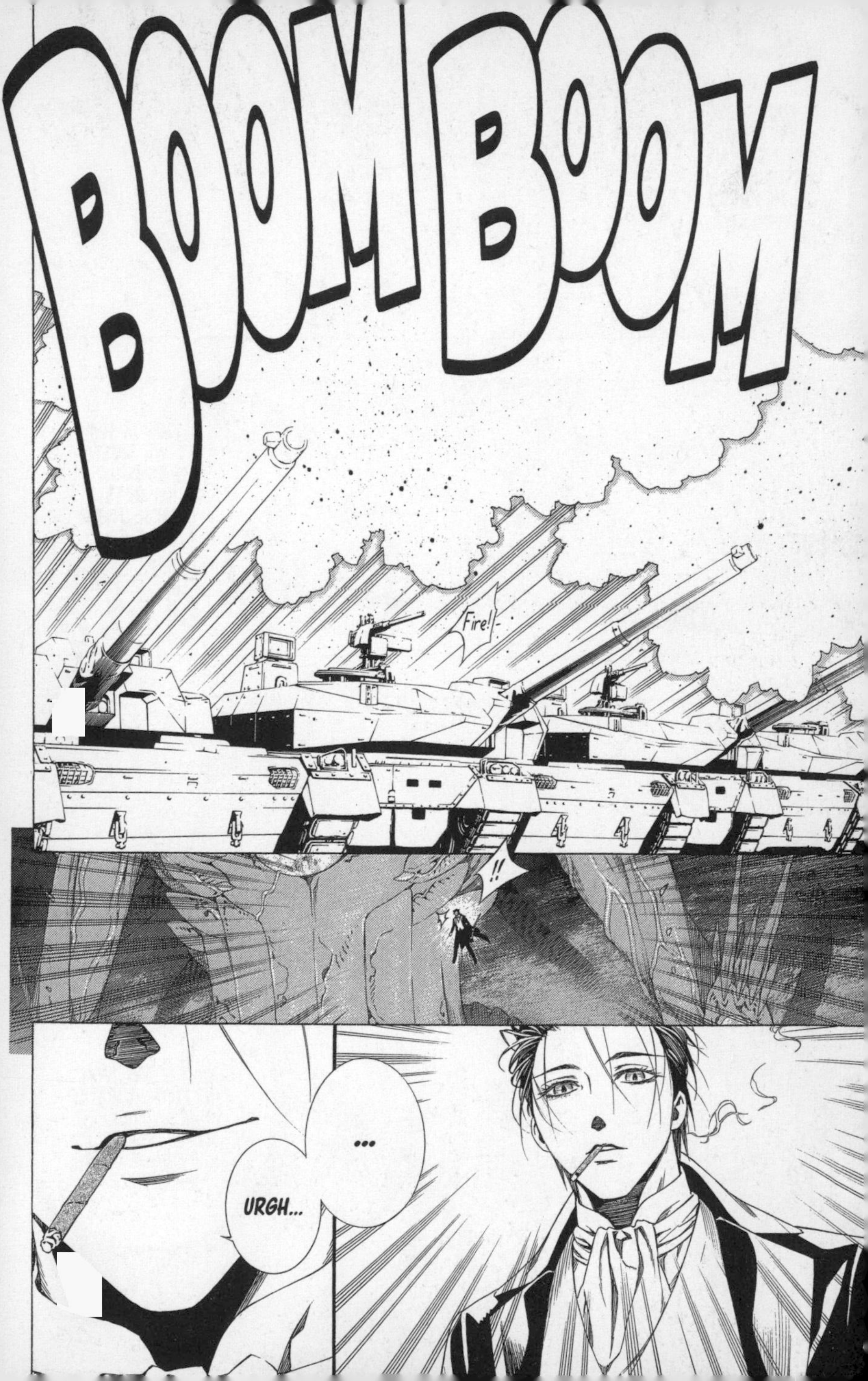
BOOM BOOM
Fire!
!!
...
URGH...

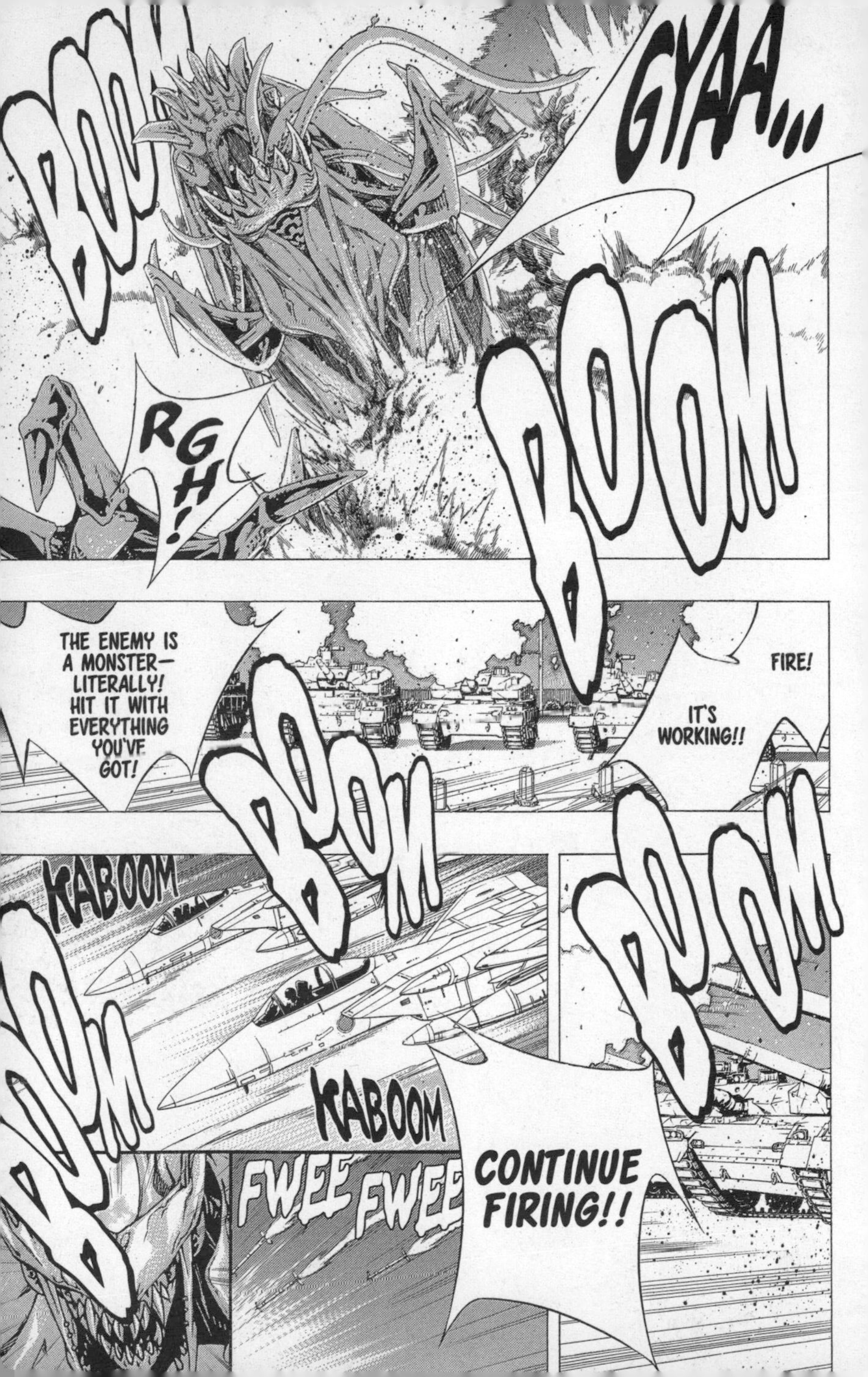
GYAA...
BOOM
BOOM
RGH!
FIRE!
IT'S WORKING!!
BOOM
THE ENEMY IS A MONSTER—LITERALLY! HIT IT WITH EVERYTHING YOU'VE GOT!
BOOM
CONTINUE FIRING!!
KABOOM
KABOOM
BOOM
FWEE FWEE

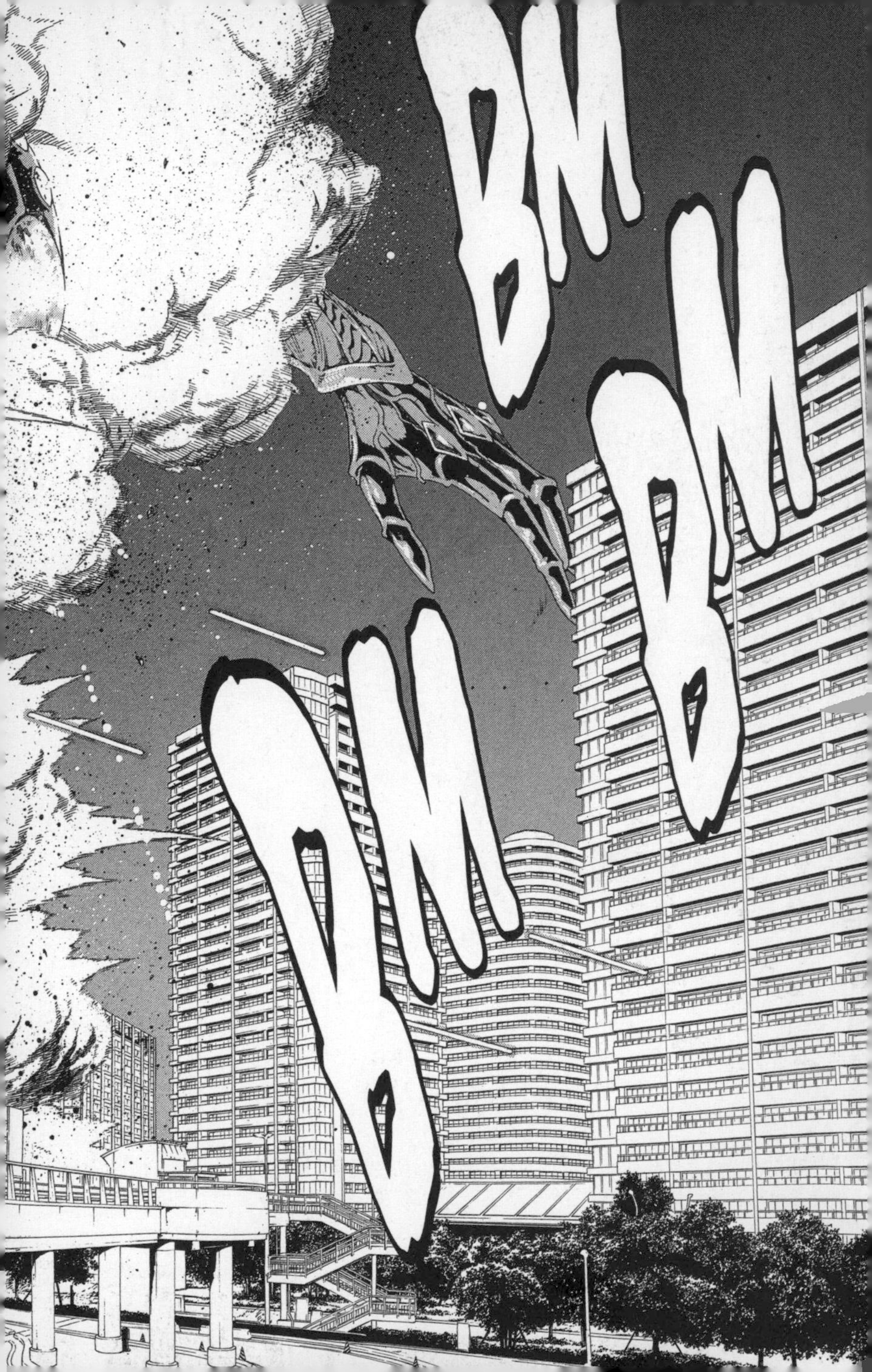
BM
BM
BM

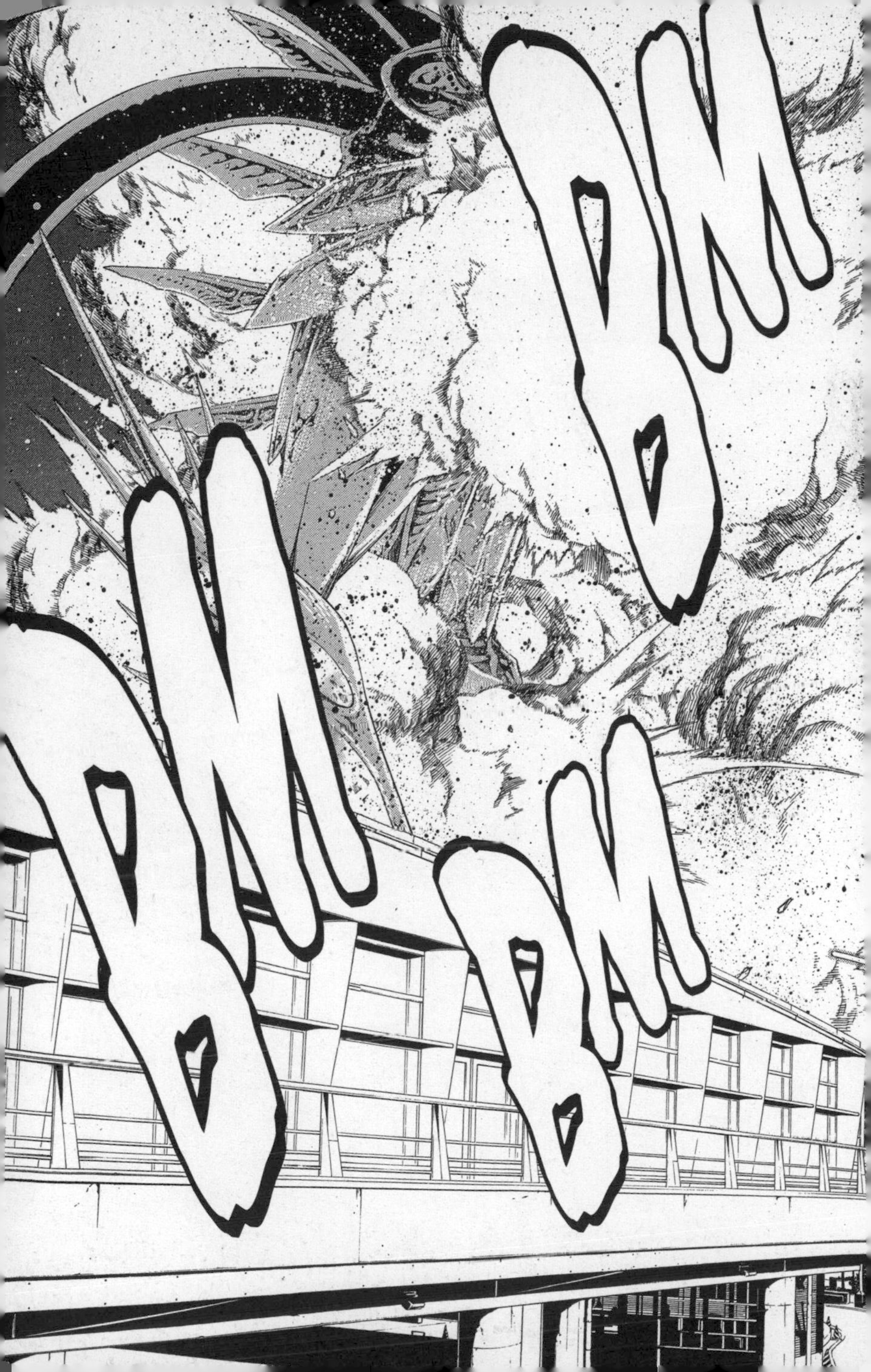
BOM
BOM
BOM

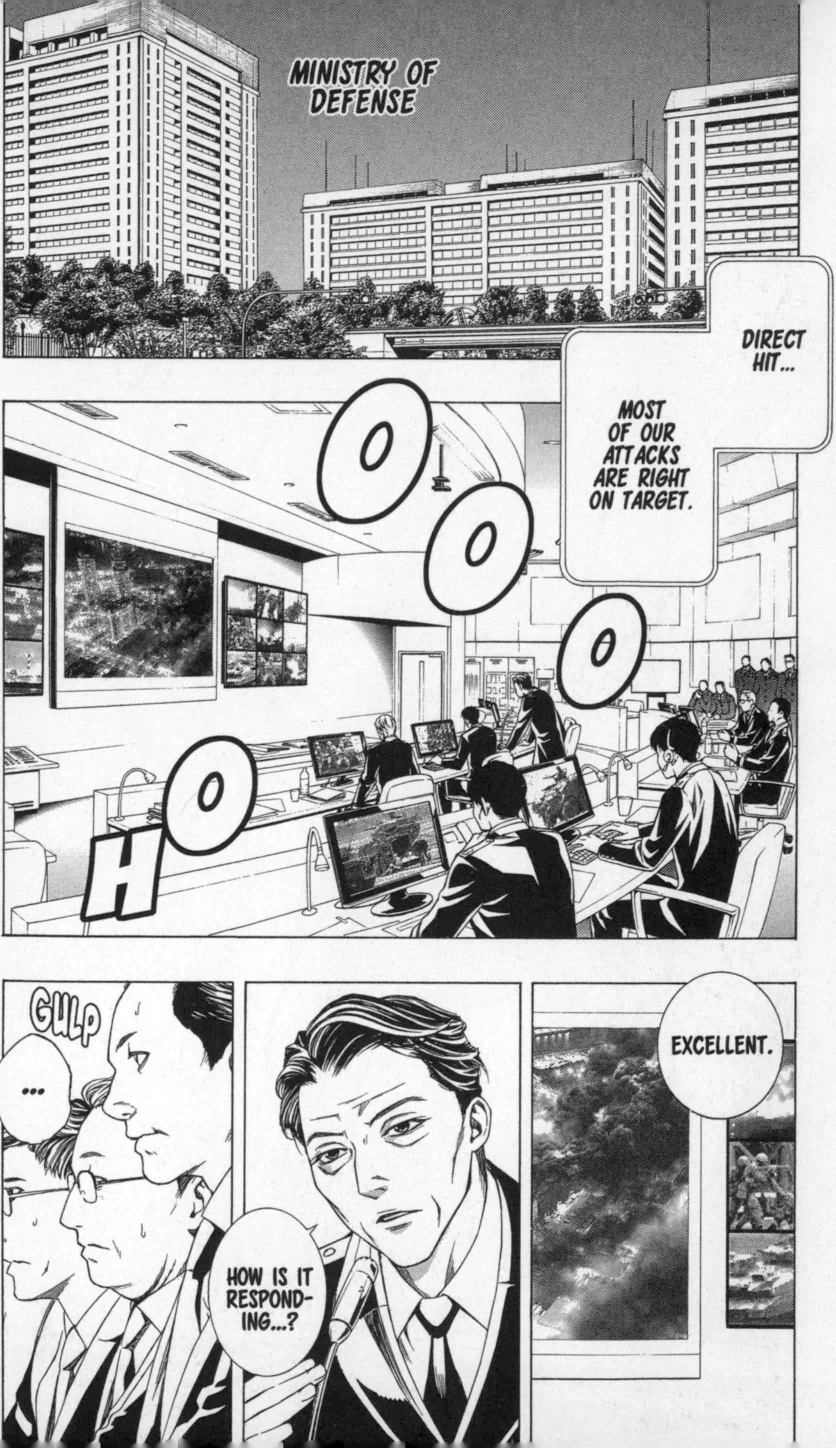
MINISTRY OF DEFENSE
DIRECT HIT...
MOST OF OUR ATTACKS ARE RIGHT ON TARGET.
HOOOO
EXCELLENT.
HOW IS IT RESPOND-ING...?
GULP
...

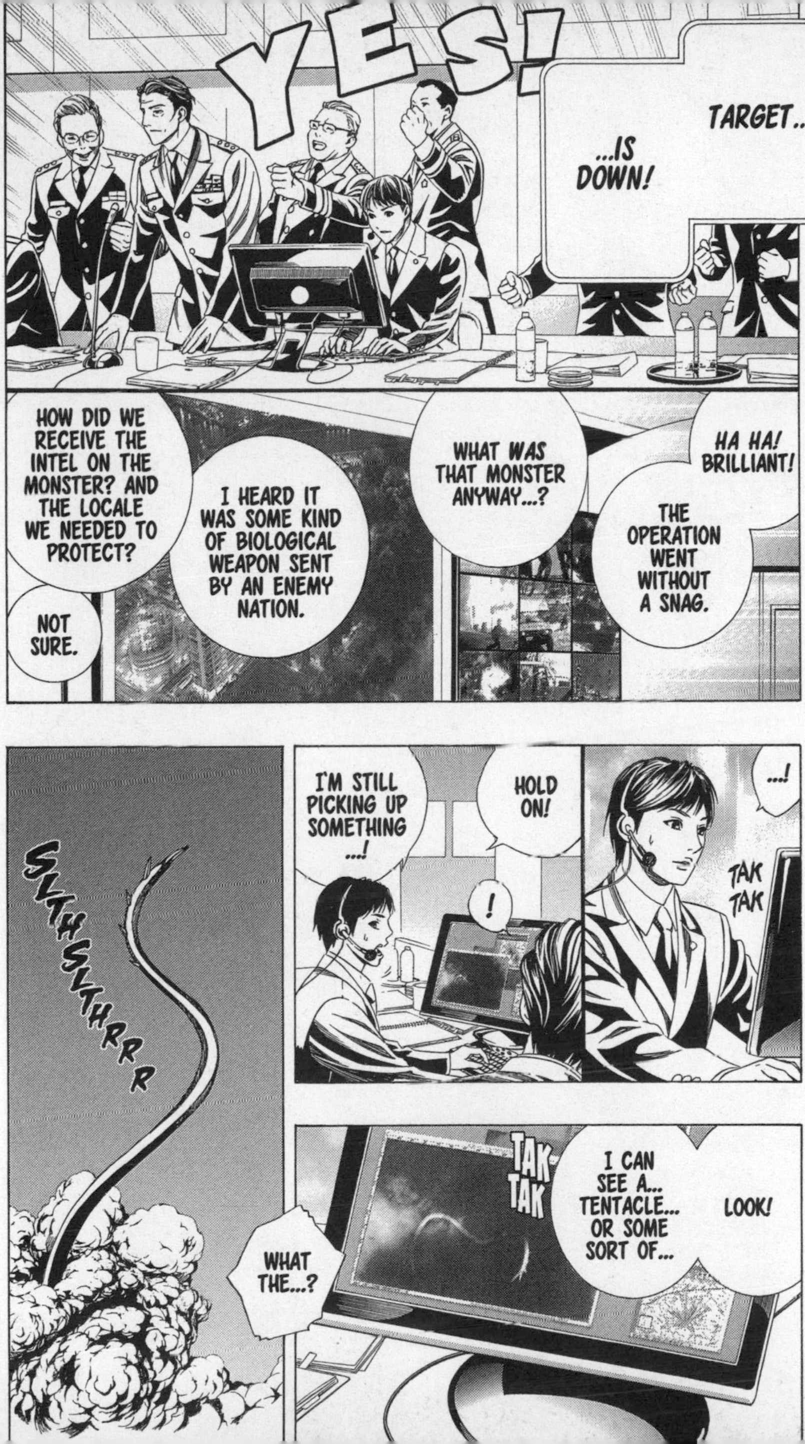
TARGET...
...IS DOWN!
YES!
HA HA! BRILLIANT!
THE OPERATION WENT WITHOUT A SNAG.
WHAT WAS THAT MONSTER ANYWAY...?
I HEARD IT WAS SOME KIND OF BIOLOGICAL WEAPON SENT BY AN ENEMY NATION.
HOW DID WE RECEIVE THE INTEL ON THE MONSTER? AND THE LOCALE WE NEEDED TO PROTECT?
NOT SURE.
...!
TAK TAK
HOLD ON!
I'M STILL PICKING UP SOMETHING ...!
!
LOOK!
I CAN SEE A... TENTACLE... OR SOME SORT OF...
TAK TAK
WHAT THE...?
SLTHSLTHRRR

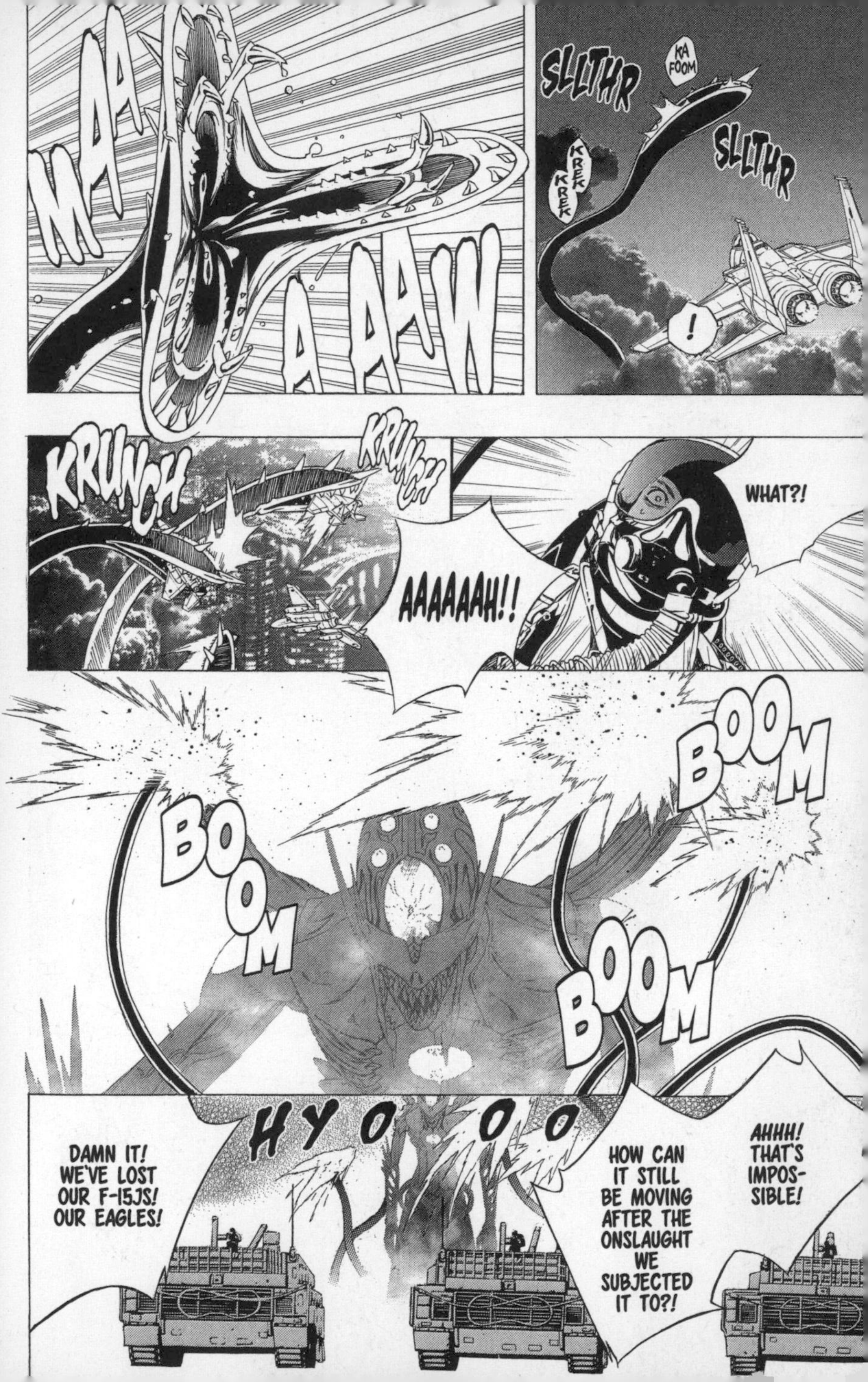
KA FOOM
SLLTHR
SLLTHR
KREK KREK
!
MAA
A AAW
WHAT?!
AAAAAAH!!
KRUNCH
KRUNCH
BOOM
BOOM
BOOM
AHHH! THAT'S IMPOSSIBLE!
HOW CAN IT STILL BE MOVING AFTER THE ONSLAUGHT WE SUBJECTED IT TO?!
HYOOOO
DAMN IT! WE'VE LOST OUR F-15JS! OUR EAGLES!

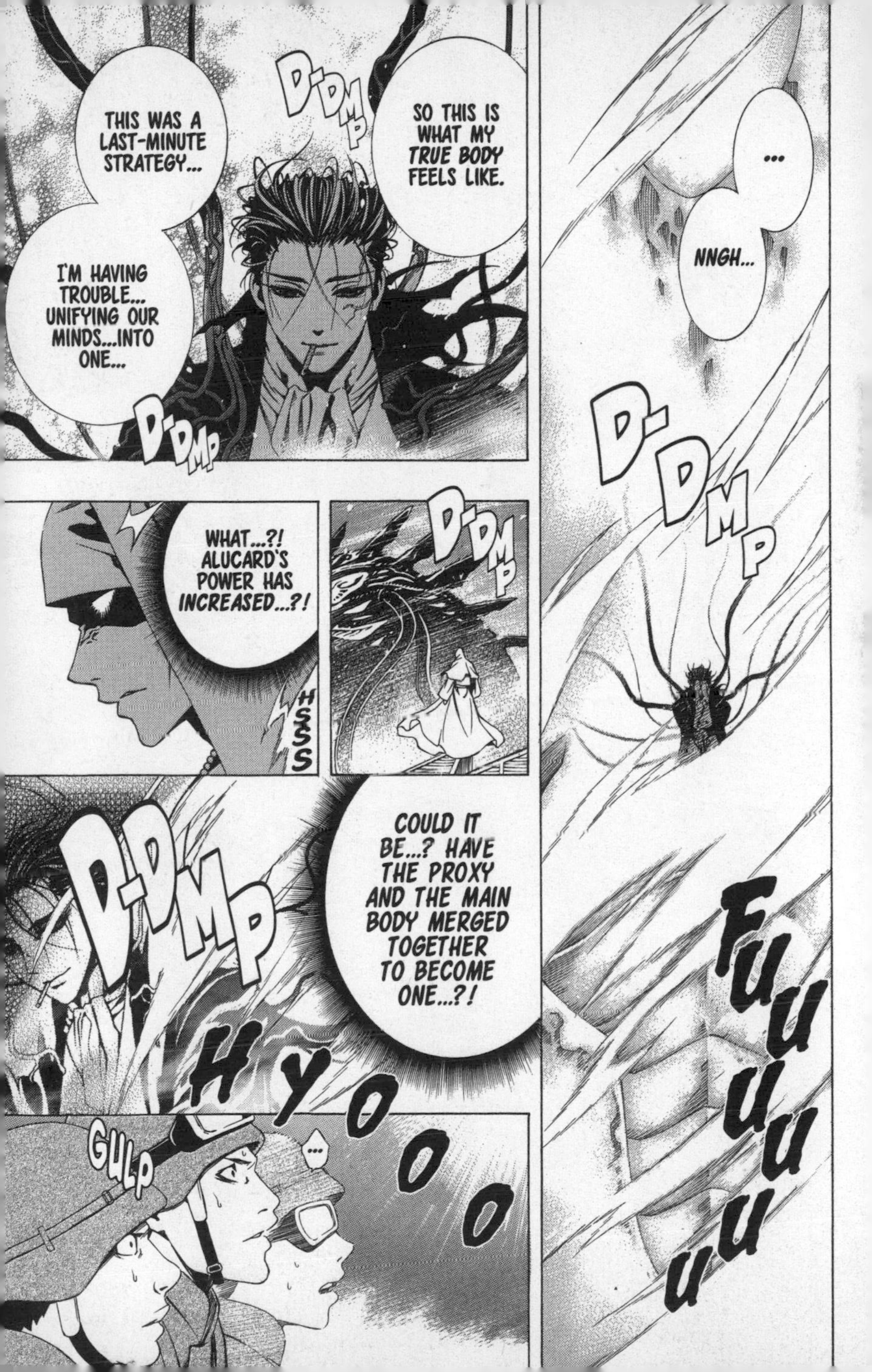
...
NNGH...
D-DMP
FUUUUUUUU
SO THIS IS WHAT MY TRUE BODY FEELS LIKE.
D-DMP
THIS WAS A LAST-MINUTE STRATEGY...
I'M HAVING TROUBLE... UNIFYING OUR MINDS...INTO ONE...
D-DMP
D-DMP
WHAT...?! ALUCARD'S POWER HAS INCREASED...?!
HSSS
COULD IT BE...? HAVE THE PROXY AND THE MAIN BODY MERGED TOGETHER TO BECOME ONE...?!
D-DMP
HYOOOO
...
GULP

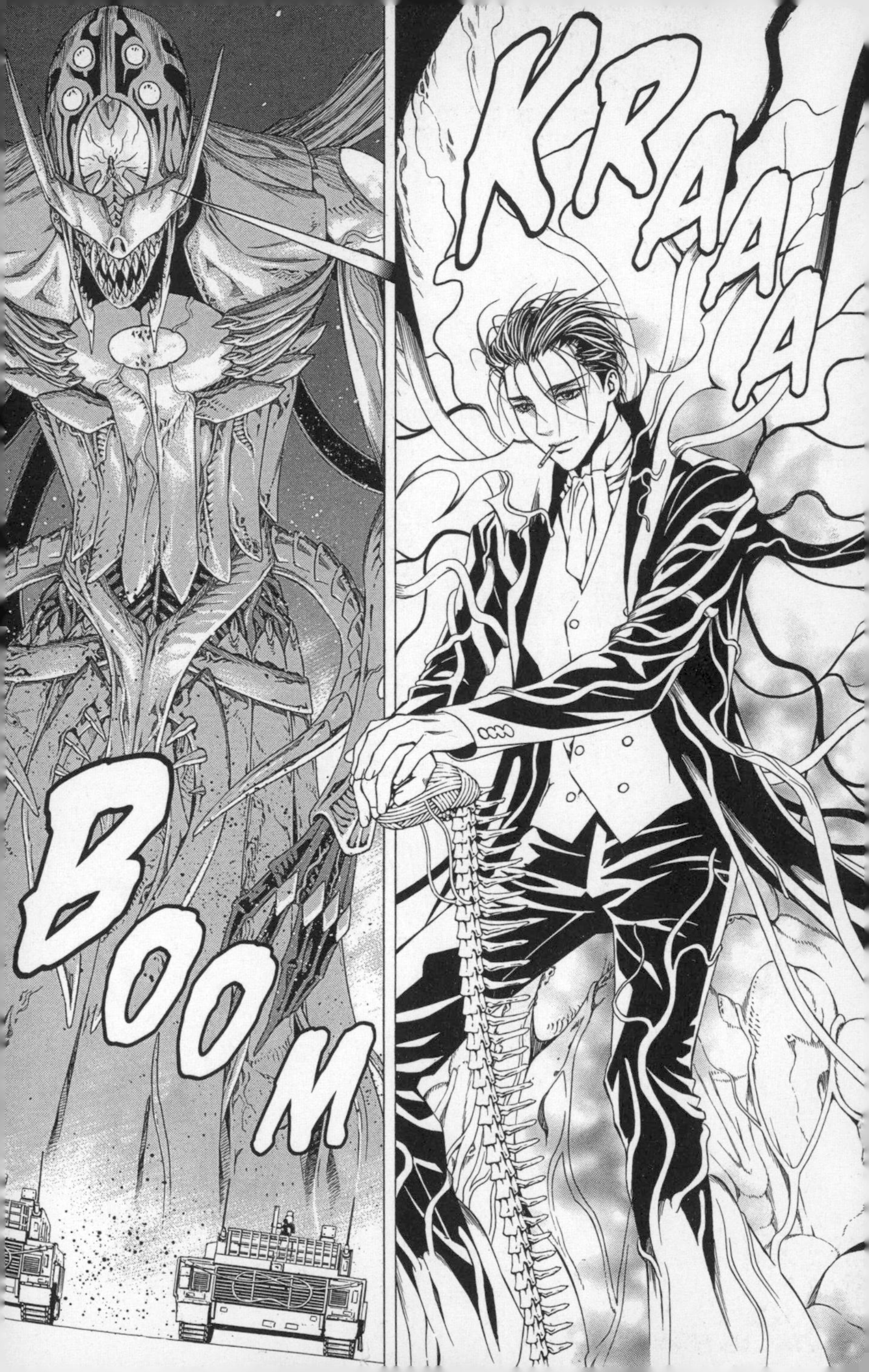
KRAAAA
BOOM

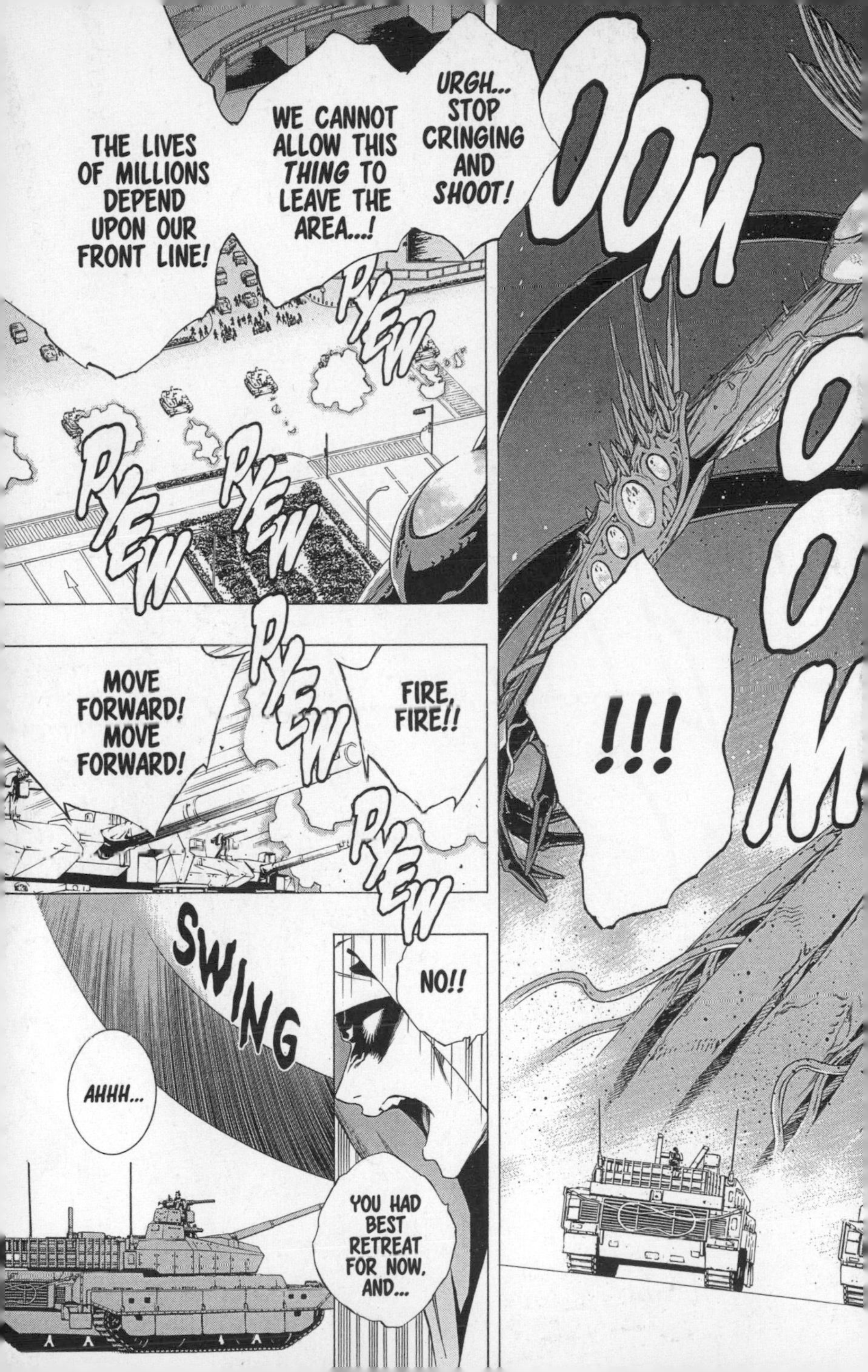
OOM
OOM
!!!
URGH... STOP CRINGING AND SHOOT!
WE CANNOT ALLOW THIS *THING* TO LEAVE THE AREA...!
THE LIVES OF MILLIONS DEPEND UPON OUR FRONT LINE!
PYEW
PYEW
PYEW
FIRE, FIRE!!
MOVE FORWARD! MOVE FORWARD!
PYEW
PYEW
NO!!
SWING
AHHH...
YOU HAD BEST RETREAT FOR NOW, AND...

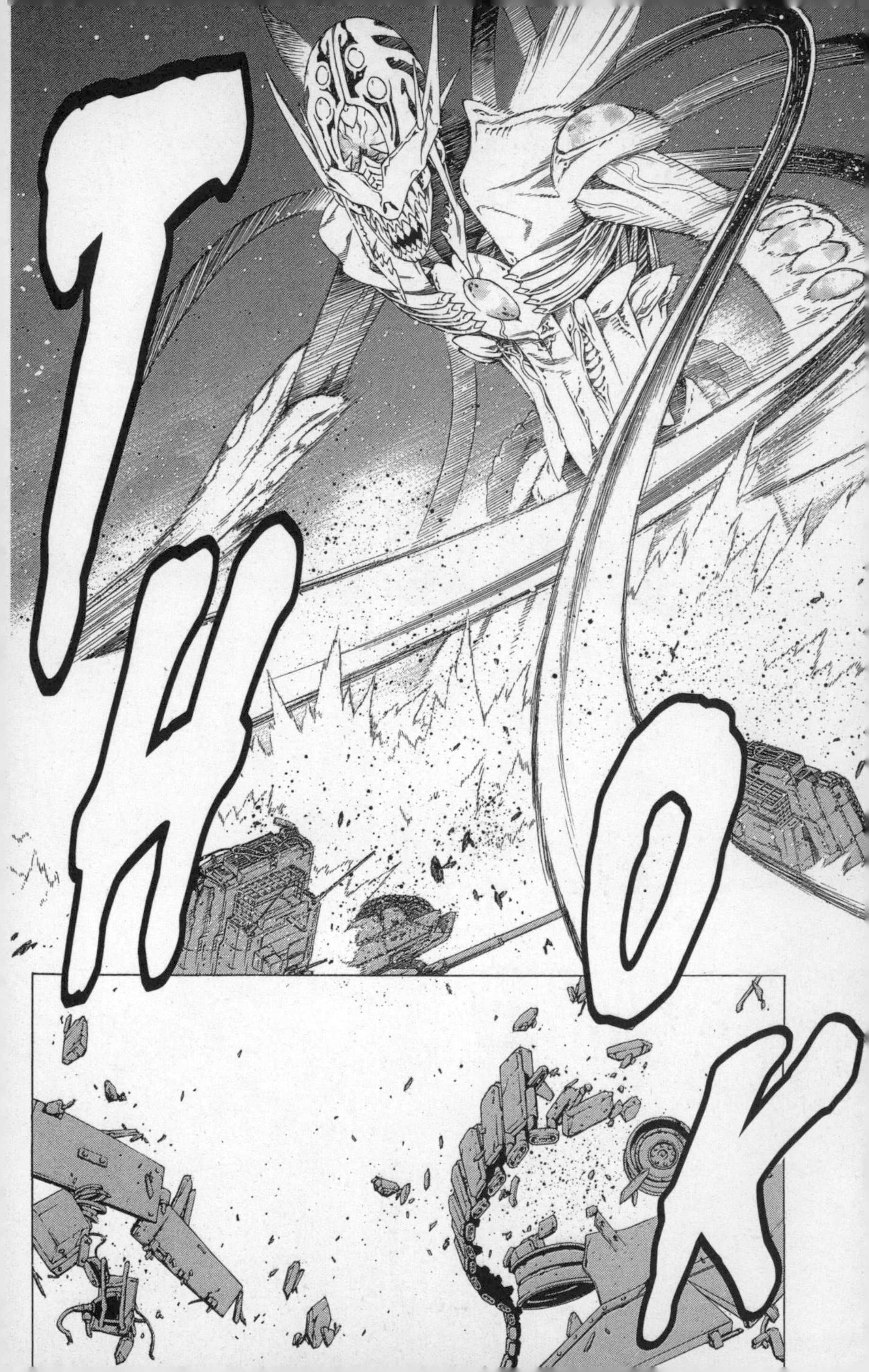
THOK

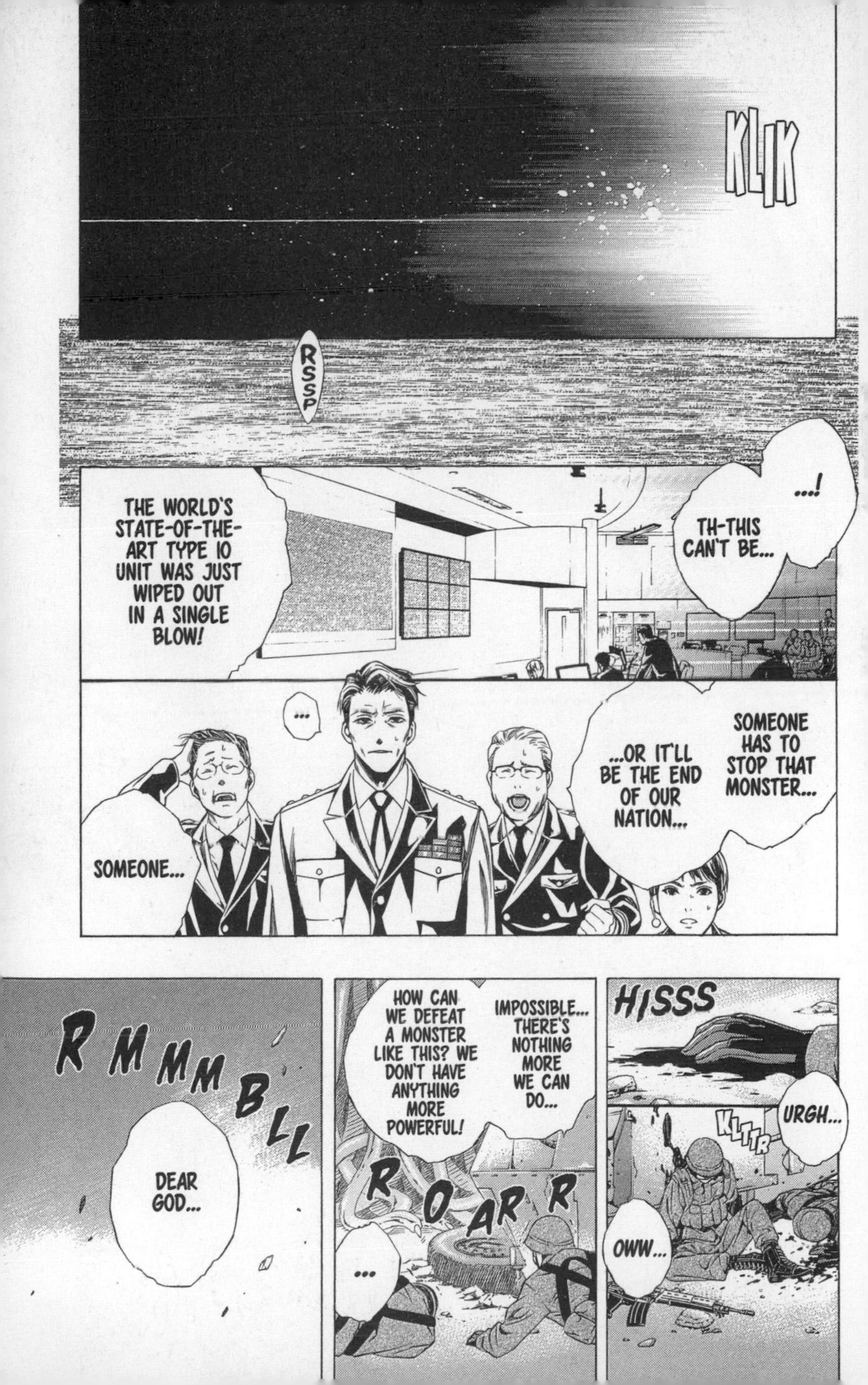
KLIK
RSSP
...!
TH-THIS CAN'T BE...
THE WORLD'S STATE-OF-THE-ART TYPE 10 UNIT WAS JUST WIPED OUT IN A SINGLE BLOW!
SOMEONE HAS TO STOP THAT MONSTER...
...OR IT'LL BE THE END OF OUR NATION...
...
SOMEONE...
HISSS
URGH...
KLTTR
OWW...
IMPOSSIBLE... THERE'S NOTHING MORE WE CAN DO...
HOW CAN WE DEFEAT A MONSTER LIKE THIS? WE DON'T HAVE ANYTHING MORE POWERFUL!
ROAR R
...
RMMMBLL
DEAR GOD...

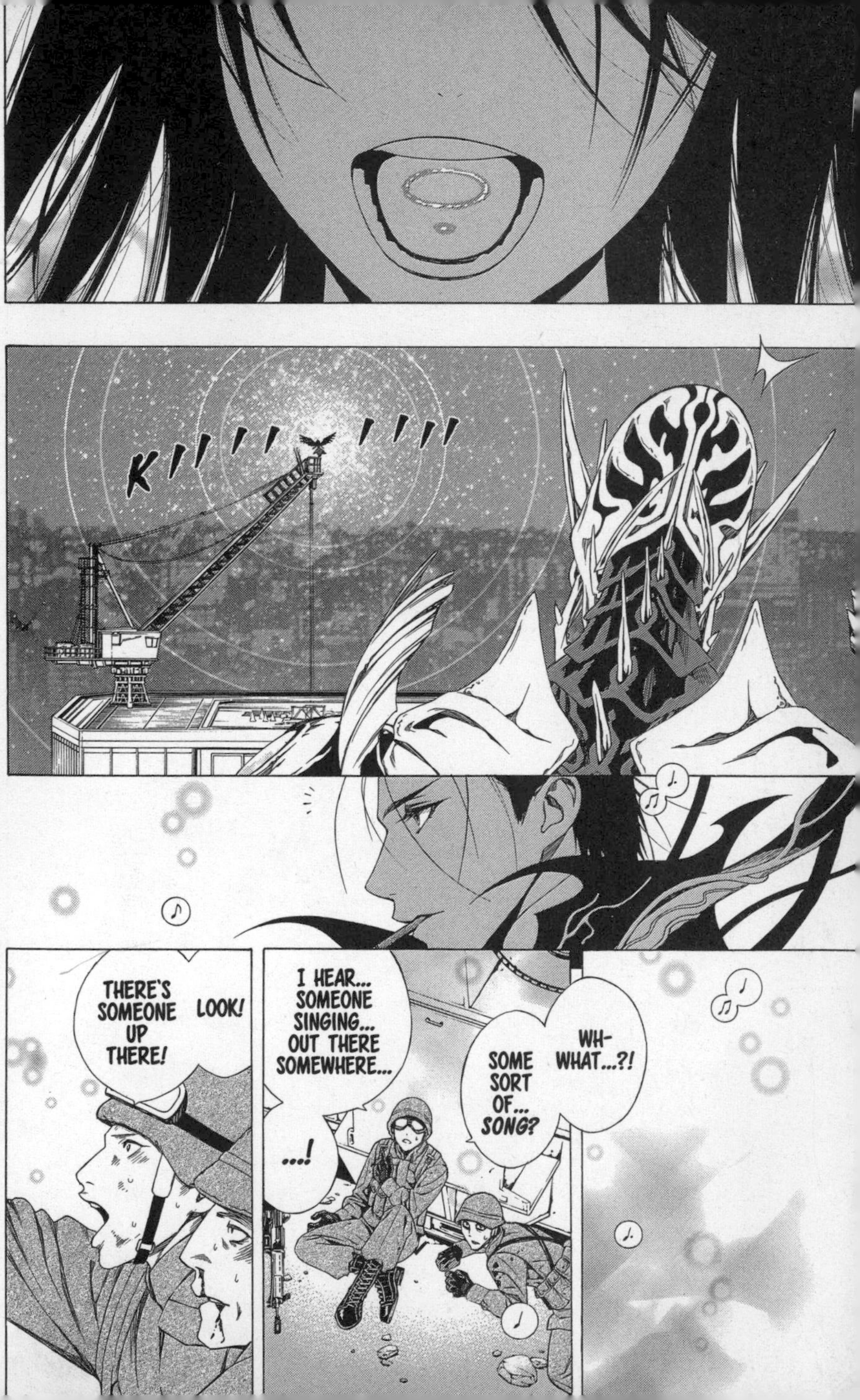
KIIII IIII
WH-WHAT...?!
SOME SORT OF... SONG?
I HEAR... SOMEONE SINGING... OUT THERE SOMEWHERE...
...!
LOOK!
THERE'S SOMEONE UP THERE!

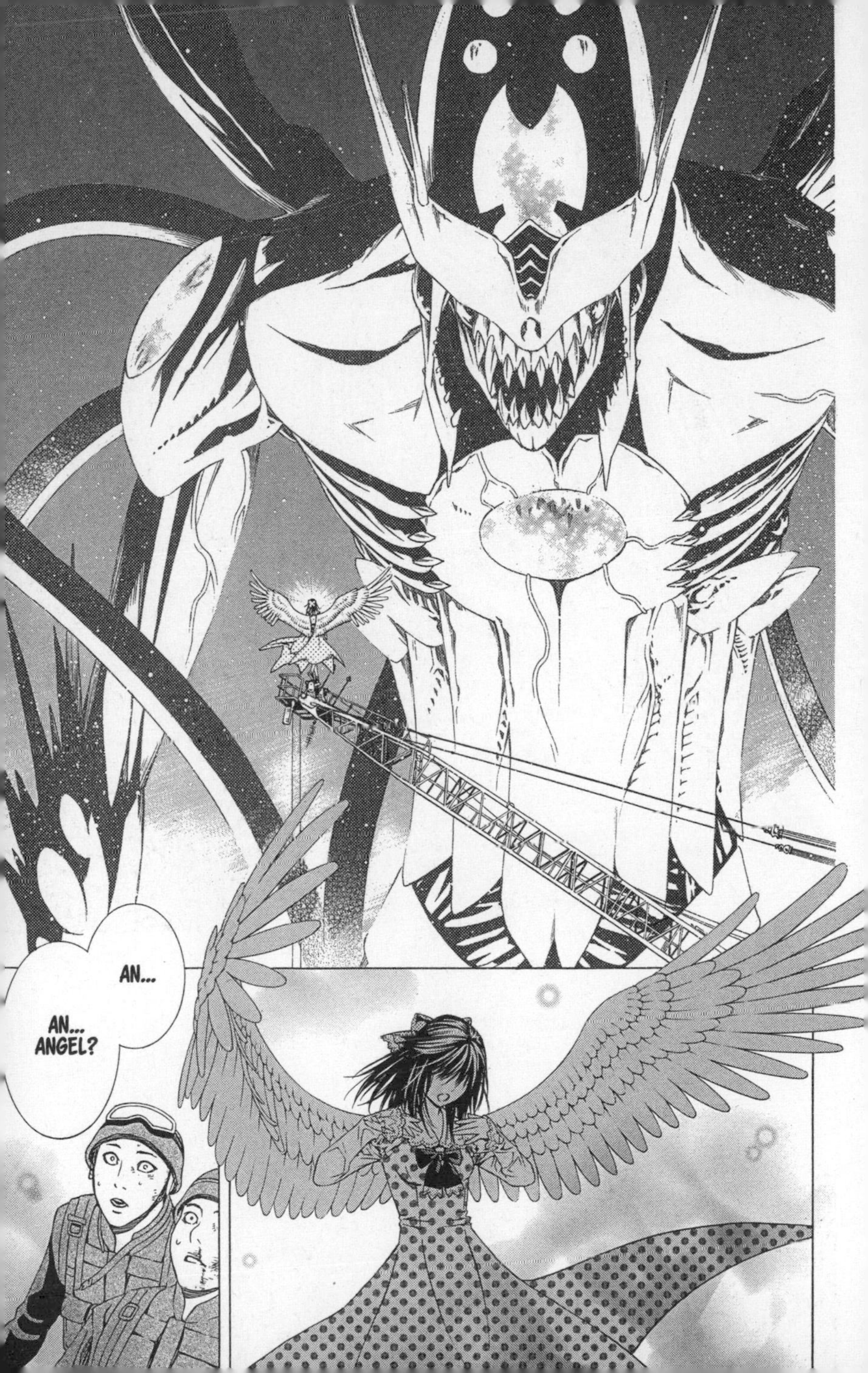
AN...
AN... ANGEL?

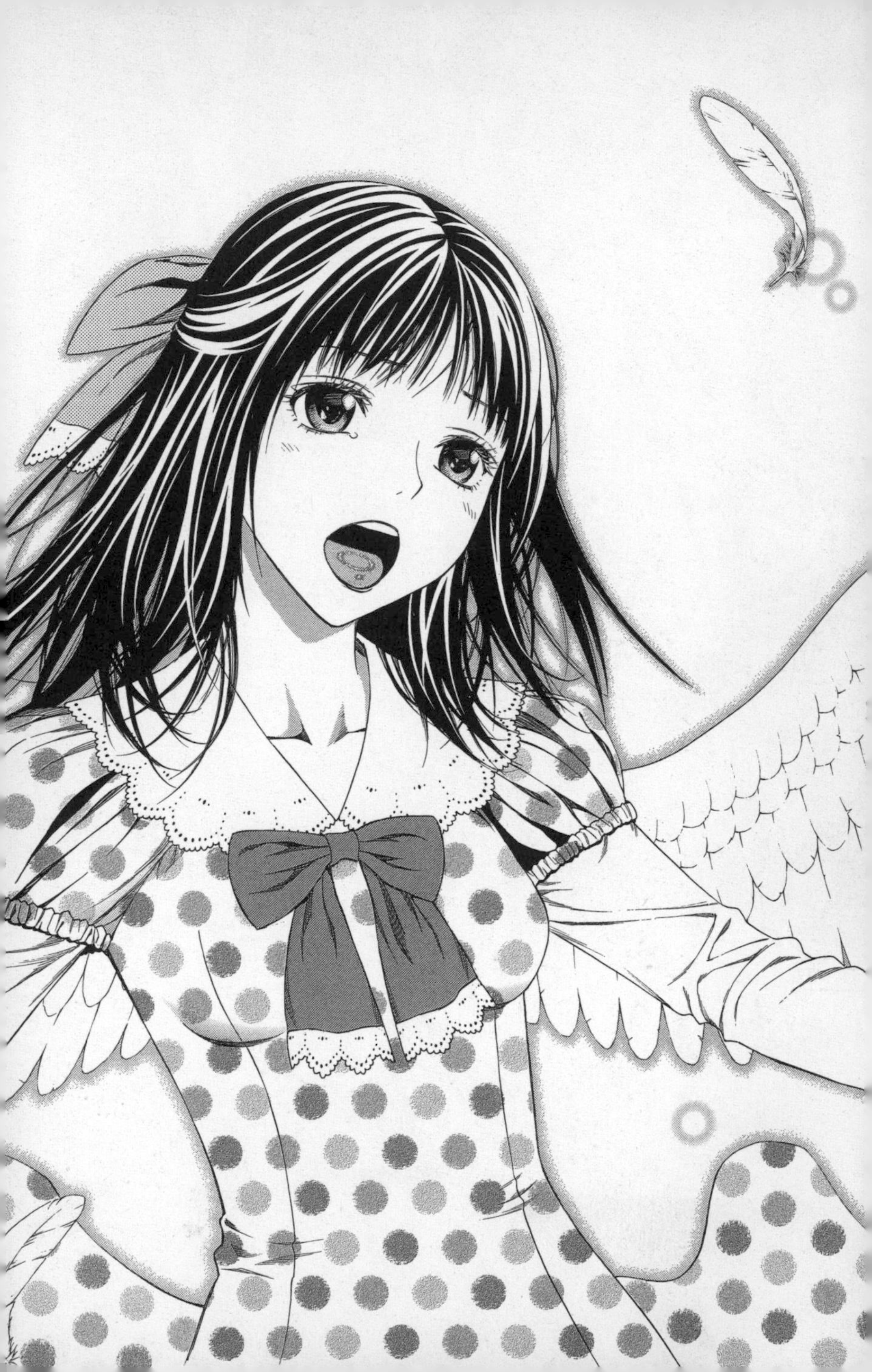

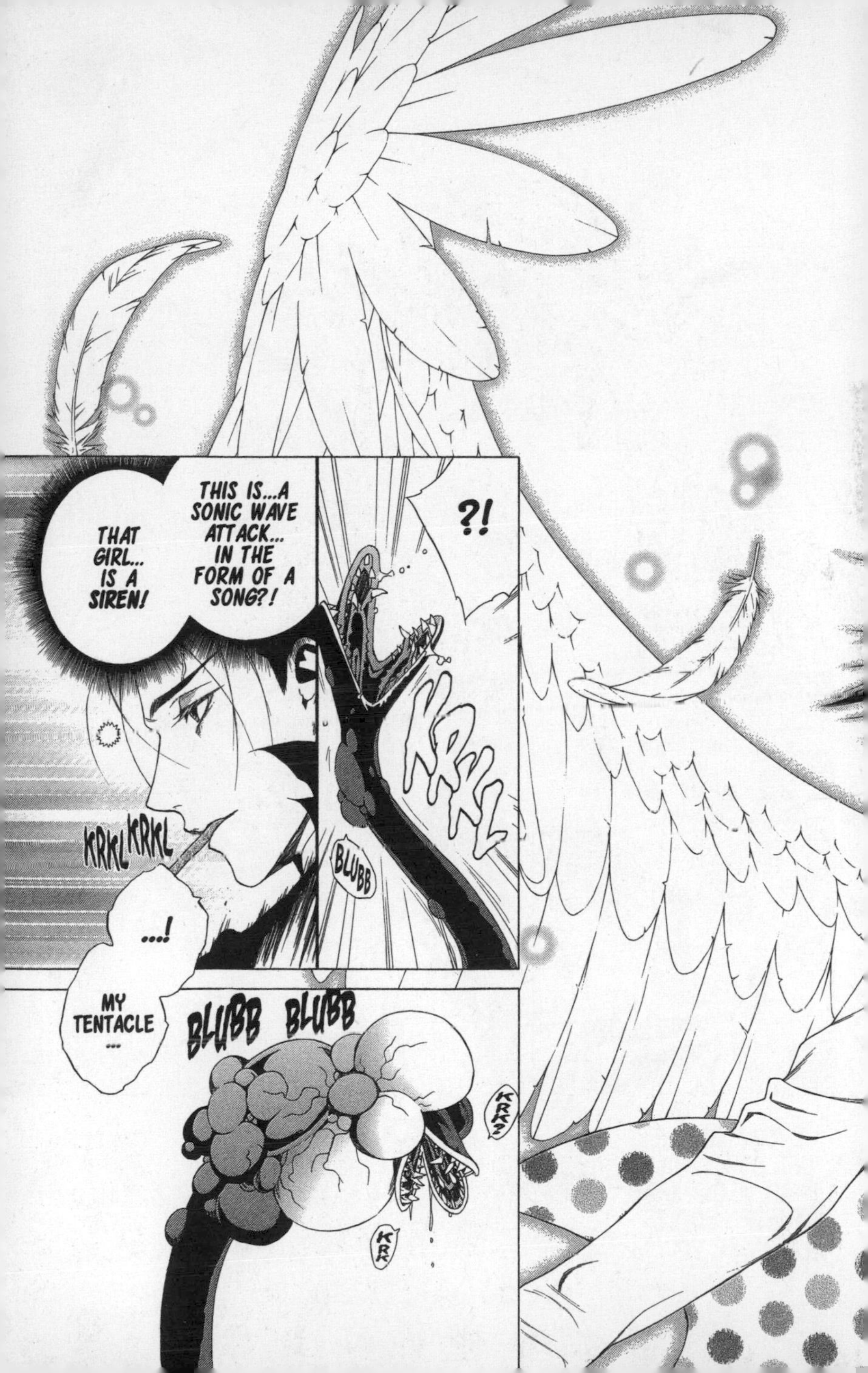
?!
KRKL
BLUBB
THIS IS...A SONIC WAVE ATTACK... IN THE FORM OF A SONG?!
THAT GIRL... IS A SIREN!
KRKL KRKL
...!
MY TENTACLE ...
BLUBB BLUBB
KRKK?
KRK

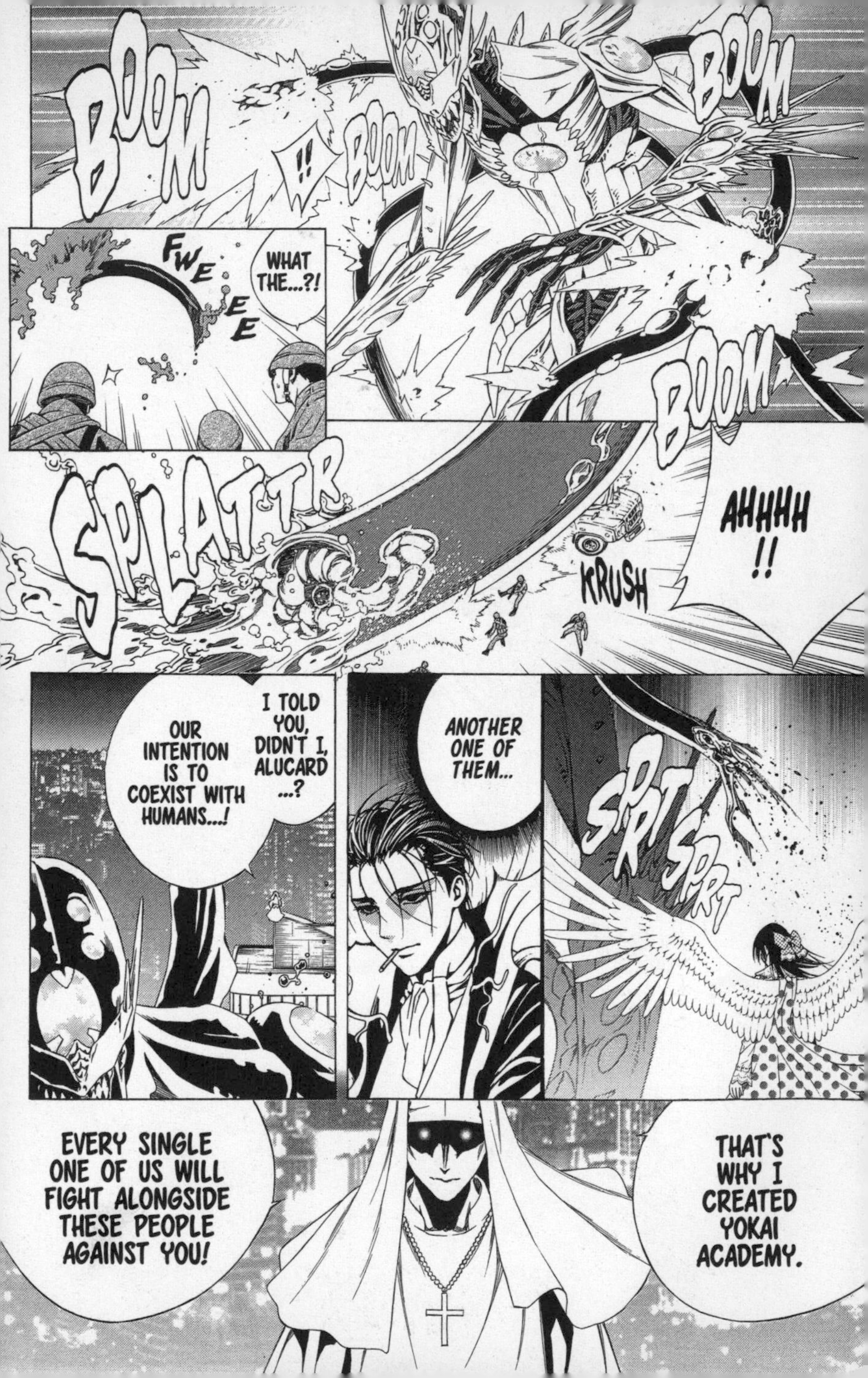
BOOM
BOOM
!!
BOOM
FWEEEE
WHAT THE...?!
BOOM
AHHHH!!
KRUSH
SPLATTR
SPRT SPRT SPRT
ANOTHER ONE OF THEM...
I TOLD YOU, DIDN'T I, ALUCARD...?
OUR INTENTION IS TO COEXIST WITH HUMANS...!
THAT'S WHY I CREATED YOKAI ACADEMY.
EVERY SINGLE ONE OF US WILL FIGHT ALONGSIDE THESE PEOPLE AGAINST YOU!

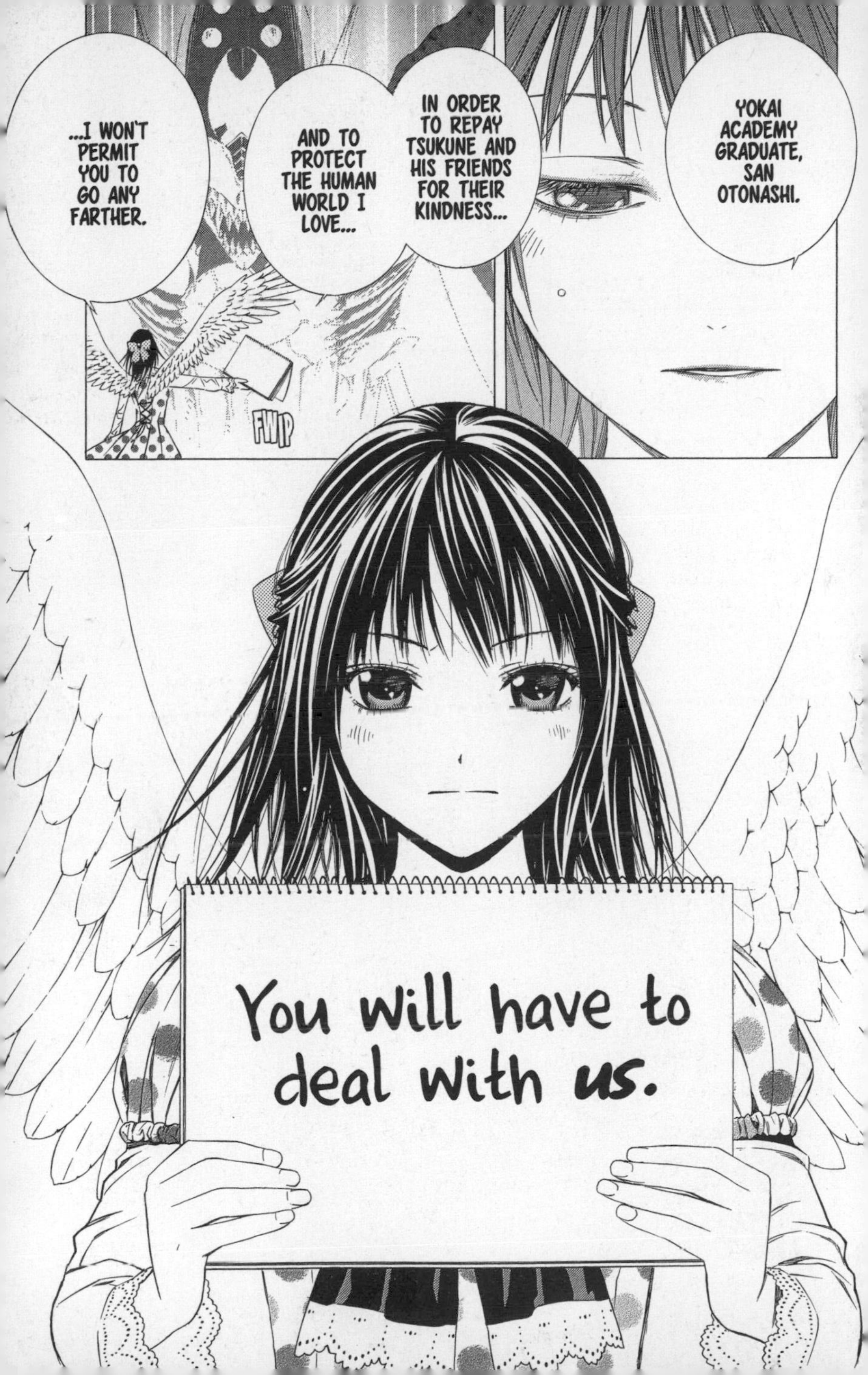
YOKAI ACADEMY GRADUATE, SAN OTONASHI.
IN ORDER TO REPAY TSUKUNE AND HIS FRIENDS FOR THEIR KINDNESS...
AND TO PROTECT THE HUMAN WORLD I LOVE...
...I WON'T PERMIT YOU TO GO ANY FARTHER.
FWIP
You will have to deal with us.

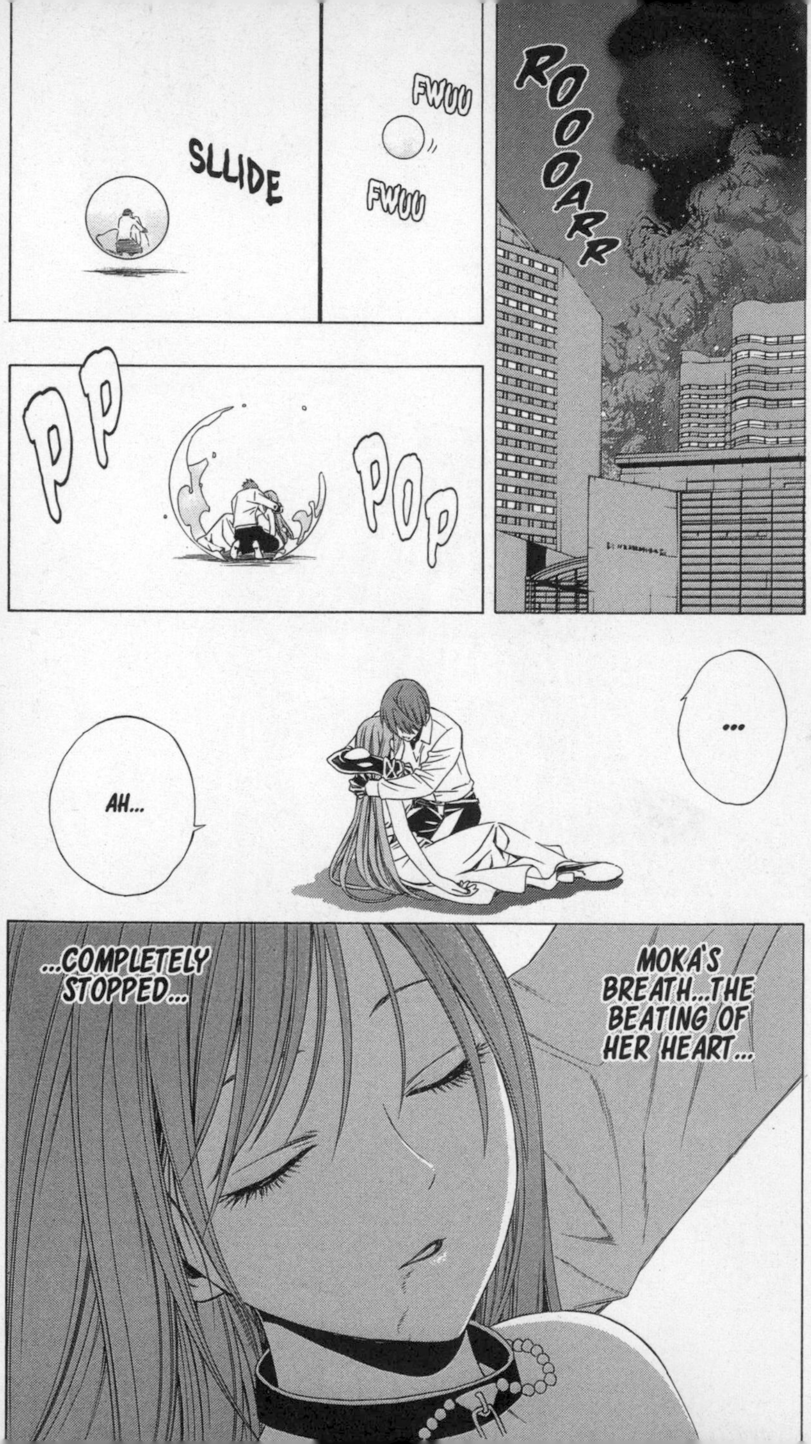
ROOOOARR
FWUU
FWUU
SLLIDE
POP
PP
...
AH...
MOKA'S BREATH...THE BEATING OF HER HEART...
...COMPLETELY STOPPED...

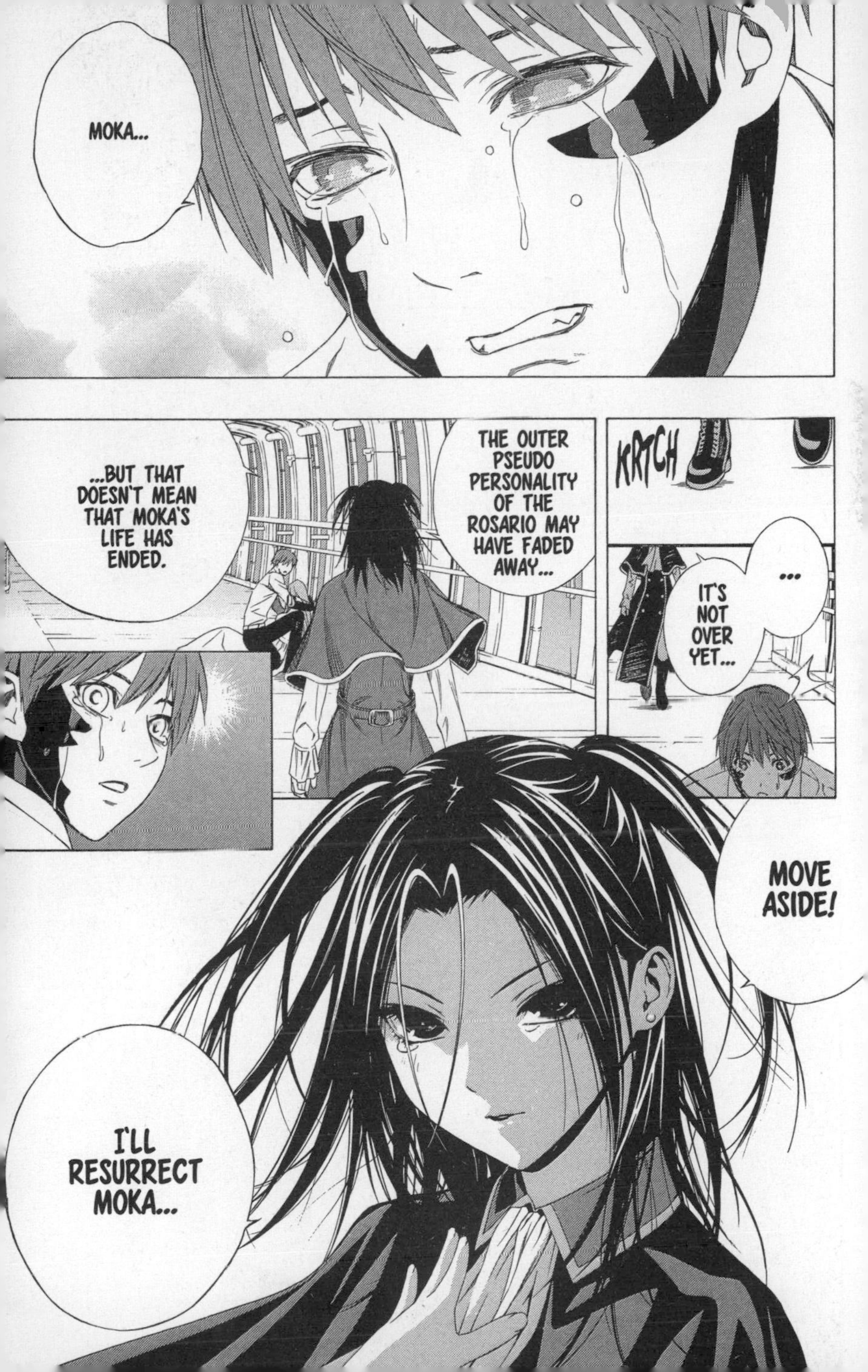
MOKA...
KRTCH
...
IT'S NOT OVER YET...
THE OUTER PSEUDO PERSONALITY OF THE ROSARIO MAY HAVE FADED AWAY...
...BUT THAT DOESN'T MEAN THAT MOKA'S LIFE HAS ENDED.
MOVE ASIDE!
I'LL RESURRECT MOKA...

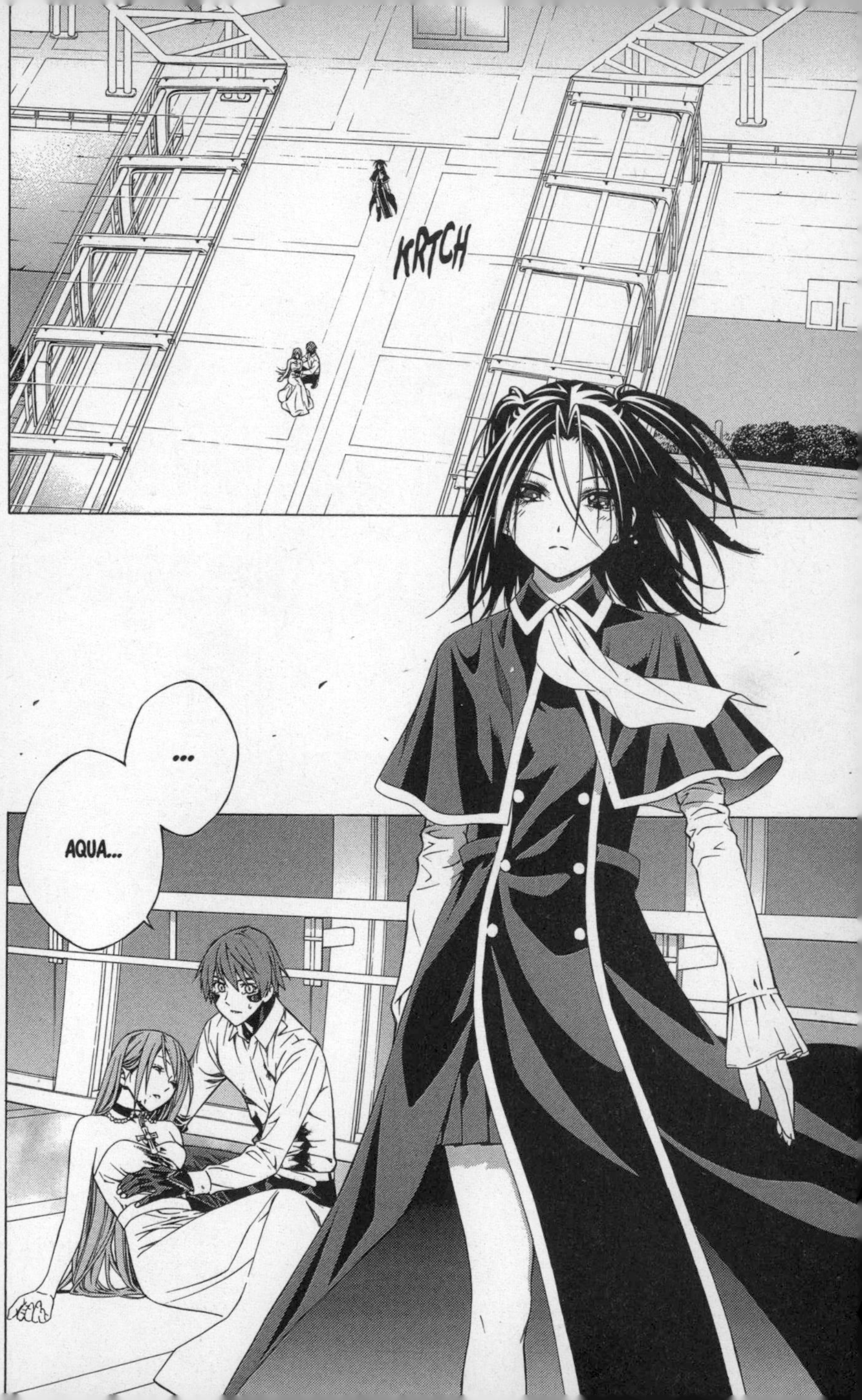
KRTCH
...
AQUA...

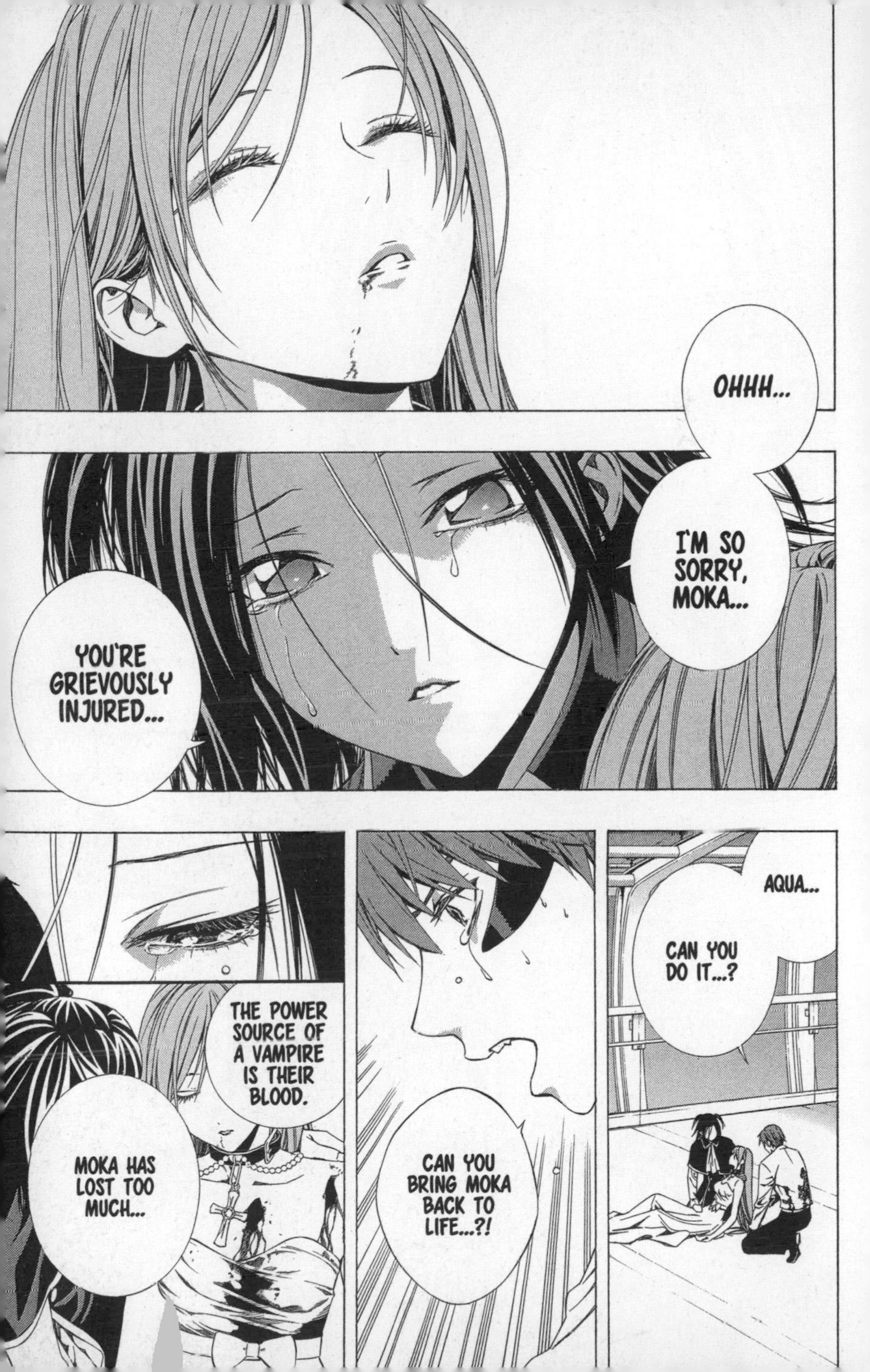
OHHH...
I'M SO SORRY, MOKA...
YOU'RE GRIEVOUSLY INJURED...
AQUA...
CAN YOU DO IT...?
CAN YOU BRING MOKA BACK TO LIFE...?!
THE POWER SOURCE OF A VAMPIRE IS THEIR BLOOD.
MOKA HAS LOST TOO MUCH...

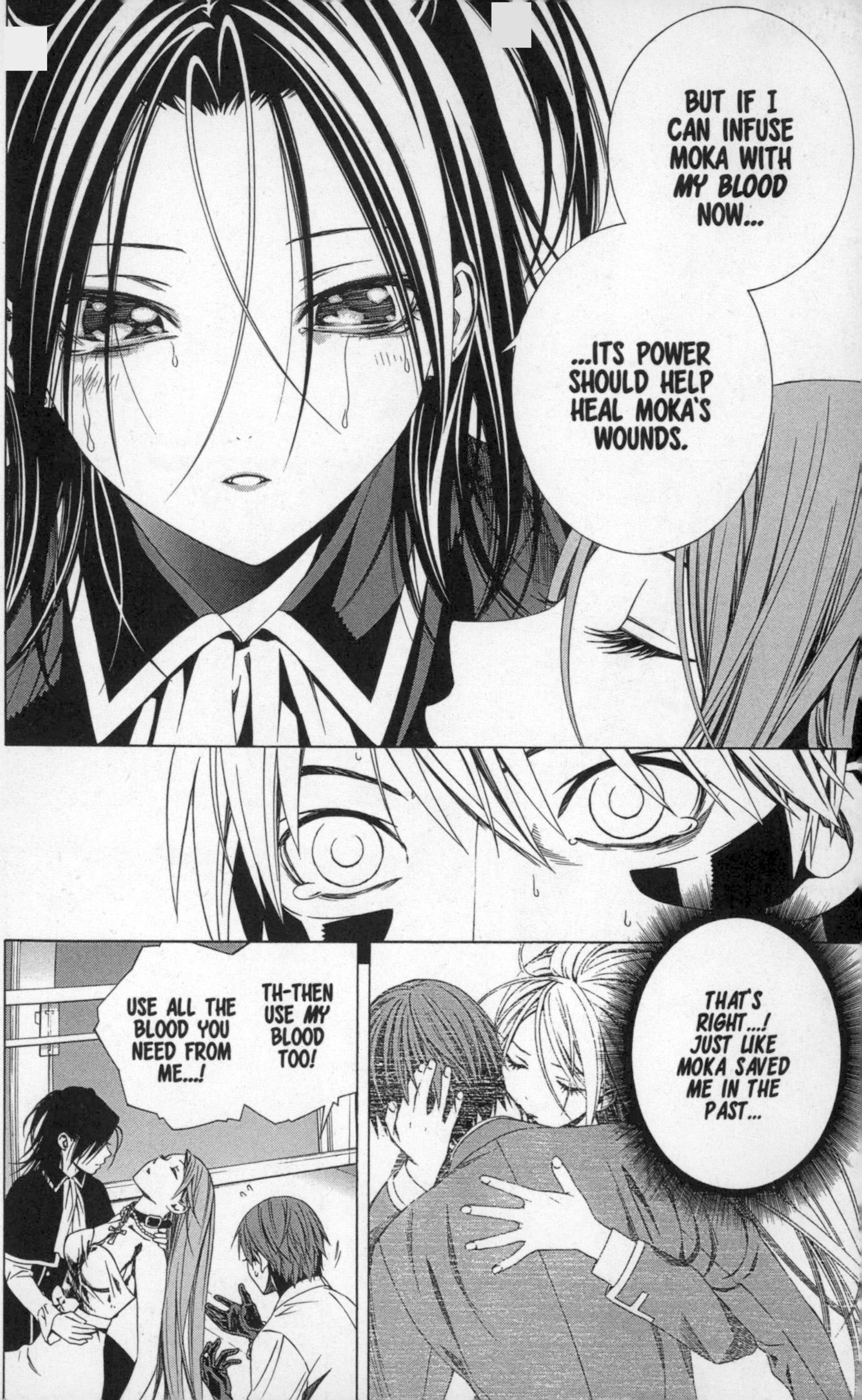
BUT IF I CAN INFUSE MOKA WITH MY BLOOD NOW...
...ITS POWER SHOULD HELP HEAL MOKA'S WOUNDS.
THAT'S RIGHT...! JUST LIKE MOKA SAVED ME IN THE PAST...
TH-THEN USE MY BLOOD TOO!
USE ALL THE BLOOD YOU NEED FROM ME...!

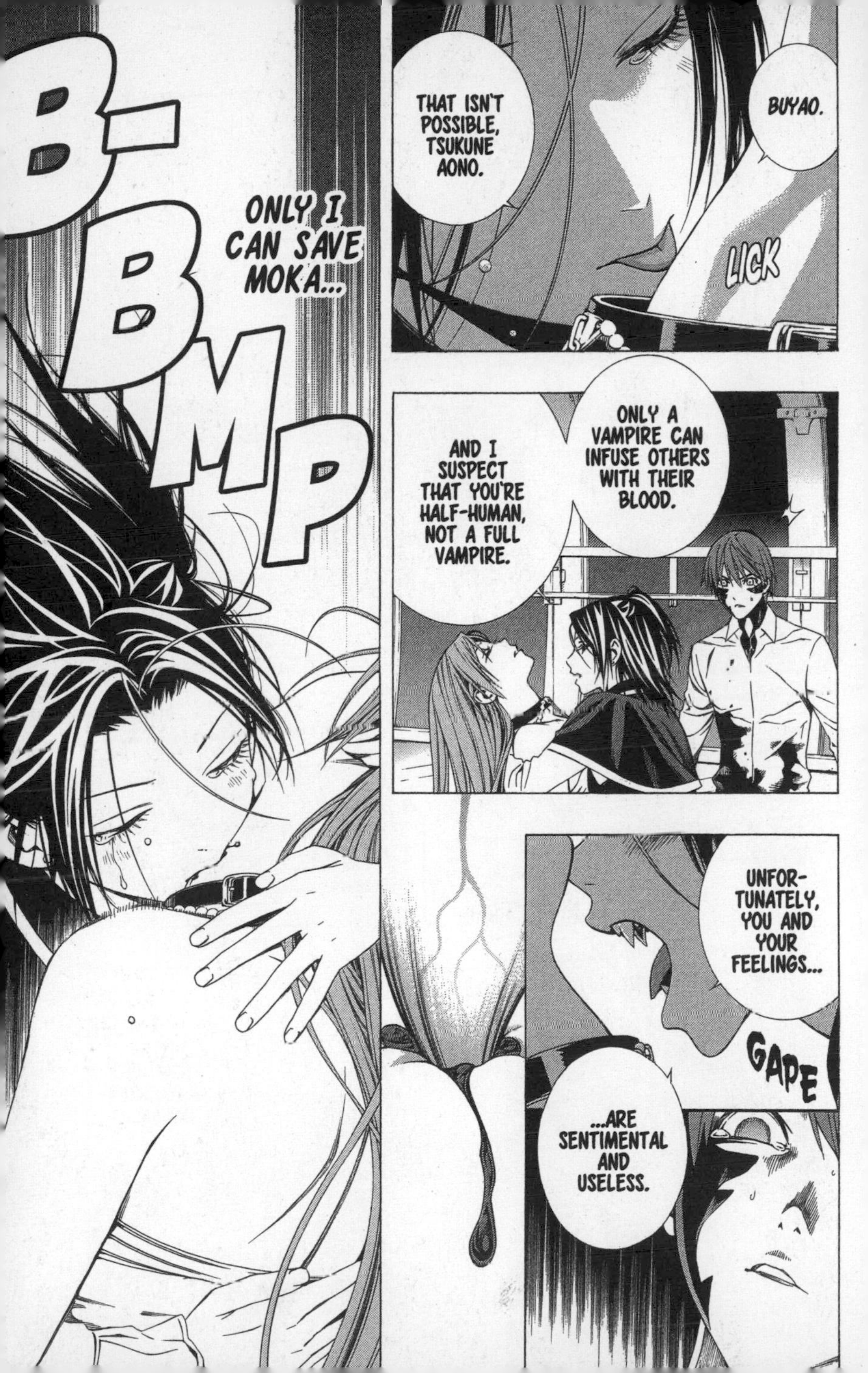
BUYAO.
THAT ISN'T POSSIBLE, TSUKUNE AONO.
LICK
ONLY A VAMPIRE CAN INFUSE OTHERS WITH THEIR BLOOD.
AND I SUSPECT THAT YOU'RE HALF-HUMAN, NOT A FULL VAMPIRE.
UNFORTUNATELY, YOU AND YOUR FEELINGS...
GAPE
...ARE SENTIMENTAL AND USELESS.
B-BMP
ONLY I CAN SAVE MOKA...

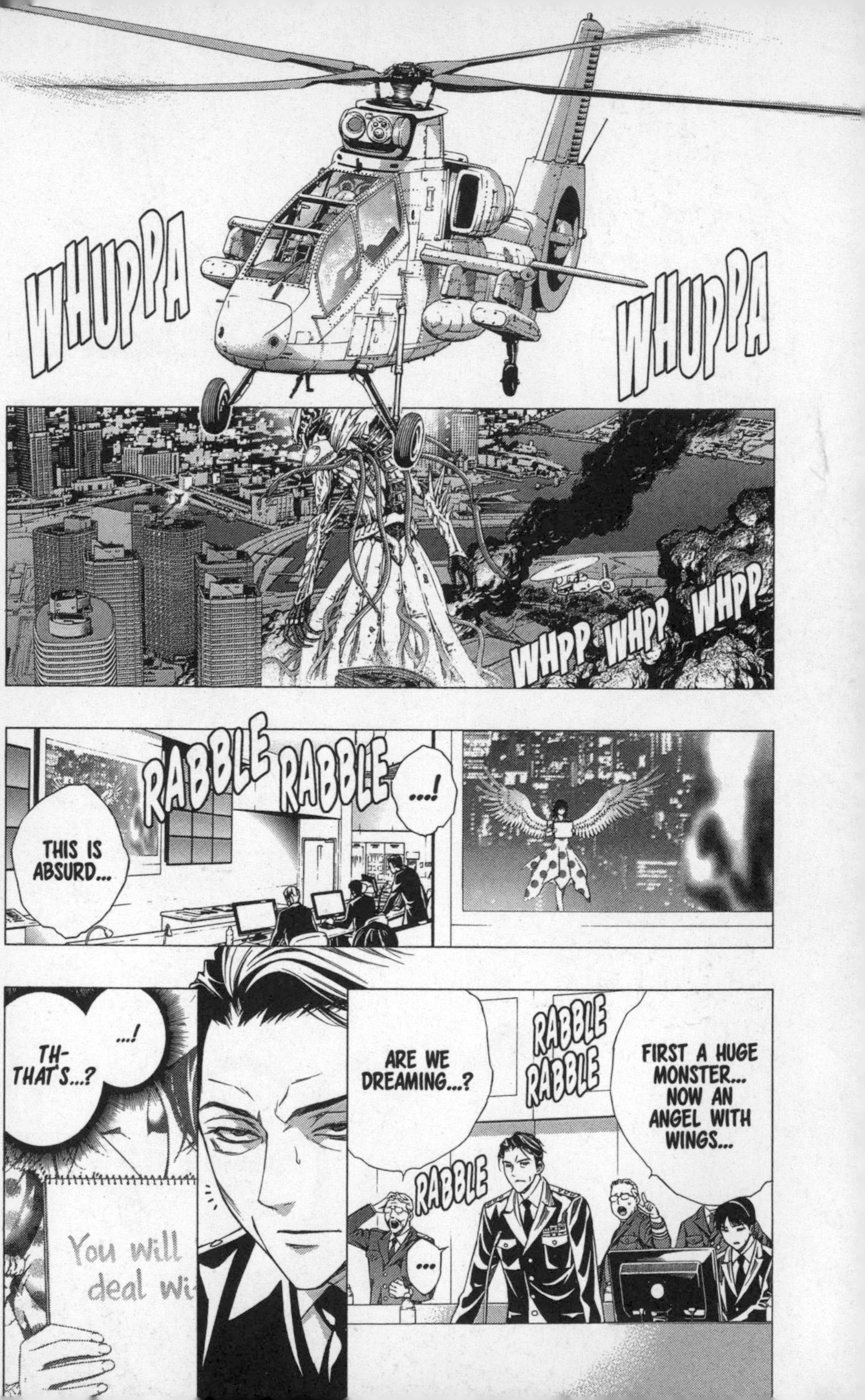
WHUPPA
WHUPPA
WHPP WHPP WHPP
...!
RABBLE RABBLE
THIS IS ABSURD...
FIRST A HUGE MONSTER... NOW AN ANGEL WITH WINGS...
RABBLE RABBLE
ARE WE DREAMING...?
RABBLE
...
...!
TH- THAT'S...?
You will deal wi-

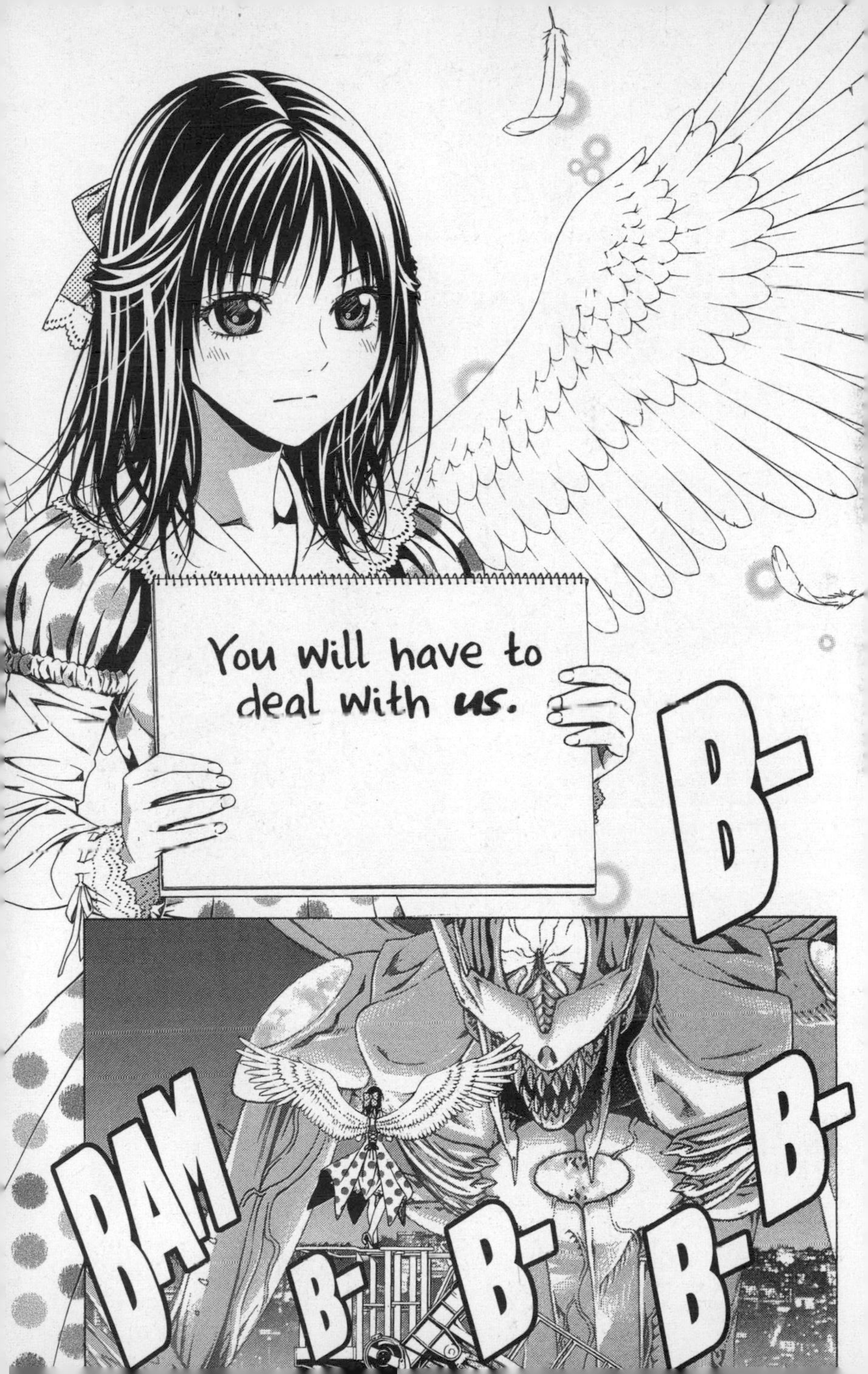
You will have to deal with us.
B-
B-B-
B-
B-
BAM

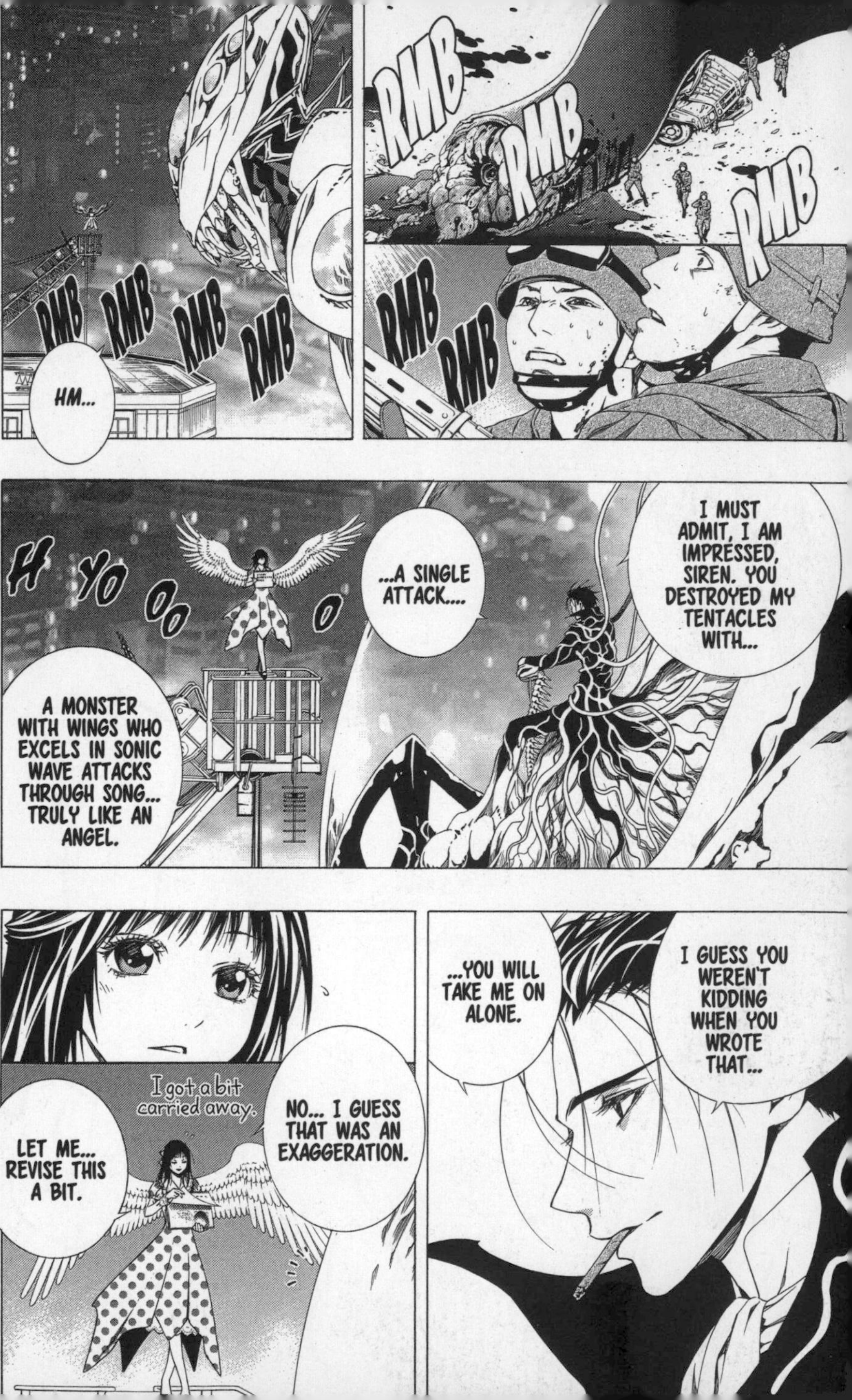
RMB
RMB
RMB
RMB
RMB
RMB
RMB
RMB
RMB
RMB
HM...
I MUST ADMIT, I AM IMPRESSED, SIREN. YOU DESTROYED MY TENTACLES WITH...
...A SINGLE ATTACK....
H YO OO O
A MONSTER WITH WINGS WHO EXCELS IN SONIC WAVE ATTACKS THROUGH SONG... TRULY LIKE AN ANGEL.
I GUESS YOU WEREN'T KIDDING WHEN YOU WROTE THAT...
...YOU WILL TAKE ME ON ALONE.
NO... I GUESS THAT WAS AN EXAGGERATION.
I got a bit carried away.
LET ME... REVISE THIS A BIT.

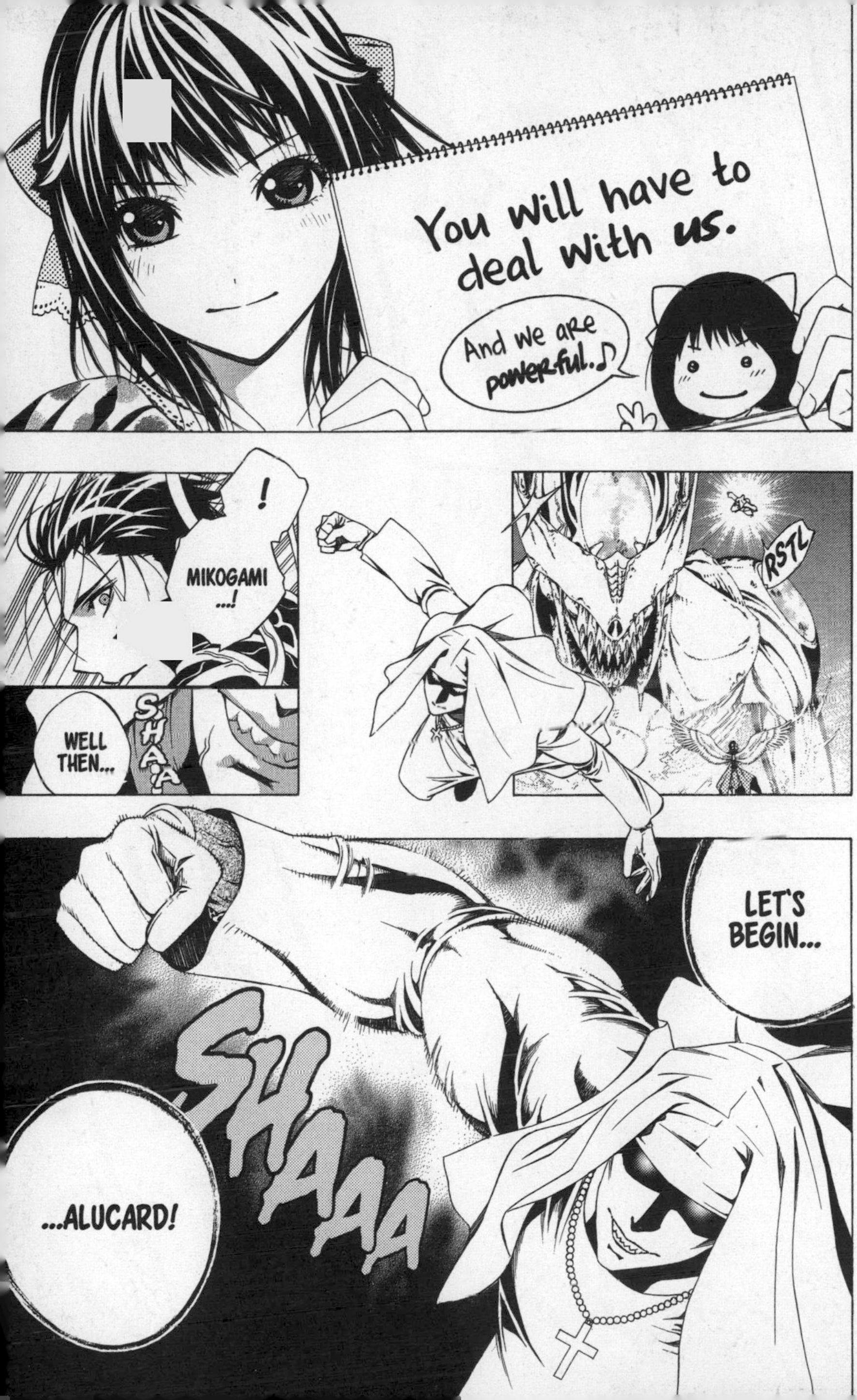
You will have to deal with us.
And we are powerful.♪
RSTL
!
MIKOGAMI ...!
SHAA
WELL THEN...
LET'S BEGIN...
SHAAA
...ALUCARD!

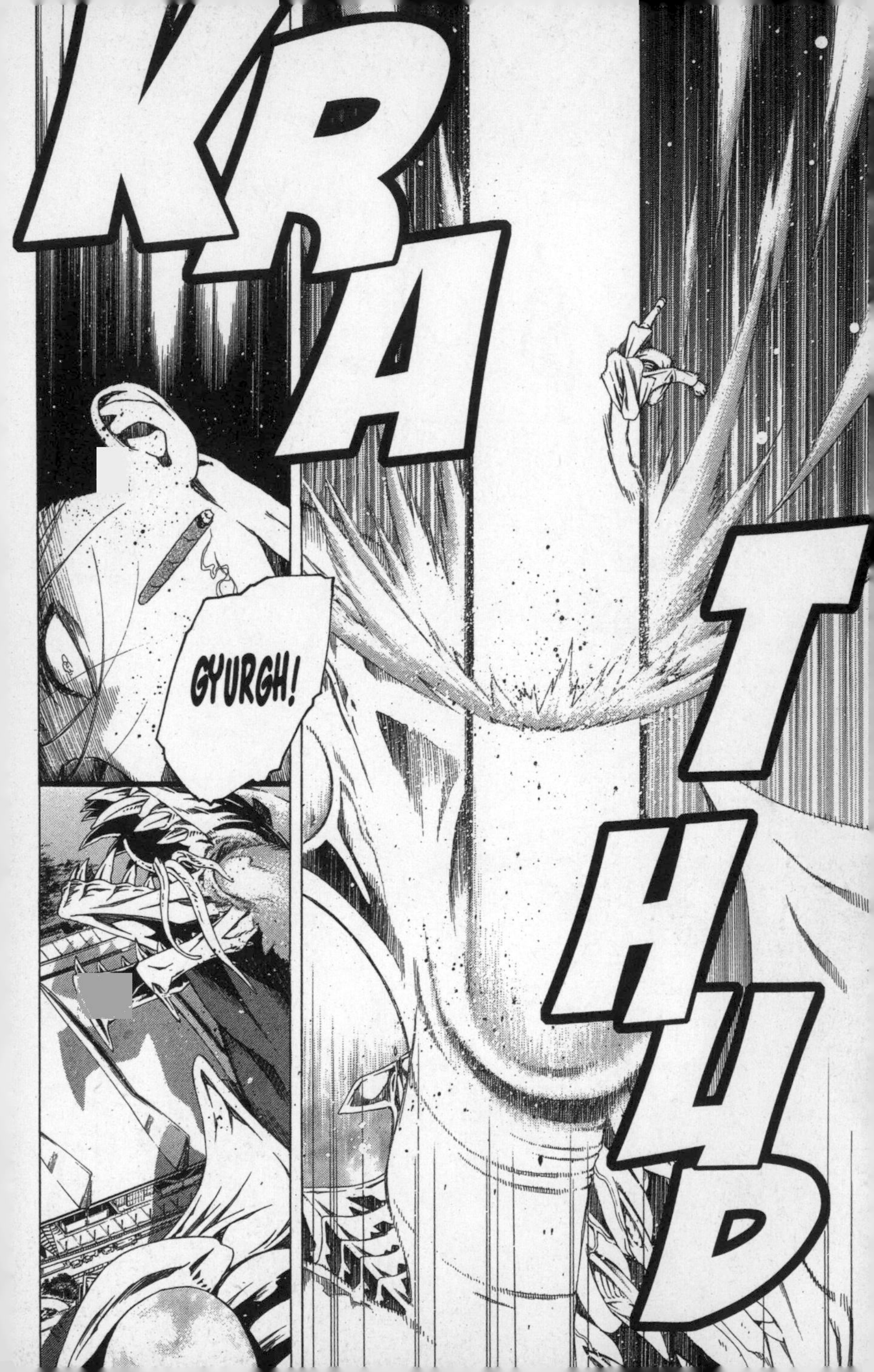
KRA
THUD
GYURGH!

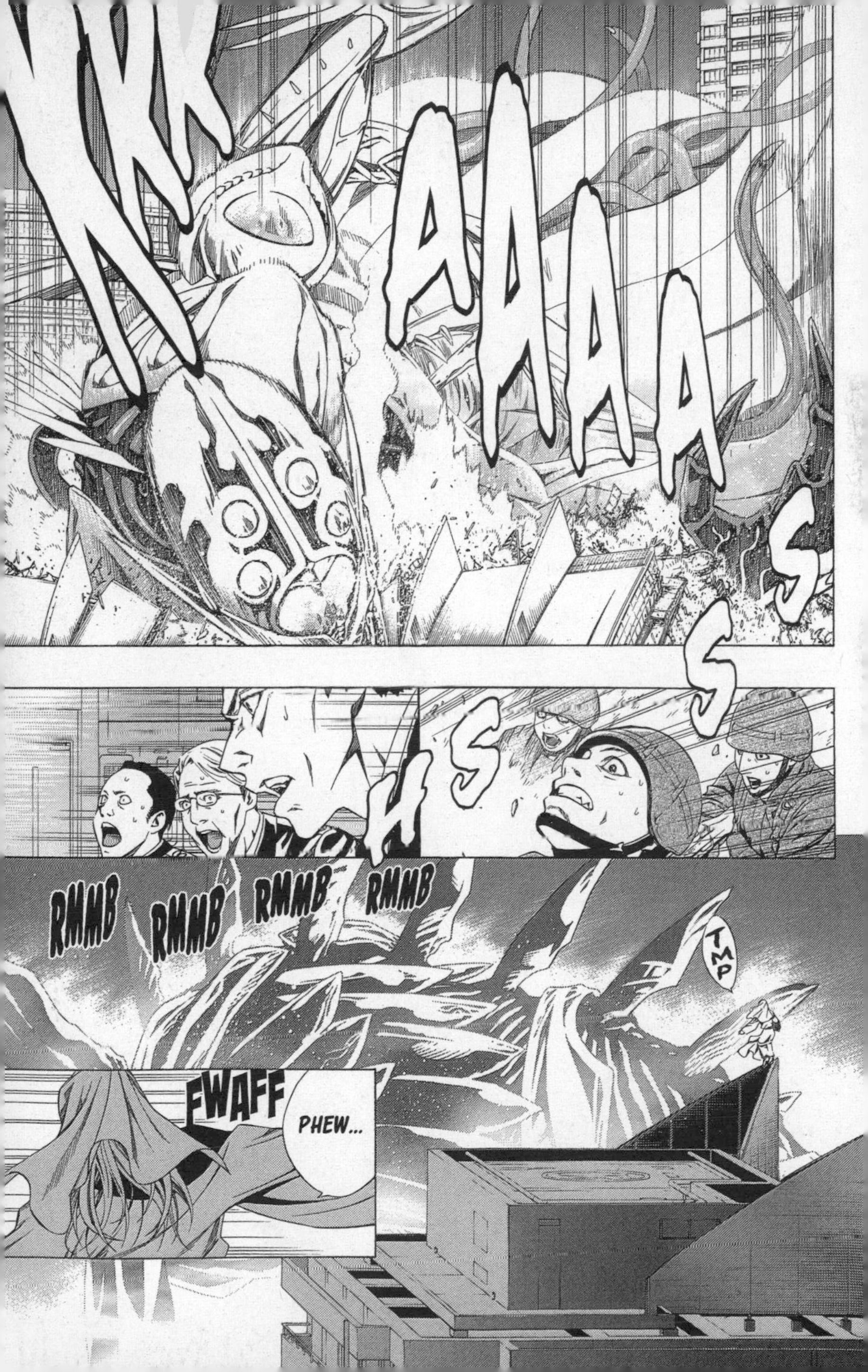
TMP
RMMB
RMMB
RMMB
RMMB
FWAFF
PHEW...

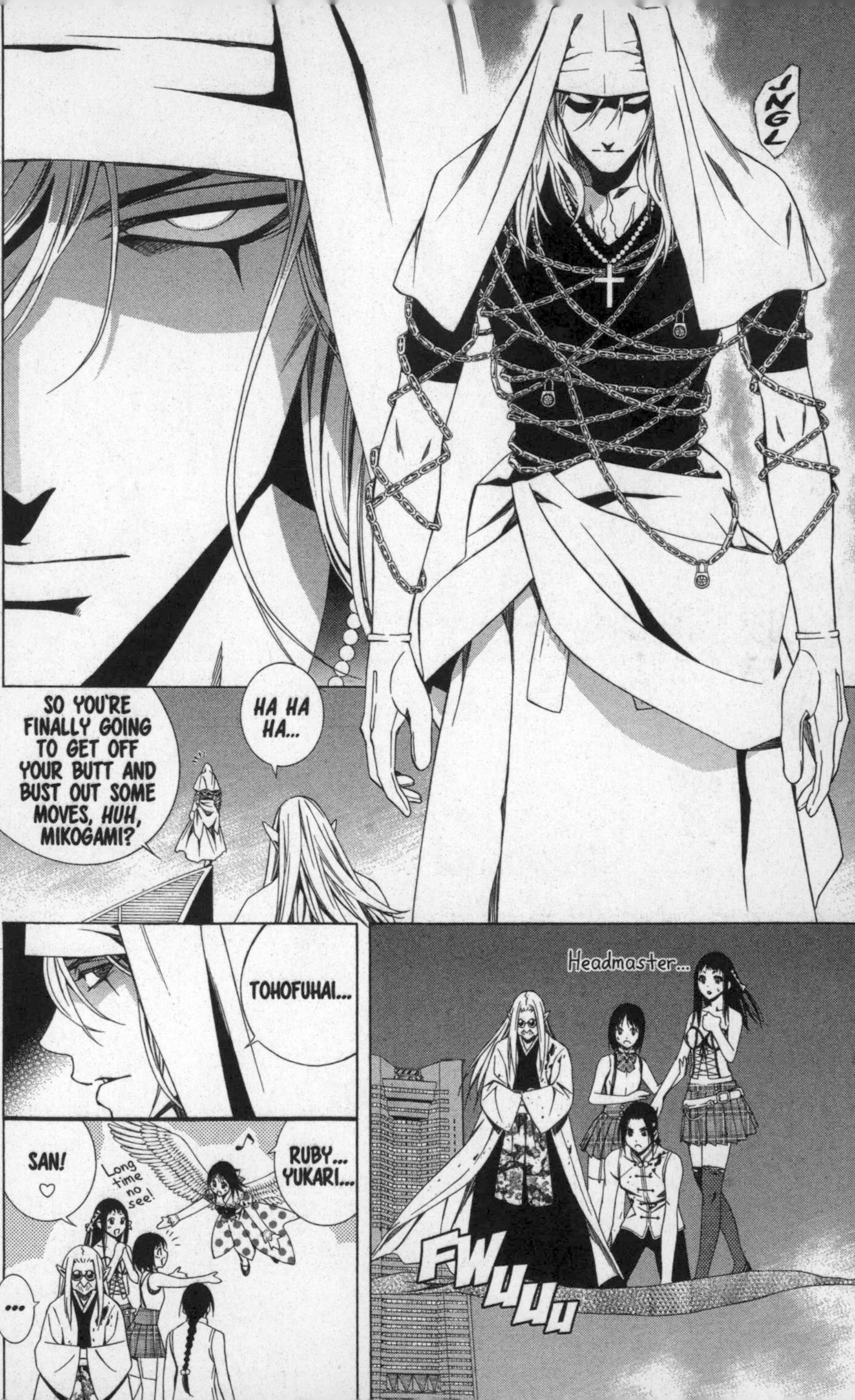
JNGL
HA HA HA...
SO YOU'RE FINALLY GOING TO GET OFF YOUR BUTT AND BUST OUT SOME MOVES, HUH, MIKOGAMI?
Headmaster...
FWUUUU
TOHOFUHAI...
RUBY... YUKARI...
SAN! ♡
Long time no see!
...

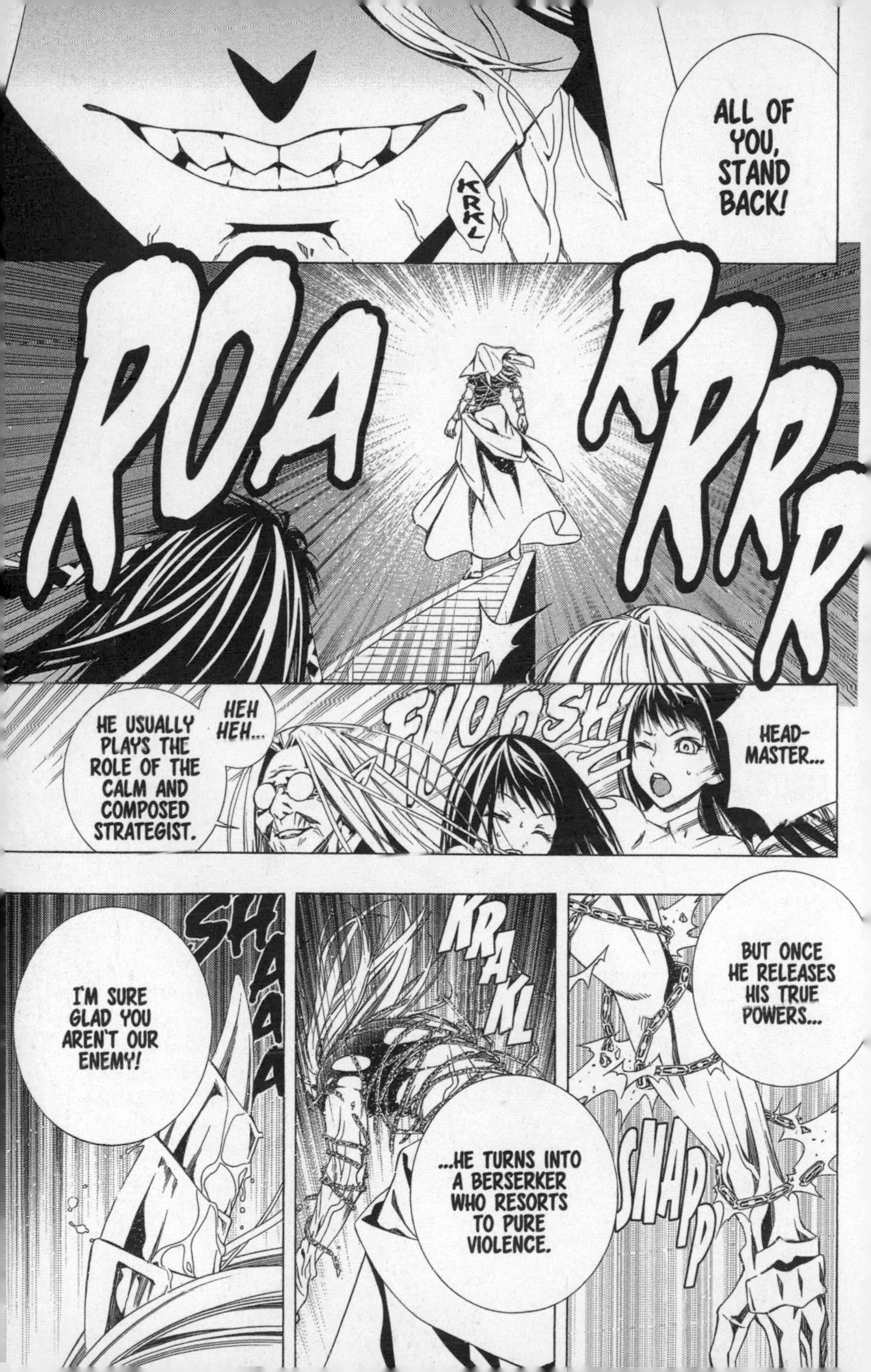
ALL OF YOU, STAND BACK!
KRKL
ROARRRR
HEAD-MASTER...
SWOOSH
HEH HEH...
HE USUALLY PLAYS THE ROLE OF THE CALM AND COMPOSED STRATEGIST.
BUT ONCE HE RELEASES HIS TRUE POWERS...
SNAP
KRAKL
...HE TURNS INTO A BERSERKER WHO RESORTS TO PURE VIOLENCE.
SHAAAA
I'M SURE GLAD YOU AREN'T OUR ENEMY!

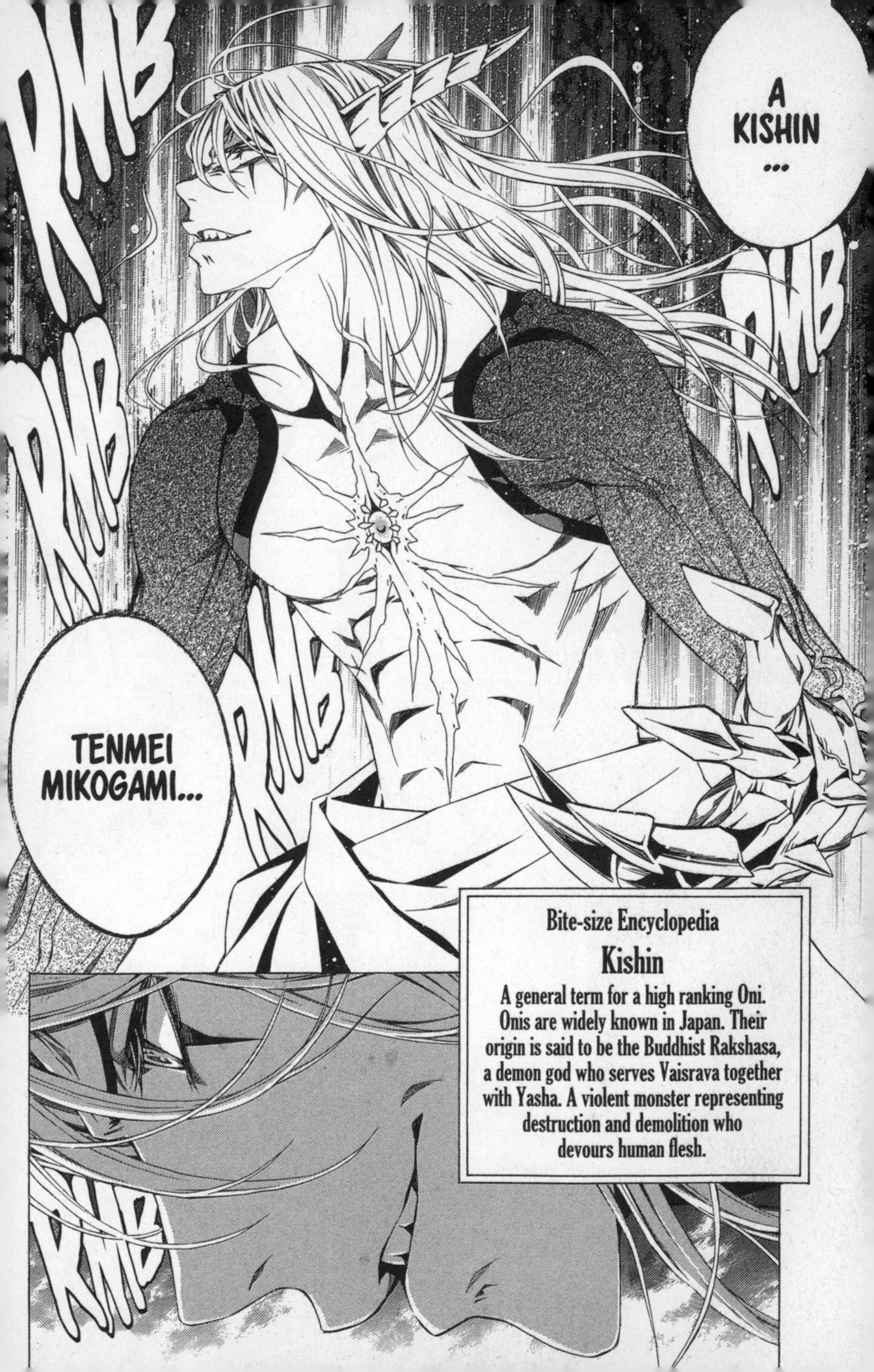
A KISHIN...
RMB
RMB
RMB
TENMEI MIKOGAMI...
RMB
Bite-size Encyclopedia
Kishin
A general term for a high ranking Oni. Onis are widely known in Japan. Their origin is said to be the Buddhist Rakshasa, a demon god who serves Vaisrava together with Yasha. A violent monster representing destruction and demolition who devours human flesh.
RMB

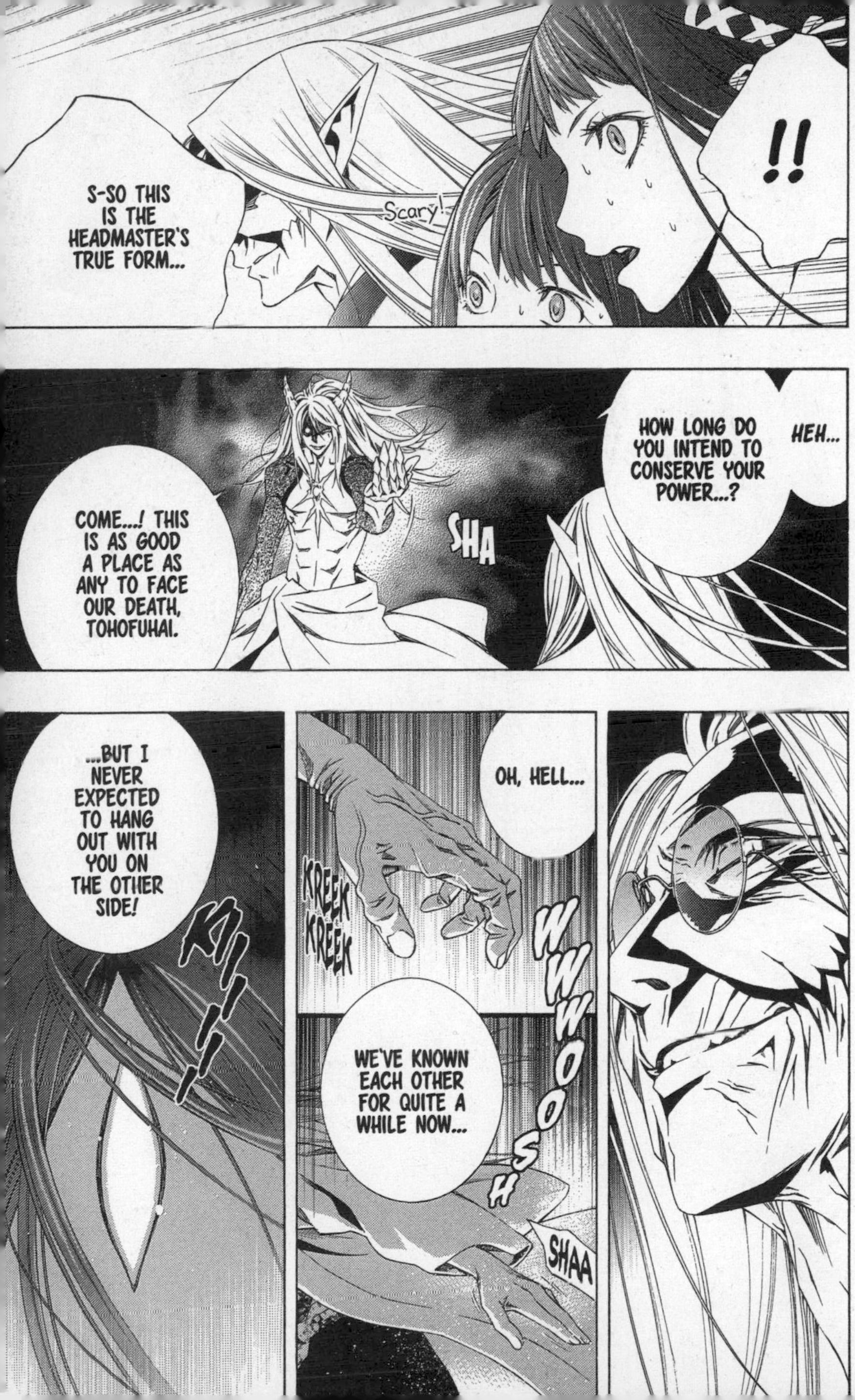
!!
Scary!
S-SO THIS IS THE HEADMASTER'S TRUE FORM...
HEH...
HOW LONG DO YOU INTEND TO CONSERVE YOUR POWER...?
SHA
COME...! THIS IS AS GOOD A PLACE AS ANY TO FACE OUR DEATH, TOHOFUHAI.
SHAA
OH, HELL...
KREEK KREEK
WWWOOOSH
WE'VE KNOWN EACH OTHER FOR QUITE A WHILE NOW...
...BUT I NEVER EXPECTED TO HANG OUT WITH YOU ON THE OTHER SIDE!
KI!!!!

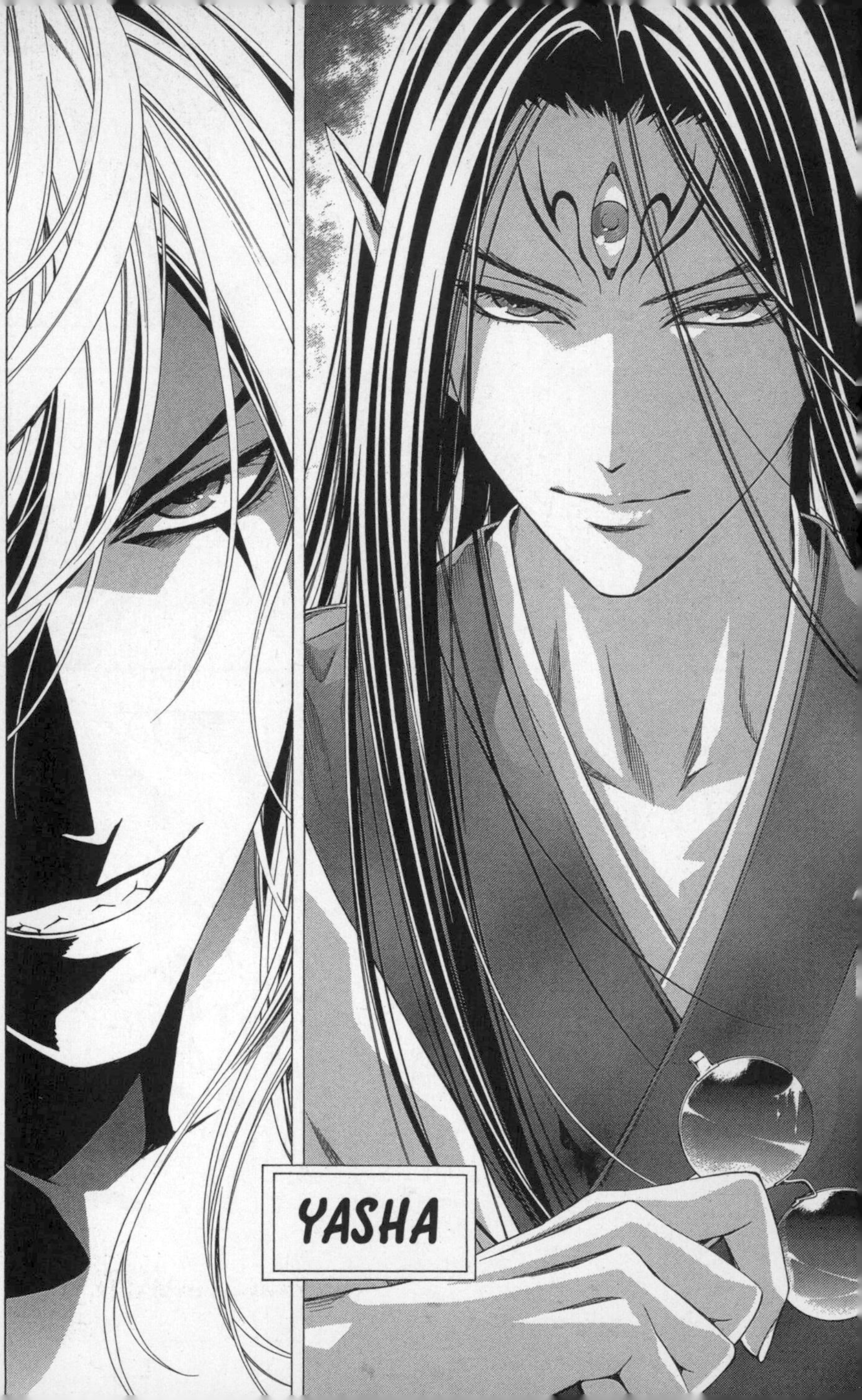
YASHA

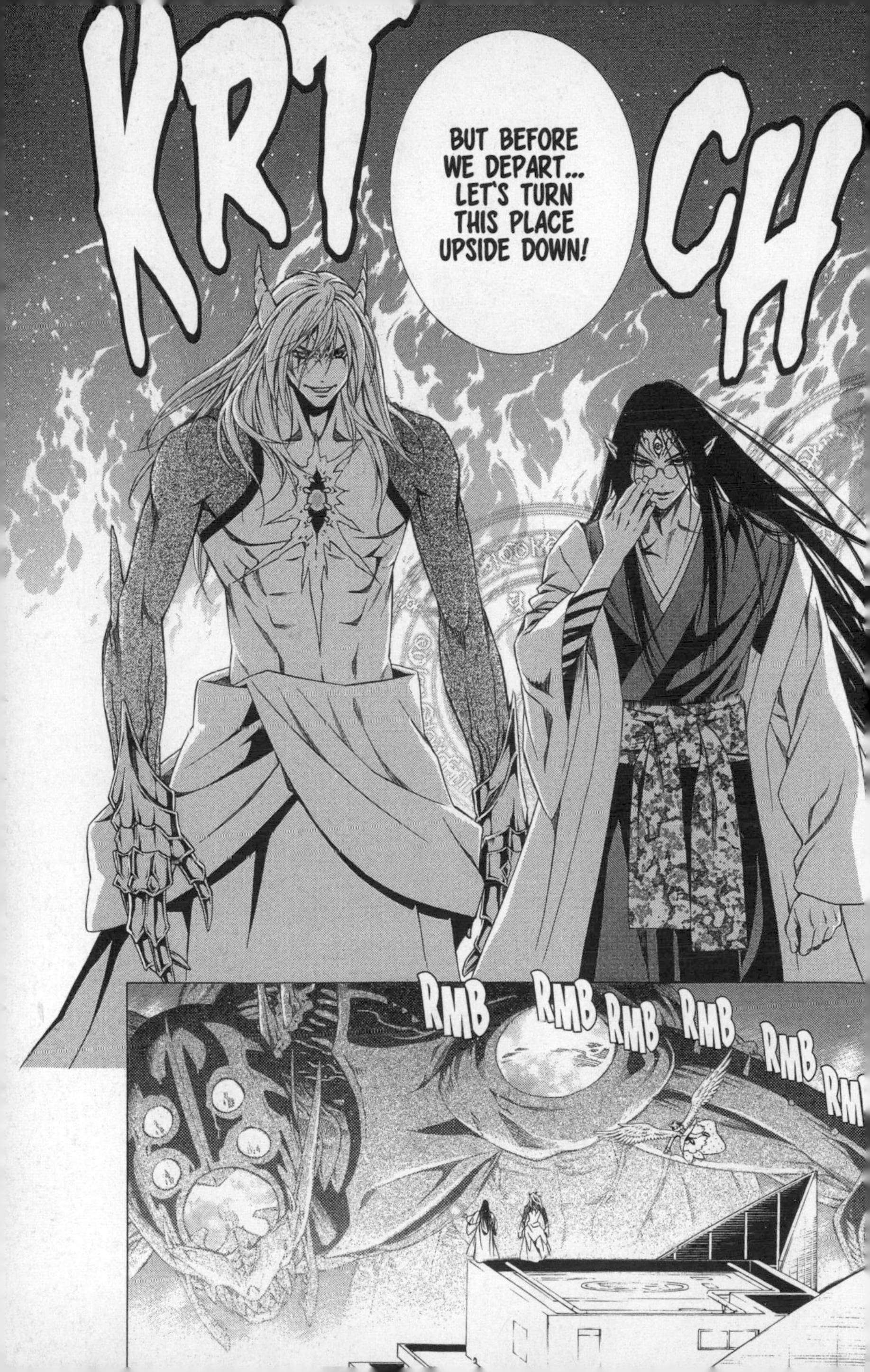
KRT CH
BUT BEFORE WE DEPART... LET'S TURN THIS PLACE UPSIDE DOWN!
RMB RMB RMB RMB RMB RM

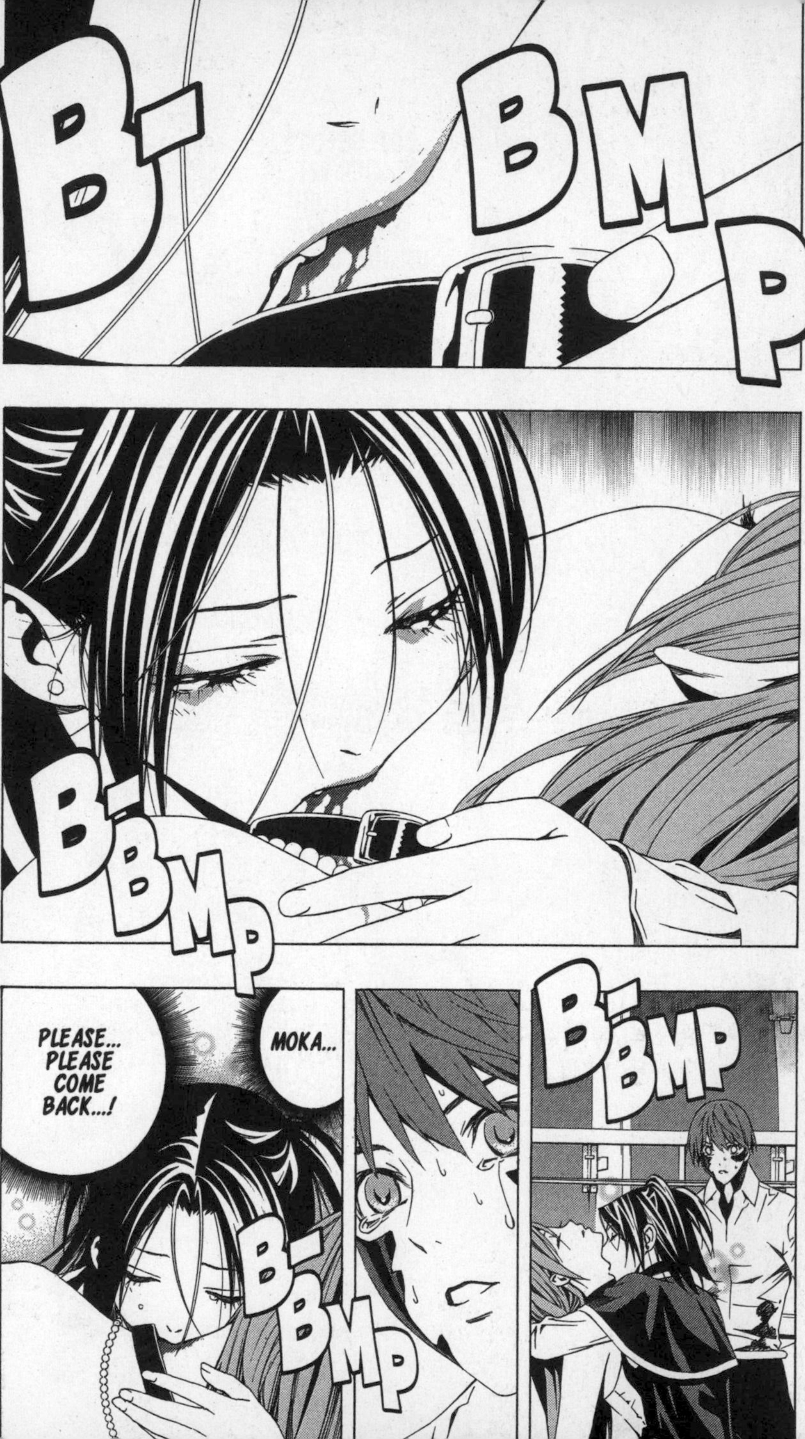
B-BMP
B-BMP
B-BMP
MOKA...
B-BMP
PLEASE... PLEASE COME BACK...!

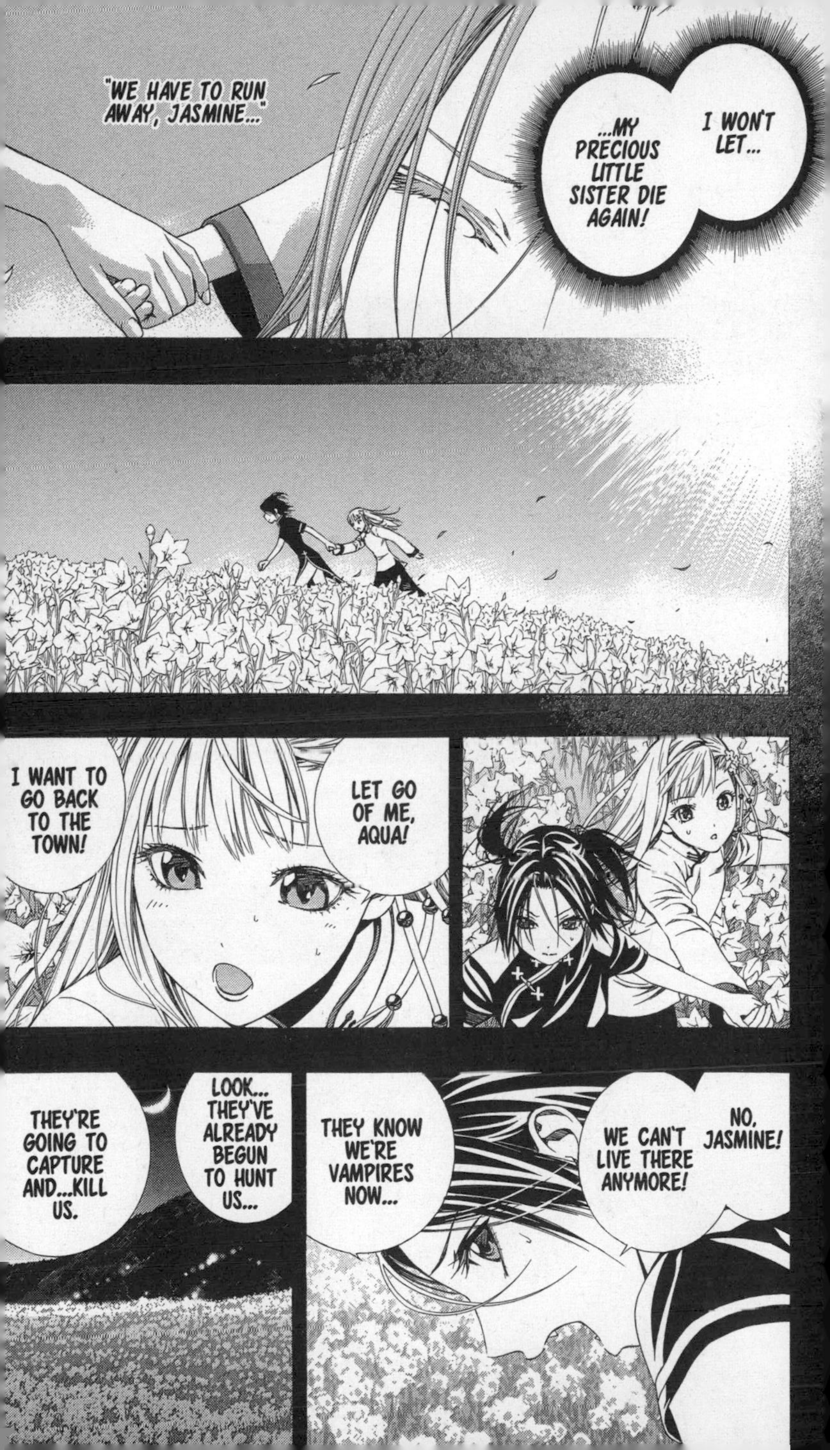
I WON'T LET...
...MY PRECIOUS LITTLE SISTER DIE AGAIN!
"WE HAVE TO RUN AWAY, JASMINE..."
LET GO OF ME, AQUA!
I WANT TO GO BACK TO THE TOWN!
NO, JASMINE!
WE CAN'T LIVE THERE ANYMORE!
THEY KNOW WE'RE VAMPIRES NOW...
LOOK... THEY'VE ALREADY BEGUN TO HUNT US...
THEY'RE GOING TO CAPTURE AND...KILL US.

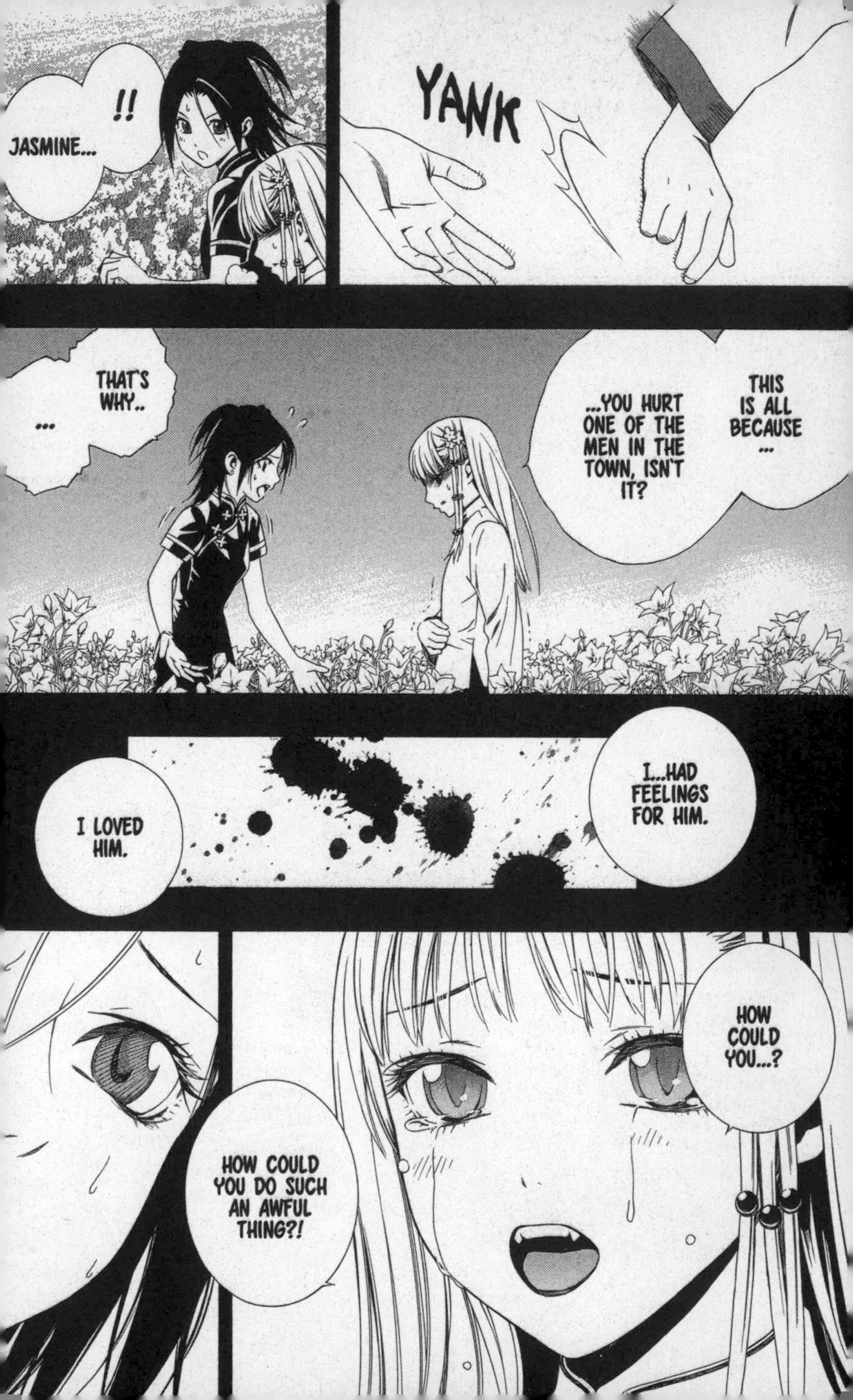
YANK
!!
JASMINE...
THIS IS ALL BECAUSE ...
...YOU HURT ONE OF THE MEN IN THE TOWN, ISN'T IT?
THAT'S WHY.. ...
I...HAD FEELINGS FOR HIM.
I LOVED HIM.
HOW COULD YOU...?
HOW COULD YOU DO SUCH AN AWFUL THING?!

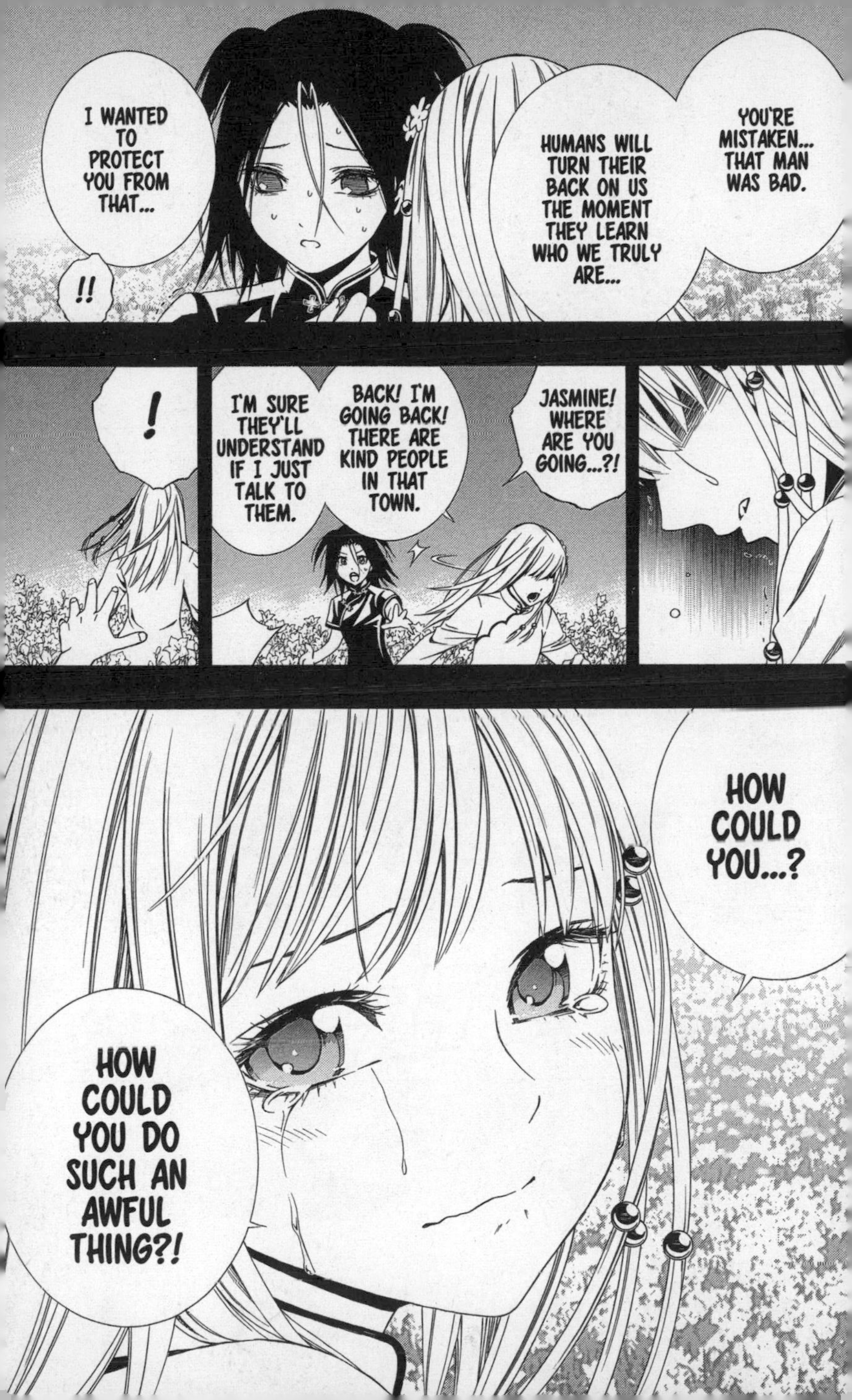
YOU'RE MISTAKEN... THAT MAN WAS BAD.
HUMANS WILL TURN THEIR BACK ON US THE MOMENT THEY LEARN WHO WE TRULY ARE...
I WANTED TO PROTECT YOU FROM THAT...
!!
JASMINE! WHERE ARE YOU GOING...?!
BACK! I'M GOING BACK! THERE ARE KIND PEOPLE IN THAT TOWN.
I'M SURE THEY'LL UNDERSTAND IF I JUST TALK TO THEM.
!
HOW COULD YOU...?
HOW COULD YOU DO SUCH AN AWFUL THING?!

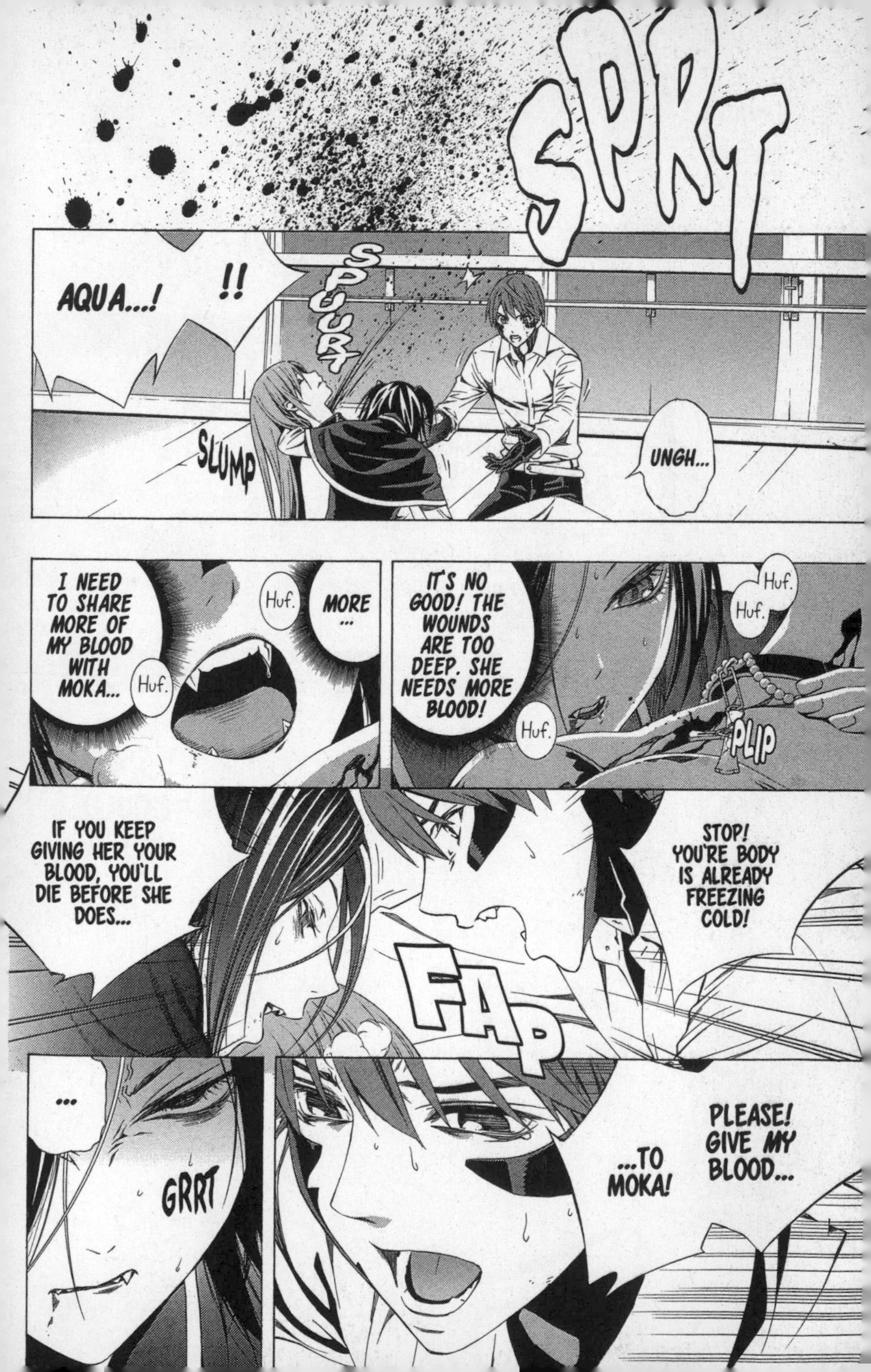
SPRT
SPURT
!!
AQUA...!
UNGH...
SLUMP
Huf.
Huf.
IT'S NO GOOD! THE WOUNDS ARE TOO DEEP. SHE NEEDS MORE BLOOD!
Huf.
PLIP
MORE...
Huf.
I NEED TO SHARE MORE OF MY BLOOD WITH MOKA...
Huf.
STOP! YOU'RE BODY IS ALREADY FREEZING COLD!
FAP
IF YOU KEEP GIVING HER YOUR BLOOD, YOU'LL DIE BEFORE SHE DOES...
PLEASE! GIVE MY BLOOD...
...TO MOKA!
...
GRRT

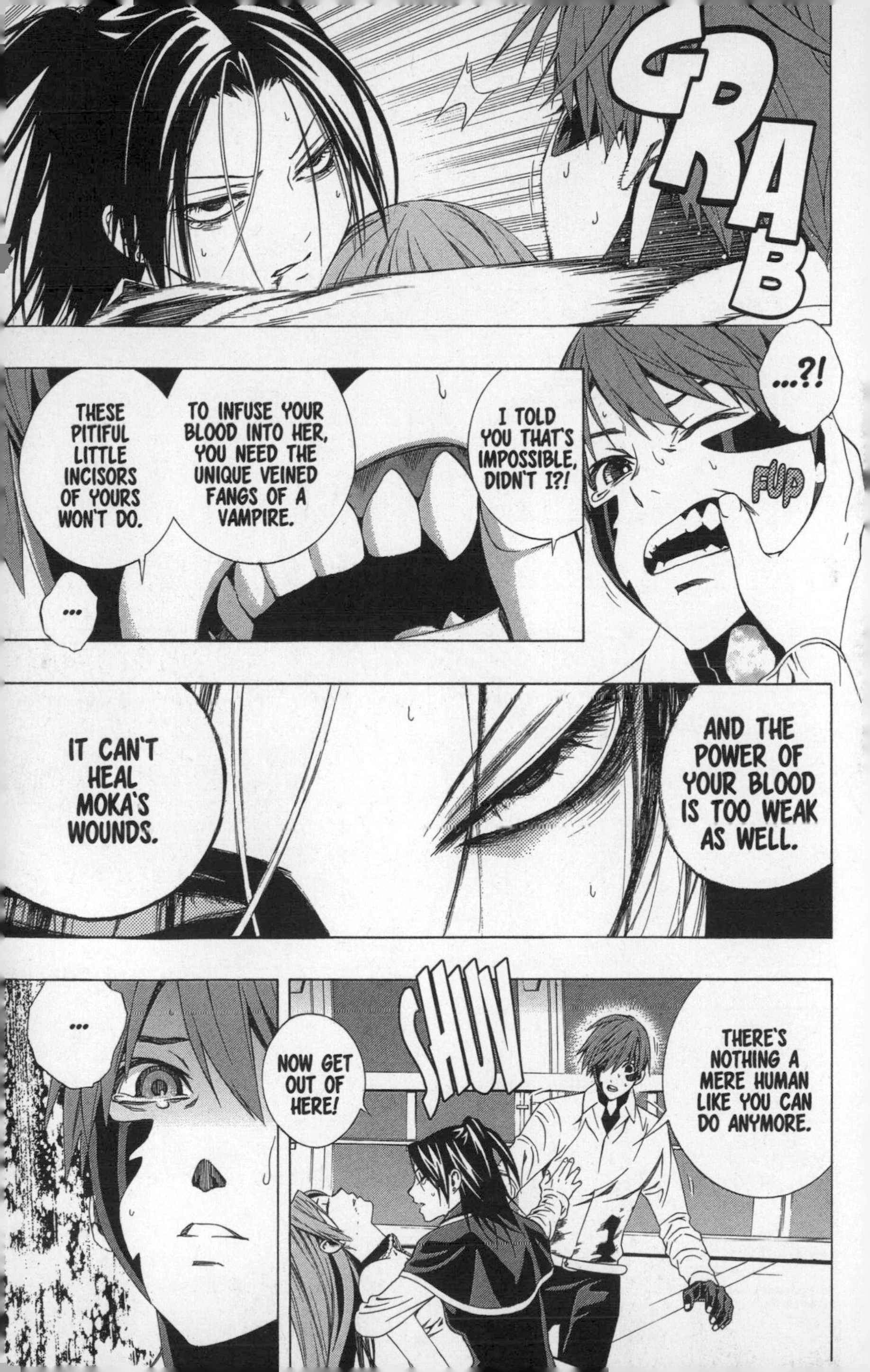
GRAB
...?!
FUP
I TOLD YOU THAT'S IMPOSSIBLE, DIDN'T I?!
TO INFUSE YOUR BLOOD INTO HER, YOU NEED THE UNIQUE VEINED FANGS OF A VAMPIRE.
THESE PITIFUL LITTLE INCISORS OF YOURS WON'T DO.
...
AND THE POWER OF YOUR BLOOD IS TOO WEAK AS WELL.
IT CAN'T HEAL MOKA'S WOUNDS.
THERE'S NOTHING A MERE HUMAN LIKE YOU CAN DO ANYMORE.
SHUV
NOW GET OUT OF HERE!
...

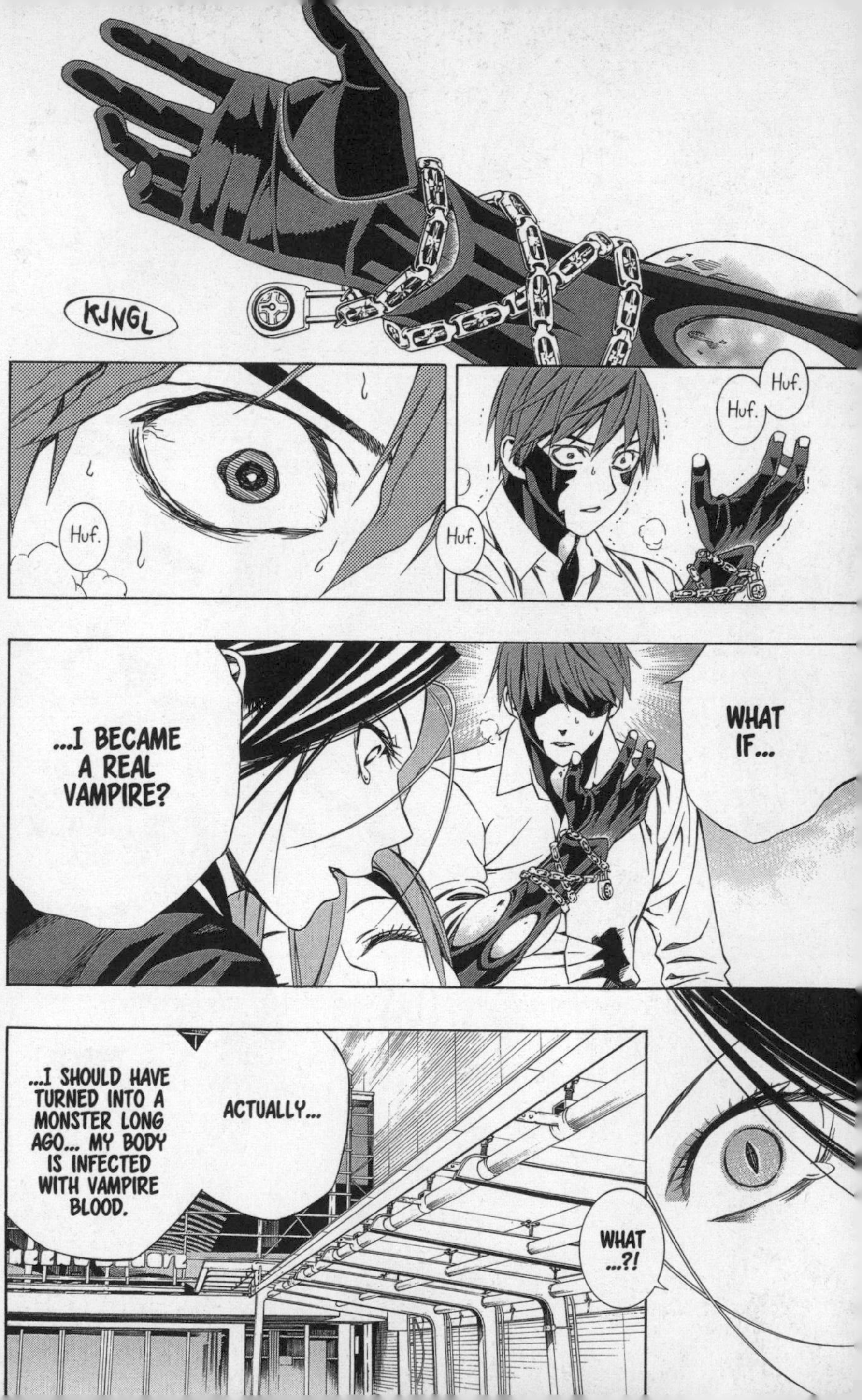
KJNGL
Huf.
Huf.
Huf.
Huf.
WHAT IF...
...I BECAME A REAL VAMPIRE?
WHAT ...?!
ACTUALLY...
...I SHOULD HAVE TURNED INTO A MONSTER LONG AGO... MY BODY IS INFECTED WITH VAMPIRE BLOOD.

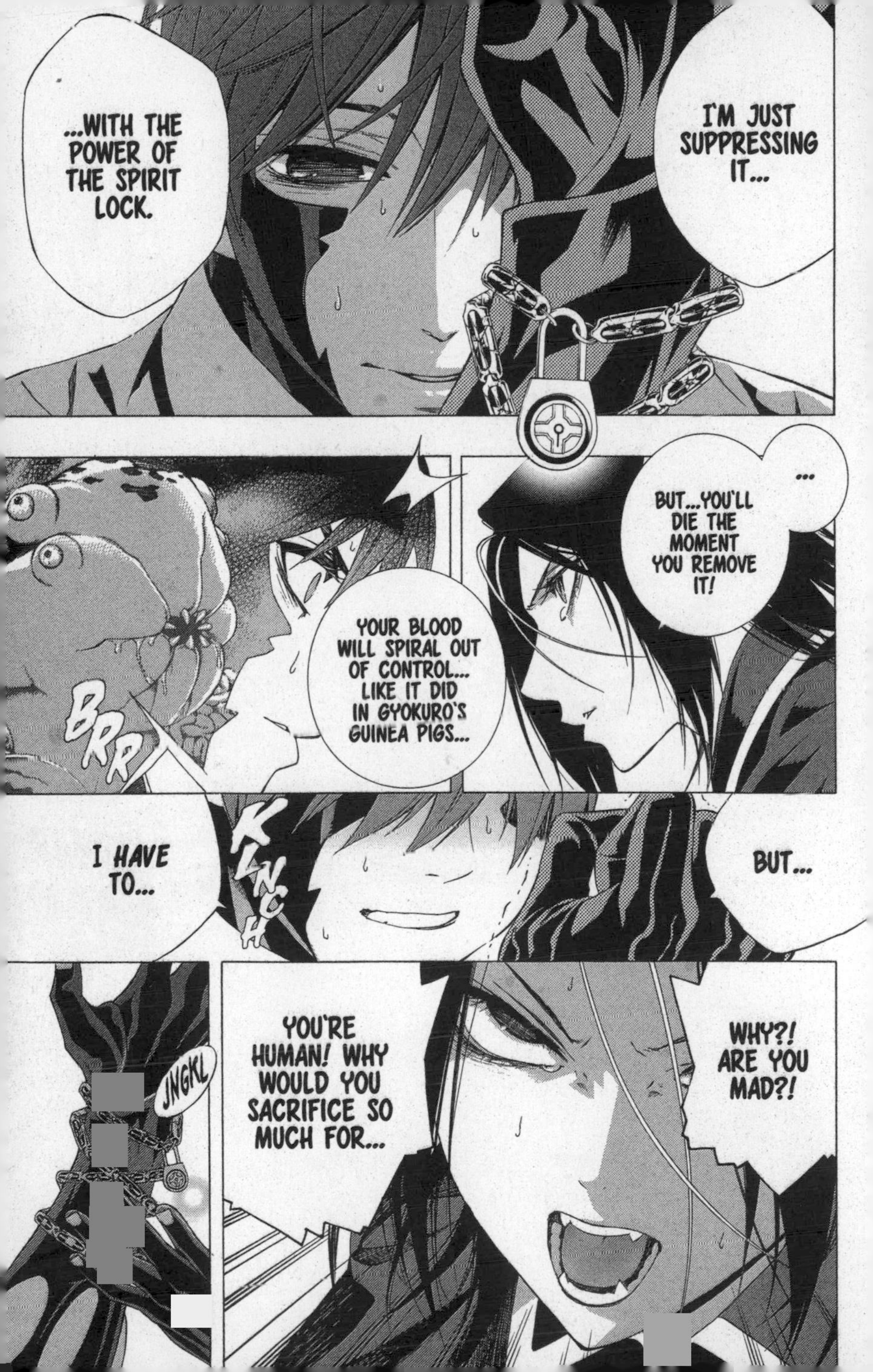
I'M JUST SUPPRESSING IT...
...WITH THE POWER OF THE SPIRIT LOCK.
...
BUT...YOU'LL DIE THE MOMENT YOU REMOVE IT!
YOUR BLOOD WILL SPIRAL OUT OF CONTROL... LIKE IT DID IN GYOKURO'S GUINEA PIGS...
BRR
BUT...
KLNCH
I HAVE TO...
WHY?! ARE YOU MAD?!
YOU'RE HUMAN! WHY WOULD YOU SACRIFICE SO MUCH FOR...
JNGKL

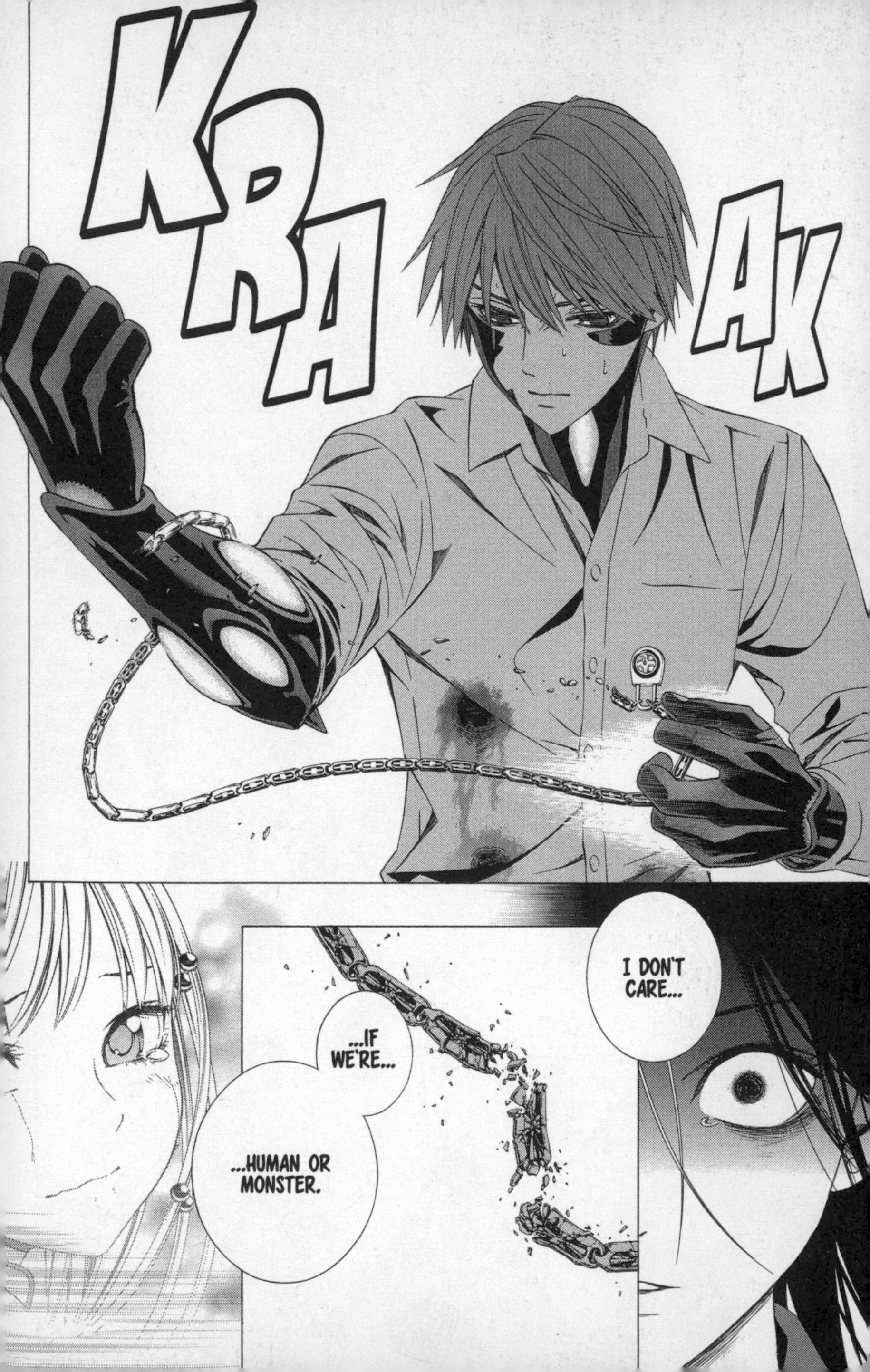
KRAAK
I DON'T CARE...
...IF WE'RE...
...HUMAN OR MONSTER.

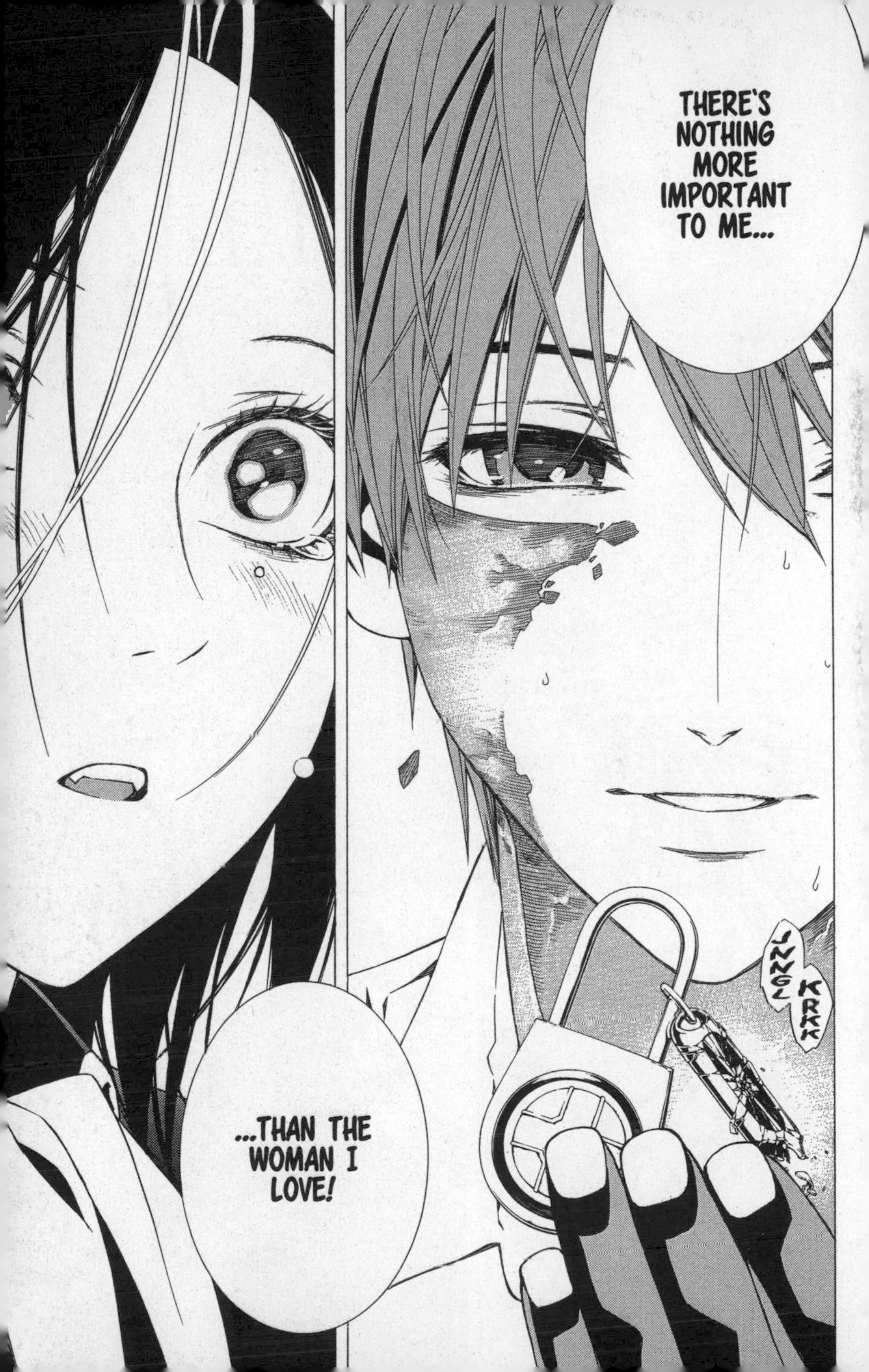
THERE'S NOTHING MORE IMPORTANT TO ME...
JNNG! KRKK
...THAN THE WOMAN I LOVE!

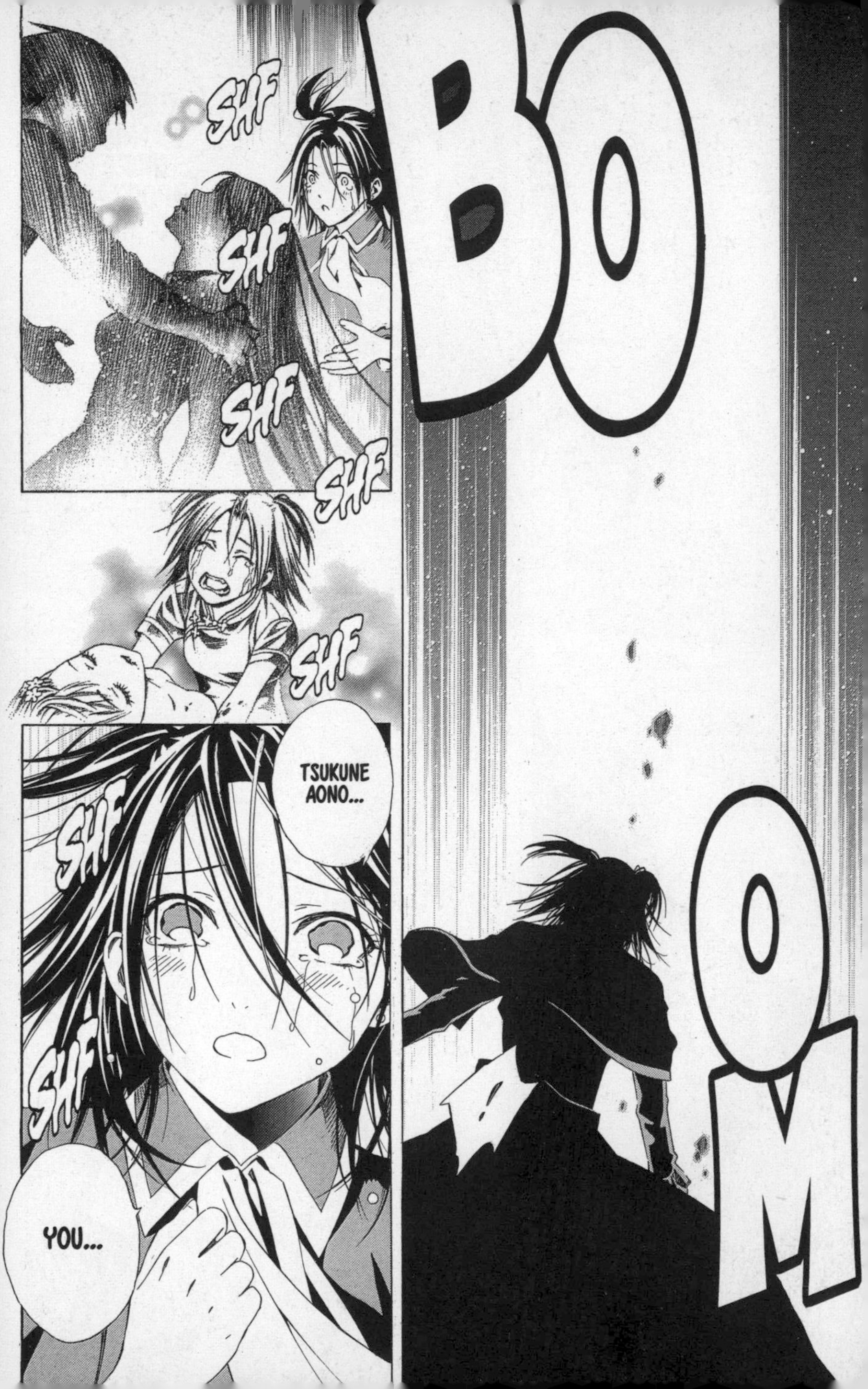
BOOOM
SHF
SHF
SHF
SHF
SHF
TSUKUNE AONO...
SHF
SHF
YOU...

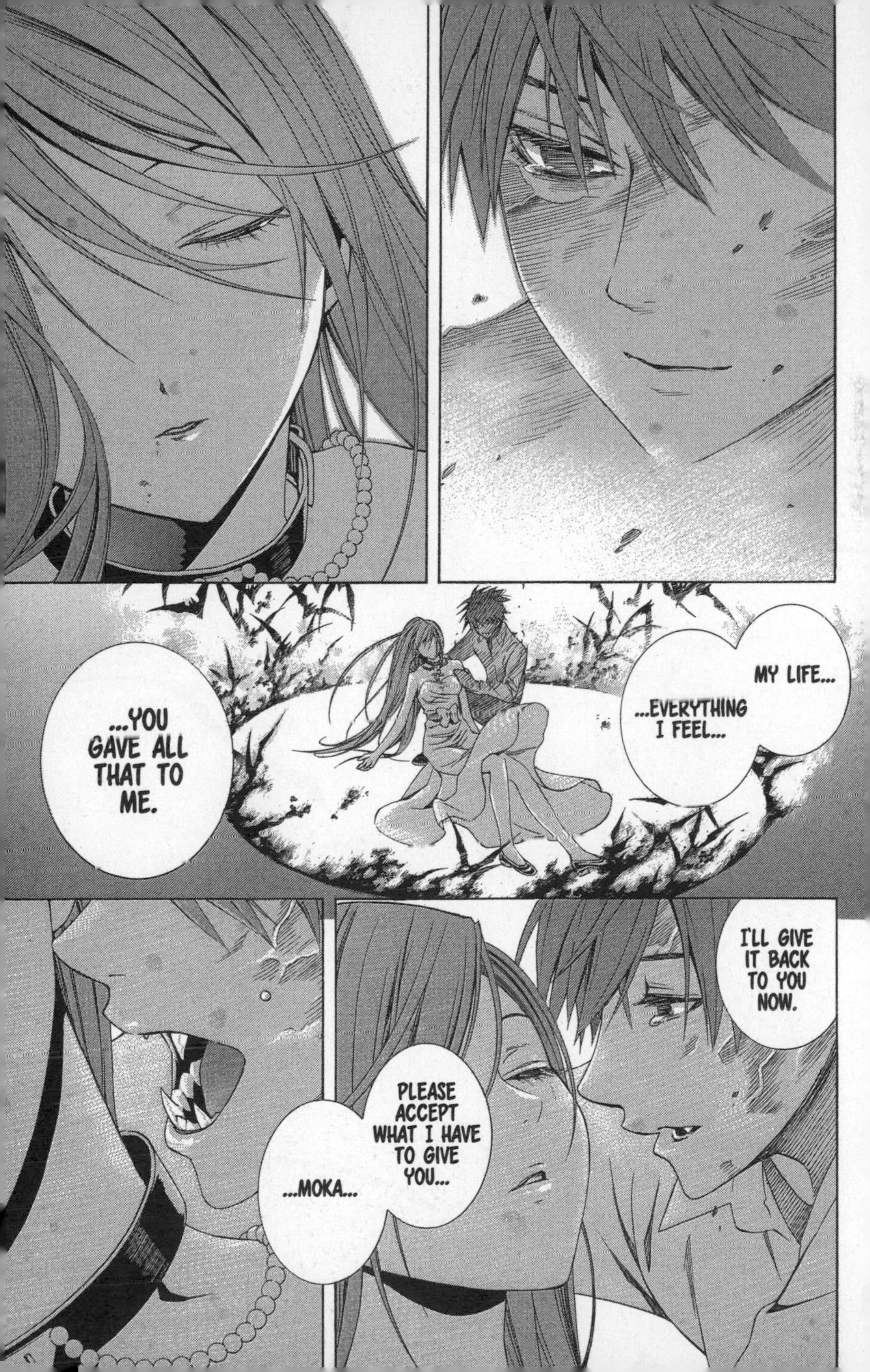
MY LIFE...
...EVERYTHING I FEEL...
...YOU GAVE ALL THAT TO ME.
I'LL GIVE IT BACK TO YOU NOW.
PLEASE ACCEPT WHAT I HAVE TO GIVE YOU...
...MOKA...

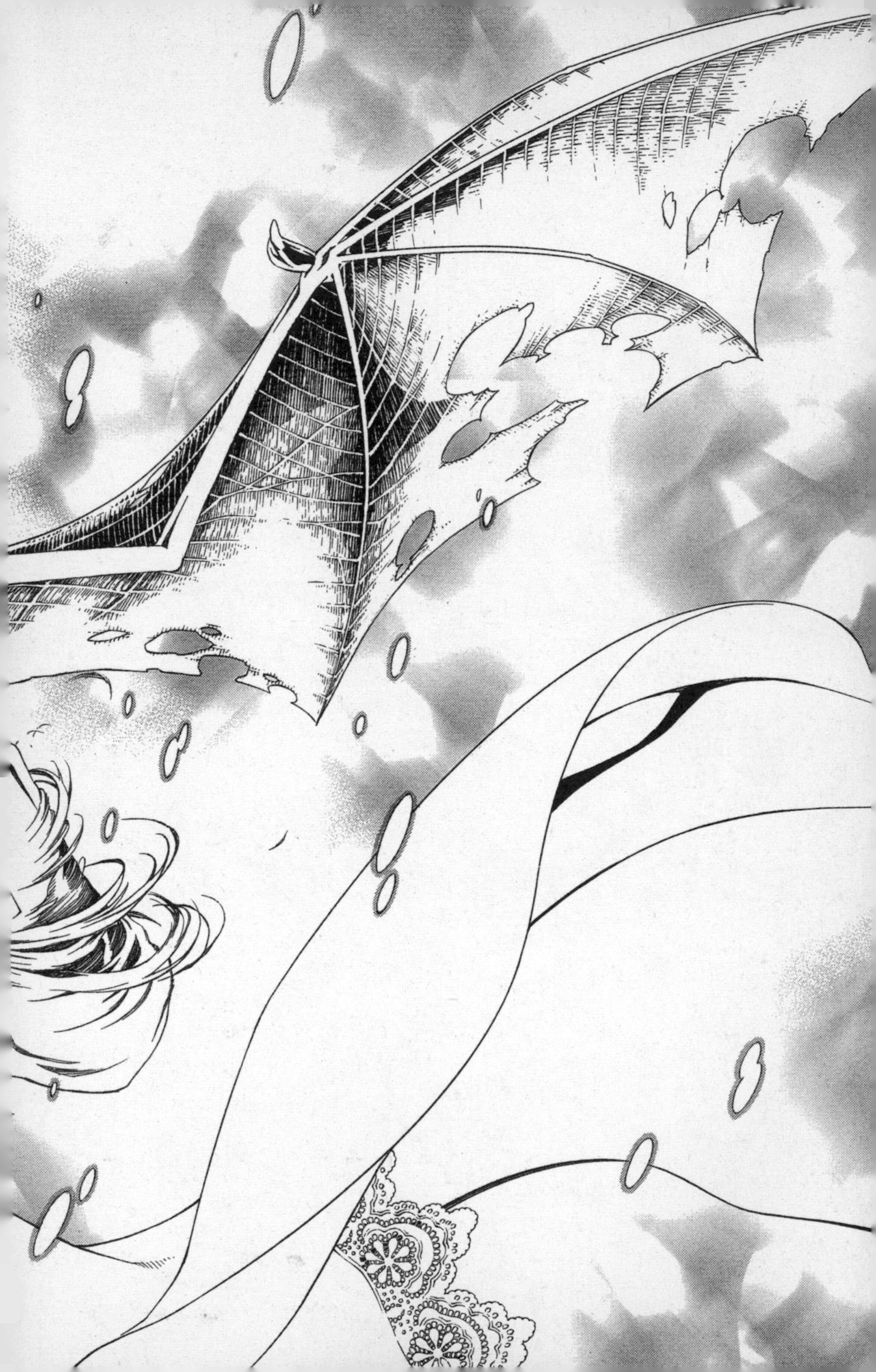

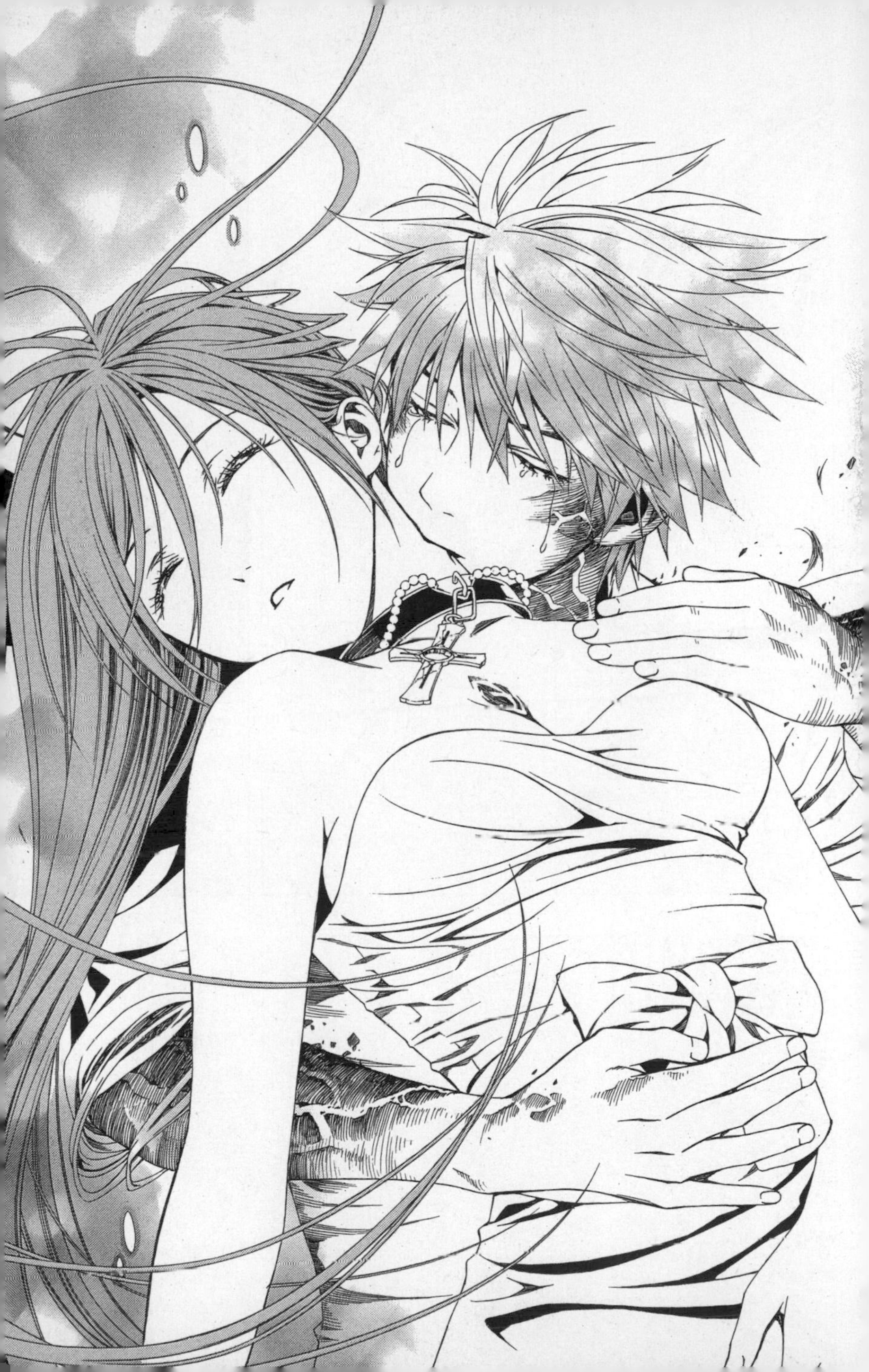

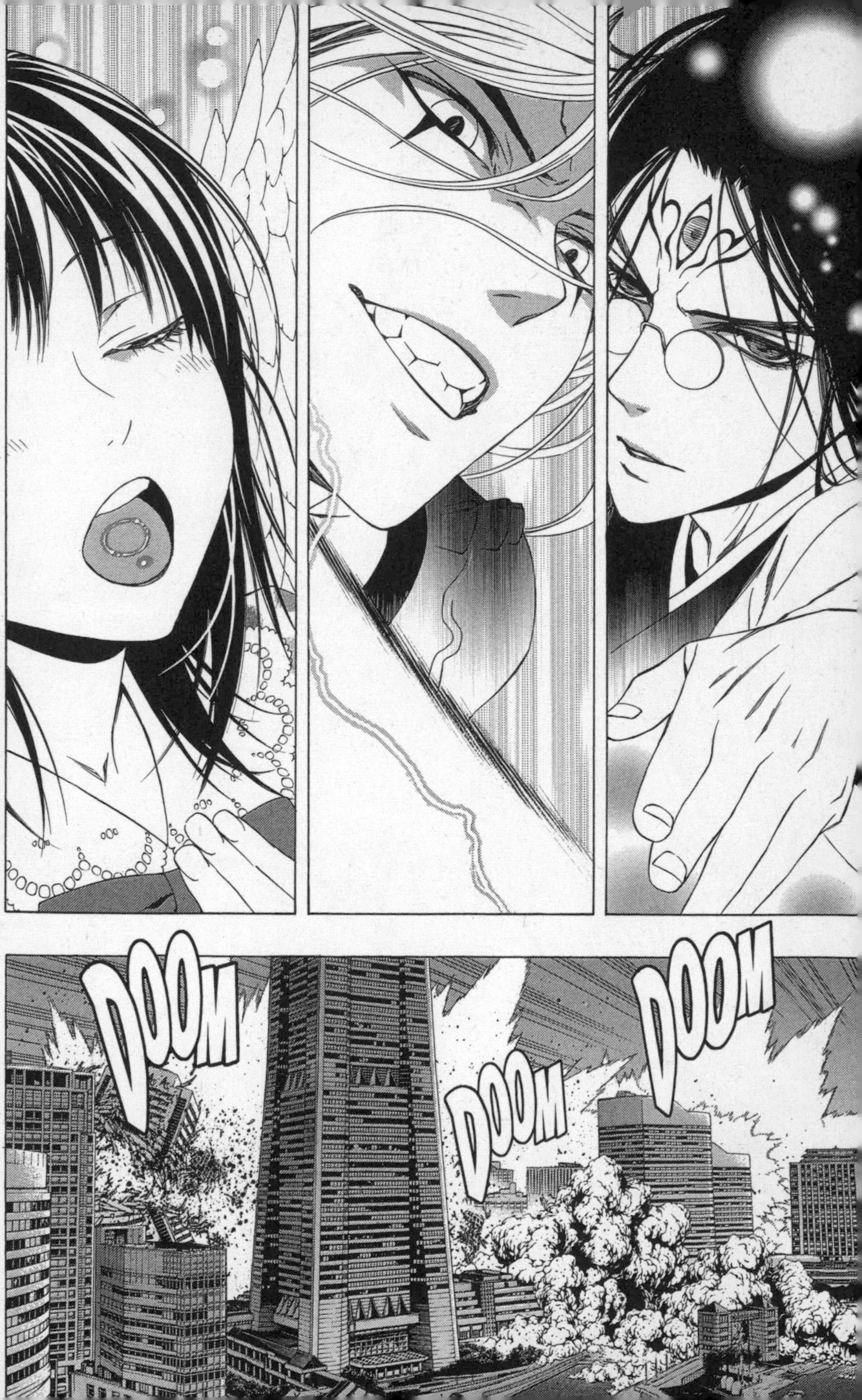
DOOM
DOOM
DOOM

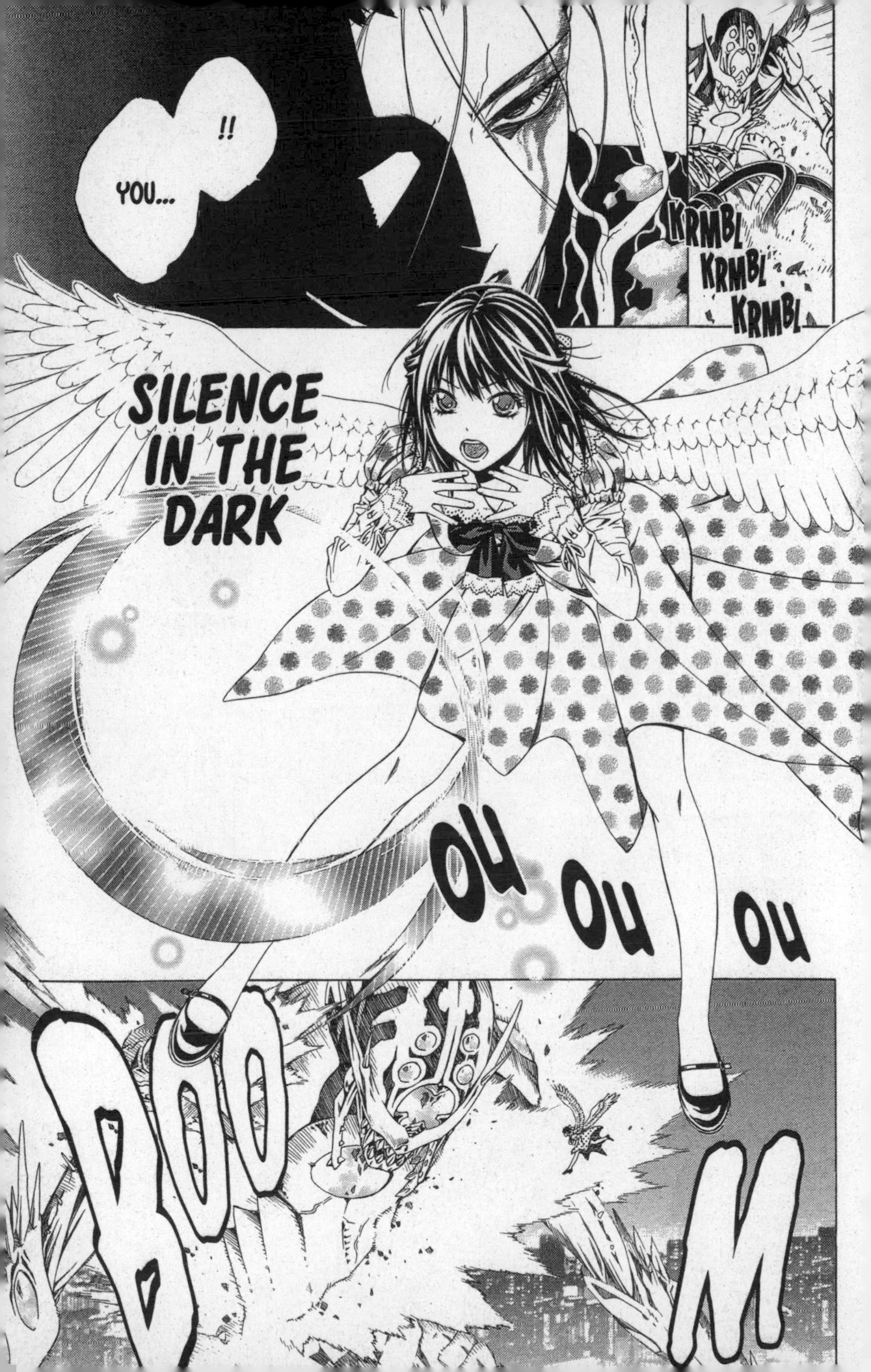
KRMBL KRMBL KRMBL
YOU... !!
SILENCE IN THE DARK
OU OU OU
BOOOM

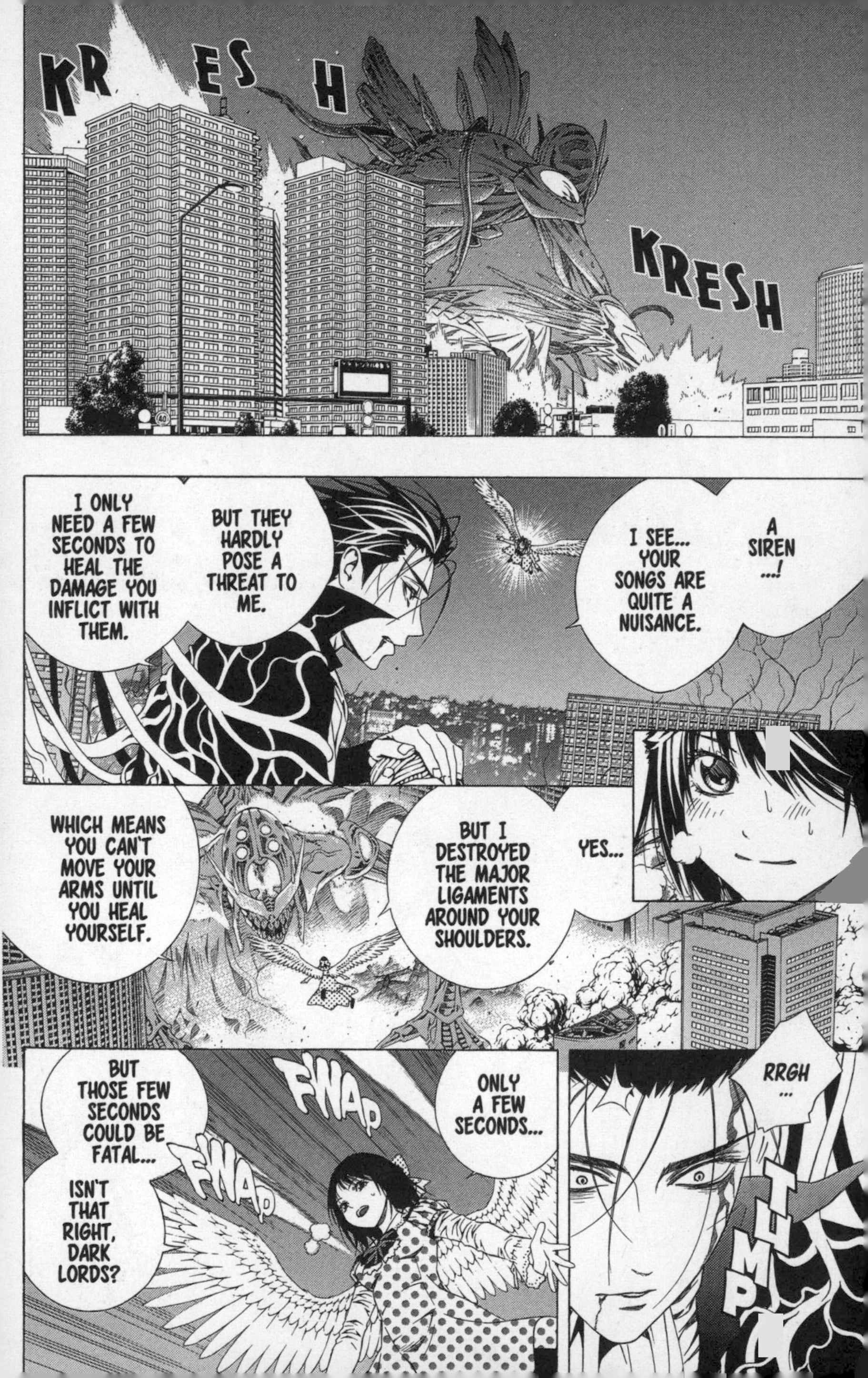
KRESH
KRESH
A SIREN ...!
I SEE... YOUR SONGS ARE QUITE A NUISANCE.
BUT THEY HARDLY POSE A THREAT TO ME.
I ONLY NEED A FEW SECONDS TO HEAL THE DAMAGE YOU INFLICT WITH THEM.
YES...
BUT I DESTROYED THE MAJOR LIGAMENTS AROUND YOUR SHOULDERS.
WHICH MEANS YOU CAN'T MOVE YOUR ARMS UNTIL YOU HEAL YOURSELF.
RRGH ...
TUMP
ONLY A FEW SECONDS...
FNAP
BUT THOSE FEW SECONDS COULD BE FATAL...
ISN'T THAT RIGHT, DARK LORDS?
FNAP

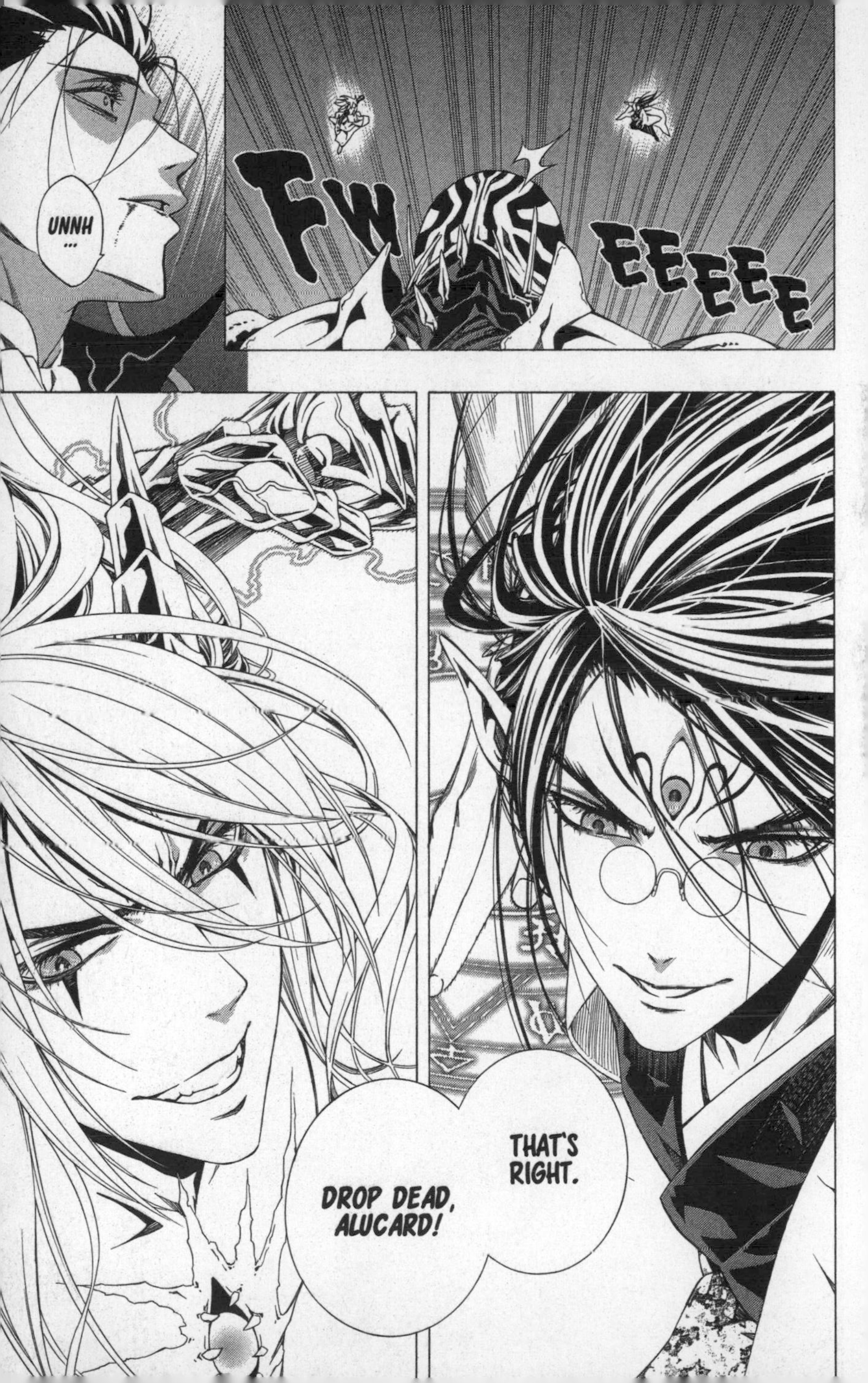
FW EEEEEE
UNNH ...
THAT'S RIGHT.
DROP DEAD, ALUCARD!

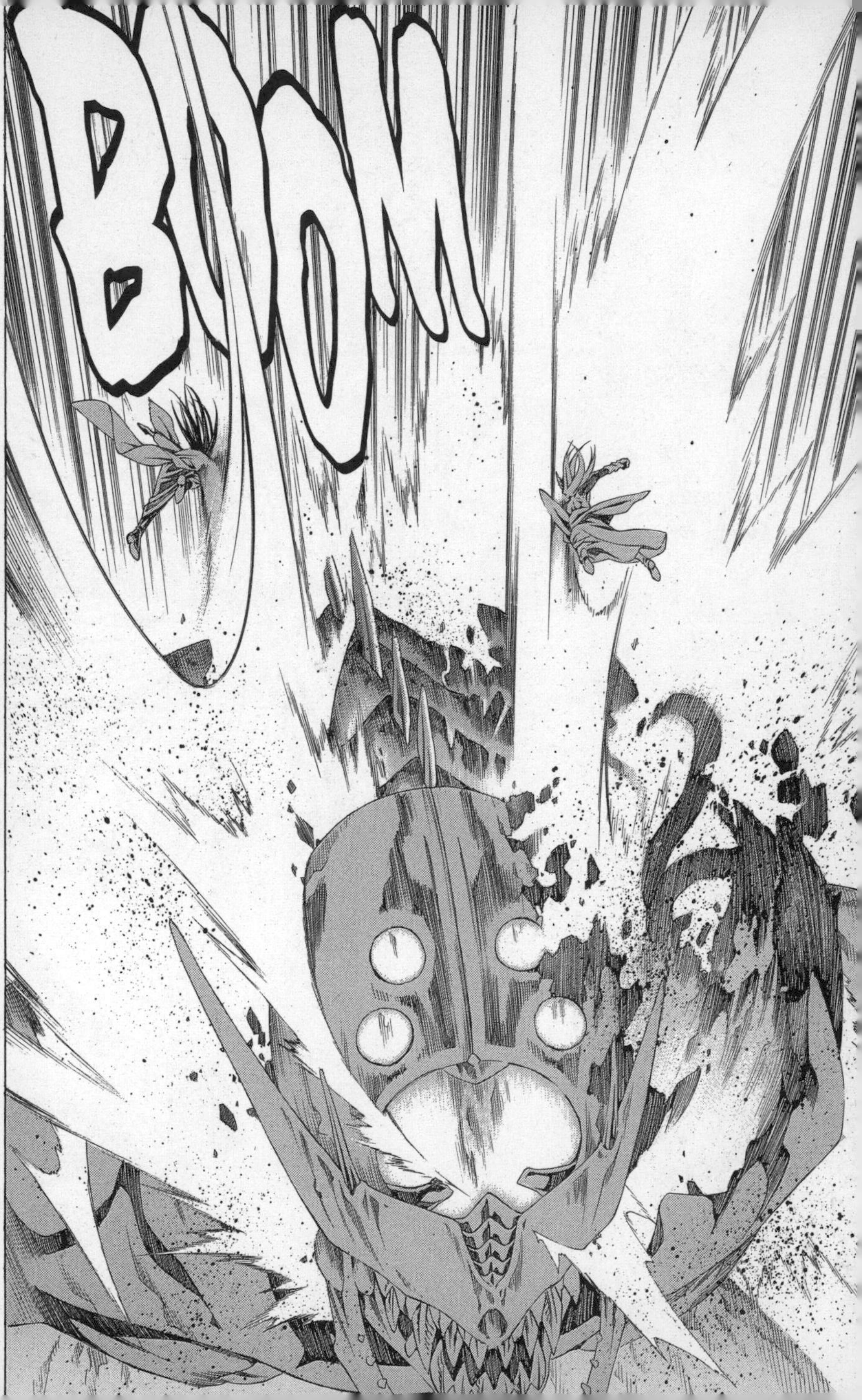
BUOM

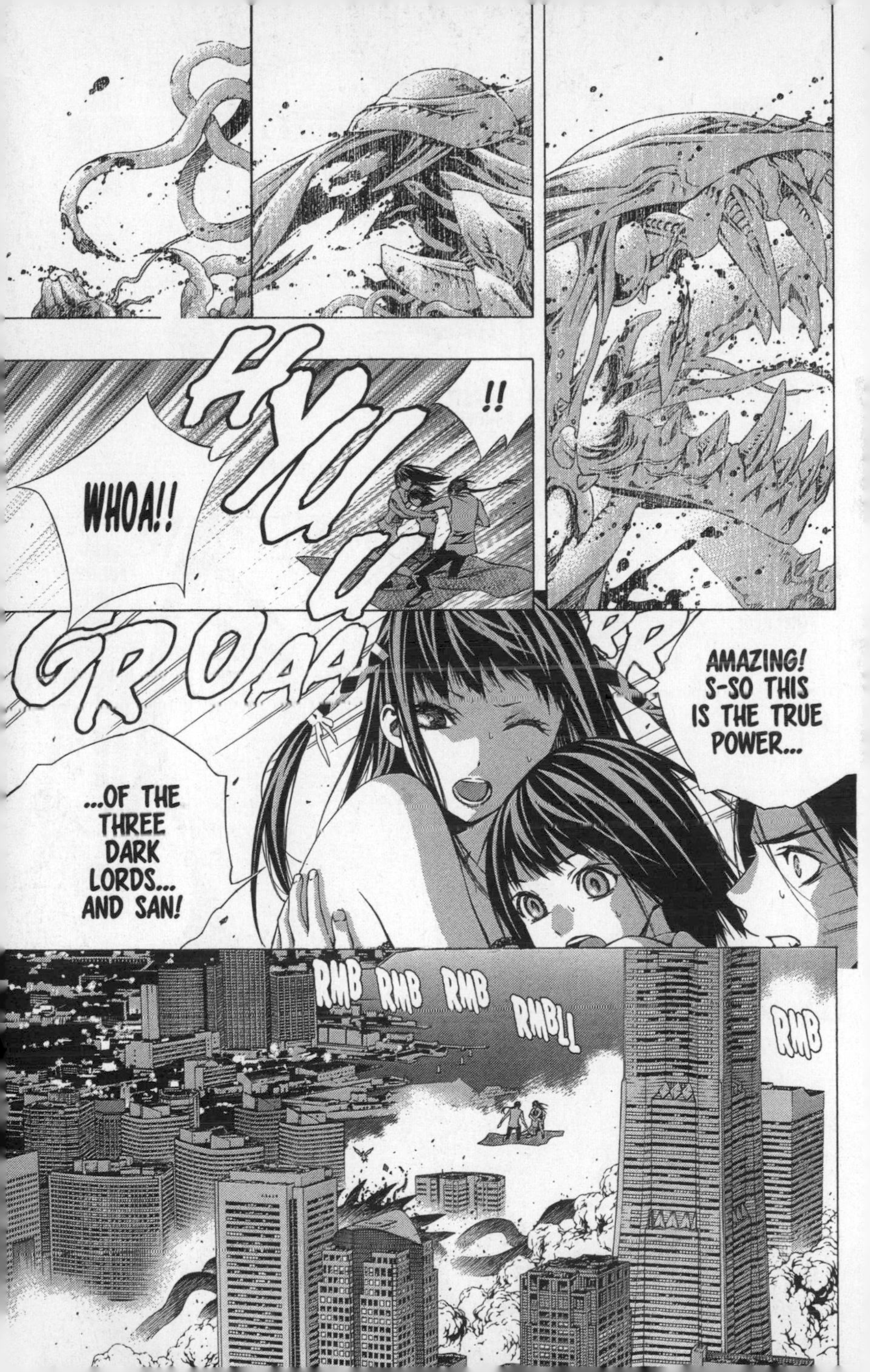

HYUUU
!!
WHOA!!
GROAARR
AMAZING! S-SO THIS IS THE TRUE POWER...
...OF THE THREE DARK LORDS... AND SAN!
RMB
RMB RMB RMB
RMBLL

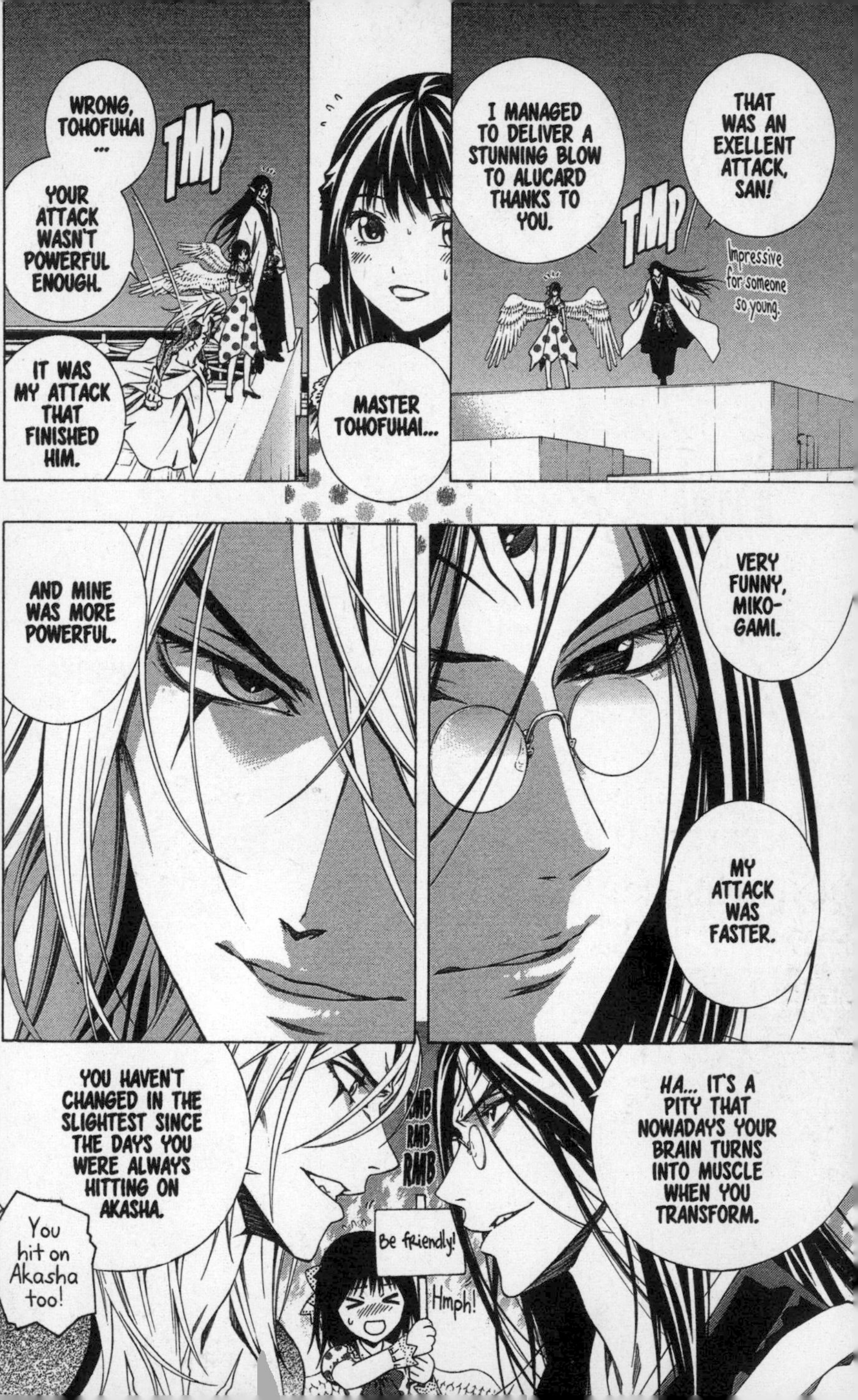
THAT WAS AN EXELLENT ATTACK, SAN!
TMP
Impressive for someone so young.
I MANAGED TO DELIVER A STUNNING BLOW TO ALUCARD THANKS TO YOU.
MASTER TOHOFUHAI...
WRONG, TOHOFUHAI ...
TMP
YOUR ATTACK WASN'T POWERFUL ENOUGH.
IT WAS MY ATTACK THAT FINISHED HIM.
VERY FUNNY, MIKO-GAMI.
MY ATTACK WAS FASTER.
AND MINE WAS MORE POWERFUL.
HA... IT'S A PITY THAT NOWADAYS YOUR BRAIN TURNS INTO MUSCLE WHEN YOU TRANSFORM.
Hmph!
RMB RMB RMB
Be friendly!
YOU HAVEN'T CHANGED IN THE SLIGHTEST SINCE THE DAYS YOU WERE ALWAYS HITTING ON AKASHA.
You hit on Akasha too!

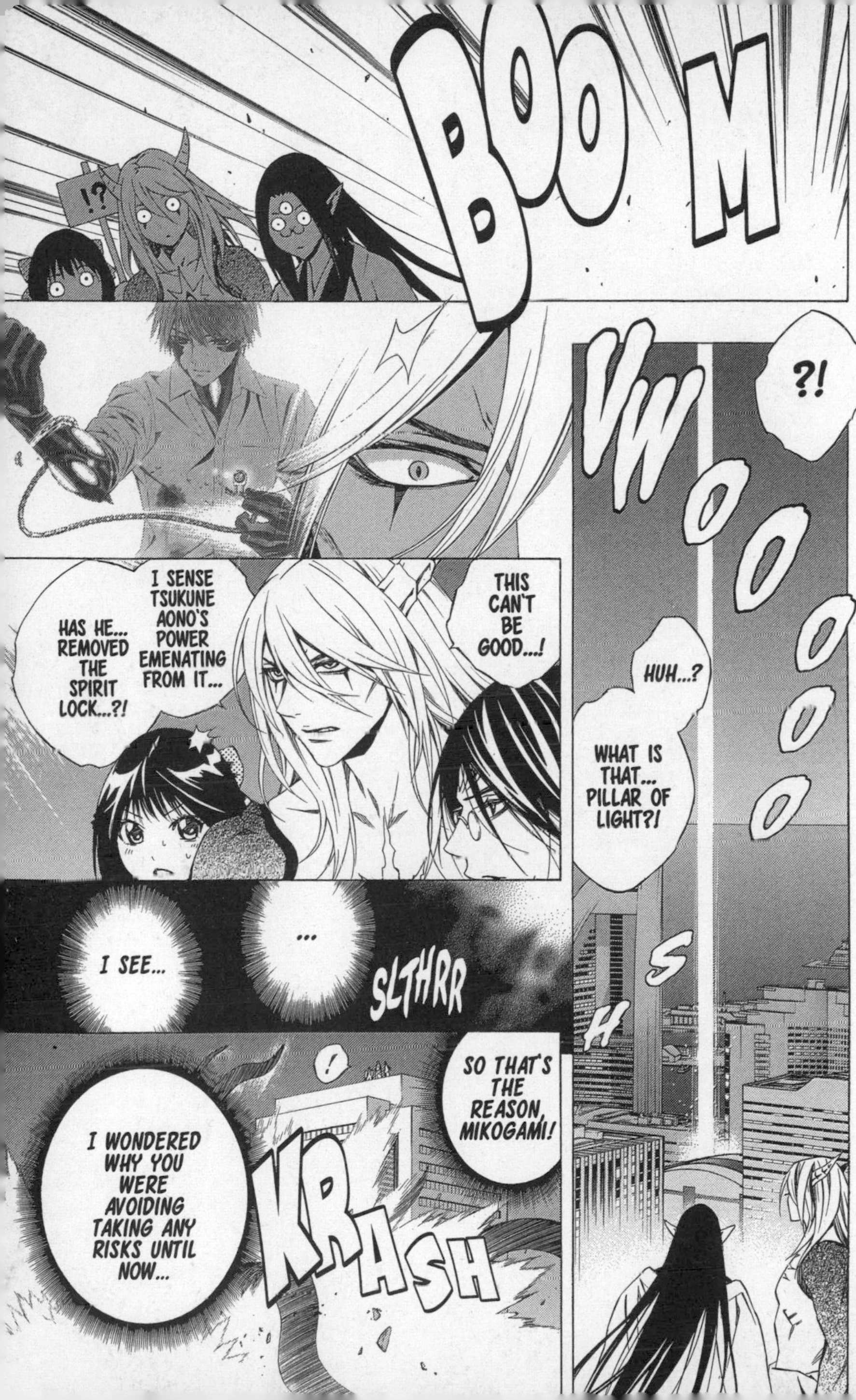

!?
BOOM
?!
VWOOOOOOSH
HUH...?
WHAT IS THAT... PILLAR OF LIGHT?!
THIS CAN'T BE GOOD...!
I SENSE TSUKUNE AONO'S POWER EMENATING FROM IT...
HAS HE... REMOVED THE SPIRIT LOCK...?!
...
I SEE...
SLTHRR
!
SO THAT'S THE REASON, MIKOGAMI!
I WONDERED WHY YOU WERE AVOIDING TAKING ANY RISKS UNTIL NOW...
KRASH

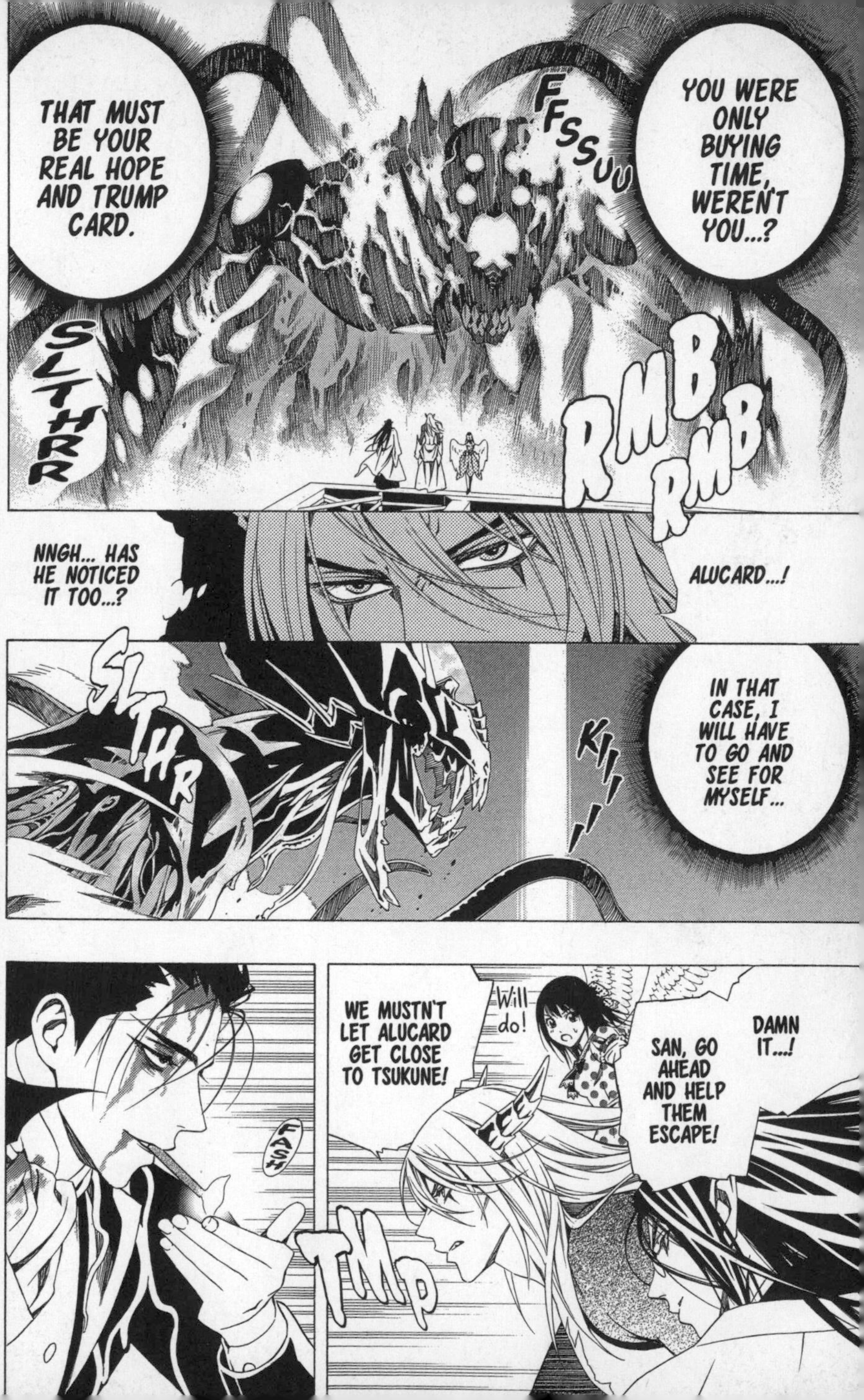
YOU WERE ONLY BUYING TIME, WEREN'T YOU...?
FFSSUU
THAT MUST BE YOUR REAL HOPE AND TRUMP CARD.
SLTHRR
RMB RMB
ALUCARD...!
NNGH... HAS HE NOTICED IT TOO...?
IN THAT CASE, I WILL HAVE TO GO AND SEE FOR MYSELF...
KIIII
SLTHR
DAMN IT...!
SAN, GO AHEAD AND HELP THEM ESCAPE!
Will do!
WE MUSTN'T LET ALUCARD GET CLOSE TO TSUKUNE!
TMP
FASH

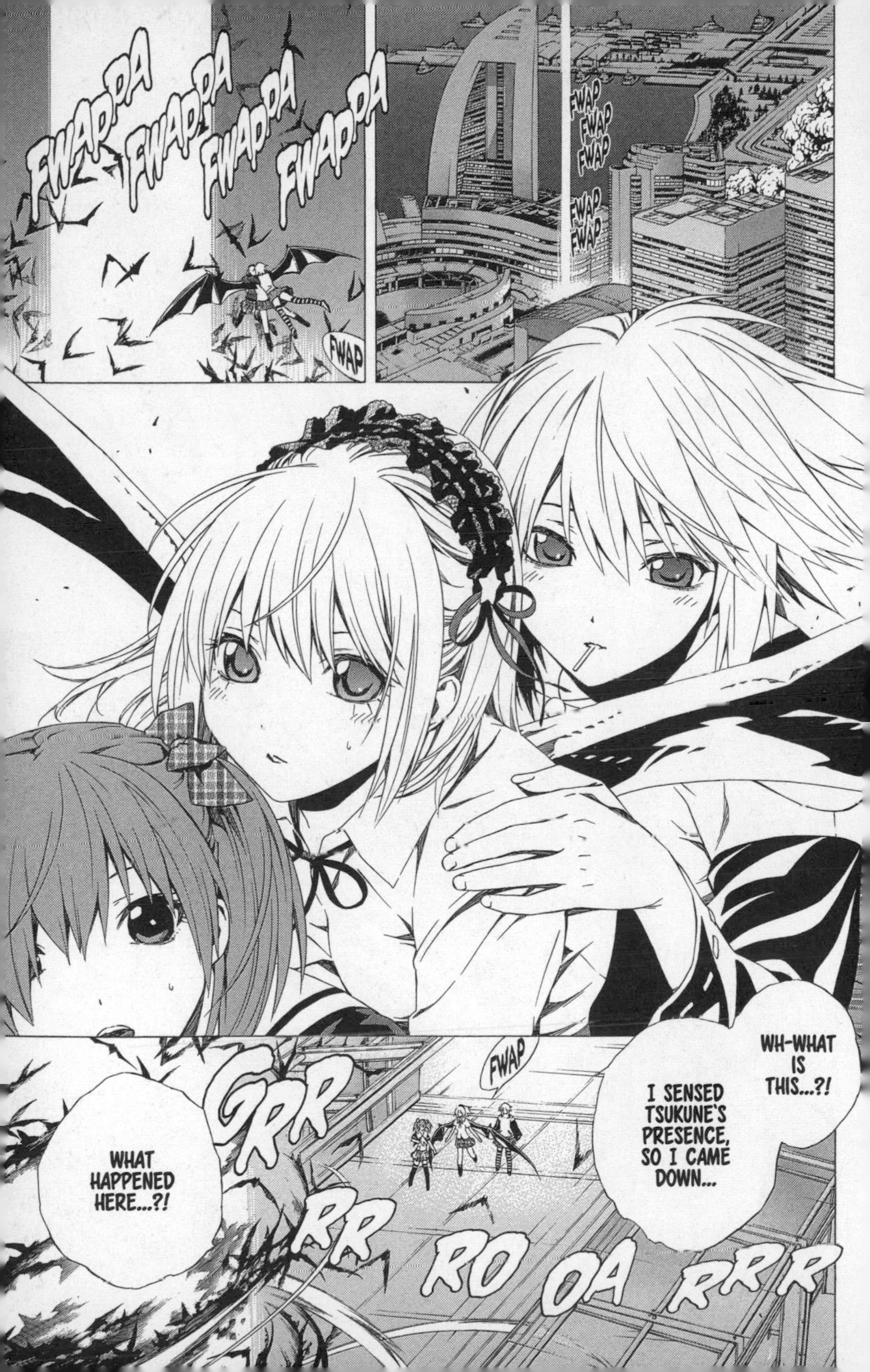
FWAP
FWAP
FWAP
FWAP
FWAP
FWAPPA
FWAPPA
FWAPPA
FWAPPA
FWAP
WH-WHAT IS THIS...?!
I SENSED TSUKUNE'S PRESENCE, SO I CAME DOWN...
FWAP
GRR
RR
WHAT HAPPENED HERE...?!
RO OA RRR

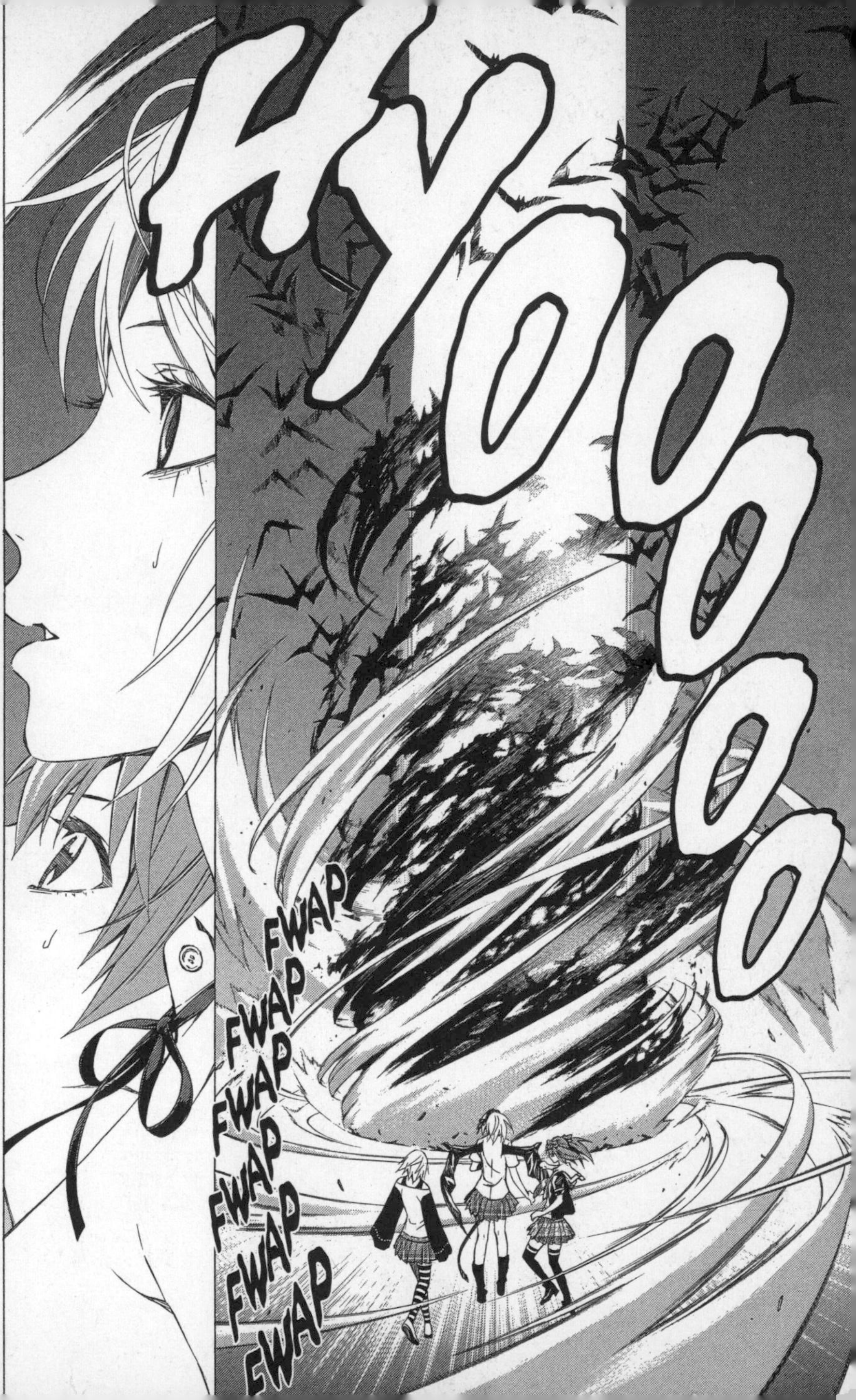
HYOOOOOOO
FWAP
FWAP
FWAP
FWAP
FWAP
FWAP
FWAP
FWAP

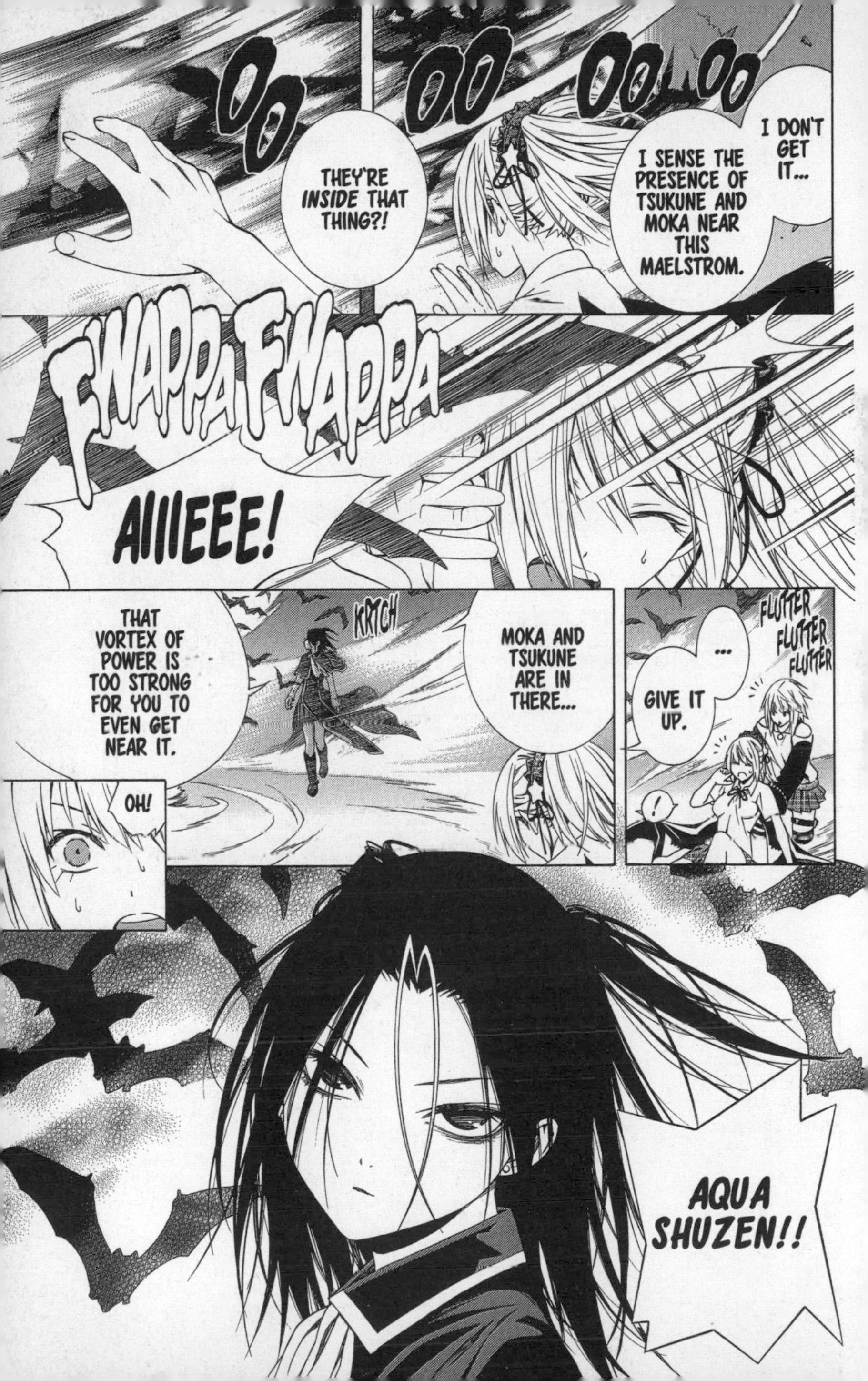
OOOOOOOOOO
I DON'T GET IT...
I SENSE THE PRESENCE OF TSUKUNE AND MOKA NEAR THIS MAELSTROM.
THEY'RE *INSIDE* THAT THING?!
FWAPPA FWAPPA
AIIIEEE!
FLUTTER FLUTTER FLUTTER
...
GIVE IT UP.
!
MOKA AND TSUKUNE ARE IN THERE...
KRTCH
THAT VORTEX OF POWER IS TOO STRONG FOR YOU TO EVEN GET NEAR IT.
OH!
AQUA SHUZEN!!

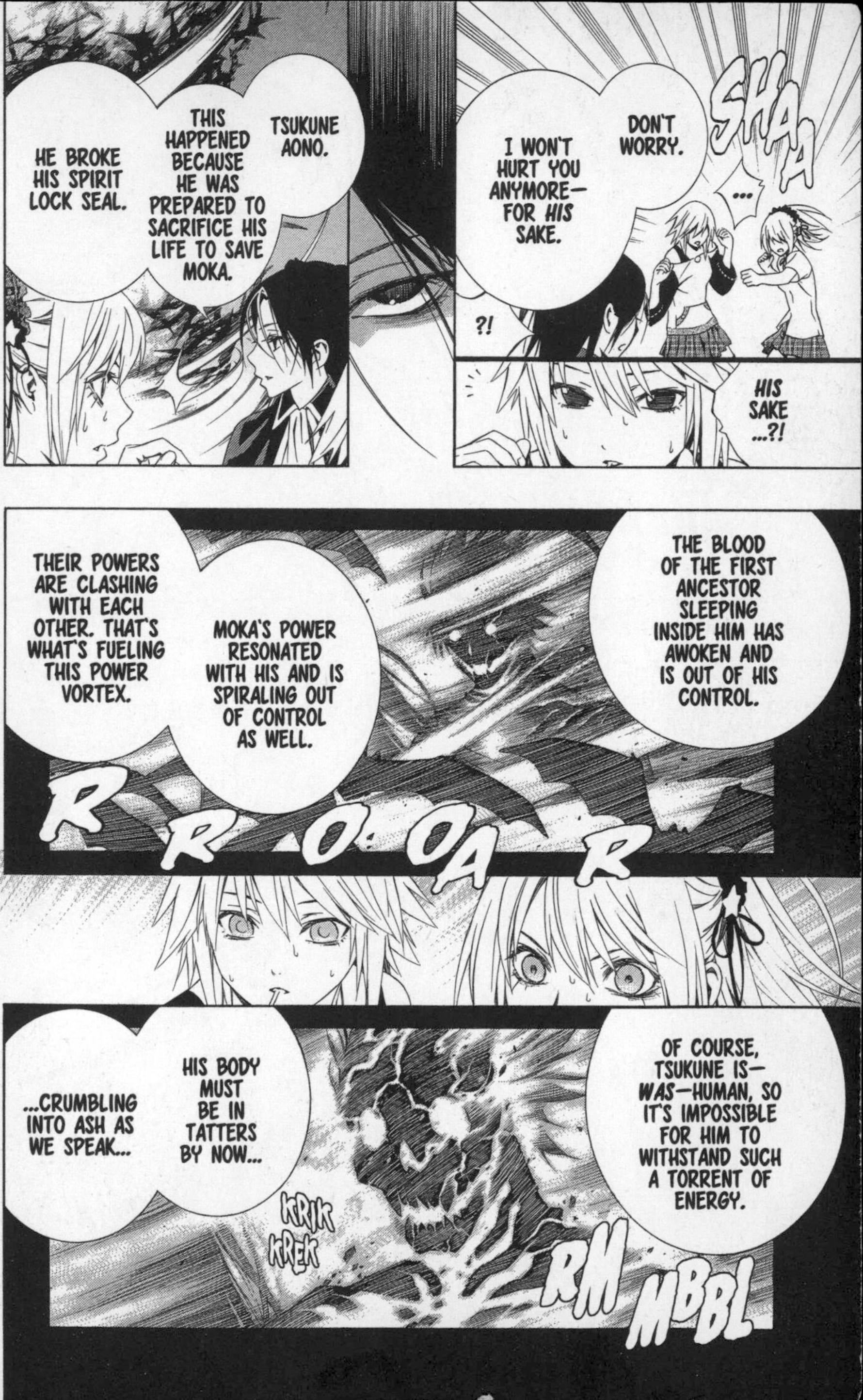
SHAA
DON'T WORRY.
I WON'T HURT YOU ANYMORE—FOR HIS SAKE.
...
?!
HIS SAKE ...?!
TSUKUNE AONO.
THIS HAPPENED BECAUSE HE WAS PREPARED TO SACRIFICE HIS LIFE TO SAVE MOKA.
HE BROKE HIS SPIRIT LOCK SEAL.
THE BLOOD OF THE FIRST ANCESTOR SLEEPING INSIDE HIM HAS AWOKEN AND IS OUT OF HIS CONTROL.
MOKA'S POWER RESONATED WITH HIS AND IS SPIRALING OUT OF CONTROL AS WELL.
THEIR POWERS ARE CLASHING WITH EACH OTHER. THAT'S WHAT'S FUELING THIS POWER VORTEX.
RROOAR
OF COURSE, TSUKUNE IS—*WAS*—HUMAN, SO IT'S IMPOSSIBLE FOR HIM TO WITHSTAND SUCH A TORRENT OF ENERGY.
HIS BODY MUST BE IN TATTERS BY NOW...
...CRUMBLING INTO ASH AS WE SPEAK...
KRIK KREK
RMMBBL

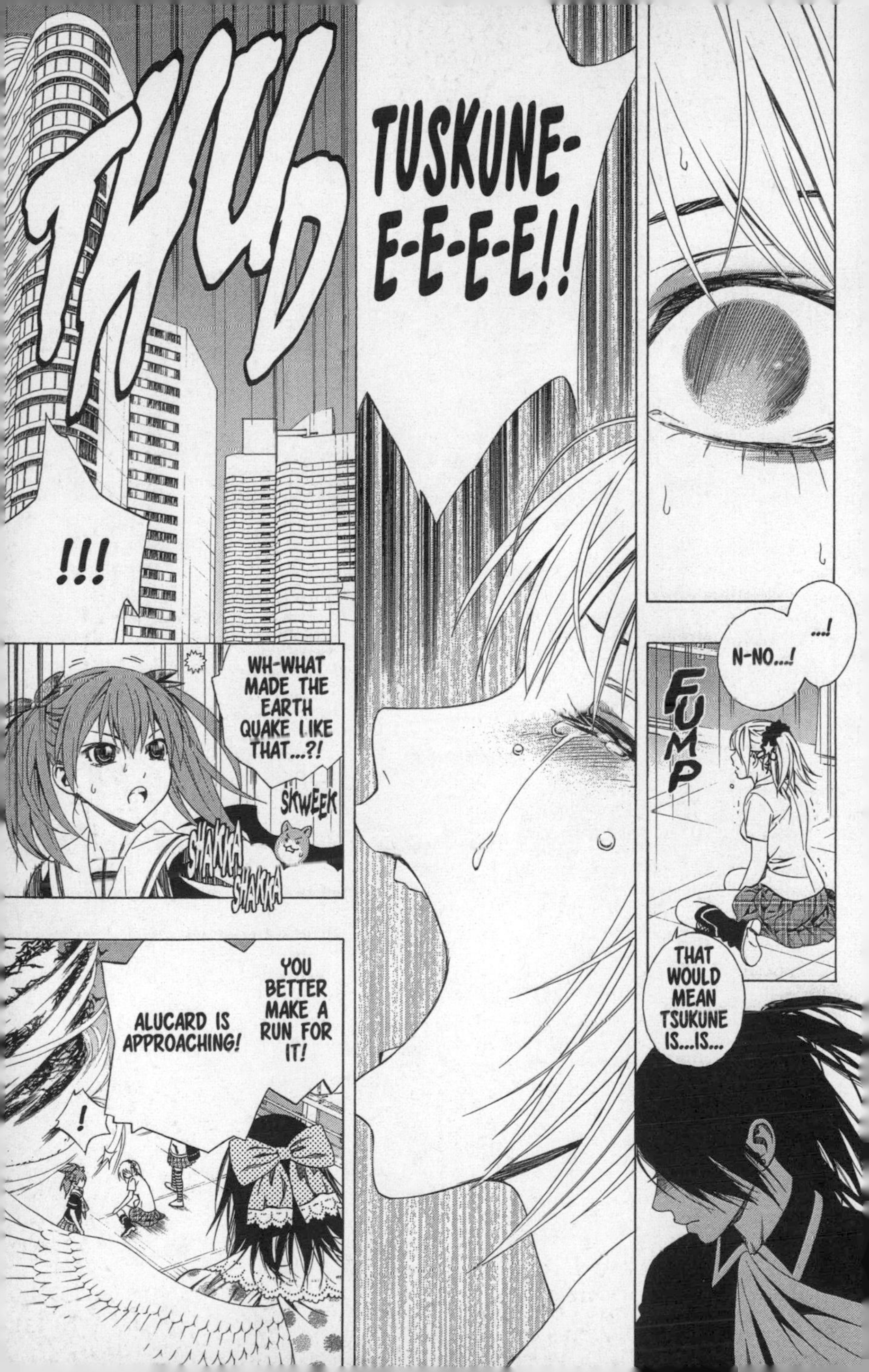
...!
N-NO...!
FUMP
THAT WOULD MEAN TSUKUNE IS...IS...
TUSKUNE-E-E-E-E!!
THUD
!!!
WH-WHAT MADE THE EARTH QUAKE LIKE THAT...?!
SKWEEK
SHAKKA SHAKKA
YOU BETTER MAKE A RUN FOR IT!
ALUCARD IS APPROACHING!
!

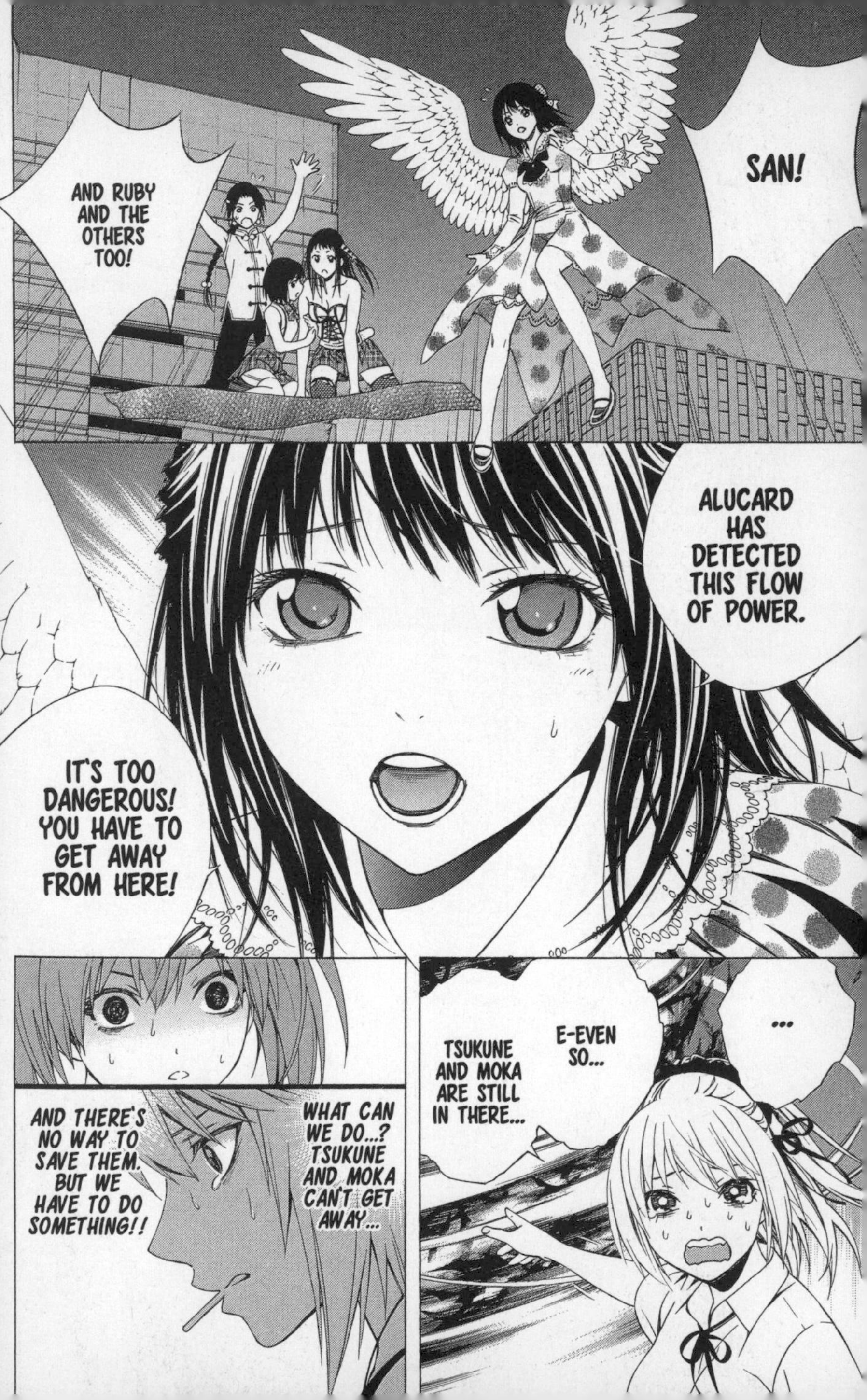
SAN!
AND RUBY AND THE OTHERS TOO!
ALUCARD HAS DETECTED THIS FLOW OF POWER.
IT'S TOO DANGEROUS! YOU HAVE TO GET AWAY FROM HERE!
...
E-EVEN SO...
TSUKUNE AND MOKA ARE STILL IN THERE...
WHAT CAN WE DO...? TSUKUNE AND MOKA CAN'T GET AWAY...
AND THERE'S NO WAY TO SAVE THEM. BUT WE HAVE TO DO SOMETHING!!

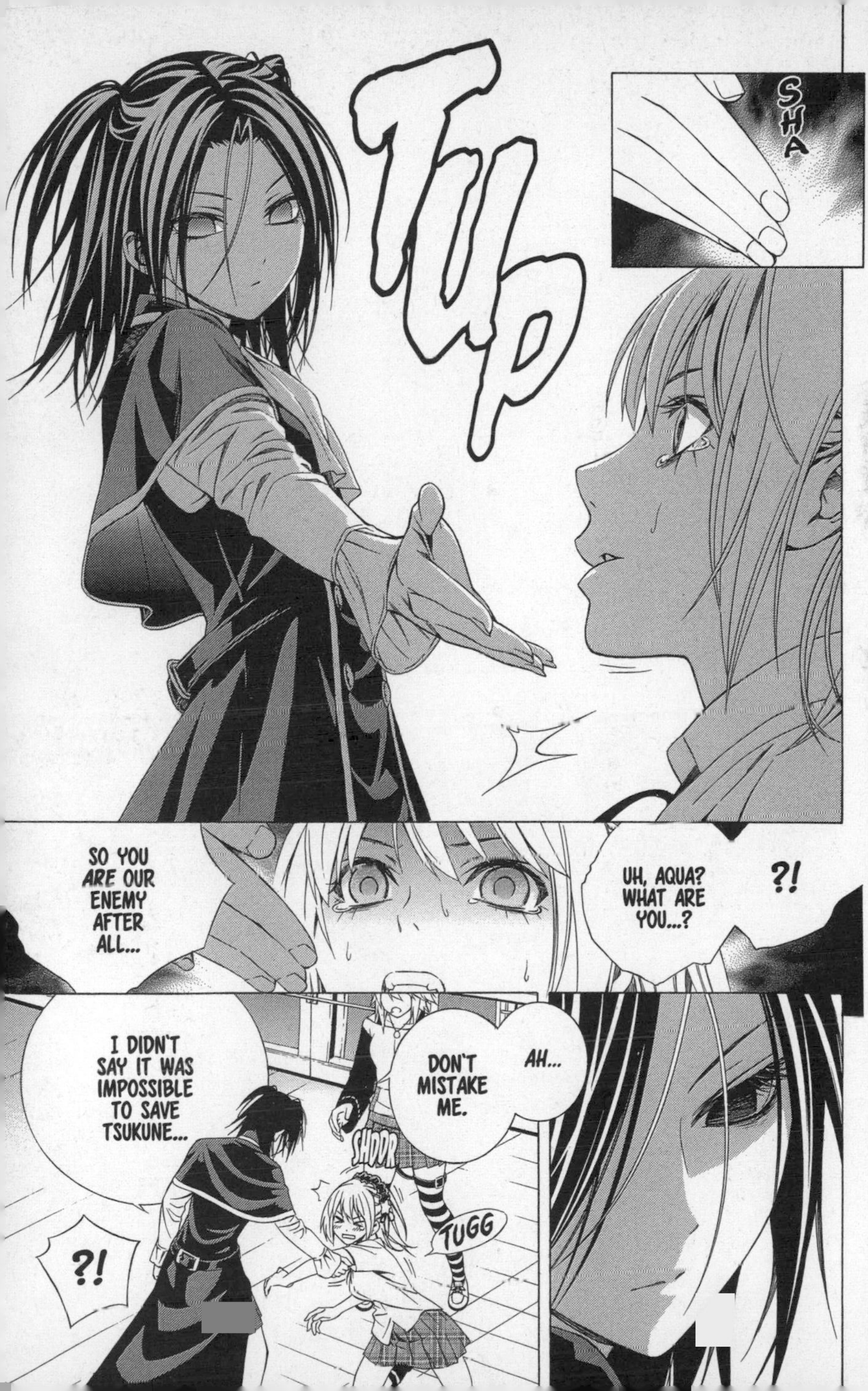
SHA
TUP
?!
UH, AQUA? WHAT ARE YOU...?
SO YOU ARE OUR ENEMY AFTER ALL...
AH...
DON'T MISTAKE ME.
I DIDN'T SAY IT WAS IMPOSSIBLE TO SAVE TSUKUNE...
SHOOR
TUGG
?!

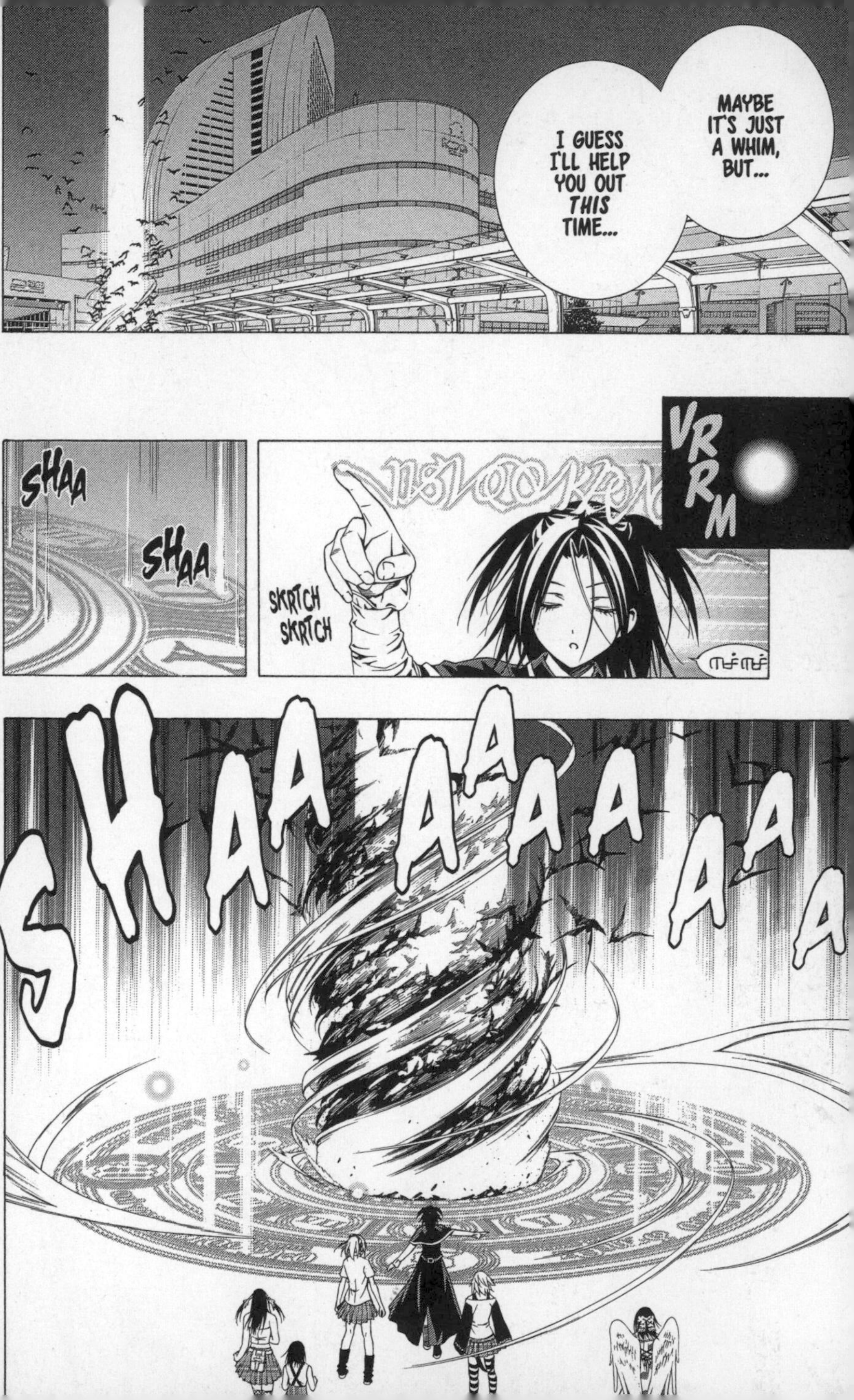
MAYBE IT'S JUST A WHIM, BUT...
I GUESS I'LL HELP YOU OUT *THIS* TIME...
VRRM
SKRTCH SKRTCH
SHAA
SHAA
SHAAAAAAAAAA

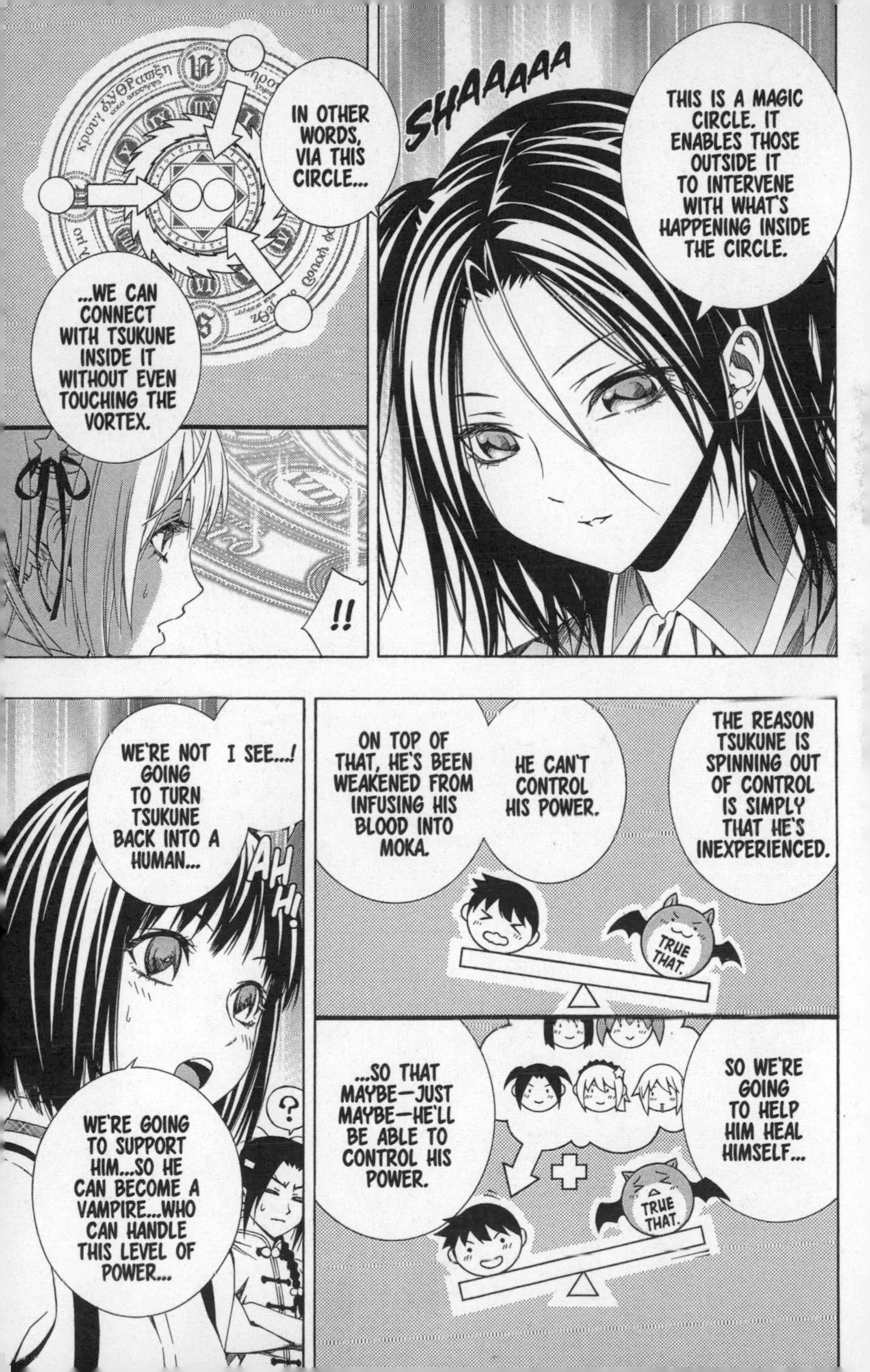
SHAAAAA
THIS IS A MAGIC CIRCLE. IT ENABLES THOSE OUTSIDE IT TO INTERVENE WITH WHAT'S HAPPENING INSIDE THE CIRCLE.
IN OTHER WORDS, VIA THIS CIRCLE...
...WE CAN CONNECT WITH TSUKUNE INSIDE IT WITHOUT EVEN TOUCHING THE VORTEX.
!!
THE REASON TSUKUNE IS SPINNING OUT OF CONTROL IS SIMPLY THAT HE'S INEXPERIENCED.
HE CAN'T CONTROL HIS POWER.
ON TOP OF THAT, HE'S BEEN WEAKENED FROM INFUSING HIS BLOOD INTO MOKA.
TRUE THAT.
SO WE'RE GOING TO HELP HIM HEAL HIMSELF...
...SO THAT MAYBE—JUST MAYBE—HE'LL BE ABLE TO CONTROL HIS POWER.
TRUE THAT.
I SEE...!
WE'RE NOT GOING TO TURN TSUKUNE BACK INTO A HUMAN...
AHH!
?
WE'RE GOING TO SUPPORT HIM...SO HE CAN BECOME A VAMPIRE...WHO CAN HANDLE THIS LEVEL OF POWER...

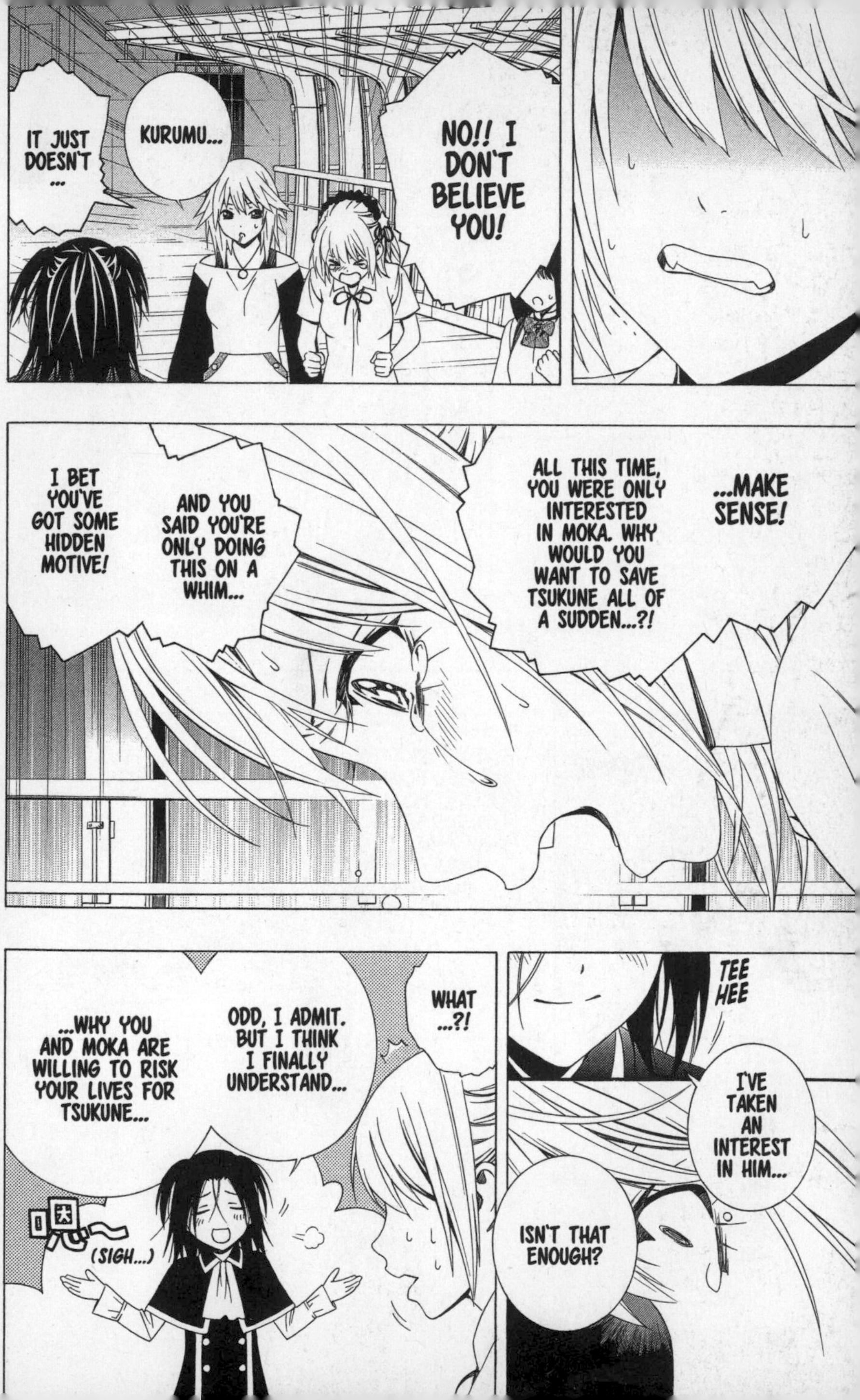
NO!! I DON'T BELIEVE YOU!
KURUMU...
IT JUST DOESN'T ...
...MAKE SENSE!
ALL THIS TIME, YOU WERE ONLY INTERESTED IN MOKA. WHY WOULD YOU WANT TO SAVE TSUKUNE ALL OF A SUDDEN...?!
AND YOU SAID YOU'RE ONLY DOING THIS ON A WHIM...
I BET YOU'VE GOT SOME HIDDEN MOTIVE!
TEE HEE
I'VE TAKEN AN INTEREST IN HIM...
ISN'T THAT ENOUGH?
WHAT ...?!
ODD, I ADMIT. BUT I THINK I FINALLY UNDERSTAND...
...WHY YOU AND MOKA ARE WILLING TO RISK YOUR LIVES FOR TSUKUNE...
(SIGH...)

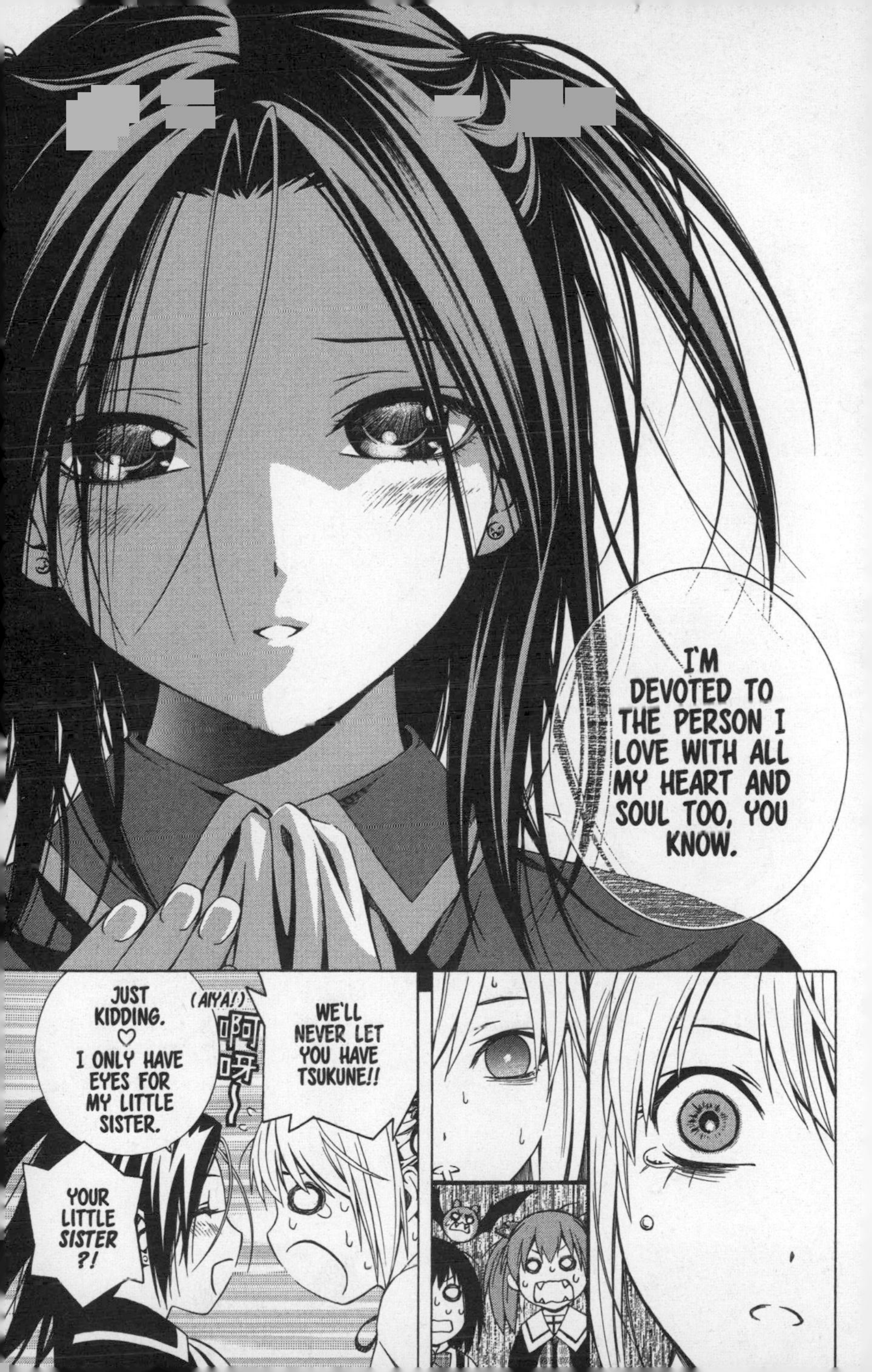
I'M DEVOTED TO THE PERSON I LOVE WITH ALL MY HEART AND SOUL TOO, YOU KNOW.
WE'LL NEVER LET YOU HAVE TSUKUNE!!
(AIYA!)
啊呀~
JUST KIDDING. ♡ I ONLY HAVE EYES FOR MY LITTLE SISTER.
YOUR LITTLE SISTER?!

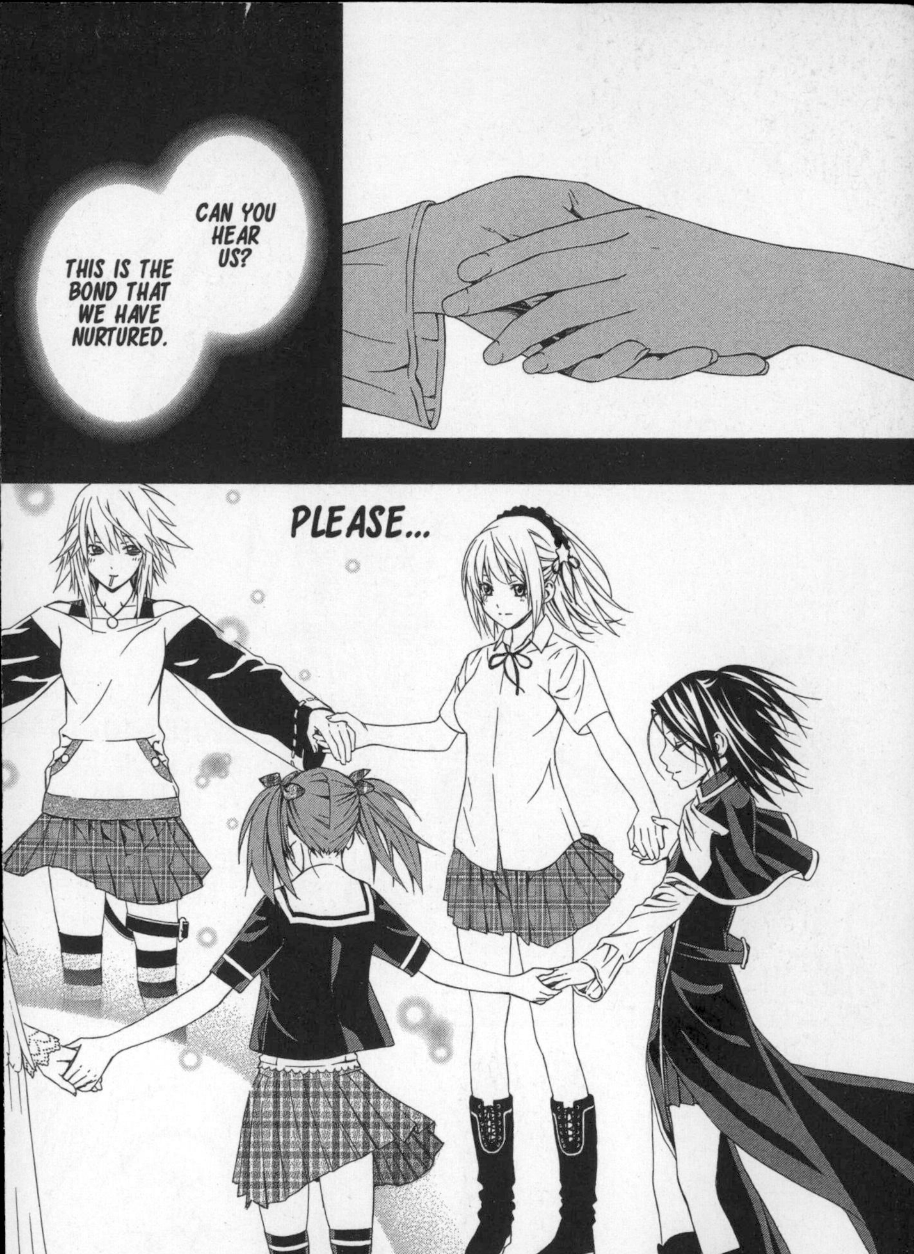
CAN YOU HEAR US?
THIS IS THE BOND THAT WE HAVE NURTURED.
PLEASE...

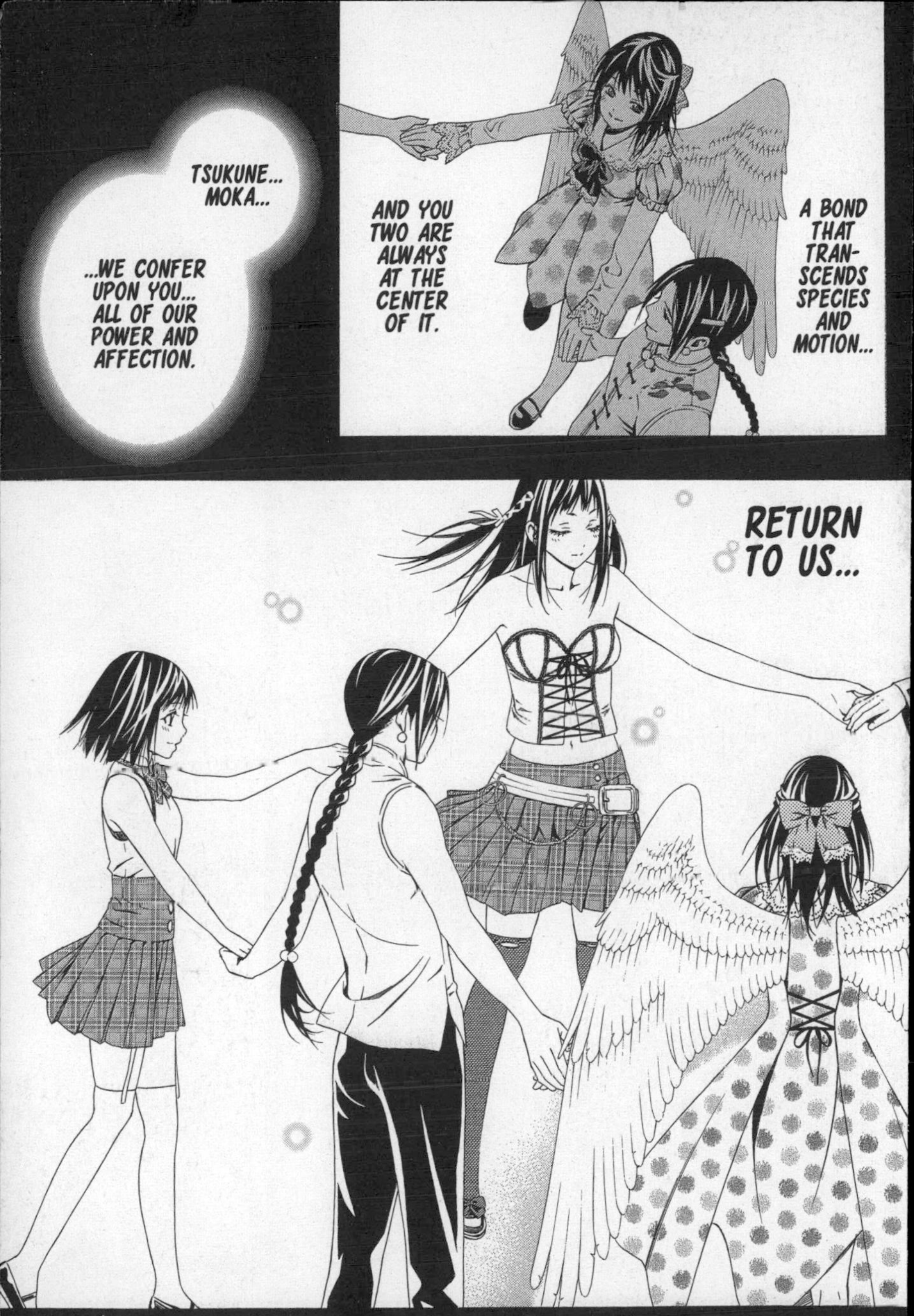
A BOND THAT TRAN-SCENDS SPECIES AND MOTION...
AND YOU TWO ARE ALWAYS AT THE CENTER OF IT.
TSUKUNE... MOKA...
...WE CONFER UPON YOU... ALL OF OUR POWER AND AFFECTION.
RETURN TO US...

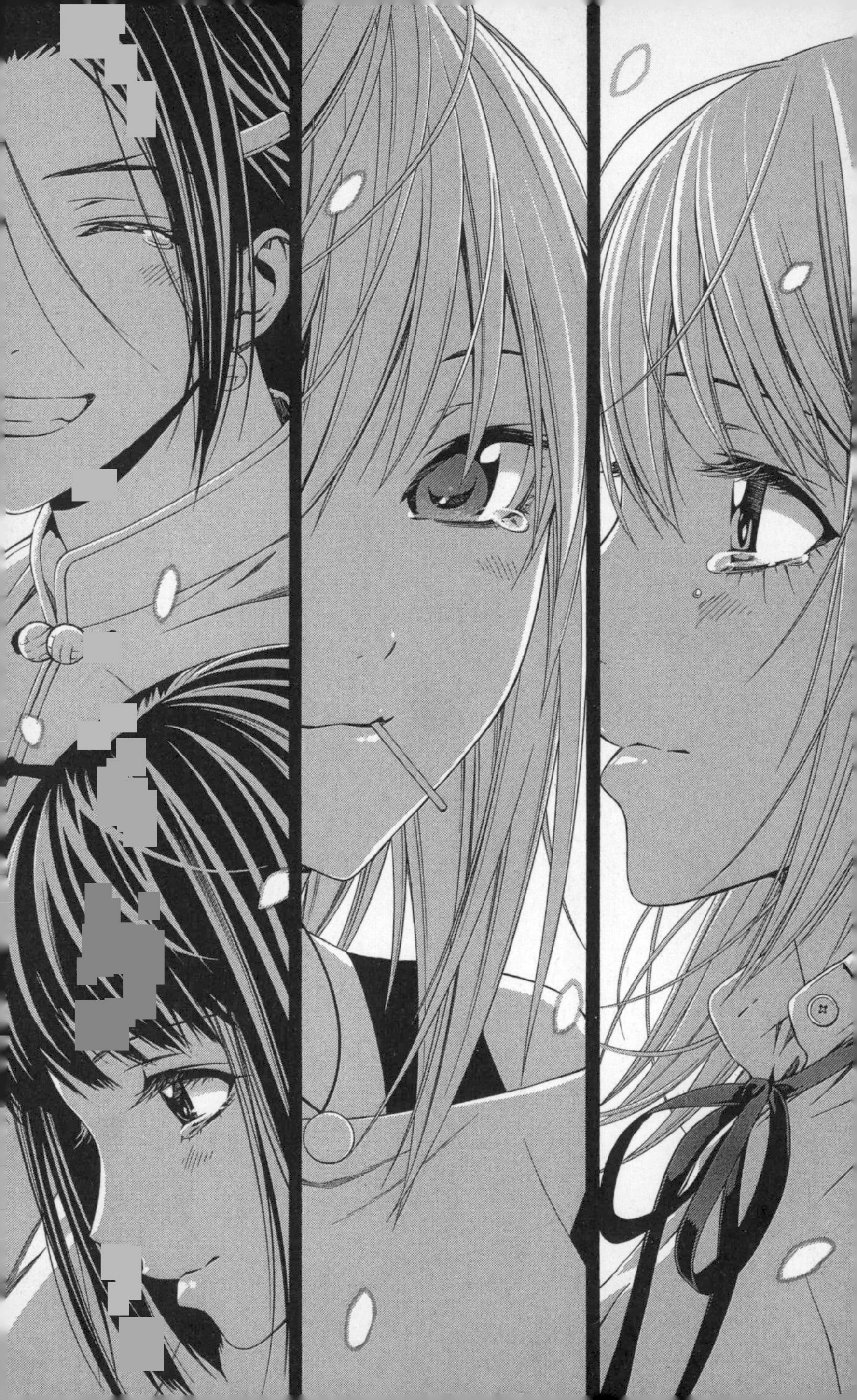

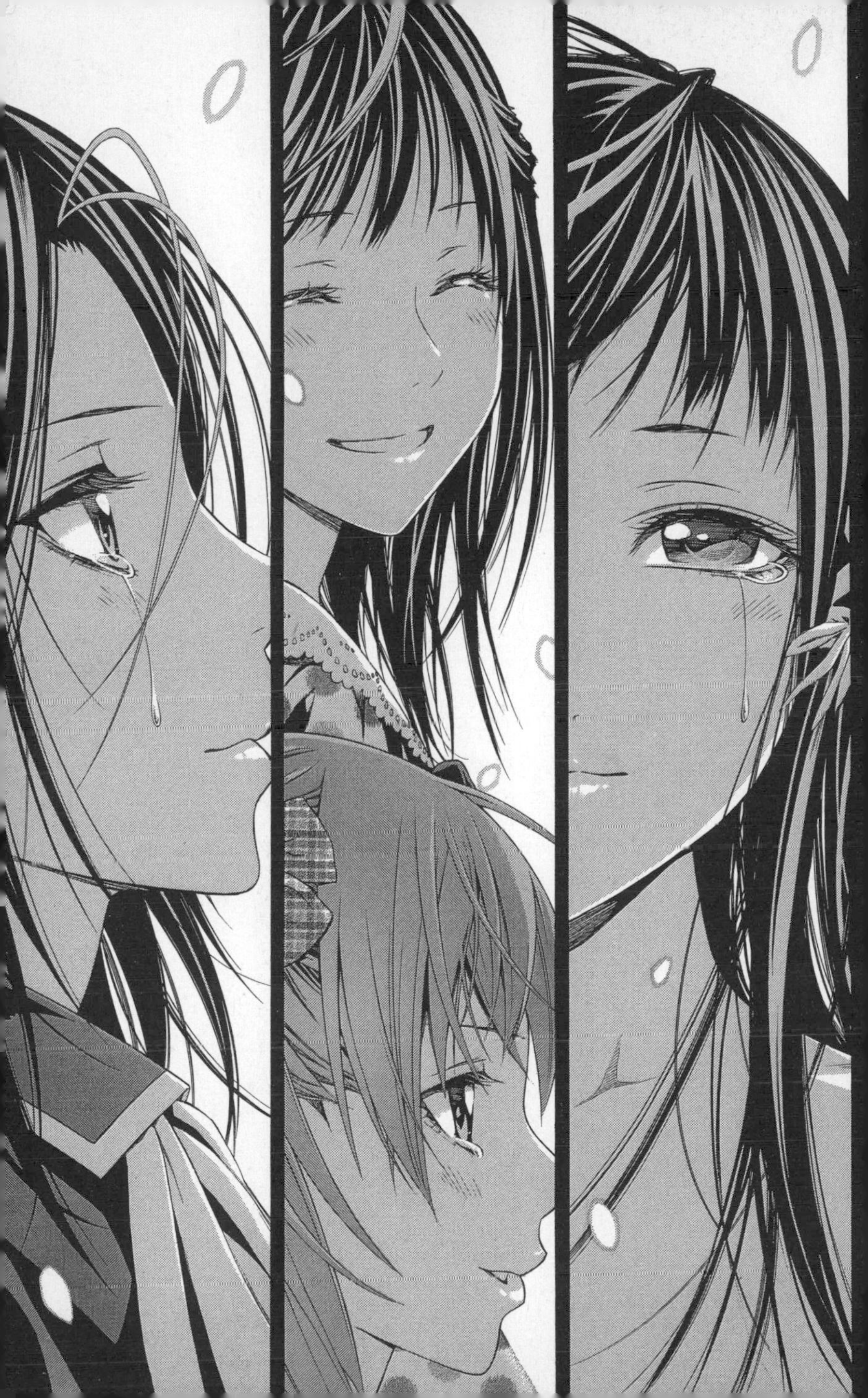

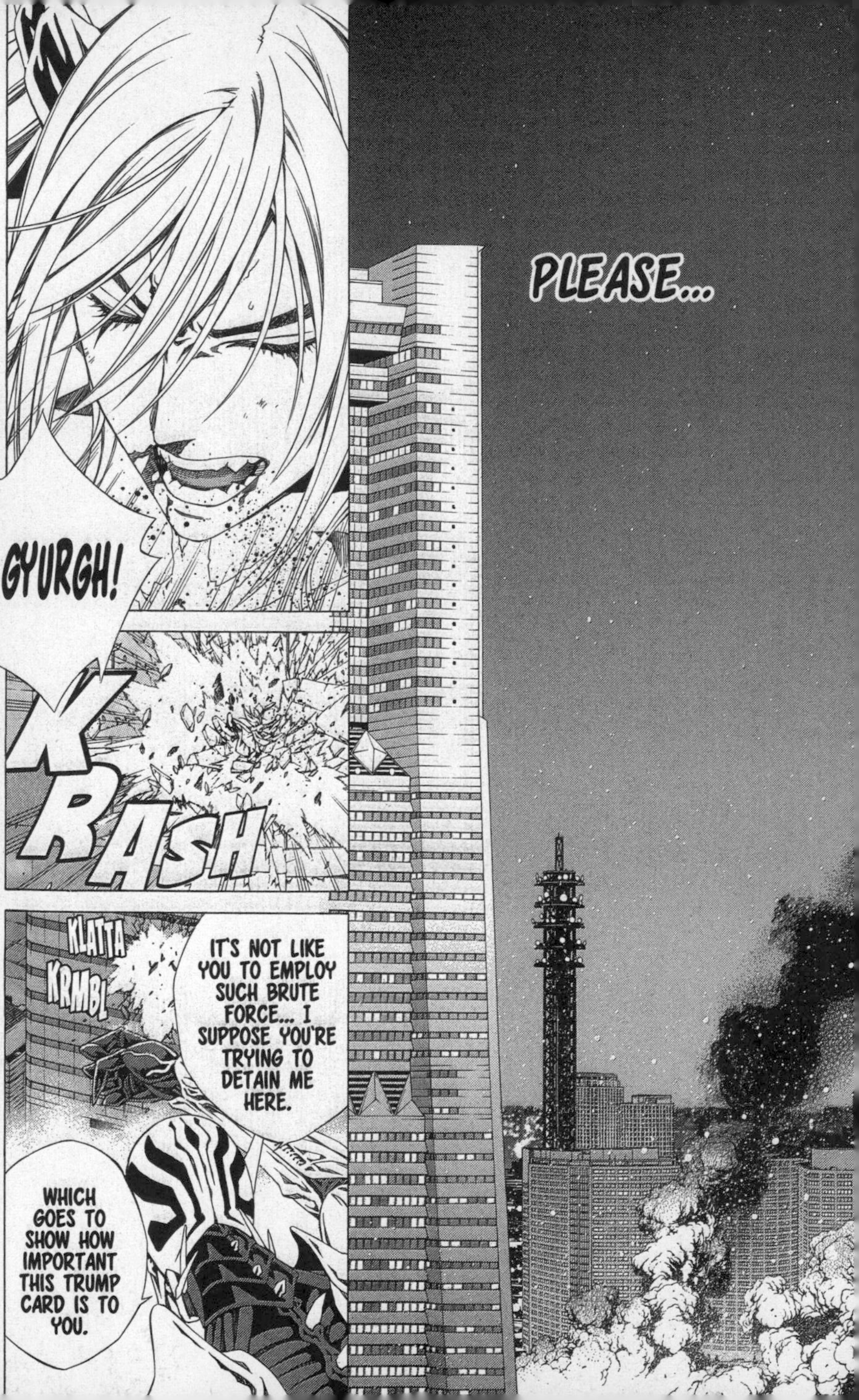
PLEASE...
GYURGH!
KRASH
IT'S NOT LIKE YOU TO EMPLOY SUCH BRUTE FORCE... I SUPPOSE YOU'RE TRYING TO DETAIN ME HERE.
KLATTA
KRMBL
WHICH GOES TO SHOW HOW IMPORTANT THIS TRUMP CARD IS TO YOU.

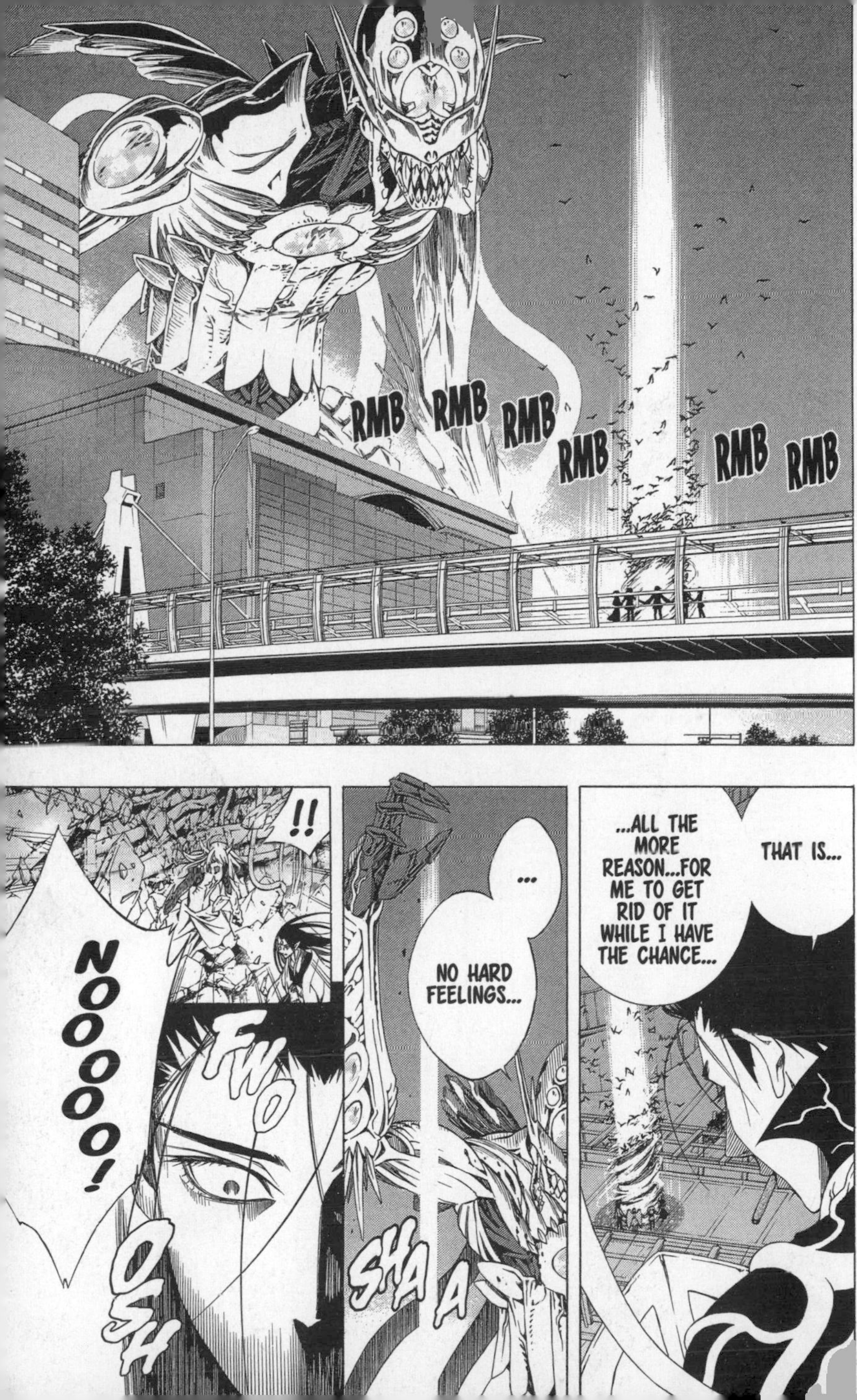
RMB RMB RMB RMB RMB RMB
THAT IS...
...ALL THE MORE REASON...FOR ME TO GET RID OF IT WHILE I HAVE THE CHANCE...
...
NO HARD FEELINGS...
SHAA
!!
NOOOOOO!
FWOOSH

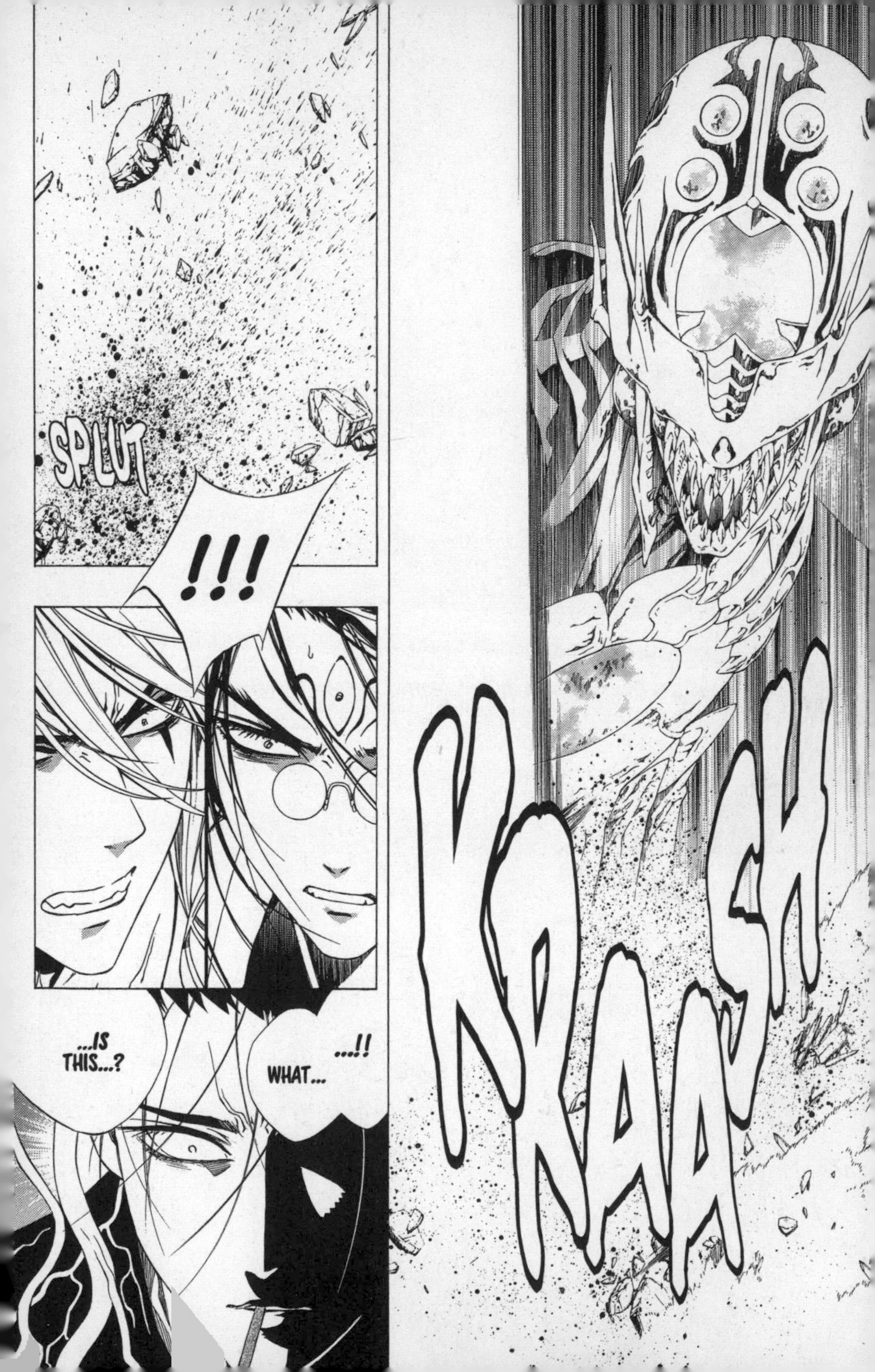
KRAASH
SPLUT
!!!
...!!
WHAT...
...IS THIS...?

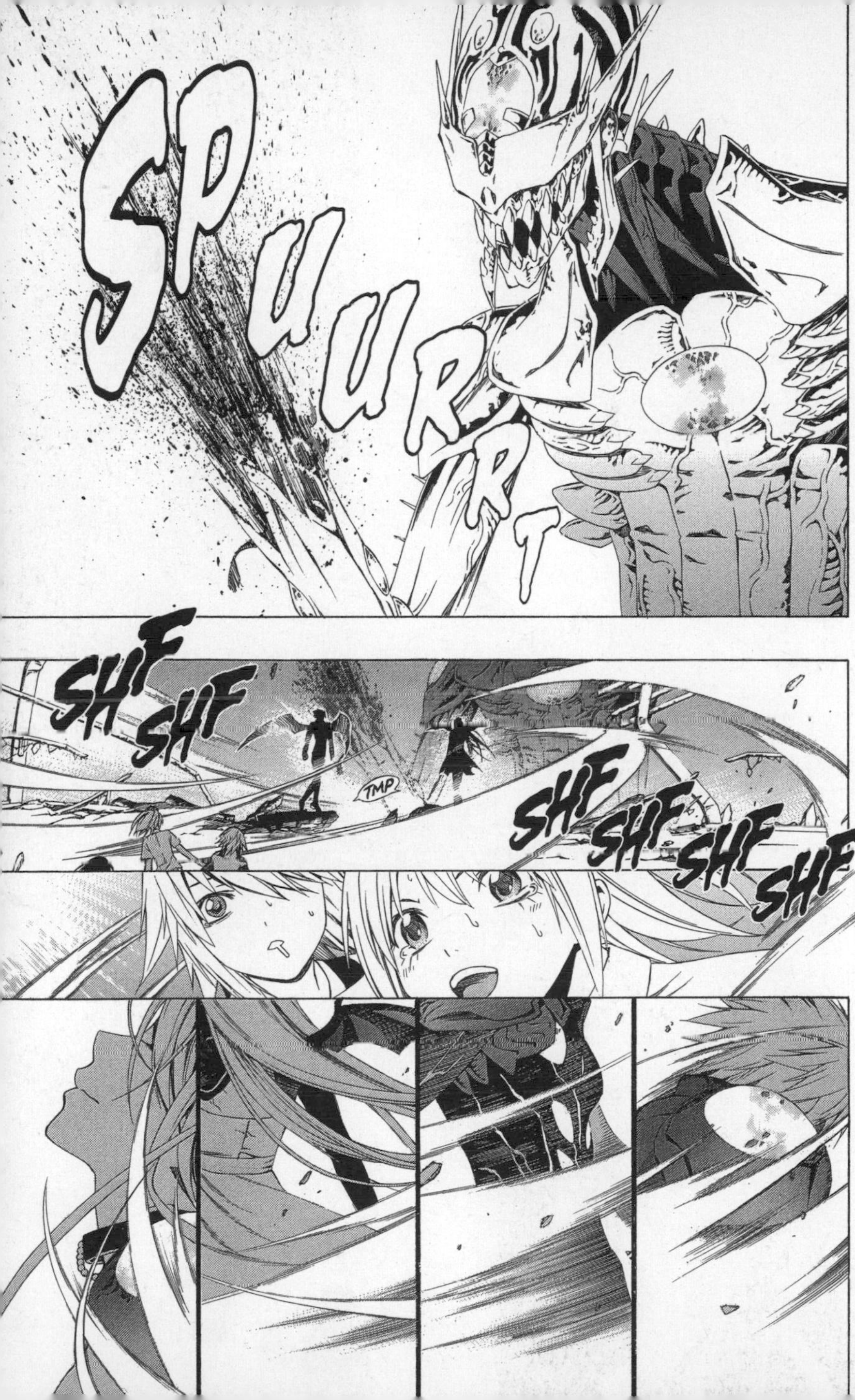
SPUURRT
SHF SHF
TMP
SHF SHF SHF SHF

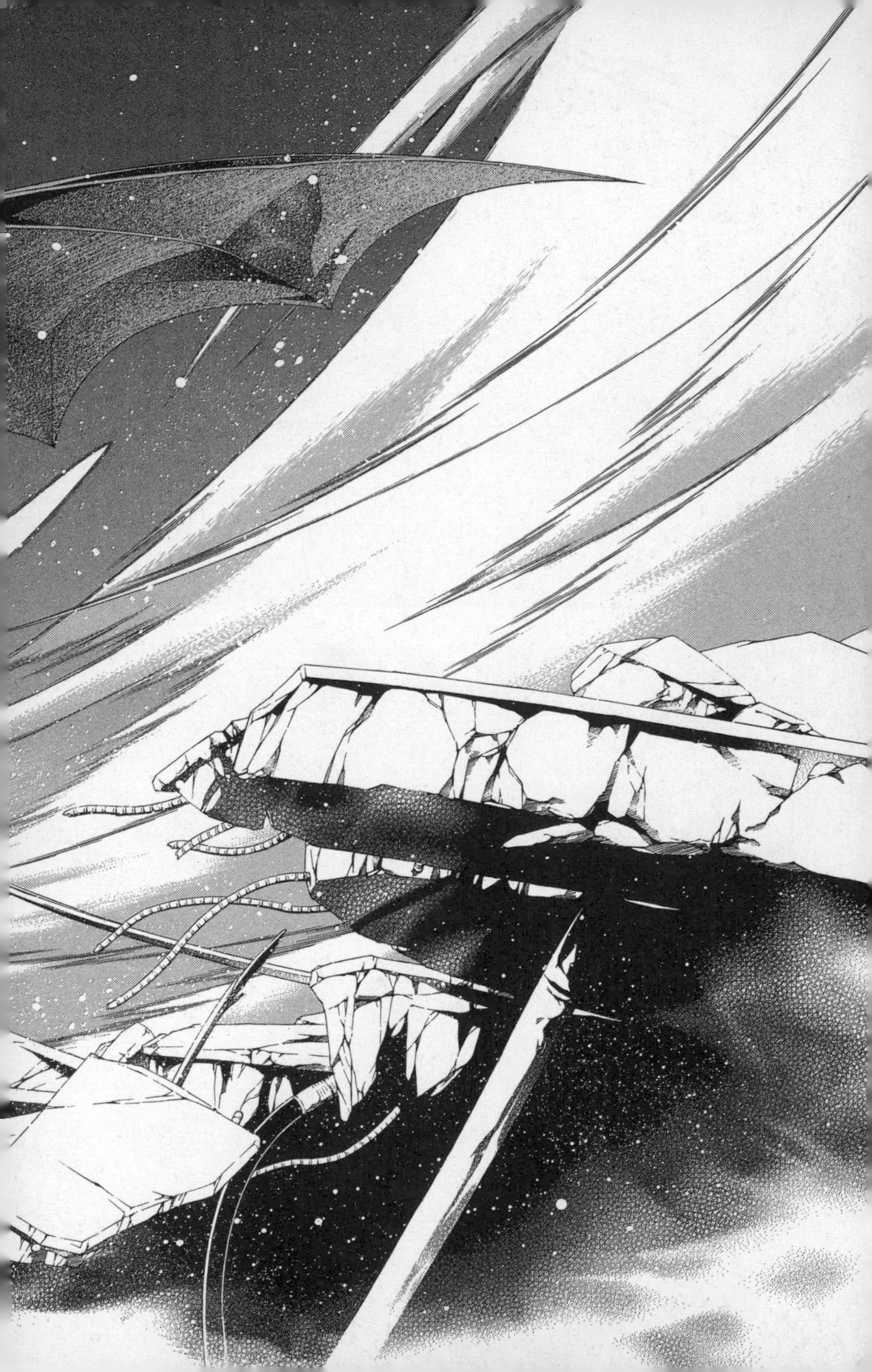

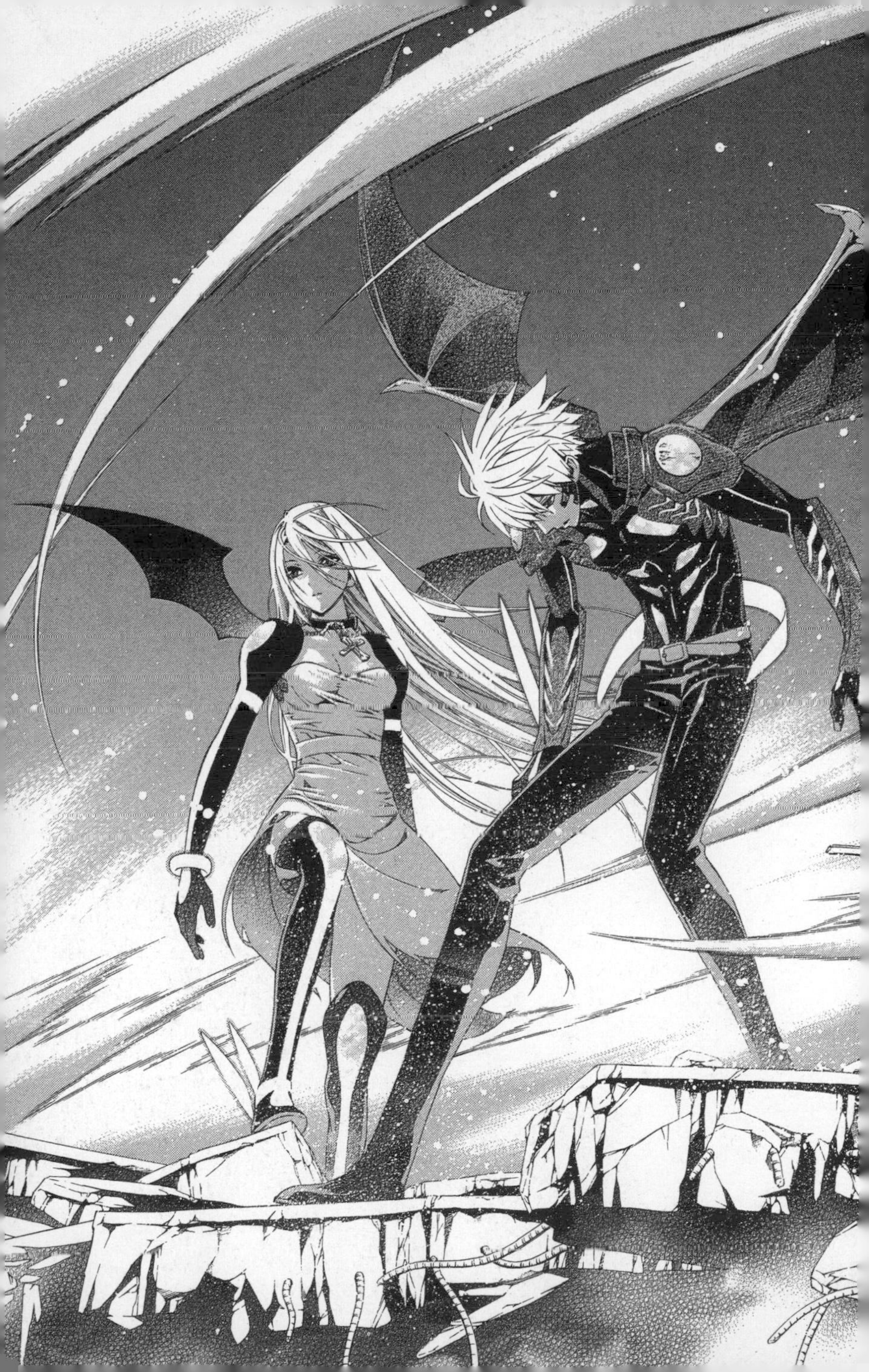

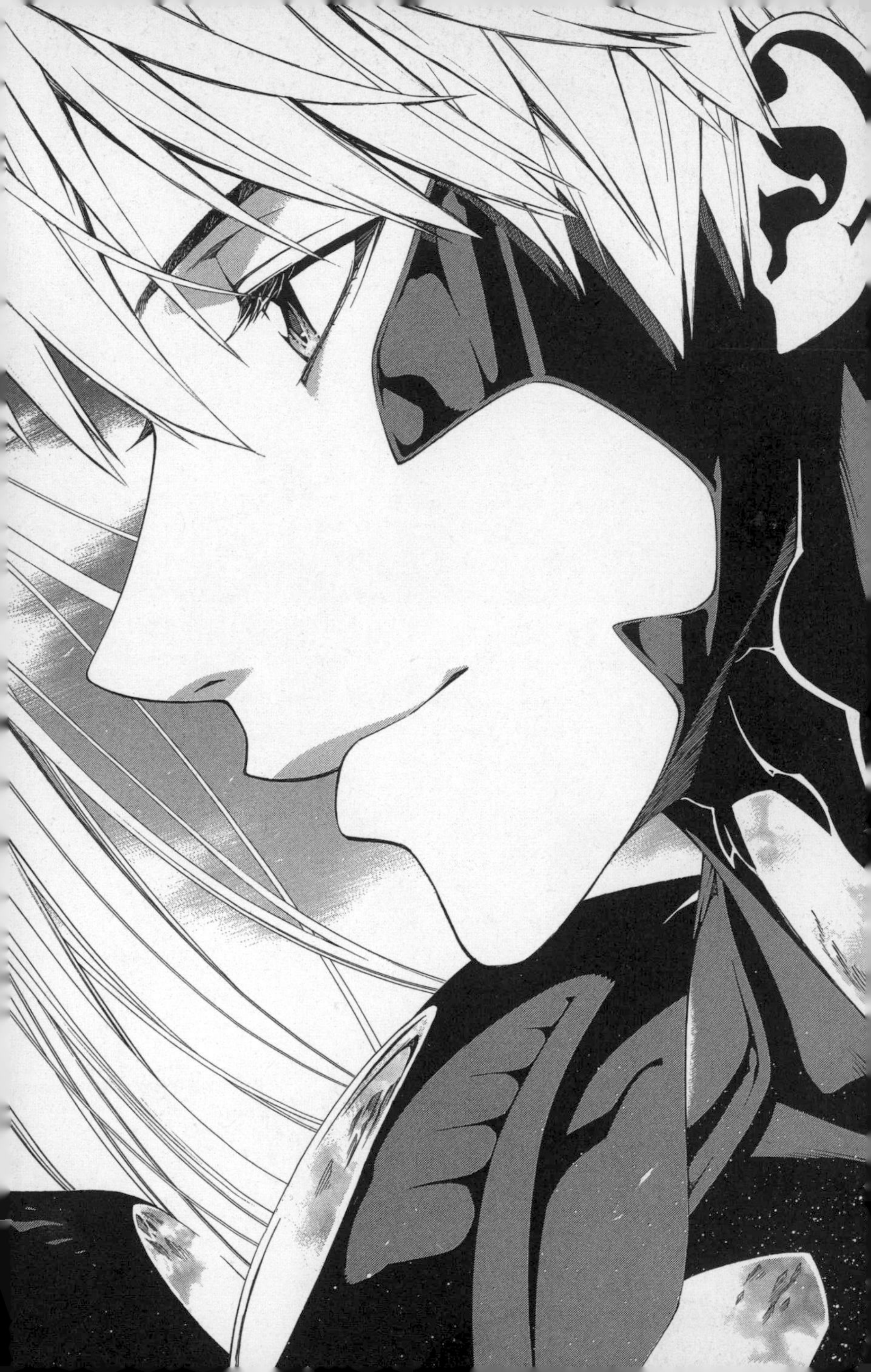

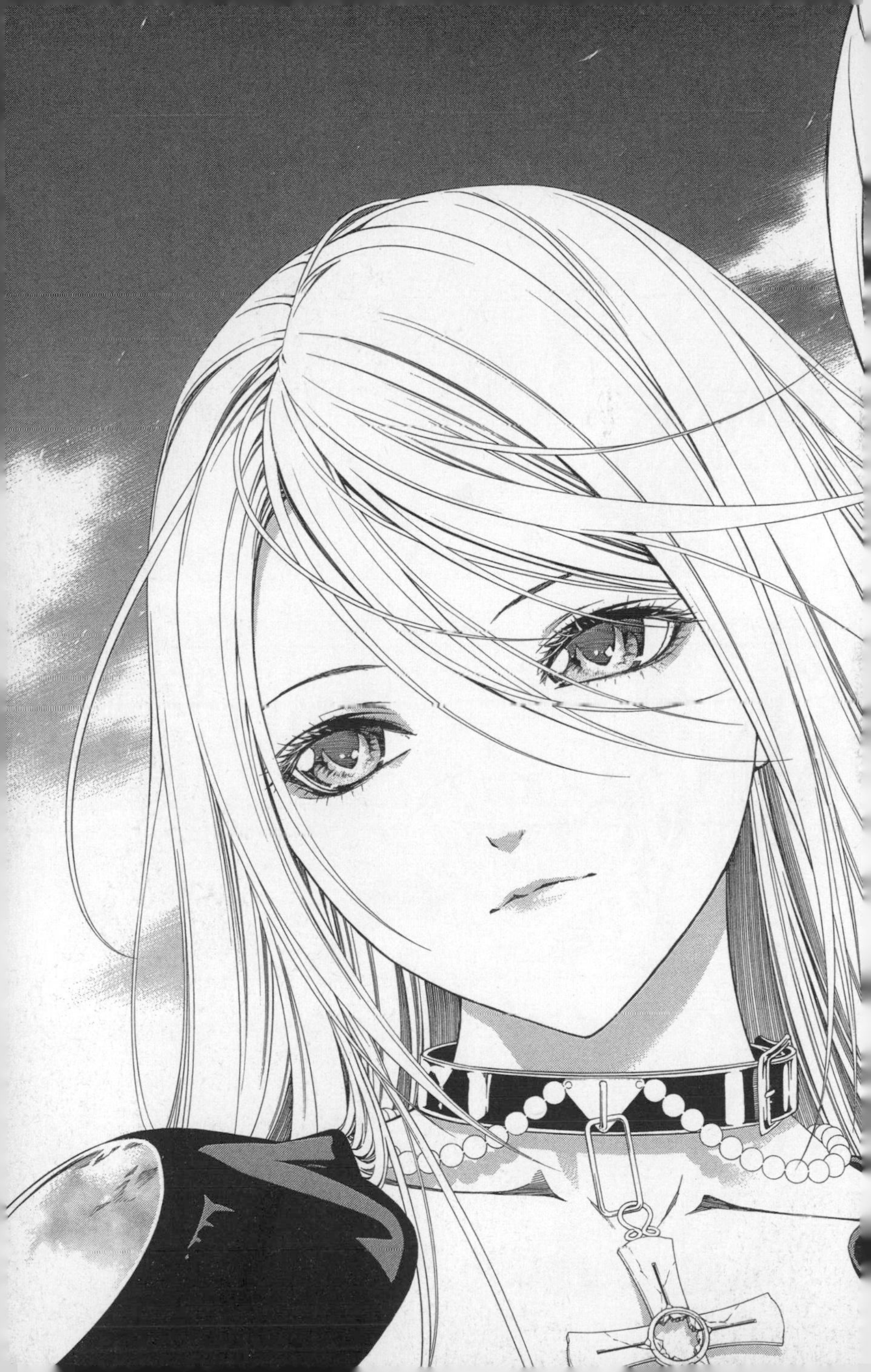

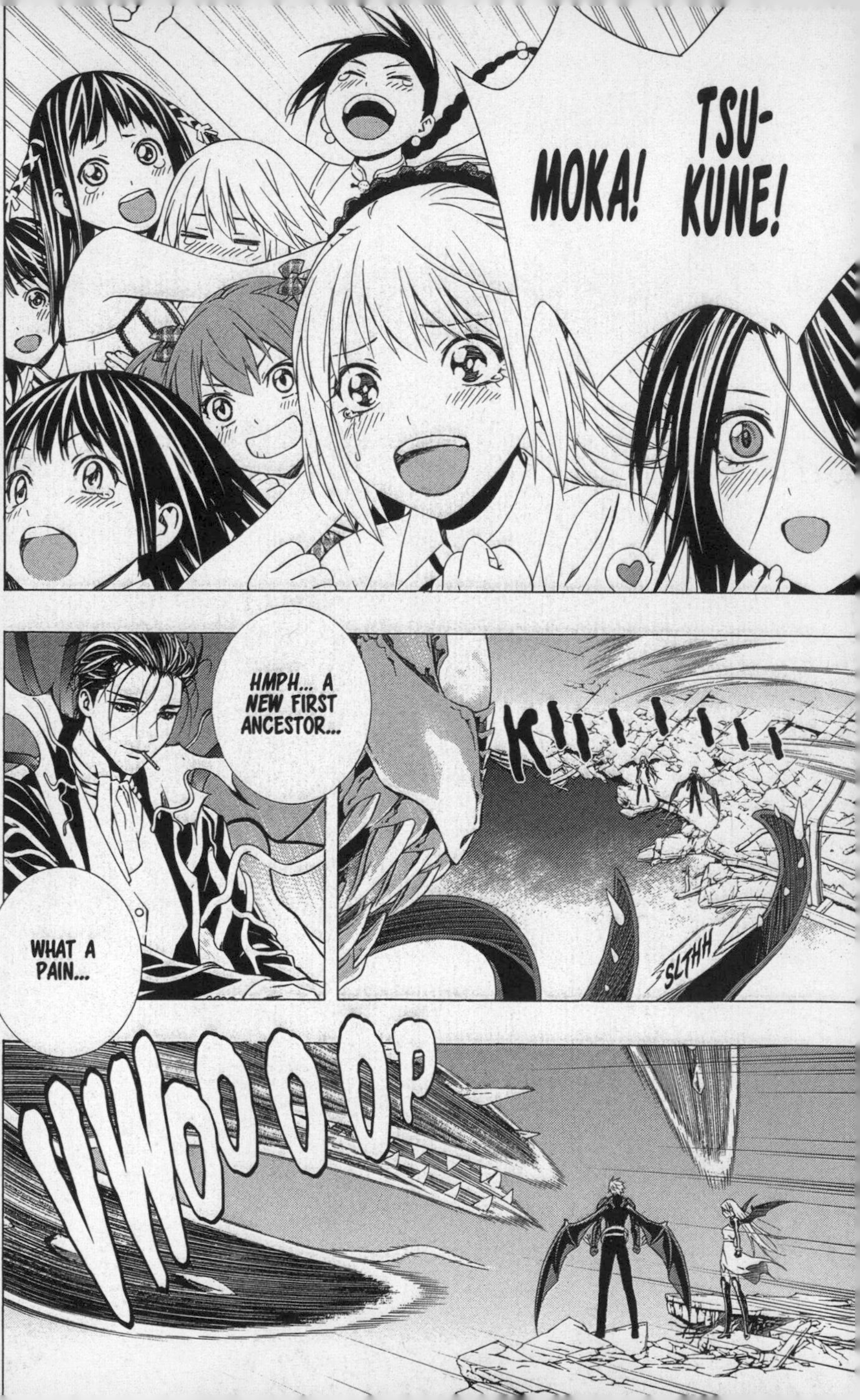
TSU-
KUNE!
MOKA!
KIIIIIII
SLTHH
HMPH... A NEW FIRST ANCESTOR...
WHAT A PAIN...
VWOOOOP

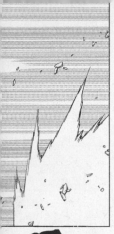

WE
RECEIVED...
YOUR
ENERGY...

THANK
YOU...

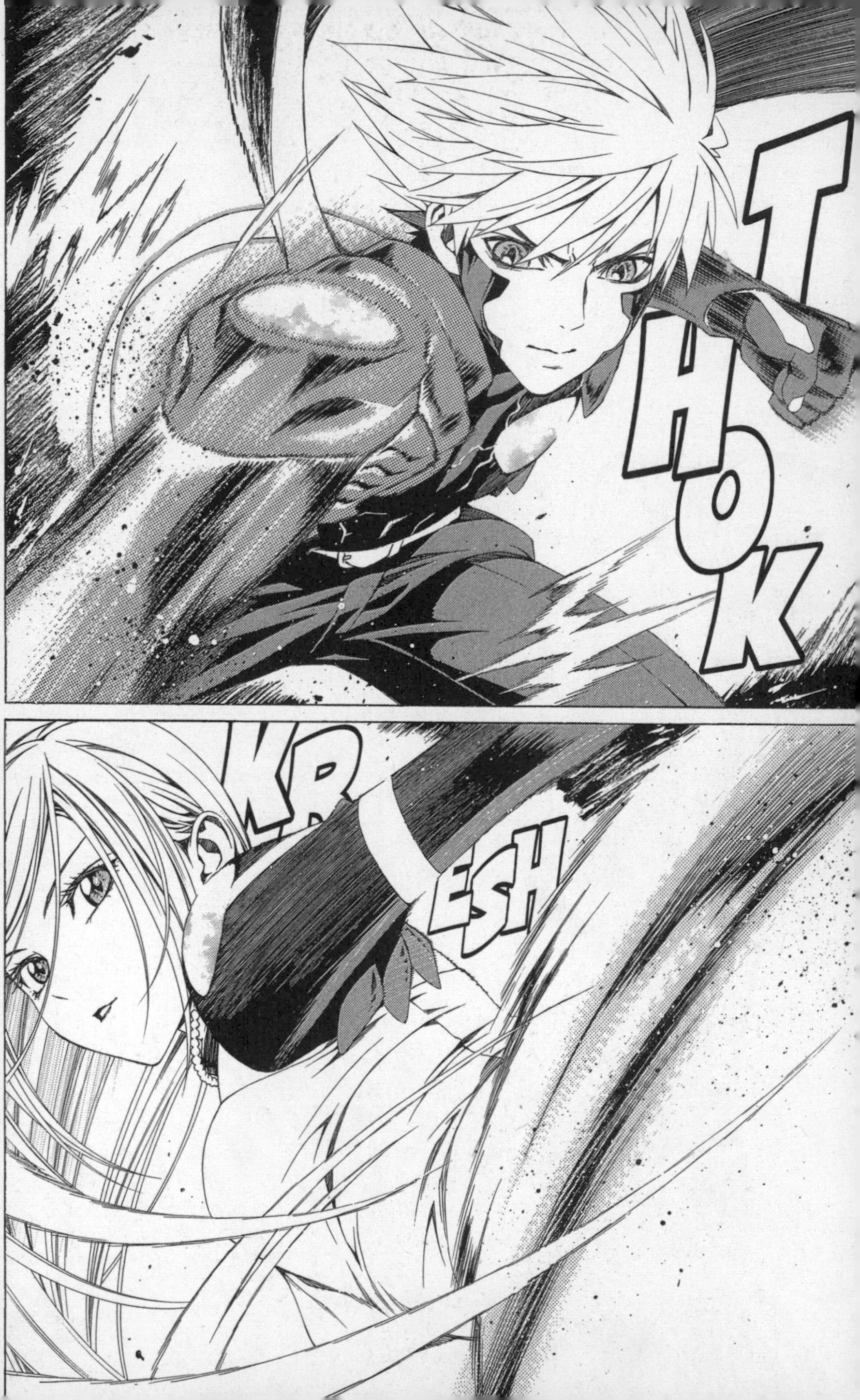
THOK
KR
ESH

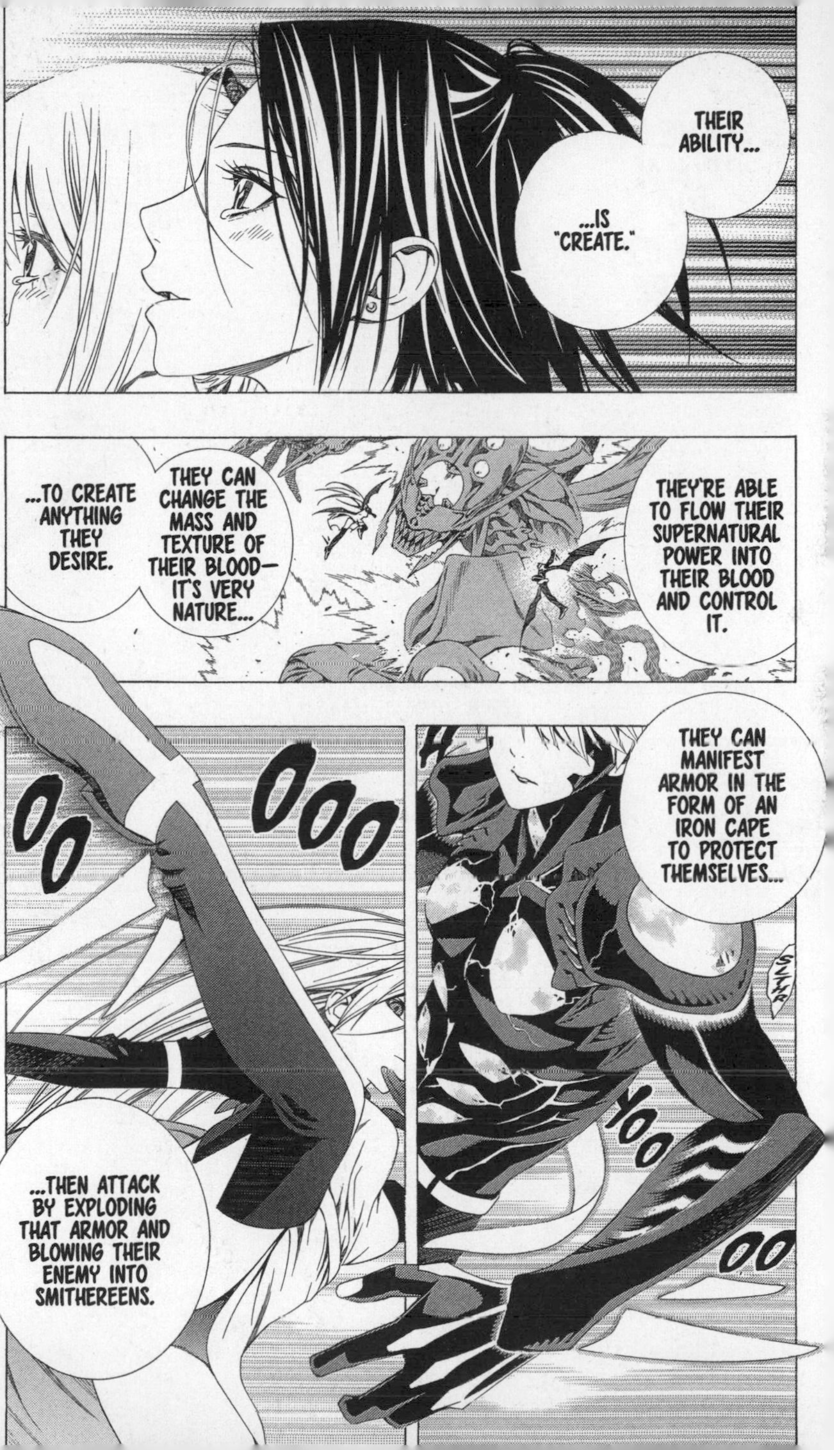
THEIR ABILITY...
...IS "CREATE."
THEY'RE ABLE TO FLOW THEIR SUPERNATURAL POWER INTO THEIR BLOOD AND CONTROL IT.
THEY CAN CHANGE THE MASS AND TEXTURE OF THEIR BLOOD—IT'S VERY NATURE...
...TO CREATE ANYTHING THEY DESIRE.
THEY CAN MANIFEST ARMOR IN THE FORM OF AN IRON CAPE TO PROTECT THEMSELVES...
SLTHR
YOOO
OO
OOO
OO
...THEN ATTACK BY EXPLODING THAT ARMOR AND BLOWING THEIR ENEMY INTO SMITHEREENS.

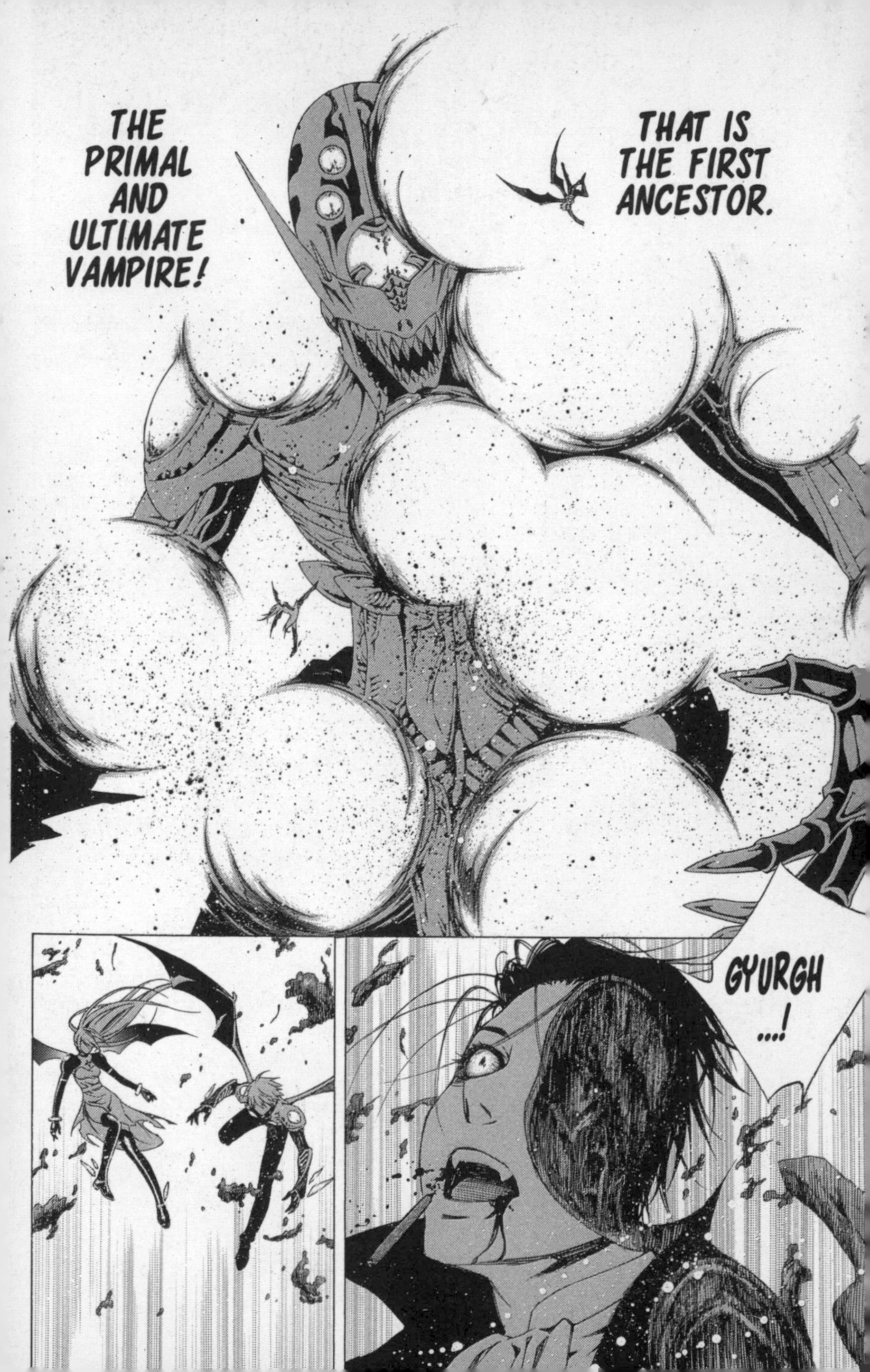
THAT IS THE FIRST ANCESTOR.
THE PRIMAL AND ULTIMATE VAMPIRE!
GYURGH ...!

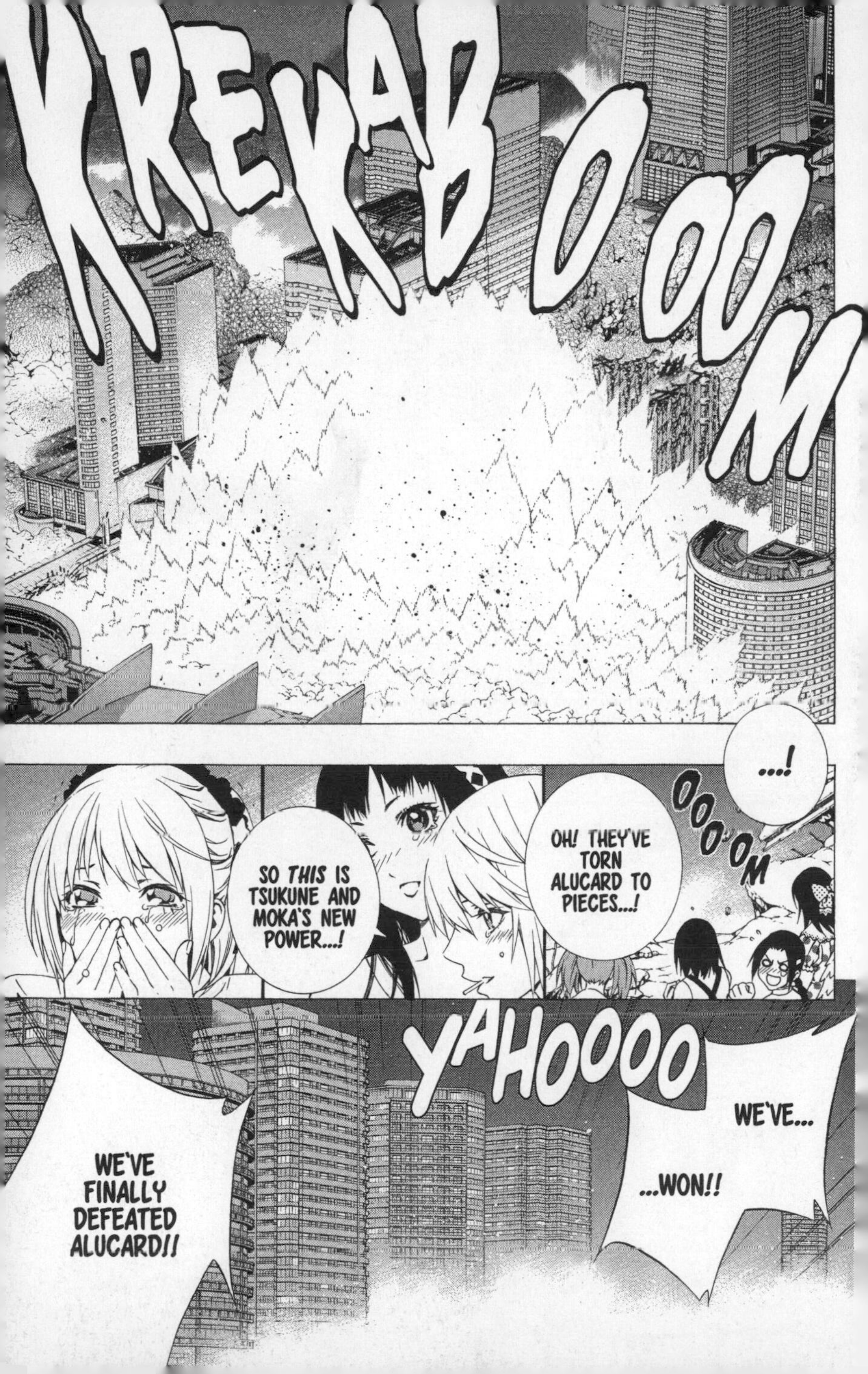
KREKABOOOM
...!
OOOOM
OH! THEY'VE TORN ALUCARD TO PIECES...!
SO *THIS* IS TSUKUNE AND MOKA'S NEW POWER...!
YAHOOOO
WE'VE...
...WON!!
WE'VE FINALLY DEFEATED ALUCARD!!

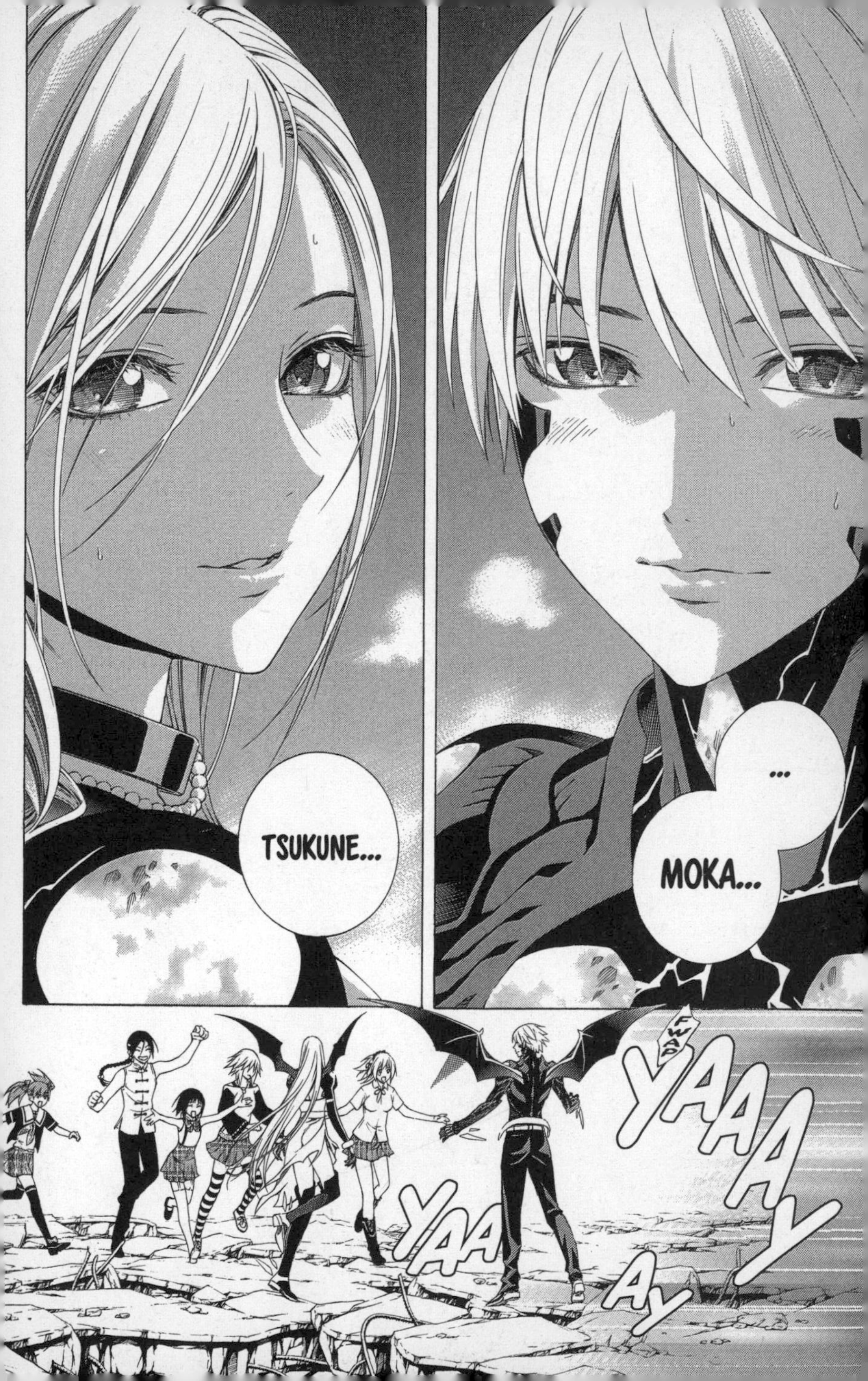
...
MOKA...
TSUKUNE...
FWAP
YAAAAY
YAAAY

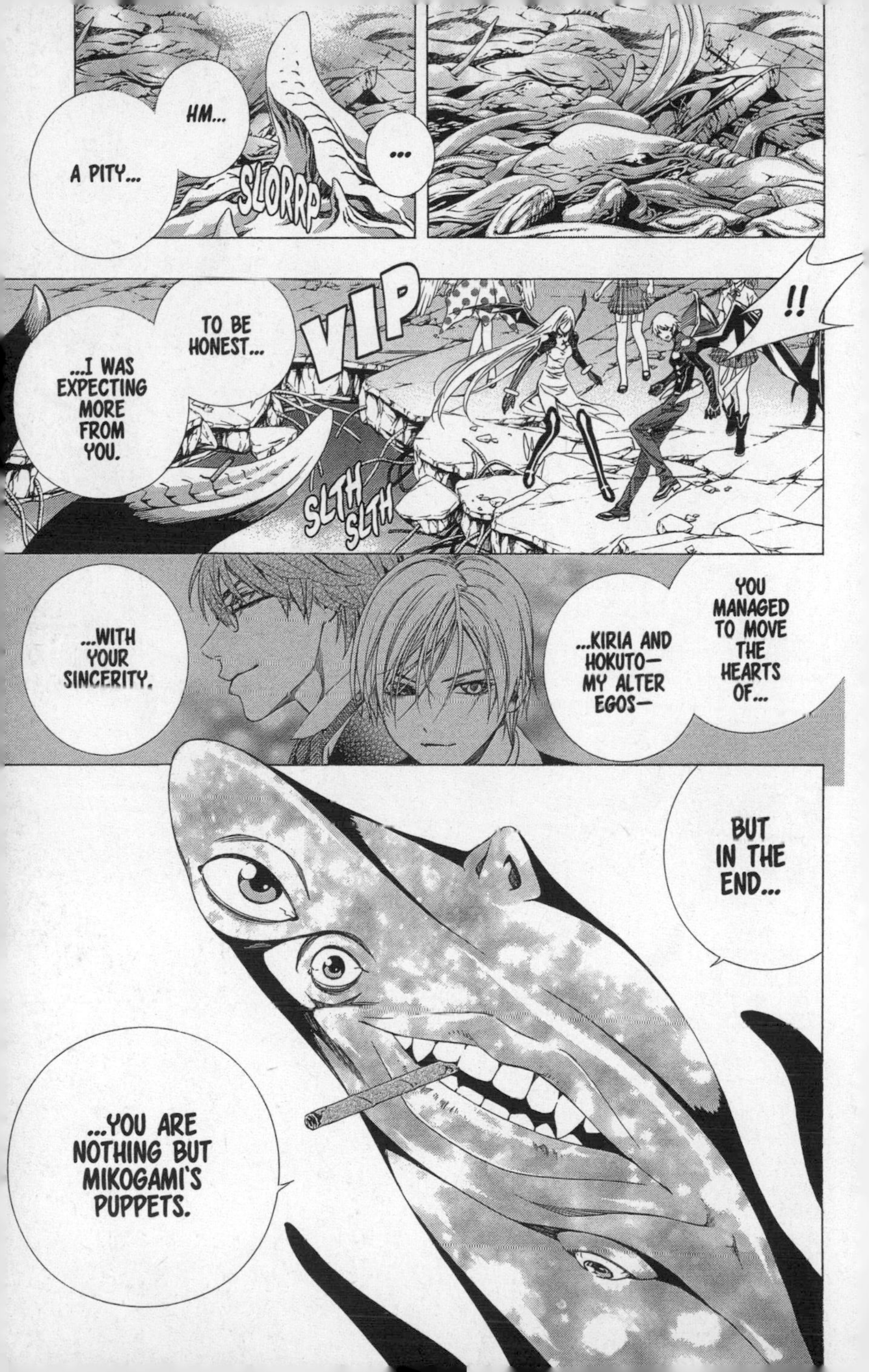
...
HM... A PITY...
SLORRP
!!
VIP
TO BE HONEST...
...I WAS EXPECTING MORE FROM YOU.
SLTH SLTH
YOU MANAGED TO MOVE THE HEARTS OF...
...KIRIA AND HOKUTO— MY ALTER EGOS—
...WITH YOUR SINCERITY.
BUT IN THE END...
...YOU ARE NOTHING BUT MIKOGAMI'S PUPPETS.

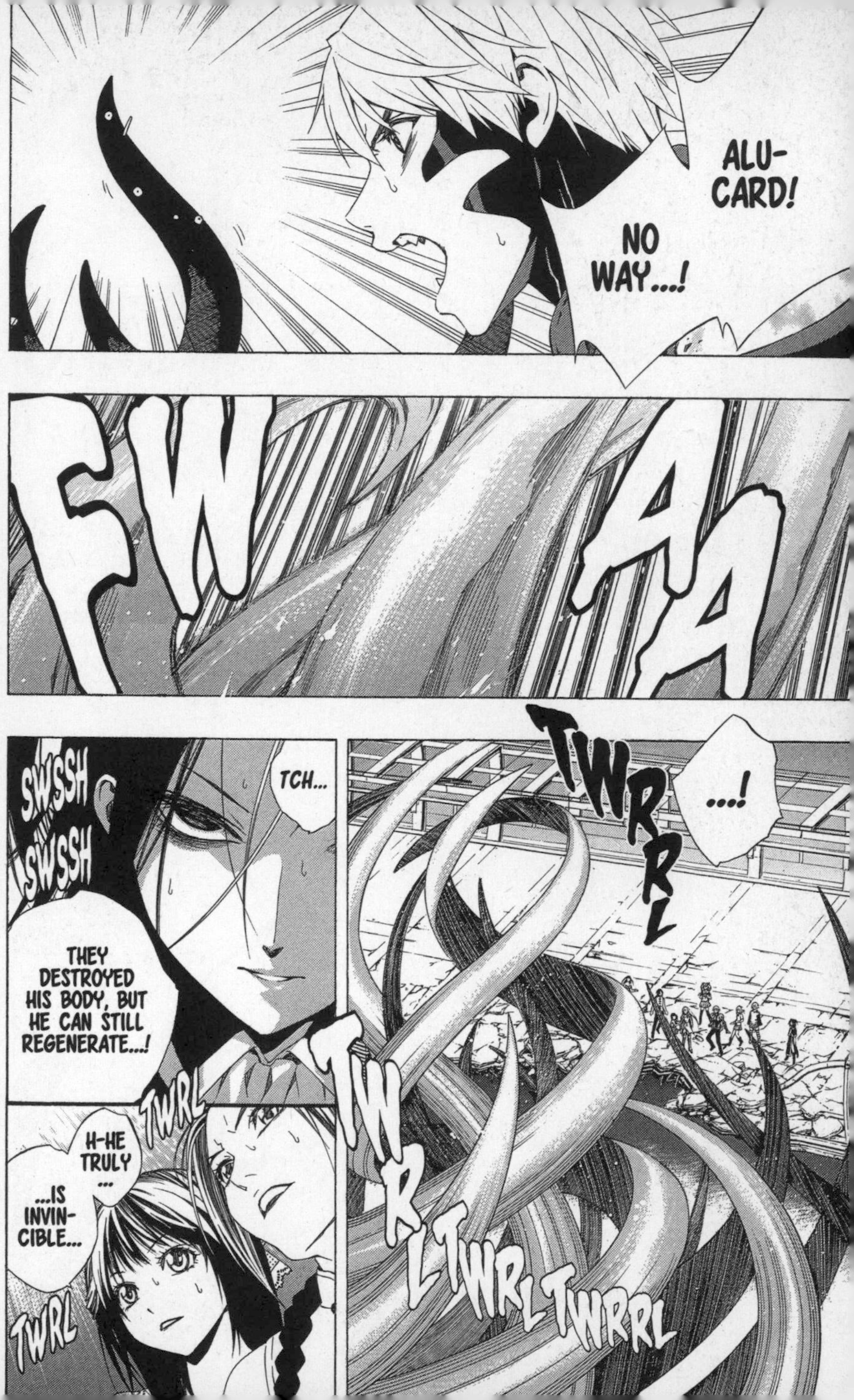
ALU-CARD!
NO WAY...!
FWA
TWRRL
...!
TWRL
TWRL
TWRRL
TCH...
SWSSH
SWSSH
THEY DESTROYED HIS BODY, BUT HE CAN STILL REGENERATE...!
TWRL
H-HE TRULY...
...IS INVINCIBLE...
TWRL

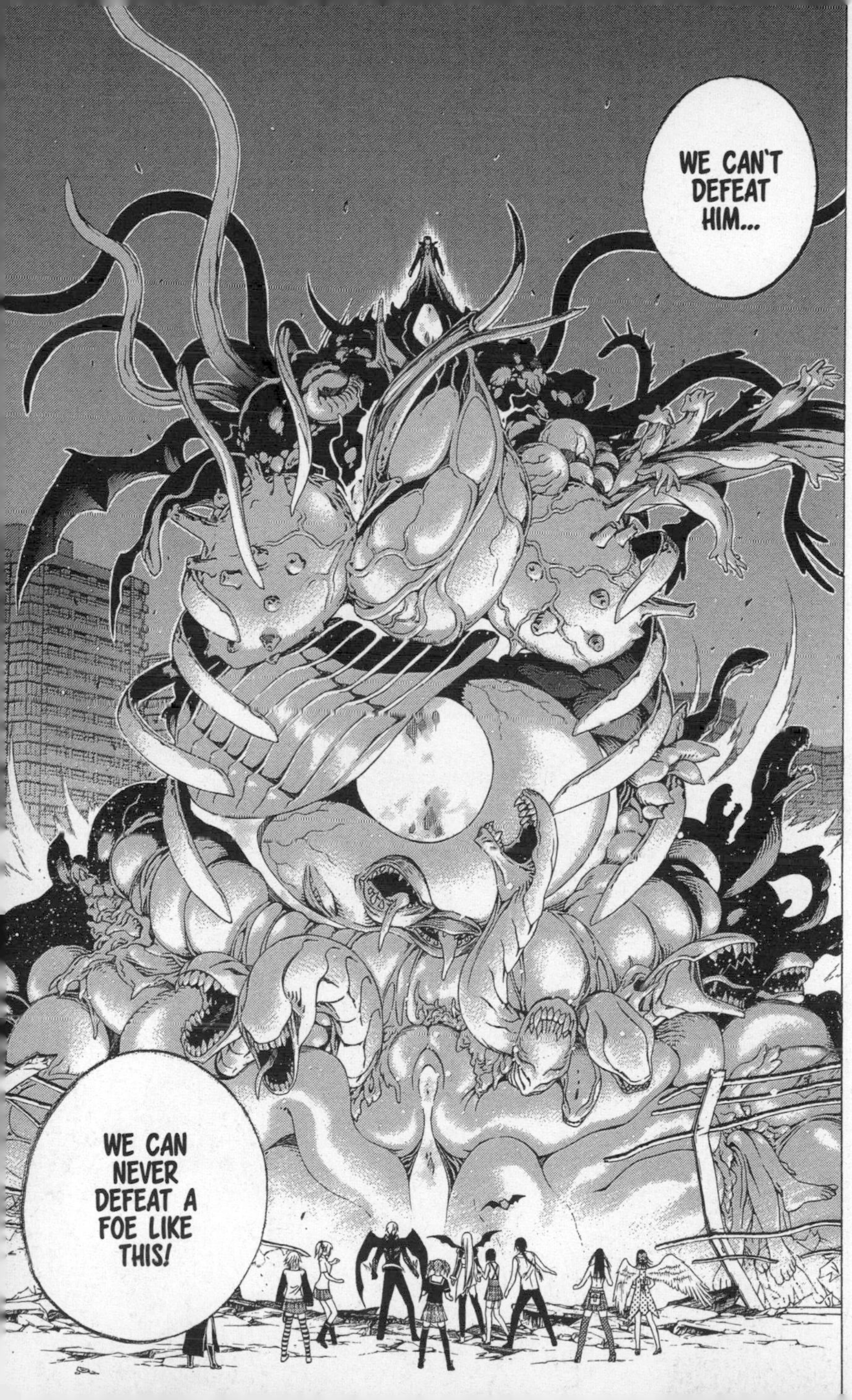
WE CAN'T DEFEAT HIM...
WE CAN NEVER DEFEAT A FOE LIKE THIS!

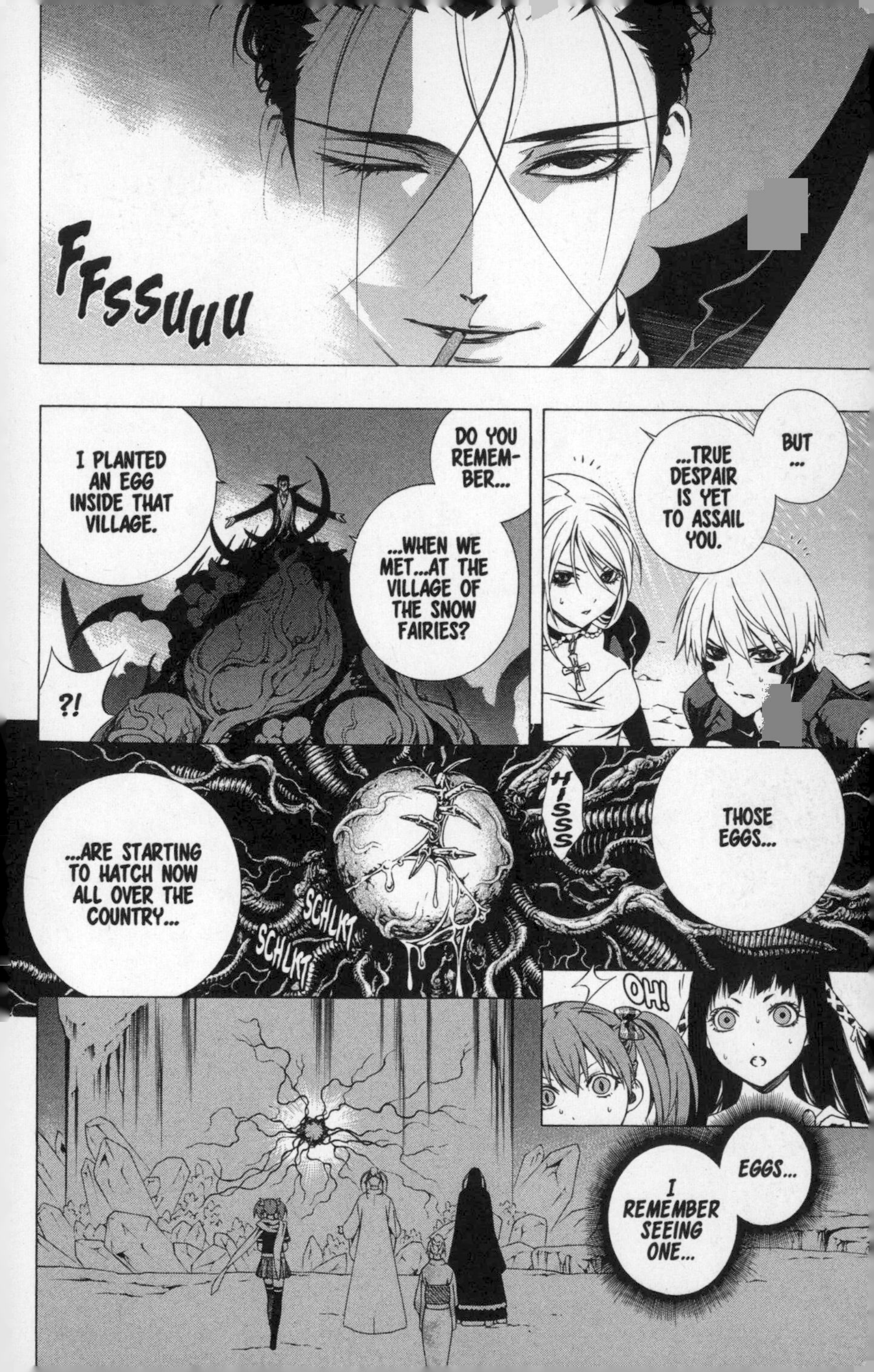
FFSSUUU
BUT...
...TRUE DESPAIR IS YET TO ASSAIL YOU.
DO YOU REMEMBER...
...WHEN WE MET...AT THE VILLAGE OF THE SNOW FAIRIES?
I PLANTED AN EGG INSIDE THAT VILLAGE.
?!
THOSE EGGS...
HISSS
...ARE STARTING TO HATCH NOW ALL OVER THE COUNTRY...
SCHLKT
SCHLKT
OH!
EGGS...
I REMEMBER SEEING ONE...

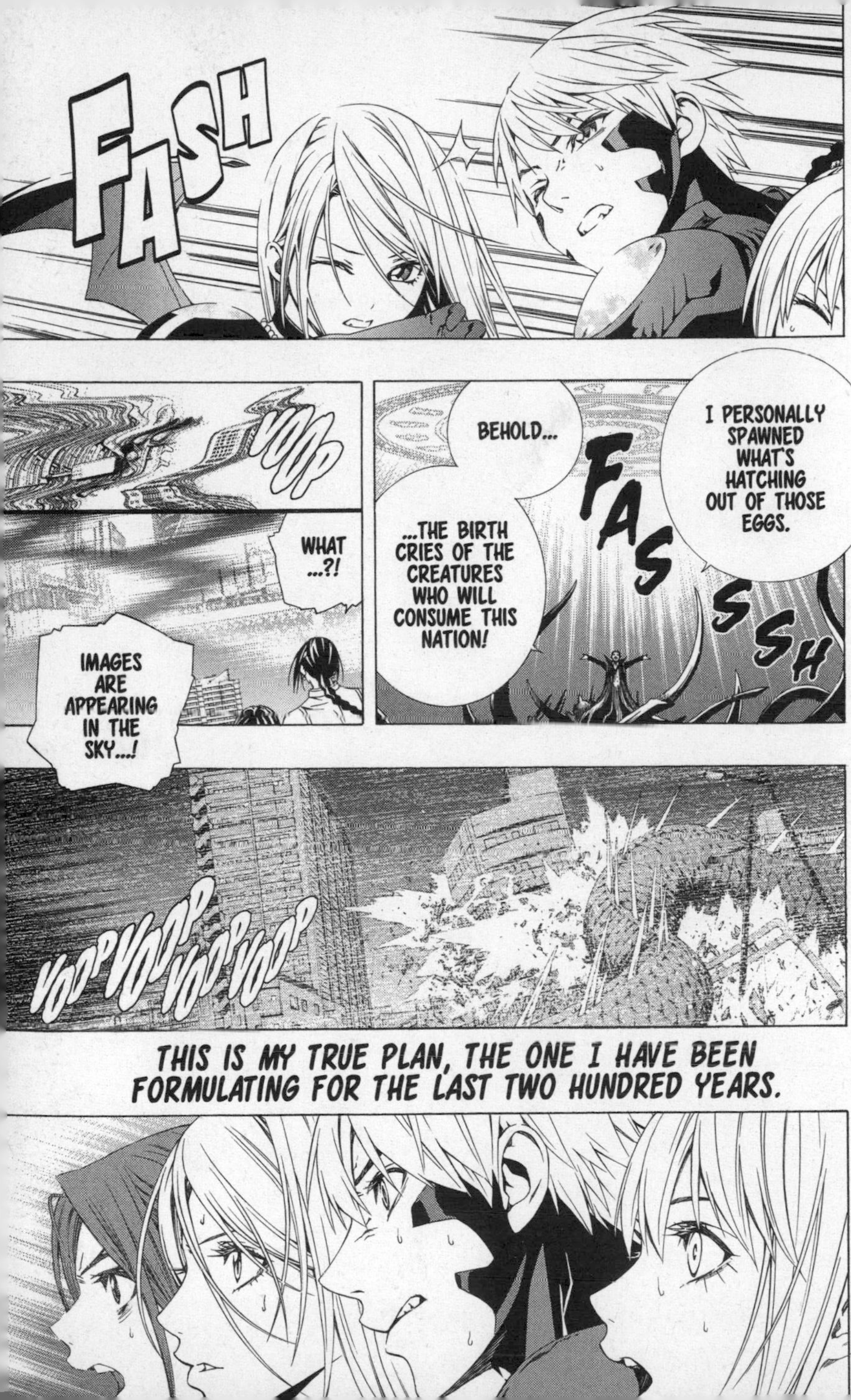
FASH
I PERSONALLY SPAWNED WHAT'S HATCHING OUT OF THOSE EGGS.
BEHOLD...
...THE BIRTH CRIES OF THE CREATURES WHO WILL CONSUME THIS NATION!
FASSSSH
VOOP
WHAT ...?!
IMAGES ARE APPEARING IN THE SKY...!
VOOPVOOPVOOPVOOP
THIS IS MY TRUE PLAN, THE ONE I HAVE BEEN FORMULATING FOR THE LAST TWO HUNDRED YEARS.

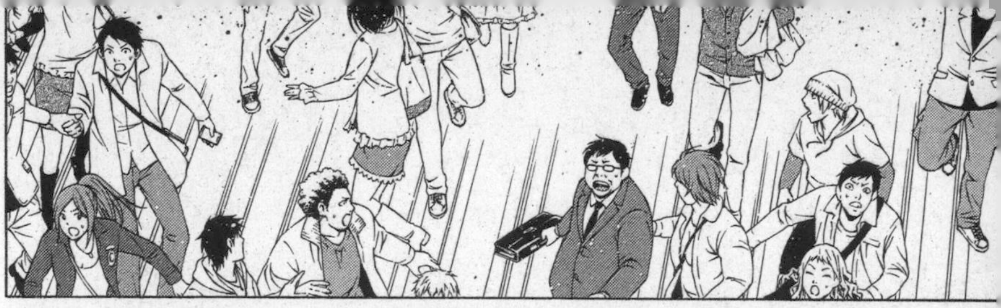

FIRST, WE WILL DECIMATE THE HUMAN POPULATION.

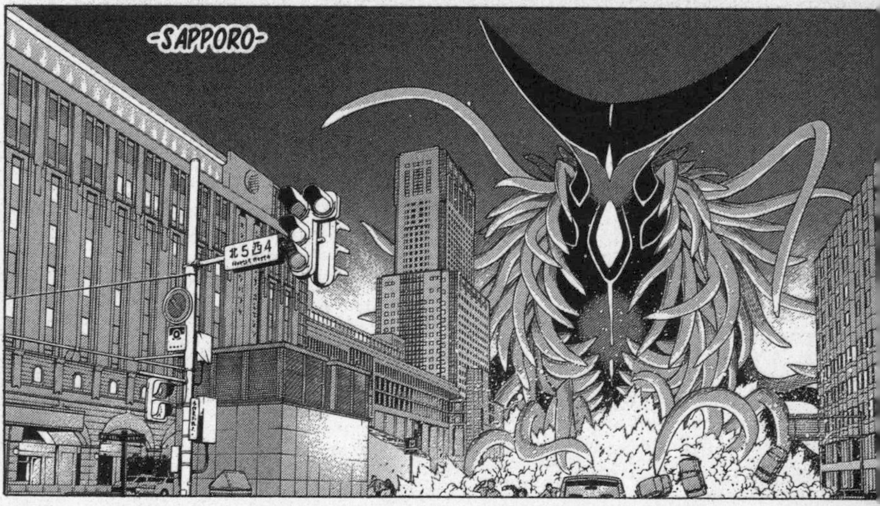
-SAPPORO-
北5西4

WE WILL DEVOUR, CRUSH AND TRAMPLE THEM.

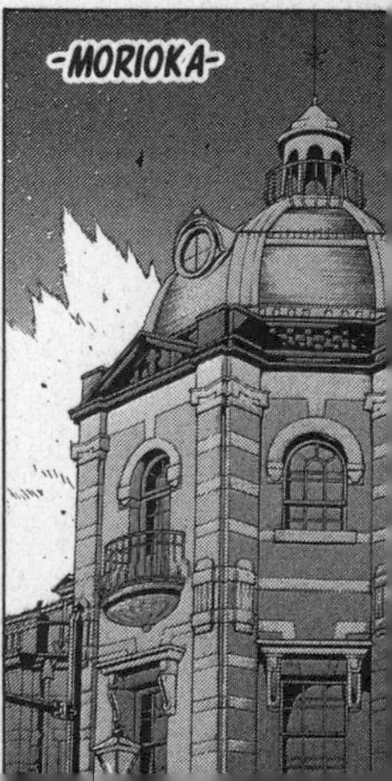
-MORIOKA-

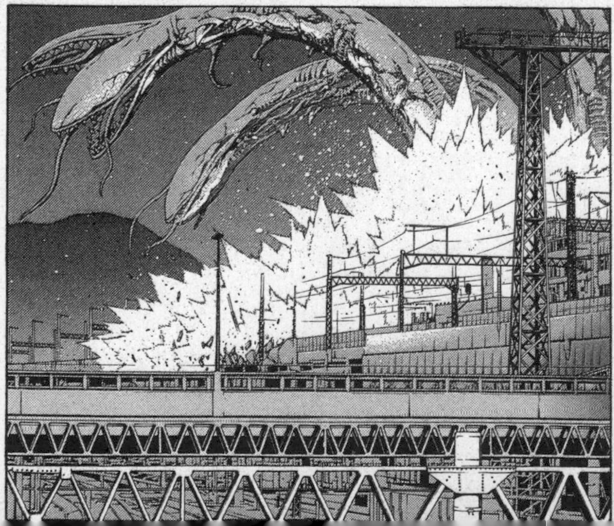

-TOKYO-

NEXT, I WILL GATHER...

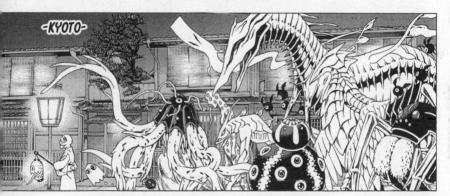

-KYOTO-

...MY KIN FROM ALL OVER THE WORLD...

-NAGASAKI-

-HIROSHIMA-

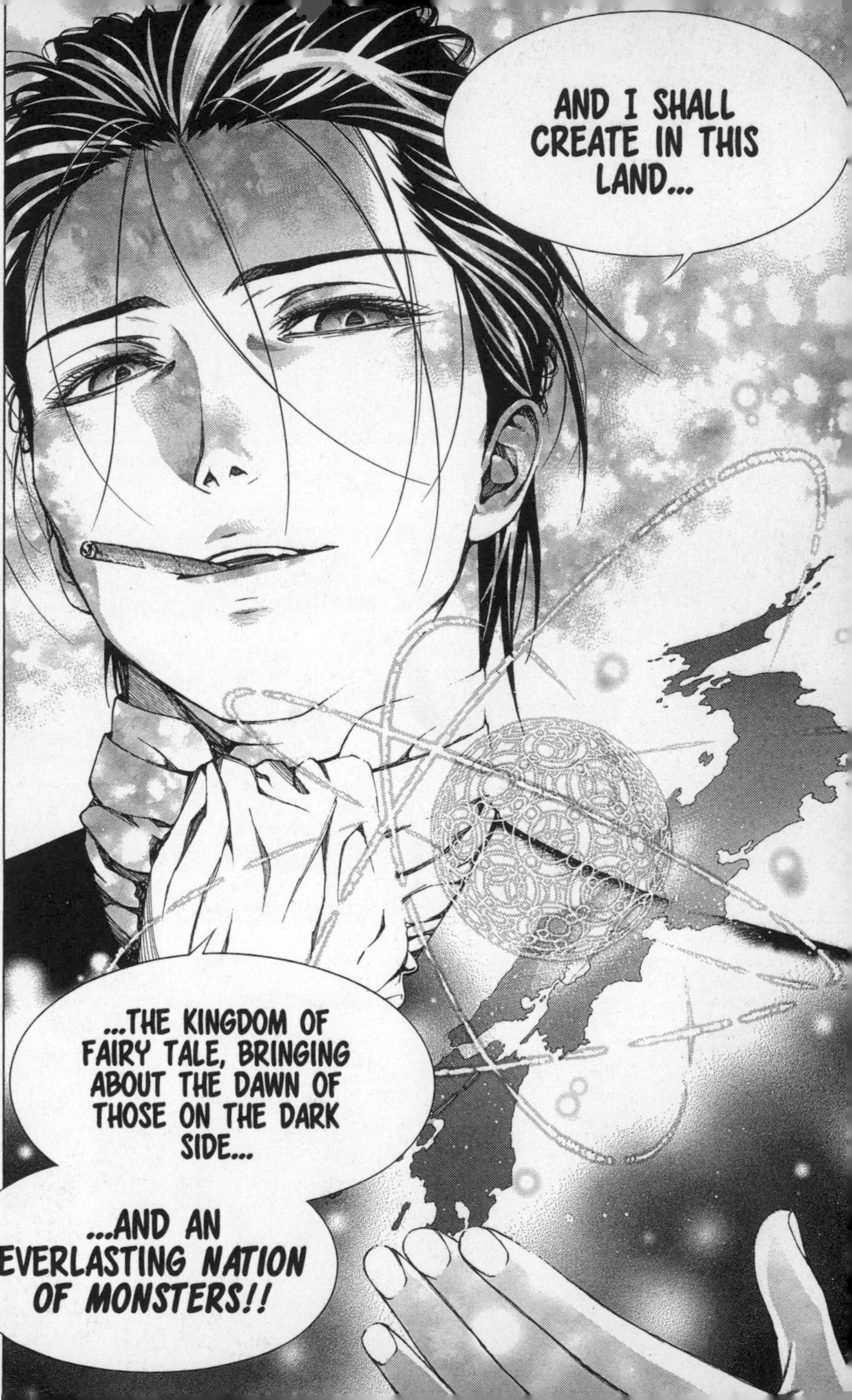
AND I SHALL CREATE IN THIS LAND...
...THE KINGDOM OF FAIRY TALE, BRINGING ABOUT THE DAWN OF THOSE ON THE DARK SIDE...
...AND AN EVERLASTING NATION OF MONSTERS!!

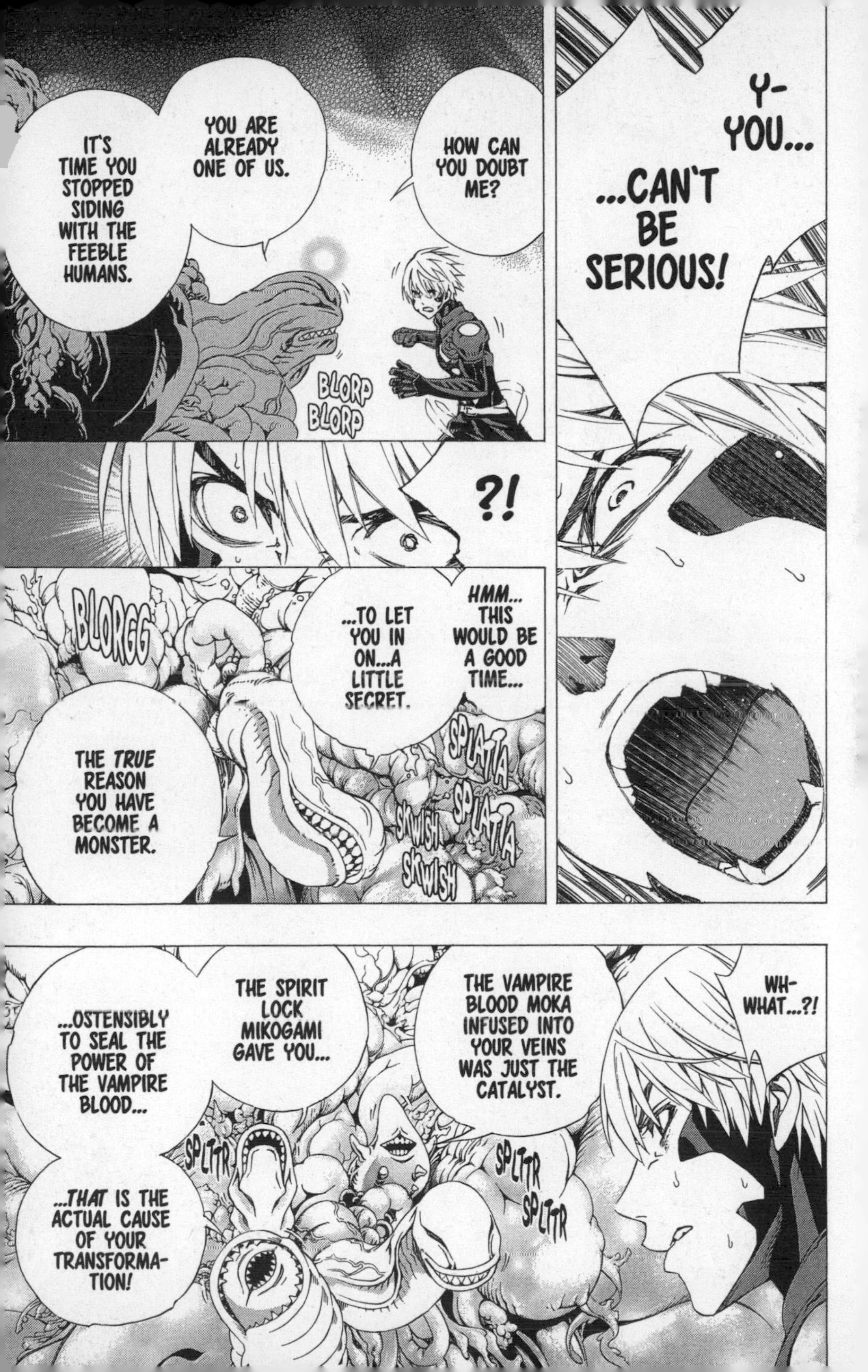
Y- YOU...
...CAN'T BE SERIOUS!
HOW CAN YOU DOUBT ME?
YOU ARE ALREADY ONE OF US.
IT'S TIME YOU STOPPED SIDING WITH THE FEEBLE HUMANS.
BLORP BLORP
?!
HMM... THIS WOULD BE A GOOD TIME...
...TO LET YOU IN ON...A LITTLE SECRET.
BLORGG
THE *TRUE* REASON YOU HAVE BECOME A MONSTER.
SPLATTA SPLATTA
SKWISH SKWISH
WH- WHAT...?!
THE VAMPIRE BLOOD MOKA INFUSED INTO YOUR VEINS WAS JUST THE CATALYST.
THE SPIRIT LOCK MIKOGAMI GAVE YOU...
...OSTENSIBLY TO SEAL THE POWER OF THE VAMPIRE BLOOD...
SPLTTR SPLTTR SPLTTR
...*THAT* IS THE ACTUAL CAUSE OF YOUR TRANSFORMA-TION!

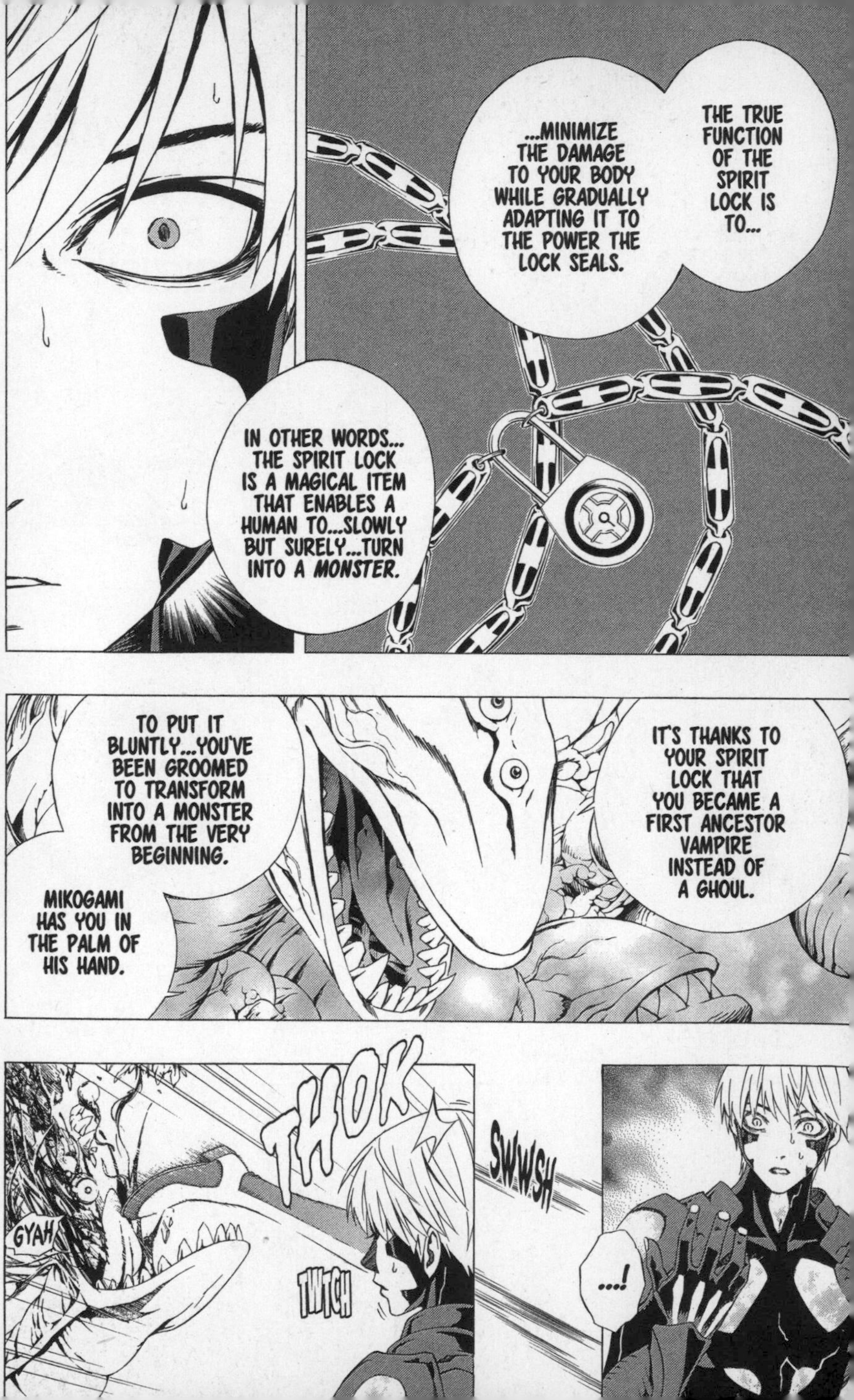

THE TRUE FUNCTION OF THE SPIRIT LOCK IS TO...
...MINIMIZE THE DAMAGE TO YOUR BODY WHILE GRADUALLY ADAPTING IT TO THE POWER THE LOCK SEALS.
IN OTHER WORDS... THE SPIRIT LOCK IS A MAGICAL ITEM THAT ENABLES A HUMAN TO...SLOWLY BUT SURELY...TURN INTO A *MONSTER.*
IT'S THANKS TO YOUR SPIRIT LOCK THAT YOU BECAME A FIRST ANCESTOR VAMPIRE INSTEAD OF A GHOUL.
TO PUT IT BLUNTLY...YOU'VE BEEN GROOMED TO TRANSFORM INTO A MONSTER FROM THE VERY BEGINNING.
MIKOGAMI HAS YOU IN THE PALM OF HIS HAND.
...!
SWWSH
THOK
GYAH
TWITCH

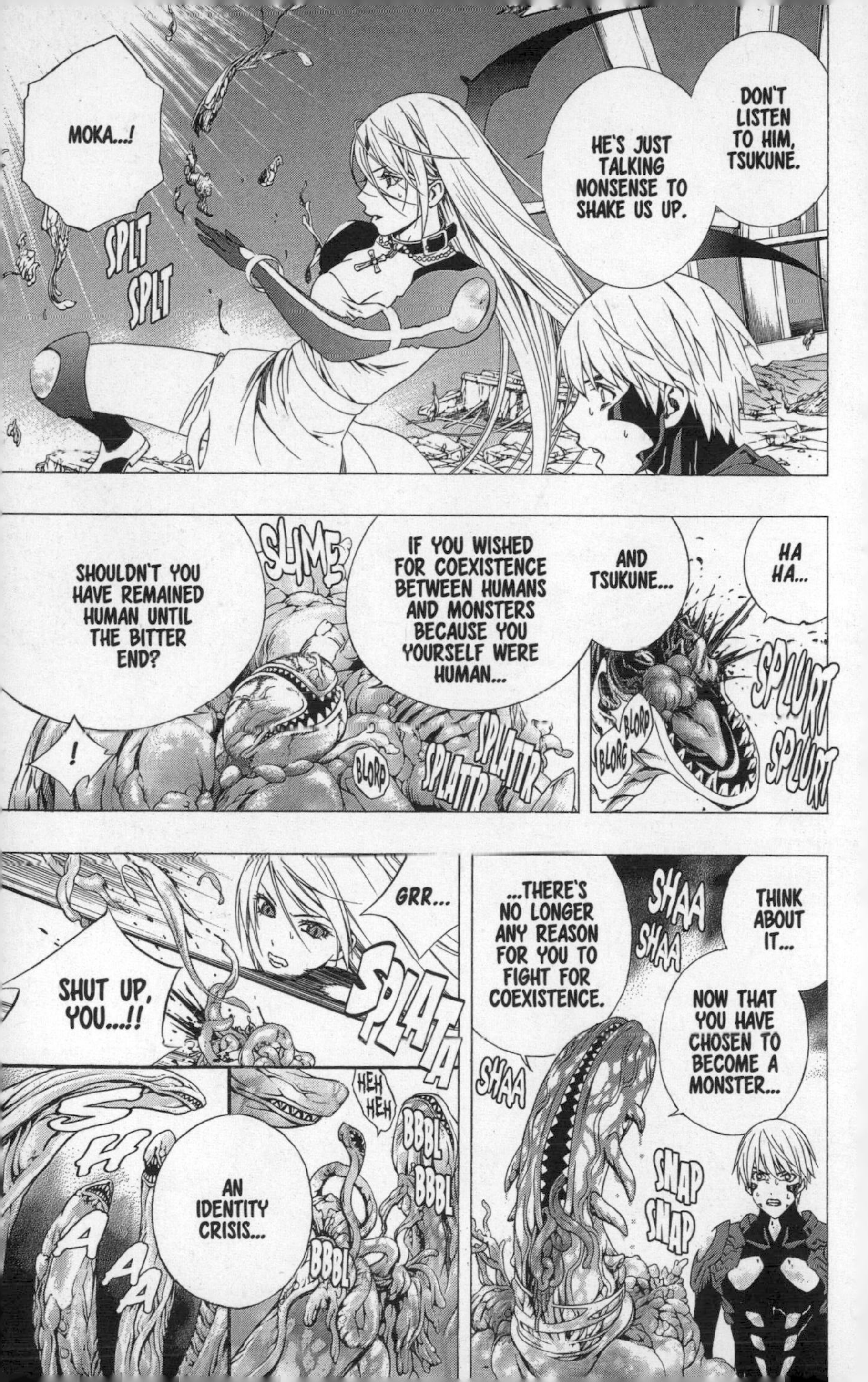
DON'T LISTEN TO HIM, TSUKUNE.
HE'S JUST TALKING NONSENSE TO SHAKE US UP.
MOKA...!
SPLT
SPLT
HA HA...
AND TSUKUNE...
SPLURT
SPLURT
BLORP
BLORG
IF YOU WISHED FOR COEXISTENCE BETWEEN HUMANS AND MONSTERS BECAUSE YOU YOURSELF WERE HUMAN...
SLIME
SHOULDN'T YOU HAVE REMAINED HUMAN UNTIL THE BITTER END?
!
SPLATTR
SPLATTR
BLORP
THINK ABOUT IT...
NOW THAT YOU HAVE CHOSEN TO BECOME A MONSTER...
SHAA
SHAA
...THERE'S NO LONGER ANY REASON FOR YOU TO FIGHT FOR COEXISTENCE.
SHAA
SNAP
SNAP
GRR...
SPLATA
SHUT UP, YOU...!!
HEH HEH
BBBL
BBBL
AN IDENTITY CRISIS...
BBBL
SHAAA

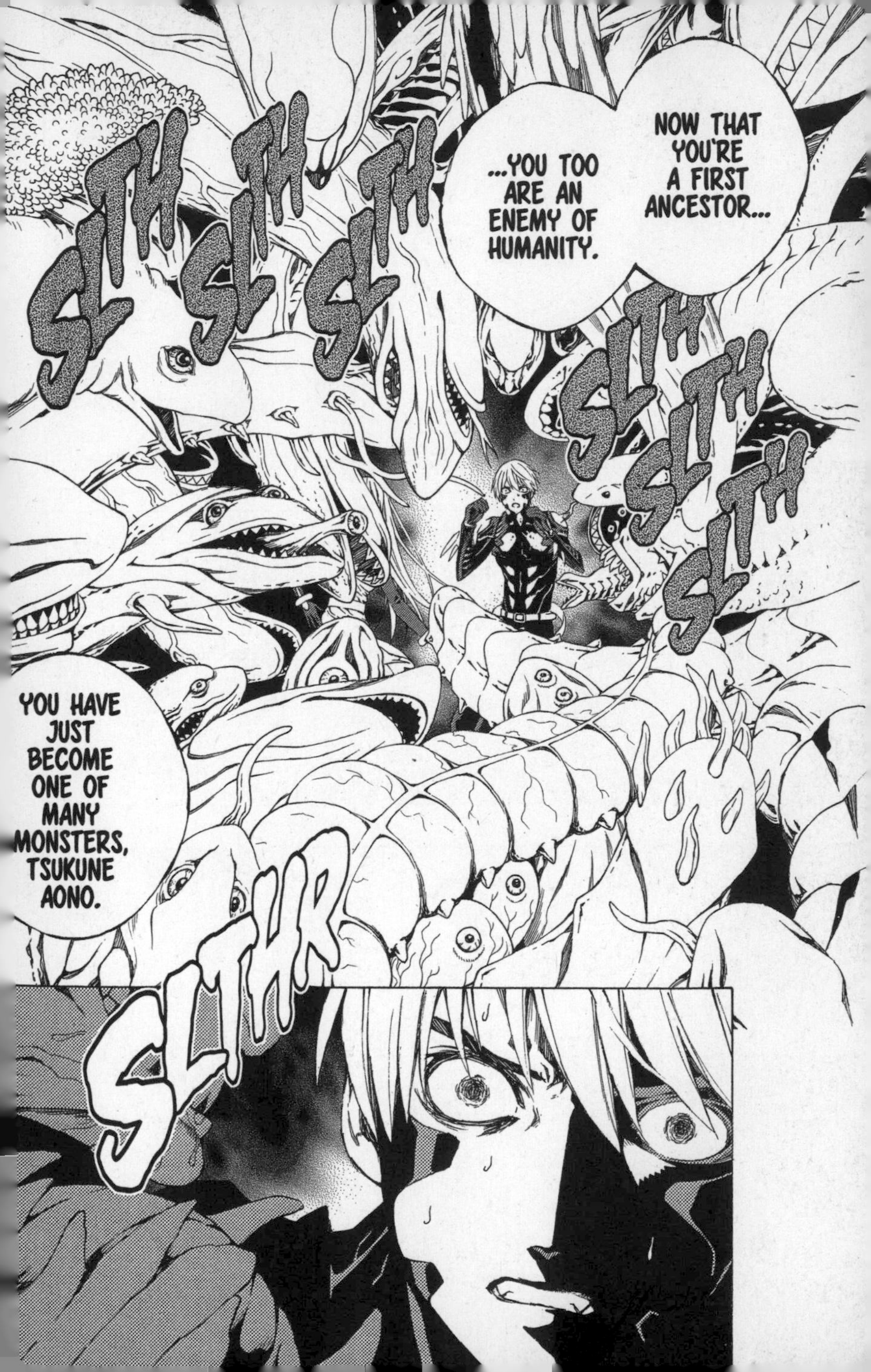
NOW THAT YOU'RE A FIRST ANCESTOR...
...YOU TOO ARE AN ENEMY OF HUMANITY.
SLITH SLITH SLITH
SLITH SLITH SLITH
YOU HAVE JUST BECOME ONE OF MANY MONSTERS, TSUKUNE AONO.
SLITHR
SLITH

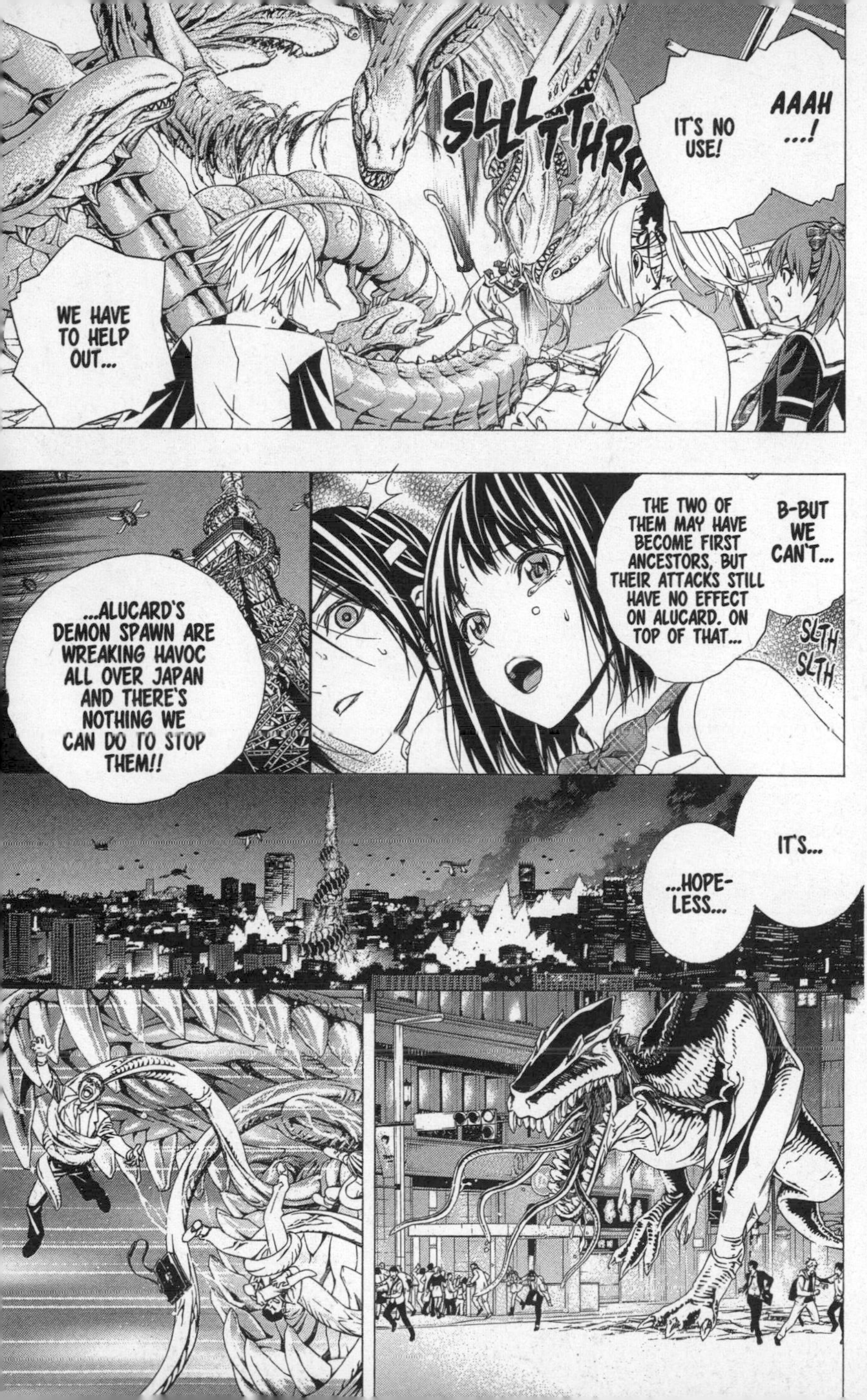
AAAH ...!
IT'S NO USE!
SLLLTTHRR
WE HAVE TO HELP OUT...
B-BUT WE CAN'T...
THE TWO OF THEM MAY HAVE BECOME FIRST ANCESTORS, BUT THEIR ATTACKS STILL HAVE NO EFFECT ON ALUCARD. ON TOP OF THAT...
SLTH SLTH
...ALUCARD'S DEMON SPAWN ARE WREAKING HAVOC ALL OVER JAPAN AND THERE'S NOTHING WE CAN DO TO STOP THEM!!
IT'S...
...HOPE-LESS...

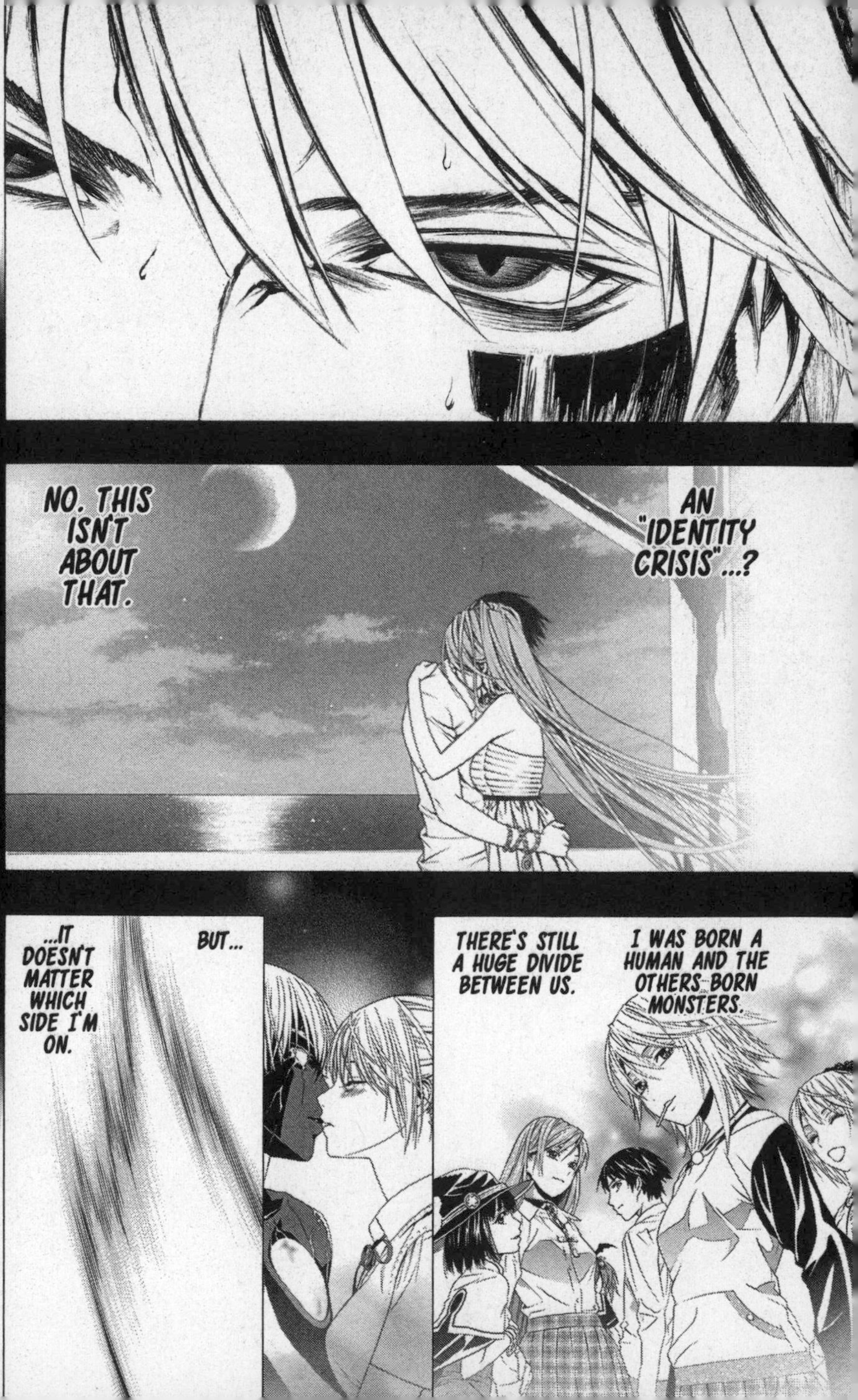
AN "IDENTITY CRISIS"...?
NO. THIS ISN'T ABOUT THAT.
I WAS BORN A HUMAN AND THE OTHERS BORN MONSTERS.
THERE'S STILL A HUGE DIVIDE BETWEEN US.
BUT...
...IT DOESN'T MATTER WHICH SIDE I'M ON.

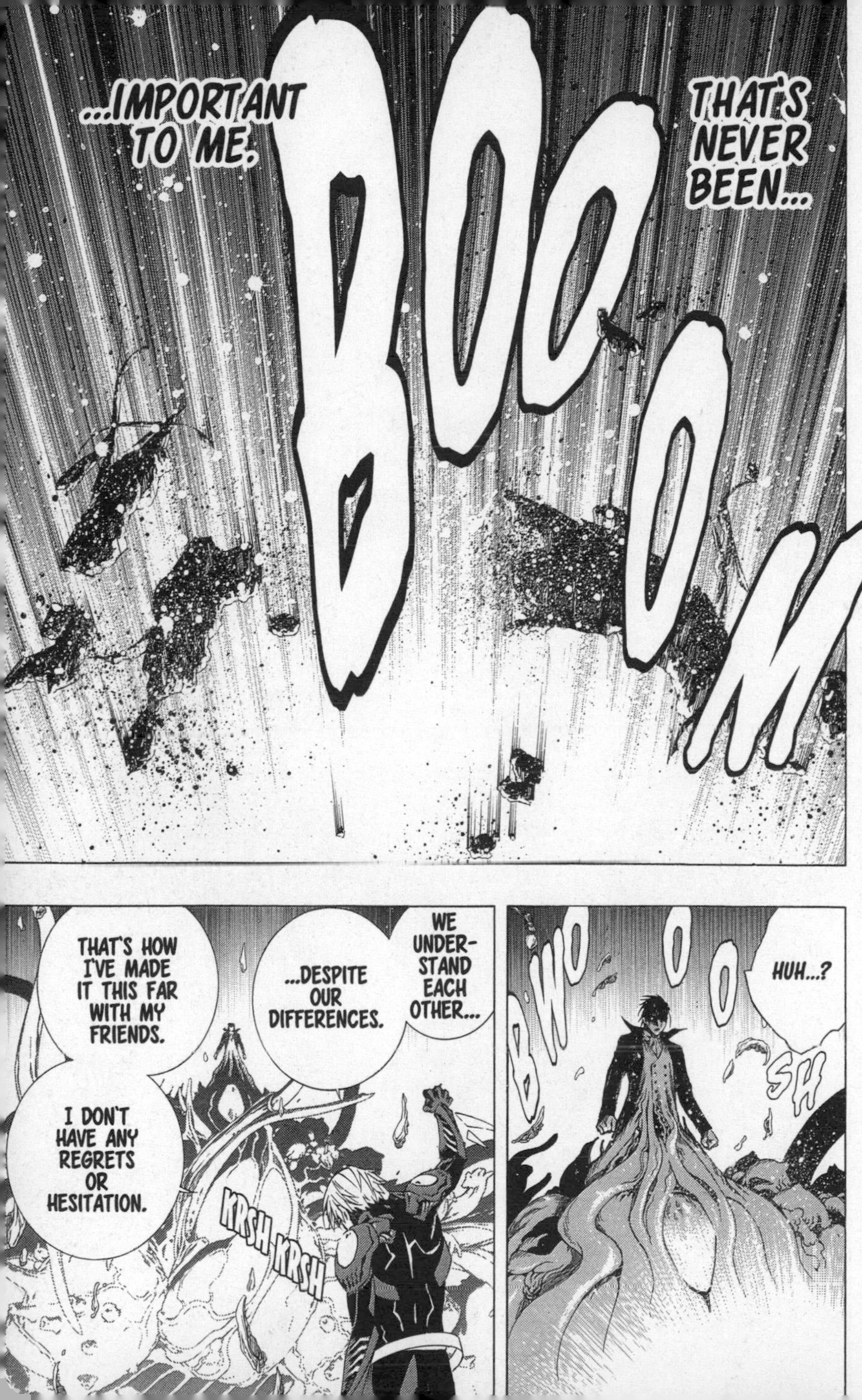
THAT'S NEVER BEEN...
BOOOOM
...IMPORTANT TO ME.
HUH...?
BWOOOSH
WE UNDERSTAND EACH OTHER...
...DESPITE OUR DIFFERENCES.
THAT'S HOW I'VE MADE IT THIS FAR WITH MY FRIENDS.
I DON'T HAVE ANY REGRETS OR HESITATION.
KRSH KRSH

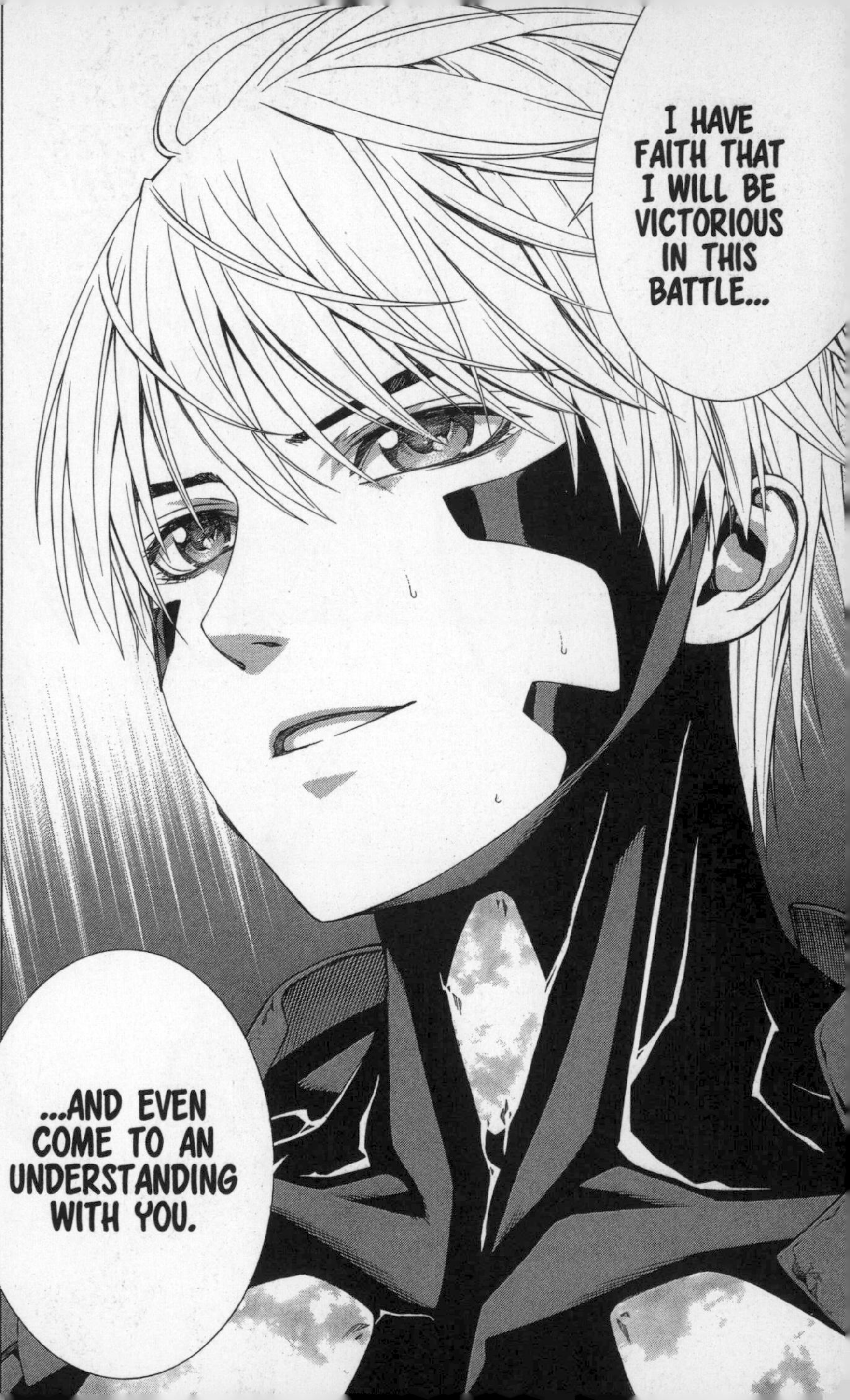
I HAVE FAITH THAT I WILL BE VICTORIOUS IN THIS BATTLE...
...AND EVEN COME TO AN UNDERSTANDING WITH YOU.

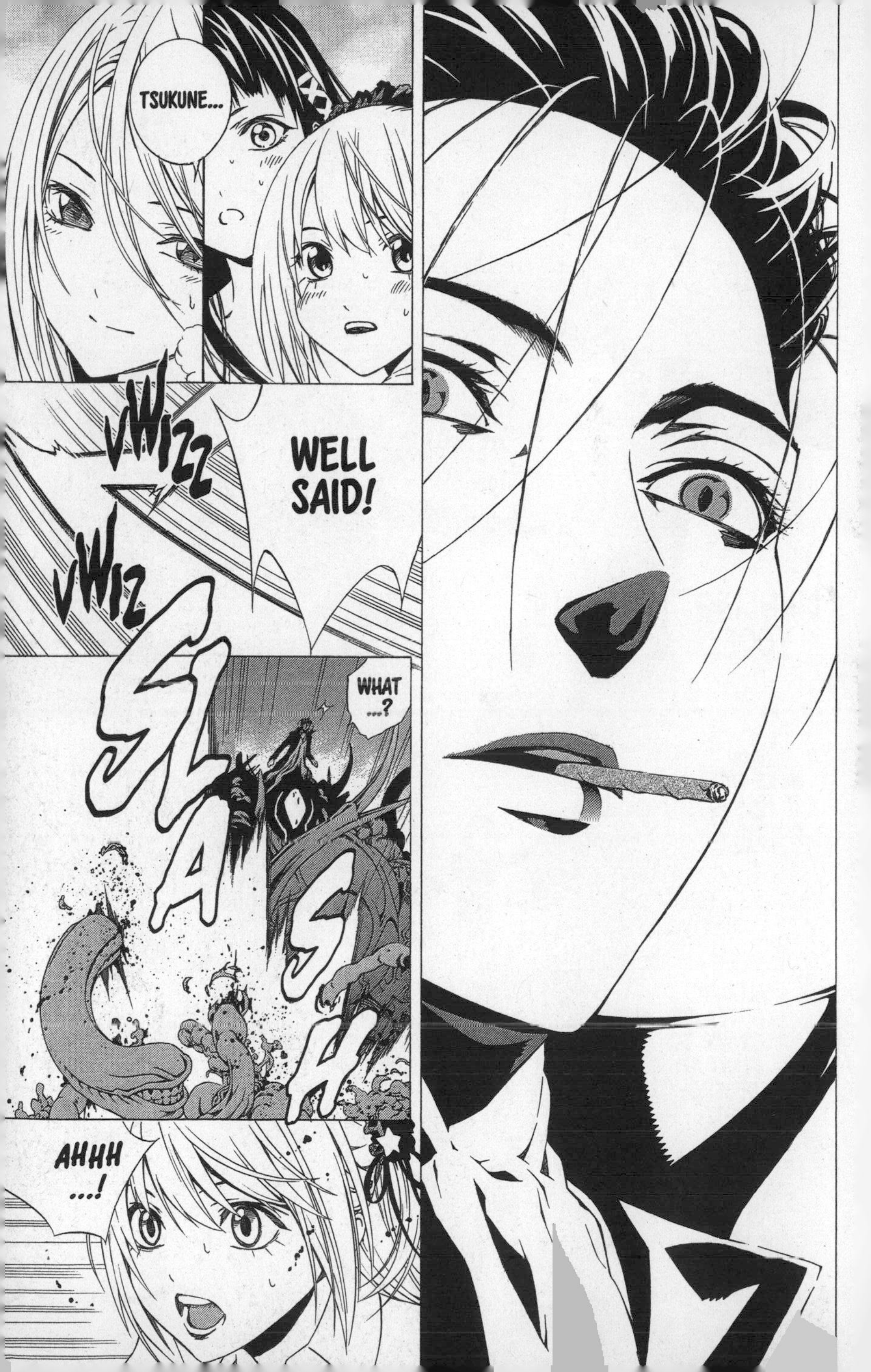
TSUKUNE...
WELL SAID!
VWIZZ
VWIZ
WHAT ...?
SLASH
AHHH ...!

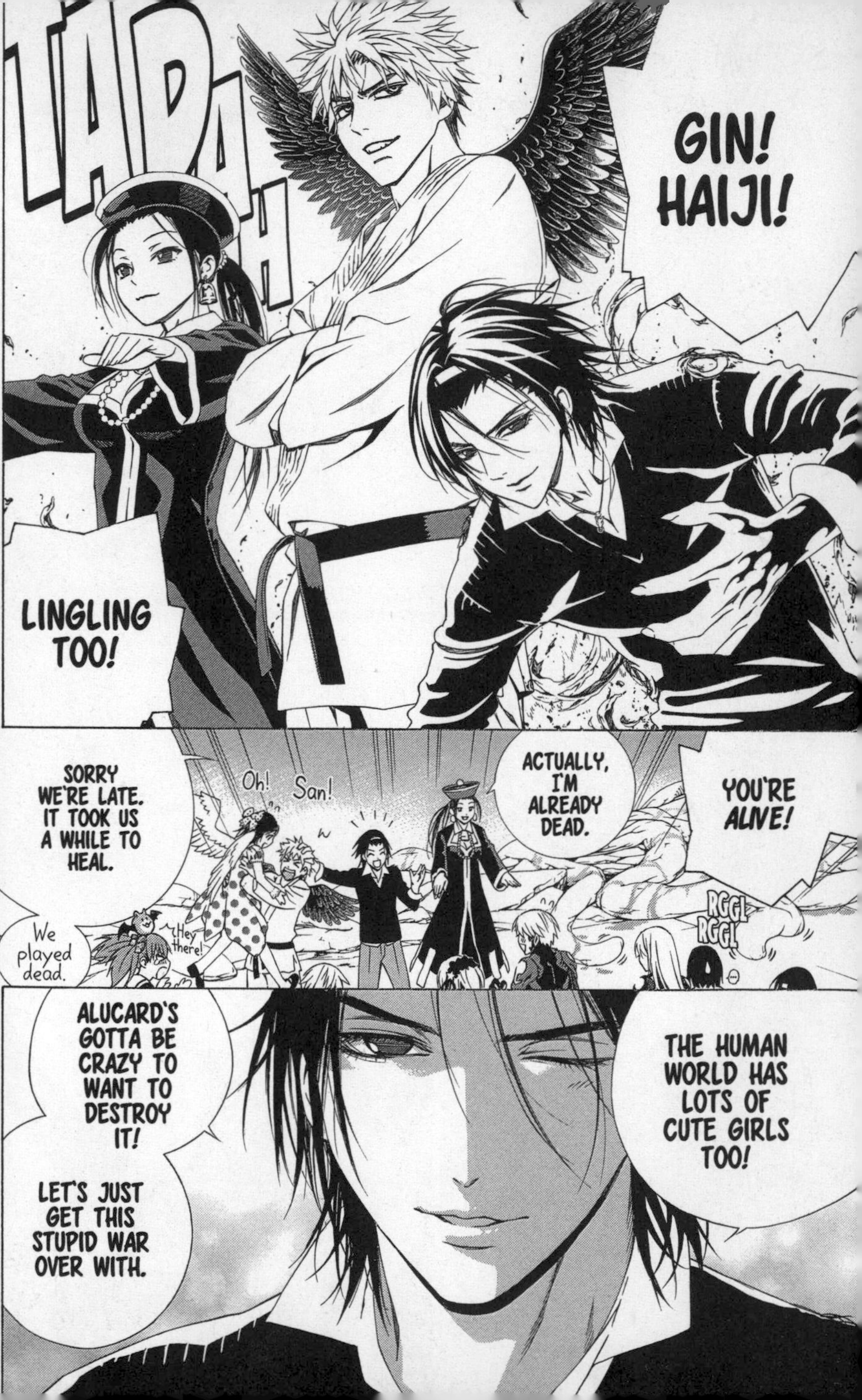
GIN! HAIJI!
TADAH
LINGLING TOO!
YOU'RE ALIVE!
ACTUALLY, I'M ALREADY DEAD.
San!
Oh!
SORRY WE'RE LATE. IT TOOK US A WHILE TO HEAL.
RGGL RGGL
...
Hey there!
We played dead.
THE HUMAN WORLD HAS LOTS OF CUTE GIRLS TOO!
ALUCARD'S GOTTA BE CRAZY TO WANT TO DESTROY IT!
LET'S JUST GET THIS STUPID WAR OVER WITH.

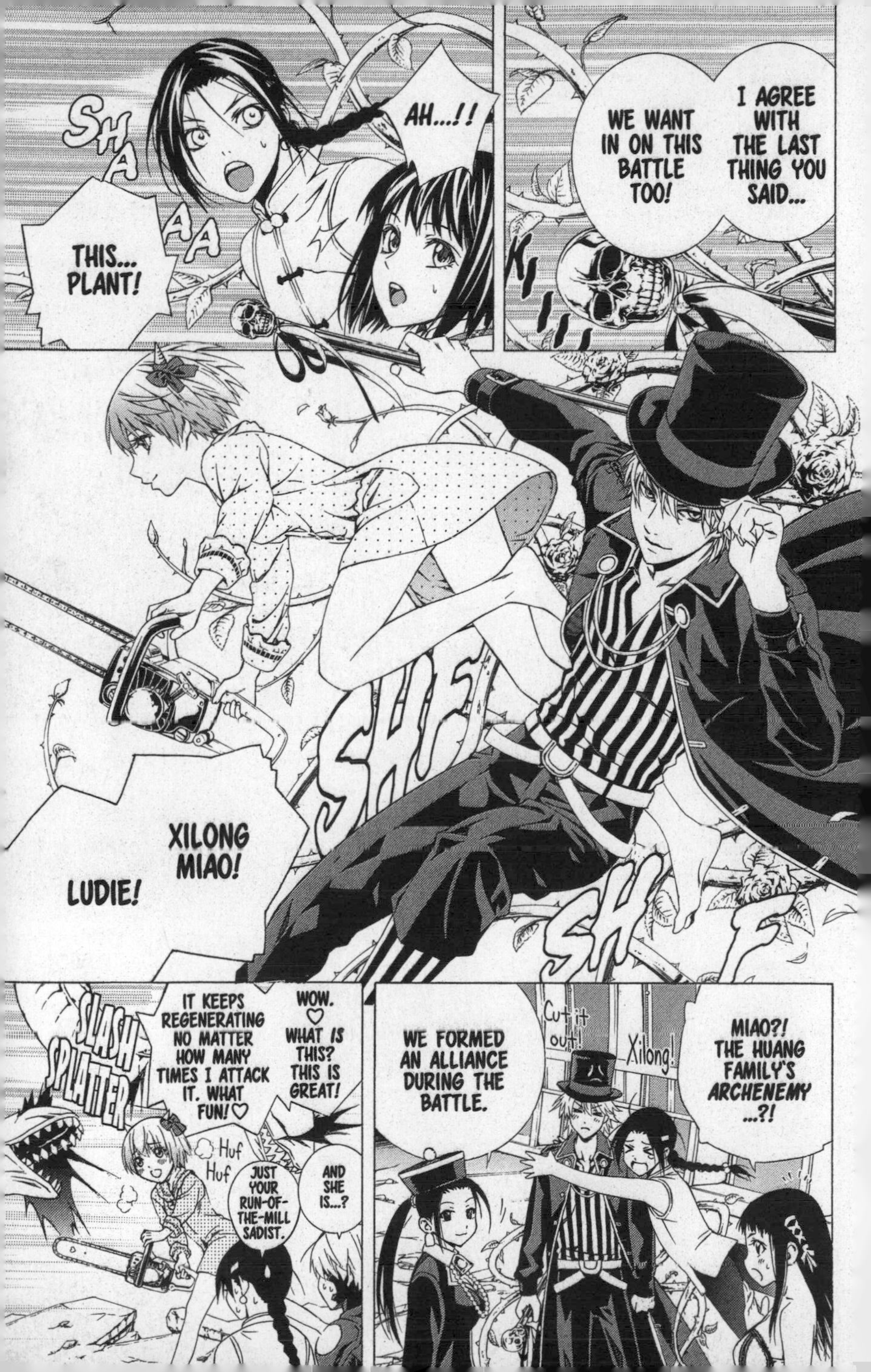
I AGREE WITH THE LAST THING YOU SAID...
WE WANT IN ON THIS BATTLE TOO!
AH...!!
SHAAAA
THIS... PLANT!
SHF
SHF
XILONG MIAO!
LUDIE!
MIAO?! THE HUANG FAMILY'S ARCHENEMY ...?!
Xilong!
Cut it out!
WE FORMED AN ALLIANCE DURING THE BATTLE.
WOW. ♡ WHAT IS THIS? THIS IS GREAT!
IT KEEPS REGENERATING NO MATTER HOW MANY TIMES I ATTACK IT. WHAT FUN!♡
SLASH
SPLATTER
Huf
Huf
AND SHE IS...?
JUST YOUR RUN-OF-THE-MILL SADIST.

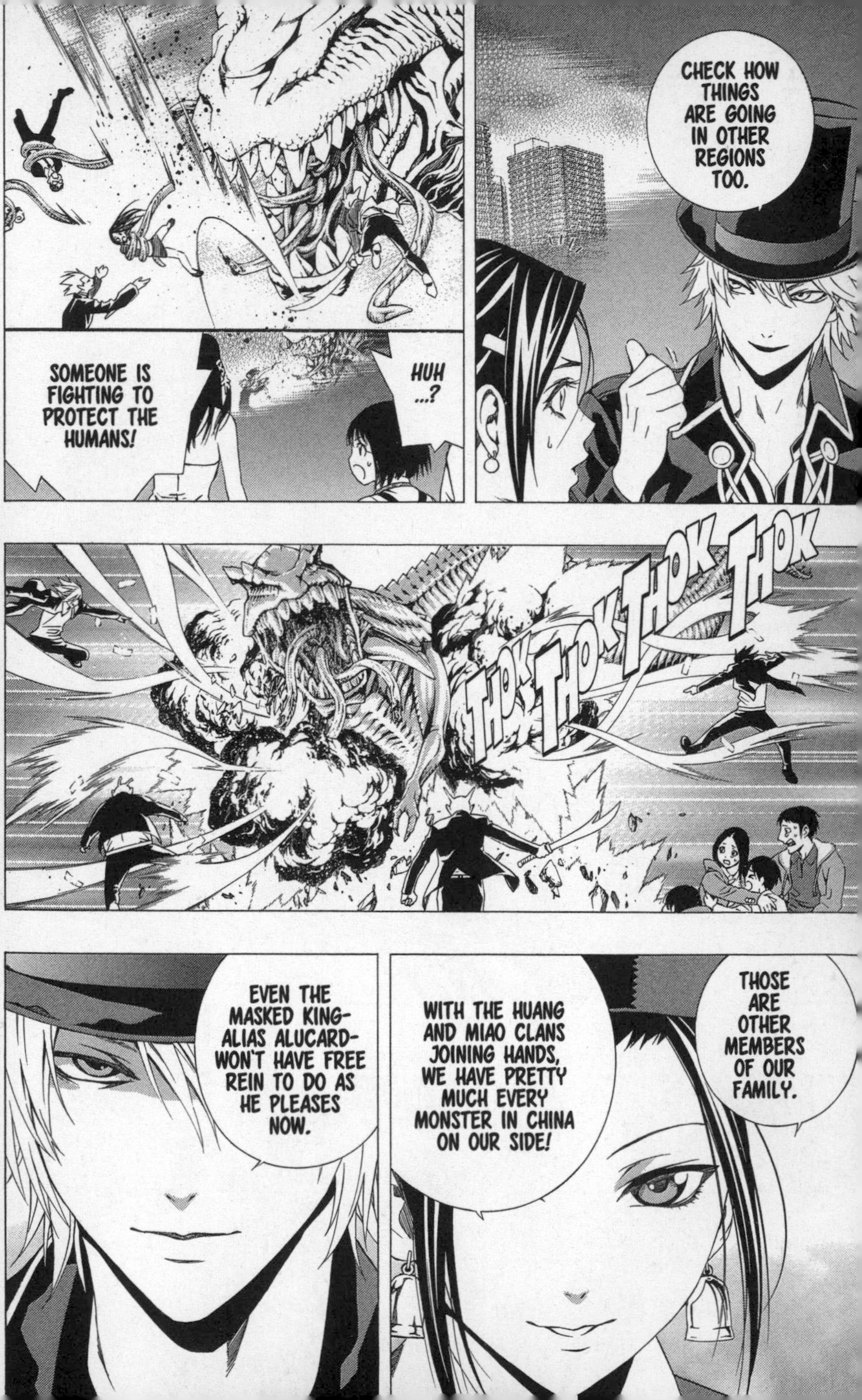
CHECK HOW THINGS ARE GOING IN OTHER REGIONS TOO.
HUH ...?
SOMEONE IS FIGHTING TO PROTECT THE HUMANS!
THOK THOK THOK THOK
THOSE ARE OTHER MEMBERS OF OUR FAMILY.
WITH THE HUANG AND MIAO CLANS JOINING HANDS, WE HAVE PRETTY MUCH EVERY MONSTER IN CHINA ON OUR SIDE!
EVEN THE MASKED KING-ALIAS ALUCARD-WON'T HAVE FREE REIN TO DO AS HE PLEASES NOW.

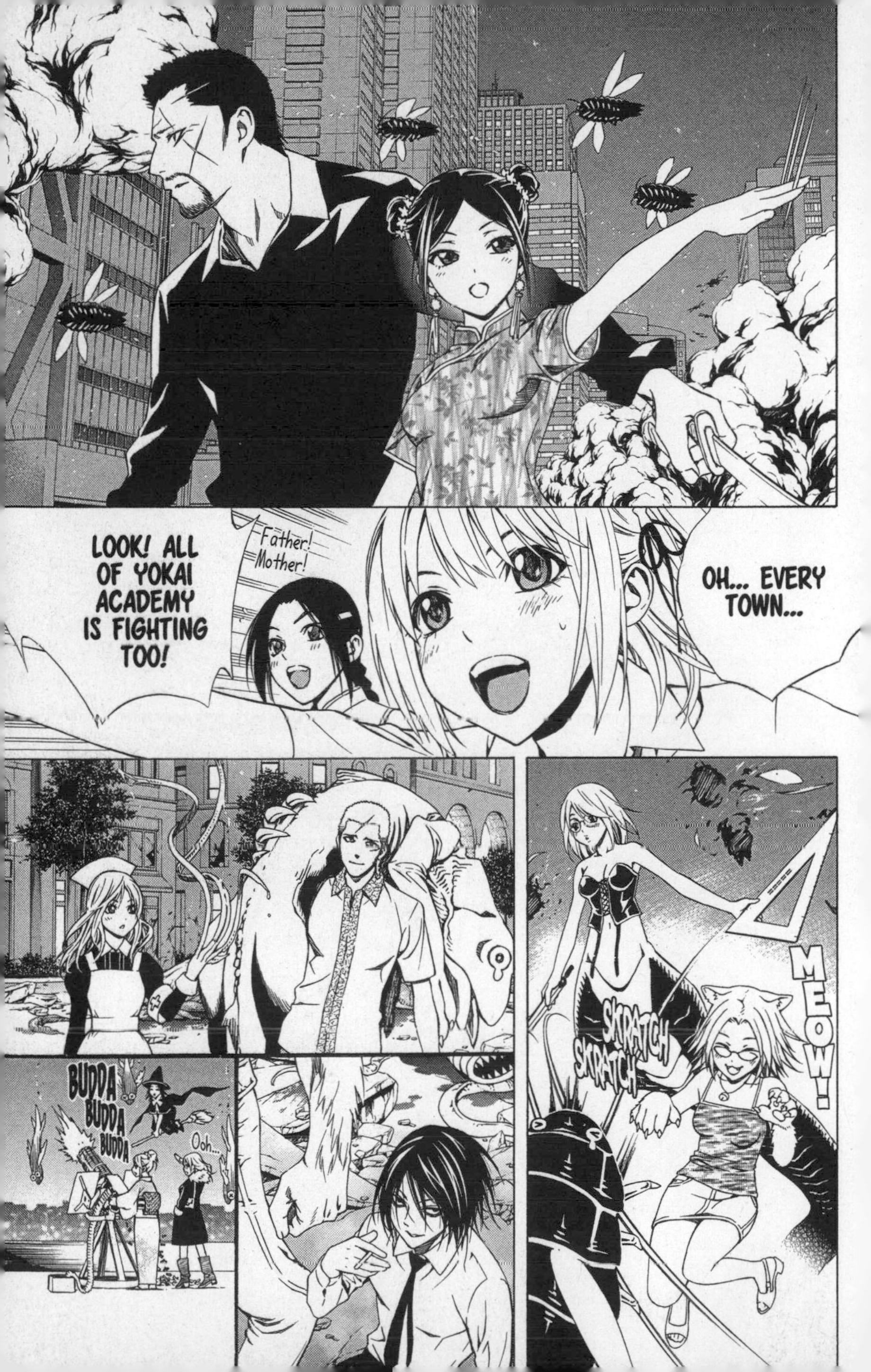
OH... EVERY TOWN...
Father! Mother!
LOOK! ALL OF YOKAI ACADEMY IS FIGHTING TOO!
MEOW!
SKRATCH SKRATCH
Ooh...
BUDDA BUDDA BUDDA

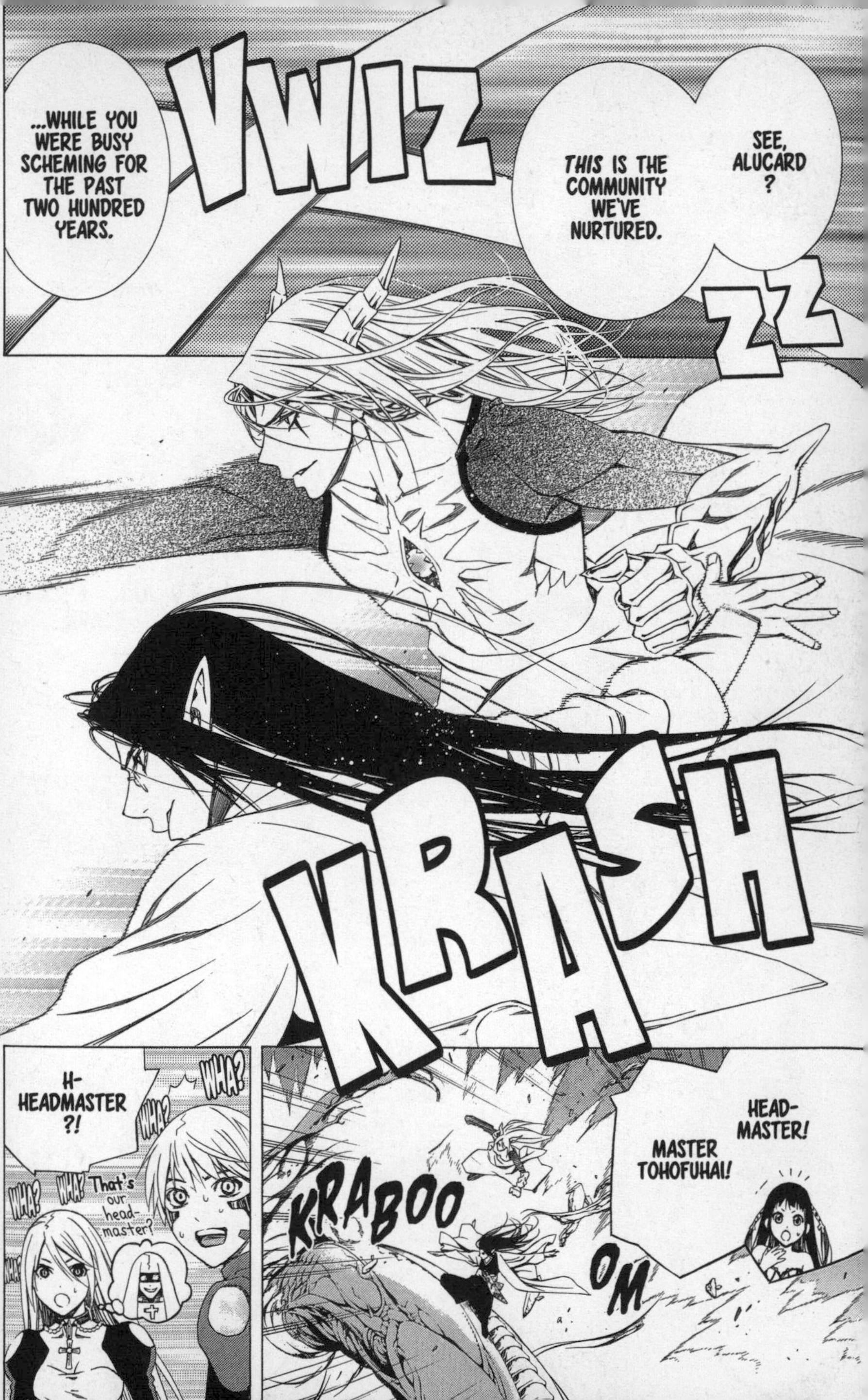
SEE, ALUCARD?
THIS IS THE COMMUNITY WE'VE NURTURED.
...WHILE YOU WERE BUSY SCHEMING FOR THE PAST TWO HUNDRED YEARS.
VWIZ
ZZ
KRASH
HEAD-MASTER!
MASTER TOHOFUHAI!
KRABOO
OM
WHA?
WHA?
H-HEADMASTER?!
WHA!
That's our head-master?
WHA?
WHA

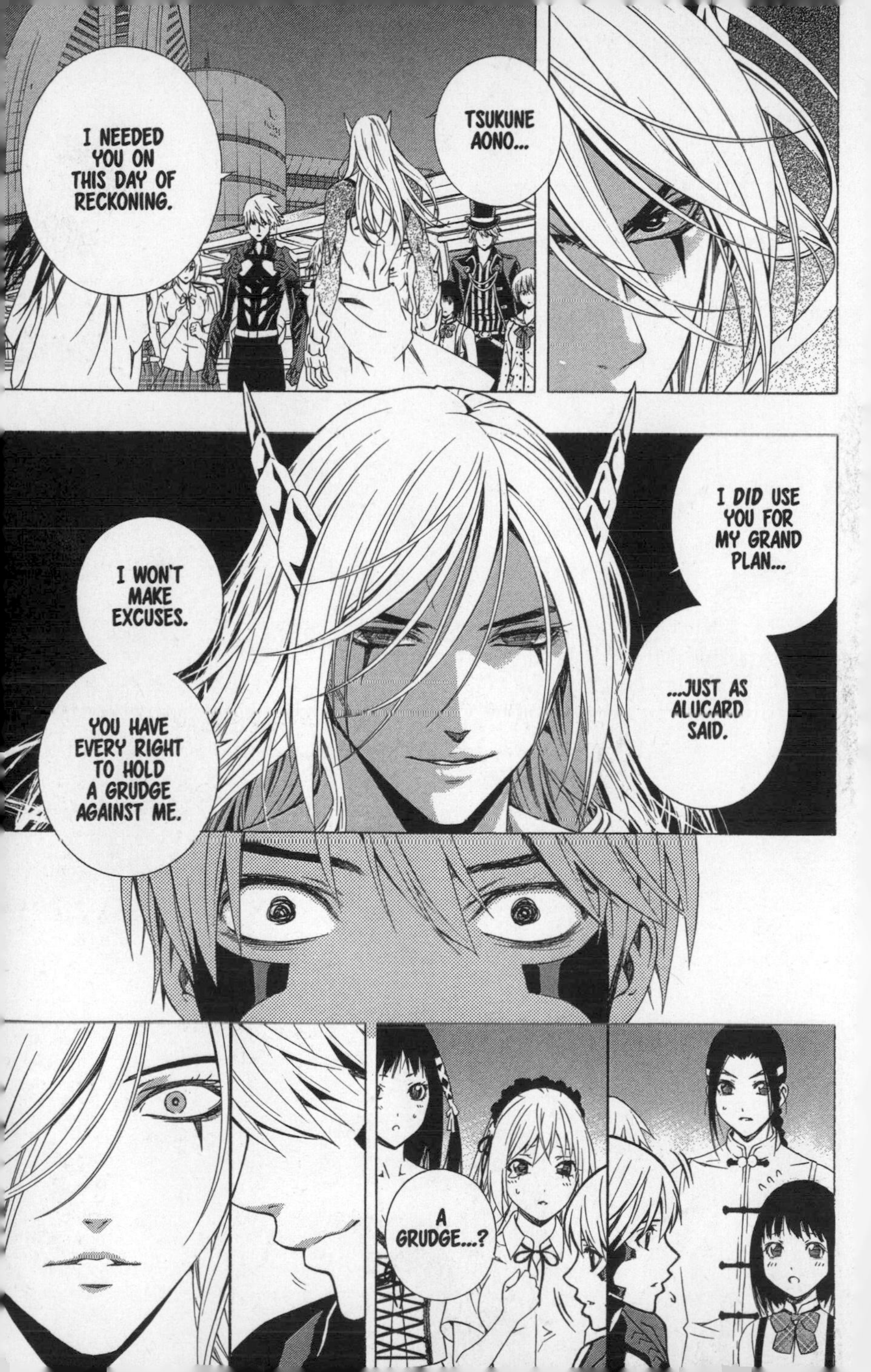
TSUKUNE AONO...
I NEEDED YOU ON THIS DAY OF RECKONING.
I *DID* USE YOU FOR MY GRAND PLAN...
...JUST AS ALUCARD SAID.
I WON'T MAKE EXCUSES.
YOU HAVE EVERY RIGHT TO HOLD A GRUDGE AGAINST ME.
A GRUDGE...?

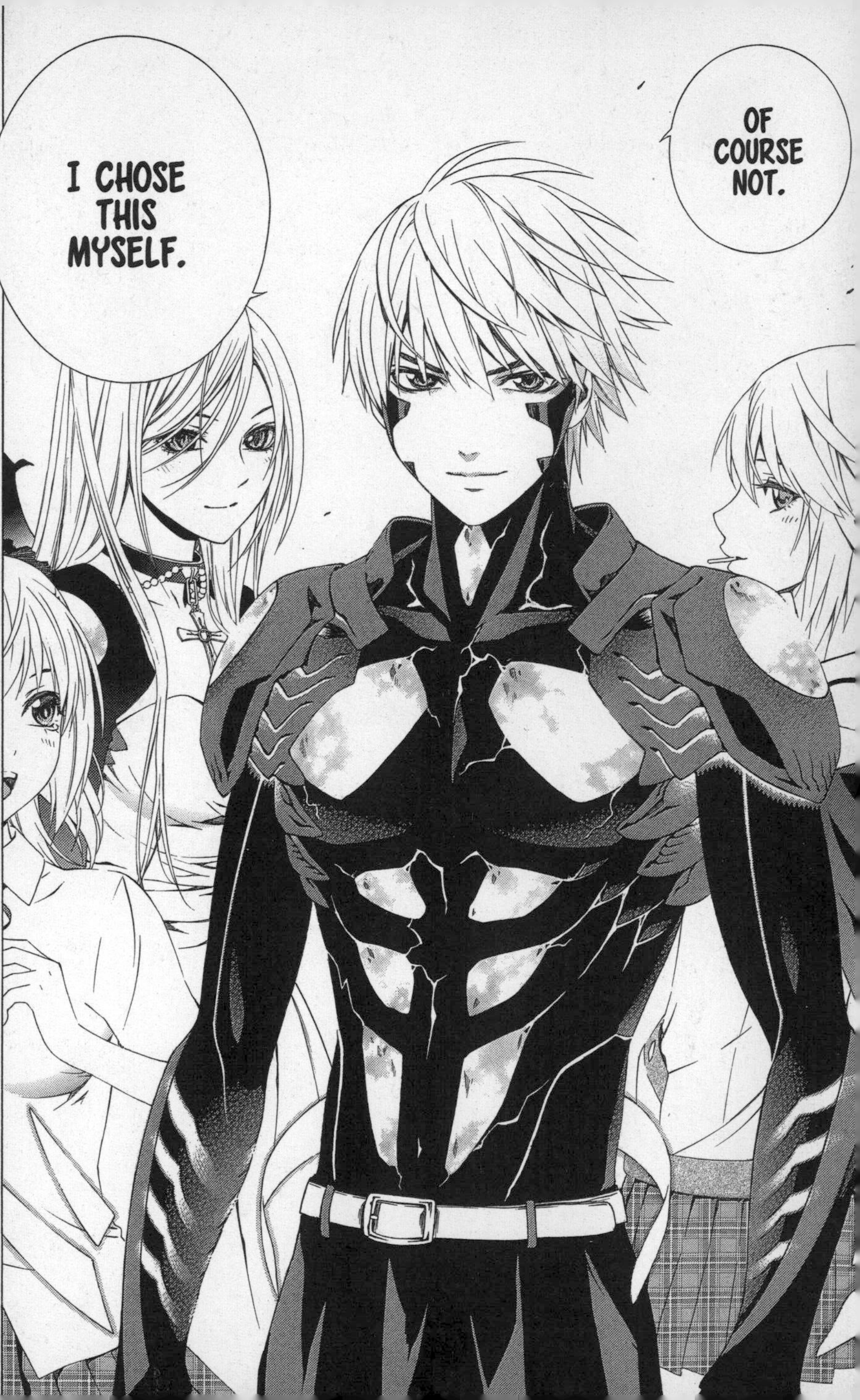
OF COURSE NOT.
I CHOSE THIS MYSELF.

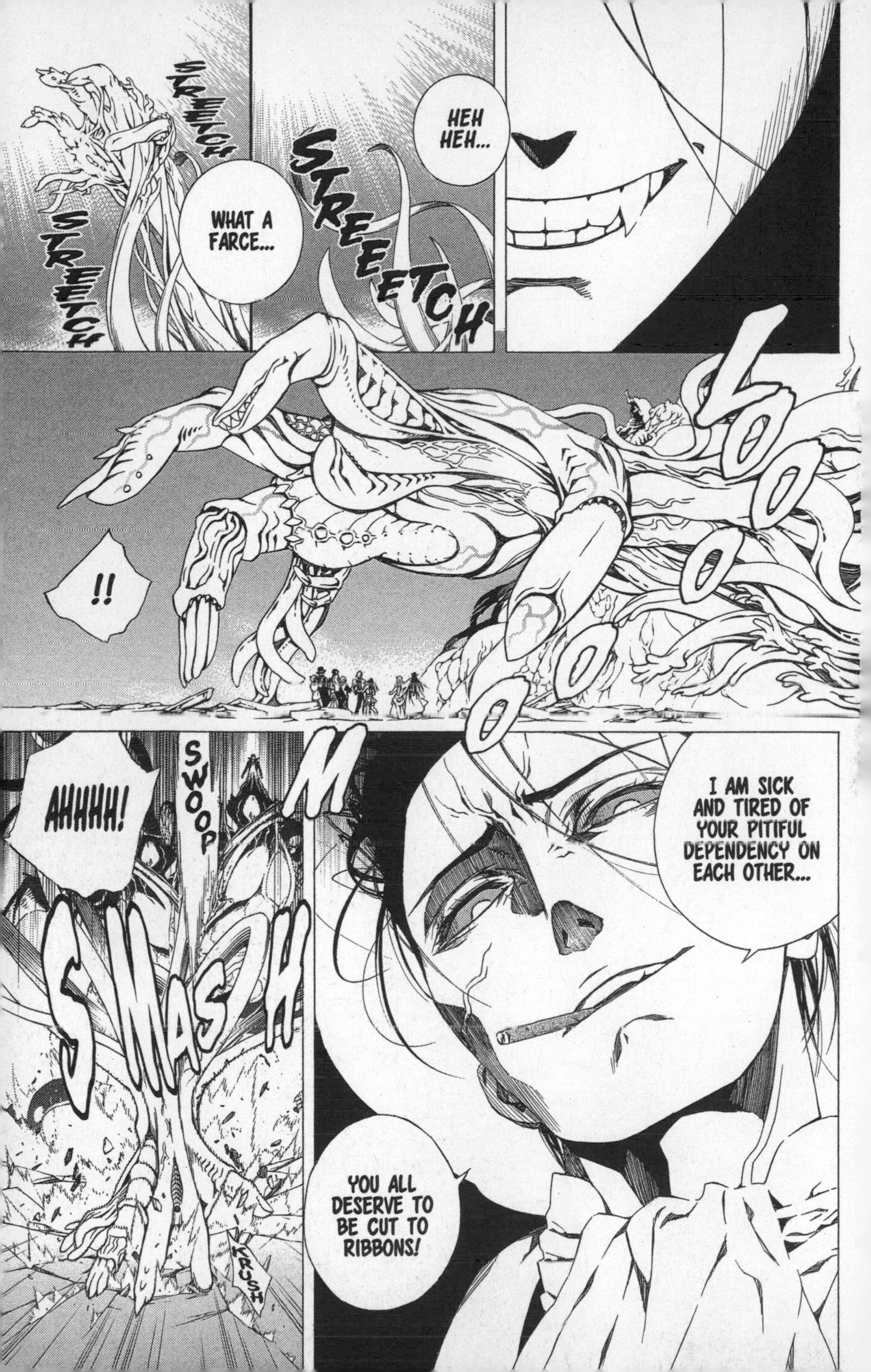

HEH HEH...
STREEETCH
WHAT A FARCE...
STREETCH
STREETCH
VOOOOOOM
!!
I AM SICK AND TIRED OF YOUR PITIFUL DEPENDENCY ON EACH OTHER...
YOU ALL DESERVE TO BE CUT TO RIBBONS!
AHHHH!
SWOOP
SMASH
KRUSH

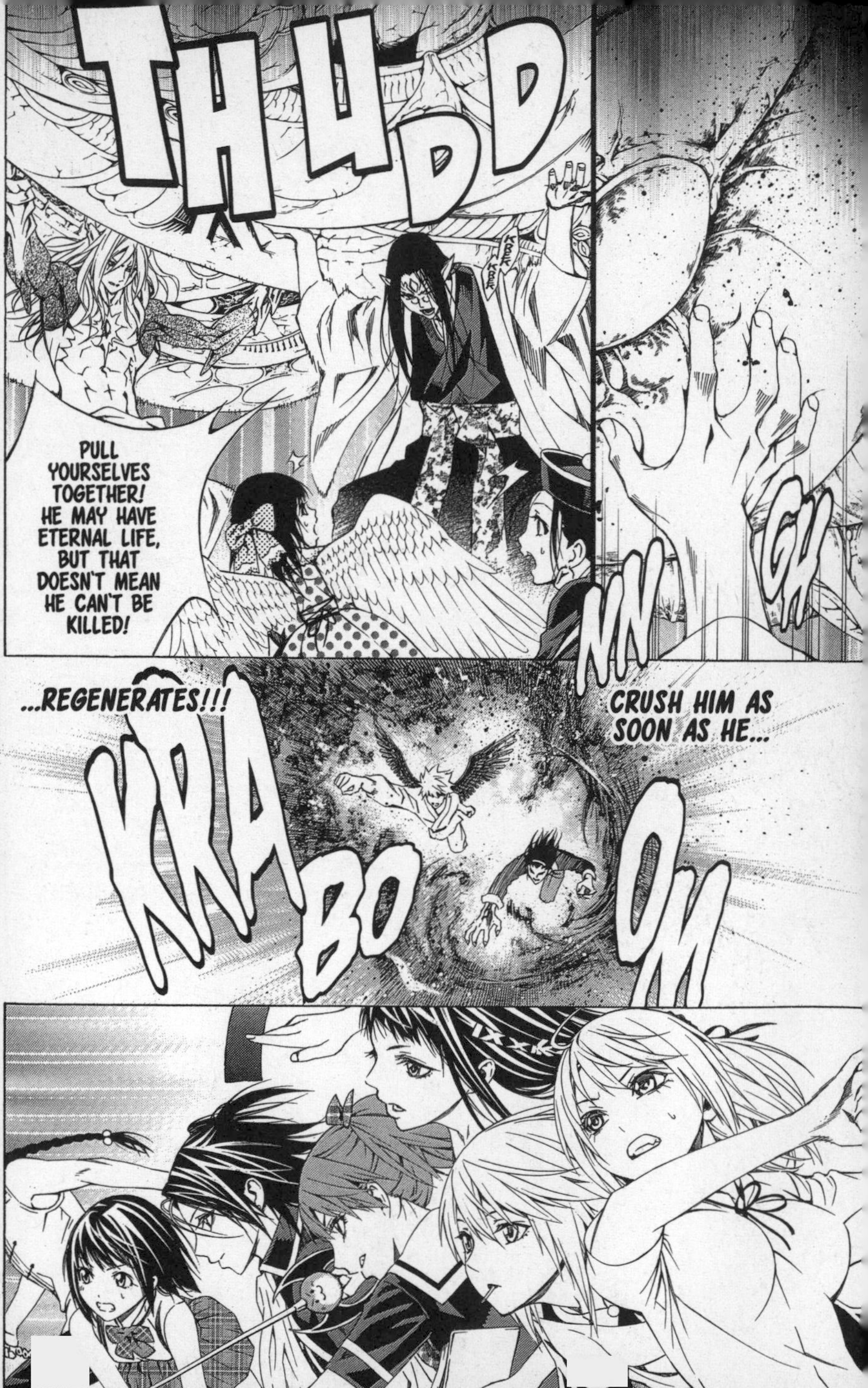
NNGH
THUDD
KREK KREK
PULL YOURSELVES TOGETHER! HE MAY HAVE ETERNAL LIFE, BUT THAT DOESN'T MEAN HE CAN'T BE KILLED!
CRUSH HIM AS SOON AS HE...
...REGENERATES!!!
KRABOOM

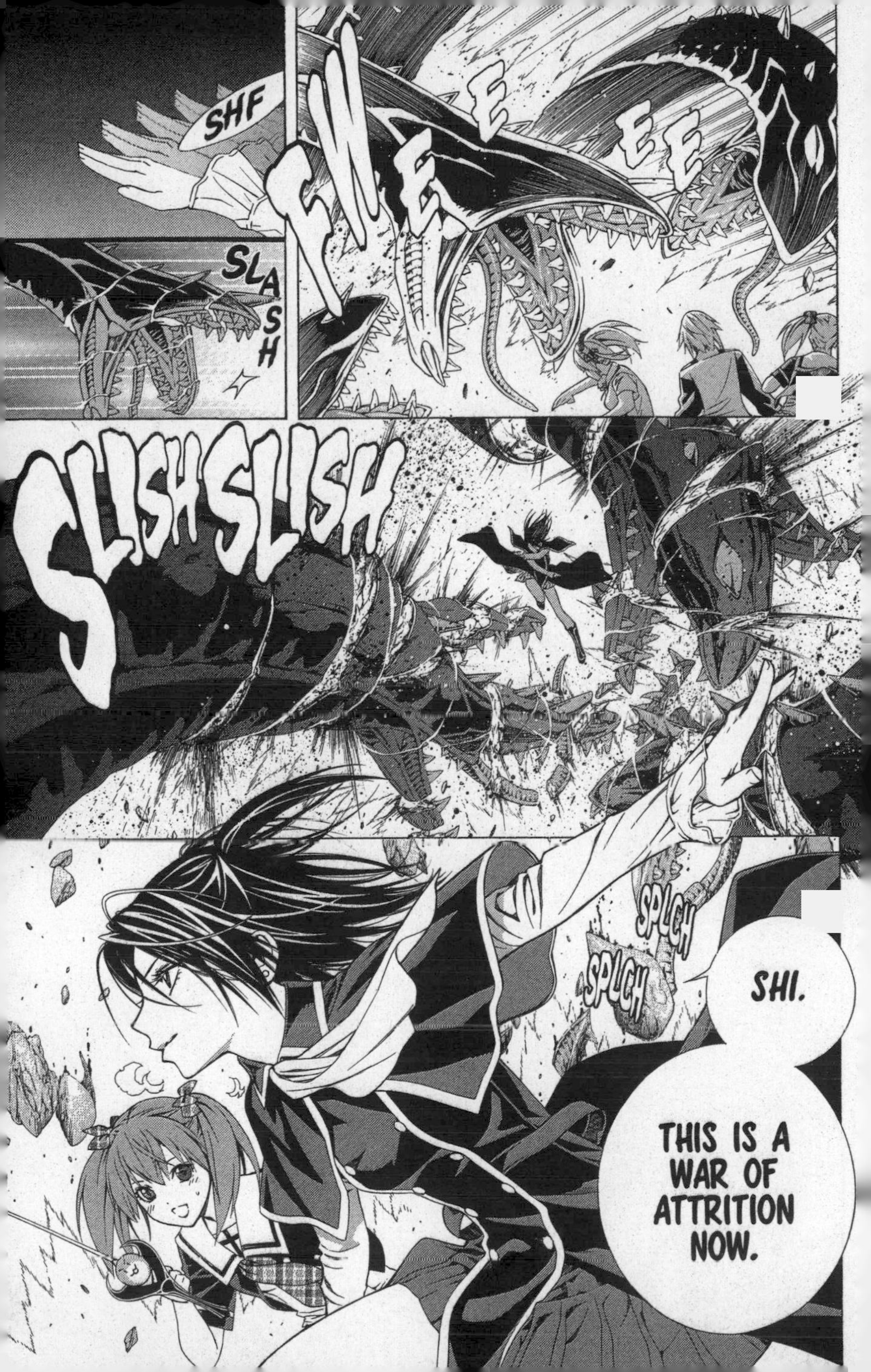
KWEEEE
SHF
SLASH
SLISH SLISH
SHI.
THIS IS A WAR OF ATTRITION NOW.
SPLCH
SPLCH

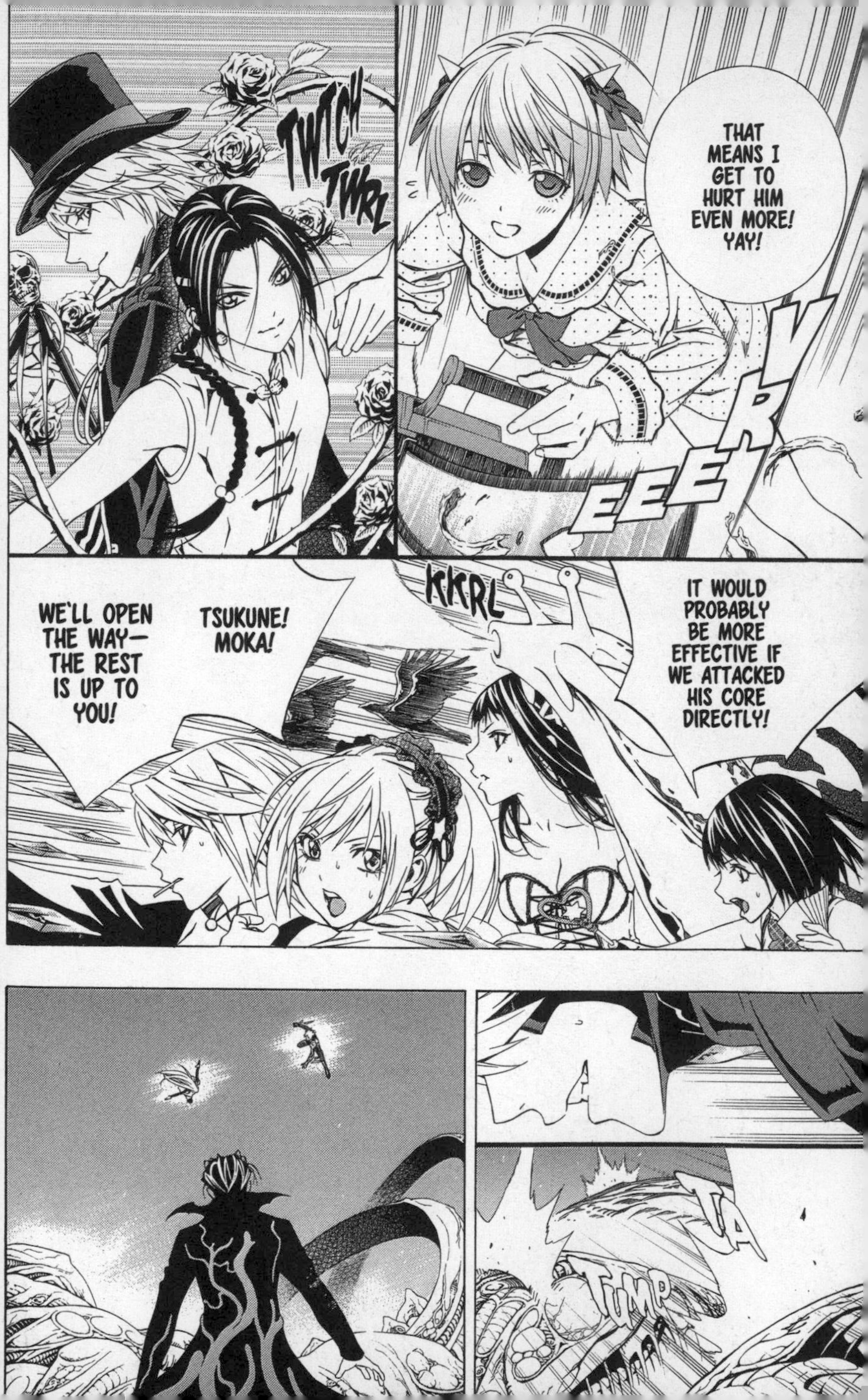
THAT MEANS I GET TO HURT HIM EVEN MORE! YAY!
TWITCH
TWRL
IT WOULD PROBABLY BE MORE EFFECTIVE IF WE ATTACKED HIS CORE DIRECTLY!
KKRL
TSUKUNE! MOKA!
WE'LL OPEN THE WAY— THE REST IS UP TO YOU!
TUMP

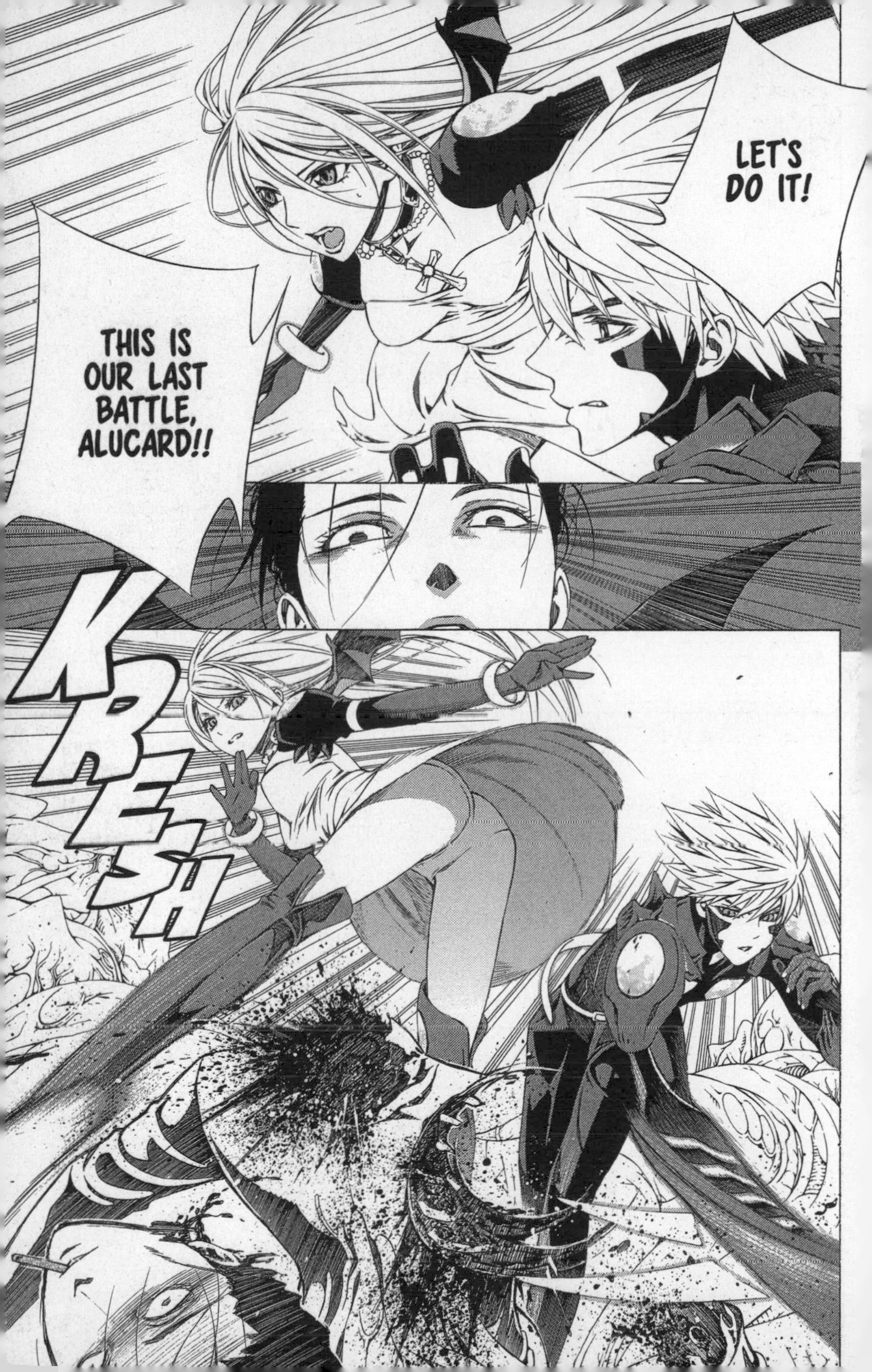
LET'S DO IT!
THIS IS OUR LAST BATTLE, ALUCARD!!
KRESH

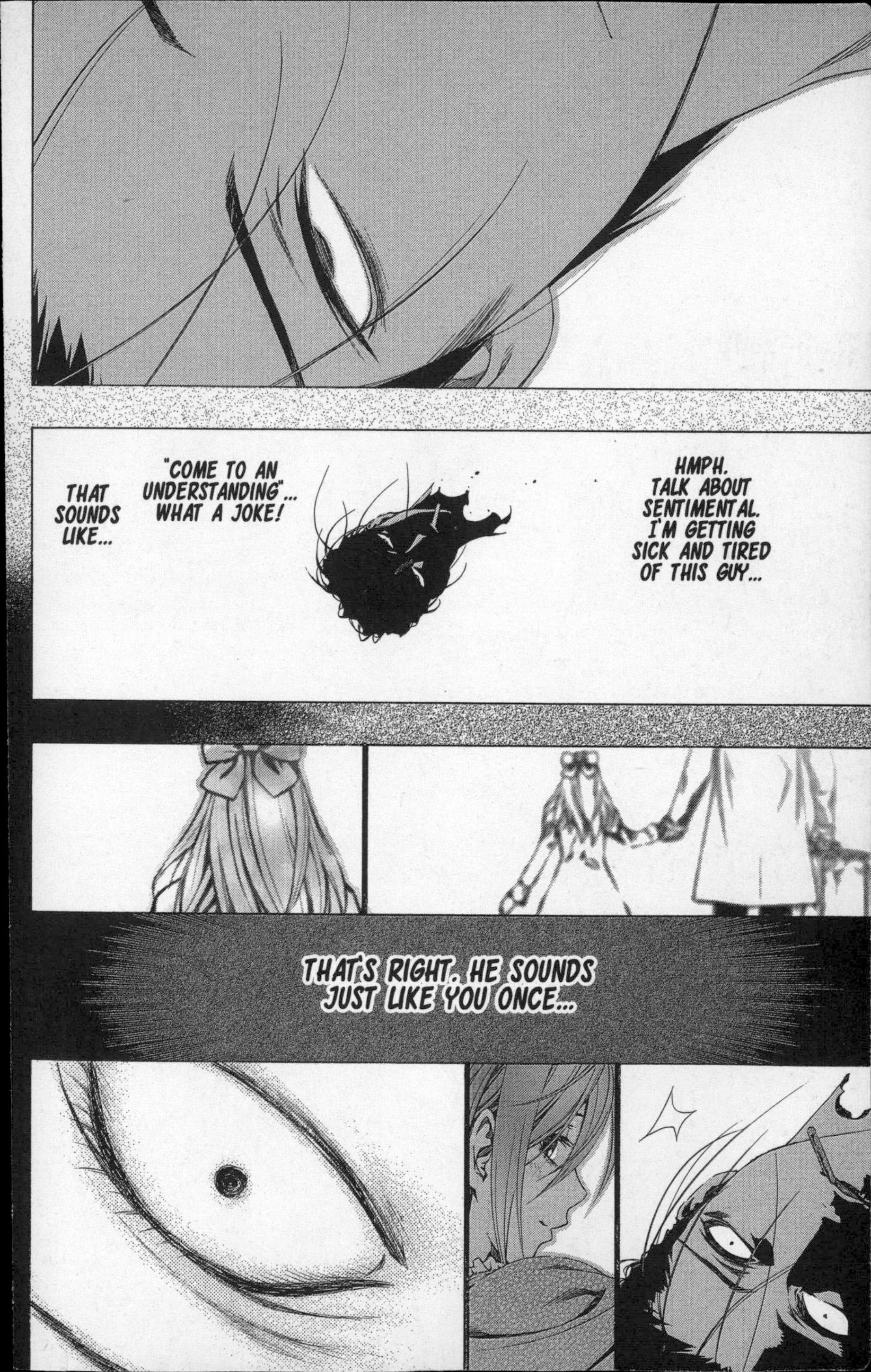
HMPH. TALK ABOUT SENTIMENTAL. I'M GETTING SICK AND TIRED OF THIS GUY...
"COME TO AN UNDERSTANDING"... WHAT A JOKE!
THAT SOUNDS LIKE...
THAT'S RIGHT. HE SOUNDS JUST LIKE YOU ONCE...

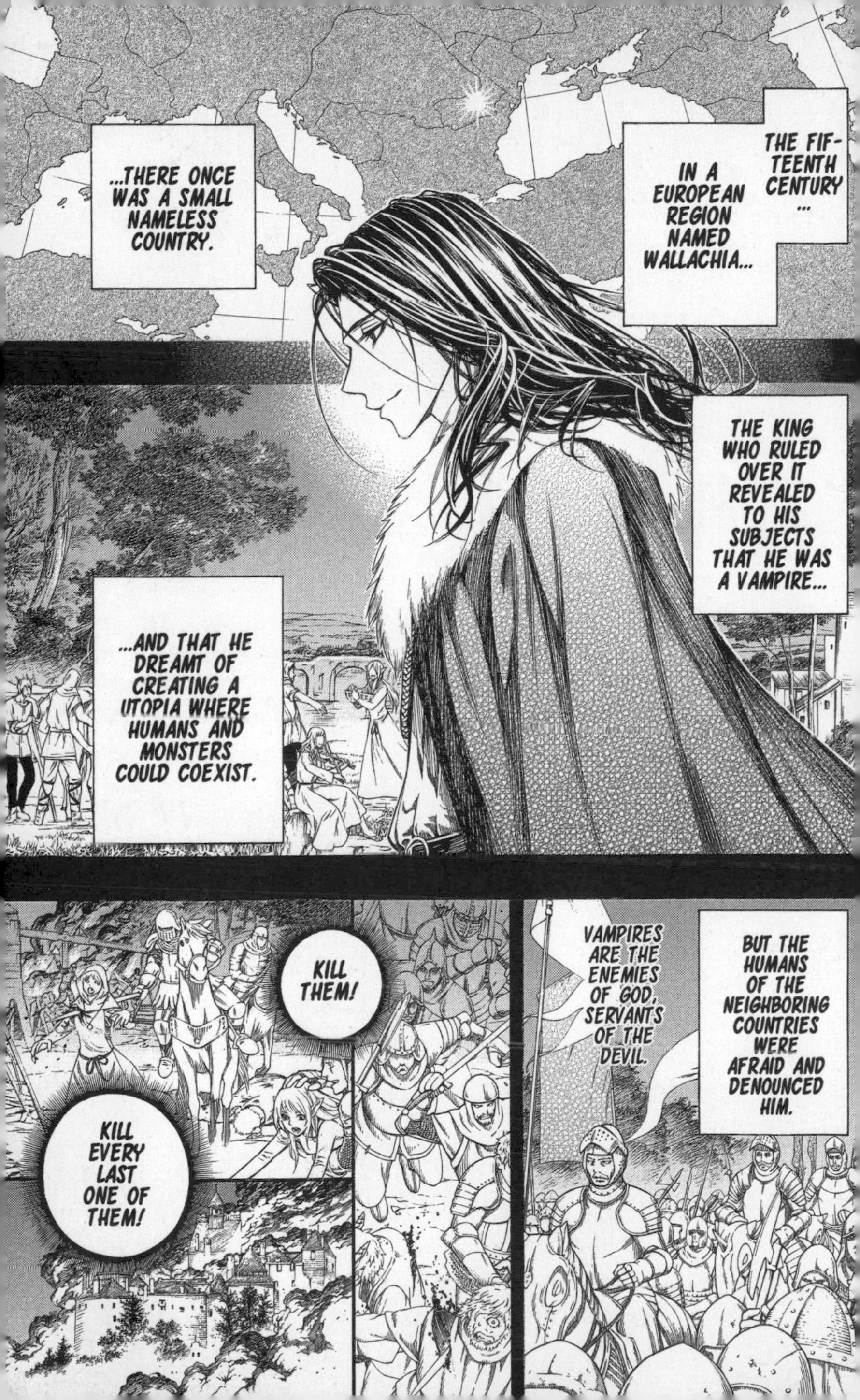
THE FIF-TEENTH CENTURY...
IN A EUROPEAN REGION NAMED WALLACHIA...
...THERE ONCE WAS A SMALL NAMELESS COUNTRY.
THE KING WHO RULED OVER IT REVEALED TO HIS SUBJECTS THAT HE WAS A VAMPIRE...
...AND THAT HE DREAMT OF CREATING A UTOPIA WHERE HUMANS AND MONSTERS COULD COEXIST.
BUT THE HUMANS OF THE NEIGHBORING COUNTRIES WERE AFRAID AND DENOUNCED HIM.
VAMPIRES ARE THE ENEMIES OF GOD, SERVANTS OF THE DEVIL.
KILL THEM!
KILL EVERY LAST ONE OF THEM!

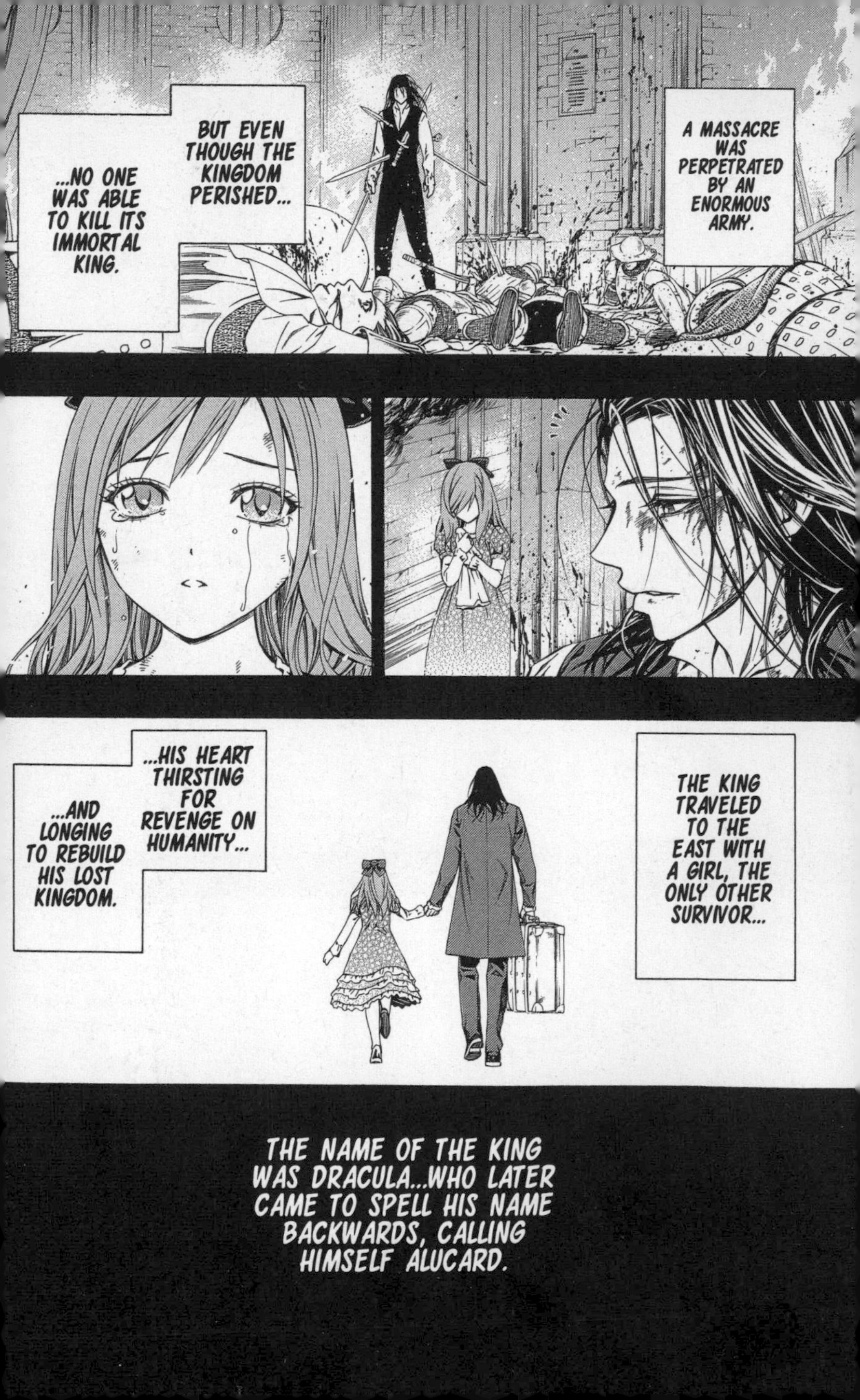
A MASSACRE WAS PERPETRATED BY AN ENORMOUS ARMY.
BUT EVEN THOUGH THE KINGDOM PERISHED...
...NO ONE WAS ABLE TO KILL ITS IMMORTAL KING.
THE KING TRAVELED TO THE EAST WITH A GIRL, THE ONLY OTHER SURVIVOR...
...HIS HEART THIRSTING FOR REVENGE ON HUMANITY...
...AND LONGING TO REBUILD HIS LOST KINGDOM.
THE NAME OF THE KING WAS DRACULA...WHO LATER CAME TO SPELL HIS NAME BACKWARDS, CALLING HIMSELF ALUCARD.

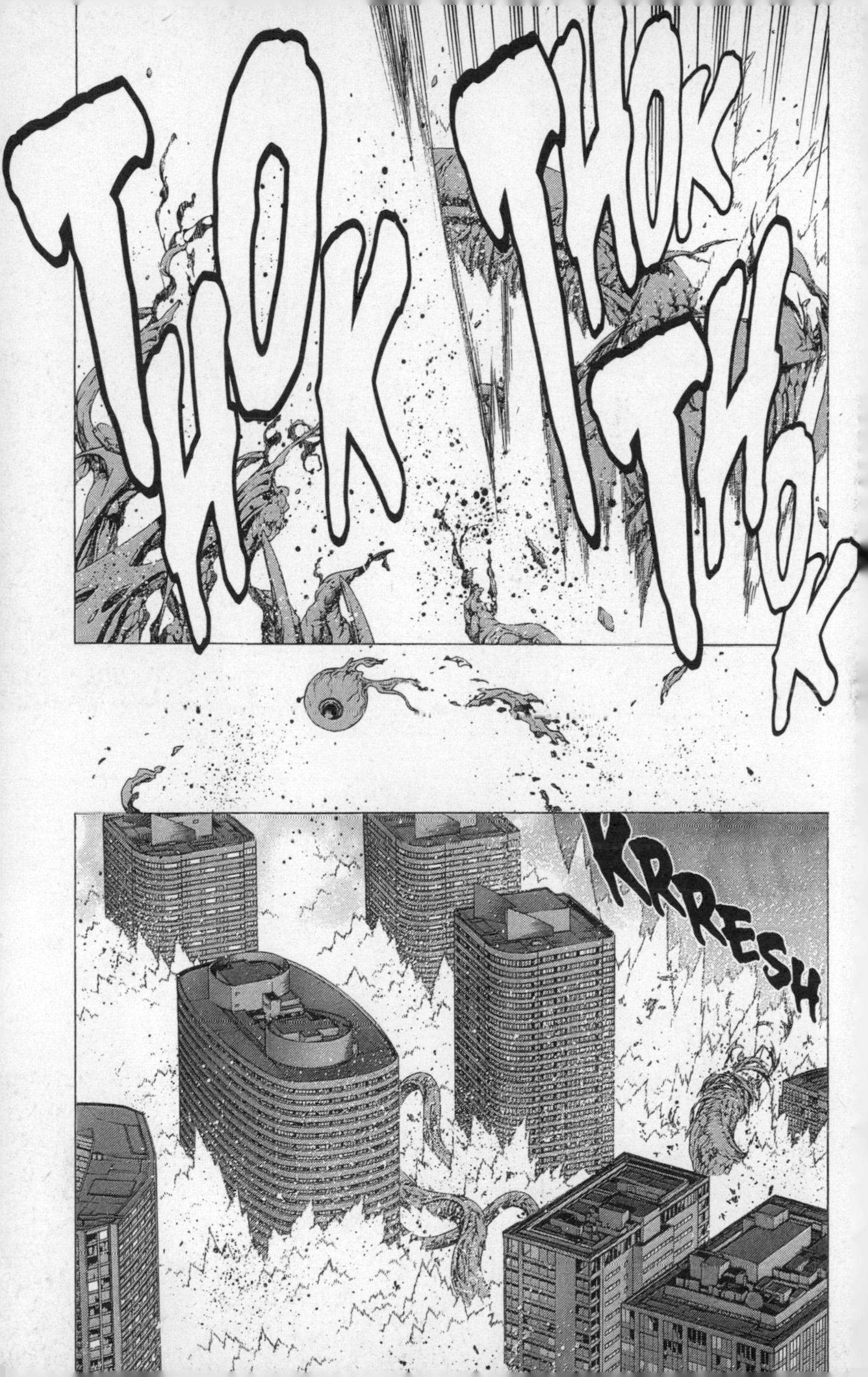
THOK
THOK
THOK
KRRESH

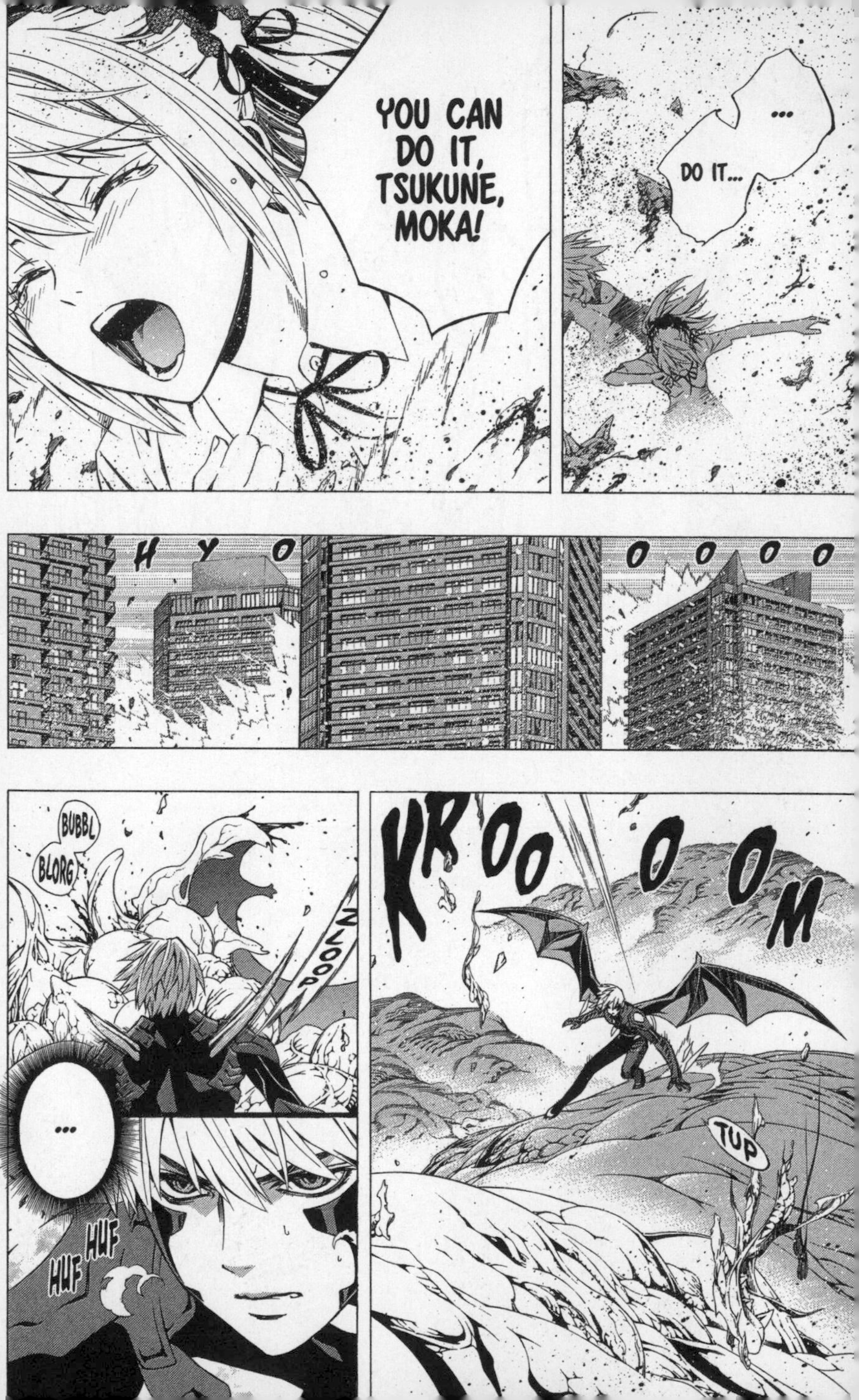
...
DO IT...
YOU CAN DO IT, TSUKUNE, MOKA!
HYOOOOO
KROOOOOM
TUP
BUBBL
BLORG
ZLOOOP
...
HUF HUF

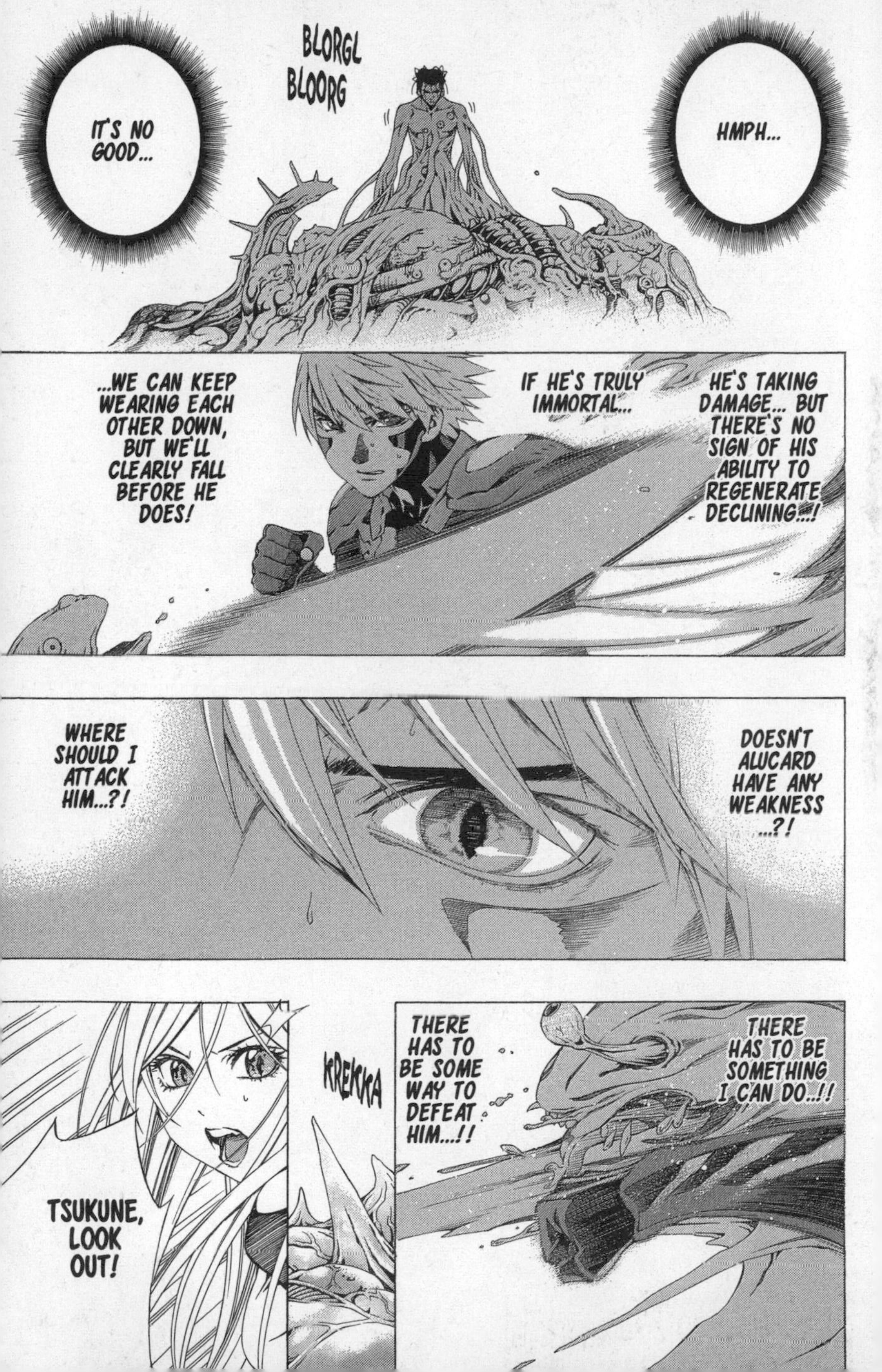
HMPH...
BLORGL BLOORG
IT'S NO GOOD...
HE'S TAKING DAMAGE... BUT THERE'S NO SIGN OF HIS ABILITY TO REGENERATE DECLINING...!
IF HE'S TRULY IMMORTAL...
...WE CAN KEEP WEARING EACH OTHER DOWN, BUT WE'LL CLEARLY FALL BEFORE HE DOES!
DOESN'T ALUCARD HAVE ANY WEAKNESS ...?!
WHERE SHOULD I ATTACK HIM...?!
THERE HAS TO BE SOMETHING I CAN DO..!!
THERE HAS TO BE SOME WAY TO DEFEAT HIM...!!
KREKKA
TSUKUNE, LOOK OUT!

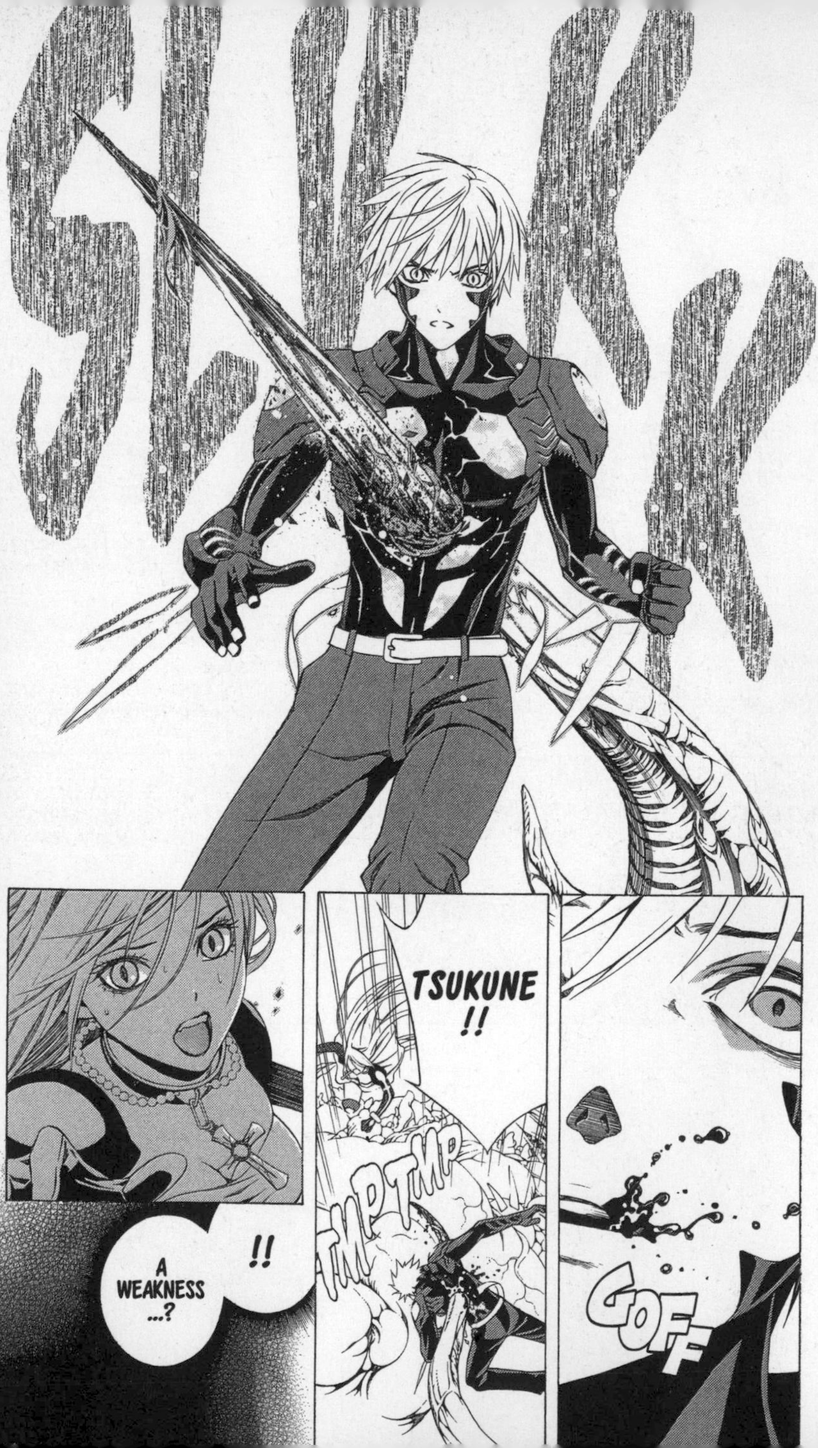
GOFF
TSUKUNE !!
TMP TMP
!!
A WEAKNESS ...?

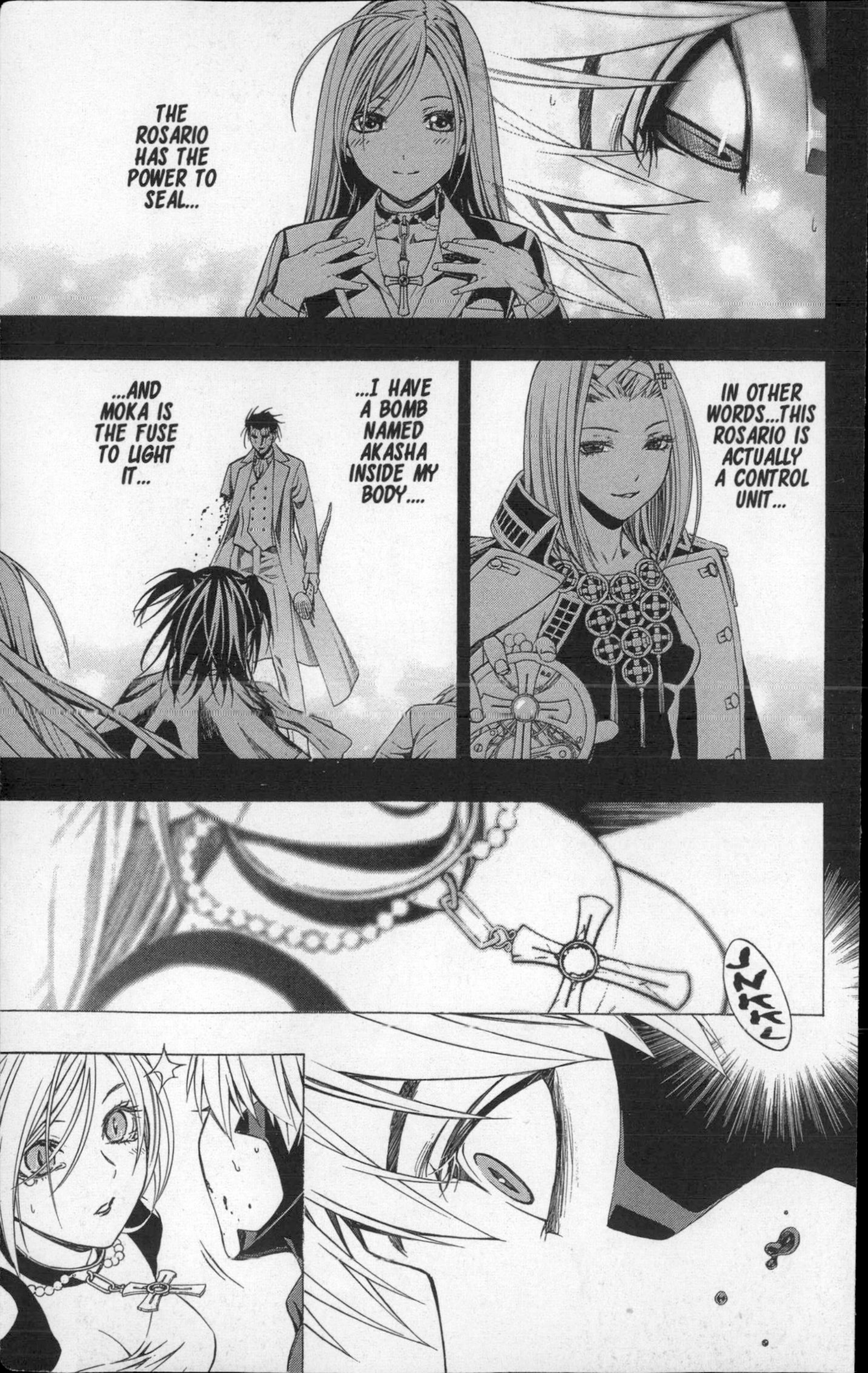
THE ROSARIO HAS THE POWER TO SEAL...
IN OTHER WORDS...THIS ROSARIO IS ACTUALLY A CONTROL UNIT...
...I HAVE A BOMB NAMED AKASHA INSIDE MY BODY....
...AND MOKA IS THE FUSE TO LIGHT IT...

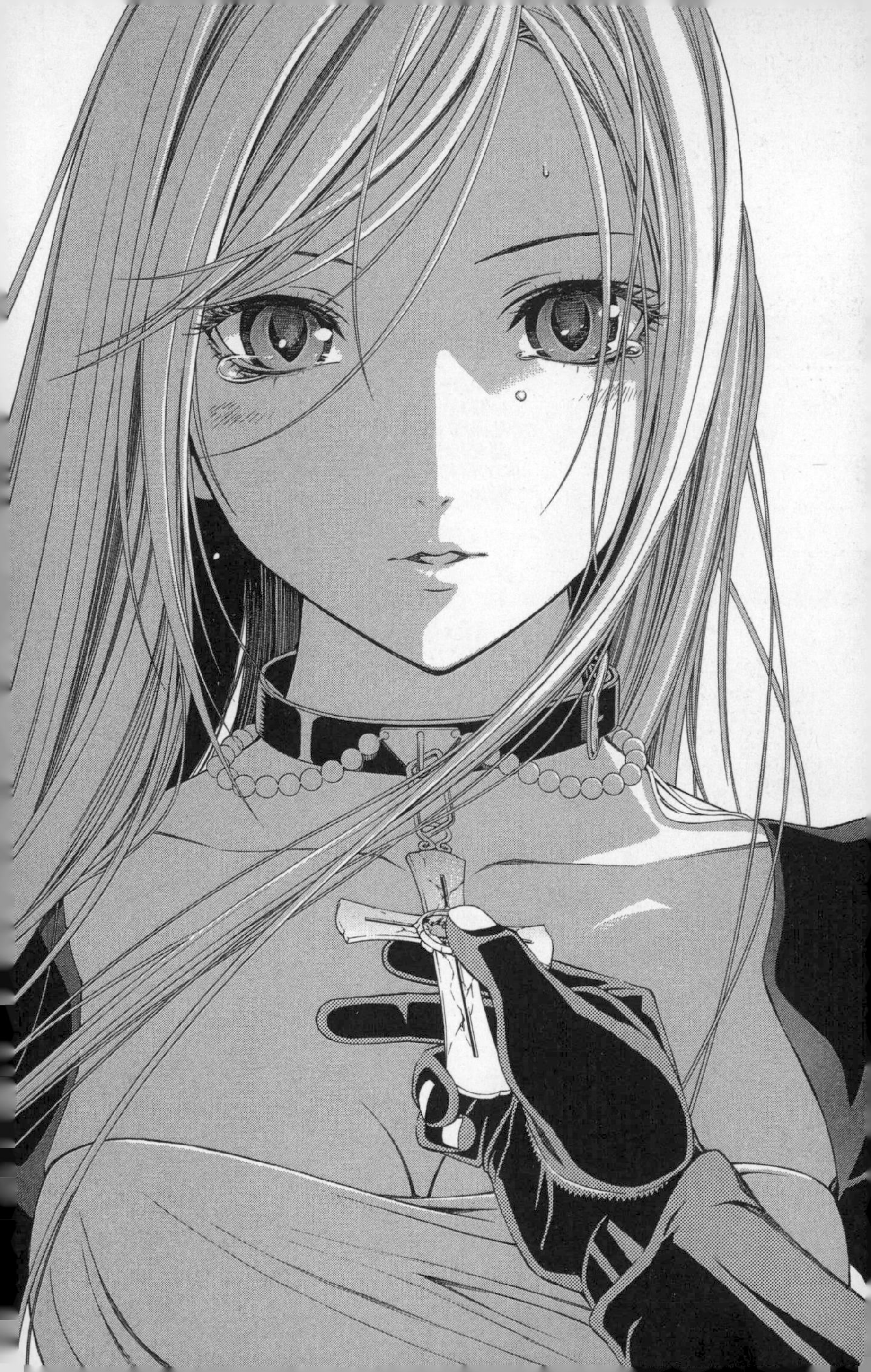

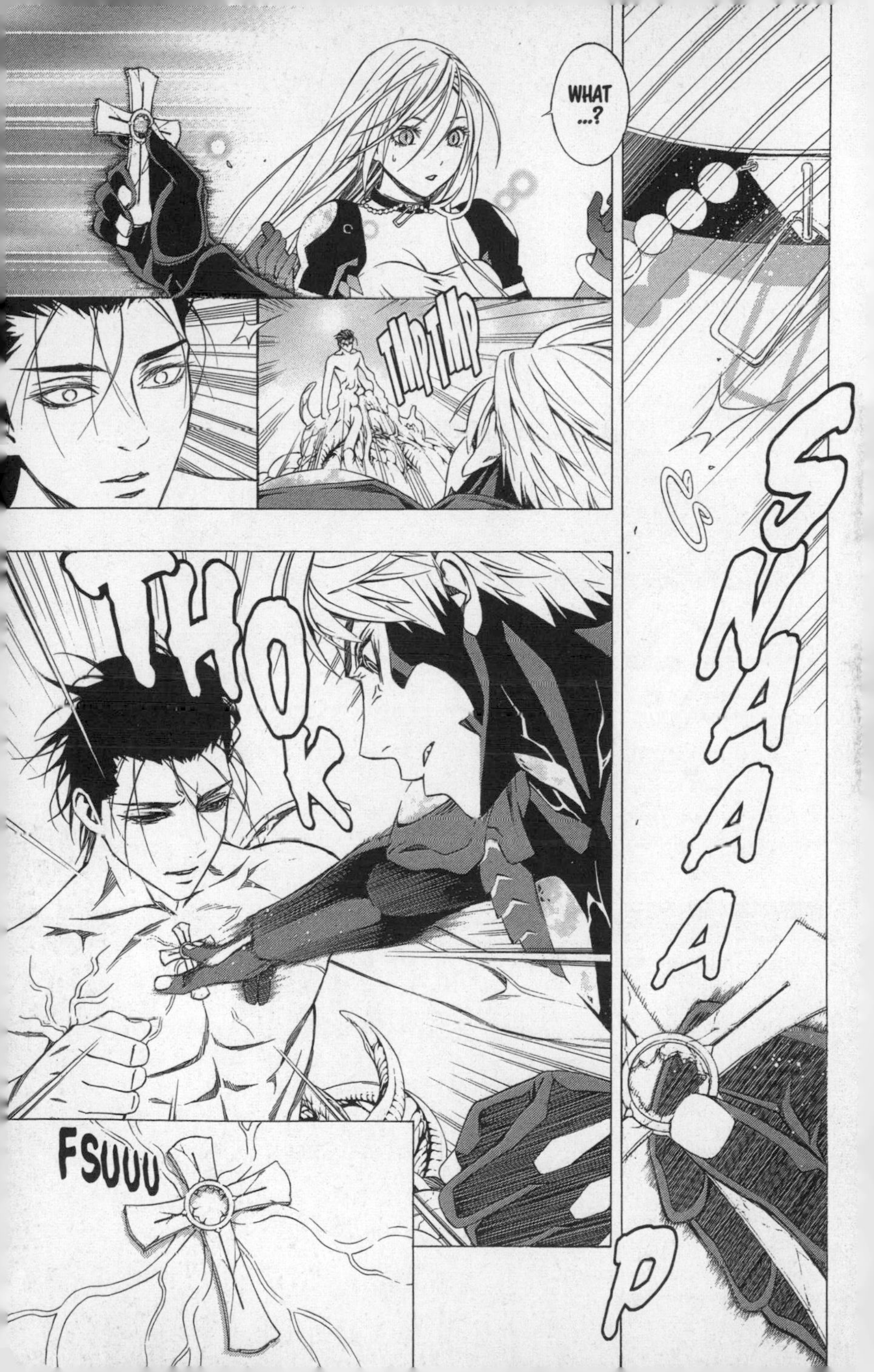
SNAAAAP
WHAT ...?
TMP TMP
THOK
FSUUU

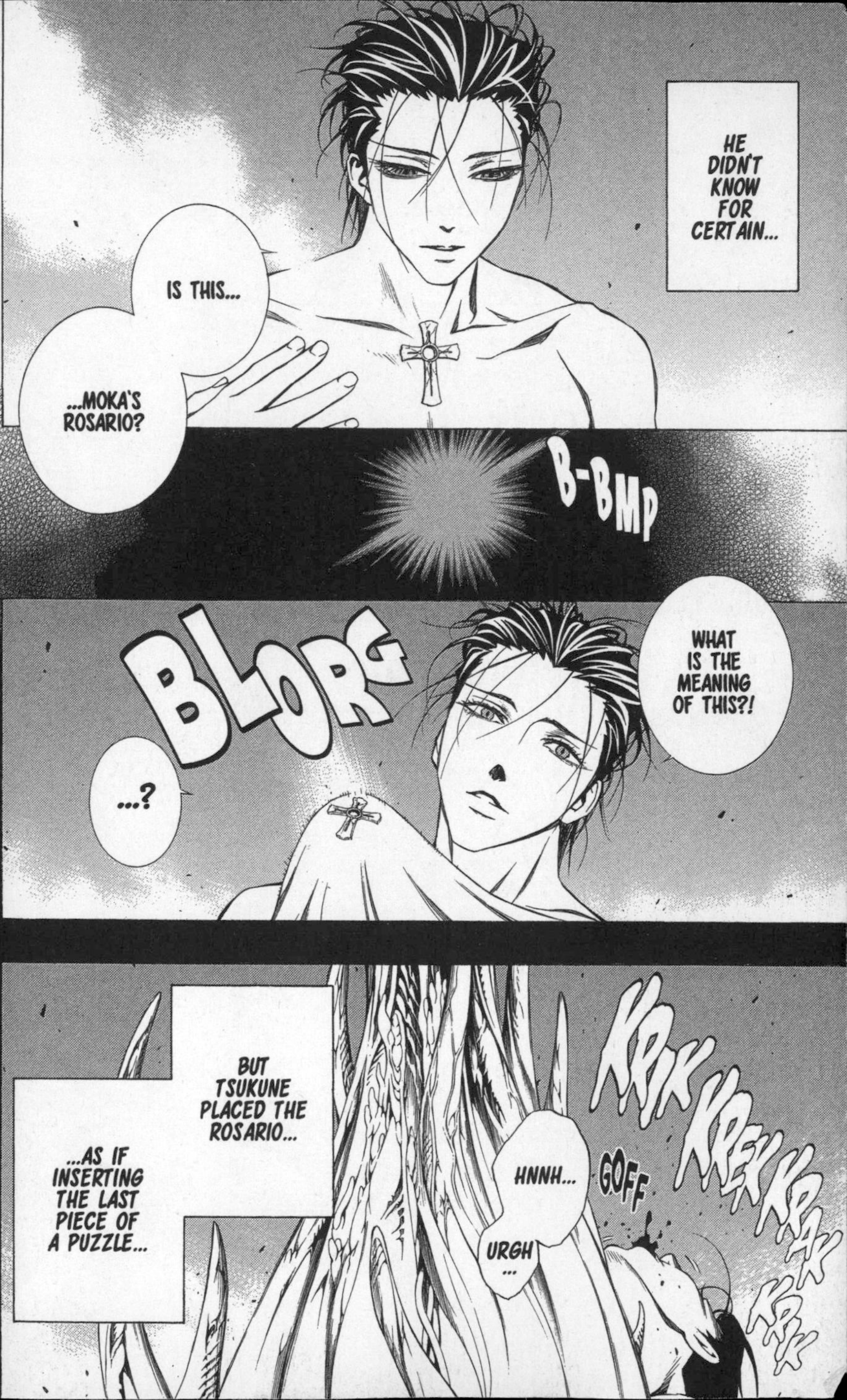
HE DIDN'T KNOW FOR CERTAIN...
IS THIS...
...MOKA'S ROSARIO?
B-BMP
WHAT IS THE MEANING OF THIS?!
BLORG
...?
KRIK KREK KRAK KRAK
GOFF
HNNH...
URGH...
BUT TSUKUNE PLACED THE ROSARIO...
...AS IF INSERTING THE LAST PIECE OF A PUZZLE...

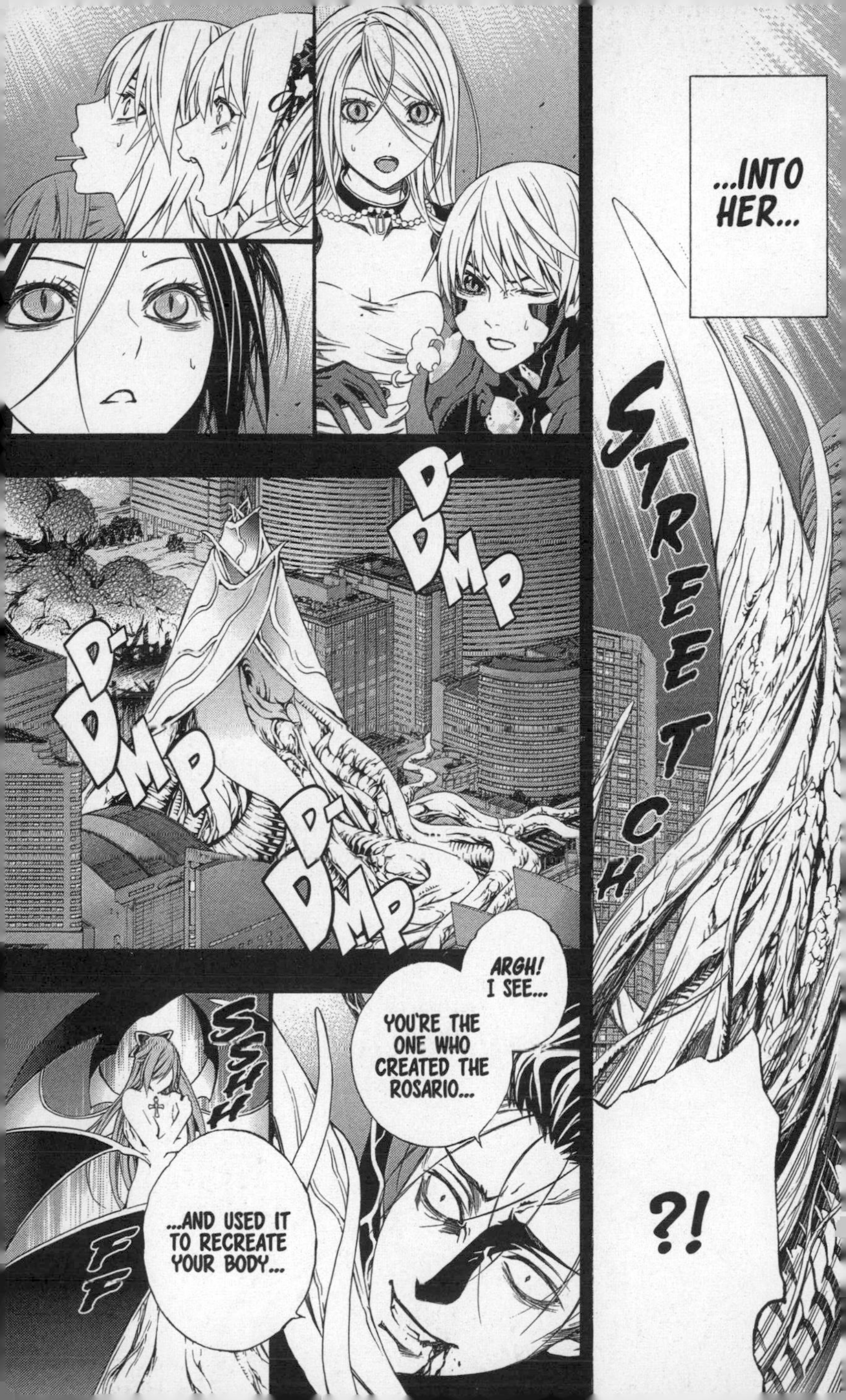
...INTO HER...
STRETCH
?!
D-DMP
D-DMP
D-DMP
ARGH! I SEE...
YOU'RE THE ONE WHO CREATED THE ROSARIO...
SSHH
...AND USED IT TO RECREATE YOUR BODY...
FF

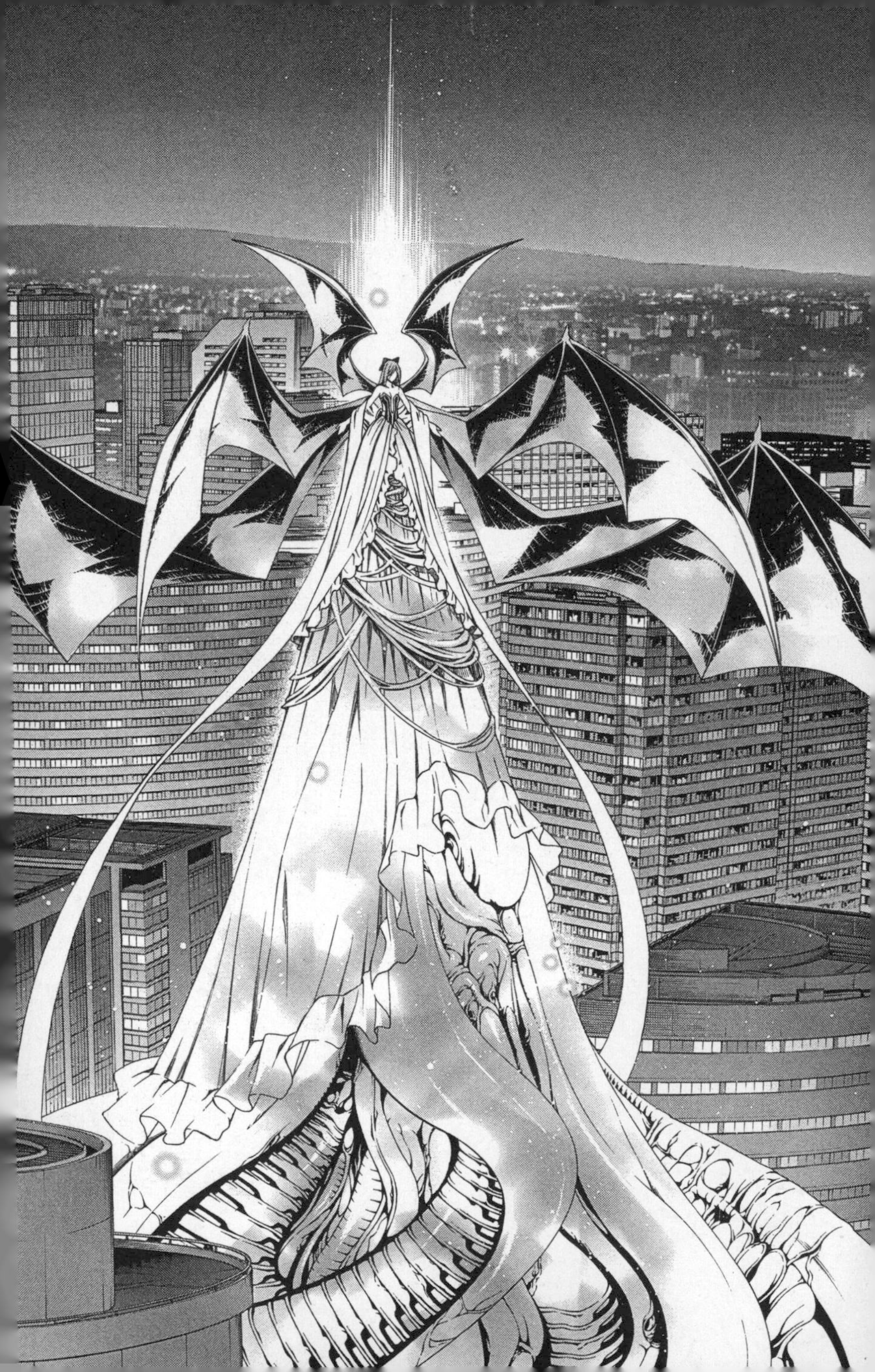

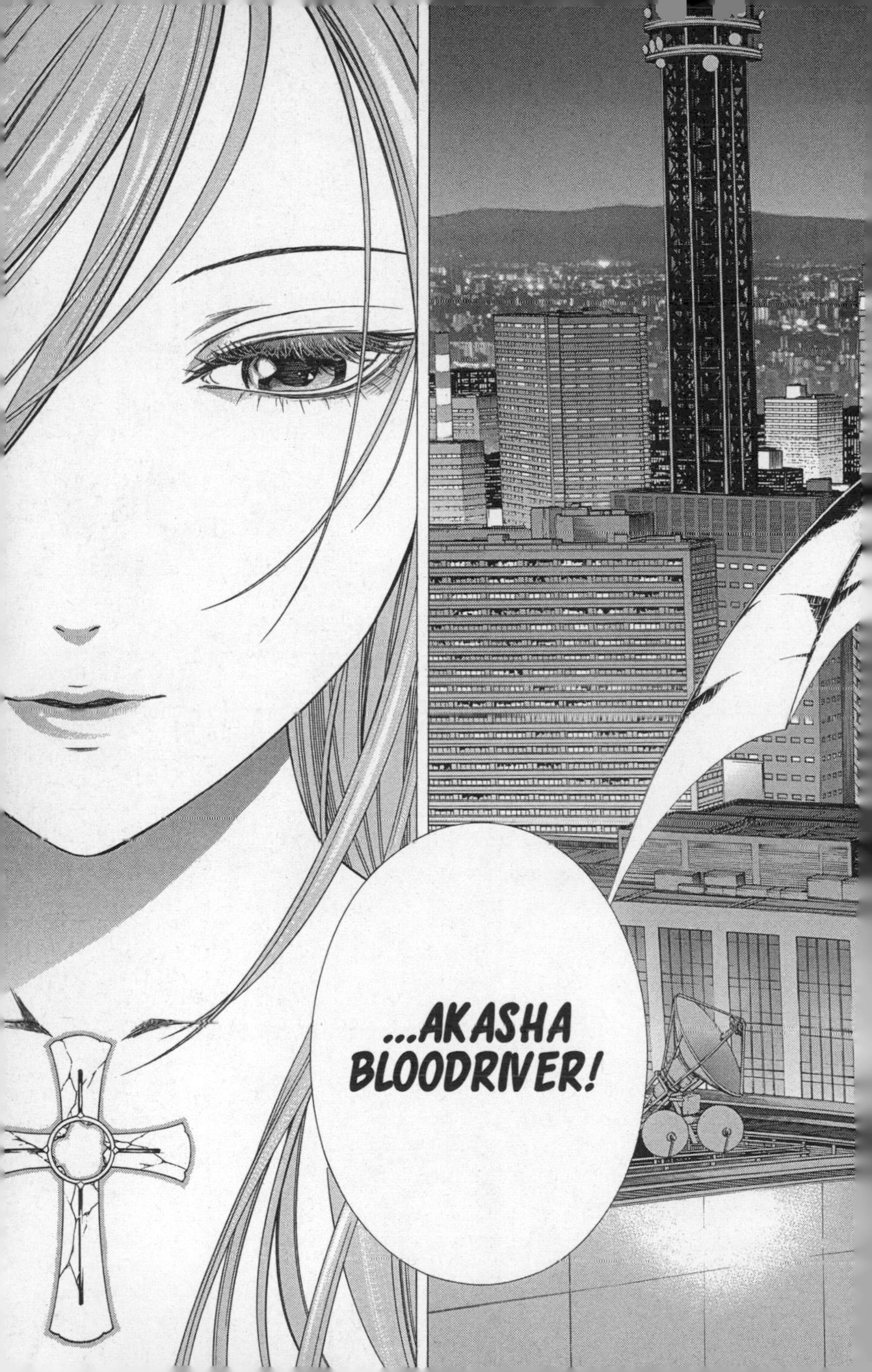
...AKASHA BLOODRIVER!

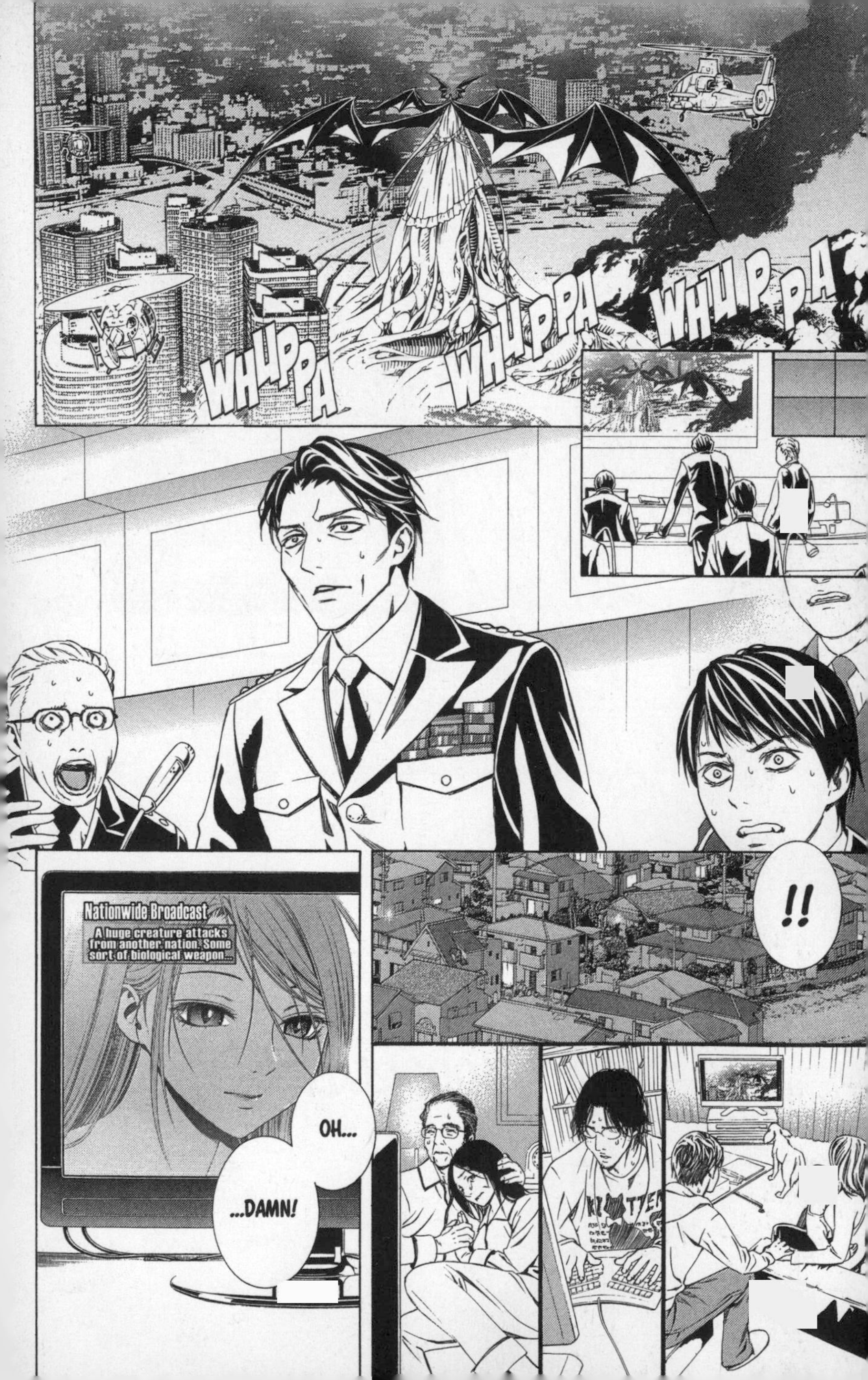
WHUPPA
WHUPPA
WHUPPA
!!
Nationwide Broadcast
A huge creature attacks from another nation. Some sort of biological weapon...
OH...
...DAMN!

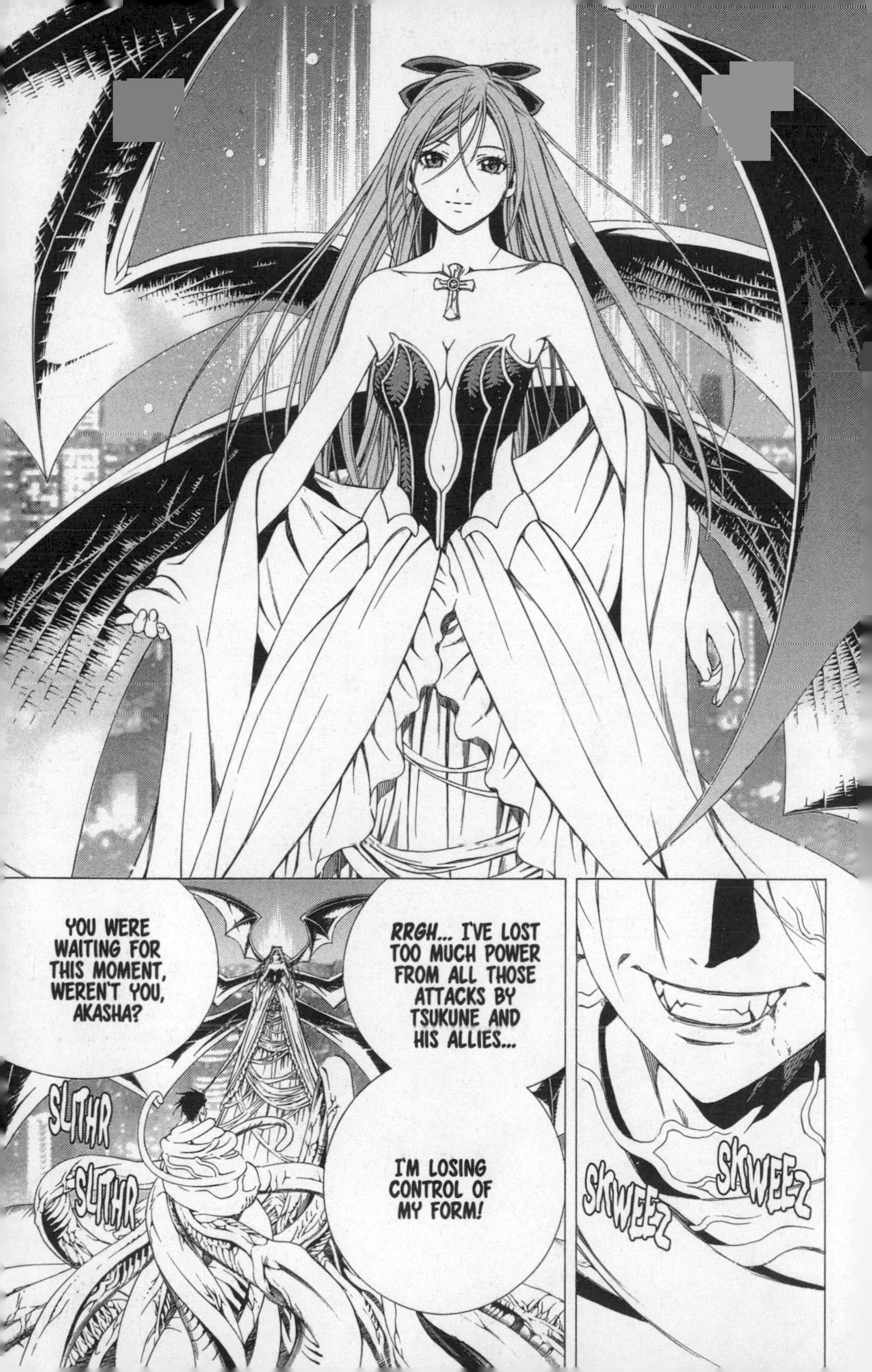
SKWEEZ
SKWEEZ
RRGH... I'VE LOST TOO MUCH POWER FROM ALL THOSE ATTACKS BY TSUKUNE AND HIS ALLIES...
YOU WERE WAITING FOR THIS MOMENT, WEREN'T YOU, AKASHA?
I'M LOSING CONTROL OF MY FORM!
SLITHR
SLITHR

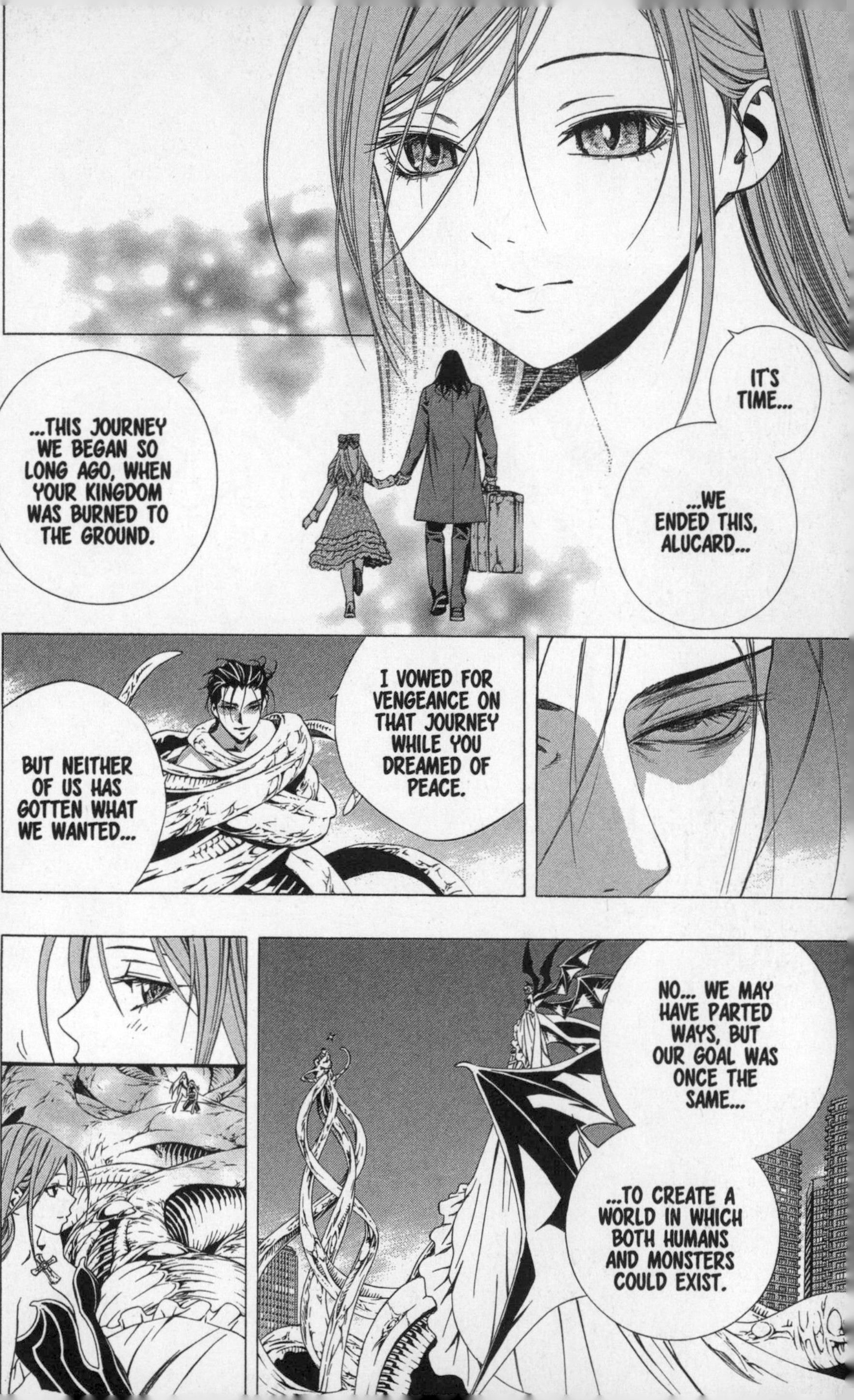
IT'S TIME...
...WE ENDED THIS, ALUCARD...
...THIS JOURNEY WE BEGAN SO LONG AGO, WHEN YOUR KINGDOM WAS BURNED TO THE GROUND.
I VOWED FOR VENGEANCE ON THAT JOURNEY WHILE YOU DREAMED OF PEACE.
BUT NEITHER OF US HAS GOTTEN WHAT WE WANTED...
NO... WE MAY HAVE PARTED WAYS, BUT OUR GOAL WAS ONCE THE SAME...
...TO CREATE A WORLD IN WHICH BOTH HUMANS AND MONSTERS COULD EXIST.

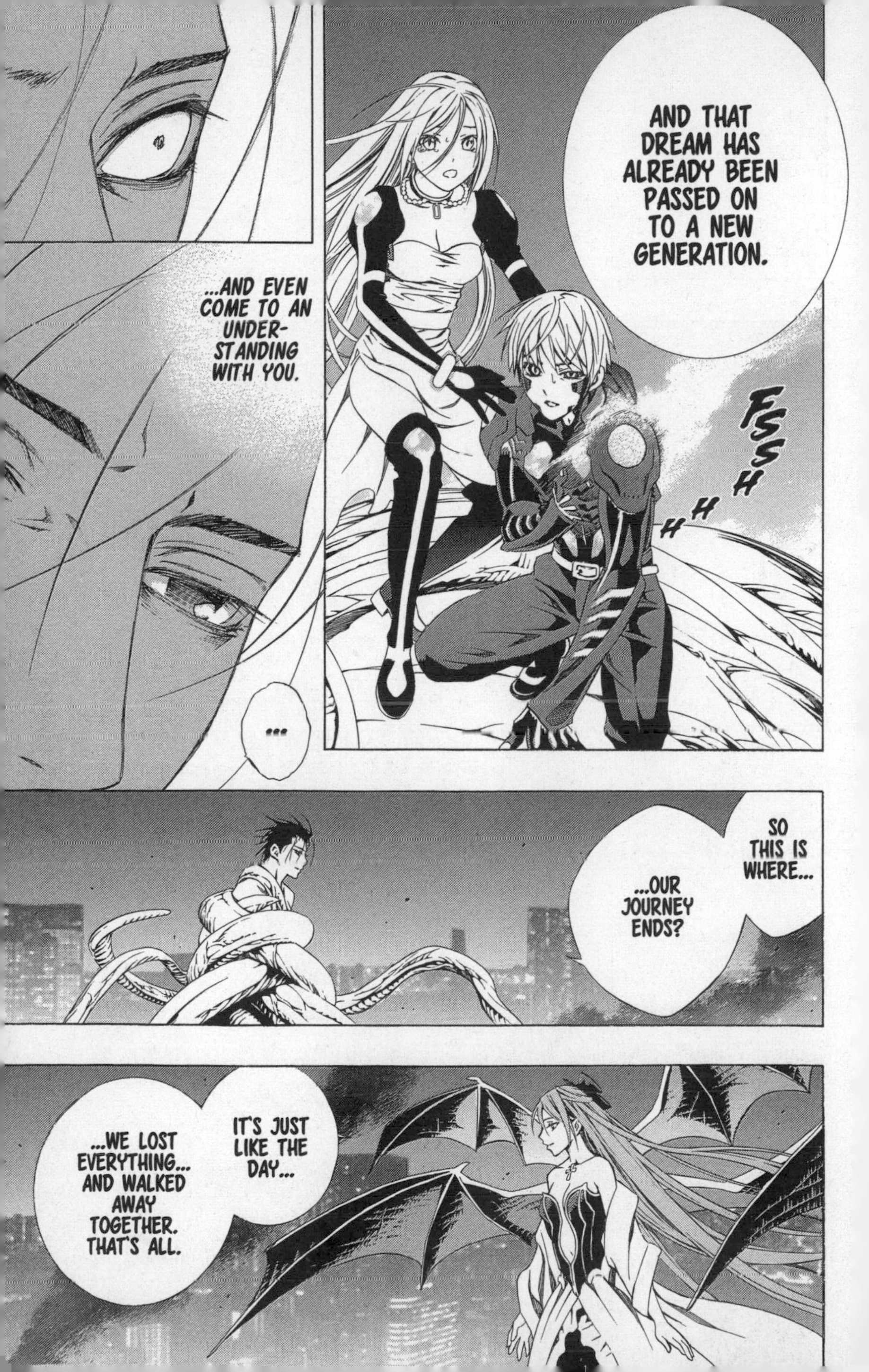
AND THAT DREAM HAS ALREADY BEEN PASSED ON TO A NEW GENERATION.
FSSHHH
...AND EVEN COME TO AN UNDER-STANDING WITH YOU.
...
SO THIS IS WHERE...
...OUR JOURNEY ENDS?
IT'S JUST LIKE THE DAY...
...WE LOST EVERYTHING... AND WALKED AWAY TOGETHER. THAT'S ALL.

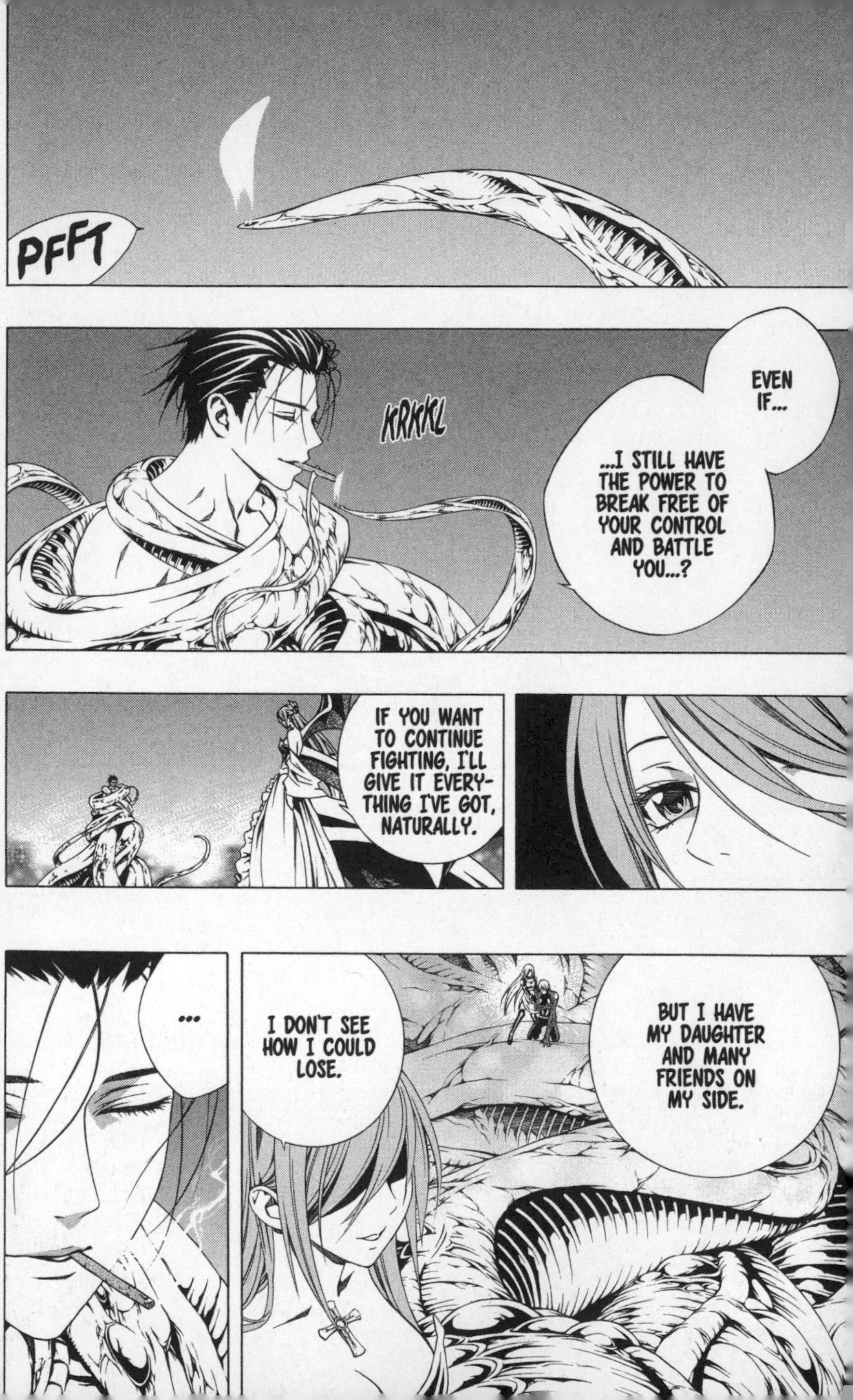
PFFT
EVEN IF...
...I STILL HAVE THE POWER TO BREAK FREE OF YOUR CONTROL AND BATTLE YOU...?
KRKKL
IF YOU WANT TO CONTINUE FIGHTING, I'LL GIVE IT EVERYTHING I'VE GOT, NATURALLY.
BUT I HAVE MY DAUGHTER AND MANY FRIENDS ON MY SIDE.
I DON'T SEE HOW I COULD LOSE.
...

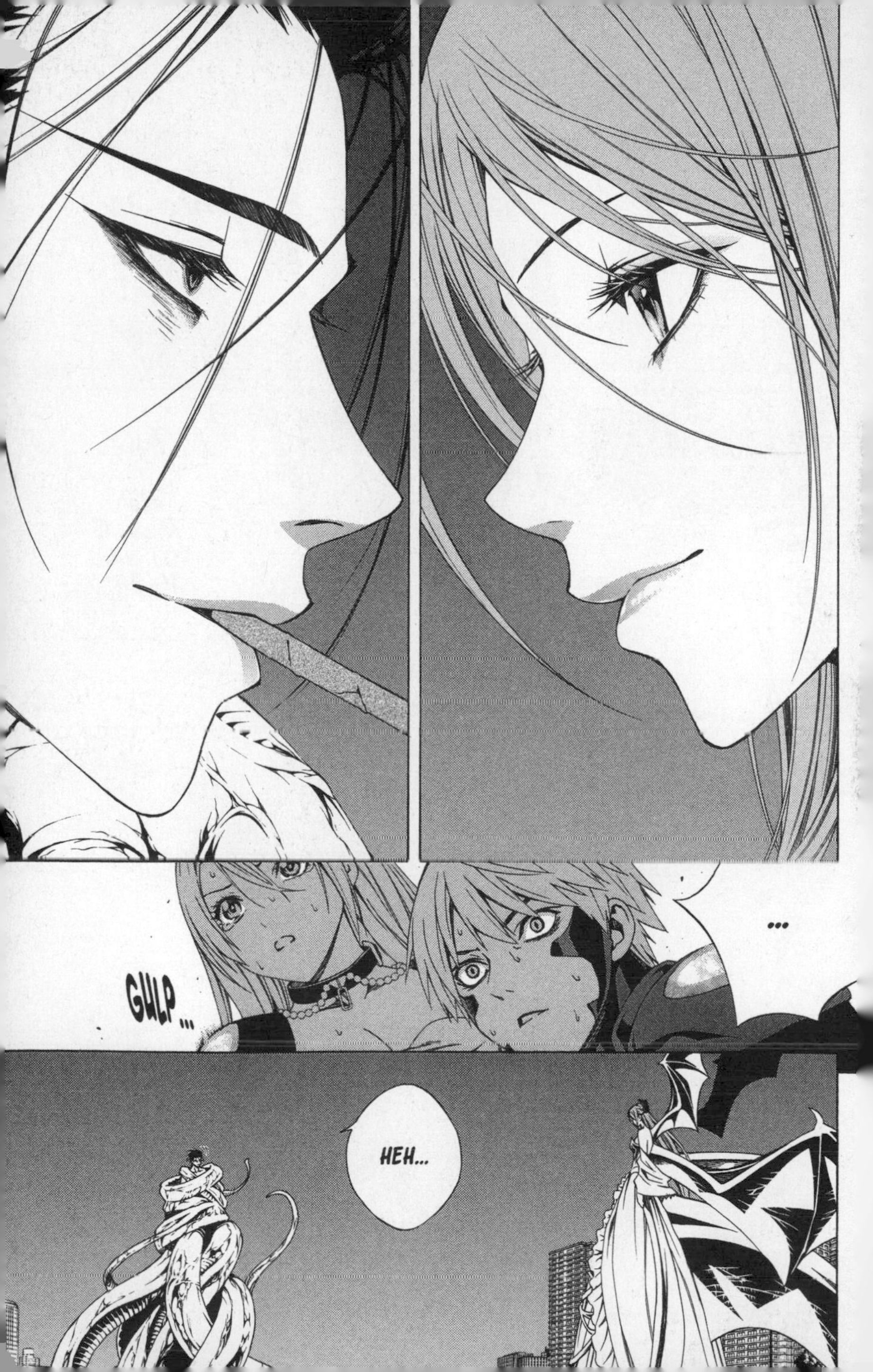
...
GULP...
HEH...

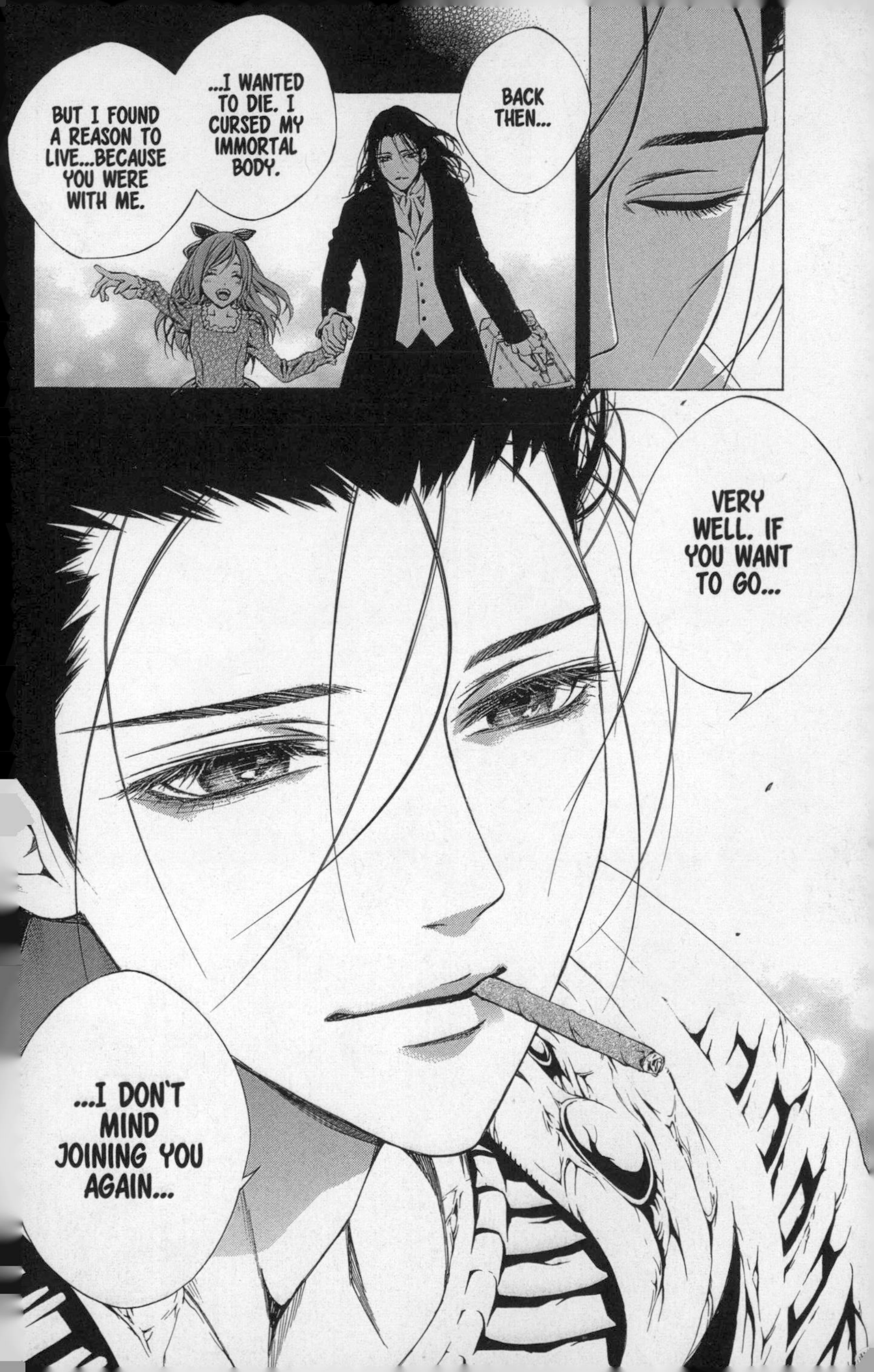
BACK THEN...
...I WANTED TO DIE. I CURSED MY IMMORTAL BODY.
BUT I FOUND A REASON TO LIVE...BECAUSE YOU WERE WITH ME.
VERY WELL. IF YOU WANT TO GO...
...I DON'T MIND JOINING YOU AGAIN...

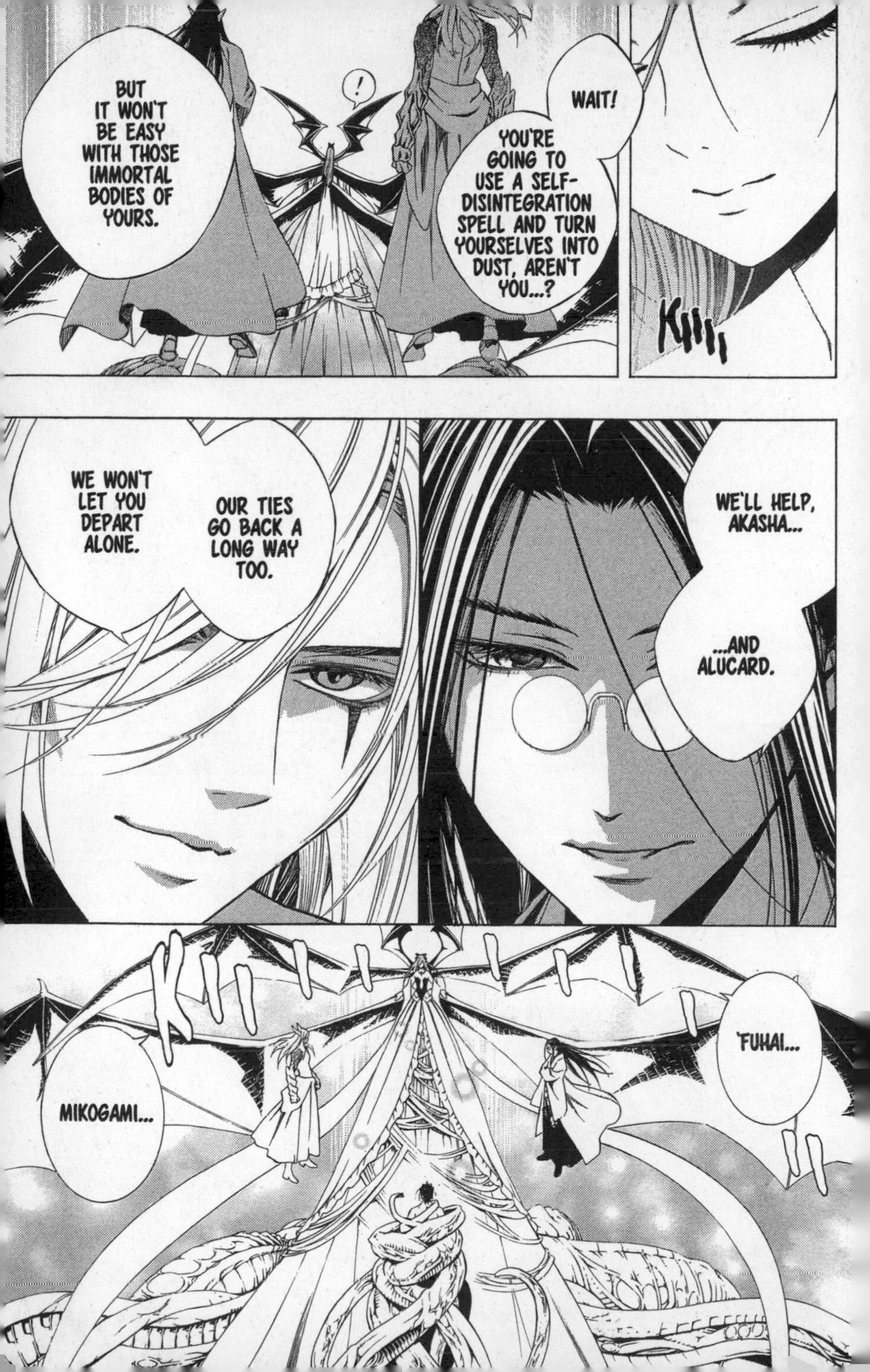
KIIII
WAIT!
YOU'RE GOING TO USE A SELF-DISINTEGRATION SPELL AND TURN YOURSELVES INTO DUST, AREN'T YOU...?
!
BUT IT WON'T BE EASY WITH THOSE IMMORTAL BODIES OF YOURS.
WE'LL HELP, AKASHA...
...AND ALUCARD.
WE WON'T LET YOU DEPART ALONE.
OUR TIES GO BACK A LONG WAY TOO.
'FUHAI...
MIKOGAMI...

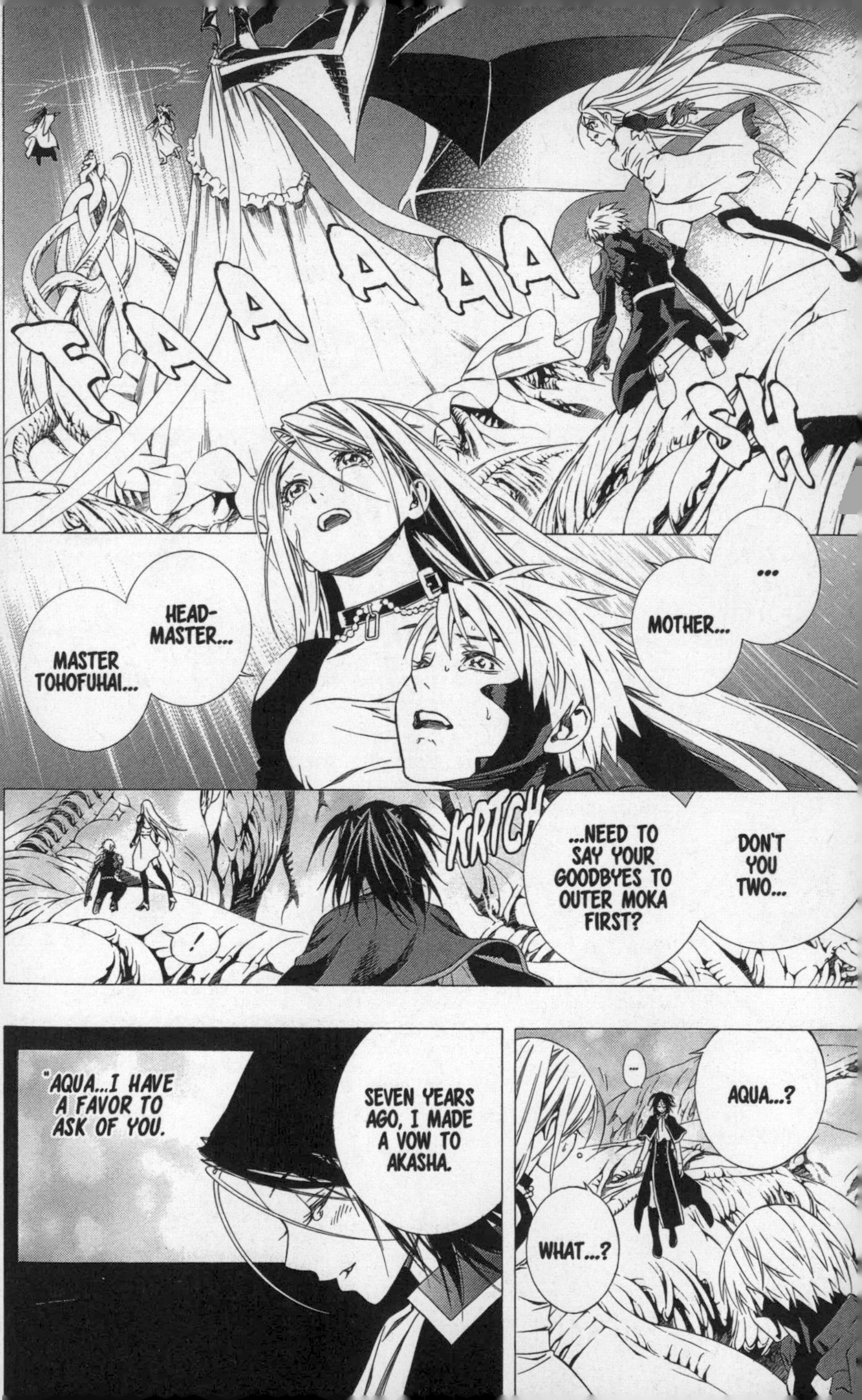
FAAAAAA
SH
...
MOTHER...
HEAD-MASTER...
MASTER TOHOFUHAI...
DON'T YOU TWO...
...NEED TO SAY YOUR GOODBYES TO OUTER MOKA FIRST?
KRTCH
!
AQUA...?
...
WHAT...?
SEVEN YEARS AGO, I MADE A VOW TO AKASHA.
"AQUA...I HAVE A FAVOR TO ASK OF YOU.

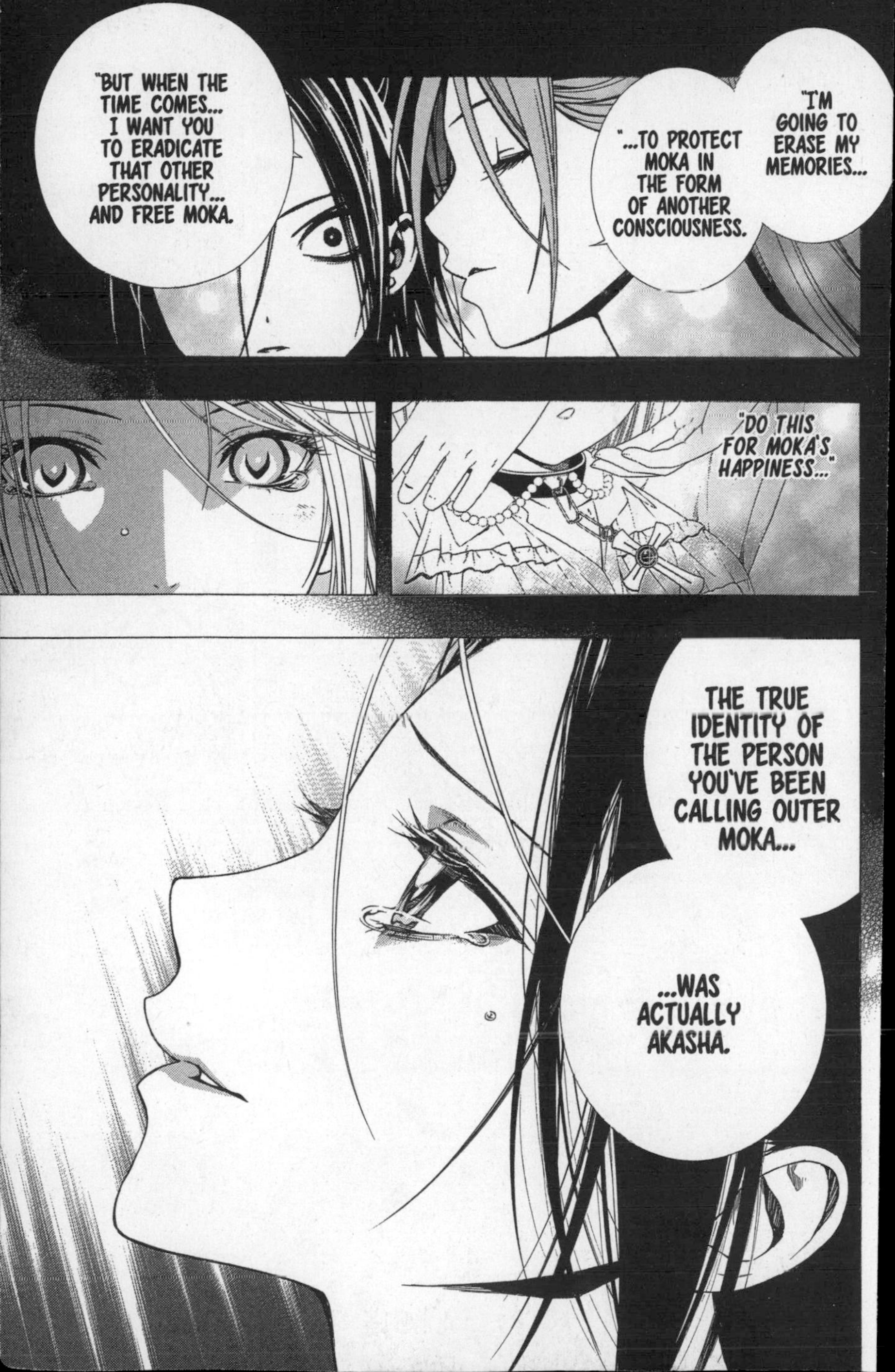
"I'M GOING TO ERASE MY MEMORIES...
"...TO PROTECT MOKA IN THE FORM OF ANOTHER CONSCIOUSNESS.
"BUT WHEN THE TIME COMES... I WANT YOU TO ERADICATE THAT OTHER PERSONALITY... AND FREE MOKA.
"DO THIS FOR MOKA'S HAPPINESS..."
THE TRUE IDENTITY OF THE PERSON YOU'VE BEEN CALLING OUTER MOKA...
...WAS ACTUALLY AKASHA.

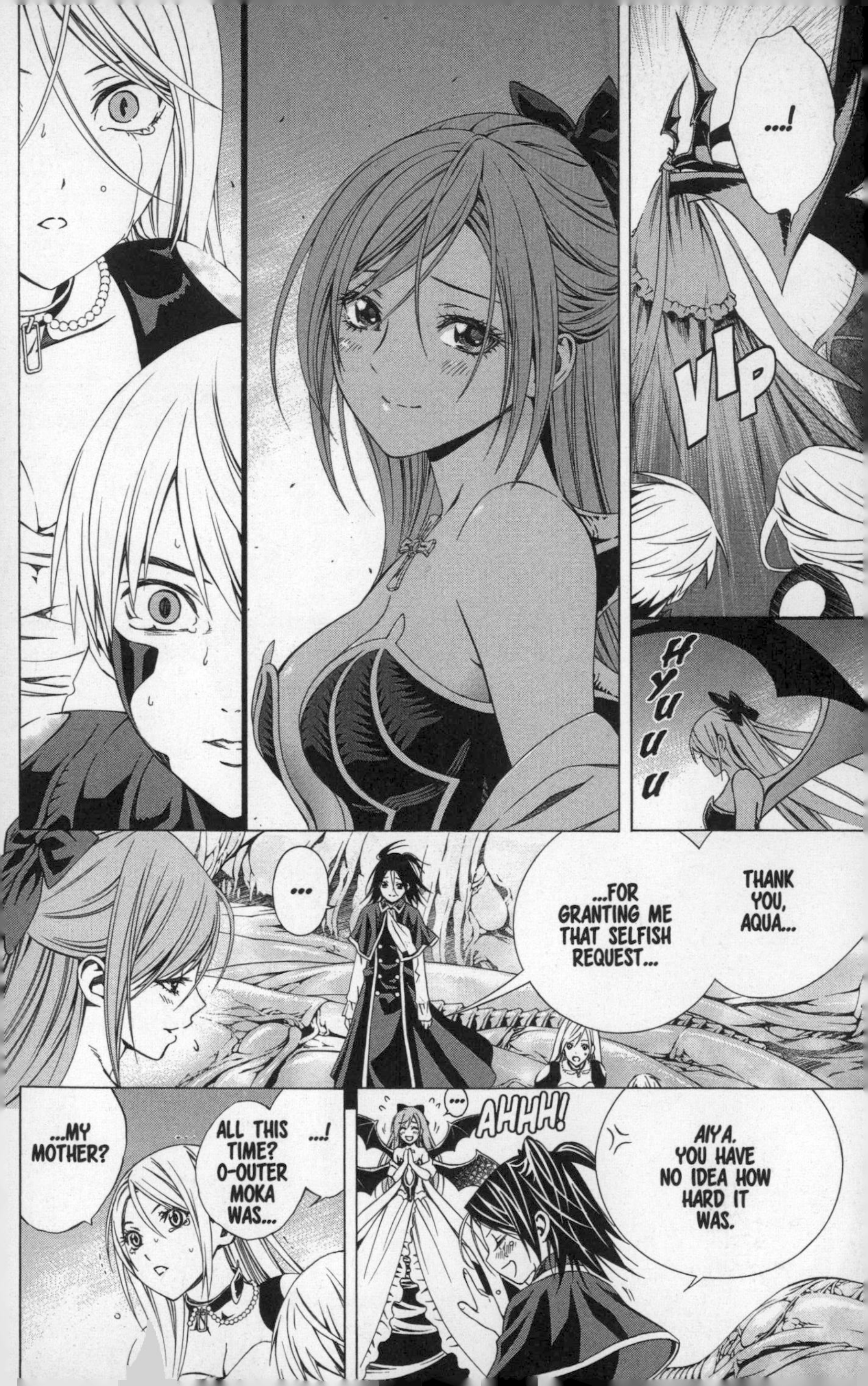
...!
VIP
HYUUUU
THANK YOU, AQUA...
...FOR GRANTING ME THAT SELFISH REQUEST...
...
AIYA. YOU HAVE NO IDEA HOW HARD IT WAS.
AHHH!
...
...!
ALL THIS TIME? O-OUTER MOKA WAS...
...MY MOTHER?

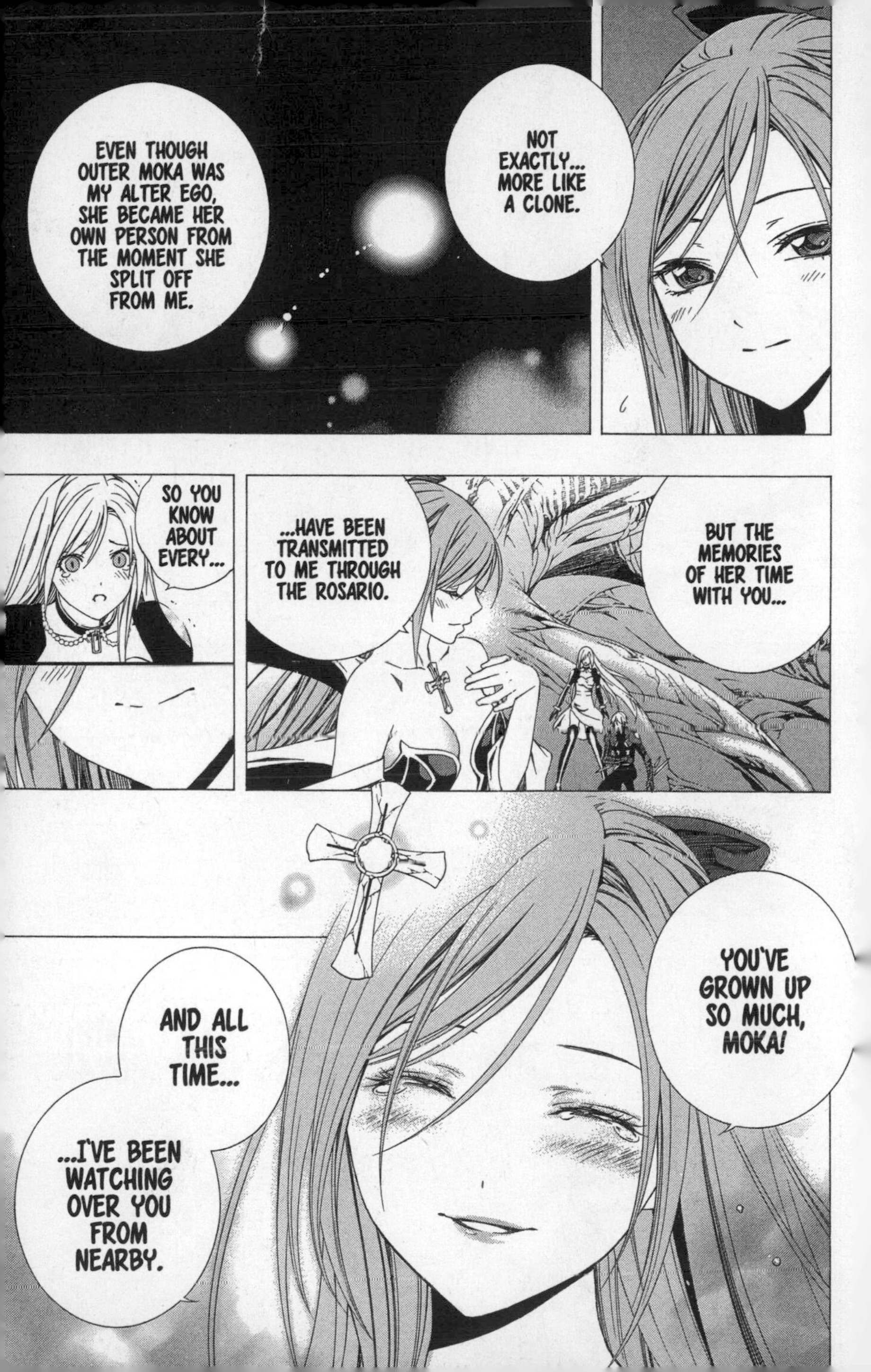
NOT EXACTLY... MORE LIKE A CLONE.
EVEN THOUGH OUTER MOKA WAS MY ALTER EGO, SHE BECAME HER OWN PERSON FROM THE MOMENT SHE SPLIT OFF FROM ME.
BUT THE MEMORIES OF HER TIME WITH YOU...
...HAVE BEEN TRANSMITTED TO ME THROUGH THE ROSARIO.
SO YOU KNOW ABOUT EVERY...
YOU'VE GROWN UP SO MUCH, MOKA!
AND ALL THIS TIME...
...I'VE BEEN WATCHING OVER YOU FROM NEARBY.

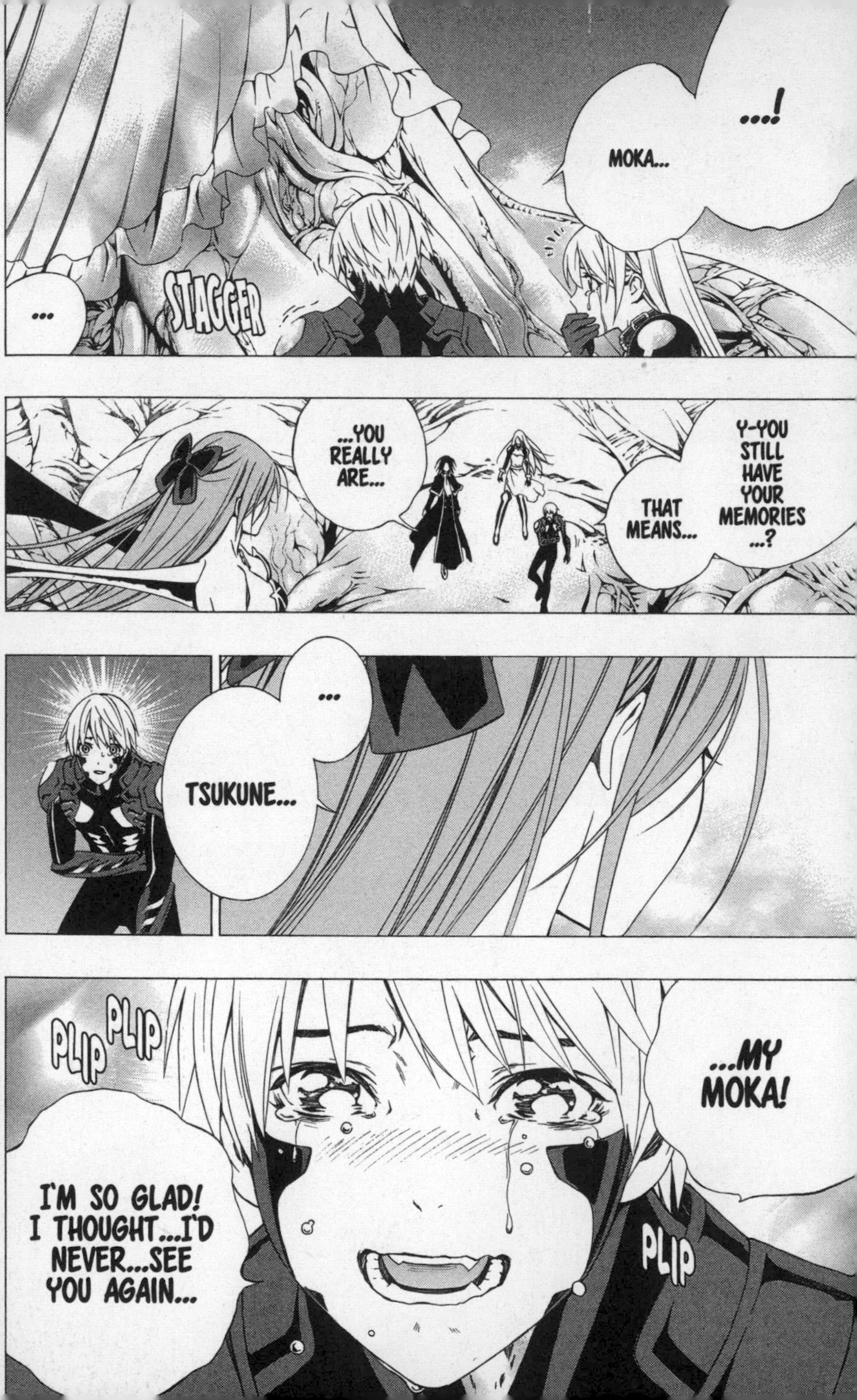
...!
MOKA...
STAGGER
...
Y-YOU STILL HAVE YOUR MEMORIES ...?
THAT MEANS...
...YOU REALLY ARE...
...
TSUKUNE...
...MY MOKA!
PLIP PLIP
PLIP
I'M SO GLAD! I THOUGHT...I'D NEVER...SEE YOU AGAIN...

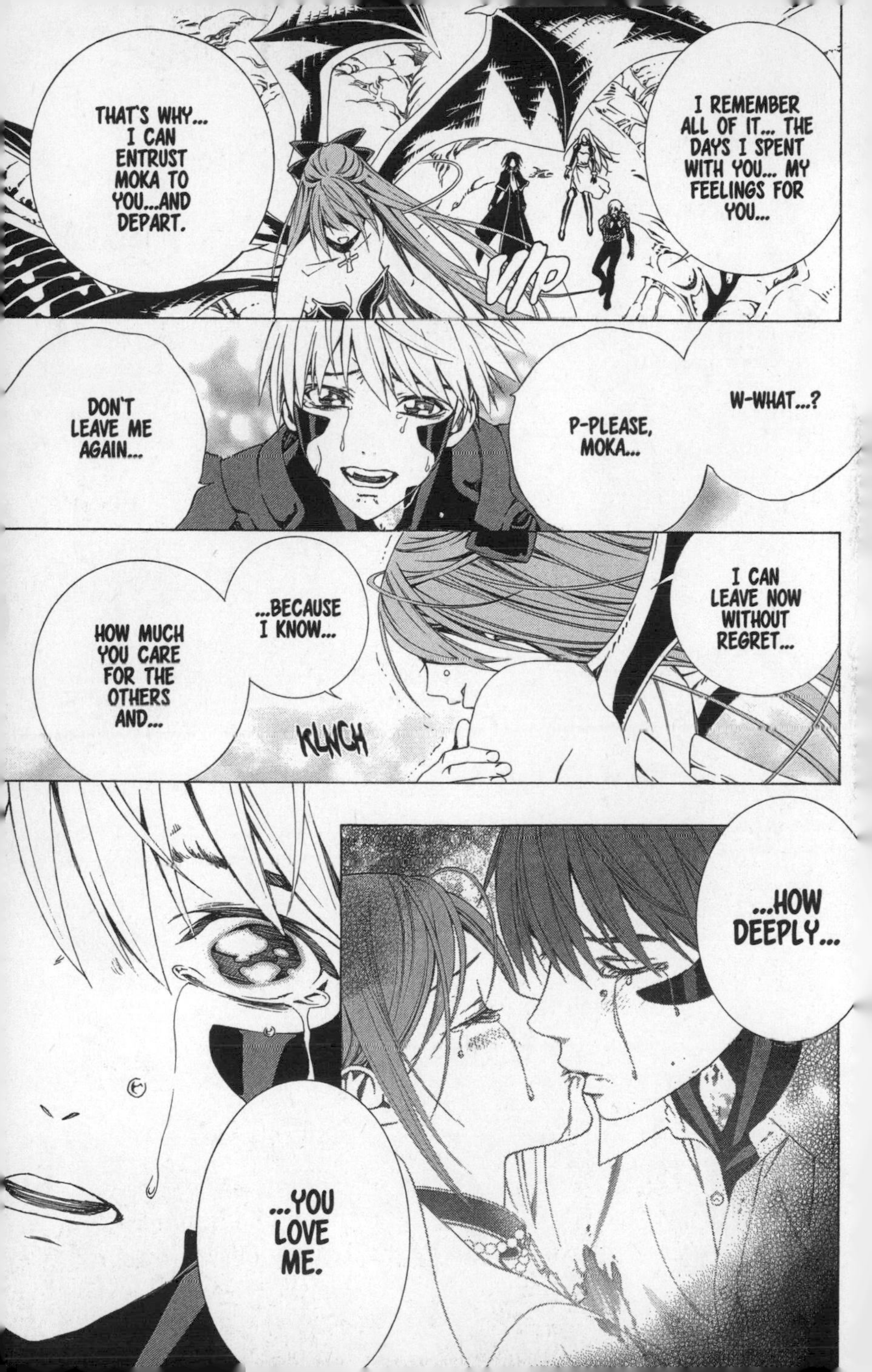
I REMEMBER ALL OF IT... THE DAYS I SPENT WITH YOU... MY FEELINGS FOR YOU...
THAT'S WHY... I CAN ENTRUST MOKA TO YOU...AND DEPART.
VIP
W-WHAT...?
P-PLEASE, MOKA...
DON'T LEAVE ME AGAIN...
I CAN LEAVE NOW WITHOUT REGRET...
...BECAUSE I KNOW...
HOW MUCH YOU CARE FOR THE OTHERS AND...
KLNCH
...HOW DEEPLY...
...YOU LOVE ME.

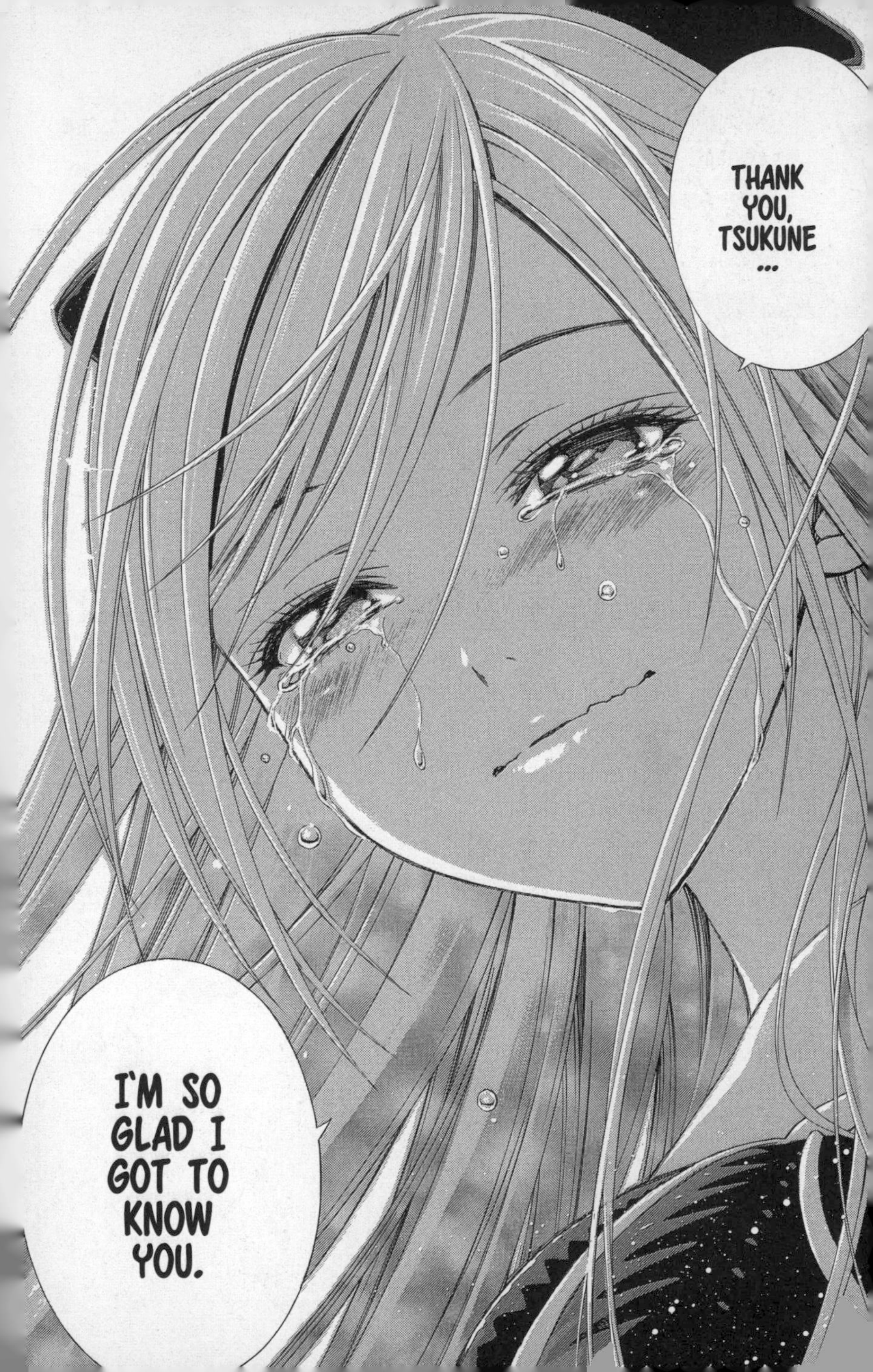
THANK YOU, TSUKUNE ...
I'M SO GLAD I GOT TO KNOW YOU.

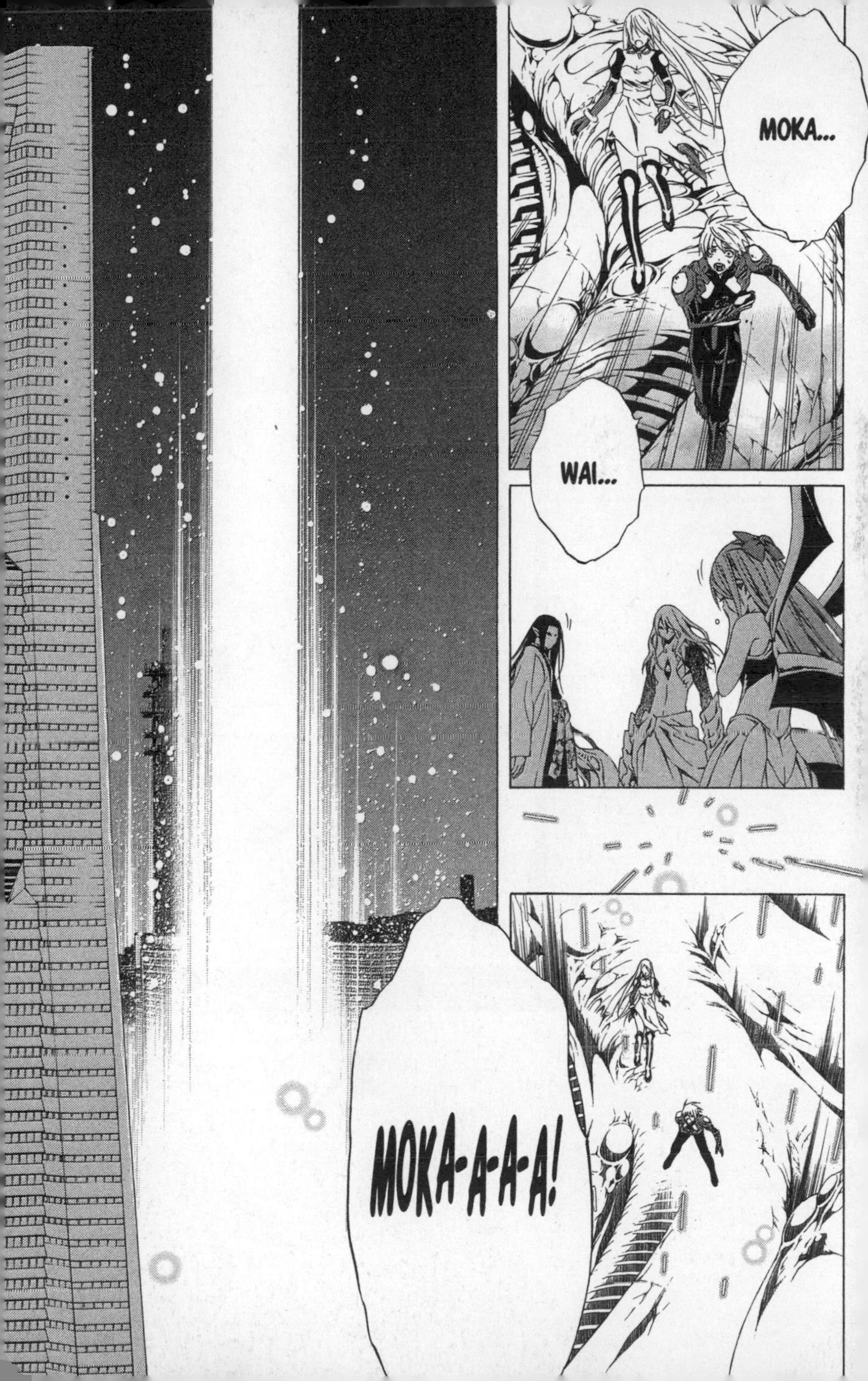
MOKA...
WAI...
MOKA-A-A-A!

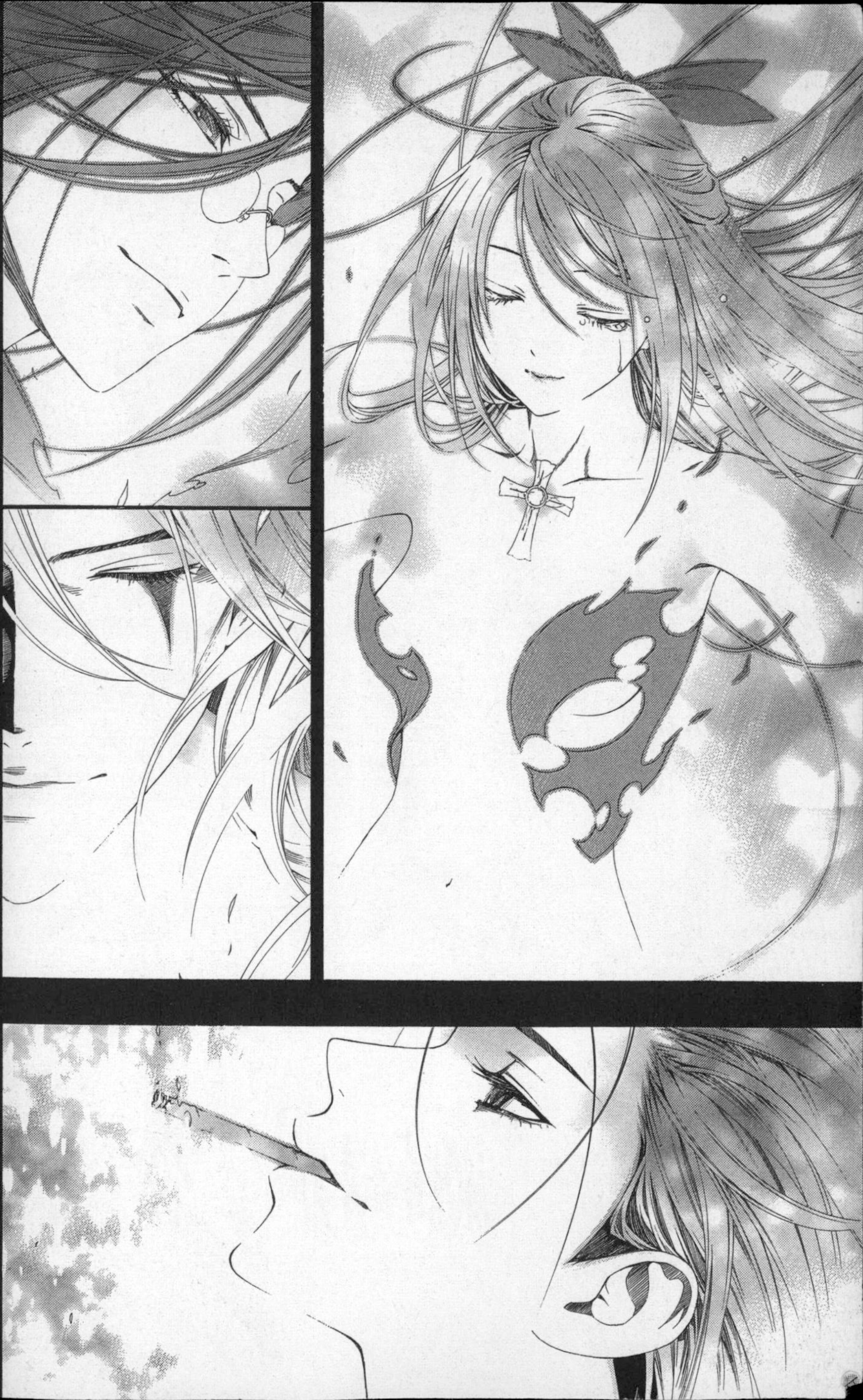

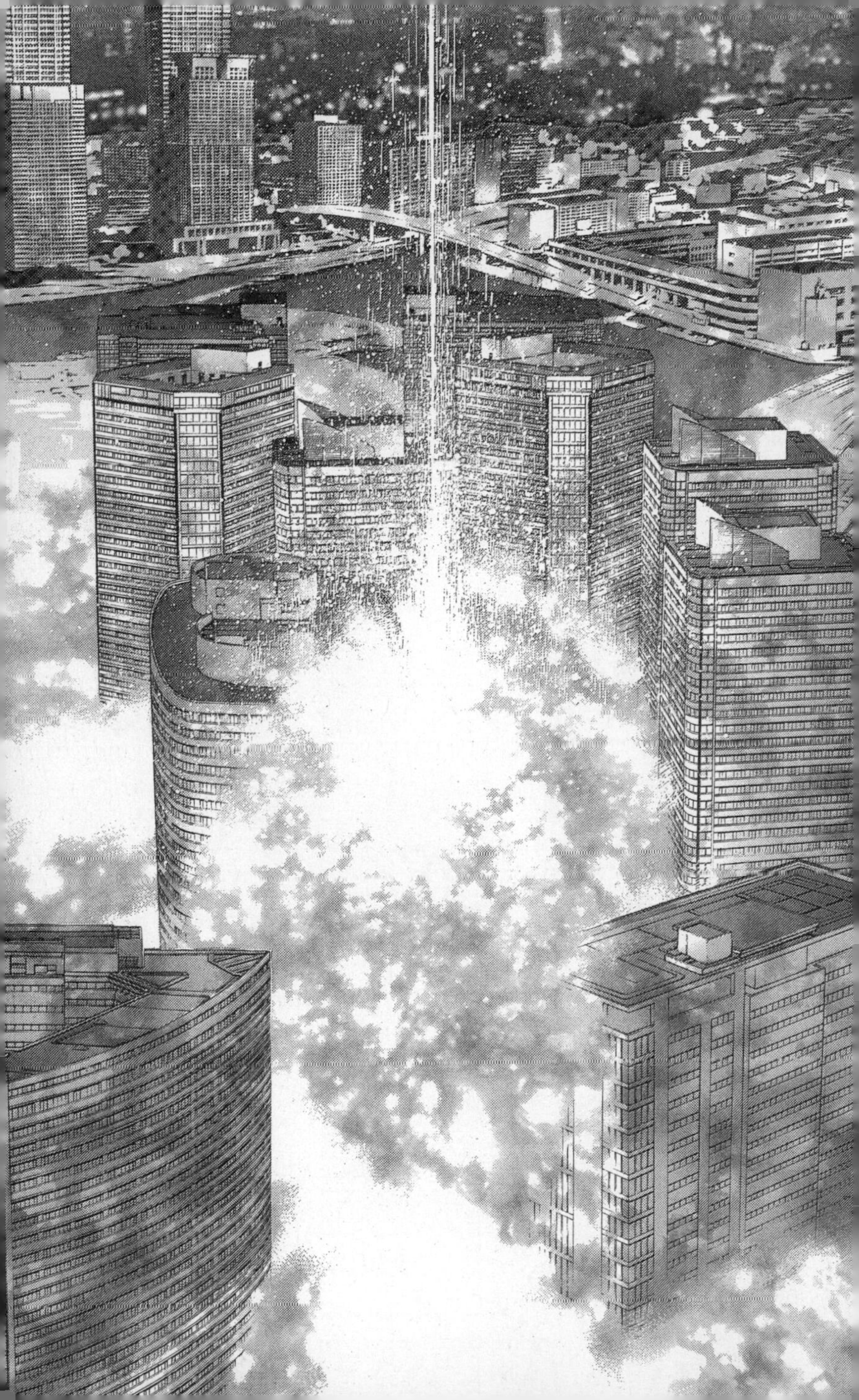

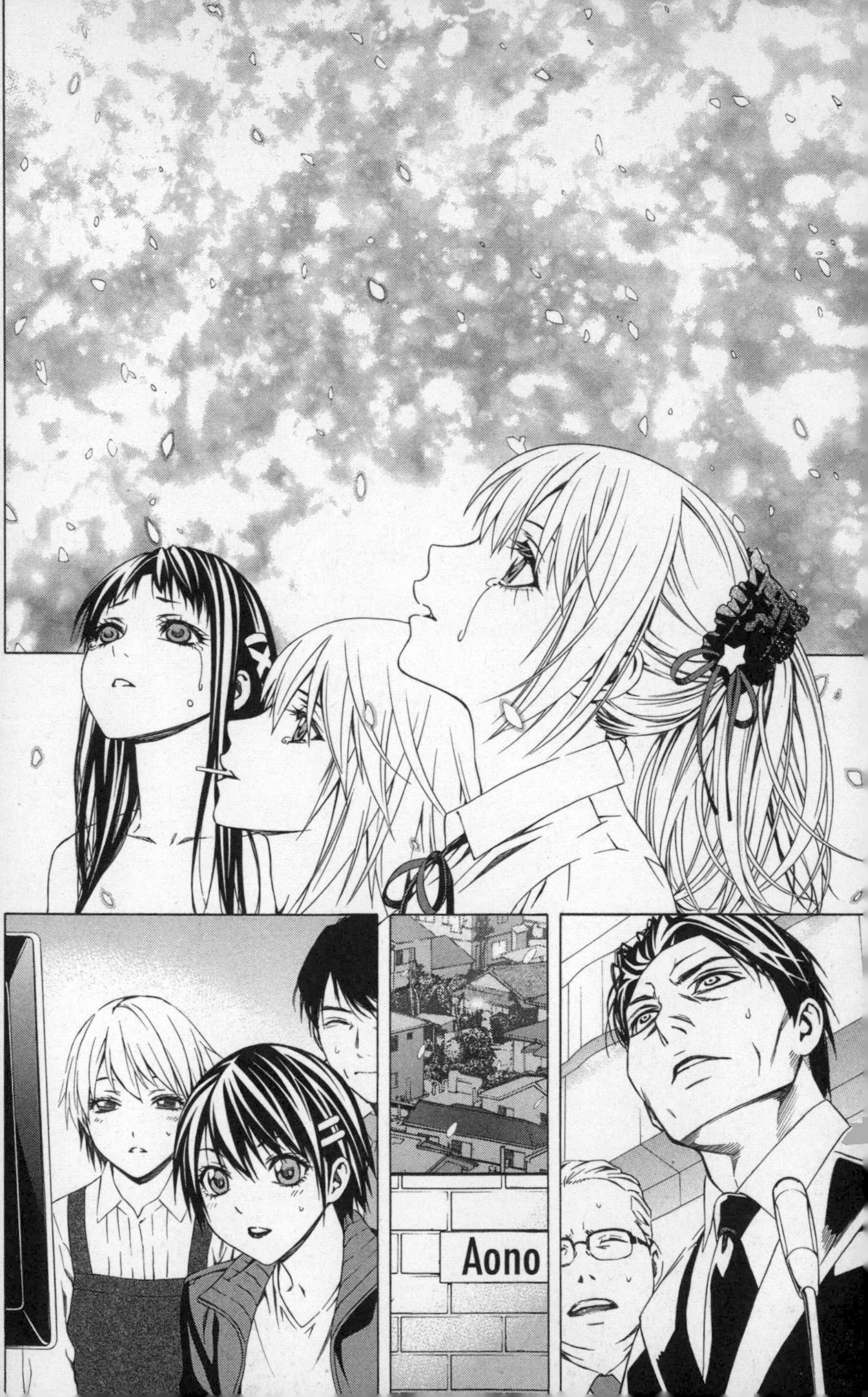
Aono

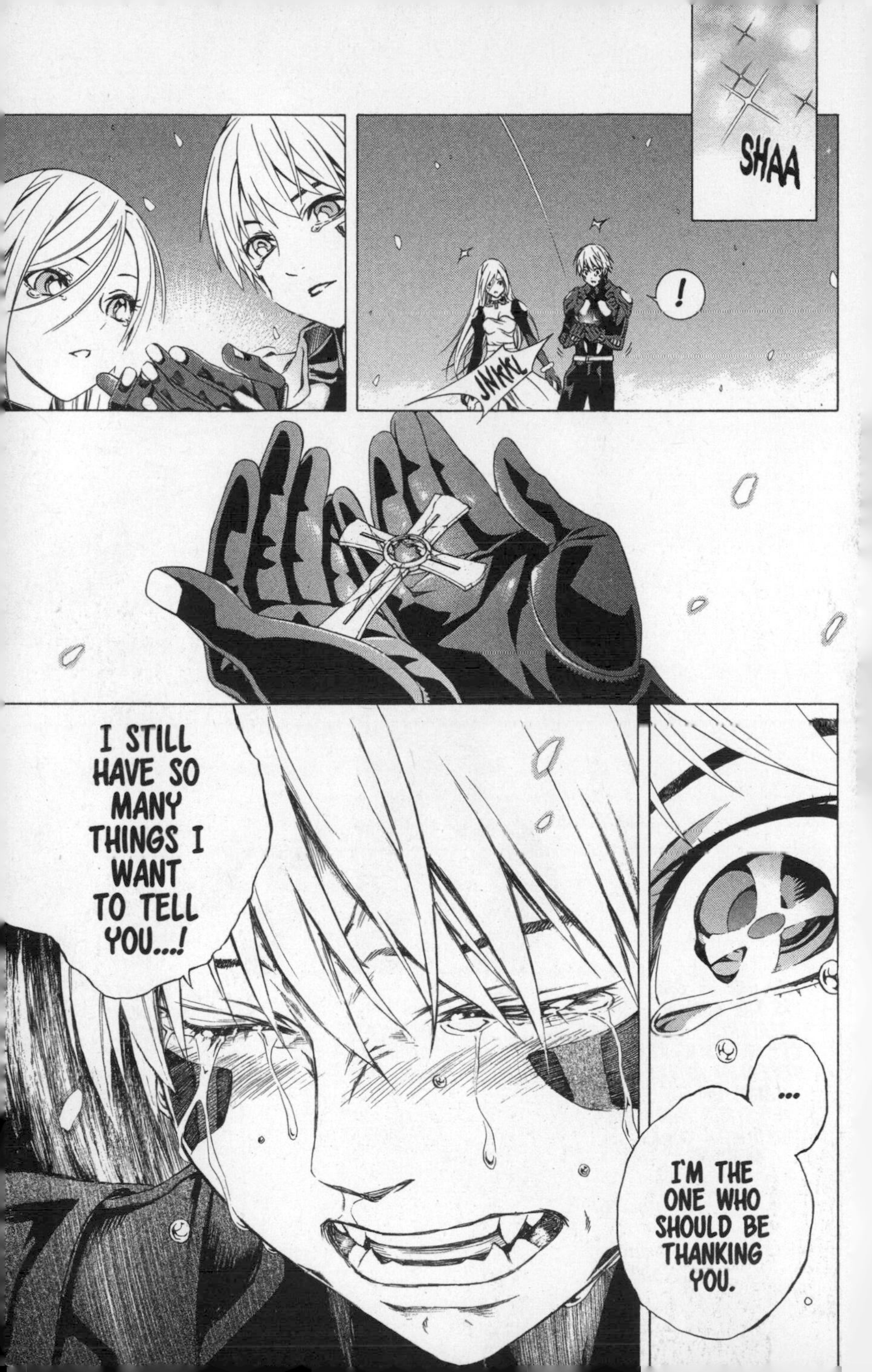
SHAA
!
JNKKL
...
I'M THE ONE WHO SHOULD BE THANKING YOU.
I STILL HAVE SO MANY THINGS I WANT TO TELL YOU...!

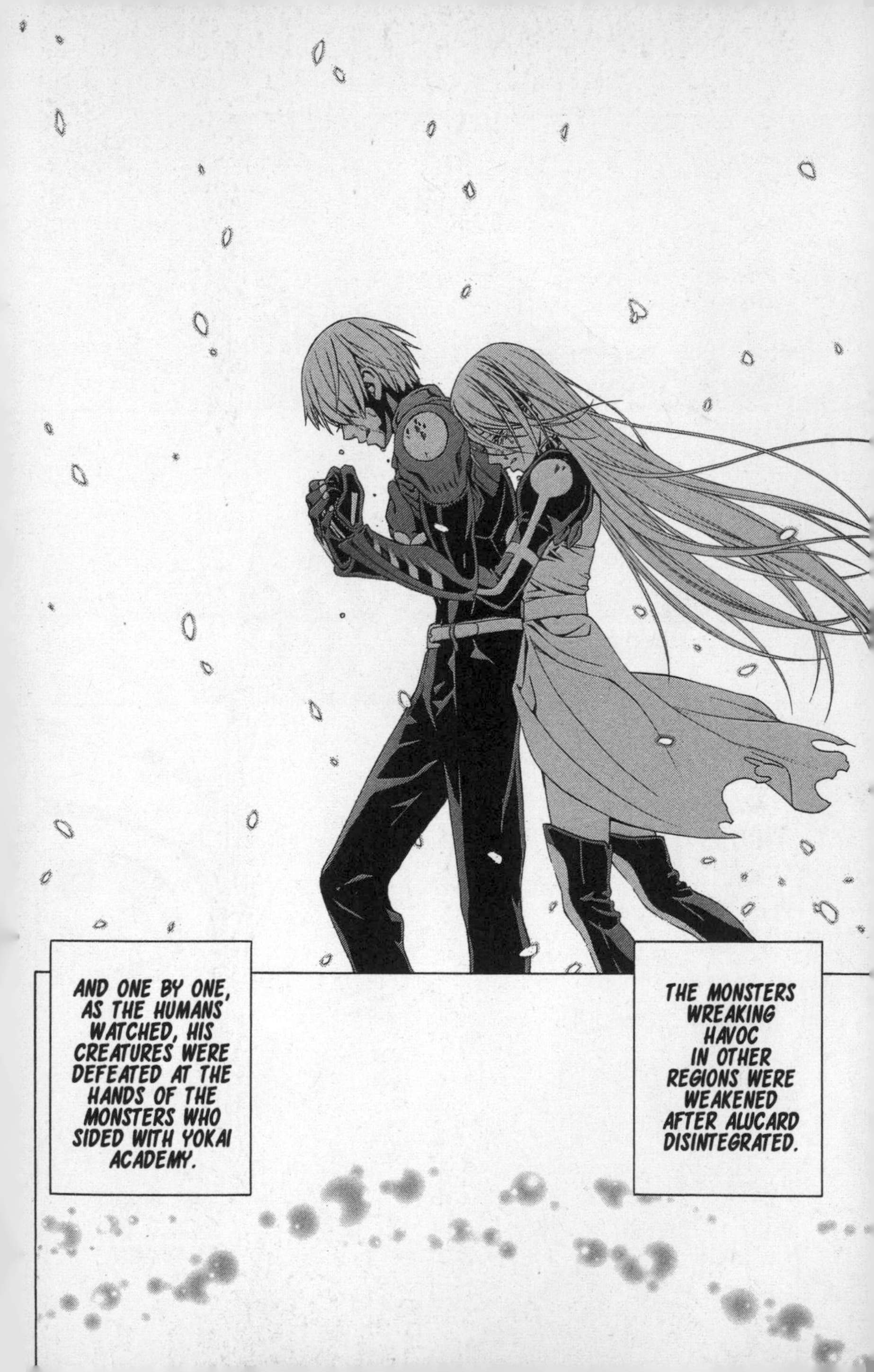
THE MONSTERS WREAKING HAVOC IN OTHER REGIONS WERE WEAKENED AFTER ALUCARD DISINTEGRATED.
AND ONE BY ONE, AS THE HUMANS WATCHED, HIS CREATURES WERE DEFEATED AT THE HANDS OF THE MONSTERS WHO SIDED WITH YOKAI ACADEMY.

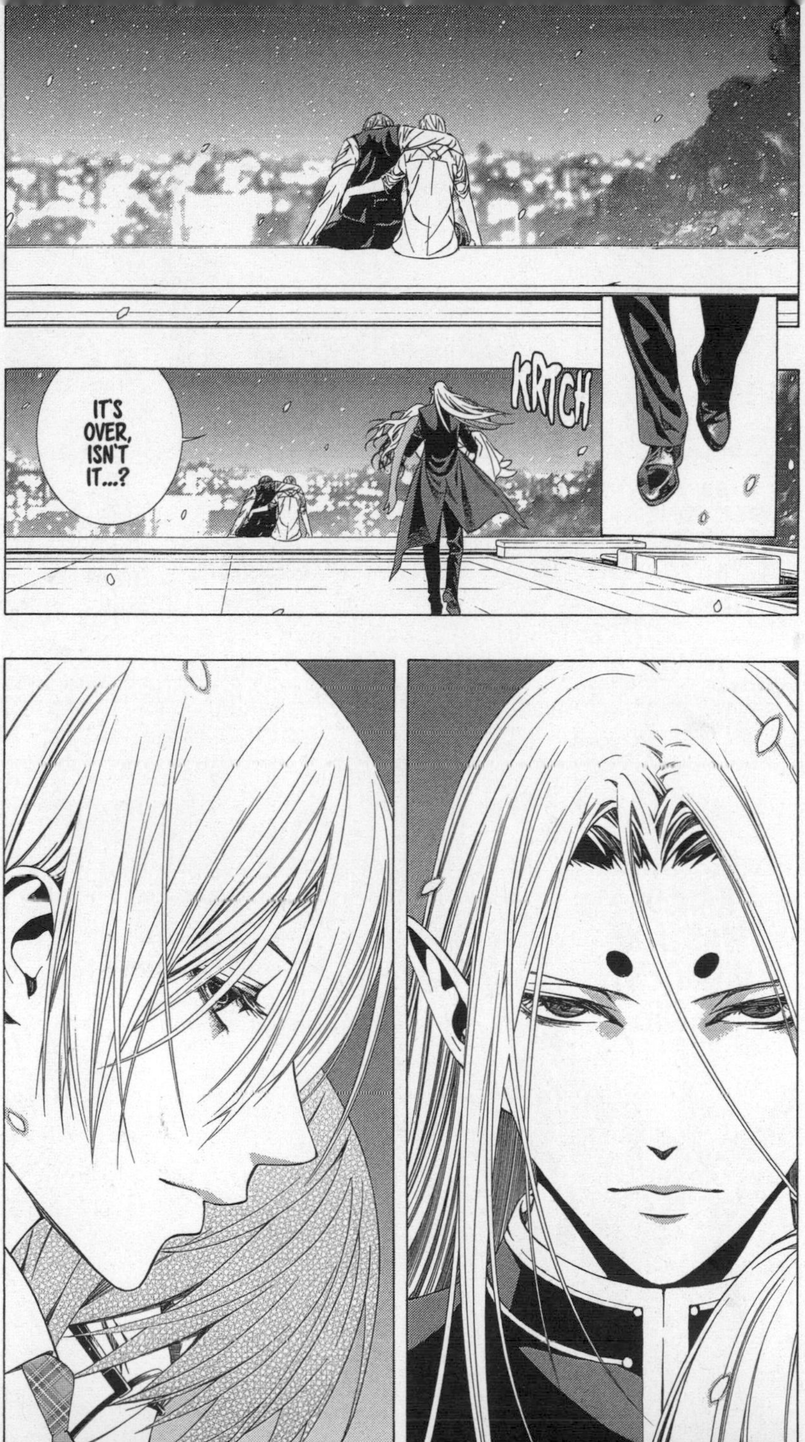
KRTCH
IT'S OVER, ISN'T IT...?

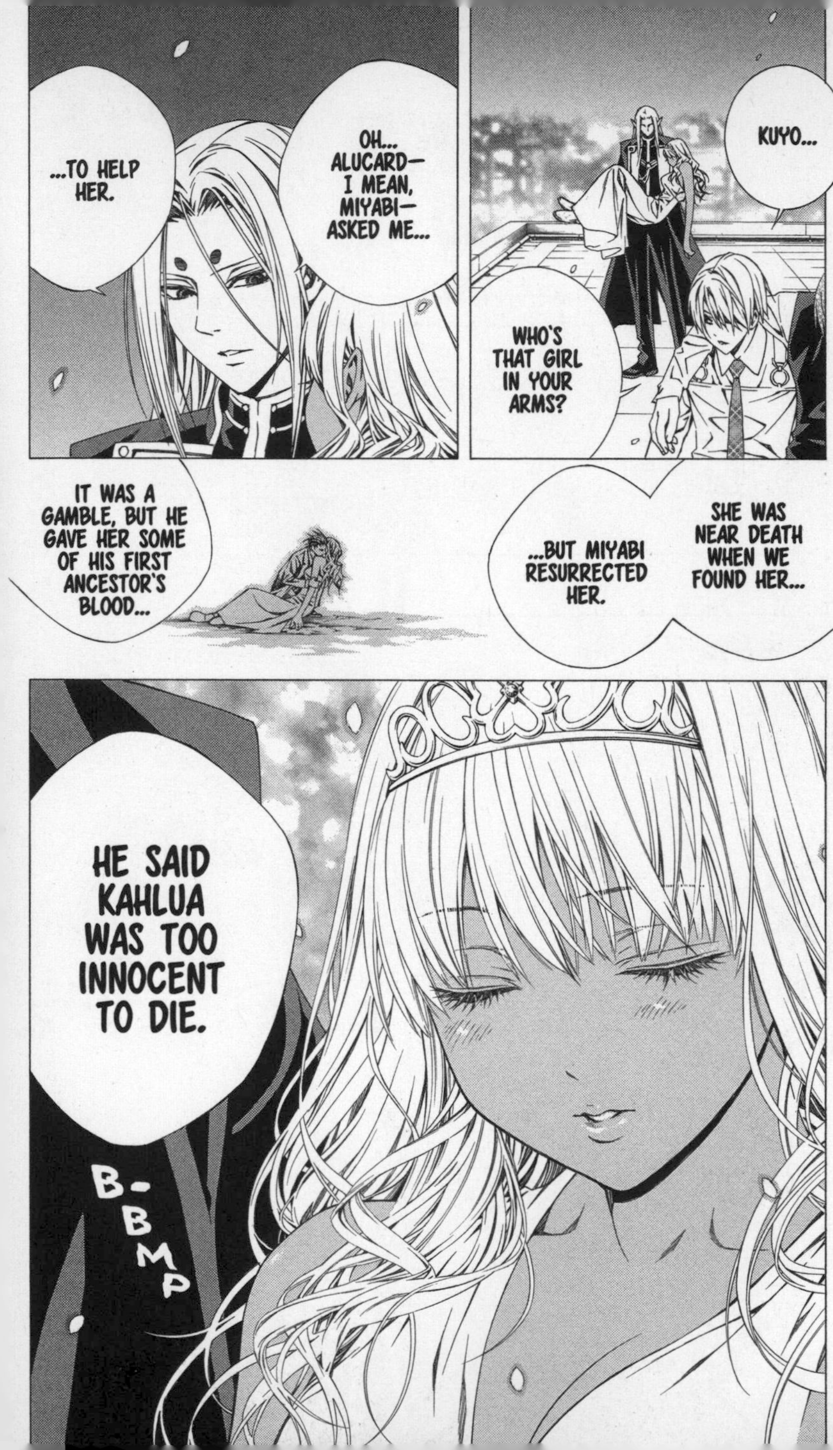
KUYO...
WHO'S THAT GIRL IN YOUR ARMS?
OH... ALUCARD— I MEAN, MIYABI— ASKED ME...
...TO HELP HER.
SHE WAS NEAR DEATH WHEN WE FOUND HER...
...BUT MIYABI RESURRECTED HER.
IT WAS A GAMBLE, BUT HE GAVE HER SOME OF HIS FIRST ANCESTOR'S BLOOD...
HE SAID KAHLUA WAS TOO INNOCENT TO DIE.
B-BMP

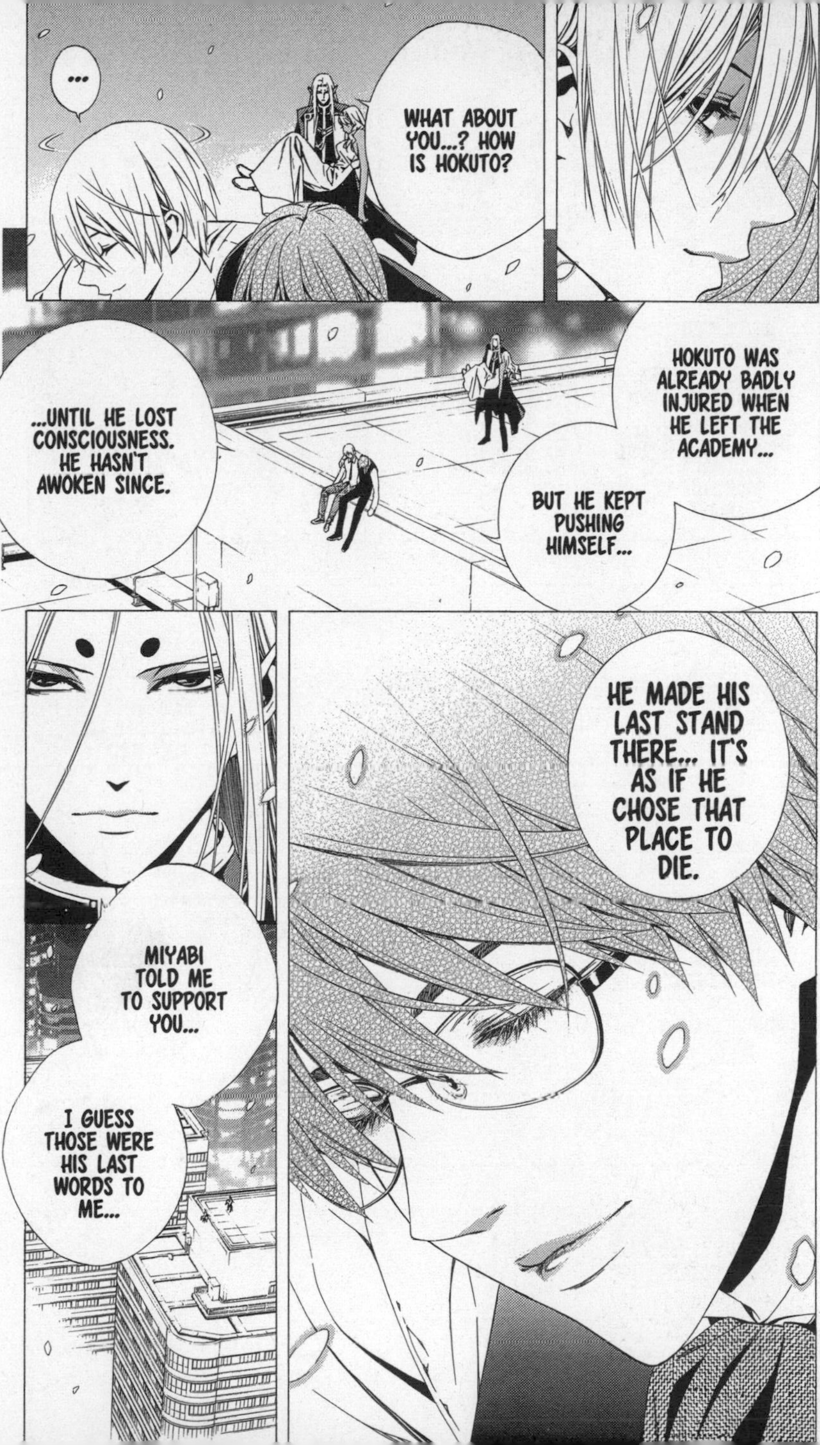
WHAT ABOUT YOU...? HOW IS HOKUTO?
...
HOKUTO WAS ALREADY BADLY INJURED WHEN HE LEFT THE ACADEMY...
BUT HE KEPT PUSHING HIMSELF...
...UNTIL HE LOST CONSCIOUSNESS. HE HASN'T AWOKEN SINCE.
HE MADE HIS LAST STAND THERE... IT'S AS IF HE CHOSE THAT PLACE TO DIE.
MIYABI TOLD ME TO SUPPORT YOU...
I GUESS THOSE WERE HIS LAST WORDS TO ME...

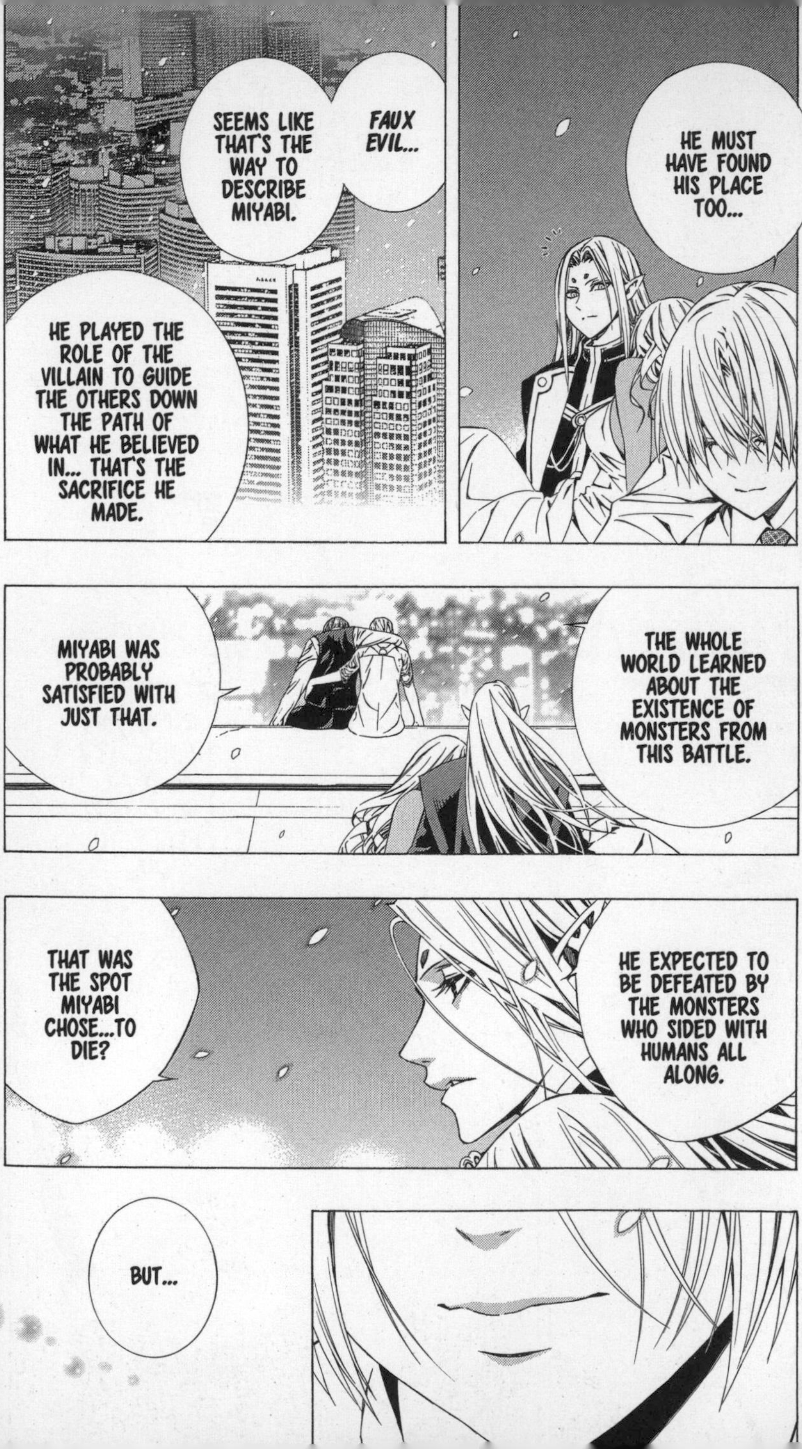
HE MUST HAVE FOUND HIS PLACE TOO...
FAUX EVIL...
SEEMS LIKE THAT'S THE WAY TO DESCRIBE MIYABI.
HE PLAYED THE ROLE OF THE VILLAIN TO GUIDE THE OTHERS DOWN THE PATH OF WHAT HE BELIEVED IN... THAT'S THE SACRIFICE HE MADE.
THE WHOLE WORLD LEARNED ABOUT THE EXISTENCE OF MONSTERS FROM THIS BATTLE.
MIYABI WAS PROBABLY SATISFIED WITH JUST THAT.
HE EXPECTED TO BE DEFEATED BY THE MONSTERS WHO SIDED WITH HUMANS ALL ALONG.
THAT WAS THE SPOT MIYABI CHOSE...TO DIE?
BUT...

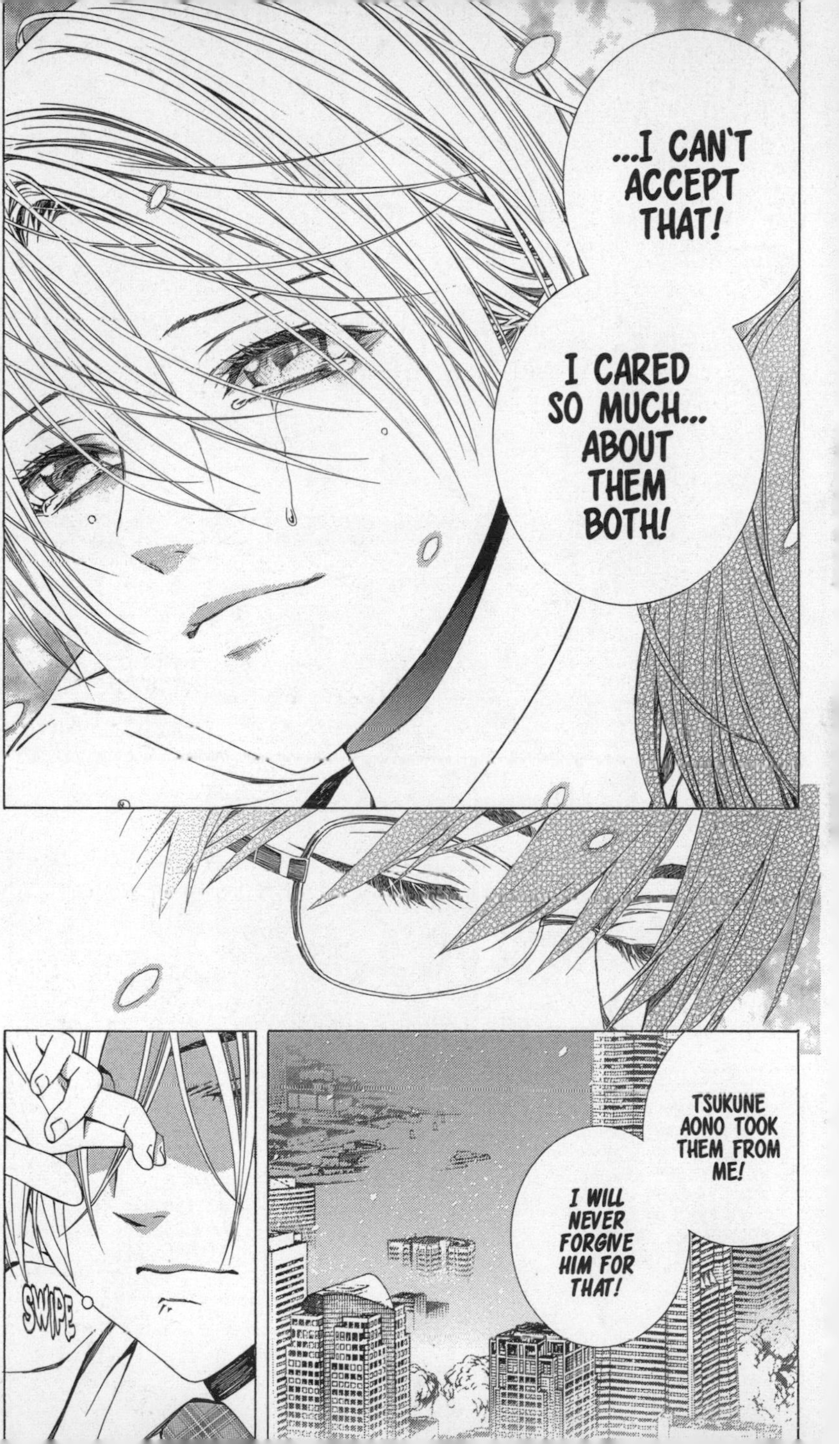
...I CAN'T ACCEPT THAT!
I CARED SO MUCH... ABOUT THEM BOTH!
TSUKUNE AONO TOOK THEM FROM ME!
I WILL NEVER FORGIVE HIM FOR THAT!
SWIPE

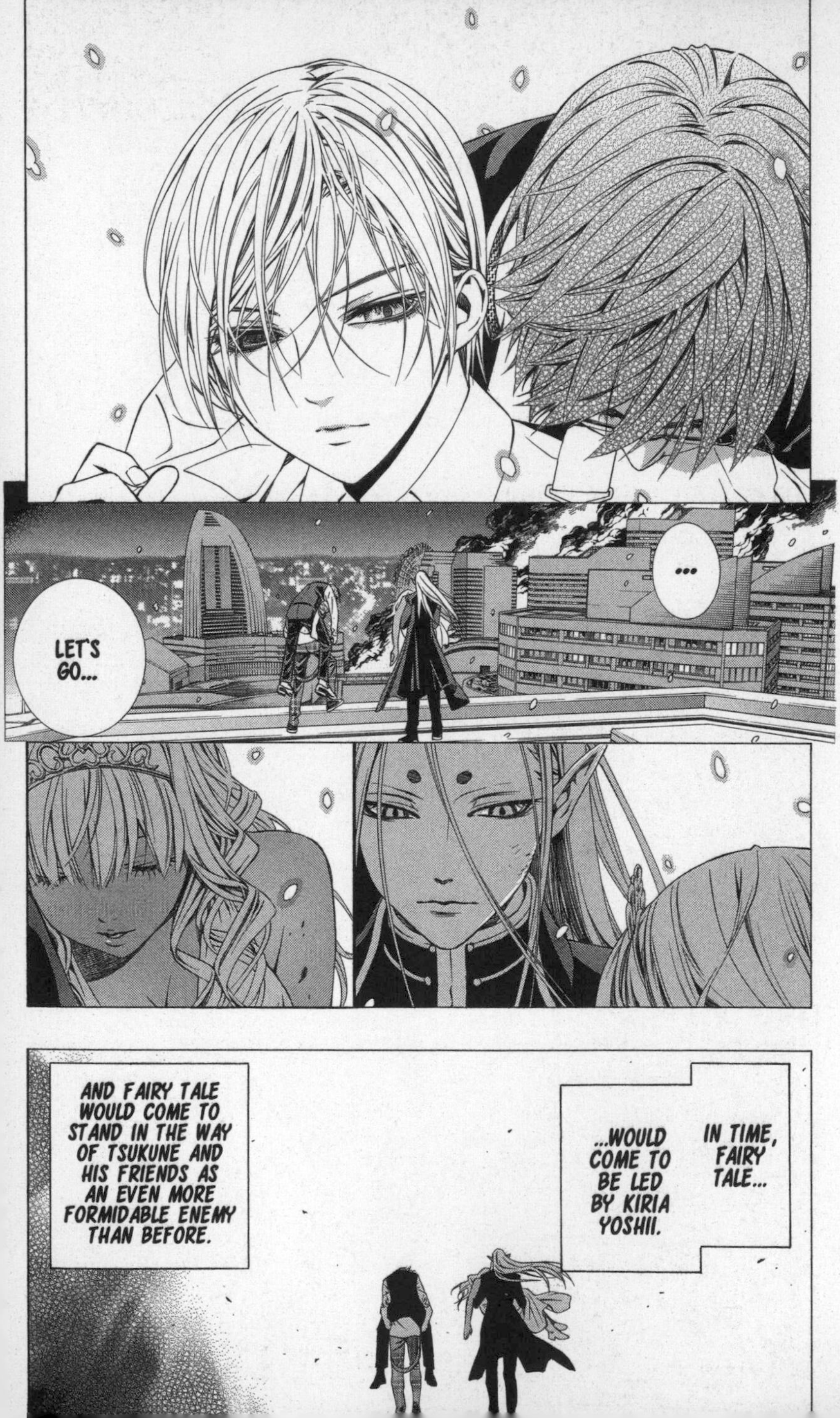
...
LET'S GO...
IN TIME, FAIRY TALE...
...WOULD COME TO BE LED BY KIRIA YOSHII.
AND FAIRY TALE WOULD COME TO STAND IN THE WAY OF TSUKUNE AND HIS FRIENDS AS AN EVEN MORE FORMIDABLE ENEMY THAN BEFORE.

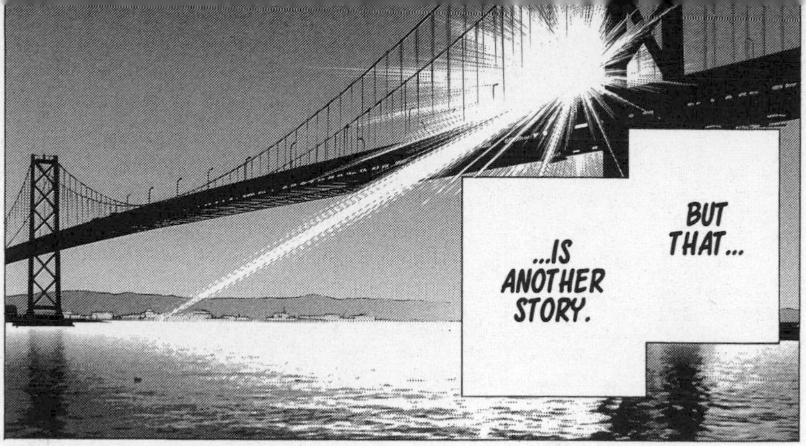
BUT THAT...
...IS ANOTHER STORY.

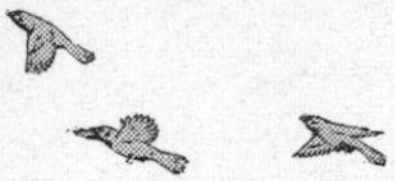

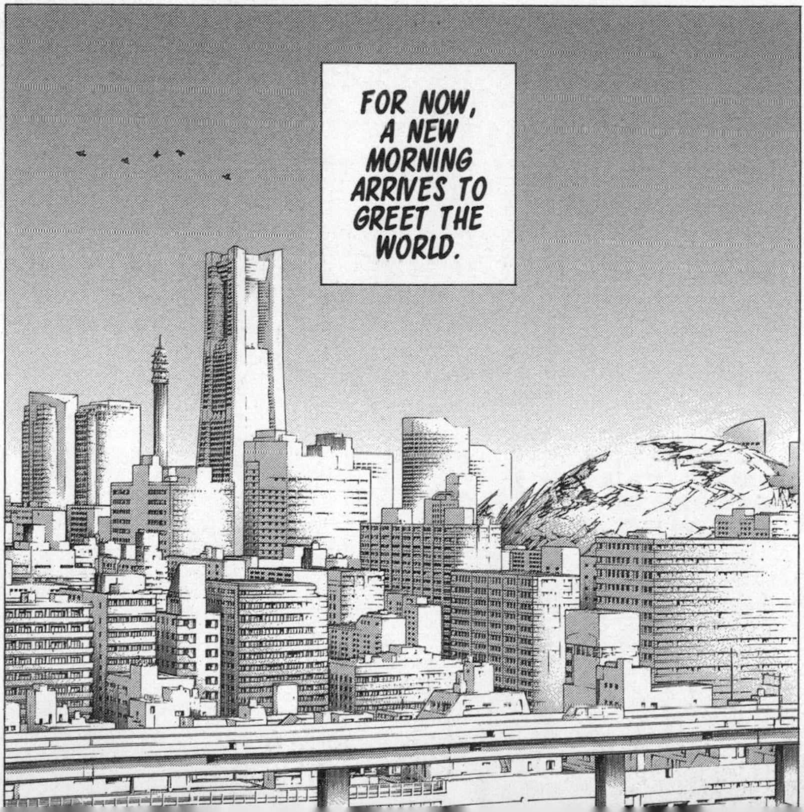
FOR NOW, A NEW MORNING ARRIVES TO GREET THE WORLD.

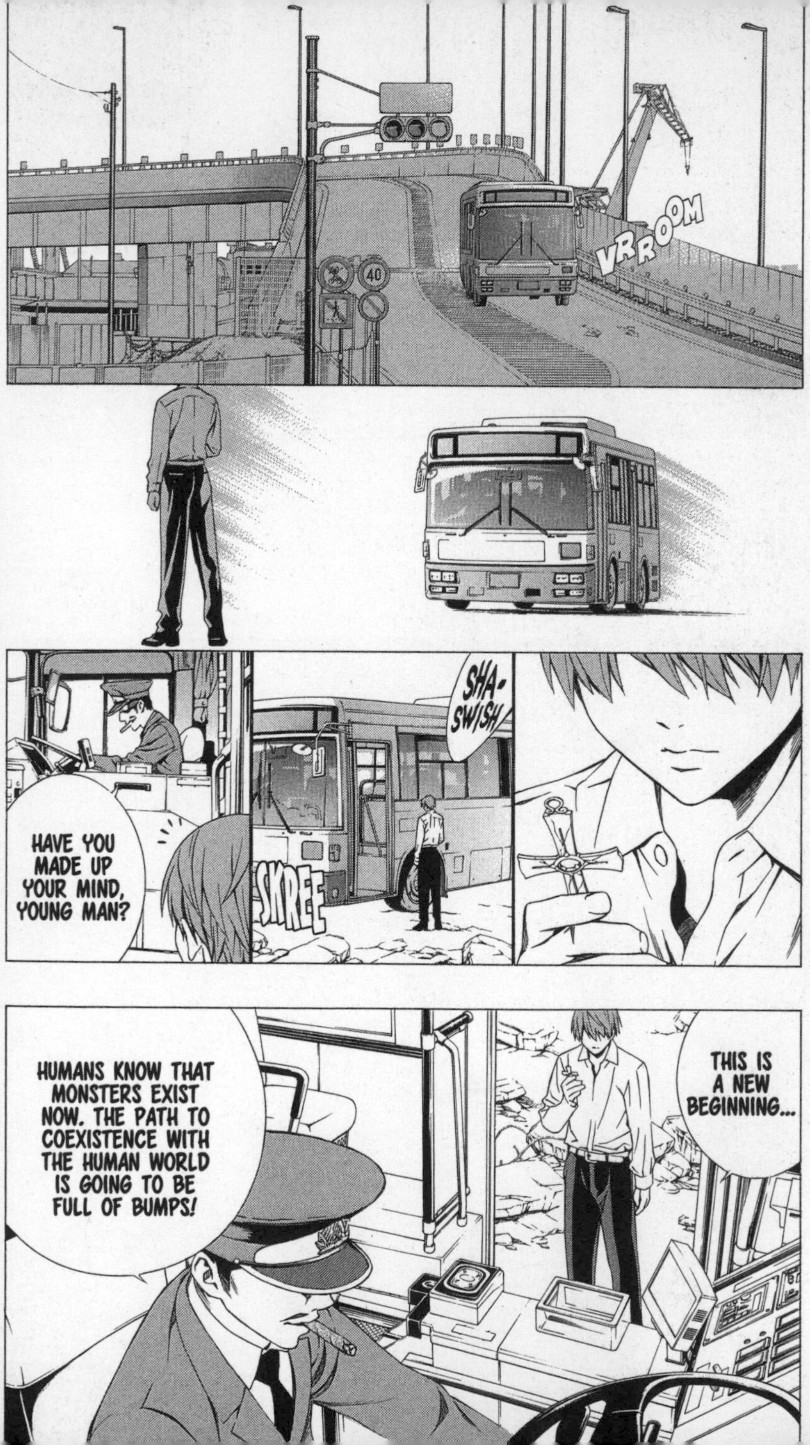
VRROOM
SHA-SWISH
SKREE
HAVE YOU MADE UP YOUR MIND, YOUNG MAN?
THIS IS A NEW BEGINNING...
HUMANS KNOW THAT MONSTERS EXIST NOW. THE PATH TO COEXISTENCE WITH THE HUMAN WORLD IS GOING TO BE FULL OF BUMPS!

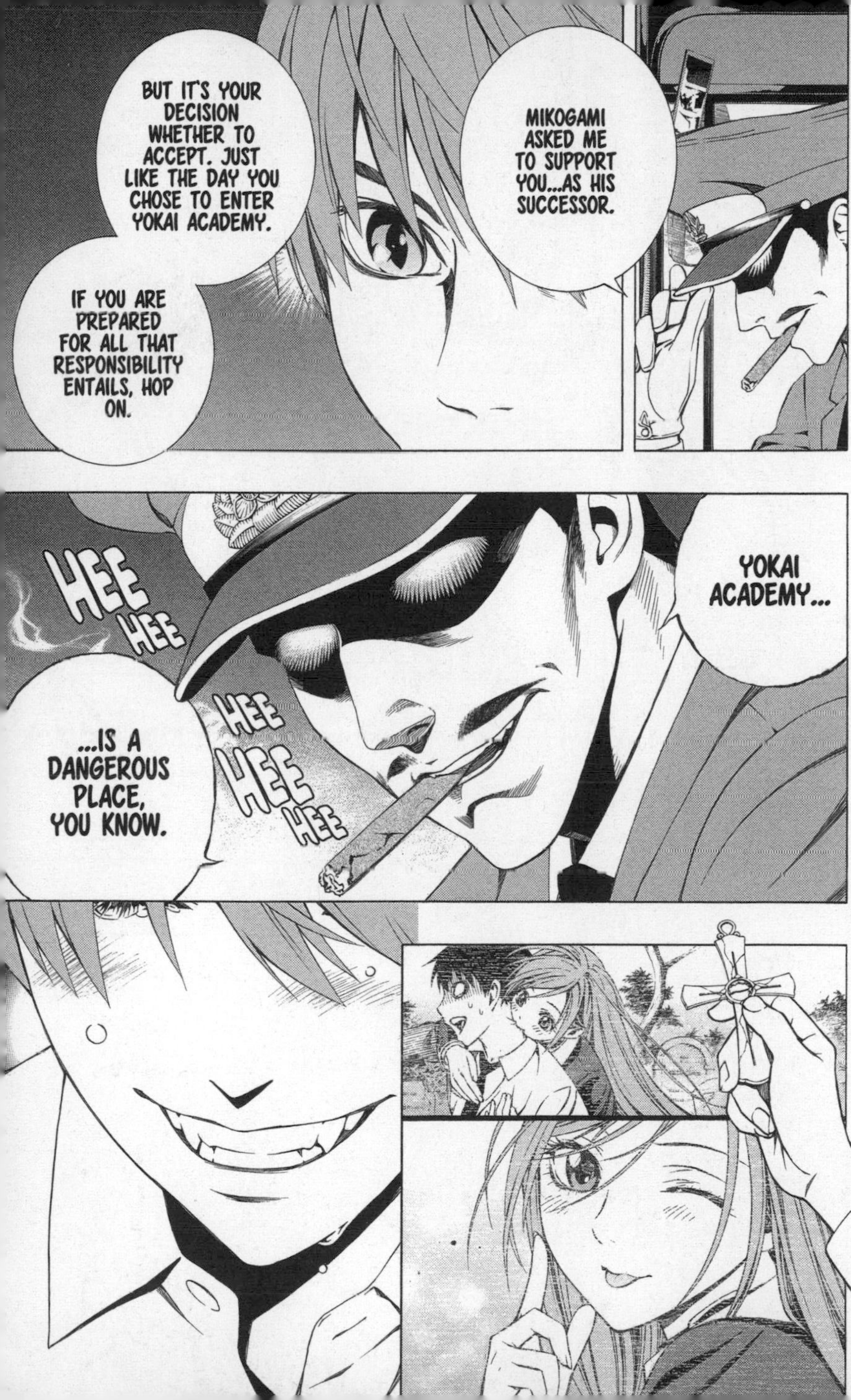
MIKOGAMI ASKED ME TO SUPPORT YOU...AS HIS SUCCESSOR.
BUT IT'S YOUR DECISION WHETHER TO ACCEPT. JUST LIKE THE DAY YOU CHOSE TO ENTER YOKAI ACADEMY.
IF YOU ARE PREPARED FOR ALL THAT RESPONSIBILITY ENTAILS, HOP ON.
YOKAI ACADEMY...
HEE HEE
HEE HEE HEE
...IS A DANGEROUS PLACE, YOU KNOW.

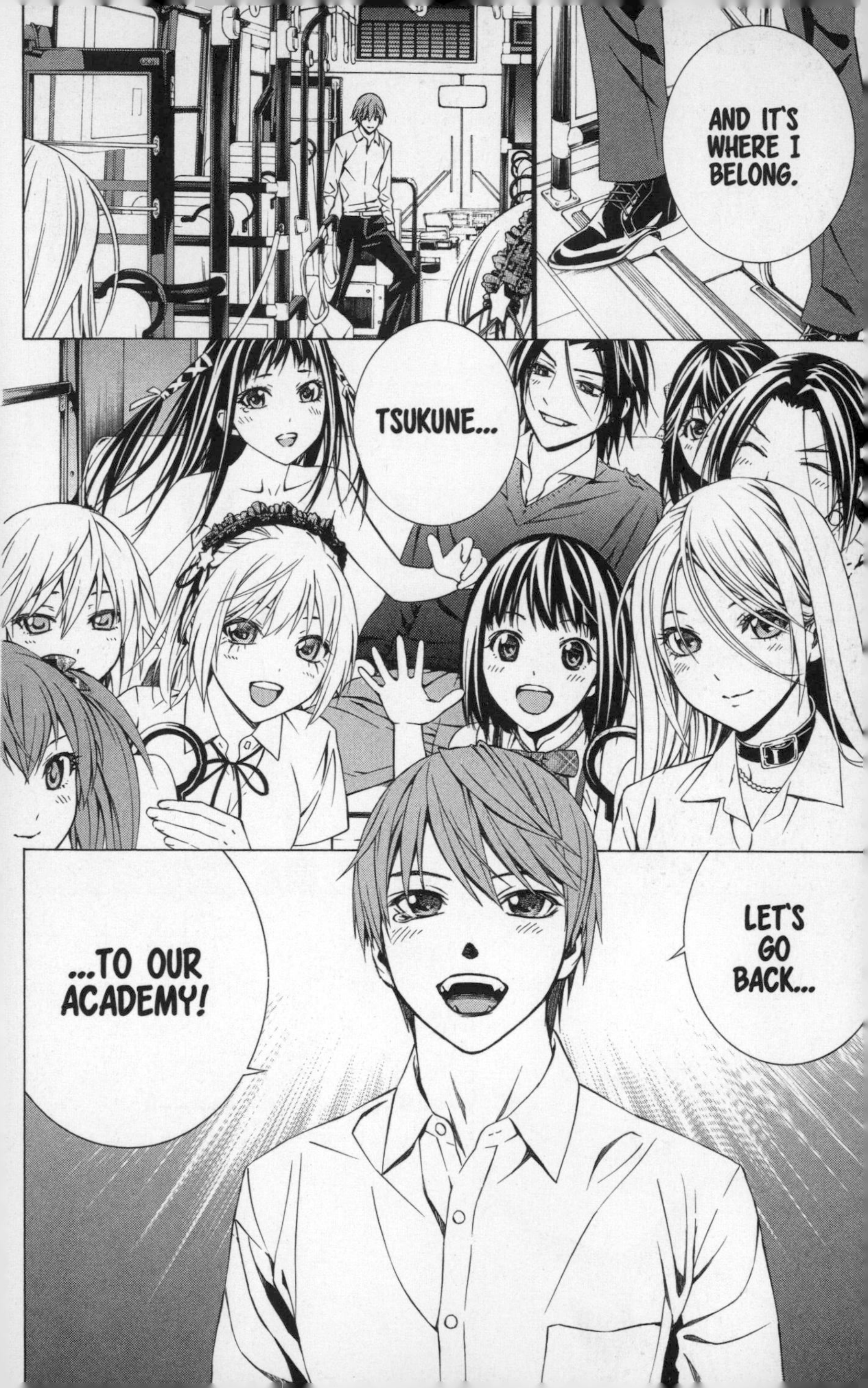
AND IT'S WHERE I BELONG.
TSUKUNE...
LET'S GO BACK...
...TO OUR ACADEMY!

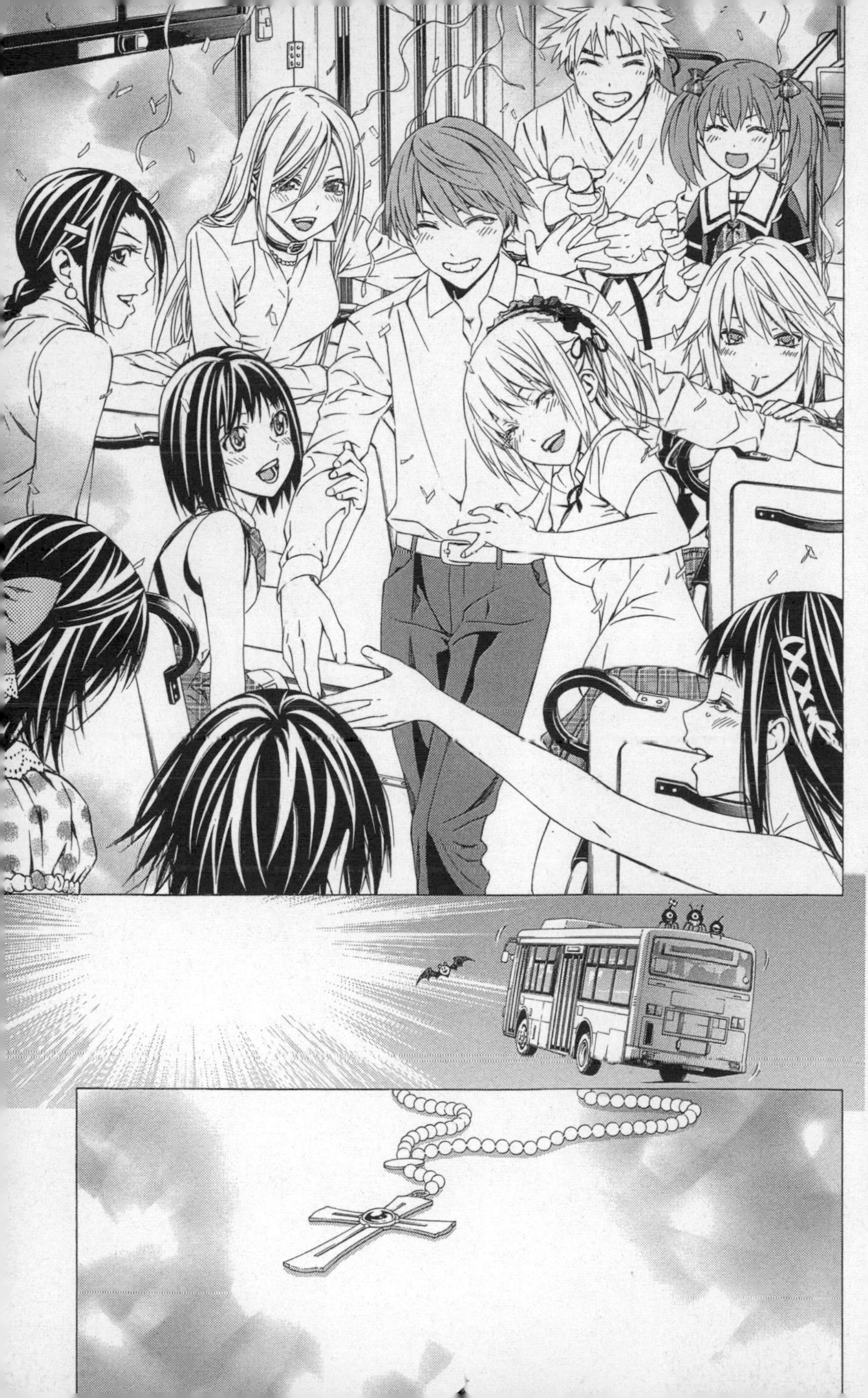

66.6: Epilogue

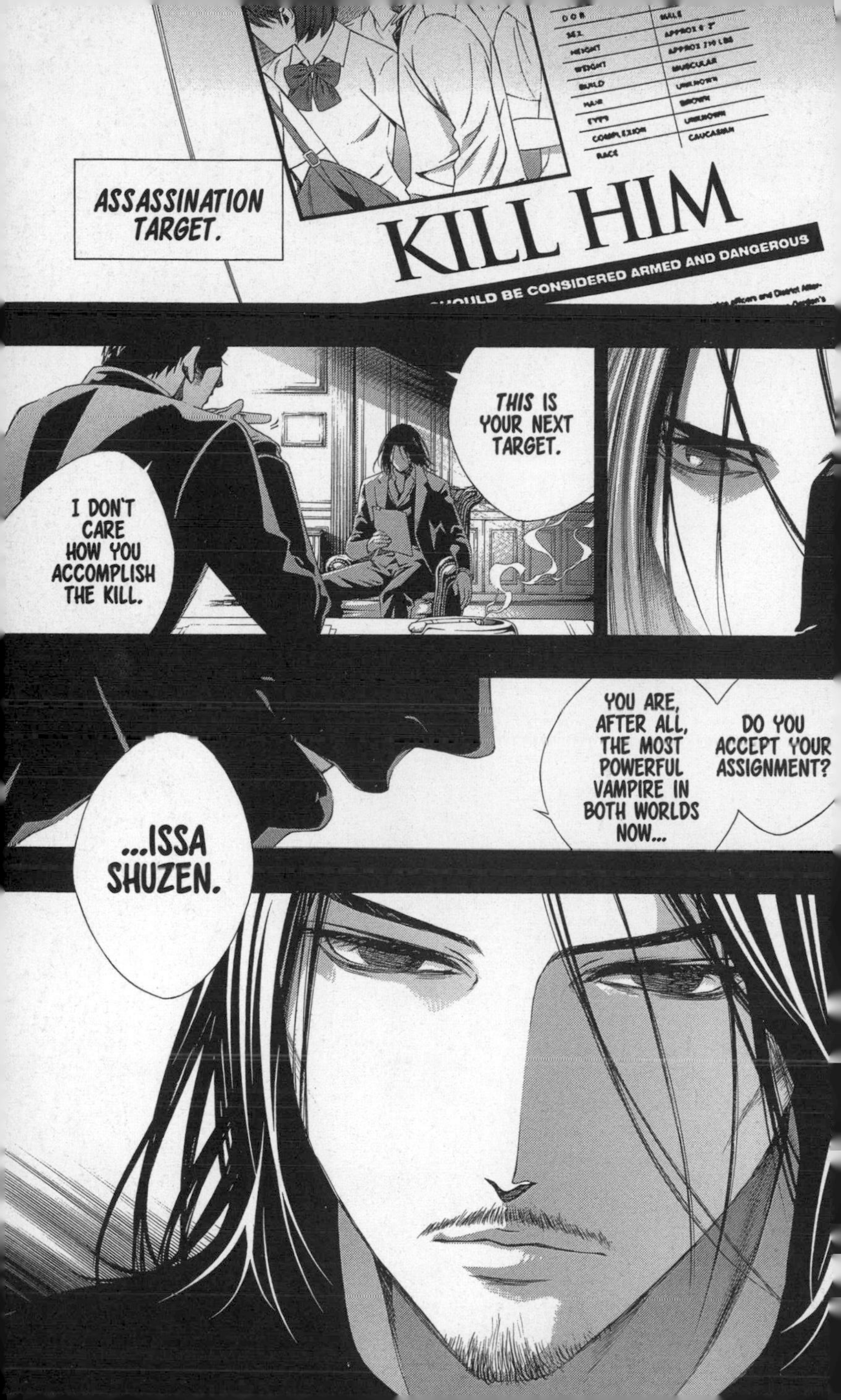
KILL HIM
BE CONSIDERED ARMED AND DANGEROUS
ASSASSINATION TARGET.
THIS IS YOUR NEXT TARGET.
I DON'T CARE HOW YOU ACCOMPLISH THE KILL.
DO YOU ACCEPT YOUR ASSIGNMENT?
YOU ARE, AFTER ALL, THE MOST POWERFUL VAMPIRE IN BOTH WORLDS NOW...
...ISSA SHUZEN.

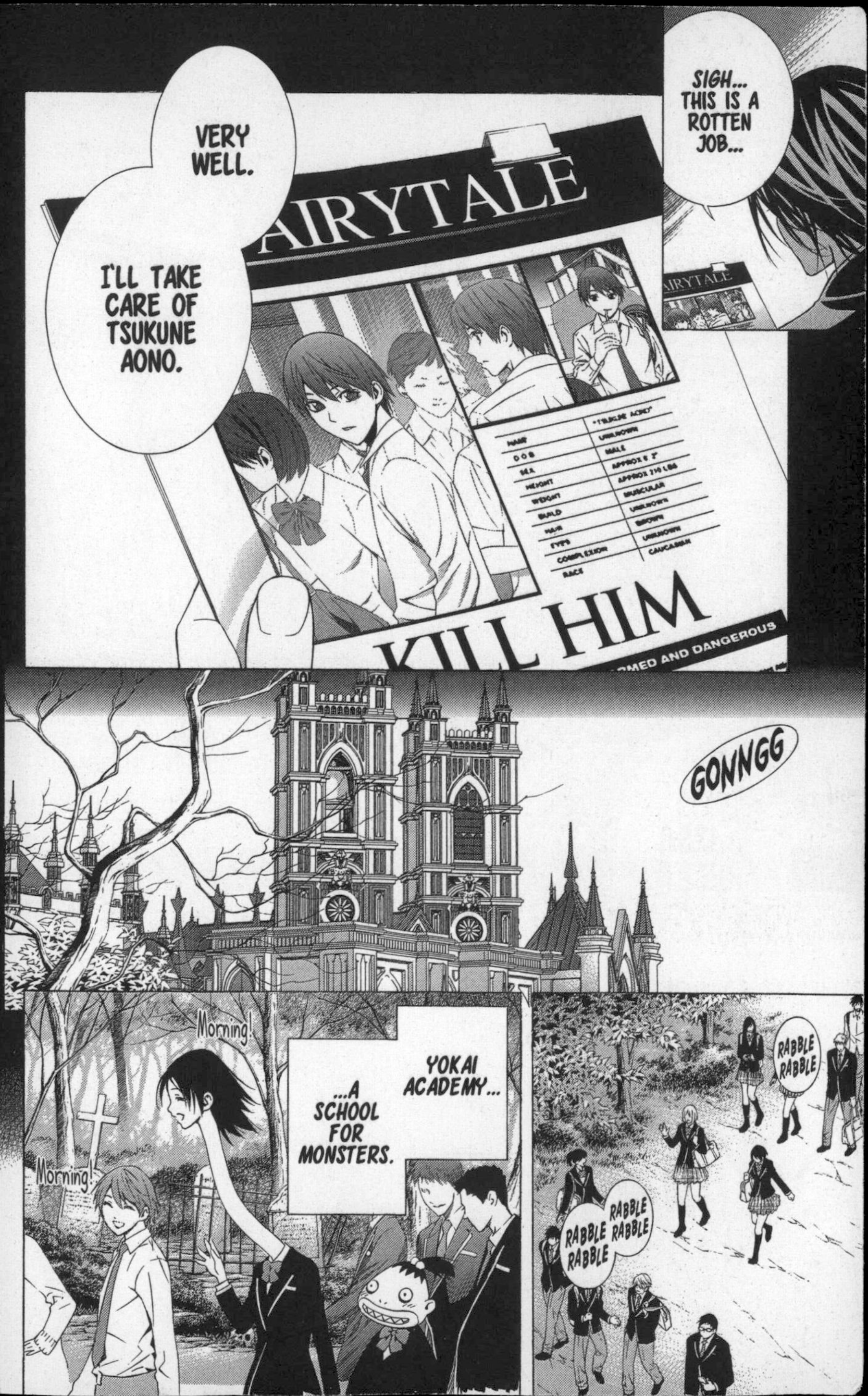
SIGH... THIS IS A ROTTEN JOB...
AIRYTALE
VERY WELL.
I'LL TAKE CARE OF TSUKUNE AONO.
AIRYTALE
KILL HIM
RMED AND DANGEROUS
GONNGG
RABBLE RABBLE
RABBLE RABBLE
RABBLE RABBLE
YOKAI ACADEMY...
...A SCHOOL FOR MONSTERS.
Morning!
Morning!

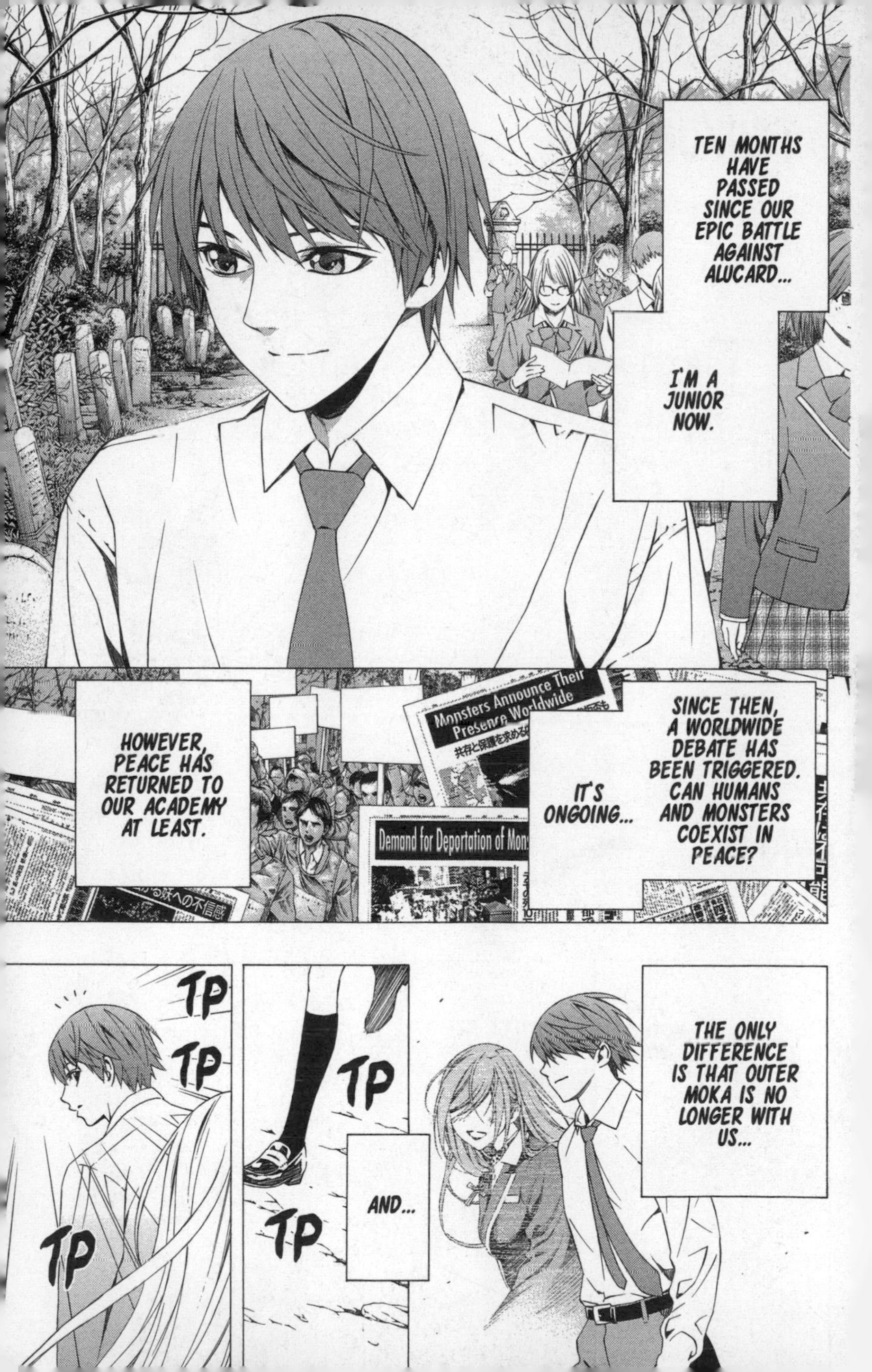
TEN MONTHS HAVE PASSED SINCE OUR EPIC BATTLE AGAINST ALUCARD...
I'M A JUNIOR NOW.
SINCE THEN, A WORLDWIDE DEBATE HAS BEEN TRIGGERED. CAN HUMANS AND MONSTERS COEXIST IN PEACE?
IT'S ONGOING...
Monsters Announce Their Presence Worldwide
共存と保護を求める
Demand for Deportation of Mons
HOWEVER, PEACE HAS RETURNED TO OUR ACADEMY AT LEAST.
THE ONLY DIFFERENCE IS THAT OUTER MOKA IS NO LONGER WITH US...
TP
TP
AND...
TP
TP
TP
TP

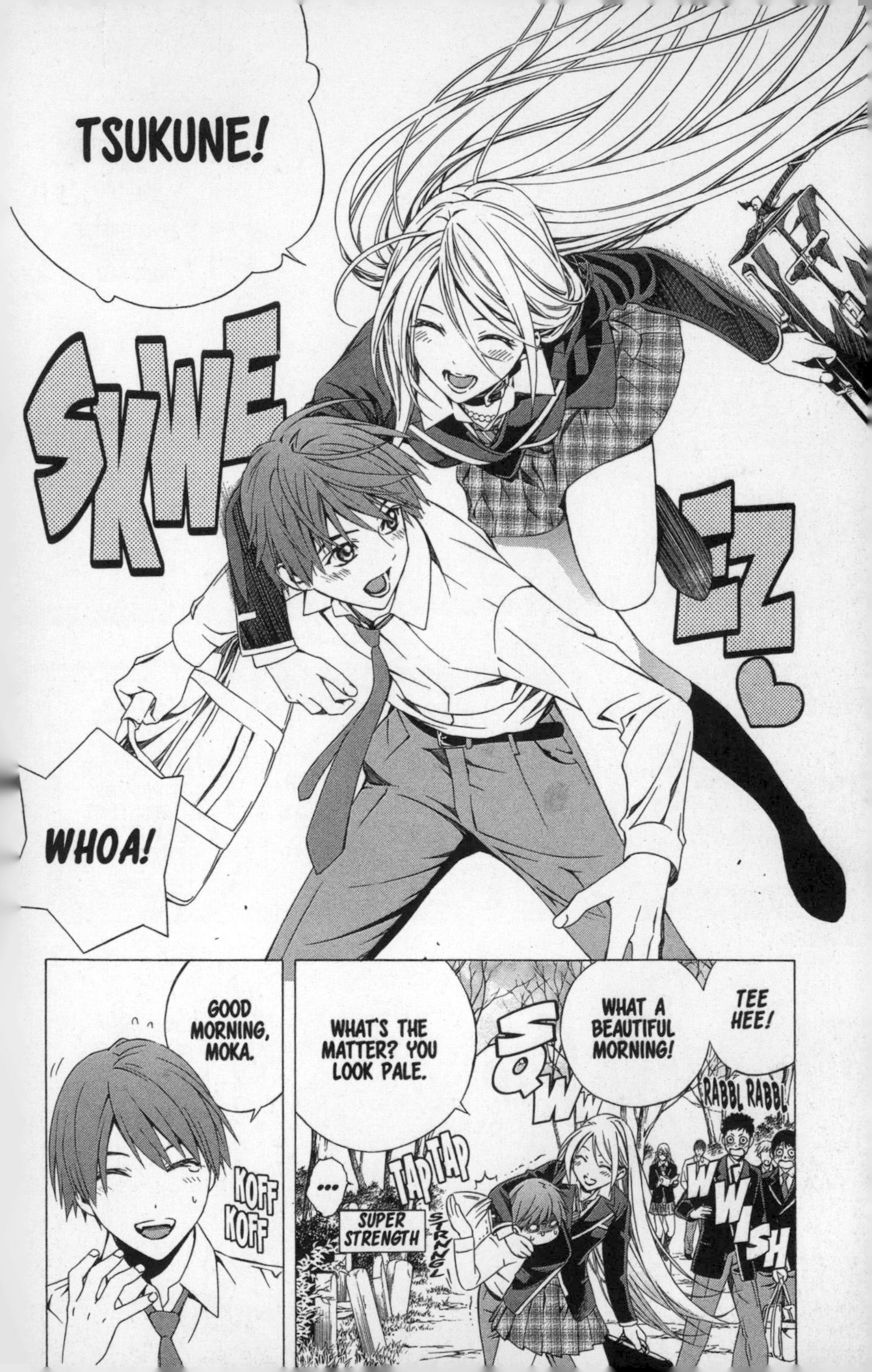
TSUKUNE!
SKWEEZ
WHOA!
TEE HEE!
WHAT A BEAUTIFUL MORNING!
RABBL RABBL
WHAT'S THE MATTER? YOU LOOK PALE.
TAP TAP
...
SUPER STRENGTH
STRNNGL
WWISH
GOOD MORNING, MOKA.
KOFF KOFF

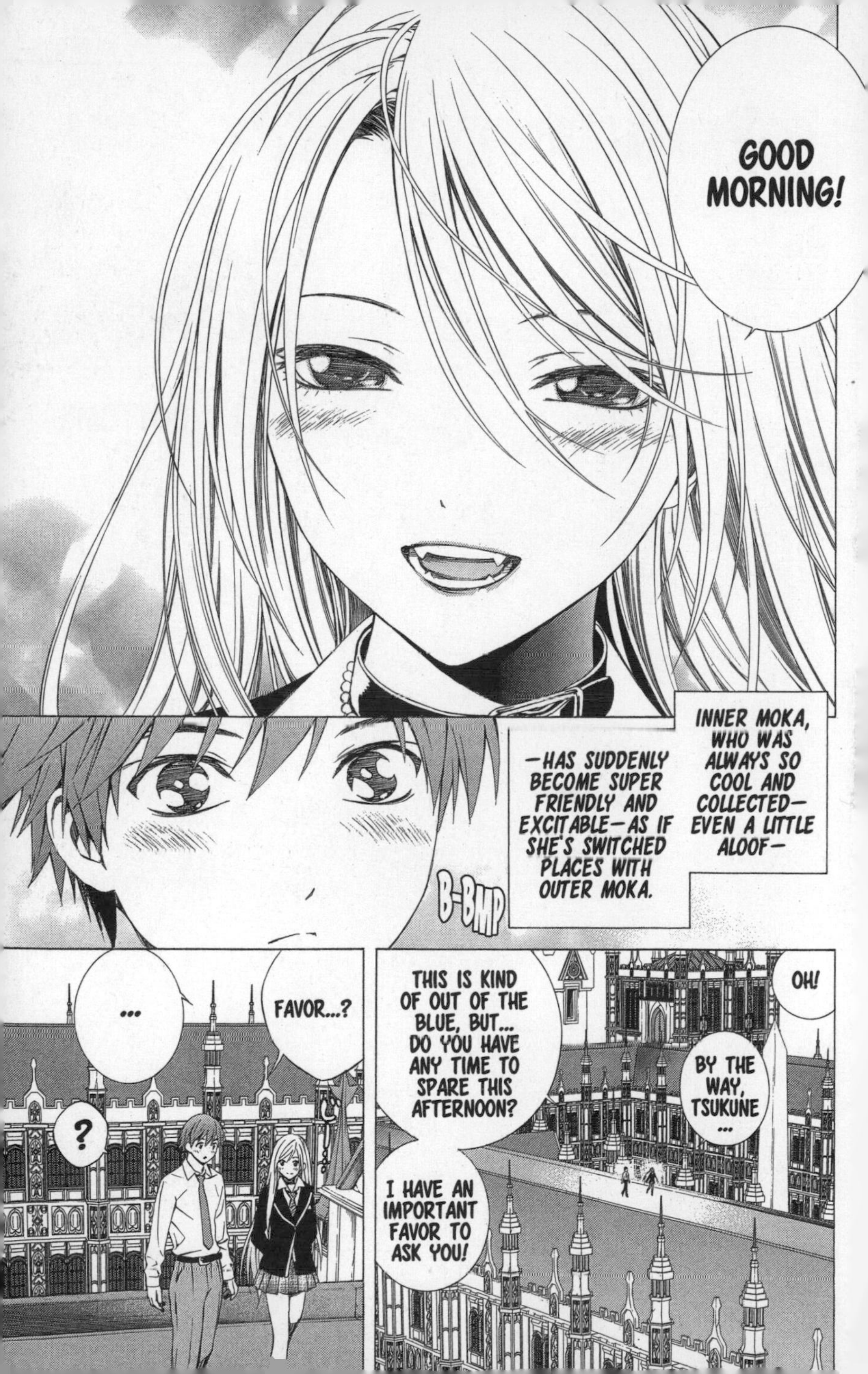
GOOD MORNING!
INNER MOKA, WHO WAS ALWAYS SO COOL AND COLLECTED—EVEN A LITTLE ALOOF—
—HAS SUDDENLY BECOME SUPER FRIENDLY AND EXCITABLE—AS IF SHE'S SWITCHED PLACES WITH OUTER MOKA.
B-BMP
OH!
BY THE WAY, TSUKUNE...
THIS IS KIND OF OUT OF THE BLUE, BUT... DO YOU HAVE ANY TIME TO SPARE THIS AFTERNOON?
I HAVE AN IMPORTANT FAVOR TO ASK YOU!
FAVOR...?
...
?

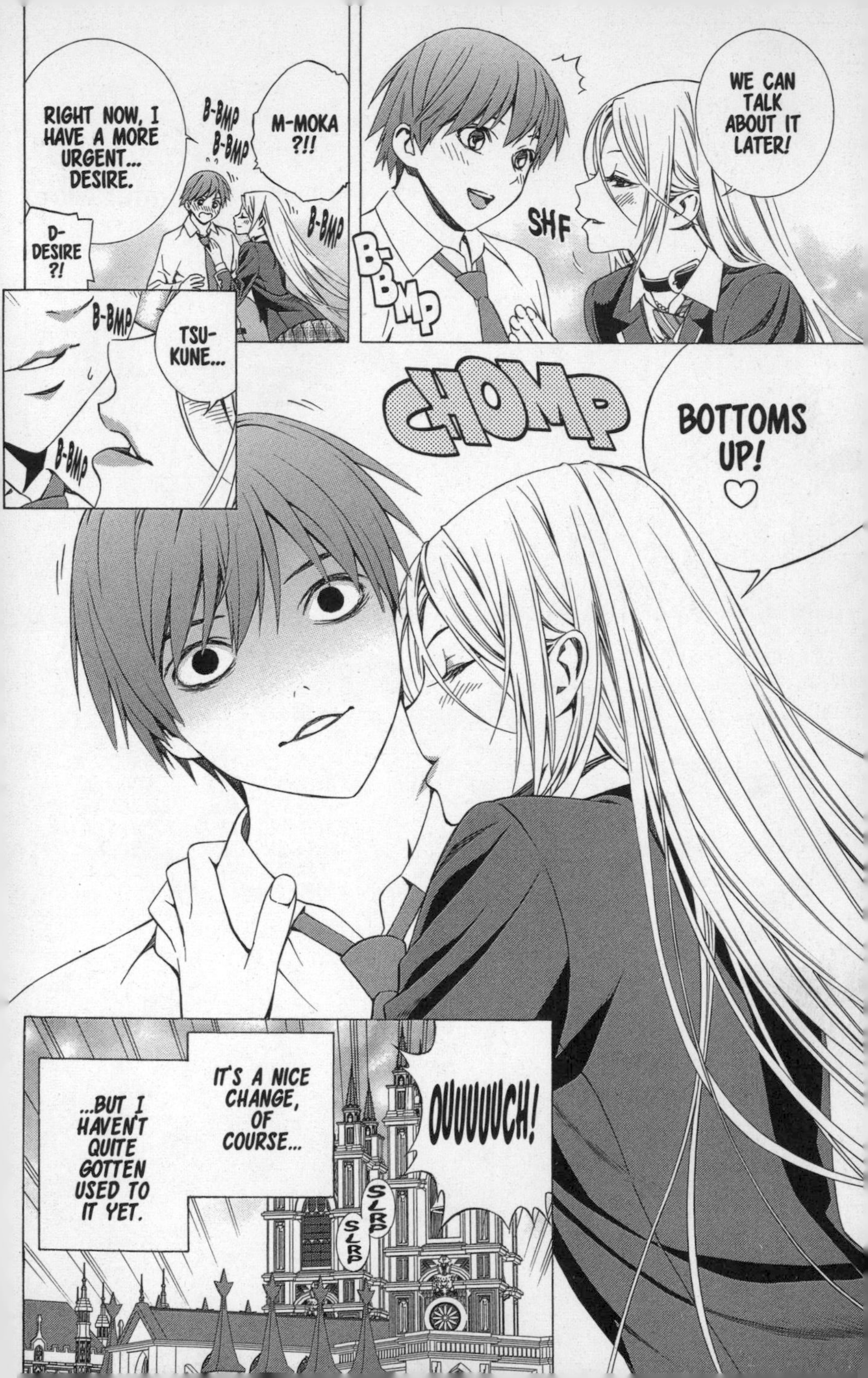
WE CAN TALK ABOUT IT LATER!
SHF
B-BMP
M-MOKA?!!
B-BMP B-BMP
RIGHT NOW, I HAVE A MORE URGENT... DESIRE.
B-BMP
D-DESIRE?!
TSU-KUNE...
B-BMP
B-BMP
BOTTOMS UP! ♡
CHOMP
OUUUUUCH!
IT'S A NICE CHANGE, OF COURSE...
...BUT I HAVEN'T QUITE GOTTEN USED TO IT YET.
SLRP
SLRP

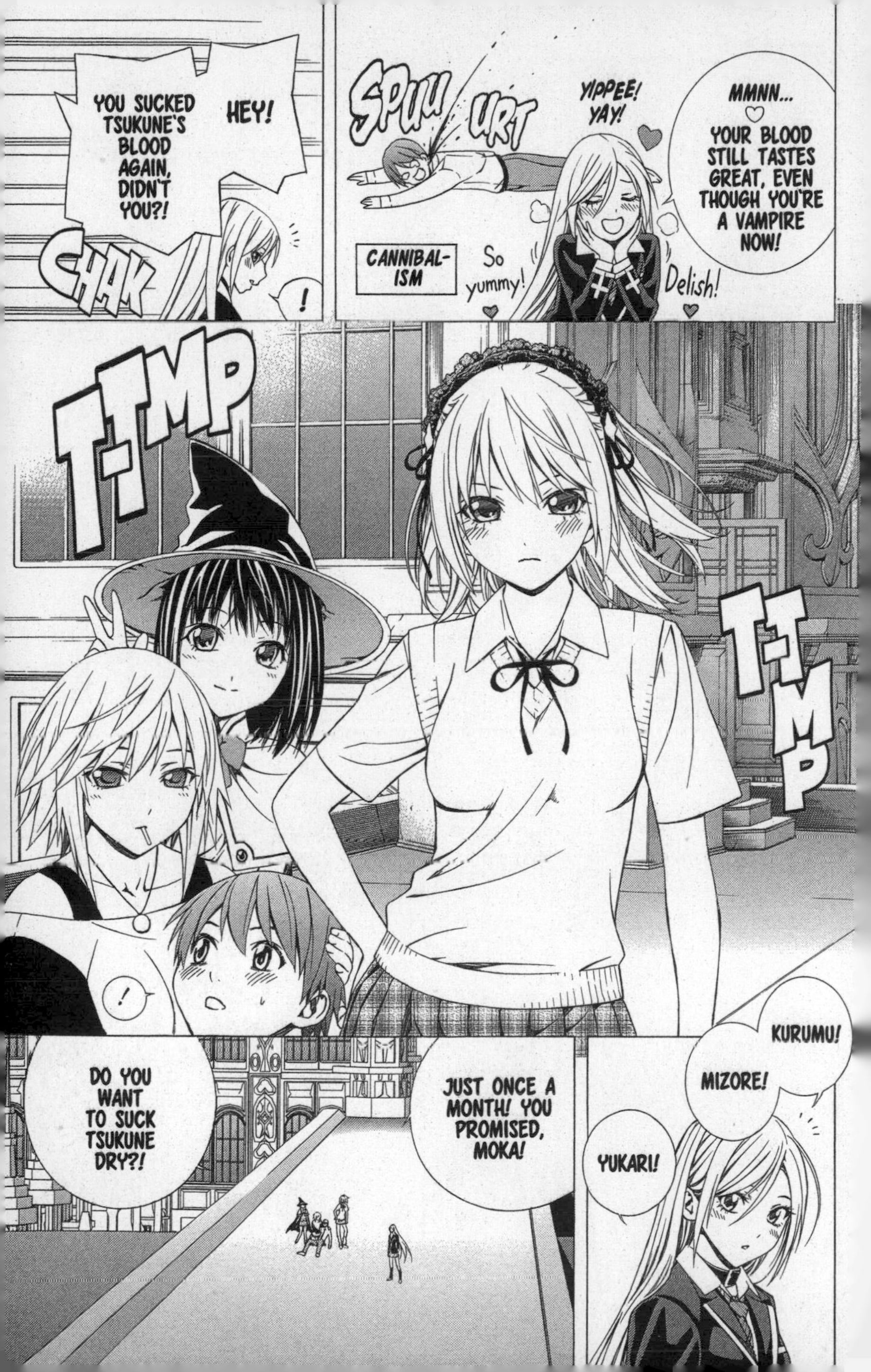
MMNN... ♡ YOUR BLOOD STILL TASTES GREAT, EVEN THOUGH YOU'RE A VAMPIRE NOW!
YIPPEE! YAY!
SPUU URT
CANNIBAL-ISM
So yummy!
Delish!
HEY!
YOU SUCKED TSUKUNE'S BLOOD AGAIN, DIDN'T YOU?!
CHAK
!
T-TMP
T-TMP
!
KURUMU!
MIZORE!
YUKARI!
JUST ONCE A MONTH! YOU PROMISED, MOKA!
DO YOU WANT TO SUCK TSUKUNE DRY?!

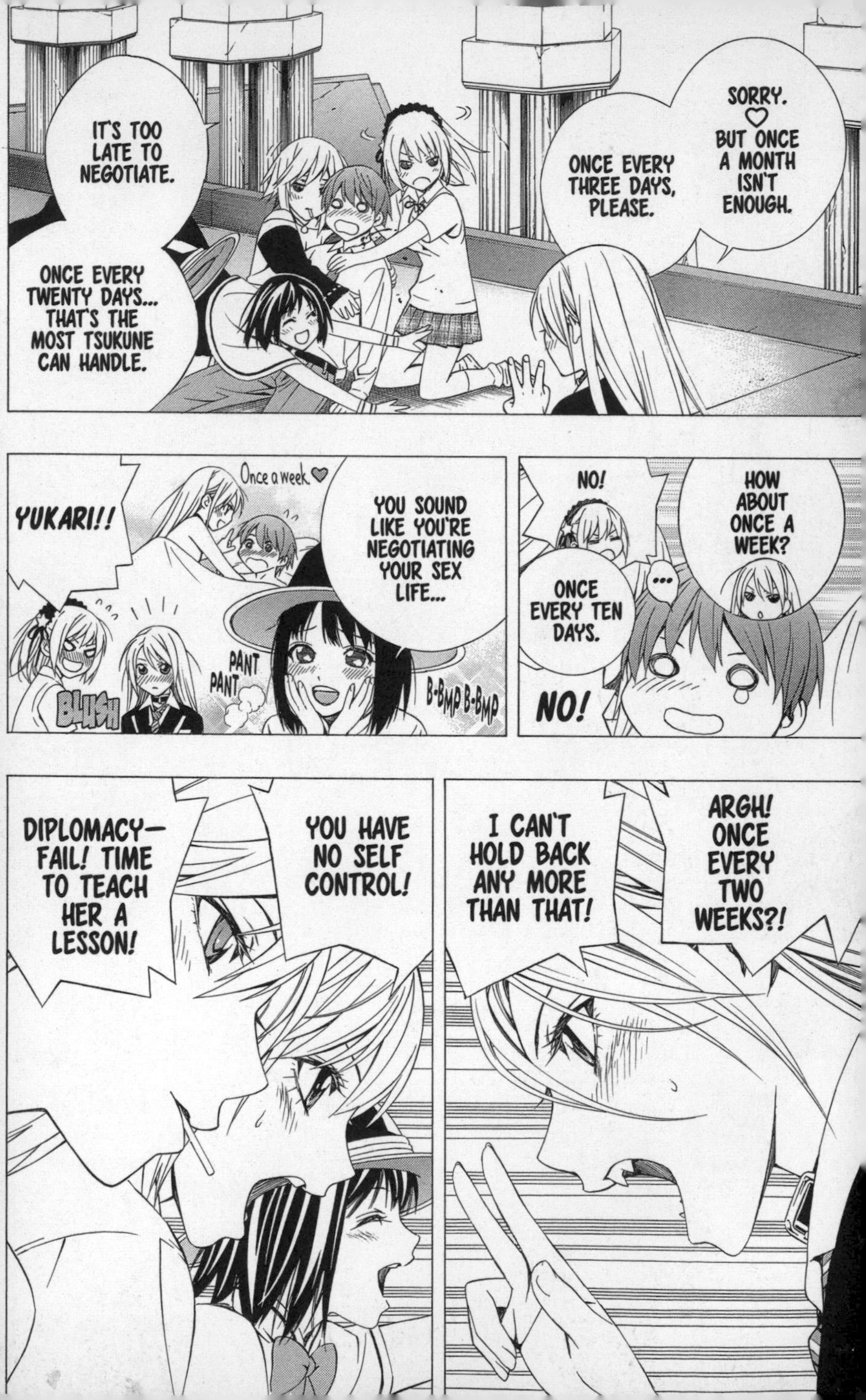

SORRY. ♡ BUT ONCE A MONTH ISN'T ENOUGH.
ONCE EVERY THREE DAYS, PLEASE.
IT'S TOO LATE TO NEGOTIATE.
ONCE EVERY TWENTY DAYS... THAT'S THE MOST TSUKUNE CAN HANDLE.
HOW ABOUT ONCE A WEEK?
NO!
...
ONCE EVERY TEN DAYS.
NO!
YOU SOUND LIKE YOU'RE NEGOTIATING YOUR SEX LIFE...
Once a week ♡
YUKARI!!
PANT PANT
B-BMP B-BMP
BLUSH
ARGH! ONCE EVERY TWO WEEKS?!
I CAN'T HOLD BACK ANY MORE THAN THAT!
YOU HAVE NO SELF CONTROL!
DIPLOMACY— FAIL! TIME TO TEACH HER A LESSON!

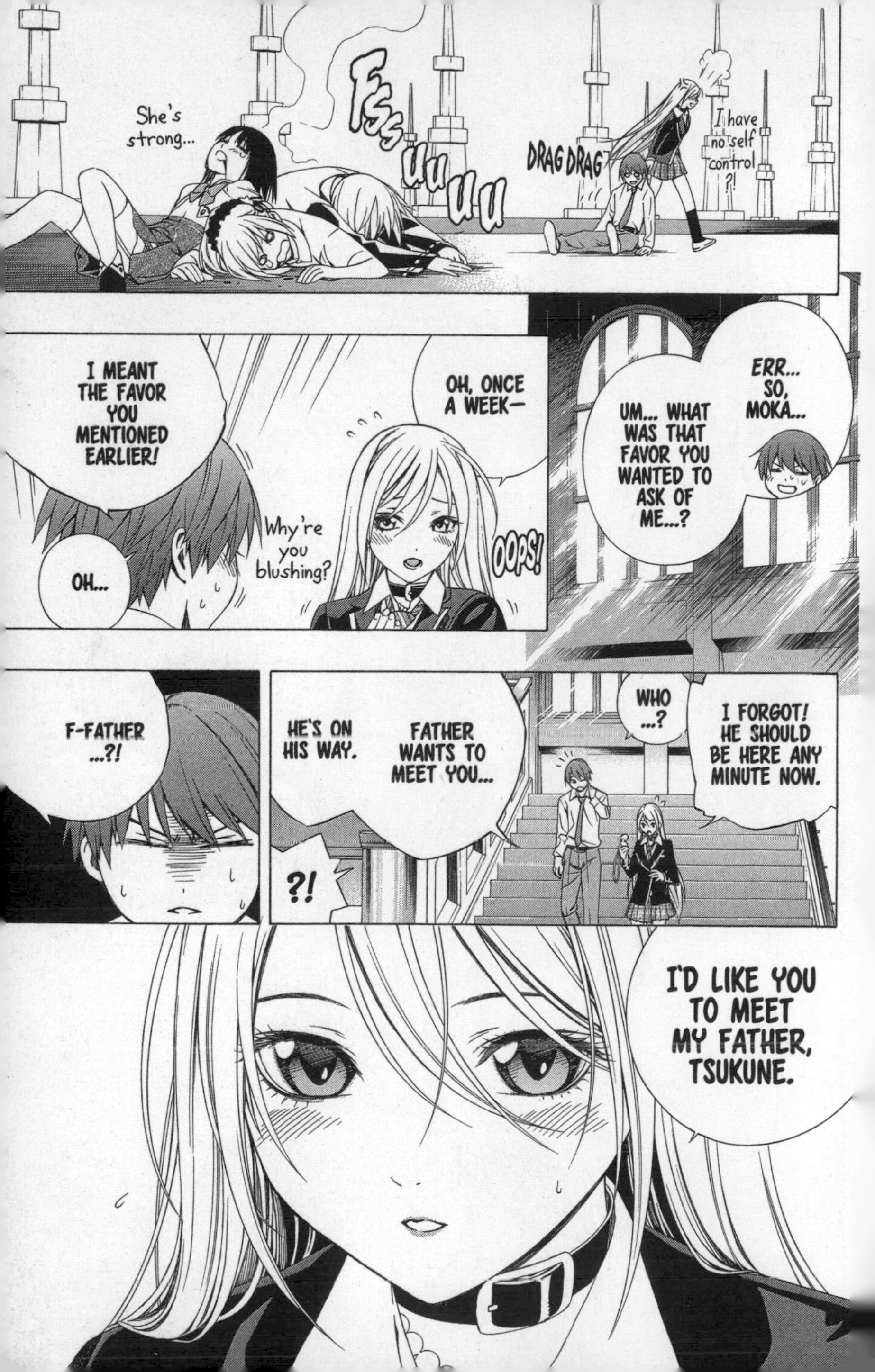
I have no self control ?!
DRAG DRAG
Fssuuuu
She's strong...
ERR... SO, MOKA...
UM... WHAT WAS THAT FAVOR YOU WANTED TO ASK OF ME...?
OH, ONCE A WEEK—
I MEANT THE FAVOR YOU MENTIONED EARLIER!
OOPS!
Why're you blushing?
OH...
I FORGOT! HE SHOULD BE HERE ANY MINUTE NOW.
WHO ...?
FATHER WANTS TO MEET YOU...
HE'S ON HIS WAY.
?!
F-FATHER ...?!
I'D LIKE YOU TO MEET MY FATHER, TSUKUNE.

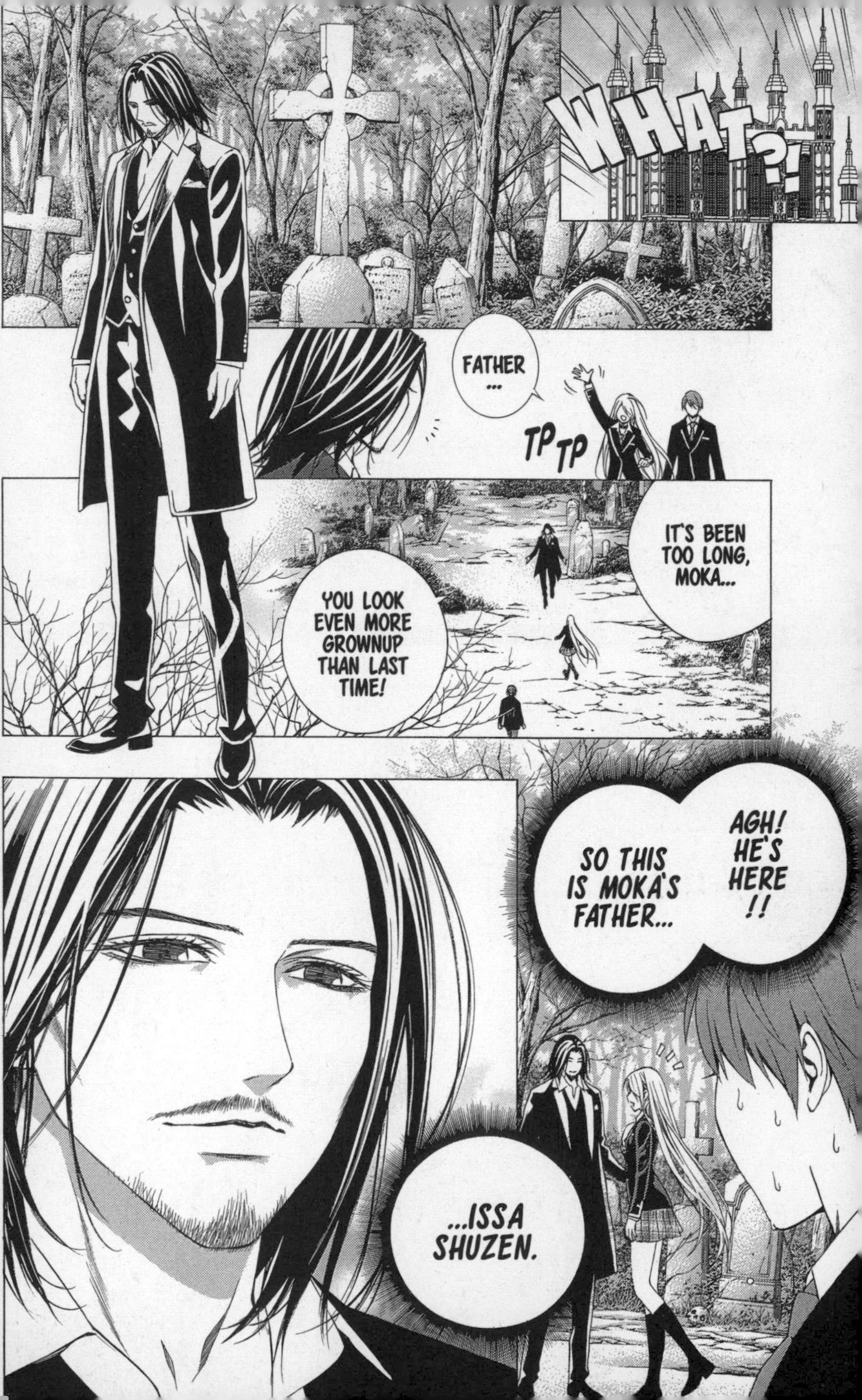
WHAT?!
FATHER...
TP TP
IT'S BEEN TOO LONG, MOKA...
YOU LOOK EVEN MORE GROWNUP THAN LAST TIME!
AGH! HE'S HERE!!
SO THIS IS MOKA'S FATHER...
...ISSA SHUZEN.

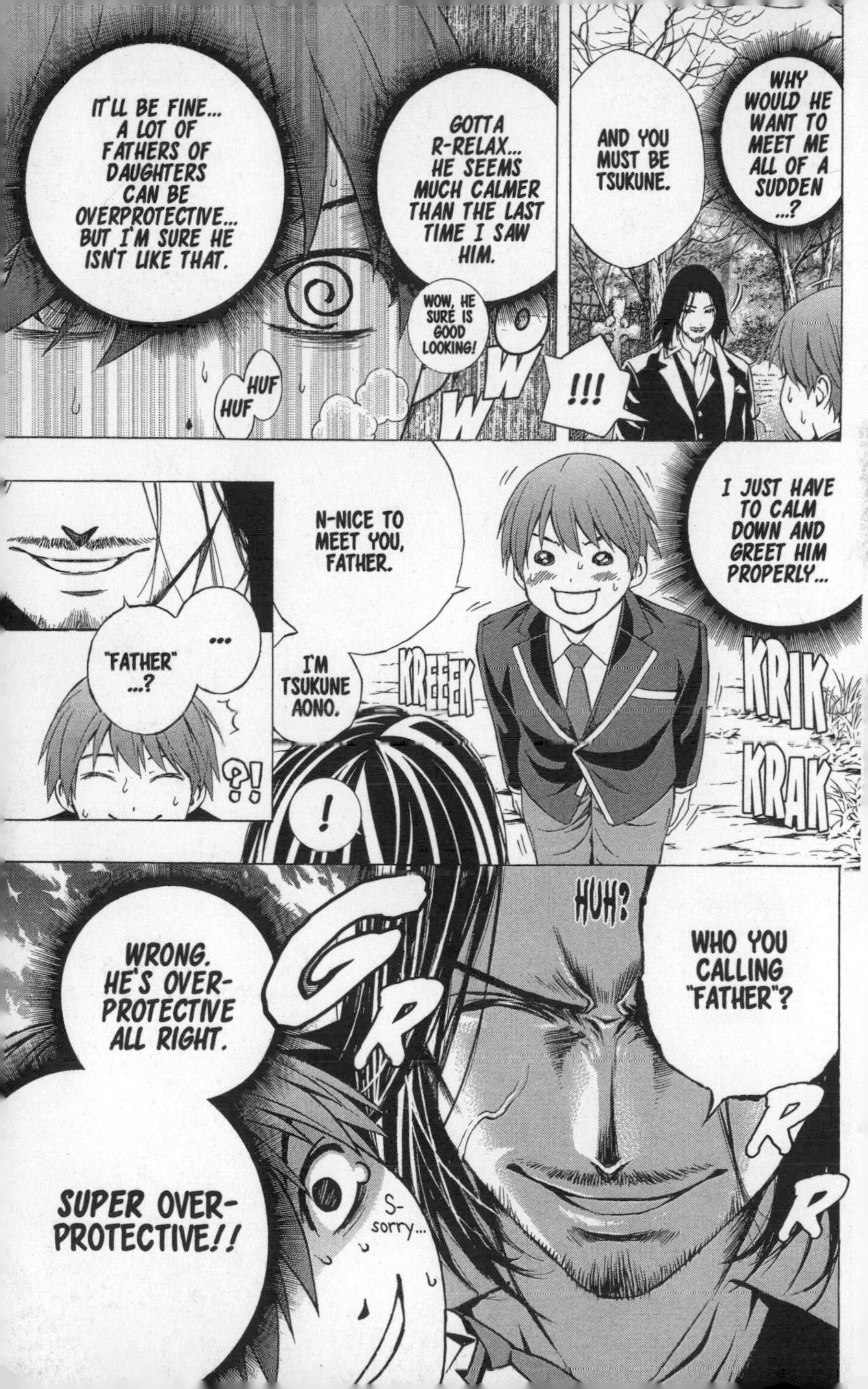
WHY WOULD HE WANT TO MEET ME ALL OF A SUDDEN ...?
AND YOU MUST BE TSUKUNE.
!!!
GOTTA R-RELAX... HE SEEMS MUCH CALMER THAN THE LAST TIME I SAW HIM.
IT'LL BE FINE... A LOT OF FATHERS OF DAUGHTERS CAN BE OVERPROTECTIVE... BUT I'M SURE HE ISN'T LIKE THAT.
WOW, HE SURE IS GOOD LOOKING!
HUF HUF
I JUST HAVE TO CALM DOWN AND GREET HIM PROPERLY...
KRIK
KRAK
N-NICE TO MEET YOU, FATHER.
I'M TSUKUNE AONO.
KREEEK
!
...
"FATHER" ...?
?!
HUH?
WHO YOU CALLING "FATHER"?
GR
RR
WRONG. HE'S OVER-PROTECTIVE ALL RIGHT.
S-sorry...
SUPER OVER-PROTECTIVE!!

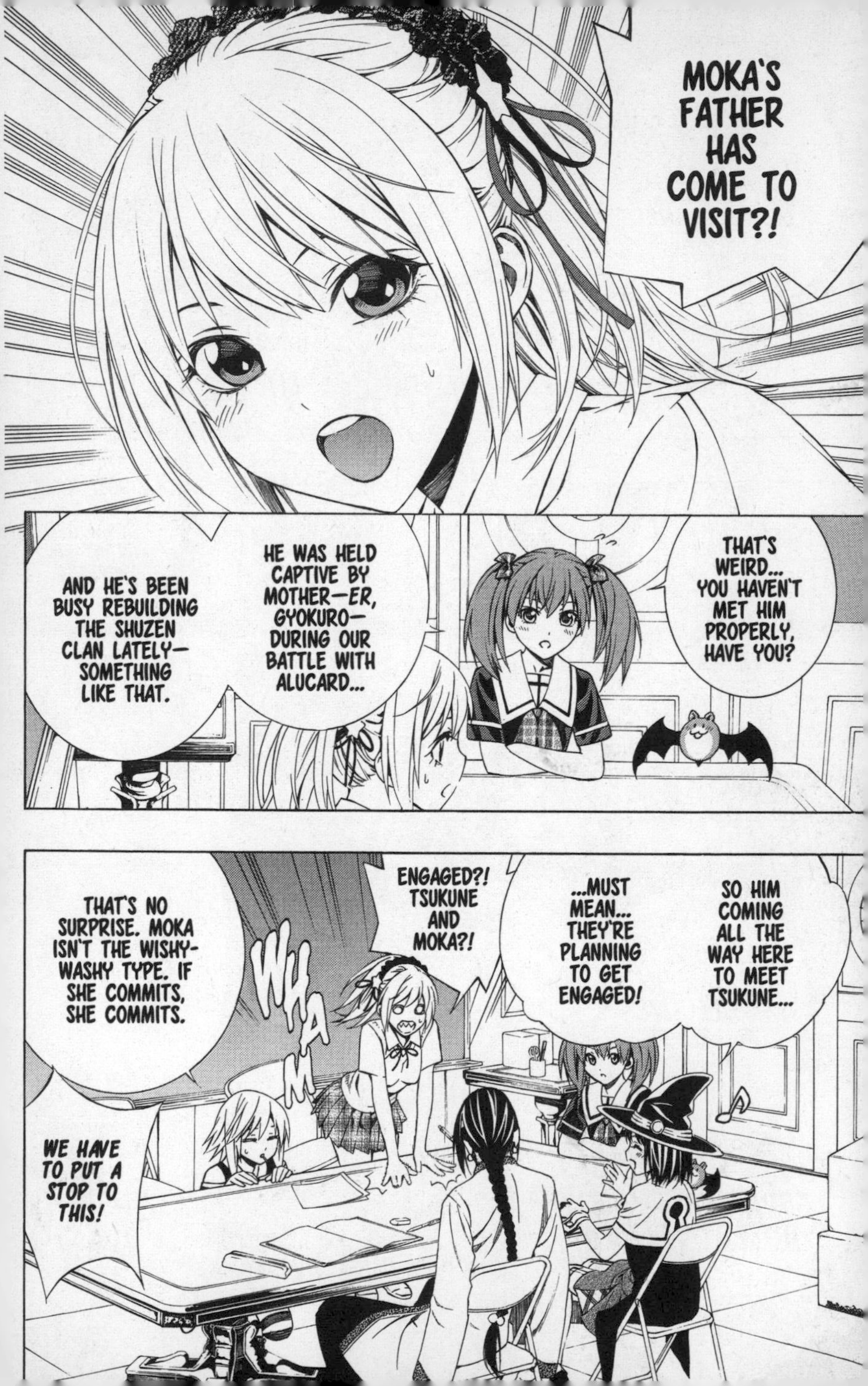
MOKA'S FATHER HAS COME TO VISIT?!
THAT'S WEIRD... YOU HAVEN'T MET HIM PROPERLY, HAVE YOU?
HE WAS HELD CAPTIVE BY MOTHER—ER, GYOKURO—DURING OUR BATTLE WITH ALUCARD...
AND HE'S BEEN BUSY REBUILDING THE SHUZEN CLAN LATELY—SOMETHING LIKE THAT.
SO HIM COMING ALL THE WAY HERE TO MEET TSUKUNE...
...MUST MEAN... THEY'RE PLANNING TO GET ENGAGED!
ENGAGED?! TSUKUNE AND MOKA?!
WHAM
THAT'S NO SURPRISE. MOKA ISN'T THE WISHY-WASHY TYPE. IF SHE COMMITS, SHE COMMITS.
WE HAVE TO PUT A STOP TO THIS!

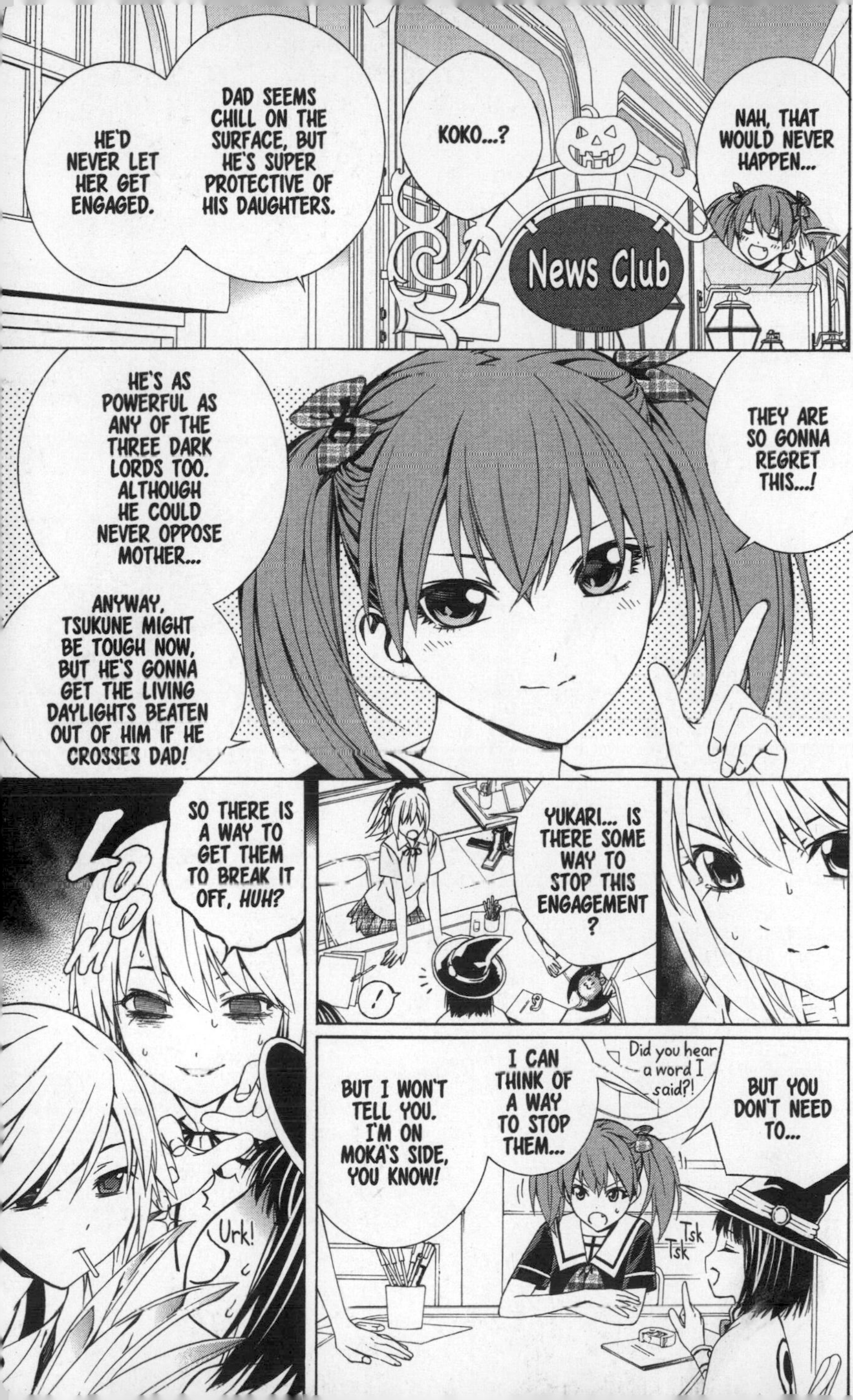
NAH, THAT WOULD NEVER HAPPEN...
KOKO...?
News Club
DAD SEEMS CHILL ON THE SURFACE, BUT HE'S SUPER PROTECTIVE OF HIS DAUGHTERS.
HE'D NEVER LET HER GET ENGAGED.
THEY ARE SO GONNA REGRET THIS...!
HE'S AS POWERFUL AS ANY OF THE THREE DARK LORDS TOO. ALTHOUGH HE COULD NEVER OPPOSE MOTHER...
ANYWAY, TSUKUNE MIGHT BE TOUGH NOW, BUT HE'S GONNA GET THE LIVING DAYLIGHTS BEATEN OUT OF HIM IF HE CROSSES DAD!
YUKARI... IS THERE SOME WAY TO STOP THIS ENGAGEMENT?
!
BUT YOU DON'T NEED TO...
Did you hear a word I said?!
I CAN THINK OF A WAY TO STOP THEM...
BUT I WON'T TELL YOU. I'M ON MOKA'S SIDE, YOU KNOW!
Tsk Tsk
SO THERE IS A WAY TO GET THEM TO BREAK IT OFF, HUH?
LOOM
Urk!

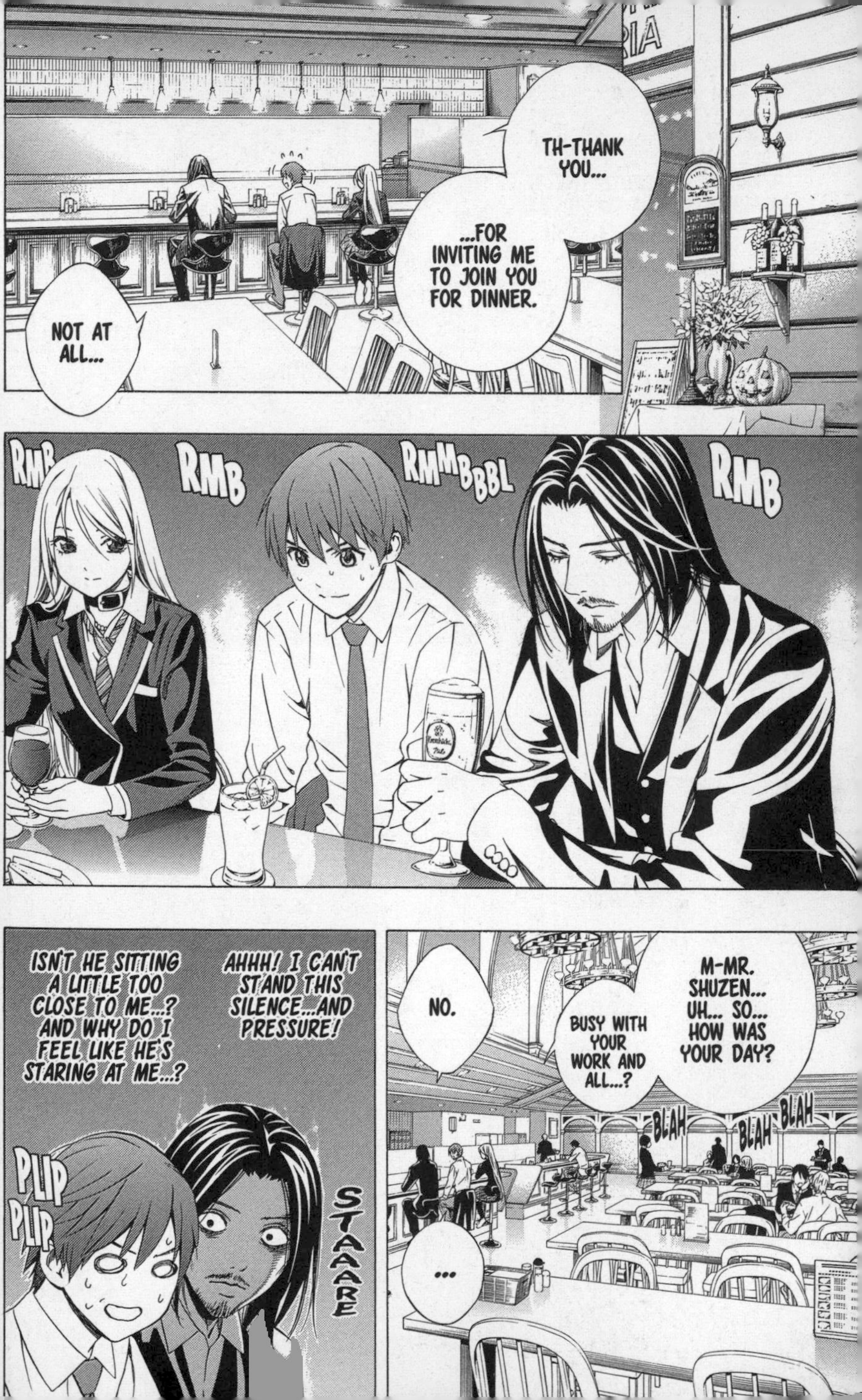
TH-THANK YOU...
...FOR INVITING ME TO JOIN YOU FOR DINNER.
NOT AT ALL...
RMB
RMMBBBL
RMB
RMB
M-MR. SHUZEN... UH... SO... HOW WAS YOUR DAY?
BUSY WITH YOUR WORK AND ALL...?
NO.
BLAH
BLAH
BLAH
...
AHHH! I CAN'T STAND THIS SILENCE...AND PRESSURE!
ISN'T HE SITTING A LITTLE TOO CLOSE TO ME...? AND WHY DO I FEEL LIKE HE'S STARING AT ME...?
STAAARE
PLIP
PLIP

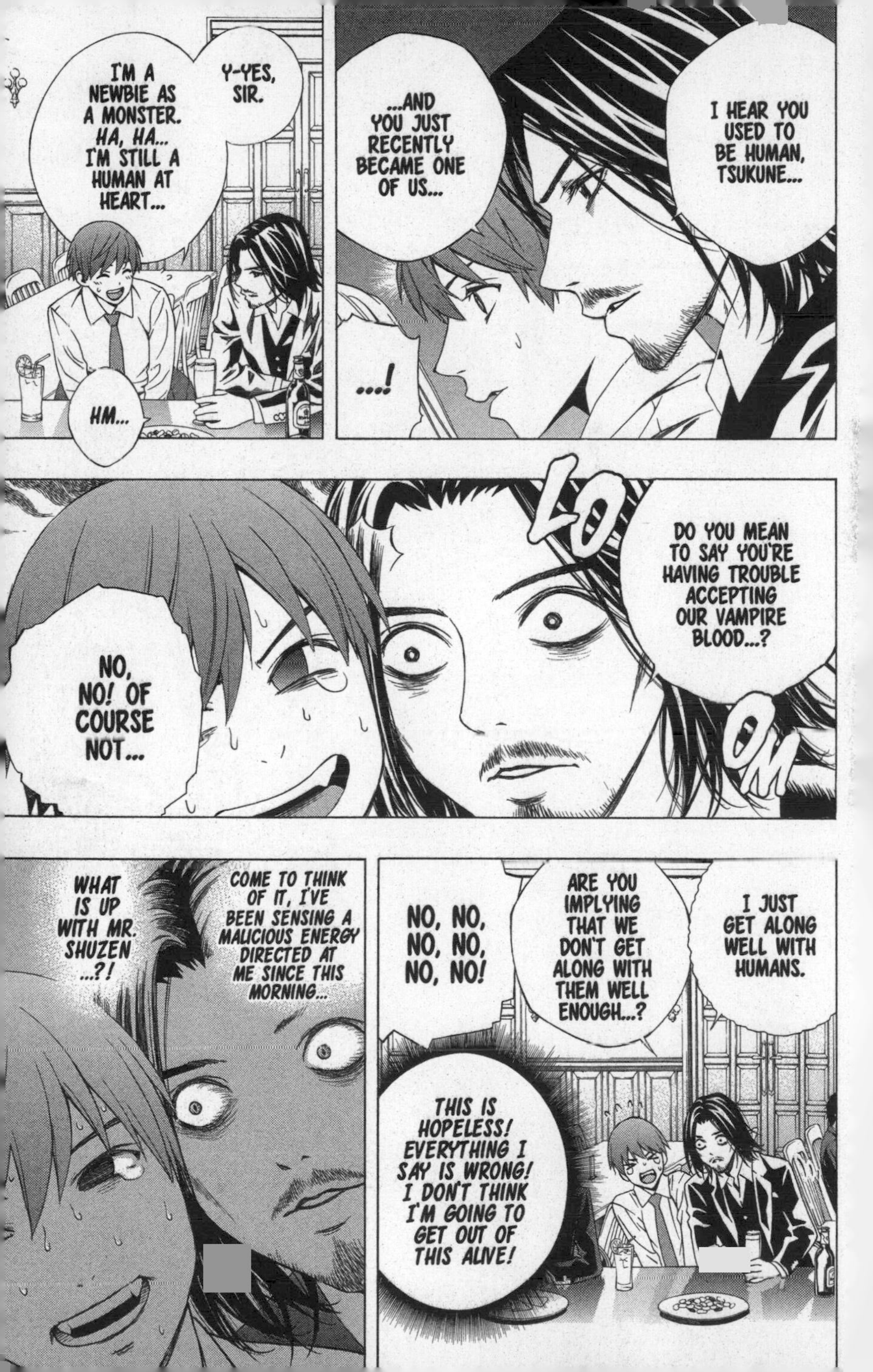
I HEAR YOU USED TO BE HUMAN, TSUKUNE...
...AND YOU JUST RECENTLY BECAME ONE OF US...
...!
Y-YES, SIR.
I'M A NEWBIE AS A MONSTER. HA, HA... I'M STILL A HUMAN AT HEART...
HM...
LO
OM
DO YOU MEAN TO SAY YOU'RE HAVING TROUBLE ACCEPTING OUR VAMPIRE BLOOD...?
NO, NO! OF COURSE NOT...
I JUST GET ALONG WELL WITH HUMANS.
ARE YOU IMPLYING THAT WE DON'T GET ALONG WITH THEM WELL ENOUGH...?
NO, NO, NO, NO, NO, NO!
THIS IS HOPELESS! EVERYTHING I SAY IS WRONG! I DON'T THINK I'M GOING TO GET OUT OF THIS ALIVE!
COME TO THINK OF IT, I'VE BEEN SENSING A MALICIOUS ENERGY DIRECTED AT ME SINCE THIS MORNING...
WHAT IS UP WITH MR. SHUZEN...?!

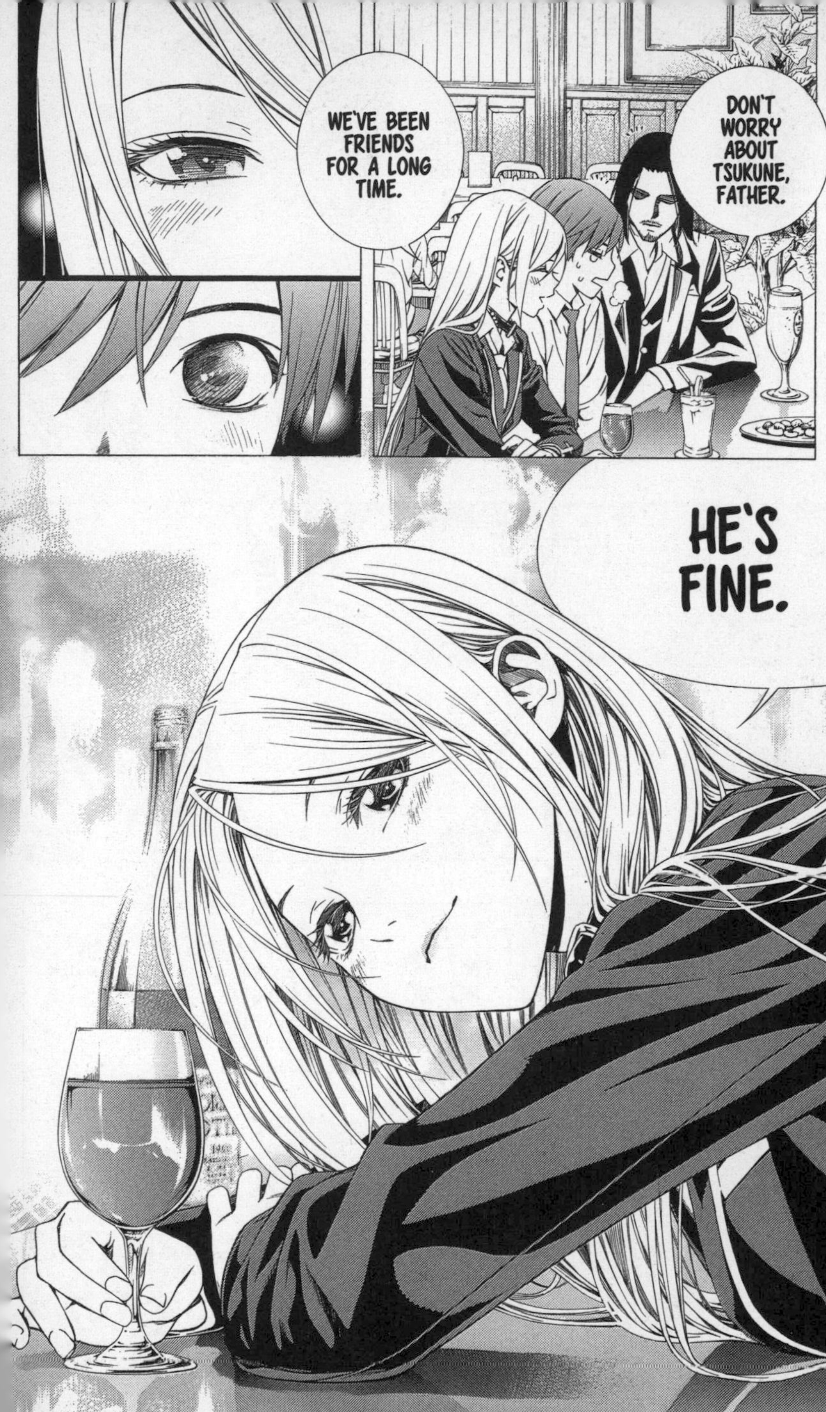
DON'T WORRY ABOUT TSUKUNE, FATHER.
WE'VE BEEN FRIENDS FOR A LONG TIME.
HE'S FINE.

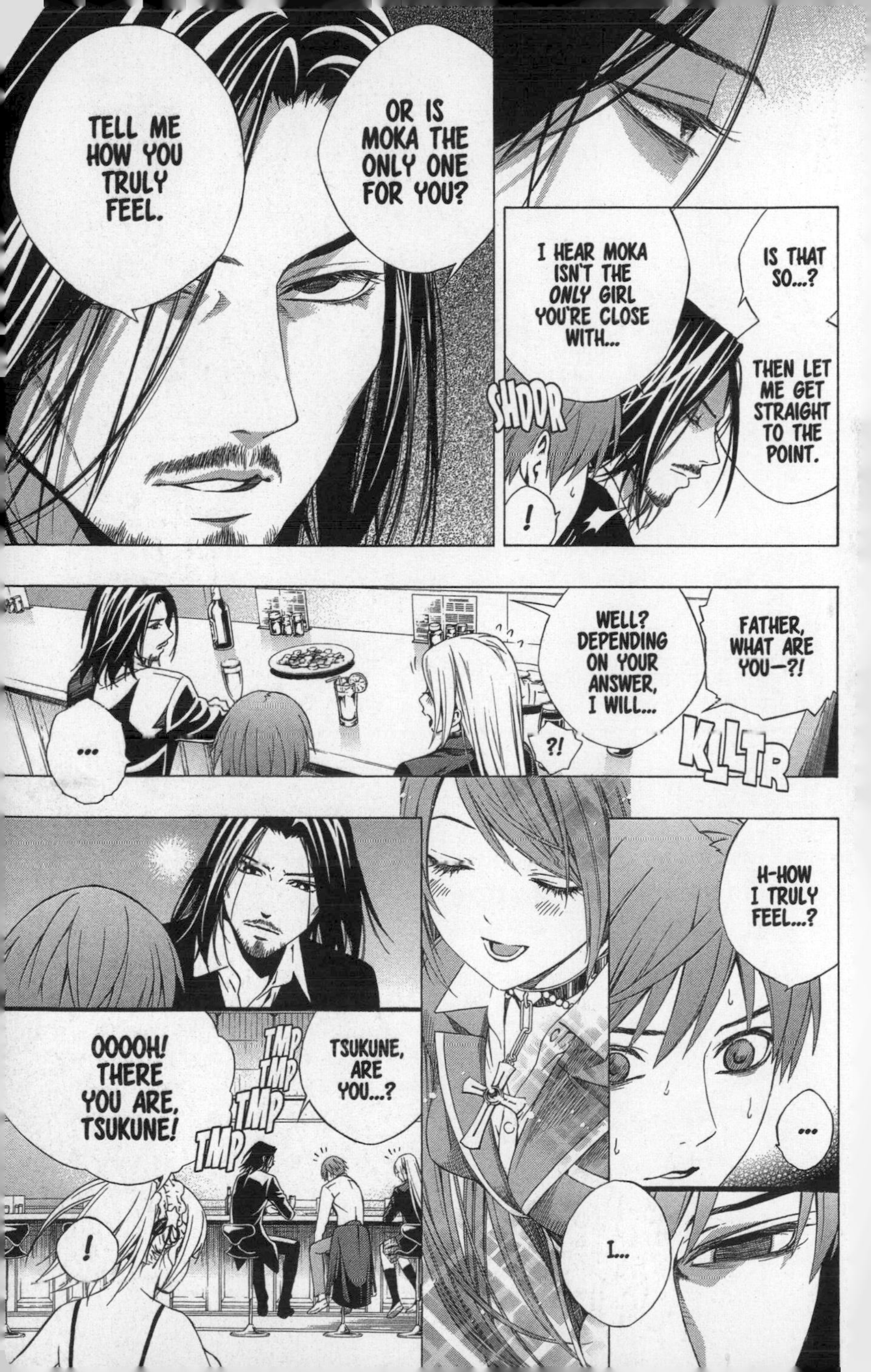
IS THAT SO...?
I HEAR MOKA ISN'T THE *ONLY* GIRL YOU'RE CLOSE WITH...
SHOOR
!
THEN LET ME GET STRAIGHT TO THE POINT.
OR IS MOKA THE ONLY ONE FOR YOU?
TELL ME HOW YOU TRULY FEEL.
FATHER, WHAT ARE YOU—?!
KLLTR
WELL? DEPENDING ON YOUR ANSWER, I WILL...
?!
...
H-HOW I TRULY FEEL...?
...
I...
TSUKUNE, ARE YOU...?
TMP TMP TMP TMP
OOOOH! THERE YOU ARE, TSUKUNE!
!

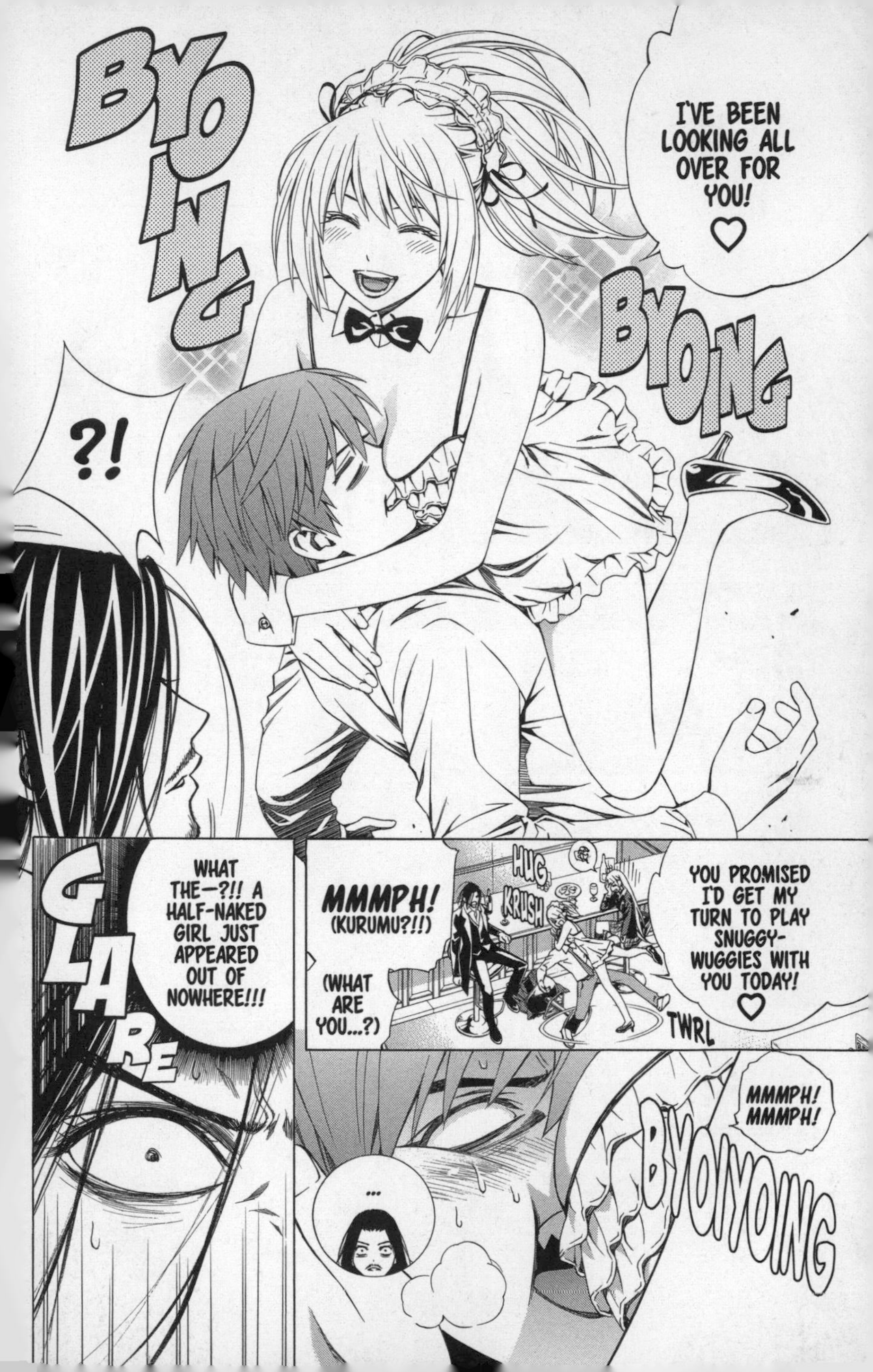
I'VE BEEN LOOKING ALL OVER FOR YOU! ♥
BYOING
BYOING
?!
YOU PROMISED I'D GET MY TURN TO PLAY SNUGGY-WUGGIES WITH YOU TODAY! ♥
HUG
KRUSH
TWRL
MMMPH! (KURUMU?!!)
(WHAT ARE YOU...?)
MMMPH! MMMPH!
BYOIYOING
...
WHAT THE—?!! A HALF-NAKED GIRL JUST APPEARED OUT OF NOWHERE!!!
GLARE

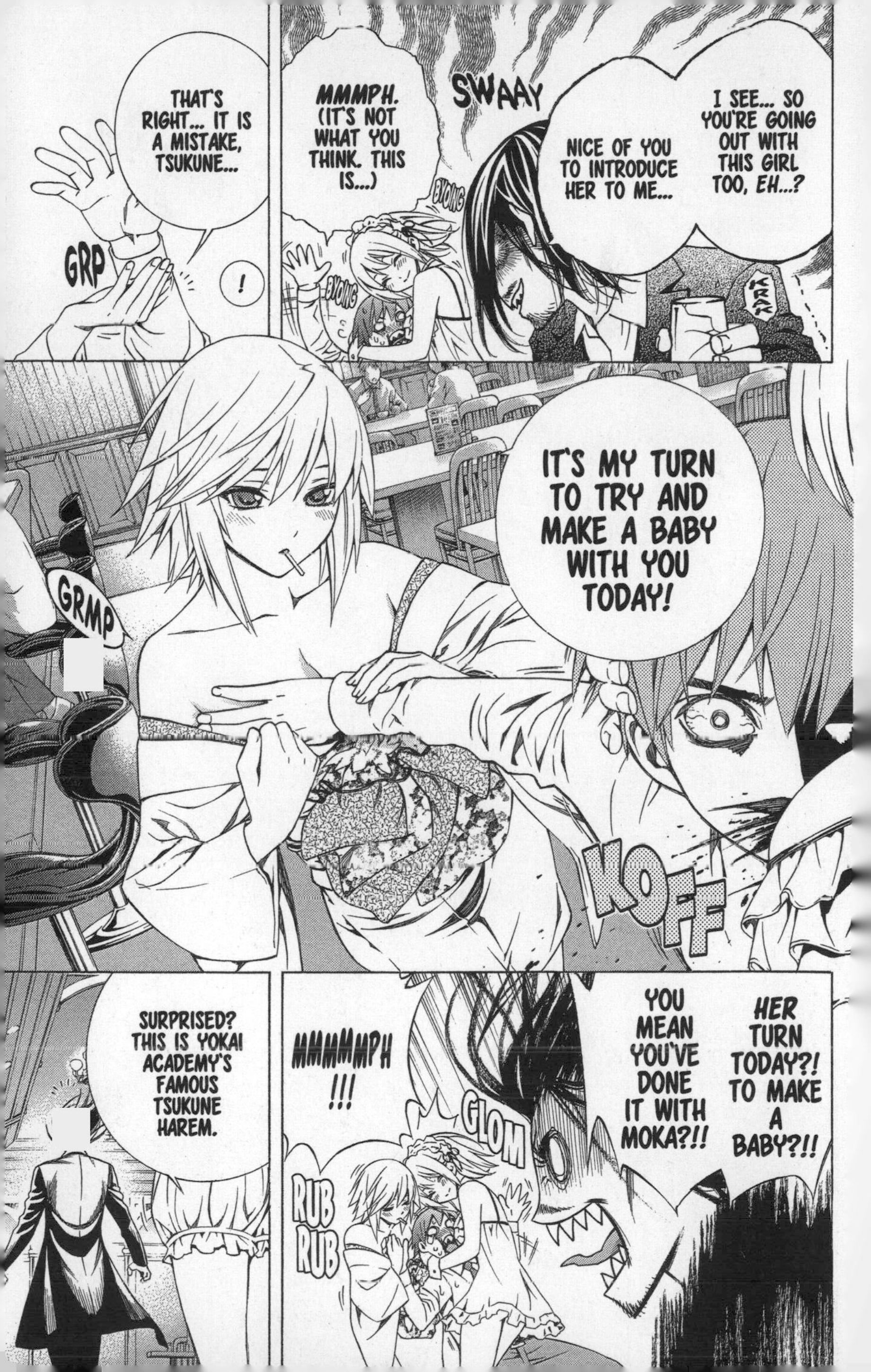
I SEE... SO YOU'RE GOING OUT WITH THIS GIRL TOO, EH...?
NICE OF YOU TO INTRODUCE HER TO ME...
SWAAY
KRAK
MMMPH. (IT'S NOT WHAT YOU THINK. THIS IS...)
BYOING
BYOING
THAT'S RIGHT... IT IS A MISTAKE, TSUKUNE...
!
GRP
IT'S MY TURN TO TRY AND MAKE A BABY WITH YOU TODAY!
GRMP
KOFF
HER TURN TODAY?! TO MAKE A BABY?!!
YOU MEAN YOU'VE DONE IT WITH MOKA?!!
MMMMMPH !!!
GLOM
RUB RUB
SURPRISED? THIS IS YOKAI ACADEMY'S FAMOUS TSUKUNE HAREM.

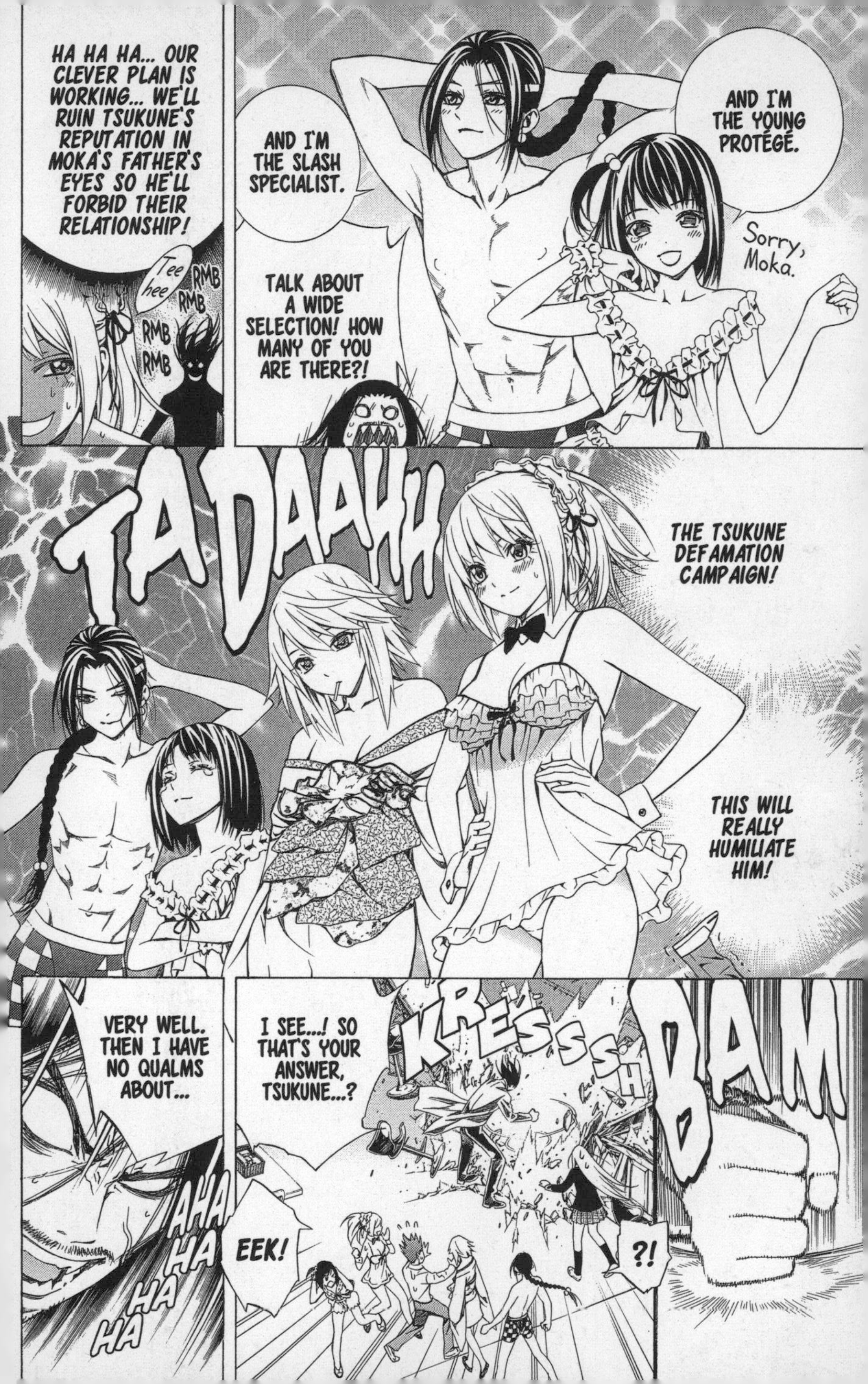
AND I'M THE YOUNG PROTÉGÉ.
Sorry, Moka.
AND I'M THE SLASH SPECIALIST.
TALK ABOUT A WIDE SELECTION! HOW MANY OF YOU ARE THERE?!
HA HA HA... OUR CLEVER PLAN IS WORKING... WE'LL RUIN TSUKUNE'S REPUTATION IN MOKA'S FATHER'S EYES SO HE'LL FORBID THEIR RELATIONSHIP!
Tee hee
RMB RMB
RMB RMB
THE TSUKUNE DEFAMATION CAMPAIGN!
THIS WILL REALLY HUMILIATE HIM!
TADAAHH
BAM
KRESSSH
?!
I SEE...! SO THAT'S YOUR ANSWER, TSUKUNE...?
EEK!
VERY WELL. THEN I HAVE NO QUALMS ABOUT...
HA HA HA HA HA AHA

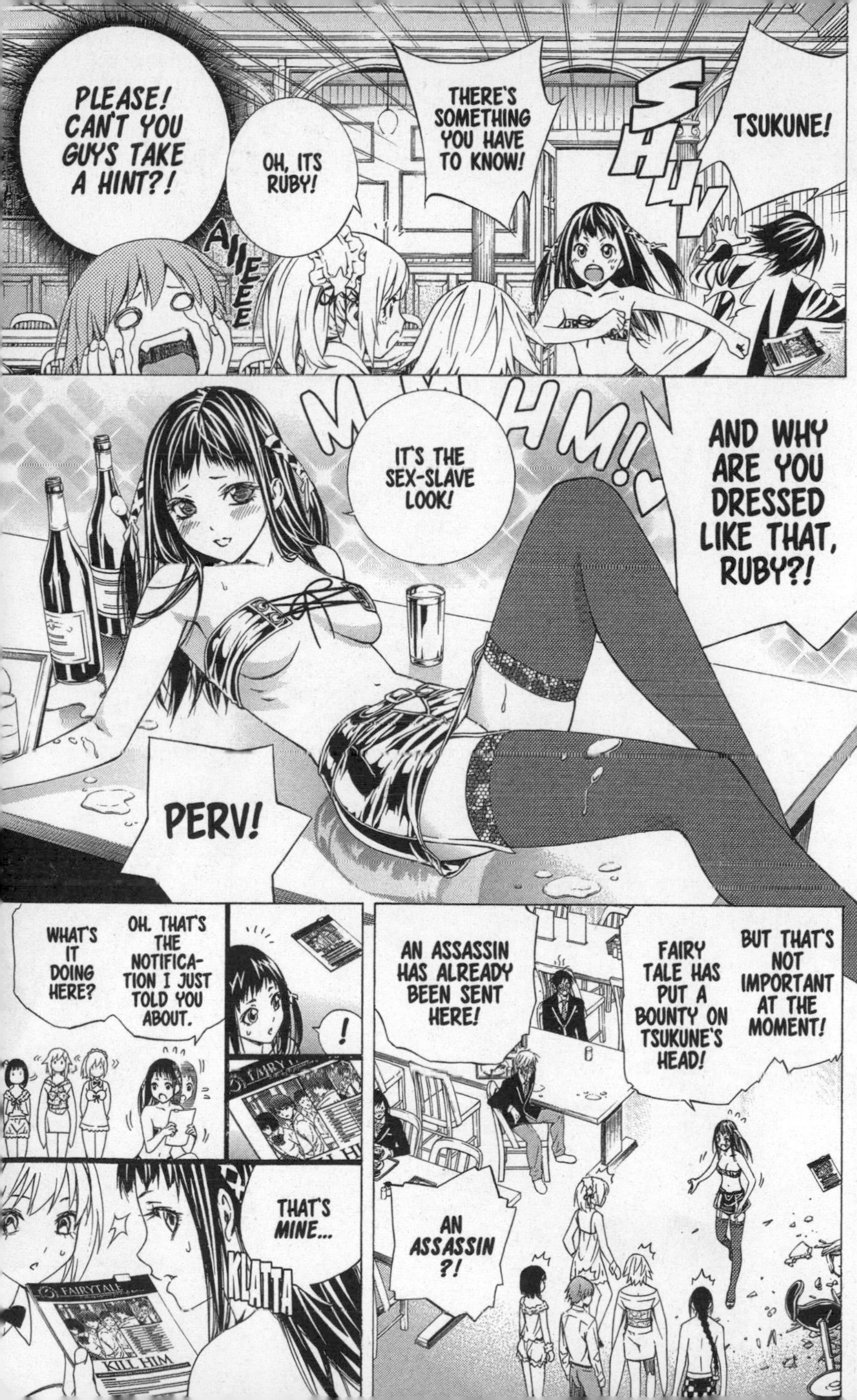
TSUKUNE!
SHUV
THERE'S SOMETHING YOU HAVE TO KNOW!
OH, ITS RUBY!
PLEASE! CAN'T YOU GUYS TAKE A HINT?!
AIIEEE
AND WHY ARE YOU DRESSED LIKE THAT, RUBY?!
HM!
IT'S THE SEX-SLAVE LOOK!
PERV!
BUT THAT'S NOT IMPORTANT AT THE MOMENT!
FAIRY TALE HAS PUT A BOUNTY ON TSUKUNE'S HEAD!
AN ASSASSIN HAS ALREADY BEEN SENT HERE!
AN ASSASSIN?!
!
OH. THAT'S THE NOTIFICATION I JUST TOLD YOU ABOUT.
WHAT'S IT DOING HERE?
THAT'S MINE...
KLATTA
FAIRYTALE
KILL HIM

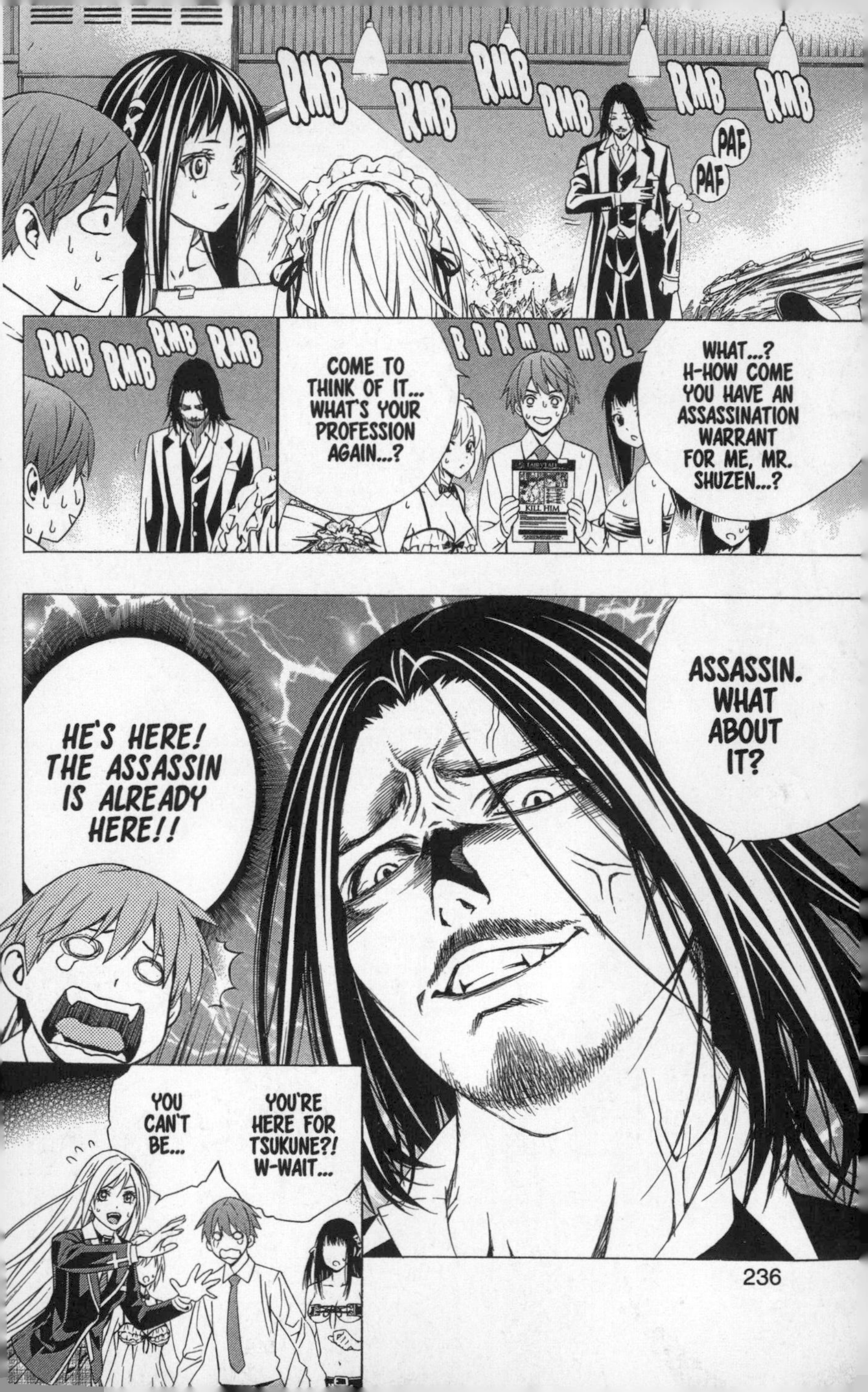
RMB RMB RMB RMB RMB RMB
PAF PAF
WHAT...? H-HOW COME YOU HAVE AN ASSASSINATION WARRANT FOR ME, MR. SHUZEN...?
KILL HIM
RRRMMMBL
COME TO THINK OF IT... WHAT'S YOUR PROFESSION AGAIN...?
RMB RMB RMB RMB
ASSASSIN. WHAT ABOUT IT?
HE'S HERE! THE ASSASSIN IS ALREADY HERE!!
YOU'RE HERE FOR TSUKUNE?! W-WAIT...
YOU CAN'T BE...

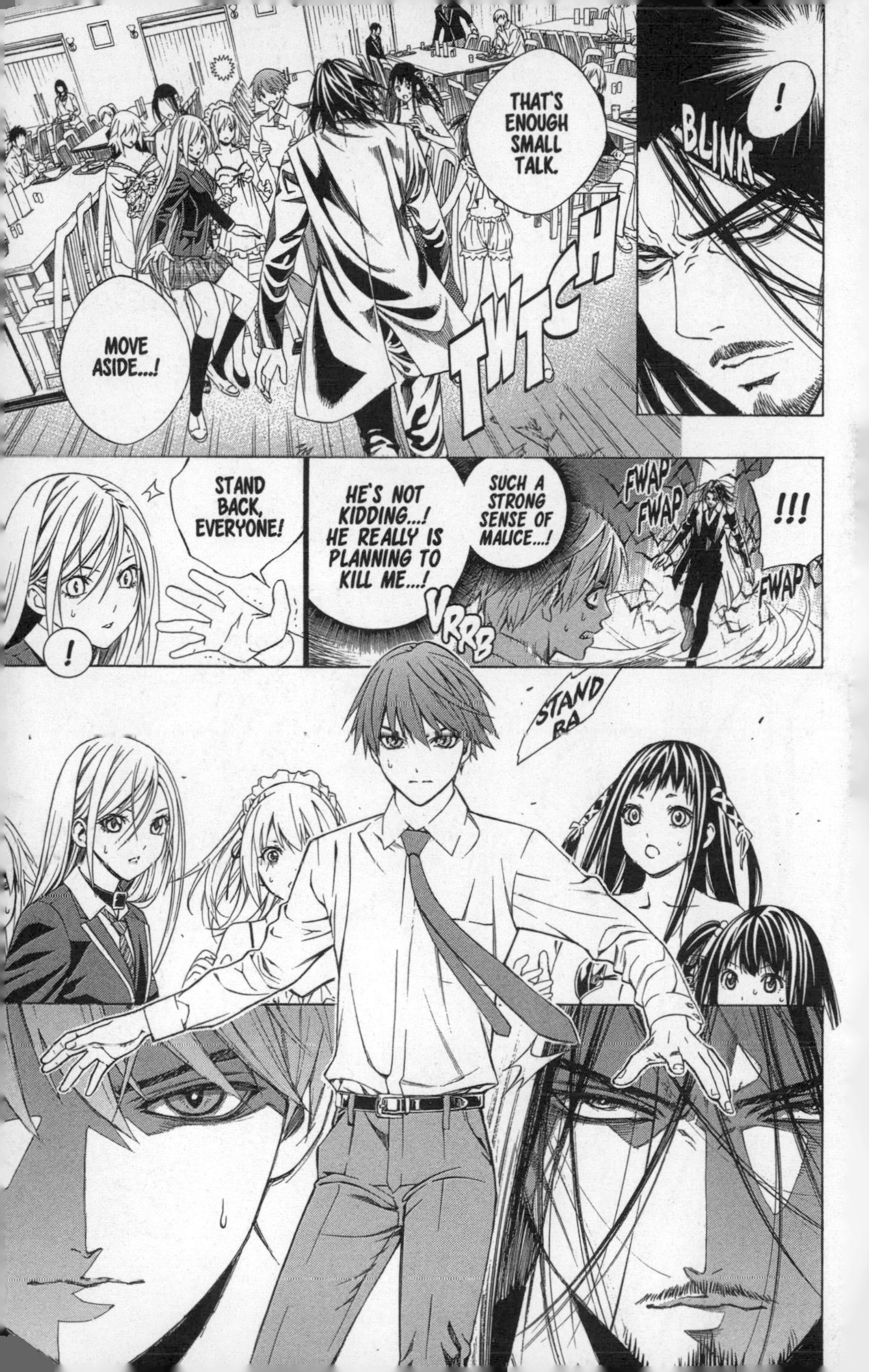
!
BLINK
THAT'S ENOUGH SMALL TALK.
TWTCH
MOVE ASIDE...!
!!!
FWAP FWAP
FWAP
SUCH A STRONG SENSE OF MALICE...!
HE'S NOT KIDDING...! HE REALLY IS PLANNING TO KILL ME...!
VRRB
STAND BACK, EVERYONE!
!
STAND RA

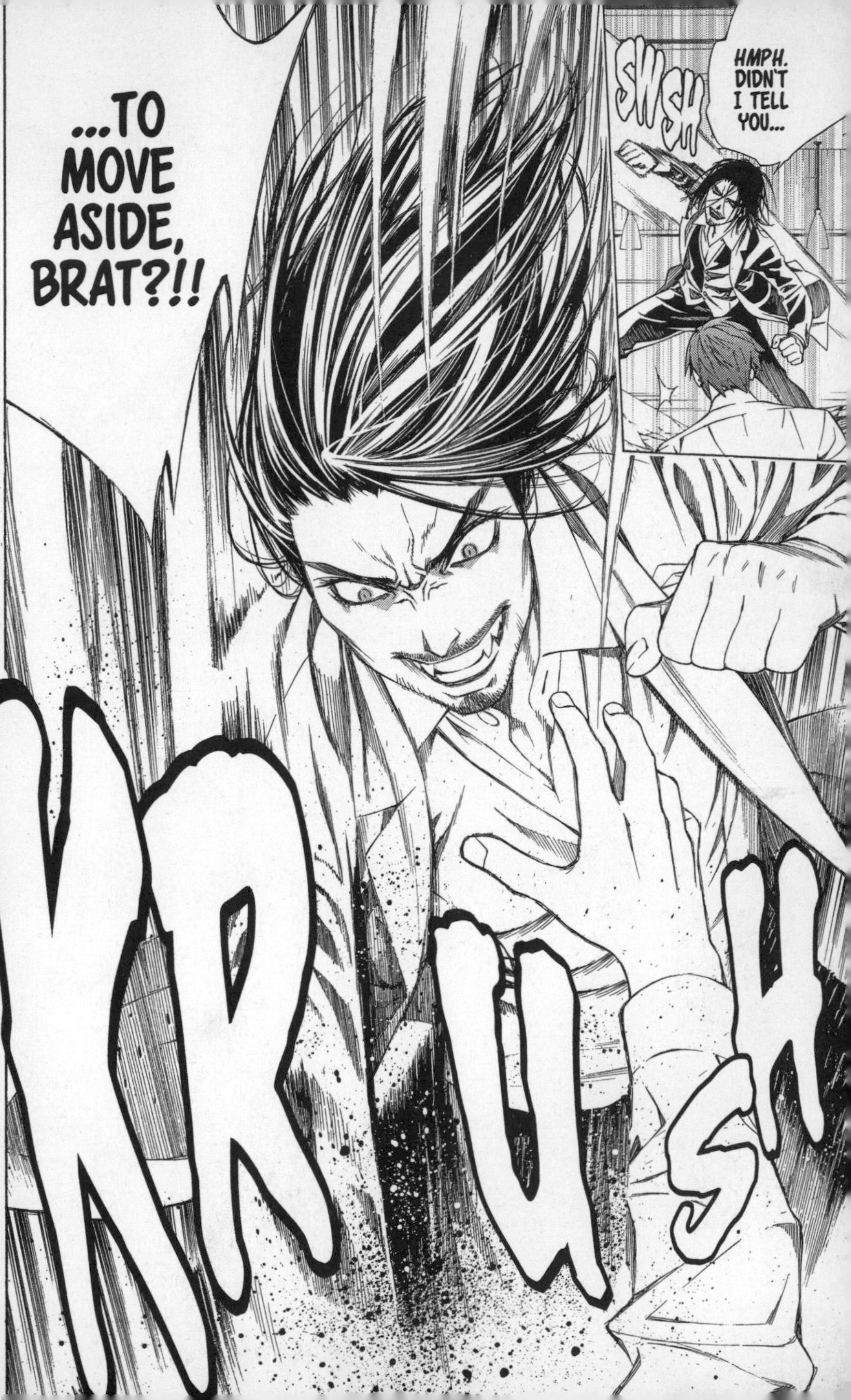
SWSH
HMPH. DIDN'T I TELL YOU...
...TO MOVE ASIDE, BRAT?!!
KRUSH

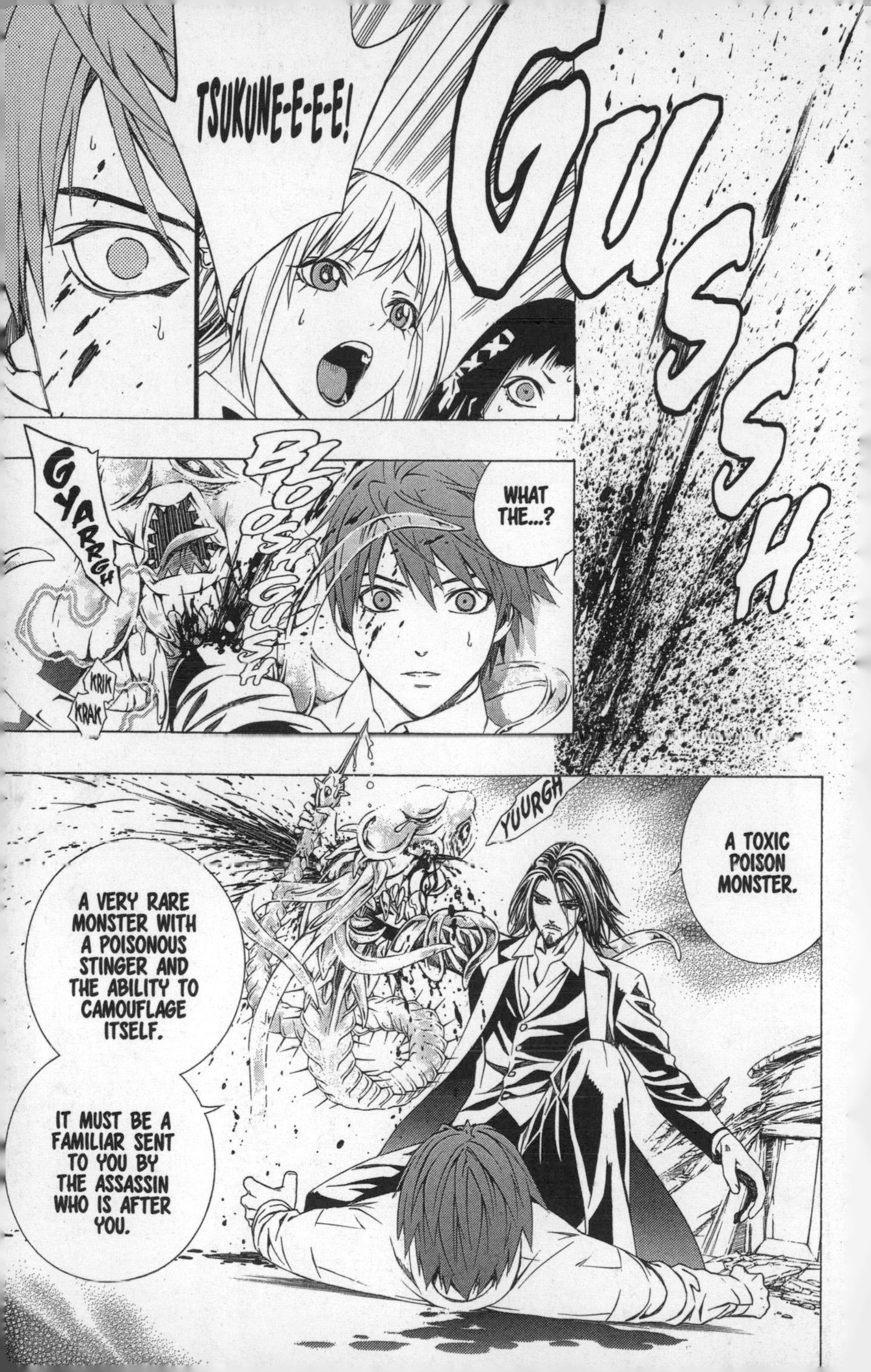
GUSSH
TSUKUNE-E-E-E!
WHAT THE...?
BLOOSH
GUSSH
GYARRGH
KRIK
KRAK
YUURGH
A TOXIC POISON MONSTER.
A VERY RARE MONSTER WITH A POISONOUS STINGER AND THE ABILITY TO CAMOUFLAGE ITSELF.
IT MUST BE A FAMILIAR SENT TO YOU BY THE ASSASSIN WHO IS AFTER YOU.

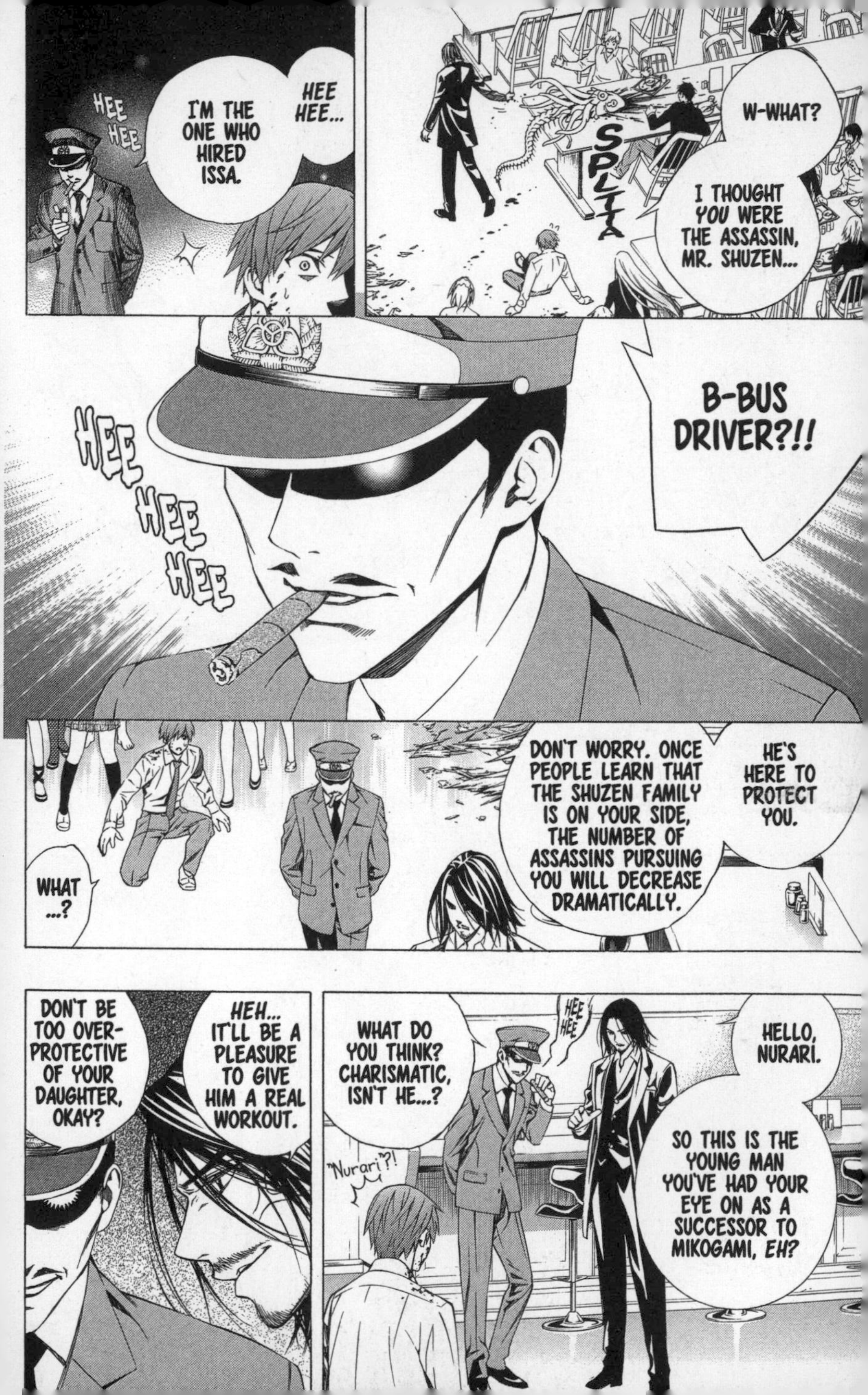
W-WHAT?
I THOUGHT *YOU* WERE THE ASSASSIN, MR. SHUZEN...
HEE HEE...
I'M THE ONE WHO HIRED ISSA.
HEE HEE
B-BUS DRIVER?!!
HEE HEE HEE
HE'S HERE TO PROTECT YOU.
DON'T WORRY. ONCE PEOPLE LEARN THAT THE SHUZEN FAMILY IS ON YOUR SIDE, THE NUMBER OF ASSASSINS PURSUING YOU WILL DECREASE DRAMATICALLY.
WHAT ...?
HELLO, NURARI.
SO THIS IS THE YOUNG MAN YOU'VE HAD YOUR EYE ON AS A SUCCESSOR TO MIKOGAMI, *EH*?
HEE HEE
WHAT DO YOU THINK? CHARISMATIC, ISN'T HE...?
"Nurari"?!
HEH... IT'LL BE A PLEASURE TO GIVE HIM A REAL WORKOUT.
DON'T BE TOO OVER-PROTECTIVE OF YOUR DAUGHTER, OKAY?

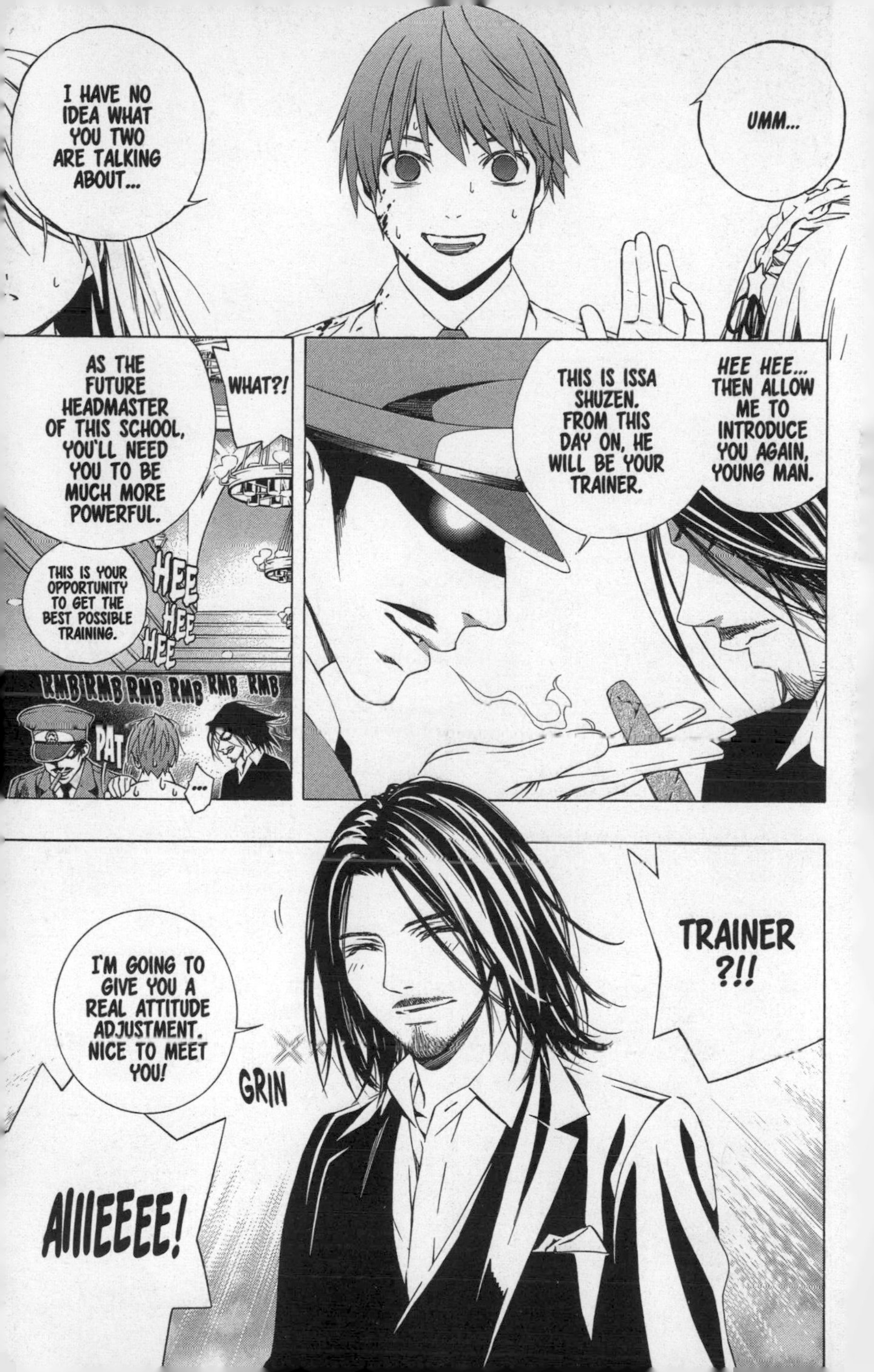
UMM...
I HAVE NO IDEA WHAT YOU TWO ARE TALKING ABOUT...
HEE HEE... THEN ALLOW ME TO INTRODUCE YOU AGAIN, YOUNG MAN.
THIS IS ISSA SHUZEN. FROM THIS DAY ON, HE WILL BE YOUR TRAINER.
WHAT?!
AS THE FUTURE HEADMASTER OF THIS SCHOOL, YOU'LL NEED YOU TO BE MUCH MORE POWERFUL.
HEE HEE HEE
THIS IS YOUR OPPORTUNITY TO GET THE BEST POSSIBLE TRAINING.
RMB RMB RMB RMB RMB RMB
PAT
...
TRAINER ?!!
GRIN
I'M GOING TO GIVE YOU A REAL ATTITUDE ADJUSTMENT. NICE TO MEET YOU!
AIIIEEEEE!

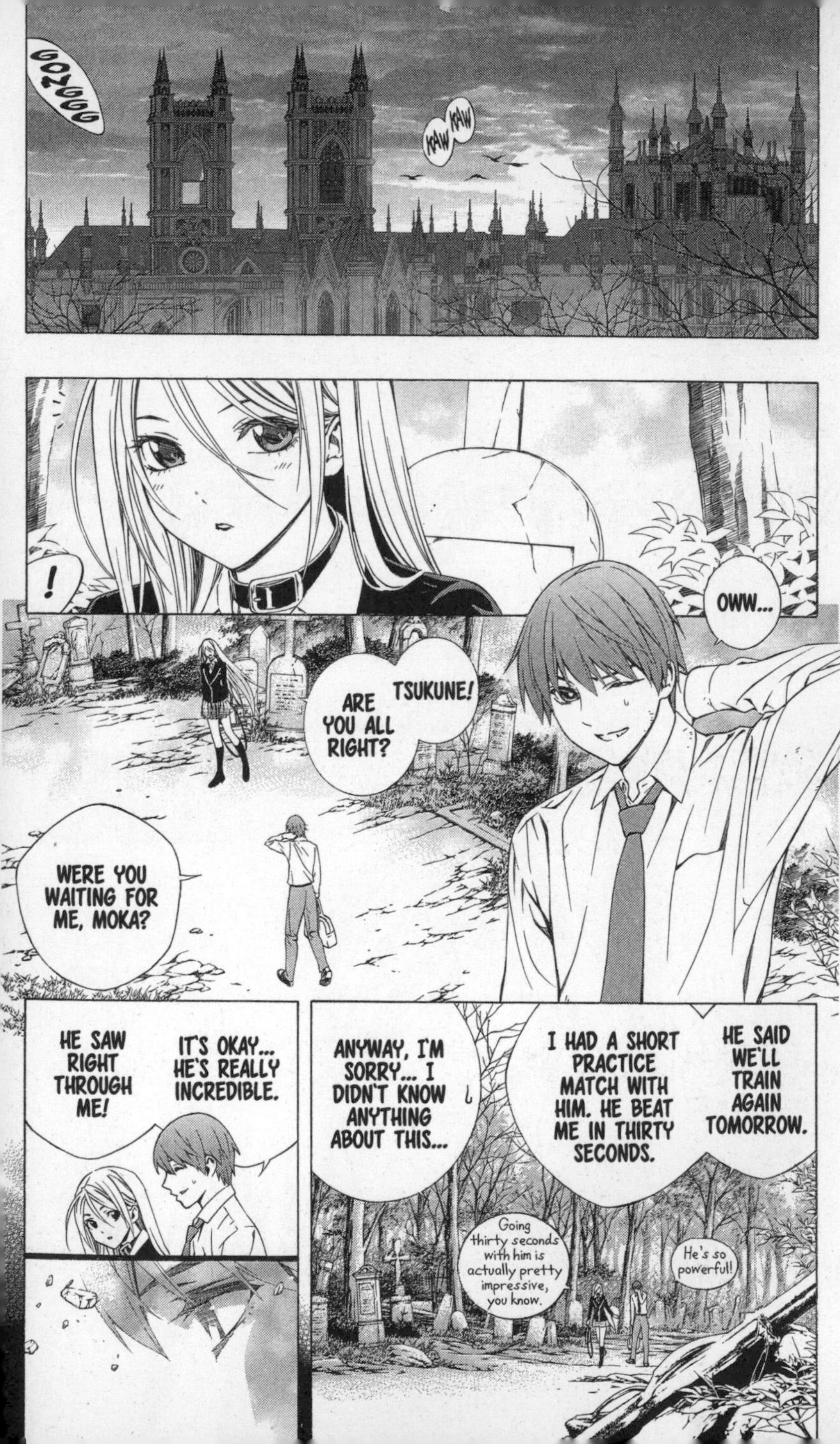
KAW KAW
GONGGG
OWW...
!
TSUKUNE! ARE YOU ALL RIGHT?
WERE YOU WAITING FOR ME, MOKA?
HE SAID WE'LL TRAIN AGAIN TOMORROW.
I HAD A SHORT PRACTICE MATCH WITH HIM. HE BEAT ME IN THIRTY SECONDS.
ANYWAY, I'M SORRY... I DIDN'T KNOW ANYTHING ABOUT THIS...
He's so powerful!
Going thirty seconds with him is actually pretty impressive, you know.
IT'S OKAY... HE'S REALLY INCREDIBLE.
HE SAW RIGHT THROUGH ME!

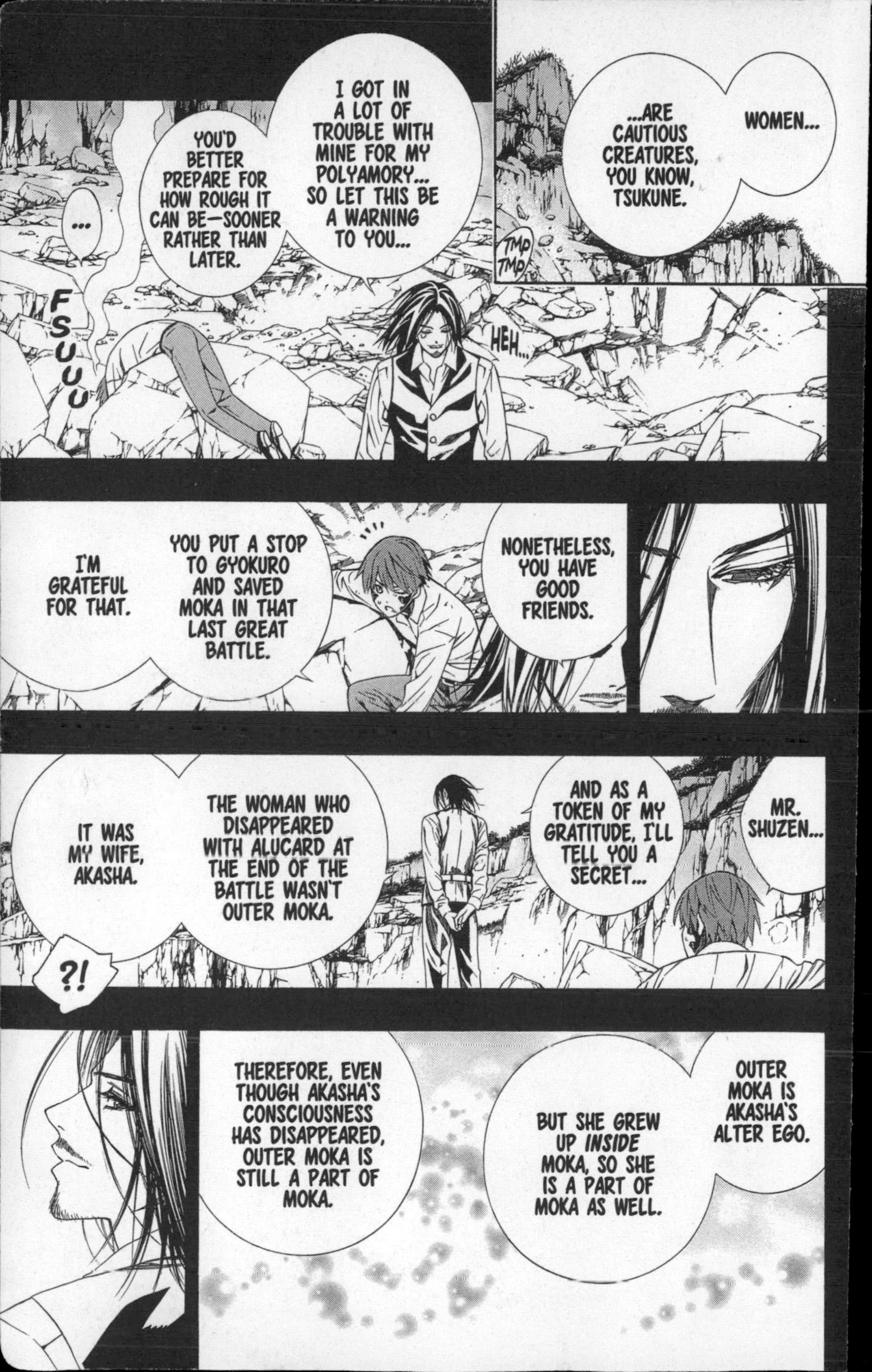

WOMEN...
...ARE CAUTIOUS CREATURES, YOU KNOW, TSUKUNE.
TMP TMP
I GOT IN A LOT OF TROUBLE WITH MINE FOR MY POLYAMORY... SO LET THIS BE A WARNING TO YOU...
YOU'D BETTER PREPARE FOR HOW ROUGH IT CAN BE—SOONER RATHER THAN LATER.
...
HEH...
FSUUU
NONETHELESS, YOU HAVE GOOD FRIENDS.
YOU PUT A STOP TO GYOKURO AND SAVED MOKA IN THAT LAST GREAT BATTLE.
I'M GRATEFUL FOR THAT.
MR. SHUZEN...
AND AS A TOKEN OF MY GRATITUDE, I'LL TELL YOU A SECRET...
THE WOMAN WHO DISAPPEARED WITH ALUCARD AT THE END OF THE BATTLE WASN'T OUTER MOKA.
IT WAS MY WIFE, AKASHA.
?!
OUTER MOKA IS AKASHA'S ALTER EGO.
BUT SHE GREW UP *INSIDE* MOKA, SO SHE IS A PART OF MOKA AS WELL.
THEREFORE, EVEN THOUGH AKASHA'S CONSCIOUSNESS HAS DISAPPEARED, OUTER MOKA IS STILL A PART OF MOKA.

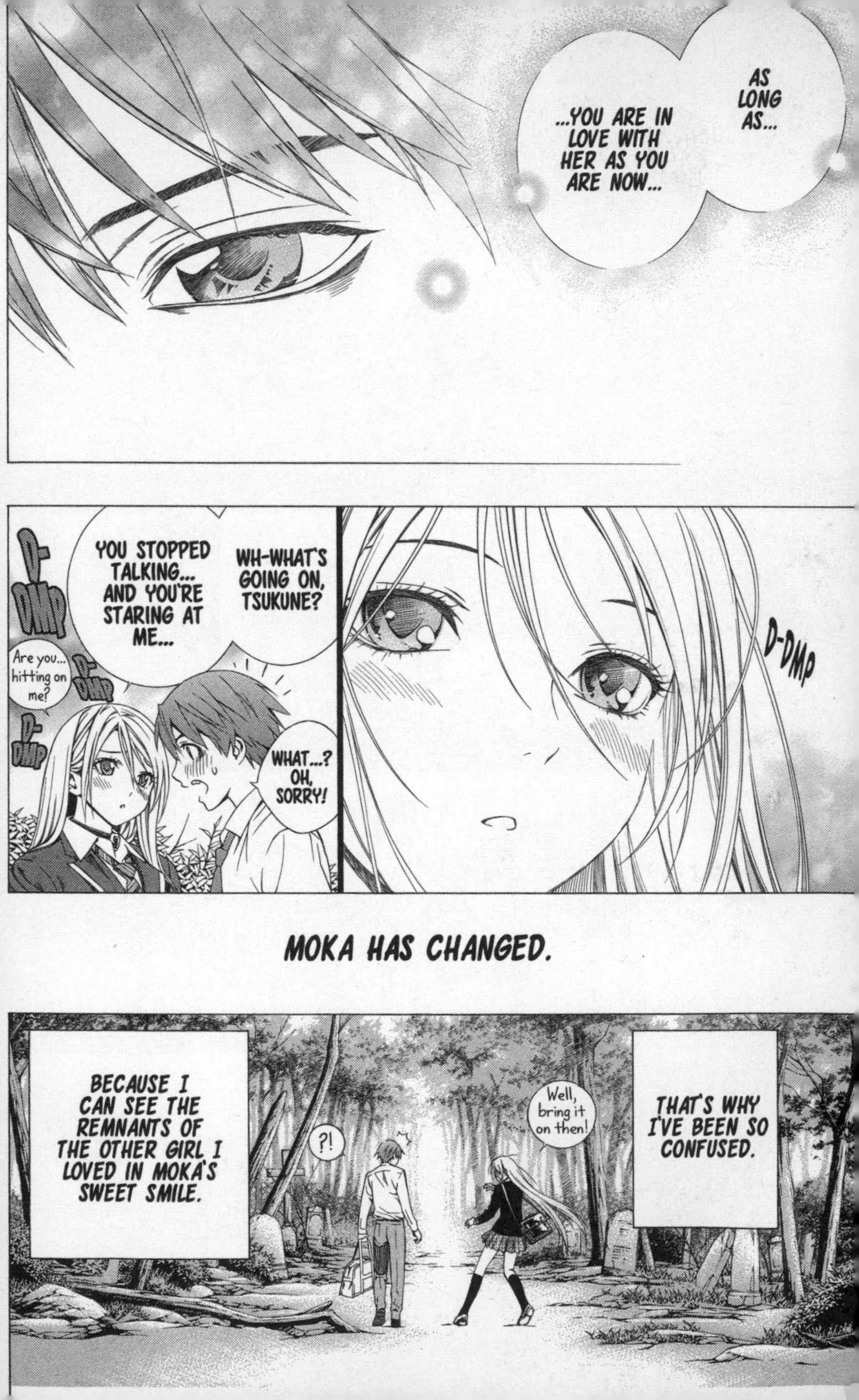
AS LONG AS...
...YOU ARE IN LOVE WITH HER AS YOU ARE NOW...
D-DMP
WH-WHAT'S GOING ON, TSUKUNE?
YOU STOPPED TALKING... AND YOU'RE STARING AT ME...
WHAT...? OH, SORRY!
Are you... hitting on me?
D-DMP D-DMP D-DMP
MOKA HAS CHANGED.
THAT'S WHY I'VE BEEN SO CONFUSED.
Well, bring it on then!
?!
BECAUSE I CAN SEE THE REMNANTS OF THE OTHER GIRL I LOVED IN MOKA'S SWEET SMILE.

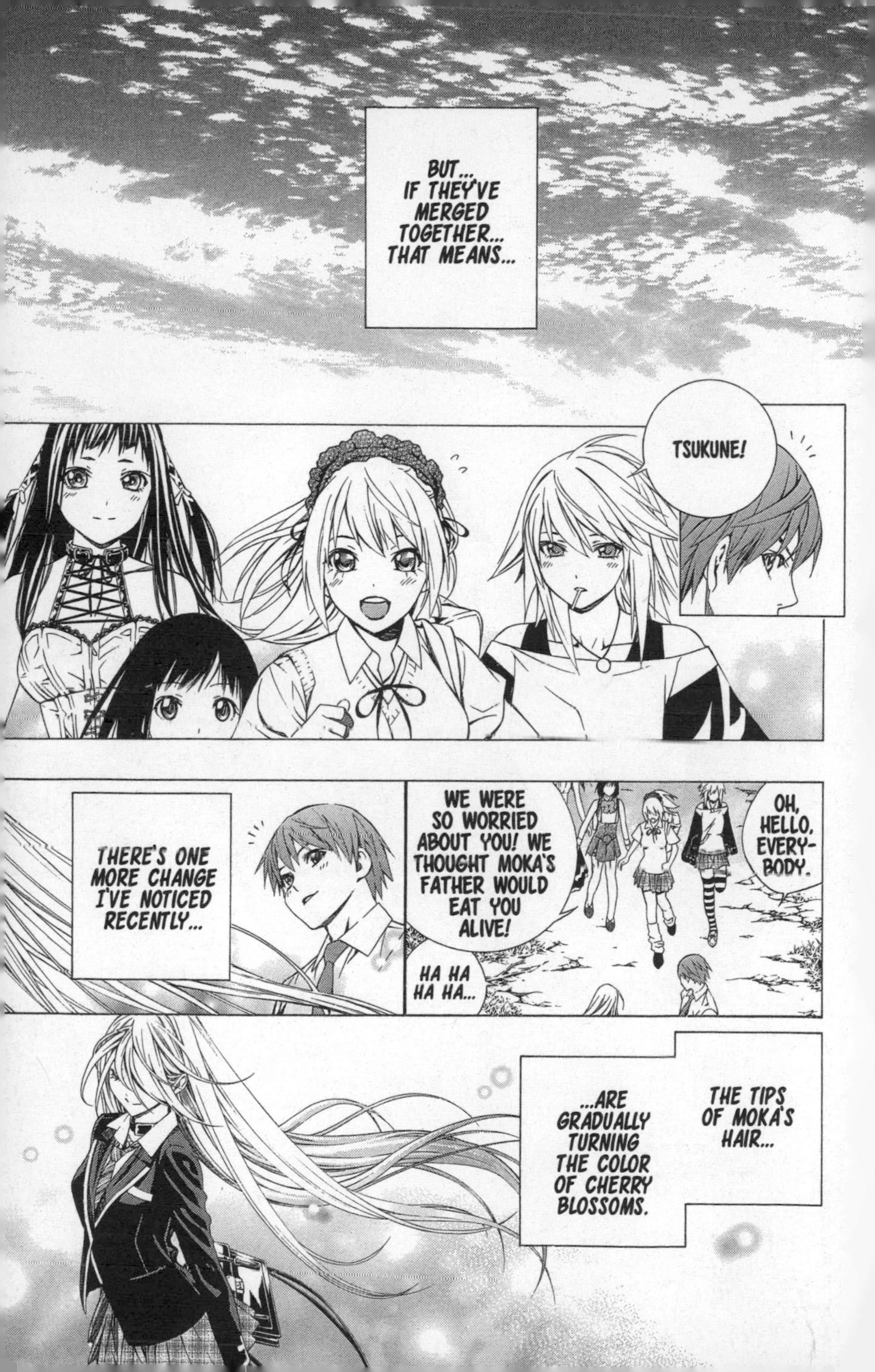
BUT... IF THEY'VE MERGED TOGETHER... THAT MEANS...
TSUKUNE!
OH, HELLO, EVERYBODY.
WE WERE SO WORRIED ABOUT YOU! WE THOUGHT MOKA'S FATHER WOULD EAT YOU ALIVE!
HA HA HA HA...
THERE'S ONE MORE CHANGE I'VE NOTICED RECENTLY...
THE TIPS OF MOKA'S HAIR...
...ARE GRADUALLY TURNING THE COLOR OF CHERRY BLOSSOMS.

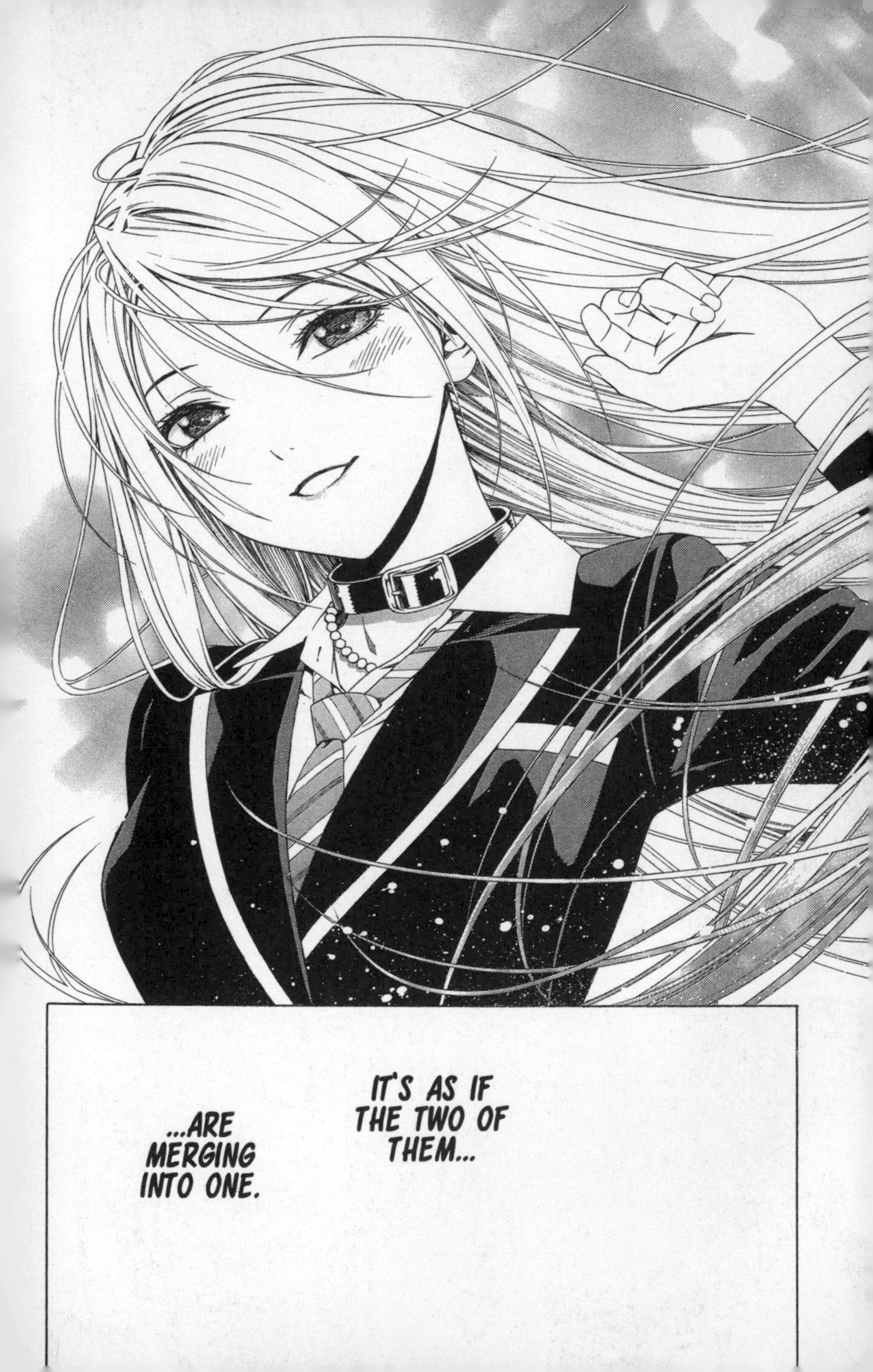
IT'S AS IF THE TWO OF THEM...
...ARE MERGING INTO ONE.

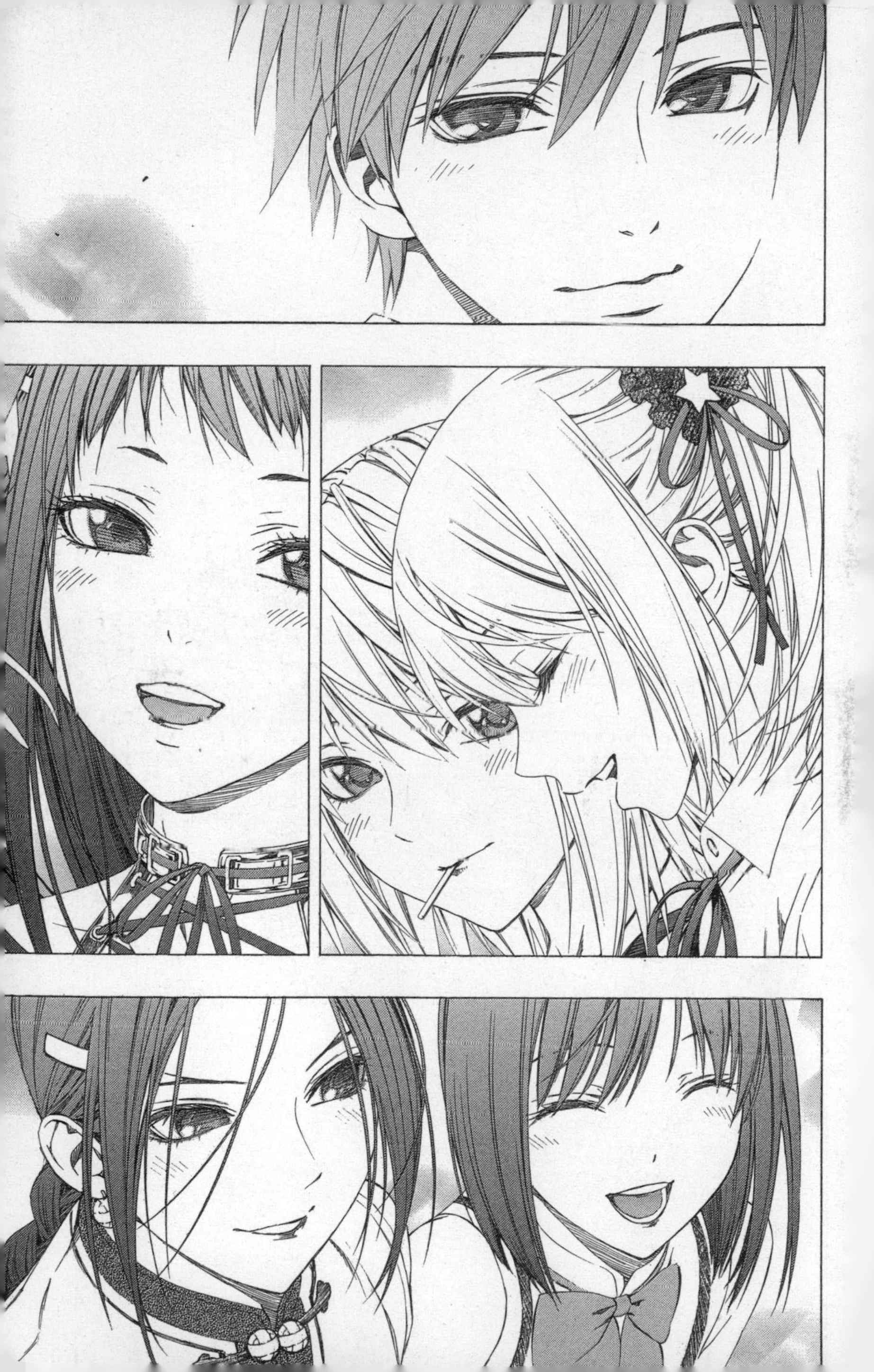

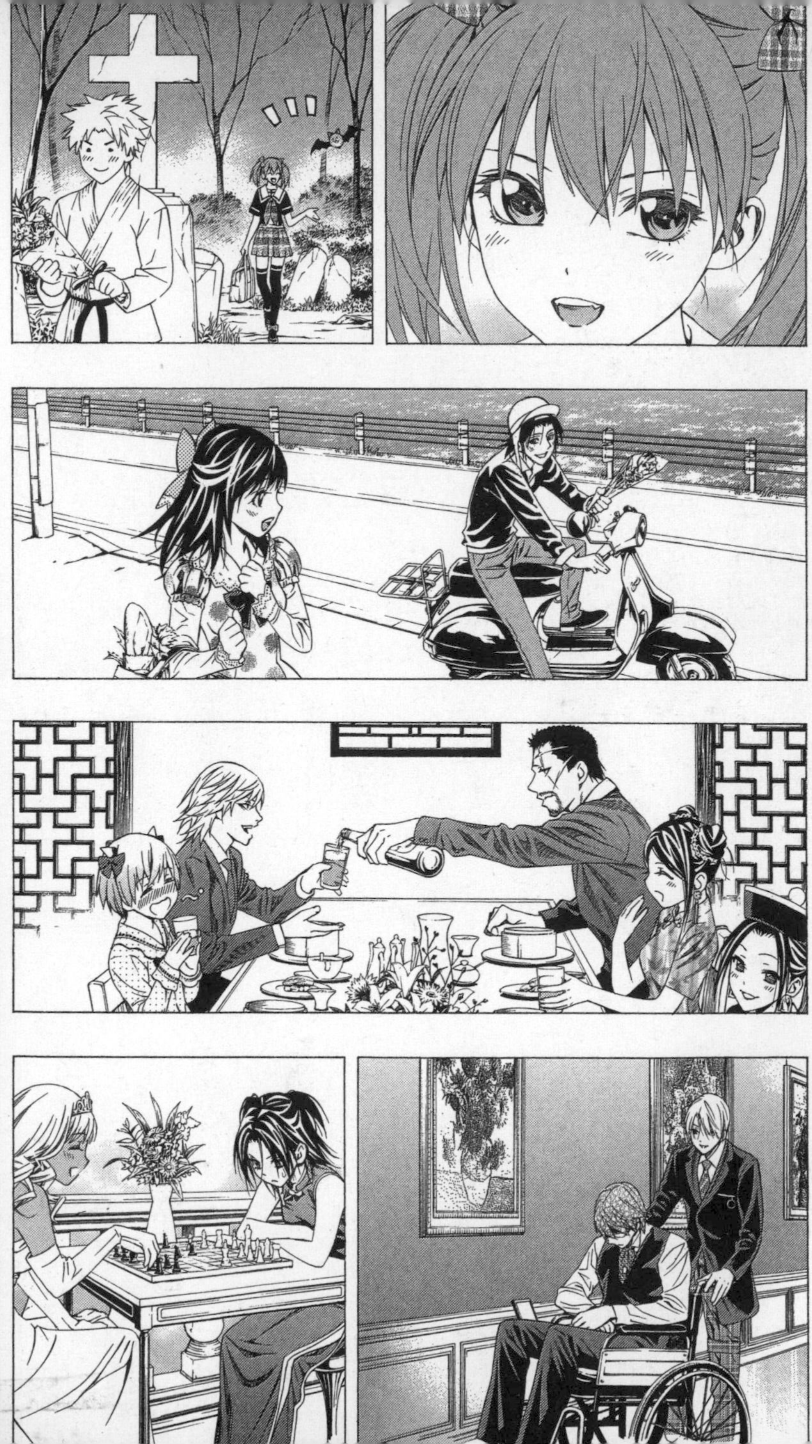

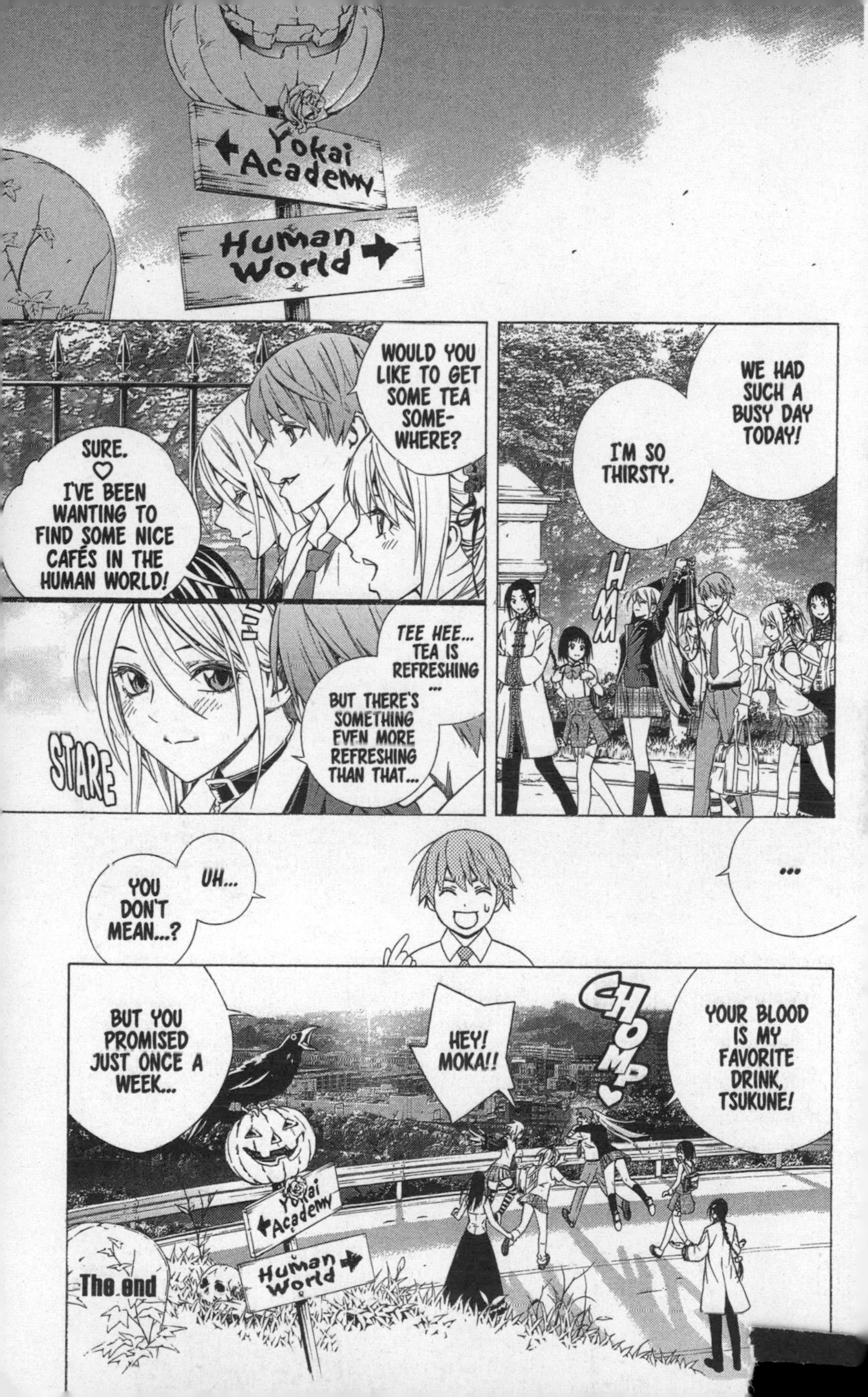
Yokai Academy
Human World
WE HAD SUCH A BUSY DAY TODAY!
I'M SO THIRSTY.
HMM
WOULD YOU LIKE TO GET SOME TEA SOME-WHERE?
SURE. ♡ I'VE BEEN WANTING TO FIND SOME NICE CAFÉS IN THE HUMAN WORLD!
TEE HEE... TEA IS REFRESHING...
BUT THERE'S SOMETHING EVEN MORE REFRESHING THAN THAT...
STARE
...
UH...
YOU DON'T MEAN...?
YOUR BLOOD IS MY FAVORITE DRINK, TSUKUNE!
CHOMP ♡
HEY! MOKA!!
BUT YOU PROMISED JUST ONCE A WEEK...
Yokai Academy
Human World
The end

ROSARIO+VAMPIRE
Season II

AKIHISA IKEDA

STAFF
MAKOTO SAITO
NOBUYUKI HAYASHI
RIKA SHIROTA

SPECIAL THANKS
YOSUKE TAKEDA
OSAMU NISHI
CHU KAWASAKI

EDITOR
SHUHEI WATANABE

COMIC
KENJU NORO

Thank you!

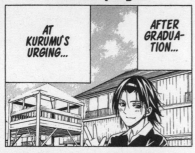

ROSARIO + VAMPIRE

Season II

EPILOGUES ♡

Meaningless End-of-Volume Theater

XIV

•Ginei's Epilogue•

AFTER GRADUATION...
AT KURUMU'S URGING...
...GIN GETS A JOB AT SAN'S INN.
I PICKED UP THE STUFF YOU ASKED FOR.
THANKS.
SZZ
NEED SOME HELP?
SURE! COULD YOU DO THIS? AND THEN THAT...
SHF
!
BUT FOR SOME REASON, THEIR RELATIONSHIP REMAINS INNOCENT.
FIRE!
...
FDGT FDGT
SPLAT SPLUT

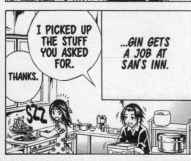

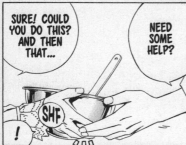

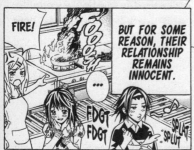

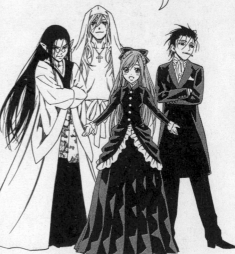

•Koko and Haiji's Epilogue•

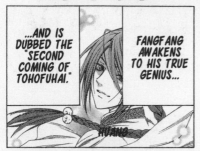

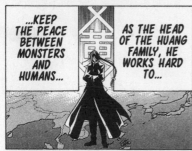

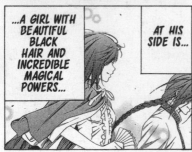

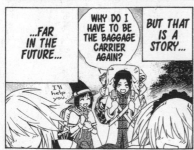

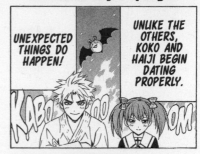

UNLIKE THE OTHERS, KOKO AND HAIJI BEGIN DATING PROPERLY.
UNEXPECTED THINGS DO HAPPEN!
KABOOOOM
OKAY, HAIJI!
TAKE ME OUT AGAIN TODAY!
SURE, KOKO!
TOGETHER WE'RE BETTER!
HA HA HA
THE PROBLEM IS...
SMASH
...NEITHER OF THEM HAS ANY IDEA WHAT A RELATIONSHIP IS.
KRASH
KRACK

•Fangfang's Epilogue•

FANGFANG AWAKENS TO HIS TRUE GENIUS...
...AND IS DUBBED THE "SECOND COMING OF TOHOFUHAI."
HUANG
AS THE HEAD OF THE HUANG FAMILY, HE WORKS HARD TO...
...KEEP THE PEACE BETWEEN MONSTERS AND HUMANS...
AT HIS SIDE IS...
...A GIRL WITH BEAUTIFUL BLACK HAIR AND INCREDIBLE MAGICAL POWERS...
BUT THAT IS A STORY...
WHY DO I HAVE TO BE THE BAGGAGE CARRIER AGAIN?
...FAR IN THE FUTURE...
I'll help you.

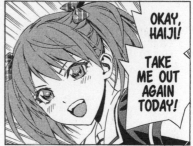

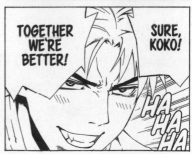

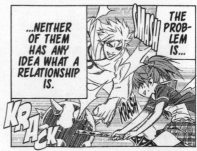

•Shuzen Family's Epilogue•

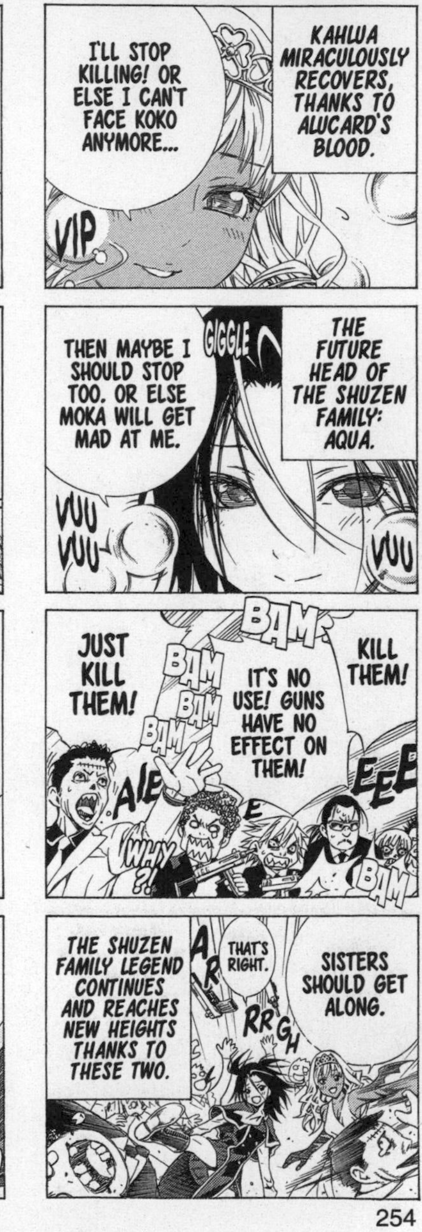
KAHLUA MIRACULOUSLY RECOVERS, THANKS TO ALUCARD'S BLOOD.
I'LL STOP KILLING! OR ELSE I CAN'T FACE KOKO ANYMORE...
VIP
THE FUTURE HEAD OF THE SHUZEN FAMILY: AQUA.
GIGGLE
THEN MAYBE I SHOULD STOP TOO. OR ELSE MOKA WILL GET MAD AT ME.
VUU
VUU VUU
BAM
KILL THEM!
IT'S NO USE! GUNS HAVE NO EFFECT ON THEM!
BAM BAM BAM
JUST KILL THEM!
EEE
AIEE
WHY?!
BAM
SISTERS SHOULD GET ALONG.
THAT'S RIGHT.
ARRRGH
THE SHUZEN FAMILY LEGEND CONTINUES AND REACHES NEW HEIGHTS THANKS TO THESE TWO.

•Fairy Tale's Epilogue•

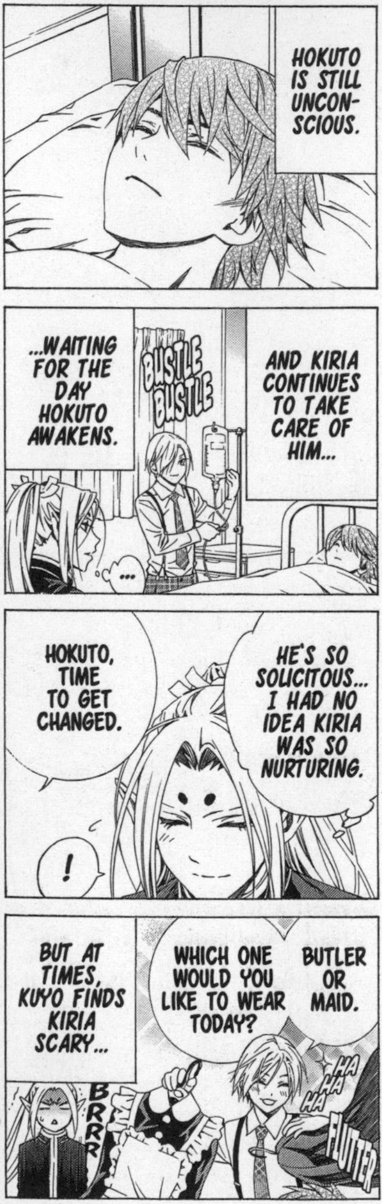
HOKUTO IS STILL UNCON-SCIOUS.
AND KIRIA CONTINUES TO TAKE CARE OF HIM...
BUSTLE BUSTLE
...WAITING FOR THE DAY HOKUTO AWAKENS.
...
HE'S SO SOLICITOUS... I HAD NO IDEA KIRIA WAS SO NURTURING.
HOKUTO, TIME TO GET CHANGED.
!
BUTLER OR MAID.
WHICH ONE WOULD YOU LIKE TO WEAR TODAY?
BUT AT TIMES, KUYO FINDS KIRIA SCARY...
HA HA HA
FLUTTER
BRRR

And What of the Other Heroines' Epilogues?

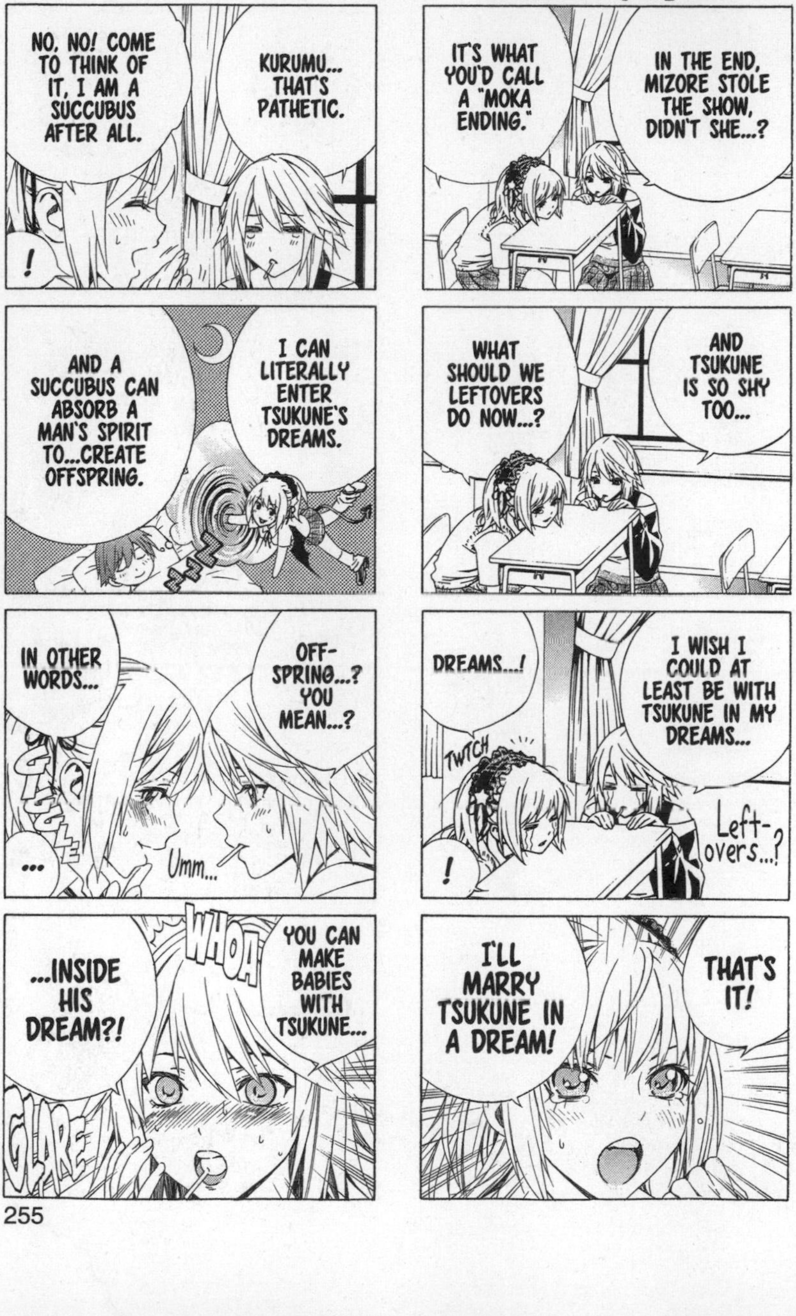
IN THE END, MIZORE STOLE THE SHOW, DIDN'T SHE...?
IT'S WHAT YOU'D CALL A "MOKA ENDING."
AND TSUKUNE IS SO SHY TOO...
WHAT SHOULD WE LEFTOVERS DO NOW...?
I WISH I COULD AT LEAST BE WITH TSUKUNE IN MY DREAMS...
DREAMS...!
TWTCH
Left-overs...?
!
THAT'S IT!
I'LL MARRY TSUKUNE IN A DREAM!
KURUMU... THAT'S PATHETIC.
NO, NO! COME TO THINK OF IT, I AM A SUCCUBUS AFTER ALL.
!
I CAN LITERALLY ENTER TSUKUNE'S DREAMS.
AND A SUCCUBUS CAN ABSORB A MAN'S SPIRIT TO...CREATE OFFSPRING.
OFF-SPRING...? YOU MEAN...?
IN OTHER WORDS...
Umm...
GIGGLE
...
YOU CAN MAKE BABIES WITH TSUKUNE...
WHOA
...INSIDE HIS DREAM?!
GLARE

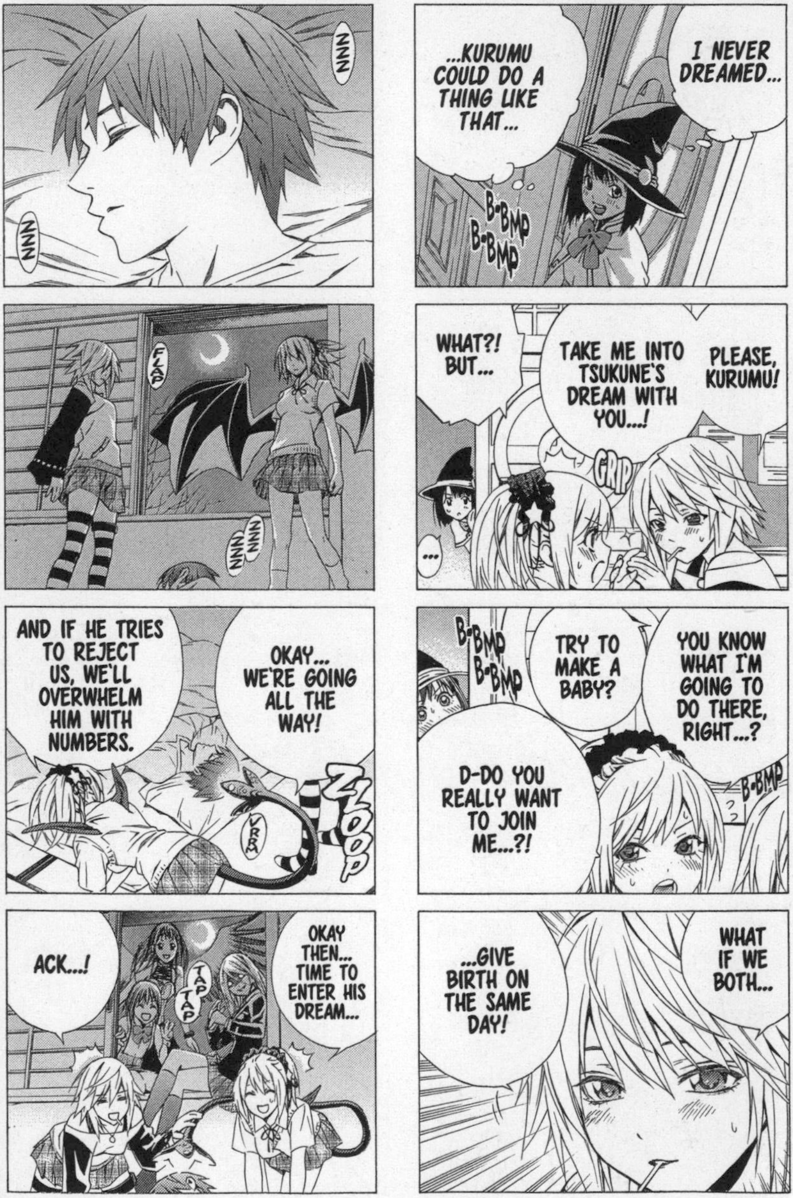
I NEVER DREAMED...
...KURUMU COULD DO A THING LIKE THAT...
B-BMP B-BMP
ZZZ
ZZZ
PLEASE, KURUMU!
TAKE ME INTO TSUKUNE'S DREAM WITH YOU...!
WHAT?! BUT...
GRIP
...
FLAP
ZZZ ZZZ ZZZ
YOU KNOW WHAT I'M GOING TO DO THERE, RIGHT...?
TRY TO MAKE A BABY?
B-BMP B-BMP
D-DO YOU REALLY WANT TO JOIN ME...?!
B-BMP
OKAY... WE'RE GOING ALL THE WAY!
AND IF HE TRIES TO REJECT US, WE'LL OVERWHELM HIM WITH NUMBERS.
ZLOOP
VRRM
WHAT IF WE BOTH...
...GIVE BIRTH ON THE SAME DAY!
OKAY THEN... TIME TO ENTER HIS DREAM...
ACK...!
TAP TAP

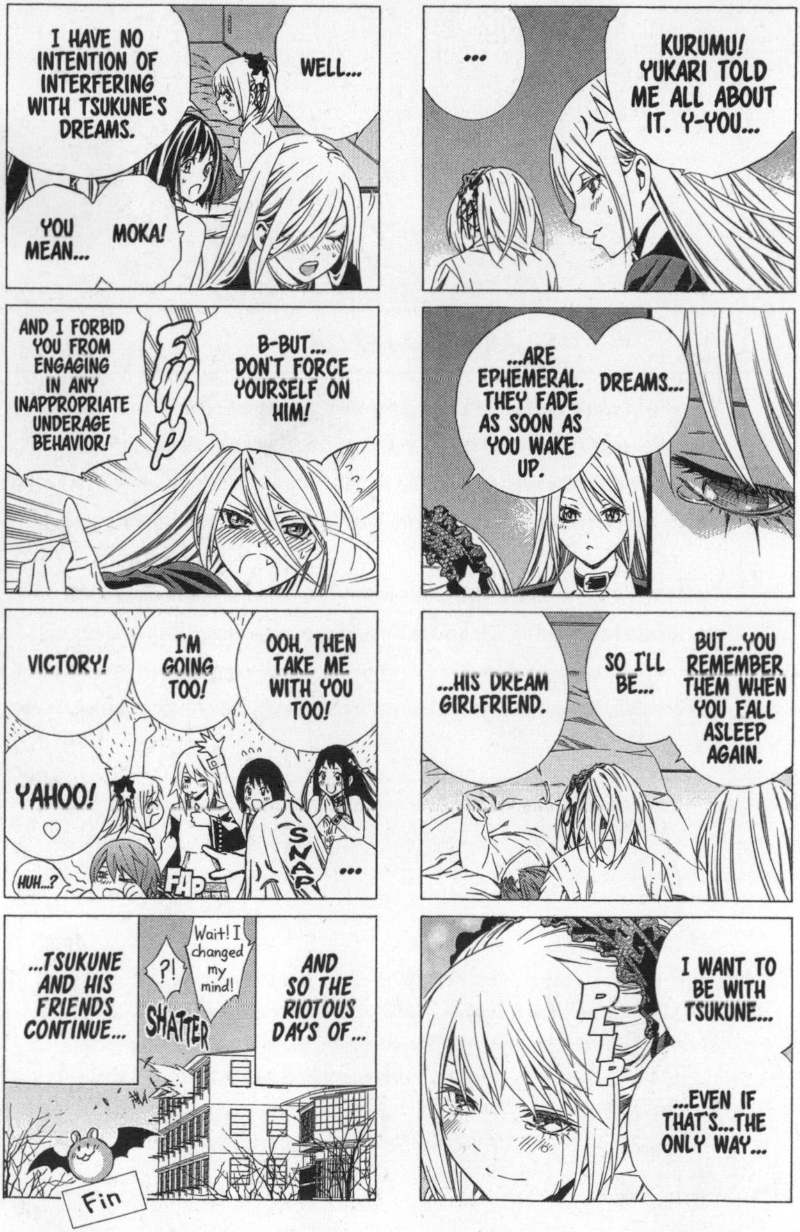
KURUMU! YUKARI TOLD ME ALL ABOUT IT. Y-YOU...
...
WELL...
I HAVE NO INTENTION OF INTERFERING WITH TSUKUNE'S DREAMS.
YOU MEAN... MOKA!
DREAMS...
...ARE EPHEMERAL. THEY FADE AS SOON AS YOU WAKE UP.
B-BUT... DON'T FORCE YOURSELF ON HIM!
FWIP
AND I FORBID YOU FROM ENGAGING IN ANY INAPPROPRIATE UNDERAGE BEHAVIOR!
BUT...YOU REMEMBER THEM WHEN YOU FALL ASLEEP AGAIN.
SO I'LL BE...
...HIS DREAM GIRLFRIEND.
OOH, THEN TAKE ME WITH YOU TOO!
I'M GOING TOO!
VICTORY!
YAHOO! ♡
...
SNAP
FAP
HUH...?
I WANT TO BE WITH TSUKUNE...
PLIP
...EVEN IF THAT'S...THE ONLY WAY...
AND SO THE RIOTOUS DAYS OF...
Wait! I changed my mind!
?!
...TSUKUNE AND HIS FRIENDS CONTINUE...
SHATTER
Fin

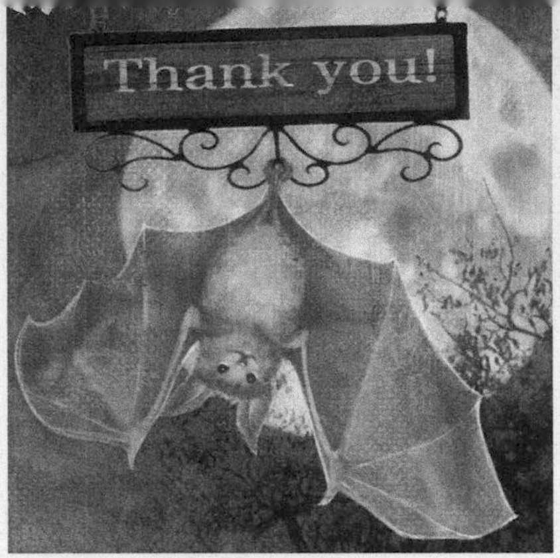
Thank you!

AKIHISA IKEDA

First of all, I would like to thank everybody from the bottom of my heart!! *Rosario + Vampire Season II* has finally reached vol. 14, the final volume! Thank you very much to all the fans who have been reading this series all the way until now, as well as the staff, editors and everyone who dealt with my impossible requests and supported me!

I said to myself, "I want the final battle to be in one volume." And because of this whim, this volume has ended up being quite thick. I hope you get more than quantity out of it!

And hopefully Tsukune and Moka's story will continue on somewhere inside your heart...!

Akihisa Ikeda was born in 1976 in Miyazaki. He debuted as a mangaka with the four-volume magical warrior fantasy series *Kiruto* in 2002, which was serialized in *Monthly Shonen Jump*. *Rosario+Vampire* debuted in *Monthly Shonen Jump* in March of 2004 and is continuing in the magazine *Jump Square (Jump SQ)* as *Rosario+Vampire: Season II*. In Japan, *Rosario+Vampire* is also available as a drama CD. In 2008, the story was released as an anime. Season II is also available as an anime now. And in Japan, there is a Nintendo DS game based on the series.

Ikeda has been a huge fan of vampires and monsters since he was a little kid. He says one of the perks of being a manga artist is being able to go for walks during the day when everybody else is stuck in the office.

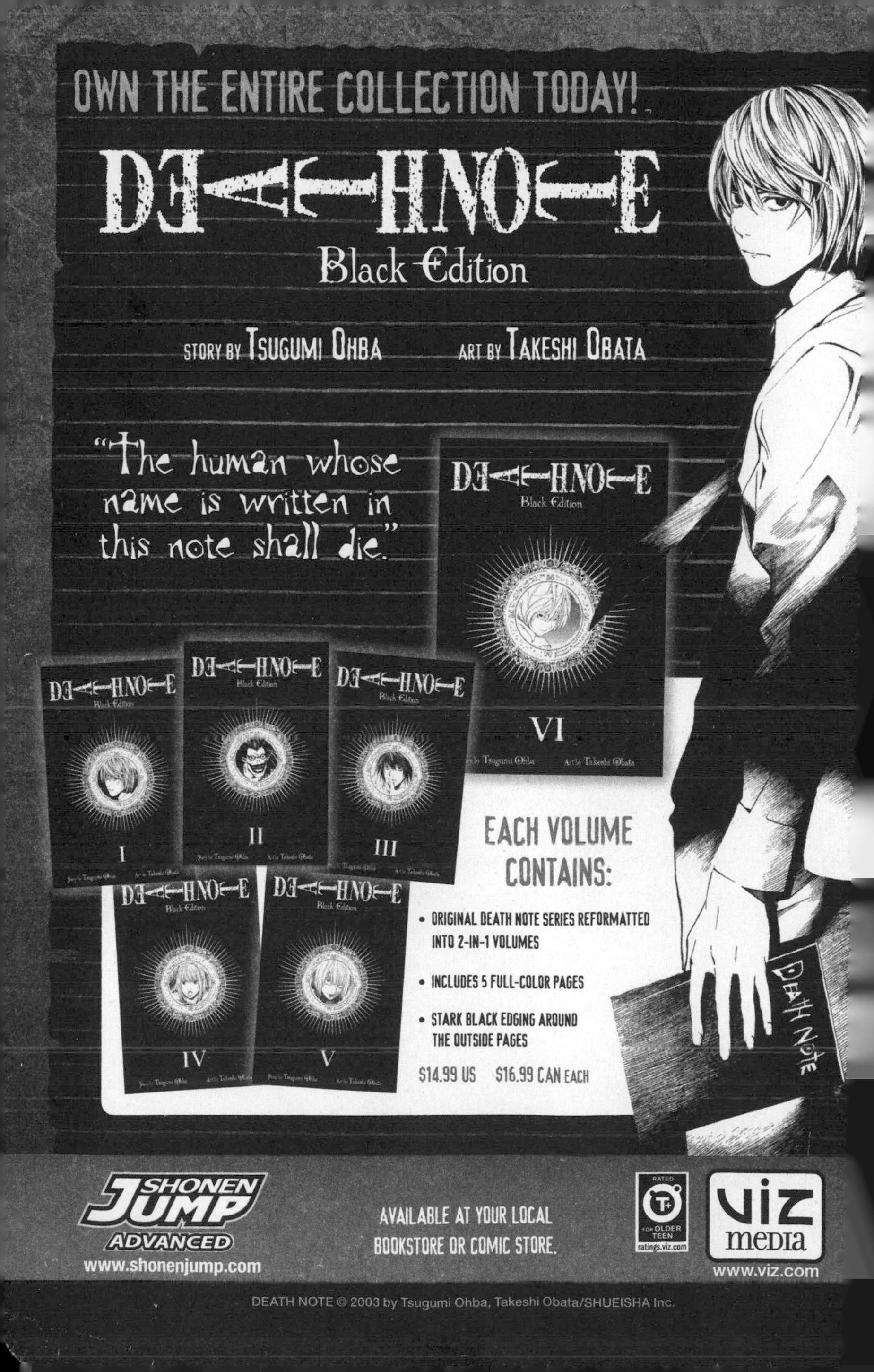
OWN THE ENTIRE COLLECTION TODAY!
DEATH NOTE
Black Edition
STORY BY TSUGUMI OHBA
ART BY TAKESHI OBATA
"The human whose name is written in this note shall die."
DEATH NOTE Black Edition VI Story by Tsugumi Ohba Art by Takeshi Obata
DEATH NOTE Black Edition I
DEATH NOTE Black Edition II
DEATH NOTE Black Edition III
DEATH NOTE Black Edition IV
DEATH NOTE Black Edition V
EACH VOLUME CONTAINS:
• ORIGINAL DEATH NOTE SERIES REFORMATTED INTO 2-IN-1 VOLUMES
• INCLUDES 5 FULL-COLOR PAGES
• STARK BLACK EDGING AROUND THE OUTSIDE PAGES
$14.99 US $16.99 CAN EACH
DEATH NOTE
SHONEN JUMP ADVANCED
www.shonenjump.com
AVAILABLE AT YOUR LOCAL BOOKSTORE OR COMIC STORE.
RATED T+ FOR OLDER TEEN ratings.viz.com
viz media
www.viz.com
DEATH NOTE © 2003 by Tsugumi Ohba, Takeshi Obata/SHUEISHA Inc.

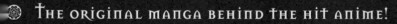

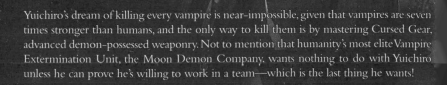

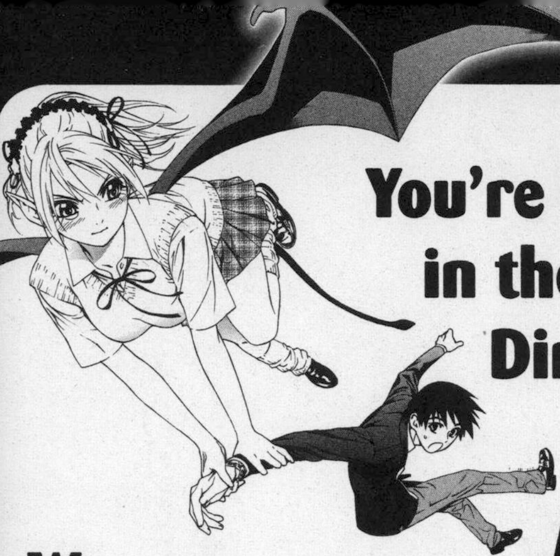

You're Reading in the Wrong Direction!!

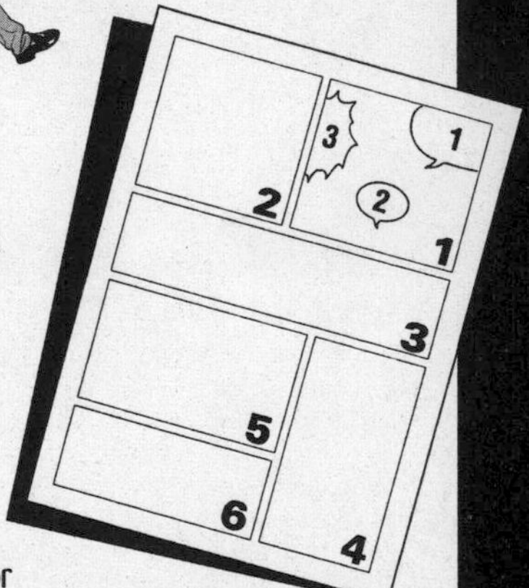
1
2
3
1
2
3
4
5
6

Whoops! Guess what? You're starting at the wrong end of the comic!

...It's true! In keeping with the original Japanese format, **Rosario+Vampire** is meant to be read from right to left, starting in the upper-right corner.

Unlike English, which is read from left to right, Japanese is read from right to left, meaning action, sound effects and word-balloon order are completely reversed... something which can make readers unfamiliar with Japanese feel pretty backwards themselves. For this reason, manga or Japanese comics published in the U.S. in English have sometimes been published "flopped"—that is, printed in exact reverse order, as though seen from the other side of a mirror.

By flopping pages, U.S. publishers can avoid confusing readers, but the compromise is not without its downside. For one thing, a character in a flopped manga series who once wore in the original Japanese version a T-shirt emblazoned with "M A Y" (as in "the merry month of") now wears one which reads "Y A M"! Additionally, many manga creators in Japan are themselves unhappy with the process, as some feel the mirror-imaging of their art skews their original intentions.

We are proud to bring you Akihisa Ikeda's **Rosario+Vampire** in the original unflop
book and let t